Contents

Nature, Culture, History
Pages 7–130

Sights from A to Z
Pages 132–369

Practical Information from A to Z
Pages 371–451

Principal Sights of Tourist Interest

Note: The above list includes only the more important places of touristic interest in Thailand which are worth seeing either for themselves or for other attractions in the vicinity. The individual sights are designated by one or two asterisks within the text of each entry.

Preface

This guide to Thailand is one of the new generation of Baedeker guides.

These guides, illustrated throughout in colour, are designed to meet the needs of the modern traveller. They are quick and easy to consult, with the principal places of interest described in alphabetical order, and the information is presented in a format that is both attractive and easy to follow.

The subject of this guide is the Kingdom of Thailand and it is in three parts. The first part gives a general account of the country, its people, language, religion, culture, economy and communications, famous people and history. A brief selection of quotations and a number of suggested itineraries provide a transition to the second part, in which the country's places and features of tourist interest – towns, villages, islands and scenery – are described. The third part contains a variety of practical information. Both the sights and the practical information are listed in alphabetical order.

The new Baedeker guides are noted for their concentration on essentials and their convenience of use. They contain numerous specially drawn plans and colour illustrations; and at the end of the book is a large map making it easy to locate the various places described in the "A to Z" section of the guide with the help of the co-ordinates given at the head of each entry.

Spelling of Thai names
The transcription of Thai names is not easy for there is no accepted system of rendering the Thai language in English. A systematic standardisation would come up against the difficulty that even in factually reliable Thai sources different versions of the same name can quite often be found.

In those parts of the country not generally frequented by tourists communication in English will sometimes be difficult. For this reason in the A to Z section of this guide Thai place names have been reproduced in blue type.

How to use this book

Following the tradition established by Karl Baedeker in 1844, sights of particular interest, outstanding buildings, works of art, etc., are distinguished by either one ★ or two ★★ stars.

To make it easier to locate the various sights listed in the "A to Z" section of the Guide, their co-ordinates on the large city map are shown in red at the head of each entry, e.g. ★Bangkok H 4.

Only a selection of hotels and restaurants can be given; no reflection is implied, therefore, on establishments not included.

The symbol ⓘ on a town plan indicates the local tourist office from which further information can be obtained. The post-horn symbol indicates a post office.

In a time of rapid change it is difficult to ensure that all the information given is entirely accurate and up to date, and the possibility of error can never be completely eliminated. Although the publishers can accept no responsibility for inaccuracies and omissions, they are always grateful for corrections and suggestions for improvement.

Facts and Figures

The "Land of Smiles", as Thailand has been known ever since it was first discovered by Europeans, continues to attract more and more visitors. The proverbial hospitality shown by its people, the varied landscape and pleasant climate – especially when it is winter in Europe – make Thailand a "must" not only for sun-worshippers but also for anyone interested in Asiatic culture. The jewels in this South Asian treasure-chest are the magnificent temples, built in a number of styles and dating from various periods, and now rubbing shoulders with examples of the ways in which the country has rapidly absorbed Western methods; the region around the capital Bangkok in particular has become a focal point of the South Asian economy. In spite of this the old traditions have remained very much alive, and it is this contrast which makes Thailand such a classical holiday venue for anyone visiting Asia for the first time.

General

Borders

Thailand borders Myanmar (formerly Burma) in the north-west and west, Laos in the north and north-east, Cambodia in the south-east and Malaysia in the south. In spite of the peace treaty signed in 1991 by the four civil war factions in Cambodia, military conflict repeatedly continues to break out in the Thai–Cambodian border region. Those contemplating travelling in this area are advised to seek current information about the situation.

Geographical location

Thailand lies between latitudes 5° 40′ and 20° 30′ north and longitudes 97° 30′ and 105° 45′ east. The capital Bangkok lies on latitude 13° 7′ north and longitude 100° 5′ east at the junction of Thailand's four main regions, the North-West (Pak Nya), the North-East (Isaan), the South-East (Pak Dai Towan Org) and the South-West (Pak Dai), in the fertile delta of the Chao Phraya, the Menam Plain, known as the "rice bowl".

The territory of Thailand covers an area of 513,115sq.km/198,115sq. miles, rather more than twice that of the United Kingdom. The maximum distance from north to south measures 1620km/1007 miles, and from east to west 780km/485 miles. Thailand is at its narrowest near Prachuap Khiri Khan, where it is only 13km/8 miles as the crow flies between the Gulf of Thailand and the border with Myanmar (Burma); the Isthmus of Kra on the Malay Peninsula is only 64km/40 miles wide. Thailand has 1875km/1165 miles of coastline on the Gulf of Thailand and 740km/460 miles on the Indian Ocean.

Capital

Bangkok has been the capital of the country since 1782, the year of the take-over by General Chakri, who later became King Rama I and founded the Chakri Dynasty which still rules today. Up until then Thonburi on the opposite bank of the Chao Phraya had been the capital. Nowadays Thonburi and Bangkok are united in one city.

The Thais gave their city the official name of "Krung Thep" (City of Angels) or "Pra Nakhorn" (Heavenly Capital). The name Bangkok was invented by Western visitors, and was probably a corruption of "Ban Makok", which stands for "village of olives".

Bangkok is the only city state in Thailand. Since it was joined with Thonburi Bangkok has been literally bursting at the seams. Originally it covered an area of only 13sq.km/5sq. miles, the boundaries of which

◀ *Great Chedi in the Wat Phra That Haripunchai in Lamphun*

can still be seen between the loop of the Chao Phraya, west of the Royal Palace, and the Krung Kasem Canal; today Bangkok has an inner city area of 6500sq.km/2510sq. miles. The widespread suburbs which were bustling with agricultural activity up until the late 19th century no longer exist; they have been swallowed up into a gigantic conurbation by urban development. Since 1960, when the figure was 1.6 million, the population of Bangkok has more than quadrupled, largely as a result of its being joined with Thonburi in the 1970s.

Topography

The varied topography of Thailand can be divided into five main areas, each of which possesses its own particular charm. The scenery is also largely determined by the climate in that particular zone; while the south has no definite rainy season – rainfall is spread more or less equally over the whole year – in the north the changing seasons are much more clearly defined. The vegetation varies accordingly; anyone travelling south to the Malay Peninsula at any time of the year will pass through evergreen tropical forests and endless rubber-tree plantations, while a marked period of drought between February and June with subtropical temperatures tends to make Central and North-Eastern Thailand appear less attractive, at least at first glance.

Central Thailand

Menam Basin

The dominant feature of Central Thailand, which stretches some 270km/168 miles north from the sea, is the Menam Basin and the River Menam Chao Phraya, which flows southwards through Thailand and enters the Gulf of Thailand in a wide spreading delta (about 20,000sq.km/7722sq. miles).

The river is the main artery of the entire country, which explains its name "Menam" ("Mother of Rivers"). It arises from the tributaries Ping, Yom and Nan which unite at Nakhon Sawan but soon disperse into a multitude of subsidiaries forming a multi-fingered delta in the middle of the Central Basin.

In the south the basin borders the sea with mountains surrounding it on its remaining sides; in the west the Central Cordillera (Tanen Tong Dan) runs from the upland area of Northern Thailand south to the Malay Peninsula; in the north lie mountainous uplands; in the south the outer edges of the Khorat Plateau (Dong Phaya Yen mountain range).

Geology

The Menam Basin is divided into two geomorphological zones: whereas an upland area with hills over 500m/1640ft rises to meet the mountains in the north of Thailand the main part of the basin is an alluvial plain with the occasional steep limestone peak towering above it, such as that at Lopburi. The central plain is geologically recent, being formed predominantly from giant masses of sediment carried by the Menam Chao Phraya. Geological boreholes indicate that the sediment reaches depths of 400m/1312ft around Bangkok. These alluvial deposits cause a considerable silting-up of the river delta, which is expanding into the Gulf of Thailand at the rate of five to six metres (16–20ft) a year.

Topography

The landscape of the wide valley is characterised by hillsides and terraces with fertile alluvial soil which has been cultivated for centuries, mainly as paddy-fields. Typical of this countryside are the many villages with wooden houses built on stilts owing to the constant danger of flooding.

The low-lying situation of the Menam Basin means that the tides reach far inland (Bangkok is only 2m/6ft above sea-level). This results in severe flooding during the annual monsoon rains of October and November with the entire plain and even large areas of Bangkok being under water. In the long term Bangkok will be seriously at risk if a further melting of the polar ice-caps should produce a rise in sea-level.

North Thailand

Broadly speaking, the line of latitude 17° north separates the north of the country from the rest of Thailand. Characteristic of this region are

Rice-growing in the Menam Basin

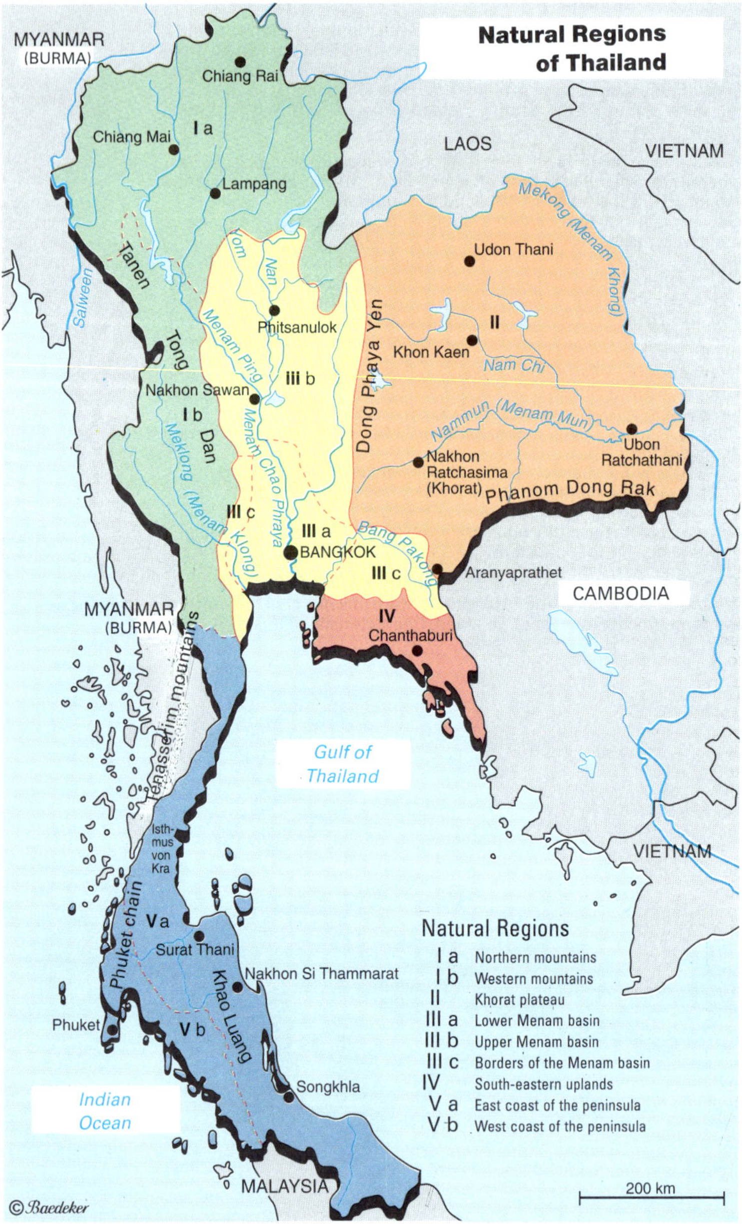
Natural Regions of Thailand
MYANMAR (BURMA)
LAOS
VIETNAM
CAMBODIA
MALAYSIA
Chiang Rai
Chiang Mai
I a
Lampang
Tanen
Salween
Tong
Yom
Nan
Phitsanulok
Menam Ping
iii b
Nakhon Sawan
I b
Meklong (Menam Klong)
Dan
Menam Chao Phraya
III c
III a
BANGKOK
Bang Pakong
III c
Aranyaprathet
Dong Phaya Yen
Udon Thani
Mekong (Menam Khong)
II
Khon Kaen
Nam Chi
Nammun (Menam Mun)
Ubon Ratchathani
Nakhon Ratchasima (Khorat)
Phanom Dong Rak
IV
Chanthaburi
Tenasserim mountains
Gulf of Thailand
Isthmus von Kra
Phuket chain
V a
Surat Thani
Nakhon Si Thammarat
Khao Luang
V b
Phuket
Songkhla
Indian Ocean
Natural Regions
I a Northern mountains
I b Western mountains
II Khorat plateau
III a Lower Menam basin
III b Upper Menam basin
III c Borders of the Menam basin
IV South-eastern uplands
V a East coast of the peninsula
V b West coast of the peninsula
200 km
© Baedeker

the foothills of the South-East Asian mountain ranges, the highest point being Doi Inthanon, some 50km/30 miles from Chiang Mai; at 2565m/8415ft it is the highest mountain in Thailand.

Topography

In the valleys of Northern Thailand the rivers Nan, Yom, Ping and Wang flow southwards. Protected from the wind, large and small basins snuggle between the mountains, providing favourable conditions for a successful agricultural economy, even though large parts of the paddy-fields have to be artificially irrigated because of the varying amounts of rainfall. For many years now reservoirs and dams have been built in an attempt to guarantee an even supply of water right through the year.

Geology

Two different geological structures determine the relief, and these in turn are the result of various mountain formations. The underlying rock of Northern Thailand dates from the Palaeozoic Age, and there are large areas of Palaeozoic limestone and slate; mountains of limestone are characterised by precipitous rocks with numerous caves and caverns.

These old mountains were again subjected to heave when the Himalayas were formed during the Tertiary Period and molten magma (which solidified into granite) was thrown up to form flat-capped mountains. Doi Inthanon is one such mountain.

Settlement

The main centres of population are the plains and basins between the mountains. The economic structure hinges mainly on agriculture, as is witnessed by the fact that most of the population live in villages rather than towns. An exception to this are the 3000 or so crude settlements which are home to the Akha, Lisu, Yao, Meo and Karen mountain tribes. Only a few of these tribesmen agreed to be re-housed under government re-settlement programmes; the vast majority have remained faithful to their age-old nomadic traditions, moving on to pastures new when the soil becomes exhausted after years of relentless cultivation. They also practise stubble-burning which has tended to denude the soil.

South-East Thailand

The south-eastern part of the country is dominated by a valley winding from west to east and a mountain range parallel to the coast, the two gradually merging into one another. The landscape is characterised by evergreen tropical forest and by mountainous granite country up to 1600m/5250ft above sea-level. Also typical of this region are the sharply-articulated coastline with its deeply-indented bays and the many islands of varying size. The numerous fishing villages along the coast bear witness to the good fishing to be had here.

It is here that the visitor to Thailand will realise his dream of tropical beaches. As a result this south-eastern region has better roads and caters more for the tourist than any other part of Thailand; seaside resorts – including the well-known one of Pattaya – are strung out along the coast like a string of pearls.

This is also an important mining area. The region around the town of Chanthaburi, 245km/152 miles from Bangkok, is a centre for precious stones, especially rubies and sapphires which are either mined or panned from the sand of the rivers.

North-East Thailand

Khorat Plateau

To the east of the Menam fluvial plain the mainly dry Khorat Plateau, with its characteristic red sandstone and slate formations, rises to an average height of 200m/656ft. The plateau, the western and southern edges of which are clearly defined by mountain chains (Dong Phaya Yen in the west and Phanom Dong Rak in the south) and which is 1300m/4270ft above sea-level at its highest point, slopes away gently eastwards in the direction of Mekong.

Geology and cultivation

Late Palaeozoic and Mesozoic limestone alternates with red Mesozoic sandstone and slate. The chalky soil is porous and parts of the sand-

Mountain landscape in northern Thailand

stone have become weathered to form the red soil typical of the tropics. The soil is not very fertile, which is why this region is often referred to as the "Poorhouse of Thailand". Some of the original vegetation – sparse forest, open savanna and grass steppes – still remains. During the rainy period the wide river valleys are almost completely flooded, providing favourable conditions for growing rice and jute.

Rivers

The River Mun flows through the Khorat Plateau on its way to join the Mekong. Dams have been built across its northern tributaries for purposes of irrigation and to produce hydro-electric power. The Mekong, 4350km/2700 miles long and the 12th longest river in the world, is largely unsuitable for shipping because of its treacherous rapids. For 600km/373 miles it forms the frontier between Thailand and Laos; two completely different ideologies and forms of society come face to face here, which has frequently resulted in military conflict in the past.

West Thailand

In the west the Central South-East Asian mountain range of Tanen Tong Dan, rising to well over 2000m/6562ft in places, forms a natural frontier with the neighbouring state of Myanmar, formerly Burma. Particularly impressive is the Sam Roi Yot chain, the "mountain range of 300 peaks", which lies on the Gulf of Thailand south of Hua Hin.

South Thailand

The shape of Thailand is often likened to an elephant's head, in which case South Thailand would be the trunk. It forms the northern part of the elongated Malay Peninsula, and its mountain backbone is a continuation of the meridional chains of North Thailand.

Location

The Menam Plain with its mountainous foothills in the west forms the northern boundary of this region, while to the west the almost inaccessible Tenasserim Mountains constitute the natural frontier with

Limestone cliffs in southern Thailand

Myanmar and in the south the San Kara Khiri Mountains divide it from Malaysia. The peninsula separates two oceans from one another; the Gulf of Thailand and the South China Sea form a part of the Western Pacific, while in the west the Andaman Sea is a periphery of the Indian Ocean. If a canal were to be built across the Isthmus of Kra, which is only 64km/40 miles wide, the distance by sea from coast to coast would be reduced by 1300km/800 miles. Although discussions are held from time to time about such a plan it is unlikely to come to fruition because of the huge costs involved.

To the south the mountains divide into two roughly parallel chains running from north to south, the Phuket Mountains and the Nakhon Si Thammarat Mountains. The highest peak at 1835m/6022ft is Khao Luang west of Nakhon Si Thammarat.

Geology

Geologically speaking, this region is almost the same as North Thailand, its mountains being foothills of the latter. Limestone was deposited on a granite base; where the granite has come to the surface, which is often the case as a result of deformative and erosive processes, flat-capped mountains have resulted. In the limestone regions, on the other hand, precipitous rock formations dominate the landscape. These towering rocks are described by geologists as tropical karst cones, their formation having been linked to the warm and moist climate. The flat top is almost always covered in thick vegetation, while the walls are mostly so steep that they appear simply as blank stone. These towers of rock often taper towards their base; the reason for this is that as it runs down rainwater attacks the stone and overhangs are constantly breaking off.

Coasts and islands

Geological occurrences have had a marked effect on the coastline. The west coast has numerous bays and islands formed from steep-walled limestone rock. The east coast with its wide beaches is most charming

An abandoned tin-mine in Phuket

and has recently been opened up to tourism. Tectonic earth movements and landslips north of Songkhla have left large freshwater lakes.

The islands, such as Phuket, are fascinating. They were formed as the result of the tilting of the Malay Peninsula when the western part sank and the eastern end rose. In the course of this tectonic movement whole mountain ranges "were drowned" in the Andaman Sea, and only the peaks of the limestone rocks, covered in thick jungle, rose out of the sea in the form of islands. A boat trip in the Bay of Phangnga is a most impressive experience.

Tin-mining

Until the collapse of the tin cartel the rich deposits of tin in South Thailand made the region economically prosperous. When tin prices fell on the world market and a large number of mines were closed as a result, e.g. those on Phuket Island, few attempts was made to fill in the mines and they remain as unpleasant scars on an otherwise extremely attractive landscape.

Climate

Tropical climate

The climate of Thailand is determined by the monsoon, which produces tropical weather conditions throughout the year, resulting in high average temperatures (over 18°C/64°F well inland), and annual deviations are always less than daily deviations. The seasons are marked by changes from rainy to dry months rather than by any temperature differences as found in Europe and elsewhere.

When to go

The "coldest" months are December and January, with average daily maximum temperatures of 25°C/77°F, this being the most pleasant time for Europeans to visit. Yet the mercury level can fall below

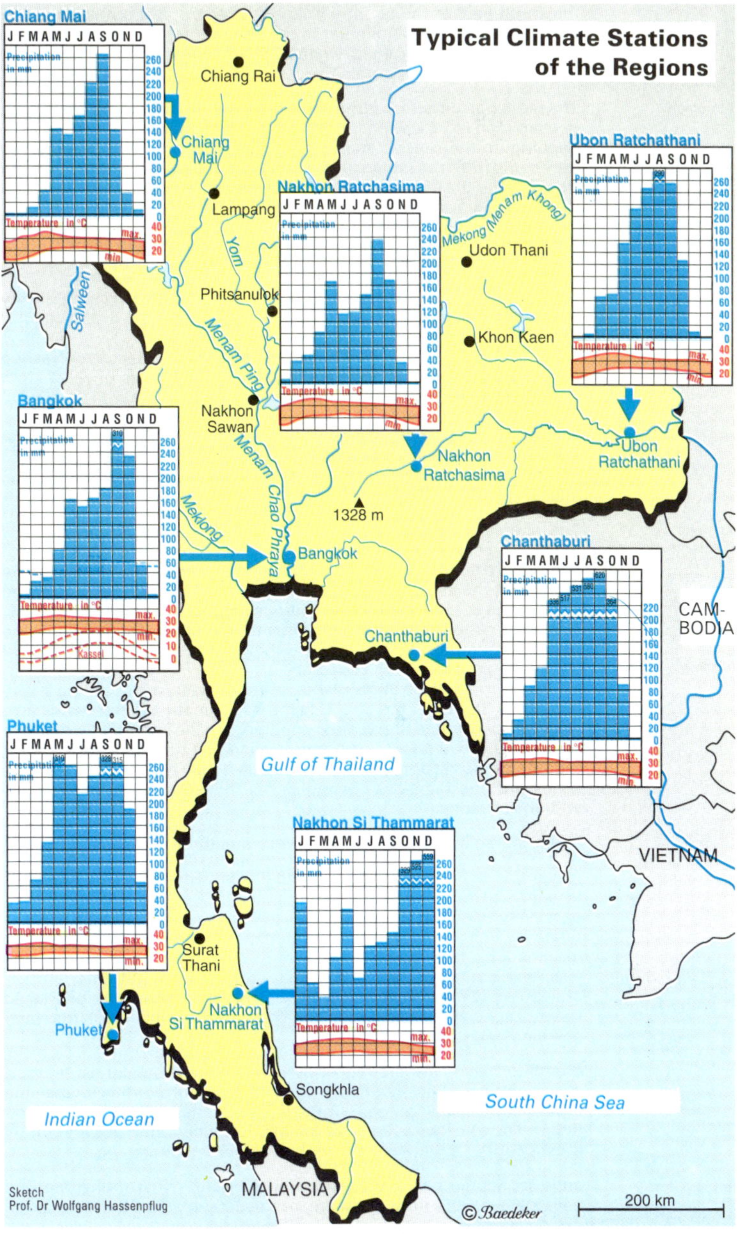
Typical Climate Stations of the Regions
Chiang Mai
Nakhon Ratchasima
Ubon Ratchathani
Bangkok
Chanthaburi
Phuket
Nakhon Si Thammarat
J F M A M J J A S O N D
Precipitation in mm
Temperature in °C
max.
min.
Kassel
Chiang Rai
Lampang
Phitsanulok
Nakhon Sawan
Udon Thani
Khon Kaen
Surat Thani
Songkhla
Salween
Yom
Menam Ping
Menam Chao Phraya
Meklong
Mekong (Menam Khong)
1328 m
Gulf of Thailand
South China Sea
Indian Ocean
CAMBODIA
VIETNAM
MALAYSIA
200 km
Sketch
Prof. Dr Wolfgang Hassenpflug
© Baedeker

10°C/50°F in the early morning during these months. It is then, too, that the south-east of the country enjoys a truly tropical but mainly very pleasant climate rather similar to the summer temperatures to which Europeans are accustomed. On the Gulf of Thailand in particular there is usually a pleasant cool breeze.

Monsoon

The monsoon determines the amount of rainfall. The monsoon climate is characterised by winds which blow from differing directions depending on the season and bring moist air masses with them when they come from the Indian or Pacific Ocean and dry air when they blow from the depths of Asia. Prevailing winds and air masses vary according to region and time of year.

Types of climate

Three different characteristic forms of tropical monsoon climate are to be found in Thailand:

1. The central region, the north and the north-east have a markedly dry climate in winter, known as the savanna climate. 83% of the country enjoys this climate type.
2. The eastern part of the south-east and the peninsula south of Nakhon Si Thammarat have a climate with only brief periods of relief from rainfall all the year round – a tropical rain-forest climate with a period of dryness. This applies to 13.6% of Thailand.
3. The east coast of the peninsula between Nakhon Si Thammarat and the Malaysian frontier has a humid climate all the year round, and no month has less than 60mm/2½in. of rain – a tropical rain-forest climate, affecting 3.4% of the country.

Climatic diagrams

The characteristics of these regions are illustrated on page 15 by means of climatic diagrams of typical meteorological stations with their yearly temperature and rainfall figures. The letters represent the months of the year. The temperatures are shown by a red band. The upper edge corresponds to the average highest daytime temperature, the lower edge the lowest night-time temperature. The height of the blue precipitation columns indicates how many millimetres of rain fall on average in the month concerned.

This form of illustration makes it unnecessary to quote so many individual figures in the text. Using these climatic diagrams it is also possible to estimate the weather conditions in the intervening regions; when doing so, it should be borne in mind that the windward sides of mountains attract appreciably more rainfall than the lee sides and that windward and lee sides change as the monsoon direction changes with the seasons.

Seasons

In the course of the year monsoons occur at three quite distinct times:

November to February is a cool time of year. The prevailing northerly to north-easterly winds originating in wintry Central Asia bring comparatively cool and dry air masses to Thailand. Accordingly there is relatively little humidity, cloud or rainfall during this period. There are months with less than 60mm/2½in. of rain, sometimes appreciably less, and not more than one or two rainy days. Night-time temperatures can fall well below 20°C/68°F. This is the best time of year to travel, especially if most sightseeing can be arranged for the early morning and the late afternoon.

March to May is the pre-monsoon period, when the highest temperatures of the year are attained. In the climatic diagrams this is when the temperature band "bulges" upward. The intense heat of the sun and temperatures often well above 35°C/95°F will be found unpleasant by most people.

June to September is the period of the south-west monsoon. The beginning of this time of the year is usually marked by the sudden

Evergreen rain-forest in southern Thailand

arrival of the monsoon accompanied by thunderstorms and violent cloudbursts followed by continuous rain. The cloud means that temperatures fall gently and humidity rises.

Rainy period

The beginning, nature and end of the monsoon rain period vary appreciably from year to year. During this time the weather is changeable, just as it is in Europe, with frequent areas of low pressure and brighter periods in between. However, amounts of rainfall are much greater than in Europe and thunderstorms much more frequent. The climatic diagrams show that monthly rainfall can be as much as 300mm/12in., even 600mm/24in., falling on 15 to 23 days in the month. The largest part of the annual rain falls in the few months of the summer monsoon. In those parts of Thailand which are dry in winter the annual precipitation amounts to between 1100 and 1500mm/44 to 60in., rising to 3000 or even 4000mm/120 or 160in. in the mountainous regions, especially in the south-east and in the Thailand peninsula.

When the monsoons change in spring and autumn the much-feared typhoons form over the tropical seas around Thailand, especially in the Gulf of Bengal, resulting in the destruction of large numbers of houses and heavy flooding.

Regions which are dry in winter

Centre (Bangkok)

This covers mainly the central region of Thailand, where high tropical temperatures persist in winter and the annual rainfall does not exceed 1100 to 1500mm/44 to 60in. It is only in the mountains which surround the central plains and hills that the rainfall amounts increase to as much as 3000mm/120in. per annum.

The climatic diagram for Bangkok clearly shows the three annual periods of its monsoon climate. From December to February the daily maxima are between 31 and 32°C/88 and 90°F; in the pre-monsoon period these then increase on average to 34 to 35°C/93 to 95°F, only to fall back to about 32°C/90°F with the onset of the south-west monsoon.

From December onwards – when on average only 2mm/0.1in. of rain falls on the one day on which it rains at all – the amount of rainfall first climbs slowly and then, with the arrival of the monsoon, abruptly until in September as much as 310mm/13in. may fall on fifteen days. In all, 1438mm/58in. falls in the course of the 88 days on which it rains.

North (Chiang Mai)

Because it is higher and further from the sea the north of Thailand is somewhat cooler and – apart from the mountains – drier than the central region. In Chiang Mai, which is 310m/1017ft above sea-level, the average annual temperature is 25.8°C/78.4°F, 1.3°C/2.3°F lower than in Bangkok. In Chiang Rai, at 380m/1247ft, the figure is 24.9°C/76.8°F.

The daily temperature fluctuations in Chiang Rai are markedly greater than in Bangkok, especially in winter and in the pre-monsoon period, when the night-time minima are relatively low (as indicated by the wide band on the climatic diagram). In the mountains near Chiang Mai and Chiang Rai it can then become very cold; when the air is dry a 1°C/1.8°F drop in temperature can be expected for every 100m/328ft increase in height.

Much of the humidity coming from the Gulf of Bengal is trapped by the Cordillera in the west on the border with Myanmar where it falls as rain, so that the region to the east thereof is the driest in the whole of Thailand. However, where air masses coming from the south climb the mountains on the northern edge of the country amounts of rainfall again increase (Chiang Mai 1332mm/52in., Chiang Rai 1837mm/72in. per annum; in both cases there are about 125 days in the year on which it rains).

North-east (Ubon Ratchathani)

The climate of north-eastern Thailand is similar to that in the neighbouring central and northern regions, but – in contrast to Bangkok – there is a more clearly defined dry period (less than three days of rain) between December and February. Also the amount of rain in September is less than that of Bangkok (on 21 rainy days instead of 23), which is explained by its being further from the sea.

Tropical Rain Forest Climate with a Short Dry Period

South-east (Chanthaburi)

In the south-east and on the Thailand peninsula rainfall amounts are noticeably higher than in the more continental north. Along the coast they increase sharply (Kap Lant 1100–1500mm/43–60in. annual rainfall, Koh Chang 3000–4000mm/120–160in.). At the Cambodian border the annual amount exceeds 3000mm/120in., and even in the driest month there are more than 60mm/2½in.

The dry winter period in this region is only short (one rainy day in December and/or two in January). On the other hand, the rainy period from May to October is long (17–25 days of rain) and heavy (between June and September alone the monthly average is well in excess of 500mm/20in., with a maximum of 620mm/25in. in September).

The early onset of the rainy season is attributable to the southern location, the heaviness of the rains, to the proximity of the sea and to the barrier effect of the mountains in the hinterland.

Tropical Rain Forest Climate

Malayan Peninsula

Further south the rainfall distribution shifts and changes in the course of the year. The dry periods are not clearly defined, with the result that a tropical rain-forest climate predominates throughout the year. The mountains and the fact that it is a peninsula mean that onshore winds carrying moist air from the sea have to climb on one side or the other, resulting in rain as they do so, while the lee-side is less moist.

East coast (Nakhon Si Thammarat)

Onshore winds from the east, which elsewhere blow only at the times of the south-east monsoons, bring rain here in winter as well, when the north is dry. The number of days of rain in Nakhon Si Thammarat is 185 per annum, one of the highest figures anywhere in the country, and even in the dry months six days of rain can be expected, with 20 to 22 in the wettest.

The chief period of rain lasts from October to January; two-thirds of the annual total of 2460mm/97in. fall during those months. Songkhla on the south of the east coast has 580mm/23in. in November. A somewhat lower rainfall peak is reached in May, when the south-west monsoon sets in bringing rain to the west coast (see climatic diagram for Phuket).

Temperatures are extremely even throughout the year, as a result of the proximity of the sea, and the heat of the pre-monsoon season is not very marked either.

The same weather pattern is repeated day in, day out. Day and night are each always twelve hours long, and the dusk and dawn periods are very short compared with those at higher latitudes such as Central Europe and the UK, each lasting only about a half an hour. As the sun rises clouds and sultriness increase, inevitably leading to thunder storms on 100 to 150 days of the year.

The tiring and oppressive sultry heat occurs when the air temperature and humidity are both high; when the air humidity measures 80 to 90% a temperature of 20°C/68°F is sufficient to produce these conditions. The most popular way to escape them is to stay on the coast, where morning sea-breezes will be found quite refreshing. The cool mountain regions will also provide relief from the sultry weather.

Heat of the sun

The tropical sun shining down from its zenith is extremely intense, and certainly visitors should not expose themselves to it for long without some form of protection. At noon, when the sun is directly overhead, a large sun-hat will suffice to protect the whole body, but the periods before and after midday, when the sun shines down equally strongly but at an angle, can be unpleasant. In the afternoon the heat of the sun is usually less owing to increasing cloud formation. In the late afternoon and early part of the night there are often thunderstorms and rain.

West coast (Phuket)

The west coast of Thailand north of Phuket as far as the Myanmar border is the country's wettest region (more than 4000mm/157in. annual rainfall). South of Ko Phuket Island the amounts reduce to between 2000 and 3000mm/80 and 120in.

The climatic diagram for Phuket shows two clear rainfall peaks. The first one in May corresponds to the south-west monsoon which arrives earlier here. As the monsoon moves further north the rain lessens somewhat, only to reach its second, even heavier and longer peak in September and October (2391mm/94in. over 181 days). Variations in temperature are minimal, as indicated by the narrow and straight band in the climatic diagram. Otherwise the daily weather pattern is the same as that for the east coast as described above.

Flora and Fauna

Flora

Thailand's vegetation can be described under two headings; whereas the north and south regions of the country are predominantly tropical forest, the agricultural land of the Menam Basin is covered in paddy-fields almost as far as the eye can see and that of the Malay Peninsula is synonymous with rubber plantations. Nearly half the country is forest; however, for a long time now these areas have no longer been the primary forests which grew here for centuries, but merely secondary forests. Uncontrolled felling, especially of fine timbers such as teak, and the lack of any proper re-afforestation planning has meant that large areas of jungle are now just bush.

The Thailand forest can be divided into two main groups, according to climate and variations in land height. In the south and south-east tropical forest predominates, whereas in the north-east and other areas of the country we find arid monsoon forests of deciduous trees.

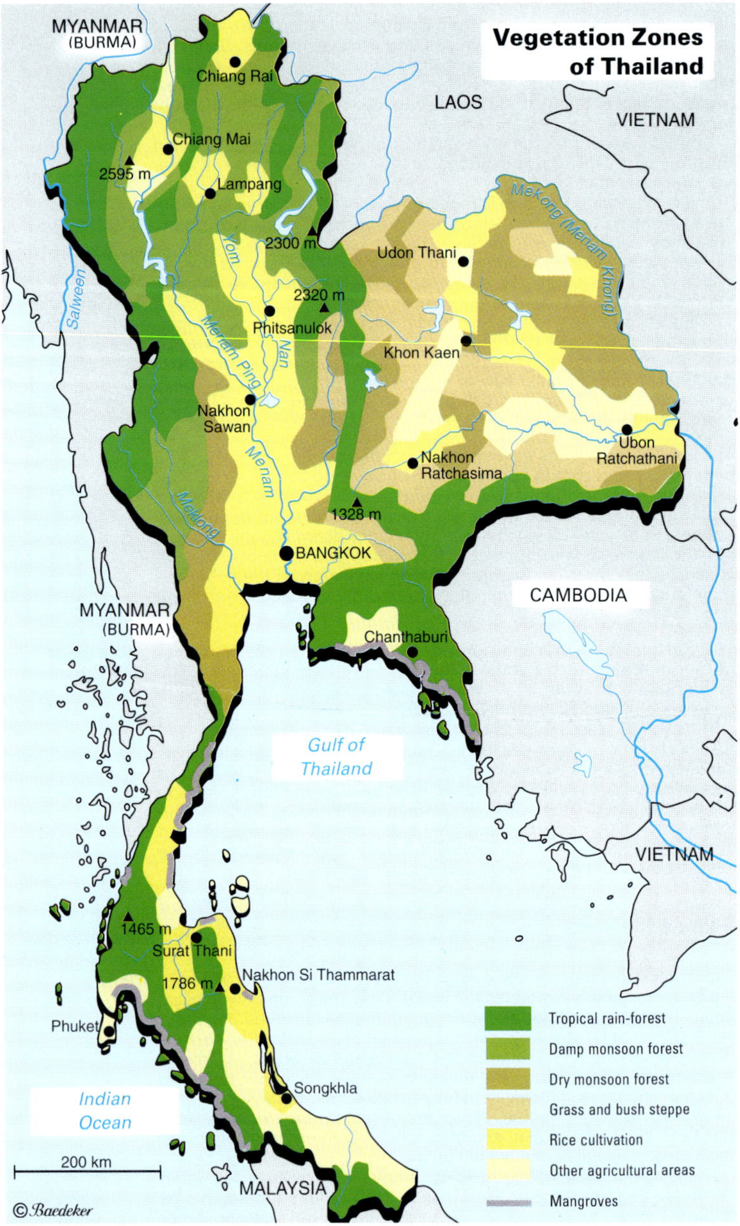
Vegetation Zones of Thailand
MYANMAR (BURMA)
LAOS
VIETNAM
Chiang Rai
Chiang Mai
2595 m
Lampang
Mekong (Menam Khong)
2300 m
Udon Thani
Yom
Salween
2320 m
Phitsanulok
Menam Ping
Nan
Khon Kaen
Nakhon Sawan
Menam
Ubon Ratchathani
Nakhon Ratchasima
Mekong
1328 m
BANGKOK
CAMBODIA
MYANMAR (BURMA)
Chanthaburi
Gulf of Thailand
VIETNAM
1465 m
Surat Thani
Nakhon Si Thammarat
1786 m
Phuket
Songkhla
Indian Ocean
200 km
MALAYSIA
© Baedeker
Tropical rain-forest
Damp monsoon forest
Dry monsoon forest
Grass and bush steppe
Rice cultivation
Other agricultural areas
Mangroves

Gum-tree plantation near Songkhla

The Khorat Plateau is somewhat unique; many years of overfelling have produced level grassy plains similar to the Russian steppes; during the rainy season the rivers overflow their banks and form swampy lakes.

Rain forest

The tropical rain forest is a primeval forest just as one imagines it. However, self-contained forests as such are still to be found only on the Malay Peninsula, the coastal strips of Southern Thailand and to the north near the Myanmar border. Experts believe that, if deforestation continues at the present rate, by the year 2000 there will be little left of the "King of Forests", not only in Thailand but in neighbouring Malaysia and Myanmar as well. The prohibition on the felling of tropical timber which was imposed by the Thai government in 1989 will in fact not change matters very much; since then imports of timber from the neighbouring countries have increased several times. It was not so very long ago that some two-thirds of Thailand was still covered in thick and unspoilt rain forest. Uncontrolled felling of the primary forests with very little re-planting and the burning of the soil as practised for centuries by the rural population have resulted in large areas being turned into scrubland. Today Thailand has to import nearly a half of its timber for building from other countries, whereas a few years ago it was self-sufficient in this respect.

The tropical rain forest is a completely impenetrable tangle of many and varied types of vegetation, which exist at various "floors". On the ground grow shade-loving bushes, ferns and small trees. The middle "storey" – mainly dipterocarpaceae, a family of evergreen plants comprising more than 40 species in Asia alone – goes up to about 25m/80ft, and above this tower the mighty yang or takhian trees, as they are known on the Malay Peninsula. The tropical rain forests are also the natural habitat of a vast range of animals of various species.

Dwarf palm

Coconut palm

Palm garden

Palms

Palm trees, of which there are numerous varieties in Thailand, are economically valuable. Coconut-palms are found mainly in the south of the country; their fruits are eaten and the refreshing milk drunk, while the shell is first dried and later used by the rural population as a cheap form of fuel. Oil from the oil-palms is exported to many countries where it is used, for example, as a raw material in the cosmetic industry.

Mangroves

The mangrove-forests in South Thailand, areas of unpretentious trees which can tolerate saltwater, are an unusual feature. At low tide the forests dry out to some extent but the deep mud makes them inaccessible. The mud becomes deposited among the tangled roots above ground, causing the coastal strips to silt up.

Economic use

There is still a large variety of different species of trees to be found in Thailand. Since the felling of teak trees was prohibited in 1988 lignified bamboo-grass has been intensively cultivated. Bamboo is used for building houses as well as for making furniture, household objects and musical instruments, while bamboo-shoots are a favourite ingredient in Thai and Chinese cooking. In addition there are pine trees, oaks and the hardwood known as yang. Another type of wood is known as rattan, a liana-like climbing and twisting palm of the rain-forest, used mainly for furniture-making. Thailand is one of the world's major exporters of rattan.

Clearing land by burning

Clearing land by burning, together with irresponsible cultivation by nomads, has also been largely to blame for the decline of the forests. For centuries tribes have moved on to pastures new after first exhausting the soil and have then proceeded to burn down the forest somewhere else. The wood-ash did admittedly act as a fertiliser, but only for a short time. As the fallow land was not re-timbered and the native vegetation re-appeared only sparsely savanna-like areas were formed, where the quick-growing bamboo predominated. It is only in recent years that an organised re-afforestation programme has been introduced in the northern parts of the country.

Flowering plants

Thailand can also boast a rich and impressive variety of flowering plants. As well as the lotus-flower and water-lily there are jasmine,

A fascinating variety of orchids in Thailand

hibiscus, luxuriant bouganvillaea and the white, yellow or red flowers of the frangipani. Thailand is the natural habitat of hundreds of different species of orchids, some of which are threatened with extinction.

Land Fauna

Thailand's fauna is particularly rich and varied in the thinly-populated western regions and in the mountains in the north, where large numbers of lemurs, jackals, various species of bear and big cats can be found. However, the numbers of tapirs, rhinos and elephants – the latter still being used today as working animals in the rough jungle – have been sadly decimated.

Elephants

There are still about 5000 Indian elephants in Thailand; in years gone by there were probably four times as many. These mighty animals

A "white" elephant in the Chitralada Palace in Bangkok

have always played an important part in Thai life, and have been depicted on the country's flag and coins. Kings fought wars seated on their backs, and reparation payments were often made by handing over giant herds of the beasts. One of the most important events in the life of Buddha was his meeting with an elephant which his wicked cousin had sent to trample him down; legend has it that it was only the power of his love which enabled the Enlightened One to save himself from being attacked.

The current role of the elephant in Thailand is far more secular. It is indispensable in the primeval forests of the north, where it is still used in forestry work even though teak trees may no longer be felled. The elephant is led by a driver (mahout) and will obey only him. Although elephants are mostly good-tempered they tend to become rather unpredictable during the winter months. The reason for this is a secretion which issues from a small hole in its head during the mating season and which tends to get into the animal's eyes. Its proverbial good memory – especially as regards unpleasant experiences – has suprised and even cost the lives of many a mahout.

The gestation period of a female elephant lasts 23 months, and it continues to provide maternal protection for a further three years. A baby elephant weighs about 100kg/220lb at birth and stands 75cm/30in. high. Elephants can live to be 100 in some cases, although the average is about 80; their best years are between 25 and 60. It is then that they work about eight hours a day, while enjoying a "holiday" during the hot months of April and May. At the age of three or so they are trained for their future work in "elephant schools". One such school, run by the state, will be found near Lampang; the best time to visit it is in the early morning.

There are also several elephant kraals at the main tourist centres (e.g. in Pattaya), where they can be observed – often posing for photographs – while being instructed and working.

"White elephants"

The "white elephant", even though – strictly speaking – there is no such thing in zoological terms, enjoys reverential status in Thailand. There are 32 special features which differentiate it from its fellows. For instance, it has twenty toe-nails instead of sixteen and has red eyes. Contrary to popular opinion, however, it is not completely white, but in fact differs only in having largish or smallish white patches on head and ears. The more such animals are found during the period of a king's reign the luckier these years are supposed to be for the ruler and his people. With sixteen white elephants, eleven of which still survive, the reign of King Bhumibol must be under a particularly lucky star!

After being caught they are declared holy elephants at a special ceremony and then kept for a while in the Dusit Zoo in Bangkok in order to acclimatise them, after which they are housed in magnificent stables in the royal Chitralada Palace (which is not open to the public) where they are lovingly cared for.

Elephant Festival in Surin

On the third weekend in November every year the colourful Elephant Festival is held in Surin. Not only does the visitor have plenty of opportunities to use his camera, he can also obtain an insight into the lives of the rural population. Many travel agencies in Bangkok offer excursions lasting one or more days.

Monkeys

Monkeys, most of whom live in packs, are to be found mainly in the many natural parks in Thailand, but sometimes in urban surroundings as well, such as in Lopburi and Wat Phra Prang Sam Yot. While most are shy of humans, some are bolder, even aggressive, and will play tricks on visitors who get too close. In Southern Thailand monkeys are trained to pick coconuts, and in tourist centres visitors may try to include them in souvenir photographs.

Working animals

Cattle, particularly the giant gaur (wild ox) and water-buffalo, are widely used, especially in agriculture, where they are quite indispensable.

Birds and butterflies

Based on a count carried out in 1991, the rain-forests are home to no less than 951 species of birds including a number which are now very rare. The best place to observe birds is in the national parks, and the Bangkok Bird Club arranges regular ornithological trips; for information write to P.O. Box 13, Ratchathewi Post Office, Bangkok 10401.

There are also a large number of tropical butterflies, some of which are rare. In order not to endanger their future it is suggested that visitors might prefer to refrain from buying preserved butterflies which they will find on sale everywhere in tourist resorts.

Also worthy of mention are the flying foxes (*pteropus vampyrus*), whose wing-span can be as much as 1.5m/5ft and which flies in swarms of thousands, as well as other flying mammals such as bats and flying dragons, including the smallest living mammal, a bat only the size of a bumble-bee, which was discovered in North Thailand.

Mosquitoes

In North Thailand especially, as well as on the islands in the south, visitors should take great care to protect themselves from the malaria-carrying mosquitoes. In these regions hotels often provide protective nets which should be used while sleeping.

Geckos

Geckos are small house-lizards which are particularly attracted by light and make a chattering noise. These little animals are completely harmless. They are welcomed in the house because they feed on pests and vermin, and are also used in games and races!

Reptiles

Giant reptiles (crocodiles, monitor lizards) as well as snakes, including some poisonous varieties such as cobras and vipers, inhabit all parts of the country. Generally speaking they are shy of humans, but nevertheless it is always wise to wear stout footwear when wading through

A female monkey with offspring

A grey-headed parrot

paddy-fields or walking through forests. Even when watching Thailand's crocodiles in a "domesticated" environment inside a protected arena great care should still be taken especially in the brackish water regions between land and sea. The most dangerous is the estuarine crocodile (*crocodylus porosus*), which can be very aggressive when faced with danger.

Animal contests

The Thai people enjoy a bet, and seem especially drawn to cock-fighting contests which are very popular especially in country districts. Specially reared birds are used for this form of "sport". The same applies to the highly-coloured fighting fish which are let loose on one another in large aquaria.

Marine Fauna

Nature Conservancy

In past years the underwater world off the coasts has been excessively exploited by Thais and tourists alike. For a long time now there have no longer been so many beautiful and unspoiled hunting grounds for divers (see Practical Information, Sport). Visitors who are keen divers should therefore act responsibly and avoid causing further damage to the beautiful world under the sea. The plundering of coral banks is strictly prohibited, and the police carry out spot-checks on returning ships and boats.

Corals

Corals are marine polyps, members of the phylum coelenterata, which protect themselves with a chalky shell. They settle mainly in large colonies in waters with strong currents warmed by the strong sun. Large coral banks can still be found off the coasts of the Andaman Sea. They are gloriously colourful – some well-travelled divers liken them to those of the Red Sea. Pieces of sharp coral are often washed ashore, so it is best always to wear rubber or plastic bathing shoes.

Fish

In the diving regions off the Thailand coast the principal fish found are puffer-fish and sticklebacks of the genera arothron and tetraodon.

A mass of coral in the Indian Ocean

A tropical fish

Evening bath for water-buffalo

Those puffer-fish which, when danger threatens, can "inflate" themselves to five times their normal size, are favourites with divers. They are also a threatened species, because the Japanese regard them as a rich delicacy ("fugu"). Their gall-bladder contains a poison which can be fatal to humans, and only those who have been specially trained and have a licence are permitted to prepare them for eating. Divers should also not overestimate the good-naturedness of the sticklebacks which can inflict a nasty wound when provoked.

Being rich in protein, fish are a valuable supplement to a rice-based diet, but unfortunately – as the result of over-fishing especially just off the coast – fishing in the Gulf of Thailand has become a rather laborious and unprofitable way of earning a living (see Economy).

Sharks

Sharks appear here and there off the Thailand coasts. Even though they normally stay well away from the shore it is still advisable to exercise care when venturing into the open sea. This is particularly true when riding on the "waterscooters" which can be hired at the bathing resorts, and those using them should not venture far from land.

Shellfish and crustaceans

Shellfish such as lobsters or crabs are a special delicacy for visitors to Thailand and are also caught in large quantities off the coasts of the islands to the south. Crayfish and mussels are also popular with the native population.

Population

Structural Details

Numbers

The population of Thailand is about 56.9 million, averaging 109.8 inhabitants per sq.km/284 per sq. mile (the figures given here are from the 1991 census). More than 80% are native Thai peoples such as the

Siamese, Chan and Lao. Important minorities include Malays, especially in the south, Chinese, Indians in Bangkok and the tourist centres, and members of hill tribes in the north.

Population growth

Not least as a result of a government birth-control programme, the annual increase in the birth-rate has been falling since the end of the 1960s; between 1970 and 1987 the figure fell by over 25%. Between 1960 and 1990 the population almost doubled, but currently the annual growth is about 1.5%. Particular difficulties were encountered among the rural population in carrying out the family planning programme. Using the slogan "That which costs nothing is worth nothing" a charge – albeit a very small one – was made by those who helped to distribute contraceptives in the villages. The United Nations are predicting that the Thai population will increase to some 80–90 million by the year 2025. Statistics clearly show the generation changes which have taken place. Today about 65% of the population are under 30, while only 3.9% are over 65. However, the percentage of older people is increasing as medical standards improve; whereas in 1960 the average life expectancy was only 50 for men and 55 for women, it is now 61 and 65 respectively.

Migration from the land

Increasing numbers of people leaving the land for the towns is causing considerable problems. One in seven of the inhabitants of Bangkok was not born in the capital. The 1991 census showed that 5.6 million people were crammed into an area of 1600sq.km/618sq. miles, with the entire conurbation of Bangkok encompassing a population of over 8 million. The number of slum dwellers is unknown as they are not registered. Thus about one tenth of Thailand's total inhabitants live in the capital city, which has a population density of 3500 to every square kilometre. In contrast, Chiang Mai, the second largest town in the country, has only about 150,000 inhabitants. The most thinly populated provinces are those of Tak and Mae Hong Son on the border with Myanmar, with only 19.0 and 12.6 inhabitants per square kilometre respectively. At the bus station the visitor can witness every morning the arrival of hundreds of new citizens drawn to the city from the poorer rural areas as if by a magnet. Like their predecessors they hope to find work and food in the "Heavenly Capital". A large number of such immigrants come from the poor north-east and the neighbouring country of Laos, where an almost common language together with a "little border trade" facilitates entering and living in Thailand.

Population Groups

Nowadays the population of Thailand is an ethnic mix which does not stop at the political boundaries. Both sides of the semi-inaccessible mountains to the west are inhabitated by hill tribes who can be said to have links with both Thailand and Myanmar. In the south lives a race closely allied both ethnically and culturally with the Malays and including a large number of Moslems. These communities are described in more detail below.

Thai (Siamese)

85% of the population can be described as Siamese. Also among the Thai people can be numbered the Chan on the Myanmar border and the Lao and Meo in the north and north-east. The origin of the Thai people has not been explained beyond all doubt. However, research has shown that they originated from the valley of Yang Tse in Southern China. They are thought to have founded the first independent kingdom called Nan Chao *c.* A.D. 650. The conquest of this kingdom by the Mongol Kublai Chan (Kubla Khan) in 1253 led to an exodus in which Thais mixed with those races that originated from China from A.D. 800 onwards and moved to the Mekong delta and settled there. In 1257 the first sovereign kingdom of Siam was founded with Sukhothai as its capital.

People of Thailand

Hill tribes

The hill tribes in the north, of Tibeto-Burmese and Sino-Laotian origin, play a special part. Six different tribes are recognised by the Thai government, which is trying to integrate the 58,000 Hmong (Meo), 40,000 Lahu, 30,000 Yao, 24,000 Akha and 18,000 Lisu. In addition there are some 246,000 Carians (see below), whose settlements can be found deep in the south of the country. The various tribes seem to get on well with one another, and their villages are often found in close proximity. Each of the peoples has its own culture and way of living, the main common factor being their belief in the supernatural and the attribution of a living soul to plants and inanimate objects.

All the hill tribes are skilled in the production of hand-made goods, and they sell their products on the markets in the towns of Chiang Mai,

An Akha woman and child

A photogenic hill-tribe child

Chiang Rai and Mae Hong Son. The Thai government runs the "Thai Hillcraft Foundation" in Chiang Rai which organises the sale of many such handicrafts, especially silverware and embroidered and woven goods. In another such institution, the "Mae Fah Luang Foundation" (named after the king's mother), young girls are trained in traditional handicrafts and young men in agriculture. They then return to their villages to teach these skills to other members of the tribe.

The elderly mother of King Bhumibol is treated with great reverence by the hill tribes, who have bestowed upon her the name of "Mae Fah Luang", or "Heavenly Mother of the King". In fact this title has secular origins, because when she visited the extreme north of Thailand she swept down in a "Bird of Heaven" (a helicopter). She has worked extremely hard to obtain subscriptions to help bring about the integration of the hill tribes, as well as founding a number of institutions which help the tribes to maintain their traditions while still enabling them to benefit from the country's economic progress.

Karens

There is considerable doubt as to where the Carians originally came from, but it is thought to be south-west China or south-east Tibet. Most Carians today live in Myanmar. Those who moved on into Thailand number among the best-integrated of all the hill tribes. Their villages are found along a line stretching from Mae Hong Son through Central Thailand and deep into the south along the Myanmar border. They originally settled in the northern mountains between Myanmar and Thailand, but were forced into the valleys by marauding tribes. They obtain their living solely from agriculture; the growing of opium is no longer an important source of income.

Akha, Lisu and Lahu

The opium-growing Akha, Lisu and Lahu tribes, living in the regions north of Chiang Mai as far as the "Golden Triangle", consider themselves culturally linked with Myanmar (Burma) and dress accordingly.

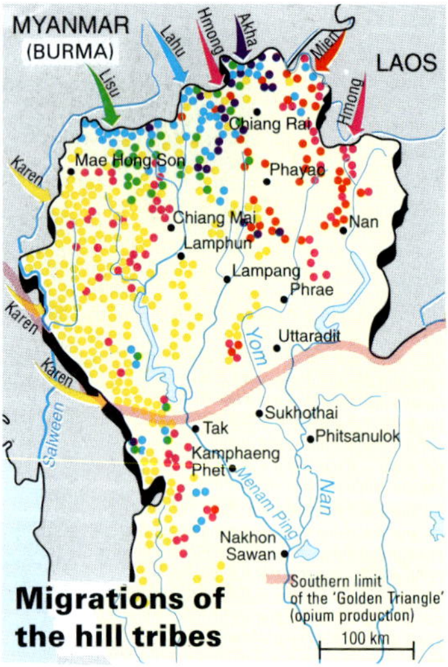

Migrations of the hill tribes

Their language belongs to the Tibeto-Burmese family of languages. While the Akha and Lahu have since the early 20th century been moving out of the South Chinese province of Yunnan across Eastern Burma and Northern Laos into Thailand, the Lisu came from the valley of the River Salween in China and migrated across Northern Burma and through Kentung.

However, those members of these three tribes who now live in Thailand form only a small part of their total number, and the majority still live where they originally settled.

The Akha feel themselves very closely linked with their ancestors, believe in spirits of all kinds and hold fiercely on to the old traditions. For example, they pray to their forefathers for food and protection from sickness and death. Their belief that one day their ancestors will return to Earth and once more occupy their villages has been a large thorn in the flesh of the Thai government in its attempts to persuade the tribe to re-settle eleswhere.

The Akha mainly make a living from agriculture, especially the cultivation of rice and vegetables, although there is still the odd field of opium poppies in some villages on the Myanmar border.

Lisu

The Lisu are dedicated to striving to obtain a position of eminence, and the children are raised in accordance with very strict principles of achievement. The – mostly large – families are based on strict patriarchal lines and village jurisdiction is in the hands of the strongest clan. They make a living from growing vegetables.

Hmong (Meo)
Yao (Mien)

The languages spoken by the Hmong (Meo) and Yao (Mien) belong to the Sino-Tibetan family, and their villages are to be found mainly in the Chiang Rai and Nan provinces. They originally came from Central China; from Laos they crossed the Mekong and, after a stay in refugee camps along the Cambodian border they entered Northern Thailand. In 1975 they found themselves the victims when the orthodox Communist Pol Pot gained power; because they had previously fought on the side of the anti-Communists they had no option but to flee from their adopted homeland. In recent years considerable progress has been made in housing them in permanent villages.

The Yao have retained the language and literature of their old homeland. The Meo live mainly from the growing of opium poppies, even though alternatives encouraged by the Thai government are gaining some ground. Polygamy is still the norm and, like the Lisu, their lives are firmly geared to the patriarchal system.

Some of the Meo and Lisu are nomadic farmers; when the soil becomes exhausted after a few years of burning and relentless cropping they move on and build new villages elsewhere.

Karen woman at the weaving-frame

Mabri (Yellow Leaves)

The Mabri, also known as the "Yellow Leaves" as a result of their custom of going naked apart from covering their private parts with a leaf, are a tribe of hunters and collective nomads whose ethnology has not been researched in any detail. To date they have resisted any attempts to encourage them to settle permanently. Some 200 live in the hills around Nan.

Moslems

There are some 1.7 million Moslems in Thailand, of which 99% are Sunnites and 1% Shi'ites. Most of them are of Arab-Malayan origin and live mainly in the southern parts of the country in the four border provinces of Satun, Yala, Pattani and Narathiwat. Some years ago they showed little willingness to be integrated into society and were a source of constant unrest, but there are now signs that the efforts made in that direction by the king's mother in particular are bearing fruit. Today not only is Islam tolerated in Thailand, it now enjoys protection under the law and its feast-days are publicly celebrated. About 100 mosques in Bangkok alone and more than 2000 throughout the country as well as 200 Koran schools bear witness to the status of Islam in Thailand (see also Religion).

Family Life and Society

The individual and society

In Asian society it is the collective community rather than the individual which is of major importance. The consequence of this view is a continual struggle for compromise and to involve as many people as possible. Putting one's own interests before those of others is unusual; the Asian always considers the needs of the community. Personality scarcely comes into play; subordination to the existing social order is considered to be much more important. The origins of this pattern of behaviour can be found in the teachings of Confucius which sees people not as individuals but as a total being. This "being" is ideally at one with the "three harmonies": harmony with the human world, harmony with nature and harmony with the spiritual world.

Muslim children in southern Thailand

Family and children

In spite of Westernisation the Thai people have retained their own cultural and social identity. The family is a closely-knit unit, often including servants and employees. The family provides security to all provided that behavioural codes based on age, sex and rank are closely observed. There are twenty times as many terms to define family relationships as there are in Western society; the particular word used describes the degree of relationship (parent, brother, sister, uncle, aunt, male or female cousin), the age ("younger" or "elder") and the side of the family ("maternal" or "paternal"). These terms are used more frequently in address than the person's actual name.

In a Thai family nobody is ever alone, even though they may sometimes seem to be so to a visitor from the West. Even in houses with several bedrooms nobody sleeps alone unless he or she expressly wishes to do so. Right from infancy the young Thai experiences this sense of togetherness. A mere whimper is enough for a child to be scooped up, soothed and rocked back and forth. As soon as it can crawl and toddle it is carried everywhere, usually naked, perched on an older sister's hip, in the crook of her arm, a position in which the little one can sleep, play and even eat whenever it wants. There does not seem to be a rigid daily routine with set sleeping times. It will seem strange to the visitor to Thailand that even the smallest children are still awake at midnight and only go to bed when they are really tired.

The children are hardly ever scolded or smacked nor is rejection used as a form of punishment. Gentle methods of conditioning are preferred; a Thai mother would never say "If you do that you will be punished!" but instead appeals to the child's sense of shame and says "If you do that the others will laugh at you!" There is an essential difference in the way Asian and Western societies bring up their children. Whereas Western parents try to encourage the child to be independent from an early age Asian parents protect their children from worries and conflict and keep them in the bosom of the family for as

"Dead to the world" – sleeping children

long as possible. The result, to a certain extent, is a collectivisation which manifests itself in later life as indecisiveness or shying away from conflict.

Bringing up girls

Girls and boys are brought up in the same way until they are six years old when preparation for their separate roles begins. For girls this consists of motherliness, shyness, selflessness and modesty. At the same time the woman is portrayed in legends as a heroine but symbolically dressed in men's clothes. Often cited are the two sisters, Chan and Muk, who disguised themselves as men during the siege of Phuket in order to trick the enemy into believing it faced a large army.

Hierarchies

Respect for their elders by the younger generation is very important in Asian societies. Grandparents command the greatest respect followed by the parents, relatives and older brothers and sisters. Total obedience is second nature to the Asian child. This later finds expression in almost unconscious suppression of one's own self so that to contradict a superior is unthinkable.

In Thailand the concept of rank is all-pervasive and every Thai is always aware of his rank in society. It is expressed even in terms of address, e.g. Khun preceding the name indicates someone of higher or occasionally similar status, never someone of a lower social position. This concept is, however, not comparable with the Indian caste system. The Thai is concerned only with his own role in life which he carries out to the letter. Yet he lives in hope of a better existence in some future life.

Role of women

The role of women in Thai society also has its roots in tradition, but has changed in recent years. True emancipation, however, in the Western sense, is limited to certain areas of employment. According to the latest figures for 1988, out of 27·5 million Thai women 11·5 million are

Heroic legendary figures: the Sisters Chan and Muk

engaged in employment! It is unusual to find women in positions of commercial responsibility although educational and career opportunities are, in theory, open to all.

King Chulalongkorn (Rama V) opened up access to all schools but equality for boys and girls was not realised until a law was passed by King Rama VI in 1921. It was 1930 before women could study law and they were barred from political office until the early 1930s. Not until 1949 did a woman from the province of Ubon Ratchathani enter Parliament, and 27 years later Loesak became the first female minister of the Kingdom, as Minister of Transport. However, in the parliamentary election in 1988 it was obvious that Thai women, often metaphorically described as the rear legs of an elephant (without which it would fall down) still had to fight to establish themselves in public life: of the 3800 or so candidates less than 10% were women.

Influence of other cultures

The observant visitor will not fail to notice that the cosmopolitan character and life-style found in Bangkok is not typical of Thailand as a whole. The majority of the people live a modest life enriched by those simple pleasures so suited to the Thai mentality. Anyone who attempts to judge Thailand merely by what he finds in Bangkok has not learned to know the country. Just a few miles from the capital will be found the rural life so typical of Asian peoples. The degree of Westernisation found mainly in the tourist centres can be attributed largely to the regents of the Chakri dynasty who were educated in the West. Rama VII, for example, was born in Heidelberg and lived in Germany for a number of years; the present King Bhumibol grew up with his brothers and sisters in Switzerland, where he also spent his student years. Later Europeans, Americans (the latter especially during the Korea and Vietnam war) and Australians employed by multi-national firms played an important part and created their own little world in Bangkok.

Sextourism

Thailand is one of the main destinations for "sextourists" from all over the world. Of the 5 million or so tourists who visit the country each year 40 to 50% are men travelling alone in search of sexual contacts.

Even though it is often asserted that prostitution (which was prohibited by law from 1960 to 1981) is rooted in the country's tradition and culture, nevertheless mass prostitution is a phenomenon of recent years. The "rest centres" set up for American servicemen during the Indo-Chinese war can be said to have been the start of commercialised sex. According to the international aid organisation "Médecins Sans Frontières" over 200,000 children and young people are forced into prostitution; in Pattaya alone there are thought to be 20,000 prostitutes of whom one half are boys and girls between twelve and fourteen years of age. The main procurers are Mafia-like organisations, frequently including Americans and Europeans, using Thai front-men. Most of the women, girls and boys are recruited by touts (some even sold by their families out of sheer desperation) and passed on to bordello-owners and pimps in all the large towns and cities. Usually these procurers tempt their victims with false promises, such as a place in a school or a job in a town frequented by tourists.

The need to resort to prostitution is mainly the result of economic and social problems. Many girls and women who become prostitutes come from the poorer parts of the country such as the north-east as well as from neighbouring Laos and Myanmar (Burma). The concentration of industry around Bangkok has led to the neglect of rural areas and to large groups of people getting badly into debt. For many women prostitution is the only way they can earn enough to feed themselves and their families; almost all prostitutes feel duty-bound to help support their relatives.

The ugly consequences of prostitution are not limited to the physical and emotional health of the individual concerned. As sexual morality in Thailand is strict (pre-marital and extra-marital sex is forbidden for women and tacitly tolerated in men) the women are regarded as social outcasts and have little chance of later being able to lead a "respectable" life. There is also the risk of being infected with Aids; according to estimates made by the World Health Organisation 4 million Thais will be infected by the year 2000.

Particularly disturbing is the increase in child and adolescent prostitution. After years of vacillation the Thai government has officially declared war on the trade and apparently really means business. Premises of doubtful repute are regularly searched, "sextourists" who have been arrested are brought before the courts and subsequently expelled from the country for life (in the majority of cases with the criminal prosecution authorities in the convicted person's home country being informed of the crimes committed). Furthermore, a number of well-known European travel operators have declared their readiness actively to combat any involvement – implied or otherwise – with child and youth prostitution.

Living Conditions

In towns

Typical of Bangkok and other large towns are the uniform houses which – apart from hotels, bank buildings and the offices of multinational concerns – are built in rows along mainly straight streets. The ground floor is often used as shops, workshops and the like which are simply closed with a roller blind in the evening, while employees and workers live on the first floor, the owners on the second and the older members of the family on the upper floor. If the family is prosperous it may have a small, mainly trellised roof garden where shadow boxing and other gymnastics take place in the morning and people socialise in the evening.

It is very rare for a Thai on an average wage to be able to afford a separate, self-contained dwelling. These tend to be reserved for the "middle classes" and are usually surrounded by high walls, often

Apartment block in Bangkok

A Thai family at their house in the country

surmounted by jagged glass – outward signs of the marked degree of security-consciousness prevalent today.

The drastic lowering of the water table in Bangkok has now made possible the construction of many high-rise buildings, which to an increasing degree are changing the face of the Thai capital. These sorts of buildings were not previously feasible because of the muddy subsoil.

In the country

Of the traditional Thai houses which were built everywhere in the countryside around the turn of the century very few remain. Although some of the traditional features are still used in house-building today, such as the pointed and crossed gable sections, they have been largely replaced by more practical and purpose-built houses. Nevertheless, the main building material used in rural areas is still wood, just as it has been for centuries.

When Ernst von Hesse-Wartegg visited Thailand in 1899 he wrote that the Thais displayed much artistic skill in building their houses, most of which were constructed without the use of metal parts or nails. The individual sections, standing on a firm base formed by teak tree-trunks rammed into the ground, were simply tied together with lengths of rope made from rattan.

The traditional Thai house is built on piles. This makes it safe from floods during the rainy season, while the space underneath can be used at other times for storage, a workshop or even as accommodation for some members of the family. Pigs, dogs and birds are often kept there, too.

Most roofs are covered with palm leaves. Even today most houses in the countryside do not have glass windows, protection from the weather being provided by wooden shutters over the windows.

Division into rooms is extremely simple; often there is only one large room which serves as sitting room, dining room and bedroom for the entire family. While electric light is now normally installed running water or even a bath is the exception rather than the rule. Large earthenware pots are kept ready full of water, often rain water which has been gathered, and even those not members of the family can take a drink from them.

Only the middle classes can dream of owning their own houses. Land prices are reasonable and plots are allocated by the authorities. The poorer people, namely those paid by the day, as well as peasants, often live near where they work in simple straw huts which provide only limited protection from wind and weather.

Health Services

Health services in Thailand have been basically reformed and greatly improved in recent years, for which Queen Sirikit and her daughter Princess Sirindhorn can take much of the credit. Nevertheless there continue to be problems with those diseases which tend to be prevalent in South-East Asia. These are headed by diarrhoea, followed by various sexual diseases, dysentery, influenza, scarlet fever and measles. Malaria, one of the most common infectious diseases in South-East Asia, on the other hand appears to have largely died out, and now only the south-east of the country can be described as a malaria region.

Improvements in health care and general welfare have also meant that epidemics and acute illnesses can be detected very quickly and counter-measures taken. In recent years there has been an intensive state programme of inoculation of children against tetanus, tuberculosis, measles, mumps and cholera.

However, statistics show that the main causes of death in Thailand are not the diseases usually associated with the Third World but rather those of the affluent society – heart disease, cancer and liver and kidney problems are more common than malaria and cholera. However, these statistics only include deaths following treatment in hospital.

Medical treatment

"Health Centers" run by the Ministry of Health play an important part in the health of the country. These are divided into four categories. Centres belonging to Class 1 must have at least ten beds and a doctor, while those of Class 2 provide basic care with the help of a trained nurse and a midwife. The 3rd class of centre are "mother and child centres" with in-patient facilities; these are found mainly in rural areas and have resulted in the number of infant mortalities in the first year of life being cut by half. The 4th class are village natal clinics.

Well-trained doctors, including many who qualified in Europe or in the United States, have their own practices or work in hospitals. As a result of salary loadings financed by the government many young doctors in particular are being attracted to the rural areas.

State and Society

Never in the course of its history has Thailand been ruled by a foreign power or nation. This is reflected in the name Thailand (in Thai: "Prathet Thai"), literally "Land of the Free". The fact that Thailand was never colonised, despite various half-hearted attempts especially by Great Britain and Portugal, was due to skilful chessboard diplomacy in particularly troubled times worldwide.

Type of state

Following a coup and the constitution subsequently promulgated in December 1932 Thailand has been a constitutional monarchy. The Thai Parliament consists of two chambers, the Senate and the National Assembly, composed of 267 Senators (mainly high officers and state officials) appointed by the King for a period of six years, and 357 elected Deputies who hold office for four years. It thus resembles the British system of government (monarch, Upper and Lower House).

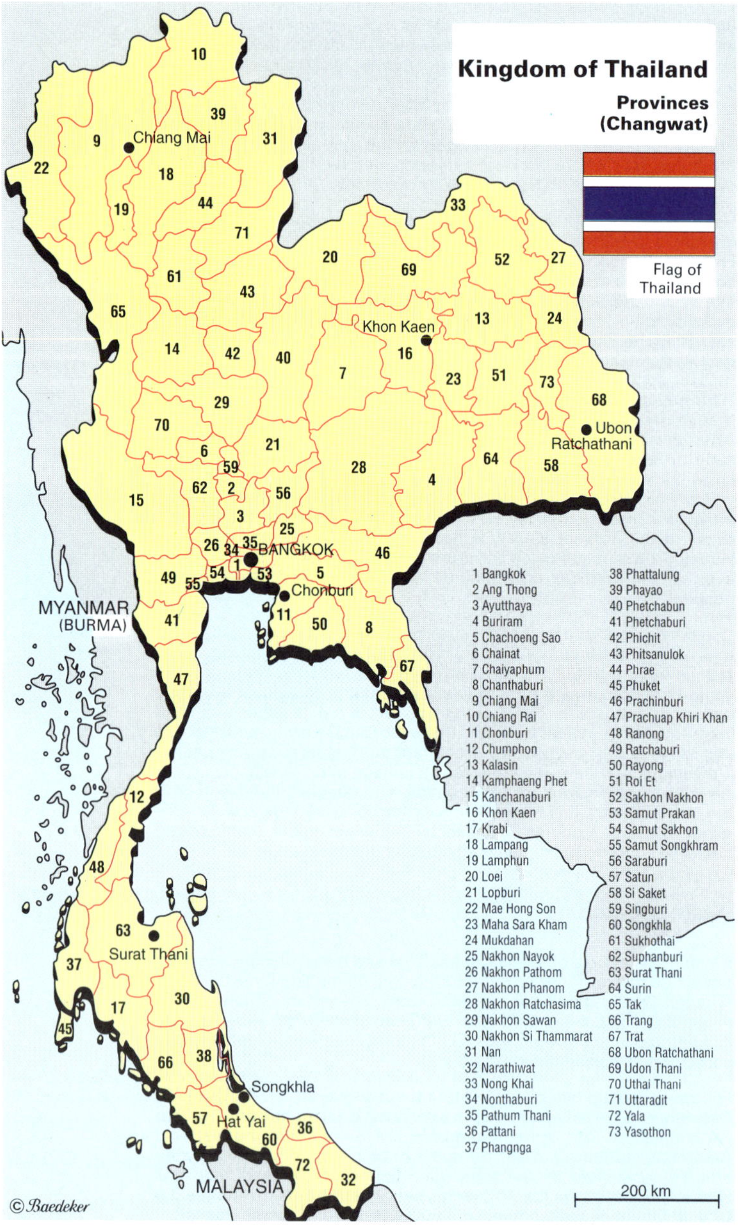
Kingdom of Thailand
Provinces (Changwat)
Flag of Thailand
1 Bangkok
2 Ang Thong
3 Ayutthaya
4 Buriram
5 Chachoeng Sao
6 Chainat
7 Chaiyaphum
8 Chanthaburi
9 Chiang Mai
10 Chiang Rai
11 Chonburi
12 Chumphon
13 Kalasin
14 Kamphaeng Phet
15 Kanchanaburi
16 Khon Kaen
17 Krabi
18 Lampang
19 Lamphun
20 Loei
21 Lopburi
22 Mae Hong Son
23 Maha Sara Kham
24 Mukdahan
25 Nakhon Nayok
26 Nakhon Pathom
27 Nakhon Phanom
28 Nakhon Ratchasima
29 Nakhon Sawan
30 Nakhon Si Thammarat
31 Nan
32 Narathiwat
33 Nong Khai
34 Nonthaburi
35 Pathum Thani
36 Pattani
37 Phangnga
38 Phattalung
39 Phayao
40 Phetchabun
41 Phetchaburi
42 Phichit
43 Phitsanulok
44 Phrae
45 Phuket
46 Prachinburi
47 Prachuap Khiri Khan
48 Ranong
49 Ratchaburi
50 Rayong
51 Roi Et
52 Sakhon Nakhon
53 Samut Prakan
54 Samut Sakhon
55 Samut Songkhram
56 Saraburi
57 Satun
58 Si Saket
59 Singburi
60 Songkhla
61 Sukhothai
62 Suphanburi
63 Surat Thani
64 Surin
65 Tak
66 Trang
67 Trat
68 Ubon Ratchathani
69 Udon Thani
70 Uthai Thani
71 Uttaradit
72 Yala
73 Yasothon
Chiang Mai
Khon Kaen
Ubon Ratchathani
BANGKOK
Chonburi
MYANMAR (BURMA)
Surat Thani
Songkhla
Hat Yai
MALAYSIA
200 km
© Baedeker

Province and city-state

Thailand is divided into 73 provinces (changwat) which are generally named after the chief town. The administration is headed by a Provincial Governor who is also the Government Deputy for Bangkok and Leader of the Provincial Administration. The provinces are subdivided into 567 districts (amphoe), which in turn subdivide into communes (tamban) with the smallest unit being the village (mu ban) which has at its head a "mayor" appointed by the provincial government. The provincial government is, subject to certain restrictions, responsible for the budget and is itself accountable to central government in Bangkok. The Bangkok government has drawn up Five Year Plans aimed at guaranteeing economic growth and direct state investments. The King has allowed himself a say in these investments, which are intended primarily to benefit agriculture in the underdeveloped regions of Thailand.

Role of the King

The King is the Supreme Head of State and in the final analysis he can determine the acceptance or rejection of a new law. However, he has not in fact exercised this prerogative for a number of years. In Thailand the "Royal Decree" is a special legislative power which the monarch can employ without the consent of Parliament.

From its origin until 1932 the Kingdom of Siam took the form of an absolute monarchy and even today the King is sacrosant. However, much has changed since Rama I came to the throne in 1782 as the first member of the Chakri dynasty. The Holy Kingdom, in which even up until the reign of King Taksin physical contact with the Royal Family was punishable by death, has had its day along with the belief in the infallibility of the monarch. Nevertheless, King Bhumibol (Rama IX) is held in great esteem by the people, who in a referendum in 1987 awarded him the title of "The Great One". In political matters, too, his word carries considerable weight: his intervention after the student riots in 1973 put to flight a number of power-hungry officers, and after the riots in May 1992 Prime Minister Suchinda felt obliged to resign after failing to receive royal support. There is little open criticism of the monarchy; even Thais living abroad have great respect for their king. The visitor is therefore strongly advised not to make any disrespectful or disparaging remarks about the Royal Family (see also Practical Information, Thai Society and the Visitor).

Rama IX (Bhumibol) is the longest-reigning monarch in the history of Thailand. Although he assumed regal office immediately following his brother's death in 1941 the official coronation did not take place until 1950 after he had completed his studies in Switzerland and married Sirikit, the daughter of a diplomat. The 42nd jubilee in June 1988 was celebrated in great style.

Role of the military

Traditionally, the military has always been the most powerful social faction in Thailand; there have been seventeen military coups d'état since 1932. Its political influence goes beyond the power it has over the armed forces; the officers themselves form an "honourable society" and many major industrial firms and service industries (e.g., two of the four television companies, the telephone monopoly, airports and the national airline, trading ports and at one time the railway too) are controlled by them. Being owned by the military can mean that a firm's political interests are protected. The army is also of course one of the major buyers of arms and supplies, and manufacturers of these commodities are only too happy to pay a "back-hander" to obtain the contracts. Corruption has always been an integral part of Thai society. Democratic movements formed mainly from intellectuals and the middle class in Bangkok which oppose the power of the military and fight for more political freedom and a more efficient administration are continuing to gain support, including that of the royal family, who have seen their former power greatly reduced under the constitution. The attempt by General Suchinda to put the protest of May 1992 down by brute force may well have rebounded on him; it would seem that by this act he lost any remaining vestige of respect among the people.

Party system

In the past governments have been formed only through the co-operation of several parties. The party system (in reality a loose association of parties) is diverse, and no one group can claim to have a monopoly of opinion. Political parties in Thailand are mostly organisations founded by interest groups, such as the army or large commercial concerns, whose main aim is simply to gain votes for their candidate; only the Palang Dharma party (the "Party of Buddhist Beliefs" led by the hopefully incorruptible former governor of Bangkok, Chamlong Srimuang) and the Communist parties can be said to have clear-cut political programmes. Communist parties are in fact banned but are active underground among students.

Political awareness

There is no overall political awareness of social class in Thailand; the voter elects a representative who is, even if only to a limited extent, able to assist him in the event of dire need. This is based on a pronounced respect – especially in rural areas – for authority and strict traditional hierarchical order. This is not the case among intellectuals with whom democratic ideals have taken root.

Foreign policy

Thailand has always been influenced in its foreign policy by the United States, which has brought in considerable investment for improvements in the infrastructure of the north-east of the country, particularly on the Cambodian border. In return for this economic aid Thailand allowed American troops to be stationed on its territory during the Vietnam war. In the course of a mood of independence towards the end of the 1970s, however, the American forces were asked to leave. Since then Thailand has followed a relatively independent foreign policy.

International membership

Thailand has been a member of the United Nations (UN) since 1946 and also of organisations affiliated to the UN. It was a founder member of the Association of South-East Asian Nations (ASEAN), founded in Bangkok in 1967, and was involved in the Colombo Plan developed in 1950, the aim of which was "to raise the living standards in member countries", based on the model of the "Marshall Plan".

Language

Thai belongs to the Sino-Tibetan family of languages, but in the narrower sense is related to Laotian, Chan and Chinese (it is still spoken today in some parts of China as a southern dialect). Many words from Pali and Sanskrit have been incorporated into the language, but these seldom occur in popular speech.

Structure of the language

Thai, also called Siamese, is like Chinese in being an isolated, monosyllabic language with only about 420 phonetically different words, so the meanings of words are determined by which of six tones is used when pronouncing them; this makes it practically impossible for a European fully to master the Thai language. Auxiliaries replace grammatical forms such as tense, gender, active, passive, etc.

The number of different consonants and vowels ranges between 50 and 82, according to Western sources, especially as there is a tendency for many symbols to change according to their position in a word, hence "l" and "r" at the end of a word are pronounced "n", at the beginning of a word both are like an "l", a double "r" in the middle of a word becomes the vowel "a" and, finally, "r" is silent after an "s", which is frequently found in religious and royal names, e.g. "Sri Ayutthaya", the "Sri" being pronounced "Si".

The written language

The Thai alphabet was introduced by King Ramkhamhaeng in 1283. In the National Museum in Bangkok visitors can see the royal declaration

A Thai reads his newspaper

inscribed on stone, the very birth-stone of Thai writing. The alphabet consists of symbols for 44 consonants and 32 vowels, of which 14 are simple vowels and the rest dipthongs. Very few changes have been made in these letters over the centuries, so that most literate Thais can decipher without too much difficulty writings which may be hundreds of years old.

Words are written without spaces from left to right; spaces are in fact inserted only at the end of sentences and before and after proper nouns.

Buddhism being predominate throughout South-East Asia this alphabet, with slight variations, has also been adopted by Burma (Myanmar), Laos and Cambodia.

Idioms

Visitors will always be coming up against the phrase "mai pen rai", meaning "that's alright or OK", "don't mention it", etc. It in fact illustrates the Thai mentality; any errors in behaviour will usually be met with a cheerful "mai pen rai".

The second linguistic idiosyncracy the "farang" (foreigner, probably a corruption of the word "français", as the French were the first Europeans Thais ever set eyes on) will come across is when he is greeted. Accompanied by a "wai", the polite form of Buddhist greeting, the Thai says "sawadi" together with "kaap" if he is a man and "kaa" if she is a woman. "Sawadi" is used as a greeting no matter what time of day it is.

The Thai language is very vivid and flowery. A Thai heart can stumble (be surprised), fall (take fright), but if it becomes damp (dschaichyn) i.e. cool it feels good and if it is full up with water (namdschai) then it is a philanthropic and compassionate heart.

Difficulties in speaking the language

Generally speaking the visitor will not need to try to speak the Thai language to any degree. If he does try to do so – with the best of intentions – his efforts will often be the cause of a lot of "sanuk" (fun).

"Sanuk" is like food and drink to the Thais, and they try to get some fun out of every occasion, and perhaps the best fun of all is to hear "farangs" trying to speak their language, since a word can have a completely different meaning if given the wrong intonation, and thus provoke gales of laughter.

Two examples will suffice to illustrate this. Just the word "mai" can mean widow, silk, wood, burning, new or stand for a question mark, depending on the tone it is uttered in. And if a "farang" actually says he has "por" (enough) to eat and over-emphasises the "o" it means it is his own father that he has eaten!

It is, however, suggested that the "farang" should at least use the "sawadi" form of greeting and express regret with a gentle "mai pen rai kaa(p)". This will certainly be met with an appreciative smile from the person he is addressing.

Some further useful expressions will be found in Practical Information, Language.

Education and Science

Early history

The first beginnings of an organised system of education came when King Ramkhamhaeng compiled the Thai alphabet in 1283. Until the 19th century the only place where instruction in the "three Rs" was provided was in the monasteries; only the nobility and members of the upper classes could afford to have their children educated by private tutors. Stone inscriptions going back to the Sukhotai Period speak of an intellectual, mainly religious form of basic education which benefited mainly the children of nobles and the clergy. For the simple folk legends and traditions handed down by word of mouth were the only way of acquiring knowledge.

Schoolchildren going home

Development of a school system

It was only in the reign of King Mongkut (Rama IV, 1851–68), who is still remembered with affection throughout Thailand, that a school system was developed which aimed at providing an education for all Thais. While the Chakri Princes continued to be taught by tutors, as they are to this day, universal educational plans for the people were worked out, with the English language as an obligatory subject. However, it was 1917 before education became compulsory for all.

Today the Ministry of Culture, formed by Mongkut's successor Chulalongkorn in 1892, is responsible for all educational and religious matters.

The present school system

Modelled on the British system, free nursery-school education is available for children of pre-school age. This is followed by six years of compulsory primary education from the age of seven; this is free, but school uniform and a part of the cost of books have to be paid for. There have been discussions for a number of years on whether to extend compulsory education to seven years. In addition to state schools private, mainly church-run bodies also provide a similar form of education. In the rural areas these are mainly Buddhist monasteries. Queen Sirikit and her daughter Sirindhorn have proved to be enthusiastic patrons of primary education.

The primary tier of education is followed by intermediate and high schools, both of which are open to all young people.

All schools, whether private or state, are supervised by the Ministry of Education. Entrance examinations for admission to technical colleges and universities are compulsory.

In addition to state schools and colleges there are a large number of educational institutions financed by the military. These schools, which include military training in the syllabus as well as general subjects, are found mainly along the coastal road between Pattaya and Sattahip as well as in the north of the country.

Monasteries play an important role in education

As many Thais cannot afford to provide their children with higher education there are a large number of charitable organisations which provide grants. Nevertheless regular schooling, especially for many youngsters in rural areas, is just not possible. Boys and girls are considered capable of working from the age of six upwards and have to labour until late at night selling flowers, newspapers or confectionery to boost the family budget; considerable numbers also provide cheap labour in factories in Bangkok. There are also some children who never go to school, these come mainly from families living in the slums.

Colleges and universities

In all there are 14 universities and technical colleges in Thailand. Of the nine colleges in Bangkok itself the largest is Chulalongkorn University, founded by King Rama IV in 1917 and now internationally recognised. There exists the opportunity for young people to enrol free of charge for a course of general studies which carries no graduation certificate at the end of it. In Chiang Mai there is an agricultural college concerned mainly with the education of young people from the mountain villages and providing them with alternatives to growing opium.

Thammasat University in Bangkok also enjoys a good reputation. Founded in 1934, this college played a special role in the student riots of 1975 and 1976. Here students initially demonstrated against the return of the former dictator Thanom Kittakachorn, who crept back into the country disguised as a monk and tried to organise underground resistance to the rule of the former rector of Thammasat University, Sanya Dharmasakti. Peaceful demonstrations against an attempt by Kittakachorn to regain power ended in a blood-bath, with the military massacring over 450 students and others. The students of Thammasat University still have a reputation as "angry young men" seeking improvements in the living standards of the people. They are in constant competition with Chulalongkorn University which is traditionally

Muslim children outside the school in Koh Panyi Village (near Phangnga)

the most respected college in the country. The King himself hands out graduation certificates at both universities.

Other colleges, some providing university courses, are to be found in Chiang Mai, Khon Kaen, Songkhla and Nakhon Pathom.

Agricultural colleges

An important role is played by establishments all over the country which provide villagers with instruction in modern agricultural methods.

Illiteracy

Thailand has made great strides in its efforts to reduce the considerable number of illiterates. In 1970 17% of adults between 35 and 40 years of age could neither read nor write; with the setting up of special schools this figure had dropped to 8% by the middle of the 1980s. There is still a problem with the over-65s, where the illiteracy rate is some 60%.

Religion

More than 92% of the population of Thailand, equivalent to 51 million people, is Buddhist, most of them believing in the Hinayana Buddhist doctrine of the "small vehicle", while some 12% adhere to Mahayana Buddhism, whose teachings are described as the "large vehicle", or sometimes Therawada Buddhism. The founder himself, the Buddha, is worshipped rather than prayed to.

While Buddhism is the state religion in Thailand others are officially recognised. These include Hindus (about 65,000, mainly Indians), Moslems (4%, mainly Malays from southern Thailand) and of course Christians (0.6%). Only 0.4% of the population is of no religious persuasion.

Buddhism

Principles

History and teachings

Buddha – the name comes from the Sanskrit and, roughly translated, means "The Enlightened One" – was born about 563 B.C. in Nepal at the foot of the Himalayas, the son of a rich landowner, and given the name Siddharta Gautama. His father also took the title of King, so that his offspring grew up as members of a noble line with the name Sakya.

Although he spent his childhood in the lap of luxury, on his three travels Siddharta became acquainted with human sorrow when he first encountered an extremely old man, then a sick person and finally experienced a bereavement. The way he was to lead the remainder of his life was decided for him when, on his fourth journey, he met a hermit who persuaded the 29-year old to give up the life he had been leading and to become a travelling ascetic seeking answers to questions about the reasons for man's existence on Earth. Legend sets out to prove how serious a decision this must have been for him by explaining that, on the very day he set out, a son was born to him.

After seven years wandering in the wilderness, meditating profoundly and seeking a middle path between abundance and ascesis, it was in his thirty-fifth year that finally, having passed through the Four Stages of Contemplation, he reached the State of Enlightenment under a pipal tree by the River Nerajara in India. He preached his first sermon in the Indian town of Benares, using as his text the principles of the Four Holy Truths, "This is Suffering", "This is the Cause of Suffering", "This is the Solution to Suffering" and "The Way to Abolish Suffering".

Three months after delivering this sermon the number of his disciples had increased to sixty, and he sent them out into the world with the words "Spread the joyful message to all you meet; no two of you are to take the same road!" During the forty-five years that followed he travelled through-out India spreading his teachings of the "Wheel of

The "Wheel of Law", set in motion by Buddha

Law" (dharmacakrapravartana). Through the strength of his merciful love he was able to avoid attempts by his cousin Devadatta to murder him, for instance by inciting elephants to charge at him. Although Buddhist tradition has it that in the year 543 B.C., in his 80th year, Buddha died and passed into Nirvana, a stage in which all earthly desires dissolve into a state of Beatitude and Eternal Rebirth, historians have in fact established the date of his death as 480 or 470 B.C.

However, the year 543 B.C. remains one of the most important dates in the Buddhist calendar. The visitor to Thailand will often come across a date arrived at by adding together the year in which Buddha is said to have died and the normal Western "anno domini" date: for example, 1993 becomes 2536 (1993 + 543) in countries practising the Buddhist religion.

Principles

The principles of Buddhism stem from the Hindu religion, from which it derived the concept of Karma, the invincible Law of the Cosmos. Karma means that the sum of a person's actions in one of his successive states of existence must be paid for in the next life. This constant cycle of lives is inevitable; according to legend Buddha himself had to complete more than 500 life cycles in varying forms. In simple terms, however, an individual can be influenced by each of these separate existences while basing his own life more or less on the principles laid down by Buddha. Those normally nearest to Nirvana, however, are the monks residing in the monasteries, who devote their whole lives to the study of Buddha's teachings. This explains why monks in Thailand are held in such high esteem.

The difference between Mahayana and Hinayana Buddhism lies in the possibilities of breaking out from the Birth–Death–Rebirth cycle. While Hinayana Buddhism maintains that every Believer must attain

Buddhist monks studying Pali scripts ▶

this state without any assistance, Mayahana Buddhism which evolved in the 1st and 2nd c. A.D. included some Bodhisattvas, men who had already reached the State of Enlightenment but remained unrecognised on earth to show others the "Eightfold Path of Knowledge" and the true road to Nirvana. Even Buddha himself, after completing his 500 life-cycles of Birth, Death and Rebirth, became a Bodhisattva before finally entering Nirvana.

It was in the 3rd c. B.C. that the first Buddhist monks, sent out by the Indian ruler Ashoke, arrived in the Nakon Pathom region, and it was here too that the doctrine as taught today evolved. The laws laid down by the Enlightened One became intermixed with elements of Hinduism, such as the Indian image of the world. One of the many versions of this image of the world stems from King Loei Thai (1299–1347). According to him the world exists within an infinite space, and is itself broken up into a material world, another pure in form and yet a third composed of intangible things. In the material world are the cold and hot Hells, and above it a flat world, with Mount Meru as its centre, inhabitated by men, animals and spirits. The uppermost of the worlds is that of the Deities, who are in a state of meditation lasting thousands of years and have laid aside all physically recognisable forms. Above these three worlds lies Nirvana, which man is incapable of describing because it is totally beyond his powers of imagination.

While pure Buddhist teaching made no reference to gods as such, over the centuries doctrines evolved which served gods of related religions, such as Hinduism. As a result parts of Hindu mythology became absorbed, such as the trinity of Brahma, the Founder of the Universe, Shiva, the god with the third eye threatening disaster, or Vishnu, the Benefactor, Guardian and Redeemer. These also appear in the Buddhist religion in various incarnations, for example Vishnu as Rama, the main hero of the epic poem "Ramayana".

Monks

Almost every Thai believer enters a monastery at some time in his life. Until 1945 this was for a minimum period of three months, but now the – normally young – Thai needs to spend only a few weeks there to enhance his knowledge of the teachings of Buddha. Previously one had to be at least 20 years of age; now even boys of ten to twelve can be seen in the temple, beginning their education there and being accepted as novices when they reach the age of fifteen. In the whole of Thailand there are about 3000 temples with an estimated 200,000 monks (Bikkhu).

Even as novices the boys have to keep the three most important rules applied to monks: they must give up all earthly possessions and beg for their living, inflict no sorrow or suffering on any fellow creature, and deny themselves any sexual pleasures. The novice is allowed to bring in only the eight utensils of an ascetic – the monk's staff made in three sections, a needle, a razor to shave his head, a strainer for water, an alms-dish and a string of 108 beads which he allows to run through his fingers during meditation.

In the early mornings in particular the streets of Bangkok are studded with groups of monks in their saffron-coloured robes (Kasaya) and with shaven heads. They collect their food for the day which they place in cotton bags, but it is not really true to call this begging, because the Buddhist faithful are happy to contribute their share of the food the monks need, as by doing so they are helping to save their own souls, and they give thanks for it by making a "wai", placing their hands together in a respectful sign of greeting.

The monks are not allowed to take anything that has previously been touched by a woman's hand, but this rule was not actually imposed by Buddha himself; as a matter of fact it was some time after his death when people tried to accuse him of having said that women have only a very small part to play in the world's affairs. Nevertheless, even today a monk will decline food or money proffered by a woman. Nuns, or

Children as temporary monks

maetschis, also live in the monasteries. They are not subject to the same rules as the monks, and are allowed to carry money and manage the running of the monastery.

Belief in spirits

Actually a feature of Animism, spirits play an important part in Thai religious life. With the express toleration of Buddha, as long as neither his teachings nor any form of life suffer as a result, the numerous gods – while remaining subordinate to the great teacher – may nevertheless use their cheerful powers to help people with their minor everyday problems and cares (provided, of course, that the person or persons concerned keep on the right side of them!).

The individual is divided into three parts, the material body (kai), an own and a free spirit (winyan and khwan). If the person succeeds in tying the khwan down inside the body this will result in good health, well-being and a successful career. This is the reason why small children have a piece of wool tied round their wrist, in order to attach the khwan to the body. After illness or death the khwan is able to leave the body, but will sometimes wander restlessly around seeking a living being in which to make its home. At every Buddhist funeral a lavish rite is performed in order to prevent the khwan returning to earth. The mountain peoples of Northern Thailand attach even more importance to spirits and perform special animistic rites.

Spirit-houses

Thais are normally extremely mistrustful of anything concerning Heaven and Earth. Buddhism is, however, a sufficiently tolerant religion to allow widespread Animism, or belief in spirits. There are, of course, both evil spirits and good ones, earth spirits (Phra Phum) as well as house spirits (Phi Ruan). In and around the house alone live nine spirits. If recognised as such, good spirits are accepted into the family, while evil spirits find their home in Saan Phra Phum, where they are

Phra Mae Torini, the earth-mother

House of spirits

pacified every day by means of suitable offerings. Evil spirits are thought to be mainly dead people who have been denied rebirth and a further step towards Nirvana.

Phra Phum is everyone's true everyday comforter, since he actually lives with people – not under their roof, it is true, nor in the shadow of a house, but very close by, usually on the north side, so that he is never overshadowed. As guardian spirit of the household his dwelling is a palace or temple-like artistically-fashioned shrine set on a post at eye-level with a narrow platform around it to hold the virtually daily offerings he receives.

At the rear of the little spirit-house will be found a wooden or clay figure of Phra Phum. Holding a fly-swat in one hand and a large book in the other, he can watch through the open front door and observe all that goes on and how people behave; he enters family events in his book and anyone showing a lack of respect is punished by nightmares or in very bad cases by being robbed, burgled or suffering a fire.

Thais can be seen bringing rice, tea, orchids or other gifts, seeking the blessing of the good spirits. On the occasion of special events or tribulations (such as illness, a birth, debt or when hoping to win the top lottery prize) Phra Phum may well receive gifts of models of horses and elephants, slaves and dancing-girls made from paper or wood.

The exact spot where the spirit-house should be placed and when is usually decided by astrologers; for example, it will be built some time before work is begun on a new house, a road or some other building, to give the spirits time to get used to their new home. In streets and roads spirit-houses are often placed at dangerous spots where accidents frequently occur.

The rites practised are mainly quite unfathomable to the lay foreign visitor. Nevertheless, a visit for instance to the Erawan Shrine on Rama I Road in Bangkok (although only a spirit-house, it is specially revered by the faithful) or Lak Muang, also in Bangkok, will be found worth-

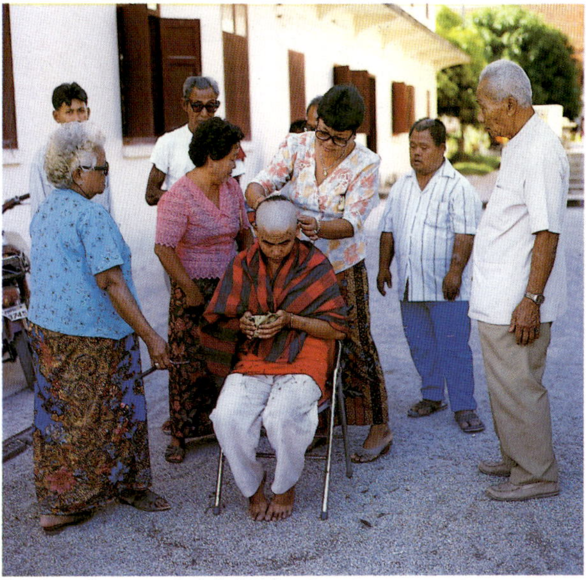

Relatives shave a novice's hair before he enters a monastery

while. Here – paying due respect and keeping a suitable distance – the visitor can observe Thais practising their religion.

Religious Practices

Buddhist ordination

For a man his greatest event – mostly before marriage – is his entry into the Buddhist Order of a temple. It is as much a feast for family and neighbours (especially the eve of the temple ceremony) as it is a religious celebration. Long before the event the young man makes the rounds of all relatives and neighbours, asking them to forgive his "misdeeds". On the eve of the ordination the whole neighbourhood (in Bangkok the congregation of the temple in question) will assemble en masse, bringing with them at least one and often two orchestras. One orchestra will consist largely of mature players, but the other will be made up of the guest of honour's friends and contemporaries, and may include jazz and pop in its repertoire. While the young people and their families stroll in the lamplight along the street or by the water's edge, feasting on rice and sweetmeats from gigantic cooking-pots, the older relatives and neighbours assemble in the home of the "Siddharta's" parents where he, in princely garb, stretches out on the floor, with just his head or elbow resting on a red velvet cushion, in front of a white-clad Brahmin (always an Indian), who reminds the young man once more of all the good things his parents have done for him.

The Brahmin will previously have been given the details by neighbours and relations and, for a fee, has made them up into celebratory poems. The older people all around break off from their betel-chewing, cigarette-smoking and tea-drinking on hearing of some particularly meritorious deed (Tambun) to utter an approving "huuii", with the young man more often than not emitting a grateful and penitent sob. This ceremony lasts several hours until midnight. The room contains only a triple-decked altar and a plaited-paper "Naga" or "Naag", the seven-headed snake which once shielded the meditating Buddha from the rain and asked to be admitted to his Order (Sangha). Although this

Away from the hectic rush of life – a monk's dwelling

was refused the "Naag" still has the consolation of knowing that on the eve of the ordination everyone is called by its name.

The celebration is resumed at an early hour the following morning, with all the friends and relations colourfully processing to the temple, singing and dancing to the sound of drums. If there is no princely steed available the "Naag" is carried on the shoulders of his peers. The others bear gifts wrapped in transparent golden paper which are piled on silver trays, and include a number of small but useful items which the young man needs for his future monastic life. The ceremonial head-shaving then takes place in the temple itself. On the third day there the young man will receive his saffron-yellow robe from his fellow monks. This occasion is excuse enough for the family to continue the celebrations without the presence of the novice himself.

Funerals

Again, as with the ordination, this is another family occasion demanding the presence of monks. The next-of-kin, dressed in mourning black or white, gather for a full seven days around the body to hear the "suffras" of the monks sitting in a row on raised padded seats or on a podium. On the day of the cremation – which may be as much as a year later, depending on the rank of the deceased – the mourners assemble in the temple precincts and receive little straw stars which, in a symbolic act, they throw to form a funeral pyre piled up with wood under a magnificent paste pagoda, which is then ignited by the most exalted guest. Only the next-of-kin attend the actual cremation, which is often only a few metres from the burning pyramid.

Animism

Whereas a Brahmin will be called in for major family events, for blessing the harvest and on the eve of a monk's ordination, everyday hope and consolation is normally sought from the stone and marble Hindu gods. For them more modest offerings usually suffice, such as a few scented candles, a garland of flowers (pyan malai) and, naturally, a humble show of respect.

A crematorium in the Wat Sutthachinda (Nakhon Ratchasima)

Tao Maha Prom, on the corner of the former Erawan Hotel in Bangkok, is especially venerated, probably because he has eight hands with which to receive gifts; however, Erawan, the triple-headed elephant (in front of the Academy of Arts, next to the National Theatre in Bangkok) and Phra Mae Torani, the Earth Mother (in the shrine opposite the Royal Hotel Klong) are also very popular. Blessings come with the water flowing through her hair during the Loy Krathong Festival in November, the highpoint of the Thai festival calendar, especially in Sukhothai.

Garlands of flowers

In the evening at every red traffic-light there are children trying to sell motorists pyan malai, the beautifully-woven garlands of sweet-smelling jasmine, orchids or roses. They are hung around the necks of people who have passed their exams or who have been given an honorary title, both to bring them luck and also as a token of respect, laid at the feet of statues of Buddha or that most earthly of all the animist spirits, Phra Phum.

Temples

Although the country's religious architecture clearly bears the stamp of the various Kings of Thailand as reflected in the religious views held at the time, almost all the temple complexes show the influence of foreign cultures as well. Missionaries or merchants trading with Thailand have left Indian or Singalese designs in their wake. For centuries the Khmer dictated the style of temple architecture along their trade routes which led them through Thailand, although over the years those in the north-east were largely abandoned and allowed to fall into decay. In the north it is the magnificently embellished buildings left by the Burmese and Laotians which are still copied today. Finally, in the 19th century, European styles were introduced, a particularly fine example being Wat Benchamabophit in Bangkok.

In temple building, however, the same thing happened as in other forms of cultural expression – the Thais often copied from neigh-

"Rhinoceros-nosed snake"

A demon as a temple guard

Kinnari (the "bird-maiden")

bouring countries, only to show themselves to be masters of the art of complementing and refining the styles of others. This explains why many temple complexes display a number of features from various eras.

Hindu temples

India during the Gupta Period (A.D. 310–500) saw the development of the free-standing temple with a tower, which replaced those in caves or rocks. The "tower-temple" consists of a cube-shaped building on a square terrace. Above the main internal structure, the cella, rises a tower, pyramidal in design and usually stepped, with relief decoration on the outside. On each of the four sides a staircase leads down to the terrace, while only one side is accessible from the cella. The oldest remaining examples of Indian tower-temples are the Shiva Temple at Geogarh, built in about the 5th c. A.D. with a tower some 13m/43ft high, the brick-built Temple of Bhitargo near Khanpur, also 5th c., and the Buddhist Mahabodhi temple – *c.* A.D. 562, tower 51m/168ft high – in Bodhgaya, where Buddha received Enlightenment. The wiharn in Wat Chet Yot in Chiang Mai is a smaller copy of the latter.

Later an assembly hall, called a mandapa, was added to the cella, and then a covered walk (antarala) was created between the cella and the mandapa. The cella porches (gopuras) were richly decorated. This established the basic form of the Hindu temple. Some elements of this style of building are still to be found in the Thai wat.

Khmer temples

In the 2nd and 1st c. B.C. the Khmer were the most powerful race in south-east Asia, and their sphere of influence extended beyond present-day Cambodia as far as Thailand and Burma. Along their trade routes, temples and other buildings of high architectural quality sprang up and many more or less well-preserved examples can still be found today, especially in the north-east of Thailand, including those in Phimai and near Prakhon Chai (Wat Prasat Panom Rung). The architects of Thailand temples copied a number of Khmer forms, including the prasat, the basic shape of which was retained while being more artistically decorated.

The design of the Khmer temple developed from the Baphnom style, which fostered the cult of the Holy Mountain (Meru) and so was

◀ *The finest example of Khmer architecture: the Prasat in Phimai* strongly influenced by the Hindu original. The Khmers showed themselves to be artistically very gifted, and the animals, human forms and plants carved on the door-posts and ledges of their temples are the work of true masters.

Prasat

The prasat, mostly a tall building with a peristyle, is like a Greek cross in plan and is normally surrounded by prangs on all four sides. It is the classical building form of the Khmer. A tower rises from where the four multi-stepped roofs converge. This tower is usually decorated with numerous statues of human beings and animals. If the building is used for religious cult or memorial purposes it becomes a prang; if it serves as, say, an audience chamber for the King or a chapel of rest, the tower ends in a spire.

An inner wall surrounds the prasat; another higher one encloses the whole temple precinct. Wide moats outside symbolise the oceans of the world, and inside there were a number of stone basins from which the priests obtained the holy water.

Wat

The word "wat" is often translated as monastery, and this is largely correct. Like medieval monasteries, the wats of Thailand provide refuge and accommodation, as well as being schools, hospitals or orphanages. In addition, however, a town's wat is often the place where festivals are celebrated.

The complex is divided into the sacral area and the monks' living quarters, normally separated from one another by a wall, known as the kampeng kheo, or "wall of jewels". The monks' quarters (khana), the large assembly hall (wiharn), a courtyard with chapels around it, the actual temple (bot) and the working areas all combine to form the temple complex. In addition, depending on the size, there may be a library, known as the ho trai, in which the sutra (writings of the teachings of Buddha) are kept, as well as one or more cloisters where the monks can stroll and meditate.

Typical buildings in a wat include the bot, wiharn, sala, ho trai and cambaria; further details of these follow. Depending on the size of the temple precincts there may be more than one wiharn, each named after the Buddha statue it contains. The chedi (or prang), typical of the Thailand wat, towers above the rest. A wat will also have a "bell-tower" (ho rakang), with a swinging drum or gong hanging in its lower floor. Frequently there will be seen dschaks (temple guards of Chinese origin), kinnari (bird-maidens), garudas (Vishnu's steeds) and other figures, almost all from Hindu mythology. Bodhi trees which stand in the temple precincts and are decorated with saffron-coloured ribbons, are particularly revered, for it was beneath such a tree that Buddha reached the stage of Enlightenment.

Bot (Ubosot)

The holiest building in the temple is the bot, or ubosot. This is where the monks' ordination is celebrated and only they are allowed to worship here; lay people must use the wiharn. Eight boundary-stones (semas) surround the holy precinct and separate it from the unconsecrated ground around it; they are usually pointed in shape and decorated with reliefs, mainly scenes from the life of Buddha. To protect them from the weather and from magical powers they are usually crowned with tabernacles in the shape of a chedi.

The bot itself is a long, rectangular building, with windows on the longer sides and the entrance always at the east end. Larger bots will have several entrances, one always larger than the others, as well as a covered walk which usually contains statues of Buddhas. The entrances and windows are often decorated with magnificent, gilded carvings or mother-of-pearl inlay. Particularly fine are the portals to temples in Northern Thailand which are usually modelled on Burmese examples. Bodies of Naga serpents form a balustrade, their heads and bodies covered in numerous tiny glass mosaics. It is a feature of these

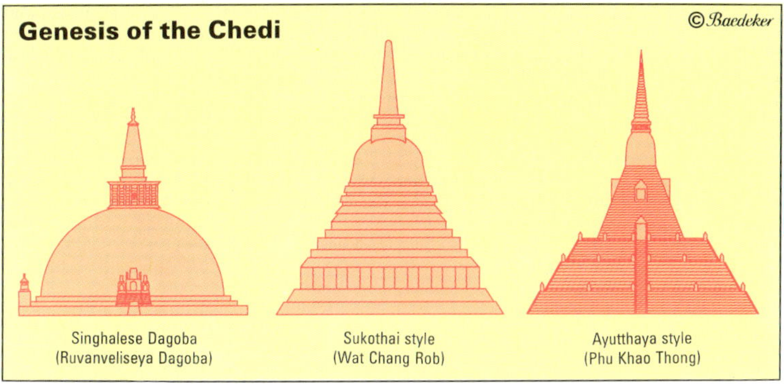

Singhalese Dagoba (Ruvanveliseya Dagoba)

Sukothai style (Wat Chang Rob)

Ayutthaya style (Phu Khao Thong)

temples that the stout walls and columns usually taper towards the top.

The stepped, slightly curved roofs are often covered with brightly-glazed tiles arranged in a certain way so as to symbolise the Naga serpent winding its way up to heaven. Small bells hanging from the eaves tinkle in the breeze, aided by small metal discs shaped like the heart-shaped leaves of the Bodhi tree.

In the larger buildings the interior is divided into three aisles, whereas the smaller have only one. On the west side, opposite the entrance, will be found the revered figure of Buddha, often surrounded by a number of other statues, garlands of flowers, offerings and a vessel full of sand in which the faithful place their joss-sticks. The atmosphere of the room is determined by the harmonious colour schemes in red, gold, blue and black as much as by the fine proportions and the fan-like timberwork, often complemented by a superbly ornate coffered ceiling. The wall-paintings normally depict scenes from the life of Buddha or from one of his earlier lives (Jataka).

Wiharn

Similar to the bot is the wiharn, where people come to offer their devotions. It, too, houses one or more statues of Buddha and is often tastefully decorated. Larger temples often have more than one wiharn.

Chedi and prang

The building which stands out and towers above the others is the chedi or prang, a typical feature of the Thai wat. The chedi (chaitya in Sanskrit) is a variation on the Indian stupa and the Singalese dagoba, the shapes of which are as laid down in one of the last requests made by Buddha. When during his last hours one of his disciples asked him what visible memorials should be erected to him he replied "Small hills of sand, like little piles of rice, something which everybody needs".

The Indian stupa and thus also the Thai chedi developed from a burial mound covering the remains of holy monks. The oldest stupas are said to have been built by King Ashoke (273–231 B.C.), for example, the four in Pattan in Nepal. The oldest include those in Anarudhapura in Sri Lanka (3rd c. B.C.), where they were called dagobas.

Stupas, prangs and chedis are not churches but cult-buildings not open to the layman, which contain the relics of Buddha and are designated as clearly defined memorials to Buddhism. In Burma, Nepal, Java or Bali the stupa is known as a pagoda, in Laos as a "that". Basically it is shaped like a semi-circle or bell and made of brick (anda), then rendered or stuccoed, with a square superstructure surmounted by a multi-stepped "parasol" roof, the symbol of holiness (chattra).

The largest chedis of particularly holy temples are crowned by a gilded spire, sometimes even one of pure gold.

In order to show deference to Buddha it is customary to walk round stupas and chedis in a clockwise direction, using a terrace surrounded by a stone balustrade (women are not allowed). There are four large gateways in all four sides of the balustrade, and the building itself is decorated with rich sculptures.

The chedi provides the best example of how the original Indian design became changed. Whereas the classical stupa is bulbous and almost plump in shape, the Thai chedi is more like a bell, with the central section often in the form of rings and the upper part coming to a point which, originally shaped like a lotus-flower, became even more slender as the years went by, and gave the original stupa that degree of elegance normally associated with Thailand.

Basically, a chedi can be divided into three sections, the substructure (maluva), the anda or barbha (where the central section is round) or harmika (where it is square), and the spire made up of "parasols" laid one on top of the other, sometimes gilded. The terraced substructure has niches containing statues of the Buddha. Whereas the Sukothai style of chedi often has elephant figures at each of the four corners, the Burmese model more often has lions. The anda, mostly round or bell-shaped and faithful to the Indian or Singalese model, may serve to symbolise the firmament of Heaven or the all-embracing principle of Enlightenment, the harmika portrays the sanctum above the world and beyond death and reincarnation, while the stylised "parasol" roof is a sign of holiness. Sometimes the individual sections melt so subtly into one another that it is difficult to distinguish them.

The interior of a chedi (not open to the layman) often houses Buddha relics and sometimes also those of kings or particularly holy monks, for example, their ashes.

The prang was also evolved from the Indian model, during the long period in which the Khmer ruled Thailand. The silhouette above the base is slender and tapers only very slightly towards its peak. Some prangs, especially those dating from the 16th c., on the other hand, are very stocky in design. Usually the prang also contains a reliquary chamber with a roofed porch situated in the centre of the building, with a flight of steps leading up to it. Most prangs are tastefully decorated and adorned with sculptures; the most impressive example is that of Wat Arun in Bangkok, and there are further beautiful prangs in Ayutthaya.

Particularly important temples are also labelled (wat) Phra Mahathat, or "Temple of the Great Holy Relic". Every royal city has or had at least one such Wat Phra Mahathat which housed in its chedi or prang a relic of Buddha, such as hair, bone or tooth. These relics are walled-up and not open to inspection by anybody.

Tip

Before entering a shrine shoes must be removed; it is considered highly improper to wear them when facing a statue of the Buddha (see Practical Information, Thai society and the visitor). On the other hand, those areas around the temple open to the public, especially in country districts, are often the place where festivals are celebrated, and some temples appear more like a market place where food, drinks and souvenirs are on sale. Birds in small cages can be purchased by the faithful and released as an act of spiritual salvation.

Sala

Salas are small, open halls built in the Thai style, with their roofs supported on columns. They are found at various places in the temple precincts, and provide resting-places for visitors.

Ho trai

The ho trai is the library containing holy scriptures and cult objects. It has a high, square substructure which protects the books from vermin and damp and which is partly surrounded by a peristyle. In Northern Thailand (for example, in Chiang Mai) there are some well-preserved

The belfry (Ho Rakang) in Uttaradit

Library (Ho Trai) in Lamphun

ho trais built of teak. A temple may have one or several ho trais, depending on its importance.

Cambaria

In the cambaria, one of plainest but most important buildings in a wat, the monks preach sermons from a pulpit between noon and 1pm. The pulpit is usually made of teak and richly decorated.

Khana (monks' living quarters)

In the khana, where the monks actually live, their quiet, reserved and strictly regulated daily life can be observed. Visitors should respect the silence and reserve observed by the monks and not disturb it by unruly behaviour of any kind, but polite conversation with English-speaking monks on the origin, calling and reasons behind their stay in Thailand is usually welcomed.

Other Religions

Islam

The history of the Sunnite Moslems in Thailand began in the 13th c., when Islam was imported into southern Siam from the Malay Peninsula. While most of Thailand's population remained true to Buddhism some small Malay communities were formed; around 1786 the Thais began to assimilate and subjugate them with scant regard for their cultural and religious traditions. Officials from distant Bangkok showed little tact or concern for the Moslems' feelings and few of them could speak the local Yawi dialect, a mixture of Arabic and Malay.

When the speaking of that dialect became prohibited and only the Thai language was permitted in schools bodies of underground resistance were formed to oppose the hated Buddhist system and the Thailand royal house; these in turn was forcefully put down by the authorities. In the 1950s and 1960s the separatist groups known as

PULO (Pattani United Liberation Organisation) and BRN (Barisan Revolutionary National) became active.

Peace was restored when the government had a change of attitude. The royal court, King Bhumibol in particular, worked to bring about integration of the Moslems and allowed the Yawi dialect to be spoken and used in schools. Women were again permitted to wear the long head-shawl, the chador, in public. The king had one of his summer residences built near Narathiwat, and he financed the building of a university in Pattani. Road signs were bi-lingual, and towns and villages bore their old names as well as the Thai version. King Bhumibol personally financed the translation of the Koran into Thai, and either he or his personal representative attends the annual celebrations on Allah's birthday. A high Islam dignitary is appointed to the Senate and is responsible for all matters pertaining to the Moslem community.

Moslem officials have a half-day off on Fridays to attend the religious service known as Djum'a and are also granted four months' holiday to make the pilgrimage to Mecca once in their lives. To avoid conflicts with the Moslem community the Thai government has prohibited publication of Salman Rushdie's "Satanic Verses".

Christianity

Christianity was introduced in the 16th and 17th c. by Spanish, Portuguese and French Jesuits. Thailand now has about 220,000 Christians who are highly regarded for their charitable and social work and for the way in which they run, with the blessing of the state, orphanages and old-people's homes, hospitals and deaf-and-dumb schools and the like. One of the oldest Catholic churches in Bangkok is the "Kalawa", built in the Neo-Gothic style and one of Thailand's 100 or so churches, half of them Protestant and half Catholic, which have been built since the 1950s in the traditional Thai style. Also of interest is the Cathedral of Notre Dame, built by French Christians in Chanthaburi and the largest

Notre Dame Cathedral in Chanthaburi

Christian church in the country. The German-speaking community in Bangkok runs an undenominational boarding-school for youngsters from socially deprived backgrounds and gives them a proper education. Other reformist faiths are also active in Thailand; the Redemptionists, for example, run a number of charitable organisations.

Hinduism and allied doctrines

Believers in Hinduism and allied doctrines total 22,000. The cosmopolitan thinking present within the Thai government and set out in the 1978 Constitution is illustrated by the great measure of freedom they enjoy. Hindi, Sanskrit and English are taught in Hindu schools alongside the obligatory Thai curriculum, and the beturbanned Sikhs maintain an undenominational school for all castes of the socially underprivileged and run caring services for the elderly and the sick.

Economy

Thailand has remained predominantly an agricultural country despite all efforts at industrialisation. Over one-third (180,000sq.km/69,500sq. miles) of its total land area is taken up with agricultural production.

Economic development

Since the early 1980s Thailand has drawn closer to the "Four Tigers", Hong Kong, Singapore, South Korea and Taiwan, countries which have become an important factor in world economy. Five Year Plans have been drawn up in an attempt to keep Thailand's finances on the right lines.

1982 was a turning-point in the country's national economy. Rice exports, which until then had traditionally been the main foreign currency earner, had to take second place to tourism. This fact led to criticism of the Five Year Plan, on the grounds that it depended too much on foreign investment. Nevertheless, in the new Five Year Plan (1992–97) an absolute priority was given to the continued development of tourism and, as a corollary, the service sector. In order to achieve the goals set, steps are being taken to facilitate the inflow of foreign capital and to encourage financial backers to invest in Thailand.

This economic buoyancy can also be ascribed to the improved political situation, which has become much more stable since the wave of democratic reforms in the early summer of 1992. The Thai government is actively striving to take advantage of its position within a region of the world which has seen continuous economic growth over a number of years. In this connection it is worth noting that Thailand is increasingly becoming the repository of money transfers from other less stable areas of Asia – a trend that became very apparent when there were large inflows of money from Hong Kong, whose status as a British Crown Colony comes to an end on June 30th 1997 when it will be returned to the People's Republic of China.

Overseas trade

In 1988 Thailand imported goods to the value of 18.6 billion US dollars, but exports were only 15.4 billion dollars. Thus, after three years of consolidation, the trade deficit continues to rise. The overseas debt in 1988 was 3.17 billion dollars, producing a total to date of some 22 billion, or 39% of the GDP. It is hoped that future overseas debts will be limited to a maximum of 2 billion dollars per annum and the balance of payments deficit to 4% of the GDP.

The European Community is well-regarded in Thailand and is its fifth most important trading partner. The country now produces many commodities such as textiles, rice, fruit and vegetables and fish which are of interest to the European market.

Mining and Energy

Minerals

Thailand has reserves of important minerals such as tin, zinc and fluorite; the south of the country forms part of the South-East Asian "tin belt" which stretches as far as Malaysia. As, following the collapse of the tin cartel, the price of tin has dropped dramatically on the world markets in recent years Thailand, being the fourth largest producer in the world, has not escaped unscathed. 303 mines (about a half) had closed down by 1986 and exports fell by 40%.

Energy production

There are no nuclear power stations in Thailand. Most of the country's energy needs are met by oil, gas and in the north (Mae Moh) brown coal. In 1988 7.3 million tonnes of brown coal were mined, and total stocks amount to 1.8 billion tonnes. In future natural gas will become increasingly important as a source of power when the vast reserves beneath the Gulf of Thailand are developed. Two power stations in Bangkok and some cement factories have already been connected to a 400km/250 mile-long pipeline, part of which is the longest undersea pipeline in the world. Consumption and export of this natural gas will bring savings and revenue worth billions to relieve the Thai balance of payments deficit for some years to come.

Following the discovery of oil reserves in the Gulf of Thailand in the early 1980s Thailand was immediately able to reduce its oil imports. 7.3 million barrels were extracted in 1988, and it is hoped that in future about one-third of the country's energy requirements will be met through domestic power sources.

Agriculture, Forestry and Fishing

Rice cultivation

Rice is the mainstay of agricultural production in this region, the "rice bowl of South-East Asia", with a maximum of two harvests a year being possible. Nevertheless, production has fallen over recent years – at present some 18 million tonnes a year are harvested from 9.4 million hectares/22 million acres, whereas in 1985 20.3 million tonnes were grown and 10.2 million hectares/25 million acres were under cultivation. In 1989 5.3 million tonnes were exported, with proceeds of 33 billion baht.

Only white rice (nas suan) is suitable for export; the brown rice (hill rice and na muang rice) grown in the north and central regions is

Tapping a rubber-tree . . .

. . . pressing the raw rubber . . .

mainly for domestic consumption. With intensive cultivation and better management the government hopes that harvests will increase in spite of reduced areas under cultivation; at present scarcely 60% of the paddy-fields are actually being utilised. Increased industrialisation, especially in the Menam Basin and in and around Bangkok, has exacerbated this fall in production.

Coconut palms

The coconut palm is intensively used. The wood is used for building houses and the nuts contain the delicious milk. The flesh can either be eaten or dried to make copra which in turn produces coconut oil, the basis for soap, cosmetics, candles and fats. Country people use the shells as a cheap form of fuel.

Forestry

Over 70% of North Thailand (30% of the whole country) is covered in thick forest. About a half is dipterocarpus forest (mainly yang trees producing wood-oil), the rest of mixed timbers, with teak predominating. This tropical rain forest has been seriously damaged as the result of indiscriminate burning, nomadic cultivation and excessive deforestation. It is to be hoped that an organised re-planting programme will save the day, but this depends to a great extent on how well the people come to appreciate the problem. The government were late in realising the seriousness of the matter and it was November 1988, following devastating floods which resulted in much loss of life and rendered thousands homeless, before a royal decree was published aimed at protecting the tropical forest. The exporting of raw timber is entirely prohibited.

Other crops

Between the early 1960s and the mid-1980s production of vegetables more than doubled and that of fruit – especially citrus fruits and bananas – increased even faster. Thailand and the Philippines are

. . . and hanging it up to dry

Fishing is one of the basic elements of the Thai economy

world-leaders in the growing of pineapples. After rice, the major agricultural exports are manioch (a tuber rich in starch), cane sugar and maize. In 1990 Thailand exported 5.7 million tonnes of tapioca (cornflour extracted from manioch) to the European Union alone. Raw rubber is an increasingly important crop; Thailand now produces 18% of the world total, putting it in third place behind Malaysia and Indonesia.

Livestock

Of considerable importance is the breeding of working animals (especially those used in the paddy-fields). The rearing of pigs, beef-cattle and poultry is largely for the domestic market, Thailand being relatively unimportant as a meat exporter.

Fishing

Fishing remains vital to the economy, with Thailand being the world's largest exporter of tuna fish. Although quotas have stagnated since 1972 the number of fishing boats increased six-fold between 1976 and 1988; by 1989 there were some 16,000 of them. In 1989 Thai fishermen landed nearly 2 million tonnes of fish for processing in the modern plants, most of which was for export. In the Bangkok region alone there are 30 fish factories working for export.

Rice farmers who supplement their income with private fishing are subsidised by the government. Experimental freshwater fish farms have been set up, with state assistance, especially in the north.

Industry

Industrialisation

Increasing industrialisation is not without its problems, the main one being the increasing drift from the land to the towns. Thousands of agricultural workers now seek work in Bangkok, especially in years when the harvests are poor. Government programmes aimed at providing subsidies in such years have so far met with a cool reception, but may help the situation given time.

These cocoons . . .

. . . become Thai silk

Bangkok

Bangkok is the industrial and commercial centre of Thailand. All the country's international and national concerns have their headquarters there and the office blocks of multinational companies and service industries dominate the city. However, the government is trying to make other regions equally attractive to industry, but first of all the infrastructure will have to be much improved.

Large numbers of modern factory units have sprung up around Bangkok, with a wide range of products, including chemical goods and those based on vegetable and animal materials. The textile industry is of major importance and exports all over the world.

Textiles

Thailand has traditionally remained one of the world's largest producers of silk. Produced mainly in two quality grades, exports amount to some 500 million baht per annum, and almost as much again is sold to visitors to Thailand. Cotton and other materials are also made. Quality-wise Thailand's textile industry can now match most of the countries with long-standing reputations, and low labour costs mean that manufacturers of international renown use it more and more as an "extended workbench".

Jewellery

Few people are aware that after Italy Thailand is the second largest manufacturer of jewellery in the world; more than 23 million pieces were made in 1989. Rubies and sapphires are mined in the south-east, and diamonds and other precious stones are sent to Thailand from all over the world for cutting and polishing. The Asian Institute of Gemmological Science in Bangkok, which provides training for budding young jewellers from all over the world, enjoys an excellent reputation.

Motor industry

Thailand does not have its own automobile industry and currently, as part of a "joint venture", vehicles are assembled from parts manufactured in Japan and Europe.

Economy

Tourism

Alongside agriculture and fishing tourism has, over the last ten years, developed into one of the major sources of income and the number of tourists is increasing annually. While most visitors come from Malaysia and Japan, the main non-Asian tourists are Americans, Germans and British, in that order; in 1993 some 5.6 million Europeans visited Thailand. In 1960 tourism netted 195 million baht compared with 83 billion baht (say £2 billion) in 1992. It has long since overtaken rice exports (1992: 35 billion baht) as the main source of income from abroad. This serves to underline the importance of tourism which employs over 600,000 people according to the most recent information.

In the Five Year Plan adopted in 1992 the government placed great importance on the continued expansion of the tourist industry. Foreign investors and Thai leaders of service industries can expect considerable state assistance in this sphere.

Sextourism

See Population, Family Life and Society

Labour Policy

Employment

In 1992 there were 31.2 million people gainfully employed in Thailand (53.2% of the population). It is estimated that this figure will reach well over 38 million by the year 2000. South-East Asia has a high proportion of children forming part of the working population. In 1980 1.44 million children and young people between 11 and 15 were engaged in paid employment, and in 1984 the figure was 1.04 million, or 20% of that age group. The bulk of the workforce are aged between 20 and 35 which reflects the structure of the population as a whole.

Low wages – the average monthly income in the Bangkok region in 1992 was 4600 baht and 2500 baht for unskilled workers – together with generous tax concessions are favourable factors from the employers' point of view and encourage them to expand.

Juvenile work: a youngster polishing diamonds

The largest potential workforce of some 17 million is still to be found in agriculture and forestry. As in the rest of South-East Asia, most industrial workers are employed in manufacturing industry; in 1982 those engaged in the service industries came only fourth in the scale, but in recent years their number has increased three or fourfold.

It is interesting to note that almost as many women as men work. The reasons for this are traditional rather than because of state incentives or social legislation.

Unemployment

Unemployment figures are difficult to judge, as they are not published regularly and include only those who are officially registered as looking for work and the sick registered with the authorities. They do not include the high number of casual workers. This resulted in a low official figure of 4.1% in 1991, compared with 7.2% quoted by the Bank of Bangkok. The number unemployed is expected to rise in the years to come as many jobs are being lost in the textile, building and agricultural industries.

In Bangkok there is a state unemployment exchange which offers its services free of charge to those looking for work.

Trade unions

Free trade unions were permitted for the first time in the history of the country during the period of great social upheaval between 1973 and 1976. Trade unions had existed since the end of the Second World War and had some successes such as a legal minimum wage, but they were under state control. Not until 1975 was there labour legislation to protect workers' rights such as maternity leave. Today there are 23 trade unions under one umbrella organisation. Farming co-operatives are particularly active in the Government's new settlement zones. Bangkok is prone to strikes and demonstrations; the most recent available statistics relate to 1981, when there were 54 strikes involving 22,000 people.

Child labour

The trade unions have been unable to take much action against the continual flouting of the employment laws to protect children under fourteen. Strictly speaking they are only allowed to help out occasionally with their parents' business. It is well known, however, that boys and girls of a very young age are obliged to contribute to the family income and work in small firms such as printers and match factories or sell newspapers and flowers for a pittance, but it is tolerated.

Communications

With a few exceptions Thailand has a well-developed communications network most of which is up to European standards.

Air travel

Bangkok International Airport, the largest in Thailand, opened in 1987 and is the turntable for almost all continental and intercontinental flights and the base for Thai Airways International. There are other international airports in Chiang Mai, Chiang Rai, Hat Yai, Phuket, Surat Thani and Ubon Ratchathani. There are plans to open up other airports for international flights in the future.

Over 35 international airlines fly into Bangkok International Airport. In 1990 it handled 15.57 million passengers (including stopovers), compared with 1.2 million in 1975, a twelvefold increase in fifteen years. This figure is expected to reach 20 million by the year 2000. The cargo terminal handles 400,000 tonnes of cargo each year. A few months after it came into service this new airport was already found to be too small and it has been continually extended ever since. A possible second large airport at Nong Ngu Hao, near Bangkok, is currently the subject of discussion.

Now only a museum exhibit: a steam-engine in Kanchanaburi

The comprehensive network of domestic flights offered by Thai Airways International means that visitors can reach all parts of the country quickly and cheaply. In addition to the above mentioned international airports Thai International and Bangkok Airways (a private airline) fly at intervals (albeit not regularly) into those at Hua Hin, Khon Kaen, Koh Samui, Krabi, Lampang, Loei, Mae Hong Son, Mae Sot, Nan, Nakhon Ratchasima, Nakhon Si Thammarat, Nan, Narathiwat, Pattani, Phitsanulok, Phrae, Ranong, Sakon Nakhon, Surat Thani, Surin, Tak, Trang, Trat and Udon Thani.

Railways

The railway network of the State Railway of Thailand (SRT) is well developed, even by European standards; 3728km/2315 miles of track link the country's towns. The main routes are between Bangkok and Chiang Mai and other major towns, with connections to Malaysia and Singapore.

Long-distance express trains are comfortably furnished with couchettes and sleeping compartments, an example being the night-train which leaves Bangkok every evening and arrives in Chiang Mai the next morning. However, a railway journey into the southern areas of Thailand can be rather uncomfortable because of the poor condition of the rails and embankments; built at the end of the 19th c. by German engineers, they are due for an overhaul in the next few years. Modern diesel engines have replaced the nostalgic old steam engines which are still common elsewhere in Asia.

Roads

Although hardly up to European standards Thailand's roads are nevertheless very good. In all there are some 50,000km/31,000 miles of roads, of which 16,700km/10,400 miles are state highways and 24,500/15,200 are country roads. All the major towns are linked by the national road network and road-signs are normally in both Thai and English.

A boat on a klong in Bangkok

Bangkok's greatest problem is that of ever-increasing traffic volumes. Only a seventh of the total population of Thailand lives in the capital yet more than a half of all vehicles are registered there, and it becomes more choked with traffic than any other city in South-East Asia. In a desperate attempt to alleviate matters at rush-hours the main streets are declared one-way streets at certain periods of the day. The swampy ground makes an underground system impossible; 60km/40 miles of multi-level rail and tollroad links which, among other things, connect the city centre and the airport, were completed in 1994. Many of the famous klongs (canals), which once gave Bangkok its name of "Venice of the East", have been sacrificed to the building of new roads, but this has produced little relief. The government's only answer seems to be to impose an import tax of up to 400% of the purchase tax on imported cars, but even this has failed to reduce the number of new cars to any marked degree, as many foreign manufacturers have got round this obstacle by setting up assembly works in Thailand itself.

Buses and taxis, including the typical Asian "tuk-tuks" and "samlors", are an important means of transport, and many bicycle rickshaws are still seen in country districts. These will take the visitor quickly and cheaply to his destination but a lungful of exhaust fumes is a non-optional extra on the three-wheeled open scooters.

Klongs

Boats and ferries are no longer as important as when the central plain around Bangkok was criss-crossed by canals, but the ferry is still the fastest way of crossing the Menam Chao Phraya, the main river flowing through Bangkok. Regular boat and ship services operate up and downstream, but although they are relatively cheap the number of passengers is steadily decreasing. It is not long ago that hundreds of thousands of people regularly travelled to work, school, university or market by boat.

Shipping

After the Klong Toey harbour in Bangkok (originally three separate harbours) began to show more and more signs of silting-up and it became clear that in the foreseeable future only ships with a shallow draught would be able to enter, plans were made to build new deep sea harbours. At present such harbours are being constructed at Laem Chabang and Map Tha Put on the south-east coast and Phuket on the south coast. The harbour at Sattahip, which is also a Thai naval base, is being enlarged. In 1992 the total volume of freight handled in the port of Bangkok was some 34.2 million tonnes (including crude oil). A modern computer-controlled centre on the East Quay prepares more than 320,000 TEU (1 TEU equals one 20ft container lorry) of goods for despatch every year.

Several times a year international cruise-ships call at Thailand's ports. They then lie at anchor either in Pattaya or Phuket or berth in the harbours of Bangkok or Sattahip.

At one time the Menam Chao Phraya was an important waterway from the Gulf of Thailand to the interior, but it has long ceased to be so. As a result of the huge amounts of mud the river has deposited its mouth is no longer deep enough to provide a channel for ships.

History

Origins of Ban Chiang culture in Northern Thailand, of which little is known.	*c.* 4000 B.C.
Monks sent by King Ashoke to region around Nakhon Pathom to spread the word of Buddha.	*c.* 250 B.C.
Probable founding of first Thai empire in Yunnan (South China).	*c.* A.D. 600
The area that is modern Thailand is inhabited mainly by the Khmer. Some smaller areas in the north-east are occupied by people from Burma and Cambodia. These can be regarded as the earliest inhabitants of Thailand.	A.D. 800 to 1100
Reinforcements move in from South China, provoked by the bellicose behaviour of Kublai Khan, grandson of Ghengis Khan.	*c.* A.D. 1200
Thai people found the first sovereign Kingdom of Siam.	1257
Reign of King Ramkhamhaeng in which Thai culture flourishes. He introduces the Thai alphabet, still used today, with elements of Indian Dewanagari script. Sukhothai becomes the first capital of the new Kingdom of Siam.	1279–98
Mengrai conquers the Kingdom of Haripunchai. Further Thai principalities (Chiang Rai and Chiang Saen) are formed.	1281
The Thai Prince Mengrai founds Chiang Mai (New Town), on the River Mae Ping, as capital of the Kingdom of Lan-Na Thai (Kingdom of 100,000 Rice Fields). The former capital of Lamphun is abandoned as it is subject to regular flooding.	1292
Following the death of Ramkhamhaeng the Kingdom is divided into principalities and Sukhothai ceases to be the capital.	*c.* 1300
Liu Thai succeeds his father Lo Thai to become Mahadharmaraya I. He displeases the rulers of Ayutthaya by preferring the religious orders to the military and is forced to recognise their supremacy. Sukhothai becomes part of their kingdom and Liu Thai is demoted to governor.	1347
King Rama Thibodi (U Thong) becomes King and Ayutthaya the capital, thereby laying the foundations for Thailand's development into the most powerful state in South-East Asia until the fall of Ayutthaya in 1767.	1350
The first Europeans – Portuguese, trading under the orders of their Viceroy, Alfonso d'Albuquerque – sail from Malacca (now Malaysia) up the Chao Phraya. The Portuguese had conquered Malacca in 1511, then learned that the country actually belonged to the King of Sayam in Ayutthaya. They are now offering him firearms and gunpowder for his war with the Burmese in return for the trading rights in Ayutthaya and being allowed to practise the Christian religion.	1512
The Burmese conquer Chiang Mai which remains under their control until the 18th c.	1556
After several unsuccessful attempts the Burmese occupy Ayutthaya but do not destroy it.	1569

1584 King Naresuan, who was able to escape Burmese imprisonment by fighting duels unarmed, regains Ayutthaya. Thailand regains its former territory after Naresuan drives out the Burmese.

1592 Sir James Lancaster, an Englishman, gives the country the name "Siam", which is what Europe is to call it for the next 350 years.

1593–1684 Ayutthaya's population reaches a million, and Europeans describe it "the most beautiful city they have ever seen" and "abounding in gold and diamonds". They pass Bangkok by, regarding it as somewhat unattractive, but soon realise that it is a hive of trading and build trading-posts on both banks of the River Manam Chao Phraya.

1605 King Ekatotsarot accedes to the throne. He puts an end to the aggressive policies of his brother Naresuan and instead promotes economic development. He imposes a business tax which earns him the name of "the greedy one" with European traders.

1656–88 The reign of King Narai of Ayutthaya. He is the first to realise that the great merchants who had been so warmly welcomed are not just trading in ivory, rice and skins, but are also bringing in arms and setting up garrisons. In 1664, with Dutch gunboats menacingly close to Bangkok's forts, King Narai is forced into an unfavourable trade treaty.

In this situation the French missionaries who arrived in 1656 are welcomed as his saviours and in 1681 the King makes first ambassadorial overtures to King Louis XIV of France. The royal fleet carrying the envoys disappears in mysterious circumstances near Mauritius, but a fresh diplomatic mission in 1684 reaches Versailles, meeting with a gracious reception.

1685 Louis XIV sends his legation to Siam in March 1685, headed by the Chevalier de Chaumont and backed up by a considerable number of Jesuit missionaries hoping to convert the Thais to Christianity.

1687–88 The first ambassadorial fleet leaves Siam, carrying on board precious porcelain from China and other parting gifts. Versailles' second envoys, Cébéret and de la Loubière, arrive in Siam with 1400 French troops as reinforcements. They and Narai's Greek Prime Minister, Phoulkon, are regarded with deep mistrust by a group of anti-Western courtiers who, led by Phra Phetraja, Commander of the King's Elephant Battalion, take advantage of the King being gravely ill to accuse Phoulkon of high treason. He is taken prisoner and beheaded. On Nari's death his adopted son, a Catholic convert whom he had made his heir, is also killed and Phetraja assumes the throne in 1688. All foreigners ("farangs") are expelled from the country which remains sealed off from the West for the next 130 years.

1689–1767 The Siamese are continually having to defend themselves against the Burmese and the only peacful interlude is during King Boromakot's reign from 1733 to 1758. There is a further flourishing of Ayutthaya Buddhism, art and culture.

1767 After a 15-month siege Ayutthaya is destroyed by the Burmese under King Hsinbyuschin (1763–76) and King Ekatat is murdered. Only a few of its population of a million survive, including 500 soldiers commanded by Phya Taksin who manage to escape via Bangkok to Thonburi. In the same year Taksin raises a further strong army, marches them to Chiang Mai and drives the Burmese out of the country.

1768 Phya Taksin declares himself King and Thonburi his capital, but he never finds time to organise it as he is involved in military expeditions fighting rebels inland and in pushing the borders as far as Laos and Cambodia.

King Taksin is condemned to death on the grounds of insanity, sewn into a silk sack and beaten to death. After his execution his friend and chief general Chao Phya Mahakasatsuck is offered the Crown and ascends the throne at the age of 45 as Rama I (Phra Phuttayodhfa Chulalok). He is the first Regent of the Chakri dynasty and transfers the royal residence to Bangkok on the left bank of the River Manam Chao Phraya. 1782

Death of Rama I, who is succeeded by his son Phra Phuttaloetla (Rama II). 1809

After 130 years Rama II resumes official relations with Europe. A Portuguese, Carlos Manuel Silveira, is granted permission to trade and build ships in Bangkok. 1818

An official English mission appears at Court under Dr John Crawford but is refused trading concessions. 1822

Reign of Rama III, remembered for his patronage of the arts and sciences. He founds the first public university at Wat Pho; attendance is free. Britain embarks on its first campaign to conquer Burma, thus freeing Thailand from constantly having to defend its western flank. 1824–51

Captain Henry Burney arrives in Bangkok with a fresh request for an English trading concession. A friendship and trade treaty is signed, but in fact only trading privileges are allowed. 1826

Captain Low develops Thai typeface and publishes (in Singapore) the first book for European visitors to Bangkok, "A Grammar of Siamese Language". 1828

US President Jackson despatches Edmund Roberts, together with missionaries and merchants, to Bangkok as American envoy. He is allowed to remain, subject to the same conditions as the British. 1833

A Royal Decree – printed on 9000 handbills – outlaws smoking and dealing in opium. 1839

Death of Rama III at the age of 63; he is succeeded by his son Rama IV (also known as Mongkut), a wandering monk from the age of 20. Rama IV promotes the educational and medical activities of the Christians in his country without becoming a convert himself. He reorganises the police and army along European lines. During his reign he passes 500 new laws prescribing equality irrespective of rank or status, better conditions for slaves, a ban on abduction and the right to religious expression. He founds the first official mint. Sir John Bowring, Queen Victoria's Governor of Hong Kong, concludes a friendship and trade treaty with Rama IV which guarantees British trade more freedom. 1851

The Prussian envoy Fritz Count of Eulenberg journeys around Siam and records his travels. 1860–61

An 8km/5 mile stretch of paved road, "Charoen Krung" ("may the city thrive") is opened to traffic. To enable it to be built some "klongs" (canals) are filled in. 1869

Dr Bradley's Mission Press in Singapore publishes the first printed plan of Bangkok. It shows four Christian churches, several mosques and over 80 Buddhist temples. 1870

Passengers are allowed to travel on the first stretch of railway line, covering the 70km/44 miles from Ayutthaya to Bangkok. 1882

1883	A single-track electric tramline runs for 10km/6¼ miles through Bangkok to the King's Palace.
1910	A railway line from Bangkok to Surat Thani is built by an engineer sent by Emperor Wilhelm II of Germany.
1916	Rama IV makes surnames compulsory.
1917	Education is made compulsory for a minimum of four years.
10.1.1920	Founding of the League of Nations. Siam is a member.
24.6.1932	Prince Paripatra, representing Rama IV in his absence, is kidnapped and an ultimatum is sent to the King holidaying in his palace at Glai Gangwon, who abdicates after making a memorable speech.
27.7.1932	A provisional constitution is drawn up, turning the Kingdom into a constitutional monarchy.
10.12.1932	The first constitution comes into force and Phya Mano Pakorn Nitihada is made the first Prime Minister.
1933	The leading reformers of the previous year divide into civilian and military camps.
1934	Out of the many new laws the people of Bangkok are particularly incensed by the decree on monogamy.
1935	Rama VII abdicates. A regency council acts on behalf of the new young King, Rama VIII, who is still at school in Lausanne in Switzerland.
14.6.1939	The name of the country, Siam, is changed to Thailand, locally Prathet Thai.
1941	The Japanese march into Bangkok, establishing their headquarters at the Oriental Hotel.
9.6.1946	Rama VIII is mysteriously shot, and his younger brother Bhumipol is appointed his successor (Rama IX).
28.4.1950	King Bhumibol marries Queen Sirikit, the daughter of the Thai envoy in France.
5.5.1950	The coronation of the royal couple.
1950–53	Korean War. Thailand contributes 4000 troops to the UN force.
8.9.1954	A defence pact between Thailand, Australia, Great Britain, France, New Zealand, Pakistan, the Philippines and the USA is concluded in Manila.
19.2.1955	The defence pact signed the previous year comes into force in the form of SEATO (South-East Asian Treaty Organisation).
1956	Bangkok becomes the headquarters of SEATO.
1957	Prime Minister Pibul is overthrown by General Sarit Thanarat who, until his death in 1963, is the "strong man" ruler of the country, with iron-willed enforcement of law and order against the Thai's yearning for individualism and freedom.
28.10.1958	Sarit's Revolutionary Party puts the country under martial law and from now on certain offences, especially those involving Communist activity, are tried by military tribunal.

The King and Queen pay state visits to the USA and 15 European countries. 1960

Marshal Thanom Kittikachorn becomes Prime Minister on Sarit's death. 1963

The military value of American "development aid" aimed, since the early 1950s, at enlarging the infrastructure in the north-east, becomes apparent. During the Vietnam War Thailand allows American bases on its soil, from which air attacks on Vietnam are carried out. 1965

ASEAN (Association of South-East Asian Nations) is founded. Member states include Thailand, Indonesia, Malaysia, the Philippines and Singapore. The aim of this organisation is to raise living standards. 1967

Prehistoric finds at Ban Chiang, bronze tools older than those found in Mesopotamia and probably the earliest ever made, throw the archaeological world into a frenzy.

Thanom Kittikachorn proclaims a new constitution, based on that of 1932 and containing democratic features but without curtailing to any extent the strong powers of the military, still effectively the strongest force in the country. 1968

Introduction of universal suffrage. 1969

The National Executive Council (NEC) makes Thanom its Chairman, suspends the constitution and dissolves Parliament, banning political parties and introducing martial law. However, the position of the King remains secure. 17.11.1971

The King proclaims an interim constitution. The NEC is replaced by a Government with a cabinet of 28 and Thanom as Prime Minister. The King appoints the 299 members of the National Assembly which has legislative powers. Two-thirds are high-ranking army officers and only a third are civilians and civil servants. However, in practice state control remains with Thanom, his son-in-law Narong and Prapass, the chief of police. 15.12.1972

Young Thais from all parts of the country assemble at the famous Thammasat University in Bangkok. Their demonstration is ruthlessly put down, leaving over 70 dead. The King is responsible for stopping the tanks from pursuing the 400,000 young demonstrators, and many students flee along the canals to the royal Chitralada Residence where they are granted asylum. Thanom, Narong and Prapass flee into exile and the King installs a provisional civil government under Professor Sanya Dharmasakti. 14.10.1973

Proclamation of a new democratic constitution and reintroduction of universal suffrage. The brothers Seni and Kukrit Pramoj, both over 70 years old and staunch anti-military democrats, take turns in leading the government. 7.10.74

Thanom returns from exile, dressed as a monk. Student demonstrations against him on the Thammasat campus and 50 students are killed by the military. 1976

The army assumes power. The constitution is suspended and a state of emergency promulgated. A 12-year plan for consolidation and a gradual return to democracy is announced. The army installs a civil government which lasts only 13 months, and in November 1977 General Kriangsak becomes Prime Minister. 6.10.1976

First conference between ASEAN and the European Community, with the aim of dismantling trade barriers. 1978

22.4.1979	General election, General Kriangsak remains Prime Minister with the Democratic Party, the country's oldest party, suffering heavy losses.
3.3.1980	Parliamentary vote of no confidence against Kriangsak, who steps down and is succeeded by General Prem Tinsulanonda.
1980	Thailand joins in the boycott of the Moscow Olympic Games.
1982	Bicentenary of Bangkok and also of the Chakri dynasty. "Rattanakosin" (City of Jewels, the first name given to the city and still commonly applied to Old Bangkok) is the scene of much celebration. Wat Phra Kaeo, lovingly restored, sees countless processions and religious pilgrimages. Rama I is posthumously awarded the title "The Great".
October 1983	Tyhoon "Kim" causes severe flooding in Bangkok.
29.2.1984	German President Karl Carstens pays a state visit to Thailand.
18.3.1984	Elections confirm President Prem Tinsulanonda in office; he is now the head of a four-party coalition.
May 1984	Pope John Paul II names Archbishop Michai Kitbunchu the first cardinal of Thailand and shortly afterwards pays a visit to the country.
12.12.1984	Heavy fighting on the north-east border with Cambodia as Thais attempt to repel a Vietnamese unit searching for Khmer Rouge resistance fighters.
15.3.1985	Thailand places large areas of its territory on the frontier with Cambodia under martial law.
9.9.1985	Unsuccessful coup by generals.
1987	1987 is declared "Visit Thailand Year" and tourism is given priority.
March 1987	89 members of the outlawed Thai Communist Party, who had long remained hidden in the frontier region between Thailand and Cambodia and had constantly sought to attack the military forces, now surrender to the police. This is seen as a great success for the Prem government which gains temporary popularity.
May 1987	After a referendum King Bhumibol receives the honorary title "The Great One", an honour which is rarely bestowed (the last time on King Rama I). Vietnamese mercenaries attack a refugee camp, killing seven and injuring 20 people. Foreign minister Savetsila meets with Shevardnadse and credits the USSR with playing an important part in resolving the conflict with Cambodia.
July 1987	Princess Chulabhorn accepts an invitation to be guest professor at the University of Ulm in Germany and gives lectures on pharmacy.
5.12.1987	The 60th birthday of King Rama IX (Bhumibol Adulyadej) is celebrated in Bangkok and an estimated 3 million people flock there from all over the country. On this date the new King Bhumibol Suspension bridge across the Chao Phraya (Menam) in the south of the city is opened to traffic.
February 1988	A ceasefire with the Cambodian government puts an end to hostilities along the border, thus paving the way for negotiations towards a peace treaty. Martial law is lifted.
July 1988	Prem decides not to continue in office. A coalition government is headed by Chatichai Choonhaven, son of a Chinese immigrant.

Uncontrolled tree-felling leads to severe floods with hundreds dead and thousands made homeless.	November 1988
Tree-felling is banned by a royal decree. Re-afforestation is to take place on threatened slopes.	December 1988
Despite the collapse of the Cambodia peace conference in Paris Vietnam withdraws its troops from Cambodia. Continued fighting with Khmer Rouge on Thailand's borders.	September 1989
Hurricane overturns American drilling platform in the Gulf of Thailand, leaving several dead. Severe damage also caused in the south of the country.	November 1989
A successful military coup, led by the generals, results in the corrupt Prime Minister Choohavan being removed from office and placed under house arrest. General Sunthorn Kongsompong forms a "Committee for National Salvation" and recommends to King Bhumibol the 59-year old diplomat Anand Panyacharun as the new leader.	23.2.1991
A series of devastating fires hits Bangkok: in early February a freight train carrying fuel explodes in the suburb of Din Daeng killing over 30 people. 6000 are made homeless by a chemical explosion on March 2nd in the harbour district of Khlong Toey. On March 4th a department store in Silom Road burns down, miraculously nobody is hurt. On March 5th 150 houses in Thonburi are destroyed by fire.	February/March 1991
The new cabinet minister Meechal Viravaidya, a successful family planning counsellor and well-known campaigner for the use of condoms, declares that "sex tourists" are no longer welcome in Thailand. A government campaign to fight AIDS is announced. In future female prostitution is to be discouraged and the fight against child prostitution stepped up.	March 1991
In the first free elections in neighbouring Myanmar (formerly Burma) the opposition party, the National League for Democracy, wins 397 of the 485 seats. The military government retains only ten seats but refuses to give up power. Democratic politicians flee to Thailand and set up a government in exile.	25.5.1991
Probably because an engine accidentally went into reverse, a Boeing 767 of the Austrian airline Lauda Air crashes soon after take-off and all 223 passengers are killed.	27.5.1991
Ousted Prime Minister Choonhavan returns from abroad and announces his intention to be active politically. Charges against him concerning embezzlement of public money are dropped; the Chart Thai party select him as their candidate for the forthcoming elections, originally planned for October 1991 but then postponed until the spring of 1992.	August 1991
In Pattaya successful peace negotiations take place between the opposing factions in the Cambodian civil war, after more than 20 years of fighting and the loss of 2 million dead. The peace treaty, which should enable the country to return to being a democracy, is signed in Paris on October 23rd. Prince Sihanouk, who has been in exile in France since he was deposed in 1970, is to return.	September 1991
In Bangkok the Conference of World Banks is held in the Queen Sirikit Conference Centre, built specially for the occasion. The main subject under discussion is the economic and financial situation in the former Soviet Union.	October 1991

November 1991	In Bangkok contracts are signed for the building of an overhead railway, which it is hoped will relieve the traffic problem. The contract is awarded to an international consortium.
January 1992	One of the last acts of the Anand government is to pass a strict law on Environmental Protection. In all this government has put 169 laws on the statute book during its one year in office.
February 1992	The rock-temple Wat Khao Phra on the Thailand–Cambodia border is re-opened to the public as a religious symbol of the peace now existing between the two countries.
March 1992	In the elections no one party receives sufficient votes to enable it to form a government. The military parties do best in rural regions, while in Bangkok the party of Chamlong Srimuang, the ex-mayor, opposition leader and ascetic Buddhist, wins 32 out of 35 seats. The military try to appoint Narong, the former Minister of Agriculture who became rich from tobacco and forestry, but he is accused by the USA of drug dealing, for which reason he was refused an entry visa to the USA in 1991.
April 1992	Although he had not put himself up as a candidate, the new head of government is General Suchinda Kraprayoon, who was behind the coup of February 1991. This was possible only as the result of a change in the constitution which he himself had introduced in 1991; at that time he assured people that he did not wish to head the government himself!
May 1992	Suchinda includes in his cabinet three politicians from the Chatichai government (which he himself had overthrown) who had been charged with corruption. This led to popular protests and mass demonstrations in Bangkok, Chiang Mai, Khon Kaen and Hat Yai.
17.5.1992	In Bangkok over 100,000 people demand Suchinda's resignation. Chamlong calls upon them to march on parliament, but this is prevented by the military.
18.5.1992	A state of emergency is declared in Bangkok and four neighbouring provinces. In Royal Square and before the Democratic Memorial in Bangkok soldiers fire into the huge crowds, resulting in hundreds of injured and dead (figures vary between 30 and 200). Chamlong and 2000 demonstrators are imprisoned.
24.5.1992	Suchinda resigns after issuing an amnesty for the officers who had ordered the shootings. Before he resigned he was asked by King Bhumibol to meet both him and Chamlong for talks during which the King sought a change in the constitution.
27.5.1992	Parliament alters the constitution to ensure that in future the head of government must be an elected member of parliament. Nevertheless King Bhumibol appoints Anand Panyarachun as Prime Minister because he is trusted by both king and people. His first short period in office is one of the most successful in Thailand's history. Anand goes to the country but it is uncertain whether he will himself stand as a candidate.
End of July 1992	Prime Minister Anand dismisses General Chief of Staff and Air Marshal Kaset and the head of the army Issaparong, who were mainly responsible for the use of force in May – a further attempt to curtail the influence of the military.
12.8.1992	The 60th birthday of Queen Sirikit, who is deeply respected by her people, is celebrated with parades and parties all over the country.

Anand does not stand in the parliamentary elections. Surprisingly, the winners are the Democratic party led by the lawyer Chuan Leek Pai, with the pro-military Chart Thai party second. Chatichai Choonhavan's comeback attempt (2000 complaints of falsifying votes are lodged against his National Development party) thus fails as does that of the puritanical Buddhist Chamlong. The five parties of the Democratic Movement who forced Suchinda to resign form a coalition government. Chuan Leek Pai is appointed Prime Minister. 13.9.1992

A hotel in Nakhon Ratchasima collapses, killing more than 200 people, while another 223, some severely injured, are rescued from the rubble. The police establish that the disaster occurred as a result of errors made in structural engineering calculations when three storeys, plus additional water-tanks on the roof, were added to the existing building. 13.8.1993

A panel of experts meets in Bangkok to advise on the highly critical traffic conditions obtaining in the city (January). The Buddhist monk Chalard Vorachat locks himself in an iron cage outside the parliament building in Bangkok and begins a hunger strike. At times as many as 15,000 demonstrators are present to support him in his demands for greater democracy. 1994

As a result of the bringing forward of parliamentary elections, Banham Silpa-archa is appointed as the new prime minister. At the same time the Chart Thai party regains power at the head of a seven-party coalition, its reputation considerably tarnished, however, by allegations of corruption and vote-rigging (July). The much revered Princess Mother dies at the age of 94 (July 18th). The whole of Thailand is beset by devastating storms, with some districts of Bangkok lying under water for days on end (October/November). 1995

A meeting is held in Bangkok of the heads of state of the European Union and ten Asian countries. The aim of the two-day conference is the lifting of trade barriers in Europe and Asia (January). 1996

Famous People

The following alphabetical list includes people of historical importance who through birth, residence, actions or death are connected with Thailand and have received international acclaim.

Eng and Chang
"Siamese Twins"
(1811–74)

The first Siamese twins known to medical science, the brothers Eng and Chan, were born in 1811 in Mae Klong in the province of Samut Songkhram, some 60km/40 miles from Bangkok, two of ten children of a Chinese fisherman and his Thai wife. Their two bodies were joined between buttocks and chest; at that time it was not possible to operate to separate them.

Until the age of eighteen Eng and Chan lived hidden from public gaze, but were then brought to the notice of one Robert Hunter, an American who was travelling through Thailand and who reported their existence to the American missionary Captain Coffin. Coffin persuaded their mother to let him take them to Europe and show them to medical experts. They would then be allowed to settle as free citizens in the United States.

In spite of their different characters and often varying opinions (which sometimes led to arguments between them) it was most surprising to find that the twins (who by now had taken the name of Bunker) were obviously well adjusted and in tune with one another in many respects. This was demonstrated, for example, by the fact they became excellent chessplayers and also learned to swim.

With the money which they earned from their public appearances they bought a plot of land in North Carolina in 1839 and built a house on it. Eventually they married; Eng's wife was Sara, Chang's was Adelade. No fewer than 22 children were the issue of this unusual union, with Sara and Adelade taking it in turns to share the marital bed for three days at a time.

Eng and Chang lived to be 63 years old. Eng died from an infection in 1874; his brother, who was in fact not ill, died two hours later.

Peter Veit
Musician
(1883–1968)

Peter Veit, the son of a Thai mother and a German father from Trier who taught music at court, was appointed Royal Music Expert (Phra Chen Duriyang) as a young man by King Chulalongkorn (Rama V). He was the first to transpose Thai music into notation, thus preserving a valuable national and cultural asset, and he also composed the royal hymn in 1932, the national anthem of the Thais (literally, The Free), the words of which are by either Luang Saranuprapan or Khun Vichit Madrah:

"Thailand is the embodiment of the blood and flesh of the Thai race.
Thailand for the Thailanders.
Thus will it ever be, because all Thais are as one.
We Thais are a peace-loving people,
But if we have to fight we know no fear.
We will not allow our independence to be
crushed by anyone.
We will give our last drop of blood for our country
and for the good of Thailand."

Alma Link
Benefactress
(1898–1964)

After being educated and trained as a nurse in Russia, Germany and England, with stops in London, Manila, Bangkok and Baghdad, in 1939 Alma married Herbert Link, a German industrialist based in Bangkok. It was here that she embarked on her life's work, and founded Thailand's Cheshire Home. Group Captain Leonard Cheshire was an RAF officer who witnessed the raid on Hiroshima. Subsequent stays in a military

Peter Feit

Rama IV

Rama V

hospital convinced him that the terminally ill without sufficient income and caring relatives needed a "home", a familiar place to turn to. Alma Link was responsible for the establishment of the first such Cheshire Home in Thailand, which transformed these ideas into a practical programme. She is the first and, so far, the only foreign woman to have had the honorary title of "Khunying" (Noble Lady/Gentleman) bestowed upon her.

Konstantin Phaulkon
Court adviser
(1647–88)

The Greek adventurer Konstantin Phaulkon was undoubtedly one of the most interesting personalities born outside Thailand to influence the country and its people. Born in 1647 in Argostólion on the Greek island of Kefallinia, the son of a poor fisherman, he soon signed on as a member of the crew of a British ship. His acquaintance with the brothers Samuel and George White, two businessmen seeking adventure and hoping to make a lot of money from trade with Asia, led him to join them.

First they worked for the East India Company, which had a monopoly over trade between Asia and Europe, and after a few years made it independent. Phaulkon went with them to Ayutthaya and was received at court mainly because of his astonishing command of the Thai language. While the story about his being shipwrecked on the Menam Chao Phraya is probably simply legend, the more probable truth is that he bribed his way into the positions first of court translator and later adviser to the liberal-minded ruler Narai. The zenith of Phaulkon's power was reached when Narai appointed him Chancellor and gave him the honorary title of Phraya Wichayen (Most Noble and Successful Gentleman). In order to persuade the King that only the French could halt the Dutch who had entered Siam by force and through influence he pursued a somewhat foolhardy policy which displeased government and court officials. Nevertheless, Phaulkon succeeded in stationing French troops at the mouth of the River Menam Chao Phraya, followed by Jesuit missionaries whom Phaulkon had encouraged in their hopes of converting the King to Christianity. This was the limit as far as the court officials were concerned, and on May 18th 1688 a group of Siamese, led by the commander of the Royal Elephant regiment, Phra Petraja (actually Luang Sorasak) took advantage of the King's serious illness to carry out a coup. Under the pretence that Narai, ill with dropsy, wished to see him on his death-bed in Lopburi, Phaulkon was taken prisoner, forced to surrender all his assets and was then executed. After the death of Narai Petraja himself ascended the throne and drove out all foreigners. For the next 130 years Thailand was closed to all western visitors.

Naowarat Pongpaibool
Poet
(b. 26.3.1940)

In 1980 the ASEAN (Association of South-East Asian Nations) annual prize for literature was bestowed by Queen Sirikit on the 40-year old Thai poet Naowarat Pongpaibool. A law graduate in 1963 from Bangkok University, he lectured at Prince Soongkla University in southern Thailand from 1971 to 1972 and is today Director of Bangkok's Bank Museum. His main interests, after many months spent as a monk, are Buddhism, traditional Thai music and social problems. It is difficult to translate his finest works into European tongues. Connoisseurs of Far Eastern culture may well be able to follow the alliteration, tone music, rich symbolism – the moon as the face of the beloved, etc. – but these are virtually untranslatable.

The Princess Mother
(1900–95)

The mother of Rama VIII and Rama IX, the present King, was tremendously active right up to the end of her life and was highly revered throughout Thailand. She was not born into a noble family; at the age of 18, because of her outstanding performance in her nursing exams, she was sent on a royal scholarship to continue her studies, especially in preventive medicine, in the USA, where in Boston Massachusetts she met the doctor who later became her husband, Prince Mahidol.

She was known as the "Royal Mother from the Sky" (Mae Fa Luang) in many of the remote villages of the northern mountain peoples, which was not a religious phrase, but one meant literally, for on her first visit she swooped down in a previously unknown "bird from the sky", i.e. a helicopter. It was the start of her campaign to bring medical care to even the most outlying parts of the country. To her credit she also succeeded in making medical practice in the provinces palatable to many young doctors, thereby wooing them away from better-paid work in the capital. After her death on July 18th 1995 – just a few months before her 95th birthday – her body was laid in state in the Dusit Maha Prasat in the Grand Palace precinct of Bangkok. More than 2½ million people came from all corners of the country to pay their respects to this tireless campaigner who fought so hard for improved living conditions for all Thais.

Rama I
(1737–1809)

Rama I, or Phra Phuttayodfa Chulalok as he was also called, reigned from 1782 to 1809, and saw himself as creating anew the self-confidence and unity of the Ayutthaya kingdom and continuing its expansion as well as preserving its cultural and spiritual legacy. A punitive expedition against Burma succeeded in his winning back Sukkothai and Chiangmai and extended his realm as far as Trengganu in what is now Malaysia. In founding the new capital he wished to fashion Bangkok in the style of Ayutthaya, its predecessor, and in order to re-create the former "Venice of the East" he ordered the digging of countless canals (including Kasem San Klong). He ordered Wat Suthat to be built to house the gilded Buddha carried off from Sukkothai, modelling it on Wat Phanam Choeng in Ayutthai. His own palace complex, which had suffered a fire, was rebuilt with the niche high up in the wall for the audience throne – Dusit Maha in the Grand Palace. As preserver of the spiritual legacy, Rama I reassembled the holy scriptures of Buddhism and produced a new edition of the "Ramakien" (the Thai version of the Indian "Ramayana" epic), enlarging upon the religious and court ceremonial of the Ayutthaya period. He was also responsible for the re-codification of the laws into the Law of the Three Seals.

Rama II
(1768–1824)

When Rama I died in 1809 he was succeeded on the throne of Siam by his son Phra Phuttaloetla (Rama II) who, while continuing his father's temple building programme, also started to construct the present Wat Arun, commencing with the monastery complex. His particular interest, however, was literature and he wrote a shortened version of his father's "Ramakien", brought the poet Sunthorn Phu to his court, and together with him produced the romance "Inao" and the opera "Kung Chan–Khun Phaen". In 1818 it was Rama II who for the first time in 130 years re-opened official relations with Europeans.

Rama III (1788–1851)

Rama III, also known as Phra Nang Klao, succeeded his father at the age of 36 and ruled his kingdom, then known as Siam, from 1824 to 1851. While trade and economic co-operation with China blossomed to its fullest extent during his reign (Chinese were granted concessions for sugar plantations and tin mines in southern Thailand), politically he was under increasing threat from European and American attempts at colonisation.

Rama IV (1804–68)

Rama IV was 46 when, as Prince Mongkut, he succeeded to the throne on the death of his half-brother, having spent the previous 26 years as a monk both wandering about Siam and as Abbot of Wat Bovornives, where he founded the strict Dhammayuttika Order which, in its dark-brown robes, can still be seen today. Unlike his predecessors who had grown up in the palace and been surrounded all their lives by courtiers, he was familiar with the cares and needs of every level of society. He has gone down in history as renewing the Buddhist faith by having the Pai source texts translated and taking the faithful back to the original teachings.

His country's greatest debt to him, however, was that as a result of his astute and speedy diplomacy, the colonial threat to Thailand was averted. The King was able to react in this way because not only did he have knowledge of the West, he had also studied Western languages, having learned English from American missionaries and Latin from a Catholic bishop. And anyone familiar with the "King and I" will know he employed an English governess to teach his children.

The king's hobby was astrology, which indirectly was also the cause of his death. In 1868 he predicted a full eclipse of the sun and while observing this in swampland he caught malaria and died.

Rama V Chulalongkorn (1853–1910)

Rama V, also known as Chulalongkorn (The Great), was educated by, among others, his British tutor Anna Harriet Leonowens, and succeeded his father at the age of sixteen. Favourably disposed to Western ways, one of his first official acts was to declare all his subjects "Thais", i.e. freemen, and dispensing with their customary obligation to prostrate themselves before their King as an act of homage although, in fact, many Thais continue to do so to this day.

In 1905 the King, considered Thailand's greatest reformer, abolished all forms of slavery. He was, however, also aware of the difficulties of emancipation, for earlier in 1874, when he had freed the children of slaves, he had said, "What is most needed today for the slaves is food and a roof over their heads; they have never been able to learn how to look after themselves", so now he ordered that every personal service had to be paid for, since the slave masters had to change their way of thinking, too.

Particularly close to Rama V's heart as King was the economic development of his country. He was the first King in Thailand's history after King Ramkhamhaeng (who visited China) to travel abroad, visiting Singapore, Java and India, where he learned modern administrative methods. On his return he established a national communications network, introducing the country's first postal service and the first railways, sent young Thais to study in Europe and America, while bringing in hundreds of scientists and engineers from abroad (preferably from countries with no colonial interests in South-east Asia, such as Germany, Switzerland, Austria, Italy and Scandinavia). He adopted the French "Civil Code" and English commercial law, but his consultative committee contained a number of Thai, Japanese and Dutch advisers.

The King's political strategy secured for his country peace, freedom and independence. Through diplomatic channels he ceded to France and England a large area of his country (Laos, Cambodia and four – now Malay – provinces) which had been conquered over a period of 650 years by his forefathers. Although the ceded area was twice the size of Austria he sacrificed not a single soldier in its defence. In return France and England accepted that Siam should be left untouched and act as a buffer state between their Asian colonies.

Rama VI
Vajiravudh
(1881–1925)

Rama VI, the eldest son of King Chulalongkorn and an Oxford undergraduate, succeeded his father as King at the age of 19 in 1910 and ruled until 1925, carrying on his father's modernisation programme (work on the rail network, electrification and water supply), and forming a Western-trained staff of advisers, while sending Thais to study and train in Europe. He continued the Europeanisation of Thailand with the founding of an English-style Boys' College and Boy Scouts. He also changed the national flag from a white elephant on a red ground to a copy of the French tricolour (blue, white and red).

The young King, with his Western education, translated the plays of Shakespeare and Molière into Thai, wrote several dramas about his own country's heroes and heroines, and founded 20 newspapers, of which two were published in Chinese, two in English and the rest in Thai. He himself made critical and thought-provoking contributions to these papers under a variety of pseudonyms.

In domestic policy he earned a name for himself by introducing compulsory education for four years and in his foreign policy he demonstrated his support for the French-British Entente by despatching to them his own personally trained 2000-strong Tiger Corps. This proved a shrewd move since it gained him Thailand's membership of the League of Nations.

Rama VII
Prajadibok
(1893–1941)

Rama VI's relatively early death at the age of 44 brought his younger brother Prajadibok to the throne as Ramam VII (1925–35). Wholly unprepared when he assumed the monarchy, this King had little zest for reform. He appointed five older princes to be his Supreme Council, and this was to relieve him of most of the burden of office and to see that there was plenty of "blue blood" in high office.

His reign was marked by financial difficulties sparked off by the world economic situation, which impacted in full on the Thai economy. Britain left the Gold Standard, a world recession set in and Thailand's rice exports, its main source of income, became too dear for the Sterling Area. Although the King twice cut back his Court budget (by about 65% altogether) this brought many dismissals with it, besides salary reductions for civil servants and the armed forces. The young intellectuals and officers who had been encouraged by his predecesor to train in Europe found there was no work for them and thus also no opportunity to implement the governmental, economic and social reforms they wanted. Those who had returned from being educated in France and Germany proved particularly turbulent and with the bloodless revolution of 1932 Rama VII became the country's last absolute monarch, his sarcastic reaction to their ultimatum earning him positive fame: "In order to maintain national order, to prevent bloodshed and revolution I hereby declare myself prepared to become a puppet king and thus to make forming a new government easier." He died childless in 1941, having abdicated in 1935. He was succeeded by his nephew Ananda Mahidol, a brother of Bhumibol, chosen by the government.

Rama VIII
Ananda Mahidol
(1925–46)

Although he had been crowned King in 1935 at the age of ten, most of Rama VIII's royal functions were performed by a Regent, so that the young King could continue his education in Switzerland. At the end of the Second World War, however, the government asked him, now 20, to return home, as they put it, "for the sake of unity". Once back the young monarch spent several months travelling around his country getting to know his people, mostly accompanied by his younger brother, Bhumibol, the present King.

Only four days before he was due to return to Europe to continue his studies Rama VIII died in unexplained circumstances in his palace bedroom in Bangkok.

Rama IX Bhumibol (b. 5.12.1927)

His majesty was born in Cambridge, USA, the youngest child (second son) of Prince Mahidol of Songkhla, the son of Rama V (Chulalongkorn). His mother, the Princess Mother, was during her life highly esteemed in Thailand. After the early death of his father in 1929 his mother settled in Switzerland with the children, where they were given an international but entirely bourgeois upbringing in a democratic setting. After the resignation of his uncle and the premature death of his brother Bhumibol unexpectedly found himself King in 1946. He changed his course of studies from law and political science to his hobby, natural sciences, and in 1950 returned to Thailand from Switzerland.

His official coronation was in Bangkok on May 5th 1950 and in 1951 he finally assumed the reins of government.

In what is now a reign of over 40 years the King has come to be called by his subjects, with affection as much as respect, "Father of the People", and the greater part of his rule is taken up with visiting by rail, road and air, as well as on foot, all parts of his country, especially those suffering natural disasters or in need of social aid.

His many development projects, which he also oversees personally, have made him the absolute embodiment of Thai integration, holding the country together and at peace.

His people demonstrated their gratitude to him by awarding him the title "The Great" shortly before his 60th birthday in May 1987. In honour of the birthday itself (5.12.1987) crowds estimated at 3 million attended a celebration in Bangkok.

King Ramkhamhaeng (1256?–1317)

King Ramkhamhaeng, probably the most popular ruler of the kingdom of Sukhothai, made quite a reputation for himself when, as a young man, he fought successfully by the side of his father, Sri Indratitya, who founded the state. When he ascended to the throne in 1275 (or possibly not until 1279) his inaugural speech laid the foundations of a modern state. The text of it is inscribed on a stone pillar found in the 19th

King Bhumibol on a country visit

Baedeker Special

The Royal Family

It was an event of a revolutionary character – just like the incidents in May 1992 which had brought Thailand under the world's gaze. Following a bloodbath caused by the military's use of armed force to suppress mass demonstrations by Thais calling for democratic reforms, King Bhumibol Adulyadej summoned the various protagonists to an audience at his residence, the Chitralada Palace. The parties emerged from the palace two and a half hours later having given the 65-year-old monarch a promise to cease hostilities. The whole audience had been beamed directly via television to an astonished nation.

King Bhumibol's achievement in bringing about a rapprochement after days of clashes was yet further proof of the high regard which the Royal Family enjoys in Thailand. The omnipresent figure of the monarch, whose picture hangs in even the tiniest dwelling, is a unifying symbol within the country, where influence is exerted not just by the king, but also by parliament and the army, the latter having attempted on seven occasions since 1932, and with varying degrees of success, to take power by a coup d'état.

King Bhumibol bears the title Rama IX, and is the ninth ruler of the Chakri dynasty, which has ruled the country since 1782. All rulers of Thailand have worked tirelessly for the welfare of their people, founding schools and hospitals, introducing technological innovations, such as the railway, and caring in particular for the rural peasantry. The King spends at least three days a week paying visits throughout the country, by which means he not only keeps himself informed of the needs and concerns of his people, but also brings about the realisation of numerous projects designed to benefit the country.

King Bhumibol with his countrymen

The Thai people are well aware of the extent to which they are indebted to their ruler – a gratitude which found its expression not least in the decision of a national plebiscite held in 1987, on the occasion of the King's 60th birthday, to bestow on him the hitherto seldom used appellation "the Great".

It is not just the King himself, however, who takes such an interest in the well-being of the Thai people, but also the whole of his family. Queen Sirikit is no less loved than her husband, the improvement of the school and education system being a cause dear to her heart. The King's mother, when she was alive, used to travel regularly all over the country, even in her advanced years. In particular she worked tirelessly on behalf of the ethnic minorities living in the mountainous areas of northern Thailand who bestowed on her the reverential title of Maeh Fah Luang (Royal Mother of the Sky). The sort of scandals that have rocked royal houses in other countries are completely unknown in Thailand.

Of the four royal children the two princesses Chulabhorn and Sirindhorn stand out; for years they have supported their mother in the discharge of her social duties. Indeed, their standing within the country is so high that the hitherto exclusively male succession to the throne has been abolished by law. It is thus theoretically possible for Prince Vajiaralonghorn not to become the next King of Thailand, but for his younger sister Sirindhorn to inherit her father's mantle. Ubol Ratana, the oldest daughter, has in fact renounced all the rights and obligations which derive from her royal birth and has married and gone to live abroad.

century among some ruins in Sukhothai; today it is in the National Museum in Bangkok.

The country's economy flourished during his period as King, and he was able to secure its borders by means of skilful foreign policy, with the result that the Kingdom of Sukhothai expanded so as to embrace almost all of what is now Thailand. However, when his son Liu Thai came to the throne after Ramkhamhaeng's death Sukhothai lost much of its former influence and power passed to the Kings of Ayutthaya.

Ramkhamhaeng invented the Thai script which has remained in use almost unchanged to this day, and which he based on the characters of the Khmer and the Mon alphabets. When he returned from his trips to China (including one to visit Khublai Khan in 1282) he brought back with him skilled Chinese craftsmen who instructed the Thais in the art of making china and porcelain. The style of temple-building also changed during his reign; this is best seen in the way additions were made to existing Khmer temples. In the field of religious sculpture artists encouraged by Ramkhamhaeng produced the soft, flowing forms so typical of the Sukhothai style. Buddha statues from this period are still considered to be among the most beautiful ever made in Thailand.

Queen Sirikit Somdech Phraborom Rajininath (b. 12.8.1932)

The present Queen, daughter of a diplomat, was fifteen when in Fontainebleau she made the acquaintance of an attractive fellow-countryman called Bhumibol, whose passions – apart from his study of natural sciences – were fast cars and jazz.

The sports car led to an accident which caused a severe eye injury but also, at his request, brought him a frequent visitor, Sirikit, to his bedside in Lausanne. After their engagement and marriage before returning to Bangkok in 1951 they were able to spend their last student year together. Like the rest of the Royal Family the Queen is also active in the social and charitable sphere. She is President of Thailand's Red Cross, as well some 150 other private and public welfare organisations. She has been primarily responsible for promoting the cause of educationally and socially disadvantaged women and children, as well as for the new direction given to traditional craftsmanship, such as weaving skills. It is to her personal credit that the home products she promotes find a market in other countries of the world as well as with tourists.

Royal children

Ubol Ratana, the oldest daughter, has long since been married and lives abroad, having renounced all her rights and duties. The other three children are Prince Vajiralongkorn (b. 1952), Princess Sirindhorn (b. 1955) and Princess Chulabhorn (b. 1957).

Prince Vajiralongkorn, who has always had a military bent, has graduated from the famous Duntroon Military Academy in Australia. His sister Sirindhorn was awarded the title "Maha Chakri" for her social, cultural and diplomatic commitment during her mother's illness, giving her equal status to the Prince. She studied for a doctorate in archaeology. The youngest Princess Chulabhorn is studying agriculture and forestry at Chiang Mai and Bangkok.

In 1979 an amendment to the constitution broke with the 700-year old tradition whereby only males of a certain age could ascend to the throne. With the consent of Parliament and the Crown Council any of the King's children may accede.

Chin Sophonpanich (b. June 1910)

The 32-storey high Bayoke Tower, one of the tallest buildings in Bangkok, is the headquarters of the Bangkok Bank Ltd and was officially opened in 1982 by the bank's founder, Chin Sophonpanich, on the occasion of his 72nd birthday, which was attended by over 4000 guests from all over the world.

Born in Bangkok the son of Thai and Chinese parents, he was sent by his father to study in Canton. However, he returned home at seventeen having run out of money and with no alternative but to do the same as thousands had done before him: carrying sacks of rice and cooking noodles in the Chinese quarter.

Four years later he had taken the first step up the ladder: he became manager of a small company selling building wood, tools and tinned food. During the Second World War he exported rice to Indonesia, opened up saw-mills and in 1944 founded the Bangkok Bank. Willing to take risks and trust an honest face even if it belonged to someone in dirty shorts and sandals, he was prepared to give credit to people who had been turned down by "respectable" banks.

Today Chin is one of the wealthiest businessmen in South-East Asia with 140 firms and companies covering the whole gamut of commercial activity. Chin has business interests in Hong Kong and Singapore, his bank finances 40% of all Thailand's exports and controls a third of the country's banking business. He still reckons exchange rates in his head – faster than a computer – and when others have just decided it is the right moment to take a profit on a commodity his ships have long since set sail for their destination. His six sons attended the best universities in America, Britain and Australia and have now taken over the day-to-day running of the businesses with Chin always available to act as adviser.

Sunthorn Phu
Poet
(1786–1855)

The Thai poet Sunthorn Phu is thought to have been born in Thonburi, his mother soon parting from his father to become a nanny at Court. Young Phu grew up in Wang Lang, a princely palace, where he learned to read and write as well as the basic art of poetry.

Sunthorn Phu had a definite inclination to "wine, women and song" – Thai verse is closely related to song in any case. This tendency led him to assume a wandering existence, constantly moving between monastery and the Court at Bangkok. He particularly frequented a monastery on the island of Klaeng, near Ravong, where his father had been abbot. Whereas Rama II had very much favoured Sunthorn Phu and had also involved him in reworking the "Ramakien" and other literary projects, with Rama III he fell out of favour. Then followed a wandering life when for eighteen years he worked as a stage narrator, jobbing poet, alchemist and monk. His finest "Nirat" works (descriptions of journeys, usually addressed to a lover) date from this period. Honour and esteem were only his again under Rama IV, when he had even more exalted titles bestowed upon him, such as Phra Sunhorn Woharn, or "Sunhorn the Enlightened One".

James ("Jim")
Thompson
Architect
(1906–74?)

The American architect James ("Jim") Thompson came to Bangkok after the Second World War as an officer in the secret service but soon resigned. He decided to settle in Bangkok and following a spell as manager of the Oriental Hotel he discovered the Thai art of silk-weaving. Thompson is responsible for the world-wide reputation enjoyed by Thai silk today. His modern methods of production also incorporated established techniques. Himself a gifted designer, he made an enormous contribution to the development of the Thai silk industry. After visiting his factories and spending an evening having dinner at his home the famous writer Somerset Maugham wrote in the visitor's book: "Not only have you created beautiful things but you have also exercised exquisite taste in building your unusual collection of art".

Thompson travelled widely throughout Thailand bringing beautiful things back to Bangkok and rescuing them from decay. One of the finest examples of his passion for collecting are the traditional Thai houses which he had dismantled on their original site and rebuilt in the capital. Only now can his far-sightedness be appreciated, as such well-preserved houses are hardly found anywhere else in the country.

At the height of his creativity Jim Thompson disappeared at the age of 61 in unexplained circumstances. During a short holiday in the Cameron Highlands of Malaysia he disappeared without trace in the afternoon of Easter Sunday 1967. Seven years later (1974) he was officially declared dead. His life's work is open to visitors at Jim Thompson's House in Bangkok and is administered by a charitable trust.

Prateep Ungsongtham
Educator
(b. 1951)

Definitely the youngest and by far the least academic person to receive the Far Eastern equivalent of the Nobel Prize, Prateep Ungsongtham was in 1978 awarded this distinction in Tokyo at the age of 27 for "personal effort in schooling slum-dwellers and their children".

Herself born into the "third biggest slum in the world" on Klong Toey waterfront she managed to learn to read and write and at the age of sixteen began giving lessons to children in her neighbourhood. When such "illegal" schools were condemned to be driven off the sites where Prateep had set them up the city fathers intervened and in 1974 requested her to carry on. Since "Miss" Prateep immediately put her prize-money, valued at about 10,000 US dollars, into a foundation, all Bangkok's civil servants think the world of her and back her projects, as do many private benefactors.

There are now nearly 2000 schoolchildren and over a dozen properly qualified teachers sitting down to lessons in buildings of stone, something unheard of in a slum. "Kru" (Miss) Prateep has made the Duang (gleam of light) Foundation with its "penny" school (at one baht per day) into a model for all the developing countries in South-East Asia. Nowadays the curriculum also includes adult education, family planning, occupational training and lessons in health and hygiene. International and national donations help to provide scholarships, terms of monastic study, sports and leisure programmes, as well as measures to help prevent juvenile delinquency and cope with unemployment.

Pierra Vejabul
Doctor
(1900–64)

Pierra Vejabul, Thailand's first woman doctor, had to leave home to achieve her personal ambition. She went to Paris where she paid for her studies by working as a cleaner. After graduation she spent some months in Berlin before returning to Bangkok in the early 1930s, where she was put in charge of the department for female venereal diseases. In those days the health authorities "tattooed" these women and girls, even when they were just children of fourteen. This slight but determined woman doctor soon put a stop to this practice and then took on all her patients' rejected babies as adopted children, as a result of which her family name and honour were taken away from her (her present name means "good patient doctor" and was given her by the Royal House, together with the honorary title of "Khunying").

Until her death in 1964 Khunying Vejabul ran an orphanage in which some 3000 children grew up to adulthood, many of them entering the professions and making their way in the world. In addition she ran her own practice and operated an occupational retraining centre on the edge of Bangkok where prostitutes who were pregnant or wanted to change their way of life could go for education and training.

Art and Culture

History of Art

The culture of Thailand has always been strongly influenced by that of its neighbours, especially India (through the Ramakien epic, for example) and Malaya. A certain degree of independence in the cultural field became apparent when King Ramkhamhaeng fostered the arts, and later – in the 16th and 17th centuries – when Ayutthaya became the cultural centre of South-East Asia and with the Khmer kingdom, Thai art spread further afield. Generally speaking, however, it seems to have been the Thai nature to adopt the culture of others and mould it to conform with their own – especially religious – ideals; right up to the present day Thais have always added their own highly developed and artistic refinements to the cultures of other peoples, but have never demonstrably created any new ones of their own.

Historical research

For many years tomorrow was always regarded by the Thai govenment as being more important than yesterday. It was not until the 1970s that there were any real signs of any scientifically-based research into the past; even then it was mainly foreign institutions which made the first move, an indication of the lack of any real sense of history among the Thai people. Until that time, for example, the curators of the Bangkok National Museum had concentrated solely on preserving important religious memorials, temples and statues of the Buddha. There was not enough interest in chance finds to lead to any organised research or properly planned archaeological digs. Much that would be of great interest and importance to Thailand's cultural development still lies hidden.

This may well arise from the fact that – after the fall of the old capitals of Sukhothai and Ayutthaya and the resultant loss of an inconceivably vast collection of important treasures – the young capital of Bangkok (founded in 1782) was alone regarded as the centre of culture and learning. It is here that the National Museum, the prime centre of art and culture, and the government departments responsible for historical research are situated. However, there are now branches of the National Museum at Ayutthaya, Ban Chiang, Chiang Mai, Chiang Saen, Khon Kaen, Lamphun, Lopburi, Phimai, Nakhon Si Thammarat and Nan, and there are plans for more to be set up in the next few years, specialising in exhibits relating to their own region which will be loaned by the parent museum in Bangkok.

The Ministry of Education and the Ministry for National Development have, with the Royal Family, been in the forefront in promoting and carrying out "cultural decentralisation" and since the 1970s the Tourism Authority of Thailand (TAT) has also pursued the same aim with the help of international donations. As a consequence large organised trips around the country have been arranged and new discoveries made which show that the provinces also possess a wealth of cultural and natural treasures.

Origins of Thai art

How culture spread from the probable country of origin of the Thai peoples, now southern China, one cannot say. What is certain, however, is that there must have been a distinctive culture, with strong Indian influence, which the Thais adapted, mixing and combining, for example, Buddhist with Brahmin and Hindu forms.

The oldest building remains discovered in what is now Thailand were not the work of the Siamese, who only came here from China

Art-historical sites in Thailand
MYANMAR (BURMA)
LAOS
VIETNAM
Chiang Saen
Chiang Rai
Phayao
Nan
Chiang Mai
Lamphun
Lampang
Phrae
Mekong (Menam Khong)
Si Satchanalai
Chaliang
Ban Chiang
Salween
Sukothai
Phitsanulok
That Phanom
Kamphaeng Phet
Meklong
Chaiyaphum
Si Thep
Menam
Phimai
Si Saket
Sanburi
Phra Buddhabat
Lopburi
Khao Phra Viharn
Suphanburi
Ayutthaya
Prakhon Chai
Bang Pa In
Nakhon Pathom
BANGKOK
Thonburi
CAMBODIA
Phetchaburi
Chonburi
MYANMAR (BURMA)
Gulf of Thailand
VIETNAM
Chaiya
Nakhon Si Thammarat
Indian Ocean
Songhkla
South China Sea
Pattani
MALAYSIA
200 km
© Baedeker

many centuries later, but rather that of the Khmer, Burmese and – to a lesser degree – Laotians.

Art Styles

Although the various religious trends over the centuries can be placed in some sort of order, it is nevertheless very difficult to separate the various Thai art styles, so the following survey can give only the broad outlines.

Dvaravati or Mon style (6th–13th c.)

The cultures of the time of the Dvaravati or Mon Dynasty – between the end of the 6th and the 11th/12th c. and when the capital during the dynasty's heyday was probably Nakhon – can best be seen in the Thailand central plain (Nakhon Pathom, Prachinburi, Lopburi) and in the north (Sukhotai and Lamphun). Although only a few buildings from this period still remain, those that do bear witness to a developing Thai culture of its own. Stupas or chedis of burnt brick, square or octagonal in plan, are already being richly decorated with pillars and window-ledges; the central section already shows the typical bell-shape, and the conical spires consist of numerous rings laid one on top of the other. Ornamentation is of terracotta and stucco. A particularly fine example of a chedi from the Dvaravati period is Wat Kukut in Lamphun. The Buddhist influence is already evident in these early examples of Thai culture; examples remain of the "Wheel of Law", based on the first sermon by the Enlightened Buddha in Benares. Buddha sculptures, at least those from the first two Dvaravati periods, appear quite clearly to be based on Indian models.

Srivijaya style (7th–end of 13th c.)

While Thai art was enjoying its first great flowering in the Dvaravati period another style was also developing, indicating that art was in fact living a "double life" at the time. In those early years at least two cultures were evolving quite separately: the Dvaravati style was devoted unmistakably to the teachings of Buddha, while the Srivijaya

Chedi from the Dvaravati period in the Wat Kukut in Lamphun

style – which originated in the kingdom of Srivijaya in the Indonesian archipelago – was initially dedicated to Hinduism. Vishnu, the multi-armed god far from his own doctrinal home, is depicted as Linga, the phallic symbol of Shiva. Influences emanating from the island of Java can be seen in, for example, the figures of Buddha at Songkhla. Towards the end of the Srivijaya period some of the Khmer style art-forms were also incorporated and numerous examples of these have survived; many excellent finds can be seen in the National Museum in Bangkok.

Khmer style (7th–13th c.)

Parallel with the styles just described there unfolded the very important Khmer style, examples of which still show unmistakably that it had a very profound effect on the cultures of the kingdoms of Dvaravati and Srivijaya. Outstanding examples are the buildings in what is known as the Angkor style of the late 9th c., named after the city of Angkor where markedly differing versions have appeared over the years. In the Khmer kingdom, which reached from Cambodia as far as Thai country at times, Hinduism and Mahayana Buddhism ruled supreme. Lopburi ranked as the most important cultural centre of Mon. The likenesses of Buddha dating from this period all depict a square face with stern features.

Not many buildings have survived from this time, but the finest and almost completely preserved are to be found, for example, in Phimai or near Phrakon Chai.

Angkor Wat style (late 12th c.)

The Angkor Wat style gained in popularity during the campaigns of conquest by the Khmer into what is now Thailand. Especially typical of this style is the Crowned Buddha seated on a wounded serpent with his head protected by a splayed-out shield in the shape of a seven-headed serpent. This form can be traced back to an old legend which says that, on the 42nd day after Buddha received Enlightenment, Muchalinda

A relief on the central prang of the Khmer Sanctuary in Phimai

Entrance to the Wat Prasat Phanom near Nakhon Ratchasima

(Naga), the King of the Serpents, spread out his many heads to protect him from the heavy rains which poured down on him all day long as he sat under a tree. As well as religious and historical themes the everyday life of the Thai is now also beginning to be depicted.

Anyone who is interested in learning more about the unique Angkor Wat style should visit the town of that name in Cambodia.

Chiang Mai style (11th–mid 16th c.)

The main centres of this cultural form are the cities of Chiang Mai, Chiang Saen and Lamphun; it is the style of the Lan Na kingdom. A distinction should be made between statues influenced by the early Chiang Saen style, which probably prevailed at the end of the 12th c. when Thai princes resided in this region, and those in the Chiang Mai style, which developed in the middle of the 14th c. some 50 years after the founding of the city from which it took its name. Some examples of the latter still remain, while hardly any of the Chiang Saen style have in fact survived.

Figures of Buddha from this period have stern, almost arrogant features, with plumpish bodies and barrel chests. Normally he is found seated on a double row of lotus leaves complete with stamens. Many Buddhas were carved from semi-precious stone such as rock crystal. Important examples have survived, such as the famous Jade Buddha in Wat Phra Kaeo in Bangkok, presumed to be from the Chiang Mai epoch.

U Thong style (*c.* 1220–1350)

Named after King U Thong, who also built a city of the same name in central Thailand, the title U Thong style embraces sculptures of certain forms which clearly differ from the contemporary Sukhotai style. There were three distinct forms of U Thong, those which show a clear Dvaravati and Khmer influence and, towards the end of the 13th c., a definite leaning to the Ayutthaya style.

Typical of all the U Thong styles is the seated figure of Buddha, whom the sculptor has depicted invoking the Earth, wearing a narrow

Standing Buddha in the Wat Si Iriyabot in Kamphaeng Phet

headband and with a length of material over his shoulders. Some experts think they can detect signs of the U Thong style in architecture as well, although it is in fact very difficult to differentiate between this and the Lopburi Khmer style.

Sukhothai style (end of 13th to early 15th c.)

The naming of Sukhothai as the capital of the new kingdom in 1279 saw the end of the dominance of the Khmer style of architecture. However, the Khmer temples were not pulled down; instead their exteriors were altered to accord with the new ideas, so it can be said that the Sukhothai is in fact only a variation on the Khmer or Lan Na styles. In spite of the intensive search for a completely new identity it could not be said to have been a completely fresh art form. It was clearly influenced by Ceylon and Burma as well as by Nakhon Si Thammarat far away on the Malay Peninsula.

Sculpture, too, was "modernised"; when the top layer was removed from some Buddha statues ostensibly in the Sukhothai style (as indicated by the use of fine and curved lines) an obvious "Khmer face" was revealed.

Sukhothai saw the first example of a Buddha pictured striding along, a pose in which the Enlightened One had never been depicted before. Unfortunately little remains today of one of the finest examples of this, in Wat Si Iriyabot in Kamphaeng Phet. This pose results from a legend according to which Buddha, after entering Nirwana, returned to Earth down a mystical staircase accompanied by Brahma and Indra after having tried to convert his deceased mother to his teachings.

The Sukhothai style is usually regarded as the most beautiful even if not the purest of Thai architectural styles. It was influenced by no fewer than nine kings, in particular by the third of them, the aesthetically-minded Ramkhamhaeng, who reigned from 1279 to 1299. Surviving examples can be found today not only in Sukhothai itself but all over Thailand as well. A particularly fine example is the Buddha figure in the northern wiharn of the Phra Pathom chedi in Nakhon Pathom. Although the body is more recent, a close inspection reveals that the head, hands and feet are from a statue of the Sukhothai period.

Ayutthaya style (*c.* 1350–1767)

The second great culture of Thailand blossomed during the time of the Ayutthaya kingdom, in which the search for new forms led to a surge of artistic creation such as had not been seen before. Although at the outset the influences of the earlier Gupta and Khmer models could be clearly seen it was not long before some almost entirely unique building fashions came to the fore, concentrating fine structuring, lofty edifices and lively decoration.

Elongated and delicate sculptural forms are also characteristic of this period. Now, too, the manner in which Buddha is depicted sets the pattern for a whole era; the very massiveness of the figures shows the importance of this realm and the self-portrayal of the ruler.

After the Burmese attacks in 1767 little remained of Ayutthaya except a vast area of ruins, giving only a faint idea of the city's former glory. There are said to have been 400 temples in the city alone; visitors described it as "the most beautiful they had ever seen".

Thonburi style (*c.* 1767–80)

It took some time for the Thais to recover from the total destruction of their culture in Ayutthaya and the development of new art forms – themselves largely based on old traditions – in Thonburi during the reign of King Taksin was slow indeed. Painting alone displayed new ideas; architecture, on the other hand, showed little change from what had gone before (see, for example, Wat Arun in Bangkok). Temples from this period are often adaptations of those in other towns in Thailand.

Bangkok or Rattanakosin style (*c.* 1780–1930)

Magnificent buildings, increasingly betraying Western influences, sprang up in the new capital of Bangkok. The rulers of the Chakri dynasty in particular made their mark as architects in the city where they resided, although their buildings are largely lacking in spiritual expression. Moreover, the Bangkok style brought little that was new; on the contrary, builders restricted themselves mainly to refining traditional styles, as evidenced by the rich decoration and lively ornamentation found in numerous temples, such the Wat Phra Kaeo in Bangkok. Many of the buildings are falling into ruin, as many temples were built of wood and emphasise the transitory nature of all earthly things; in recent years determined efforts have been made to save these buildings.

In order to document historical continuity some famous statues from all eras and from all over the country have been assembled in Bangkok. Only in painting were there signs of a progressive influence, as can be clearly seen in a number of Bangkok temples.

Contemporary art

Since the 1930s attempts have been made to emulate modern Western artists. However, that does not apply so much in the field of temple-building, where traditional forms are still used, even though modern building materials – such as the Italian marble used in Wat Benchamabophit in Bangkok – may be employed.

Since about 1960 an increasing amount of Thai art has been discovered in the outlying provinces, and since 1975 such finds and the areas where they were discovered have systematically been made available to the new generation of art students as well as to tourists. There is a general feeling of nostalgia and a return to traditional Thai styles, with some additions, such as introducing perspective in paintings.

The Fine Arts

Early history

In contrast to today the early days of Buddhism saw no statues of him at all; in fact, it seems that any attempt to produce paintings or idols of the Enlightened One would have been severely frowned upon. Sym-

A monumental figure of Buddha in Sukhothai

Wall-painting in the Wat Phra Kaeo in Bangkok (restored)

Buddha Figures

Mon style

Khmer style (13th c.)
Buddha as a physician

Lan Na style, late 15th c.

Sukhothai style

Thai style 12th/13th c.
Suphanburi/Sankhaburi

Ayutthaya style

bols such as lotus-blossoms depicting the beauty and complete harmony which appears to come from nothing, the Bodhi tree as the Tree of Enlightenment, the Wheel of Law, the holy footprint or the stupa were considered sufficient to instil into the faithful the Buddhist teachings and way of life.

However, some researchers in Ceylon (Sri Lanka) are said to have thought that there were Buddha statues as long ago as the 3rd c. B.C., when Buddhism made its triumphal march through Asia under the Indian King Ashoka. However, with the arrival of Mahayana Buddhism this view became less fashionable, especially outside Ceylon. What is clear is that, as time went by, people began to want something more than parables and symbols and expressed a wish for the Buddha (and the Bodhisattvas, the Enlightened One as he remained on earth) to be shown in a more recognisable form.

The earliest known likenesses of Buddha date from the 1st c. B.C. They came from the kingdom of Kubhana in northern India during the reign of King Kanishka, a keen patron of the arts, and also in the towns of Mathura and Ghandara, important centres of Indian art at that time. In the latter an art style developed which was probably strongly influenced by artists from Persia, which then formed part of the kingdom of Alexander the Great; it is therefore known as the Greco-Buddhist style.

Essential features of Buddhist sculpture

These early statues show the Buddha in a standing or sitting position, and already appear to incorporate the established principles of proportion, attributes and gestures which were to continue to be used in statues of him in the centuries which followed. Perhaps these forms were borrowed from a pre-Buddhist book of astrology and were meant to illustrate a superhuman and metaphysical personage.

Depicting the Buddha in this way no doubt sprang from the desire to create a "correct" likeness that would stand the test of time and would

Figure of Buddha: Khymer style (Lopburi)

Sukhothai style (Sukhothai)

rise above mere worldliness and finiteness and show the way to true Enlightenment. The physical proportions are based on cosmic ratios. The transfigured body of Buddha displays 32 principal characteristics (later increased by a further 80). Examples of these are the growth on the top of the head (Ushnisha, the symbol of Omniscience), which comes to a point in Thailand, is conical in shape in Cambodia or elsewhere may resemble a flickering flame; the curl (Urna) between the eyebrows, frequently represented as a spot or as a precious stone radiating light in many colours; the hair on the head, styled in small curls or waves, and the halo (the symbol of Energy) above the head or over the whole of the body. The body is sexually neutral, the palms of the hands and the soles of the feet often display the "Wheel of Law" (e.g. set in mother-of-pearl), and usually the Buddha is wearing only a simple monk's robe with the right shoulder left bare. The face, normally oval in shape, is peaceful and relaxed, often with a serene smile. Buddha's noble birth is indicated by the long ear-lobes, for only the rich could afford the heavy ear-rings which would stretch them to that extent.

Statues of the Buddha display little evidence of the careful study of the physiological structure of the human body and of movement which is so evident in, for example, Greek sculpture. To the Hindu mind, movement is an expression of the sensorial and fertile energy within the body; thus it becomes perfectly natural for Vishnu, for example, normally to be portrayed as a multi-armed god or for other gods to have several heads.

There have been very few changes made since the very early Buddha statues; the sculptors continue to be guided by traditional principles rather than indulge in free expression. Nevertheless, the artist's own religious experiences do often find expression in his work, which otherwise is always anonymous.

In accordance with ancient tradition, new figures of Buddha have life breathed into them at a festival of dedication, when the spirit of Buddha is thought to enter the statue. Nine very symbolic articles are then built into the body; a broken statue is considered worthless, for it will have lost its strength. The same applies to those which have lost their heads, which explains why the Burmese "beheaded" hundreds of Buddha figures when they sacked Ayutthaya in 1767.

Postures of Buddha

The Buddhist religion recognises four possible positions in which to portray the Buddha: standing, sitting, striding and prone. There are five variations of both the sitting and standing positions, with precise methods of holding the hands, each of which has its own symbolic meaning. The prone position symbolises the moment when Buddha enters Nirwana, and sometimes also that of his death. Many variations on the classical positions stem from the sign language used in Indian (and Thai) dances and mean little to the lay visitor.

The standing positions are: standing upright and straight; with the hip turned inwards (double bend); head, body and legs form angles (triple bend); one leg oustretched and one slightly bent (lunge position) and one leg slightly bent and one drawn up towards the abdomen (dance position).

The classical sitting positions are: cross-legged, with the soles of the feet not visible (cross-over position); cross-legged, soles of feet visible

Postures and Gestures of Buddha

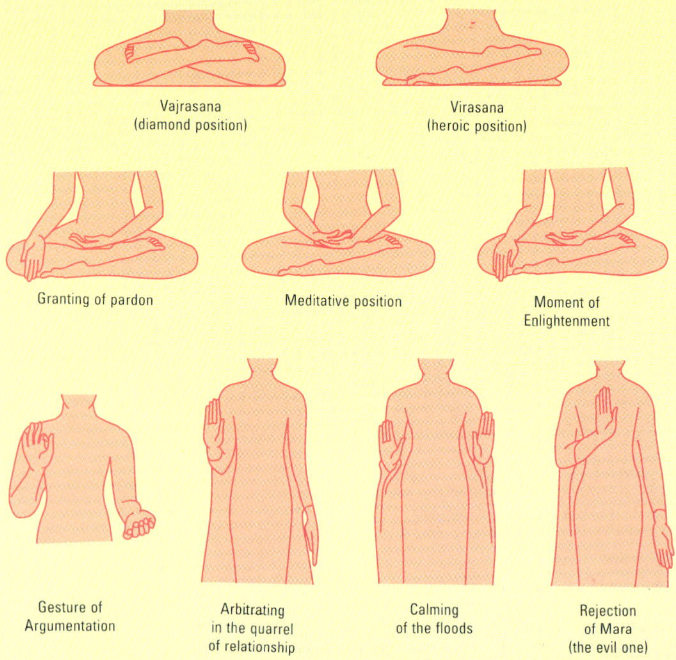

(diamond position, lotus position, meditation position); one leg tucked under, the other hanging straight down (relaxed position); sitting in the European manner, with both legs hanging down (typical of the "Buddha of the Future", or "Maitreya"). Quite often Buddha sits on the body of the Naga serpent, a demi-godlike creature from Indian mythology which lives in a legendary beautiful kingdom in the Underworld. Muchalinda, one of the Naga kings, protected Buddha when he was meditating in a heavy rainstorm by spreading out his five (sometimes depicted as seven) heads over him like a fan.

Typical of the Thai Buddha are the delicate, finely-moulded hands. The main hand positions, the "fixed seals" (mudra) to which the sculptors devote considerable attention, include the gesture of Fearlessness or Giving of Protection (abhaya-mudra, where the right hand is raised, with its palm facing forward), and that of Adoration or Worship (anjali-mudra; the hands are raised with palms together and fingers slightly bent – this hand position is found especially in portrayals by disciples of Buddha).

The gesture of Appealing to Earth (bhumisparsa-mudra), in which the right hand hangs down, palm facing backwards, above the crossed legs and an extended finger points to the ground, is derived from a legend. It is said that when Buddha was deep in meditation Mara, the Wicked One, appeared and attempted to prevent his attaining Enlightenment. As a witness to his virtue Sidharta Gautama (Buddha) called up the Earth Goddess Thorani by scratching the ground with his finger tips. Thorani's hair became full of water, for after every good deed Gautama offered up water to her. Thorani then wrang out her hair, the resultant flood swept Mara and his helpers away and Gautama became the Vanquisher of Mara (maravijaya).

In the gesture of the Turning of the Wheel of Law (dharmachakra-mudra) the hands are placed upon the breast, palms facing each other, thumbs and index fingers touching, the remaining fingers slightly stretched and spread out. This gesture reflects Buddha's first sermon following his Enlightenment.

In the dhyana-mudra or samadhi-mudra, the gesture of meditation, both Buddha's hands lie in his lap, one on top of the other, with the palms facing upwards.

The gesture of Fulfilment (karana-mudra) shows the index and small fingers stretched upwards. The middle and ring fingers are bent and covered by the thumbs.

The typical gesture of the Universal or Original Buddha, the most mystical Buddha of the Vajarayana school (adibuddha) is often shown in unity with the temporal principle (sakti). His arms are crossed on his chest and in his hands he holds a bell and a thunderbolt.

Bodhisattvas

Bodhisattvas, found only in Mahayana Buddhism, are more slender than most figures of Buddha and are also sexually neutral. They wear a crown on the head and jewellery on the neck, chest, arms and legs. The upper body is unclothed apart from a ribbon or shawl across the shoulders. The poses are more relaxed than those of Buddha statues and therefore cannot be universally classified. An attempt has been made to put them into eight basic groups, of which the most popular are the bodhisattva avalokiteeshvara (Protector from Danger) and bodhisattva maitreya (Buddha of the Future). The first of these is an incarnation of a definite type of Buddha, so the front of his crown is adorned with a small figure of Buddha. He often holds a lotus blossom, so has been named bodhisattva padmapani ("He with the Lotus Blossom in his Hand"). In his crown (jatamukuta) the bodhisattva maitreya wears a stupa symbol.

Bodhisattvas often have many arms and legs, apparently intended to illustrate their supernatural spiritual and physical powers. The eleven-headed bodhisattva, for example, has a thousand arms which embrace its body like a spoked wheel.

Garuda figure in the Wat Phokhaokaeo near Ubon Ratchathani

Brahman deities

Of the Brahman deities those most frequently portrayed are Brahma, Shiva, Vishnu, Indra, Ganesha and the goddess Lakshmi, usually in a typically Thai version. Brahma, the Omniscient and Omnipresent One and Founder of the Universe, has four crowned heads pointing to the four points of the compass and four hands holding a staff, a pitcher containing water from the River Ganges and a rosary. Shiva, with a serpent across his shoulders or with a beast of burden, the bull Nandi, is a dancing god symbolising Becoming and Passing Away, or alternatively his Linga (phallus) is worshipped in the form of a stone pillar several metres tall. Frequently he is seen with his wife Parvati. Vishnu, the Receiver of Life, is found either astride Garuda the Bird King (with the head, wings and beak of an eagle but the body of a man) or seated on the Serpent of the World or with his wife Lakshmi who is often shown seated on a lotus blossom with more such flowers or leaves in her hands. Other Indo-Brahman statues show Indra, the Invincible One, who defeats all enemies and restores natural order, the thunderbolt (Vajra) and the three-headed elephant Erawan, as well as the god Ganesha who, although somewhat low in the hierarchical order, is said to bring luck; he has the head of an elephant and four hands holding a lotus blossom, a shell, a discus and a club.

Materials

From the outset the fine arts in Thailand have included both free-standing sculptures as well as reliefs such as figurative and ornamental decoration (including plant themes) on buildings. The materials most often used are sandstone and limestone; less common are bronze, jade, rock crystal and stucco. Metal is often gilded.

◀ *Buddha in the Wat Traimitr in Bangkok, one of the finest figures of Buddha in Thailand*

Theatre

In contrast to Western cultures, if we exclude dance and music it has to be said that true theatre as such has not really taken off in Thailand, even though there exist some excellent translations of plays by Molière, Shakespeare and Goethe, among others. Thai theatre is an amalgam of dance, pantomime, music and song, and this is what the Thailander craves every time he attends. This means that the problem areas which form part of any Western tragedy hold no interest for the Thai Buddhist; in fact he would almost be against such a thing, because for him it is almost a religious taboo to present personal sorrows and differences to the public gaze. The same goes for music; anything in the form of an aesthetic entity – such as Mozart or the "Nutcracker" ballet suite – always attracts a full house, but the reverse is true of Richard Strauss, Wagner or even modern free dancing.

Lakon Nai, Kon

The Thai word for theatre is "lakon". There are four main categories, the most important of which is lakon nai, or indoor theatre, commonly known as "kon". Originally restricted to royal palaces, it now forms the main repertoire of the Bangkok National Theatre. Actors and actresses train for a year as dancers and musicians in a school attached to the theatre which ranks as a college. The pupils are chosen when aged between eleven and fourteen from schools all over the country, after strict tests of talent and application.

All male roles depicting rank, such as princes or kings, have always been and continue to be filled by young actresses, while demons and animals – especially monkeys – are acted by acrobatically-trained male graduates of the college. The main theme of this classical dance drama is based on episodes from the "Ramakien" (see Literature). Every Thai child grows up familiar with the colours and designs of the costumes

Thai theatre: a synthesis of four elements

and headgear worn by the actors and knows that the masks hide only demons and animals; the "goodies" no longer wear them, and briefly inform the audience who they are. Sixty-eight gestures – mainly movements of hands and head – hint at words unspoken, especially those linked with sorrow or eroticism.

Nang Yai, Shadow-theatre

The second category of Thai theatre is shadow-theatre (nang yai). Until the end of the absolute monarchy these pictures artistically impressed on buffalo-hide measuring at least three feet square performed both a festive and popular function: when a royal cremation ceremony took place on the Sanaam Luang, the royal meadow in front of the Grand Palace in Bangkok, these pictures would be raised on bamboo poles over 20m/66ft tall in front of the fire to illustrate dramatic scenes from the Ramakien. Today this theatrical form has been almost completely superseded by the cinema. When, from time to time, it is wished to honour a deceased teacher from the National Theatre College, they no longer use Nang Yai pictures painted on buffalo hide; instead, the graduates themselves are the actors and "entertain" the mourners.

Nan Puppet shadow-theatres

Puppet shadow-theatres (nan), on the other hand, have continued to flourish, especially in southern Thailand, but also at local festivals and in temple gardens in Bangkok itself. Just as artistically stamped out in leather, but measuring only 20 to 50cm/8 to 20in. high, these figures are manipulated in front of a cotton screen illuminated from the rear. The people involved, usually members of the same family, consist of a reciter, who explains what is going on, a musician and one or two who manipulate the puppets. They position 100 or more figures on the stage and move them in turn as required. There is no question that this form of puppetry originated in Indonesia and Malaysia, but restricting it to black and white figures and silhouettes and a few epic themes is genuine Thai, which above all keeps to the Thai style of script, verse combined with prose.

Making shadow-theatre puppets from buffalo hide

Lykay

Probably the most popular form of theatre, however, is Lykay, a mixture of operetta, cabaret and circus effects conjured up by the effective use of colour and light. Scarcely comprehensible to anyone not fluent in the language and familiar with local politics, however, at first glance the Westerner may see little in it to interest him, but the fact that it attracts large audiences of all ages and classes of people shows that it has a fascination all of its own.

Puppet shows

The fourth form of Thai theatre, puppet shows, will be available to the brief visitor to Thailand only if he is well acquainted with somebody locally, because they are usually put on only at private parties and the like, which would not normally be advertised or open to foreigners and strangers.

Dance

Traditional Thai dancing goes back over hundreds of years. As with theatre, young girls throughout the country are selected by means of strict tests and then trained in Bangkok for several years until they reach artistic maturity. Promising young girls are also taught dancing skills by older women in their villages, which itself ensures that traditions are passed on in this field.

Country folk in particular need no excuse to dance, be it at seed-sowing time or to celebrate the harvest. Dances with a spiritualist background play an important part in the lives of the mountain dwellers in particular.

Fortunately the sense of tradition is sufficiently strong in Thailand for dances still to be performed in the original way, even when it just is for the benefit of tourists.

A dance with bamboo poles

Dancing with bamboo poles

Dancing with bamboo poles is the most classical dance of all and has become known throughout the world as the result of being performed by touring dance groups from Thailand. Four pairs of male dancers each have two bamboo poles and beat them against one another in time to the music. The pairs of dancers stand in the middle and move alternately between the poles when they are apart or to the sides when they are closed. This dance requires great skill and musicality.

Finger-nail dance

Finger-nail dancing originated in northern Thailand. It was performed almost exclusively on important festival occasions and sometimes during state visits. Today it forms an important part of performances put on mainly for the benefit of tourists and photographers in, for example, the Rose Garden near Nakhon Pathom or in "Old Chiang Mai" in the town of that name.

On the tips of their fingers the dancers wear long, pointed "thimbles" made from gilded paper or silver. As with all Thai dances, the various hand and finger positions (of which there are dozens) all have a different meaning, most of which will be unintelligible to the uninformed foreigners in the audience.

Candle dance

Symbolically-speaking, the candle dance is similar to the finger-nail dance described above, except that instead of thimbles the dancers carry lighted candles; this dance can be most impressive, especially when performed in complete darkness.

Dance of the magic hen

The dance of the magic hen is one the oldest dances in Thailand and is seen mostly in the north of the country. It is based on an old game about disputes between two towns in North Thailand, and portrays just a small part of it dealing with love, death and mourning. Contemporary choreography is of more recent date, having been arranged by Chao Darasmi in the 1920s.

A "figure-nail" dance

Dances of the mountain peoples

The mountain peoples of North Thailand have also jealously guarded their traditional dances for many hundreds of years. However, their dances are based less on history and old tales and more on animistic or mystical themes.

A good example of such dances is the one where the spirits of their ancestors are exorcised. During the short performance the said spirits are invited to take possession of the bodies of the dancers and to enjoy to excess the fun and pleasure of the dance. The dancers are usually relatives of the ancestors whom they desire to honour (see Population, Hill tribes). When the dancer utters a sharp cry that is an unmistakable sign to the onlookers that the spirit has taken possession of him; when the dance is over the spirit will have had its fun and will then leave the body of the dancer.

Literature

Until well into this century Thailand literature was restricted almost entirely to Court circles, something created by the aristocracy (kings in particular) for the aristocracy. Subjects covered, too, were those favoured by the Court: academic verse, tales of journeys and voyages ("Nirat"), rowing ballads, epic poems and books teaching language and literature. All early works were in rhyming verse, and it was not until the Bangkok period that prose works began to appear.

Much of Thai literature was lost for ever as a result of the destruction of Ayutthaya by the Burmese in 1767; most of the little that was saved is now hidden in archives awaiting research.

In 1283 King Ramakhamhaeng composed a Thai alphabet which is still in use today and has proved to be the most significant milestone in the history of original Thai literature. The king used it to draft his own declaration of accession to the throne, engraved in stone and now housed in the National Museum in Bangkok; it was also probably he who compiled a poem on the modes of moral behaviour to be followed in the different situations one meets in life. The description of the Buddhist cosmography ("Traiphum") is attributed to his successor, Liu Thai (1347–68) and the description of life at the Sukhothai Court is probably by one of the ladies-in-waiting.

Court literature

Typical subjects covered in Court literature – many of which also found their way into the country's music (see entry) – include love stories filled with romance, plotting and intrigue and always with a hero who survives daredevil adventures. Many of the stories are enriched with settings based on fantasy, religion or myth, and some were based on ancient folklore subsequently enriched and changed as the result of later events in Thailand's own history.

Religious traditions, stemming mainly from Indian literature, have always played an important role. Mahabharata and Ramayana both form part of world literature, as do the old Javanese poem of Inao and numerous legends from the Jataka, the 500 lives of Buddha.

Mahabharata (Indian poetry)

Mahabharata probably has its roots in history, namely, the struggle between the Pandava and the Kaurava for supremacy in the region around what is now Delhi. This particular event has, however, become intermixed with numerous other poems, myths about gods and heroes, love stories and religious and philosophical discourses which have little to do with its true roots. The whole work consists of 110,000 verses dating from somewhere between the 4th c. B.C. and the 4th c. A.D.

Inao (Javanese poetry)

The Javanese dramatic poem describes the adventures of the Prince with the Glass Dagger who finally succeeds in winning the hand of the beautiful Princess Busba.

Ramakien (Thai poetry)

The epic poem Ramakien is the Thai version of the Indian Ramayana ("To the Glory of Rama"), which had probably been written in the 3rd c. B.C. Its central theme is the struggle between gods and demons, a sort of knightly epic of 24,000 lines. In two books added later the hero becomes an incarnation of the god Vishnu who, in the form of Rama, comes down to earth for the seventh time in order to destroy the demon-king Ravana. He becomes born one of the three sons of the King of Ayodhaya (a city on the River Sarayu in northern India) and falls in love with the king's daughter Sita who is abducted by a demon-king who forces her to live with him. After all kinds of adventures Rama succeeds, with the help of the King of the Apes, in freeing Princess Sita. However, the people are against their union even though Sita, as a sign of her innocence and virginity, rises unharmed from a burning funeral pyre. Fifteen years after Rama had disowned her he takes her back when he recognises twins which were born to Sita as his own sons. Again Sita protests her innocence, saying that the Earth will open up if she is lying. The Earth does open up and swallows Sita.

The final outcome varies; the Indian version says that Rama and Sita are reunited in Heaven, whereas in the Ramakien this happens on Earth. In the eyes of the Thais the Ramakien is a timeless tale which, made into a theatrical play by several kings, is today performed on Buddhist Holy Days.

Literature in the Ayutthaya period

Literary accomplishment blossomed during the Ayutthaya period. In "Yuon Phai" King Boroma Trailokanat (1448–88) describes the victory over Chiang Mai, and in "Mahachat", also in verse form, the last of Buddha's previous existences. The epic poem "Phra Lao" by an unknown poet (possibly King Boroma Trailokanat or even King Narai) tells of the love of Prince Lao for two princesses in a hostile country, ending with the deaths of all three. The sentimental descriptions go into great detail and provide a deep insight into the lives of the characters.

One of the great patrons of Thai literature was King Narai, who invited many artists and writers to his Court in Lopburi, including the poet Sri Phrat. The latter also wrote the love stories "Anirut" and "Kamsuon Sri Phrat". The theme of such stories is always the same: obstacles are put in the way of the lovers, they are separated but find one another again after numerous adventures. The reign of Narai also saw the writing of "Cindamani", a manual of language and literature, as well as the travel poem "Thawathosamat", describing what the traveller saw in his year-long wanderings through the country.

Writings in the Bangkok period

After the fall of Ayutthaya Thai literature also faded away for a time, even though King Taksin worked on four episodes of the Ramakien for the Lakon Theatre.

A new literary surge took place under the rulers of the Chakri dynasty. Rama I, for example, produced the only complete version of the Ramakien epic in the Thai language. One of his sons, Poromanuchit Chianrot, made a name for himself as a prolific writer, including a biography of Buddha and the novel "Naresuan" which describes the duel between King Naresuan and the Crown Prince of Burma.

A high point in the more recent history of Thai literature was reached during the rule of King Rama II when he made Sunthorn Phu from south Thailand the Court Poet. Sunthorn is the country's foremost writer, famous for his vivid imagination and poetic language. His masterpiece is "Phra Aphaimani", comprising 24,500 verses and telling of the loves, struggles and adventures of a prince. The theme is traditional, it is true, but the language breaks away from traditional rigid forms and adopts a more folksy style. Sunthorn also wrote a travel poem, several tales written in prose, as well as academic poems for ladies and princes. In conjunction with King Rama I he produced a revised edition of the romantic novel "Khun Chang, Khun Phaen" which had been first written during the Ayutthaya period, and the King himself compiled several episodes of the Ramakien and of the Inao for the Lakon Theatre, and wrote five plays for the Folk Theatre. Under King Rama III Sunthorn Phu fell into disfavour and spent eighteen years as an itinerant preacher, alchemist and monk; later, however, Rama IV bestowed on him the honorary title of "Phra Sunthorn Woham", the equivalent of "Lord Sunthorn, the Enlightened One".

Later kings also made names for themselves as poets. Rama IV wrote "London", describing his impressions on a trip to that city; Chulalongkorn (Rama V) reports on his second journey to Europe in "Klai Ban" (Far from Home), actually a collection of letters to his daughter. Considerable linguistic skill was displayed in translating some of the stories from "A Thousand and One Nights".

However, it was Rama VI who proved to be Thailand's most prolific author. He wrote 54 plays for the theatre, including the very popular "Mathana Patha" (The Killing of the Rose), epic and lyrical works as well as political treatises. He also made a name for himself as a translator of a number of Shakespeare's dramas and sonnets.

Contemporary literature

Contemporary Thai literature is linked to reality, is based on European patterns and deals with present-day problems. 1932 was the year when Thailand published its first constitution and the absolute monarchy was changed into a constitutional one; many of the stories written after that date deal with the lot of the peasants and criticise social conditions.

In addition a unique lyric form has evolved, represented by such names as the teacher and writer Magut Araridi (b. 1950), Nimit Bhumithavorn (1935–81) and the housewife who writes as a hobby, Man-Nan Ja.

For his outstanding services to the literature of Thailand the author Naowarat Pongpaibool (b. 1940; see Famous People) was awarded the ASEAN Prize for Literature in 1980.

Music

Thai music is related to that of other South-East Asian countries. Although the Thai people originated in Canton in southern China it is unclear to what extent Thailand's music is individual or part of the culture of the Sung dynasty. However, it is clear that Chinese, Indonesian and Indian influences play an important part. Traditional Thai music was always linked to the Court and the nobility; popular music is much simpler and more research needs to be done to see whether it is in fact related to Court music in any way.

Musical principles

An established musical system has been known only since the Bangkok period; for many centuries music entered Asian cultures only as a means of portraying and conveying ancient legends and stories and changed little over the years following the Ayutthaya period.

Seven full notes make up the Thai scale, there being no semi-tones such as, for example, the harmony we know in Western music. A melody will normally employ a scale of only five notes at the most. Apart from some theatrical songs which are in 7/4 time, the metre of Thai music is normally in 2/4 time. Only three tempos are used, one slow, one medium and one fast, with the middle tempo effectively forming the metre and melody; the slow tempo is produced by halving the number of beats to the bar, the fast tempo by doubling them. The half-tempo serves to accentuate the rhythm of the melody and the double-tempo embellishes it without really adding anything fresh. The main melody is established and played by only one instrument, the round "wong yai", while the remaining instruments repeat it or play variations on it.

Ensembles and instruments

The traditional Thai orchestra, the "Phipat", consists of a minimum of five ("khruang ha") and a maximum of fifteen ("khruang yai") musicians playing an equivalent number of different instruments. It accompanies practically everything that can be described as festive, attractive to watch or even sensational, ranging from temple and Court ceremonies by way of classical dance and drama to the popular "lykay" at annual markets, shadow-theatres ("nang yai") or sporting competitions.

Percussion instruments play an important part. Melodic instruments include the xylophone (the tall, boat-shaped "ranat el" and the less tall "ranat thum") with wooden rods, the metallophone ("ranat el lek", "ranat thum lek") and semi-circular gong-like xylophones, the "khong wong yai" and "khong wong lek". Cymbals, gongs and drums supply the rhythm. In addition the orchestra may employ wind instruments such as the "pi", a bulbous oboe with four reeds, and the bamboo flute known as the "khlui", string instruments like the "so duang" and "so u" (tubular fiddles) as well as "chakhe" (zithers) and "krachapi" (lutes).

Contemporary music

In recent years Thai music has undergone marked changes. Modern music is very Western-orientated, even though its themes still reflect the country's rich tradition and culture. Peter Feit, the German-born music teacher at the Court of King Rama V, was responsible for transposing much of Thailand's older music into Western notation and thus preserving it for posterity.

A number of Thai composers, including King Bhumibol himself, have mastered several wind-instruments. In the schools most children learn to play the triple-reeded bamboo flute, the "ang dalung"; beggars frequently play this instrument in the streets.

To the Western ear Thai popular music appears somewhat sentimental; the register of the male voice is usually very high. On the other hand, native folk music – often combined with ambiguous humour and always with dancing – is lively and full of rhythm. The tourist will find a higher standard of music in the night-clubs, for example, where the bands are usually composed of local musicians.

Western music

Although Thailanders have shown an interest in Western classical music for a long time now Thai symphony orchestras have been in existence for only a short time. The Bangkok Philharmonic Orchestra and the Bangkok Symphony Orchestra have a good reputation, as have the Bangkok Music Society and the Bangkok Combined Choir. Guest performances by European or international ensembles are comparatively few and far between, and tickets for these are very quickly sold out.

Traditional Sports

Kaeng Wau (Kite-flying competitions)

From the middle of February the Sanam Luang area opposite the Grand Palace in Bangkok is used as a practice-ground for the annual "Kaeng Wau" kite-flying contests, the winner of which is awarded the coveted Royal Cup donated by the King. The contests, which are held in conjunction with chess tournaments, reach their climax in the second half of April. Then huge crowds of onlookers place their bets, eat, drink and follow the events with expert enthusiasm. The Thai kite-fight represents a "celestial" version of the battle of the sexes; the male kite is known as "chula", the female as "pak pao". They are man-sized with a wing-span of more than three feet and are artistic masterpieces with prices to match. The strict rules state that the framework has to be of bamboo poles, if possible three years old, and artistically overlaid. Visitors interested in kite-flying can obtain further details from the Thai Kite Heritage Group, c/o Ron Spaulding, 47 Metheenivet Lane, Soi 24, Sukhumvit Road, Bangkok 10110.

Takraw: a favourite game with young people

Takraw
(Ball-game)

In Takraw the player has to propel a ball, 12cm/5in. in diameter and made of basketwork, through the air using any part of his body except his hands and get it either into his opponent's net which is suspended from a loop 2·75m/9ft high or – another variation of the game – over a 2·5m/8¼ft high net into the opponent's court. This latter "net-Takraw" form of the game is the one agreed upon by all the Asiatic countries taking part in the "ASEAN Games". In Thailand, however, the more popular form is "circle-Takraw", with six or eight players and either with or without a net suspended from a loop in the middle of the circle. When played this way the players stand in a circle an equal distance away from each other. The longer the ball remains in the air the more involved become the contortions of the players, and the higher the ball is headed and the more varied the leaps and parts of the body used to propel the ball, the higher the points scored. A particularly high score is obtained with a "catch-throw", with the foot kicking the ball through a loop formed by the player's own arms, either when jumping up in the air or with the loop being formed behind his back. The ball is "dead" if it touches hand or arm or lands on the floor. The game lasts 40 minutes and there is no rest period.

For a small payment visitors can obtain a ball and try it for themselves. The minimum required is nine different ball exercises, including throwing the ball round the body or rolling it over various parts of the body. Anyone playing solo who can keep the ball off the ground for ten to twelve minutes is up to performing in a European circus and quite good even by Thai standards.

Another variation of the game requires a playing strip measuring 50 by 3m/165 by 10ft along which the player races with the ball, again remembering that it must not be touched with the hand.

The inventors of this wonderful ball-game were two brothers named Dang and Dii who – with true Chinese acumen – made a prosperous business out of it, exporting it and giving demonstrations throughout

Thai boxing, a popular sport

the USA. Dang is said to have been able to keep the ball in the air, using all parts of his body except his hands, while interchanging between lying, sitting, standing and walking. That was about the year 1900; before that a similar game had been played but using a ball made of feathers or bamboo strips and varying in size. In King Naresuan's time (*c.* 1579) the balls must have been extremely big, because elephants used to play "football" with them with criminals condemned to die rolling about inside.

Nowadays there is nothing so macabre about Takraw. The Ministry of Education, numerous clubs and the King himself all patronise the game which, at minimal cost, provides maximum fitness, team spirit and great spectator-appeal. Net-Takraw can be watched at the National Stadium and at Hua Mak Stadium in Bangkok. At the same time "circle-Takraw" has rapidly become an annual super-tournament held on the Sanam Luang in the city, where a member of the royal family awards the major trophy, the Royal Cup, to the winning team.

Krabee-Krabong (Sword-fighting)

The origins of the Thai version of sword-fighting go back many hundreds of years to duels between men – often royal personages – riding on the backs of elephants. Although modern fire-arms superseded this form of battle it was nevertheless jealously preserved as late as the beginning of this century, when King Chulalongkorn ensured that all the princes received instruction in this form of self-defence. King Chulalongkorn himself often practised the "Sword Dance" on elephant-back, not in a duelling sense but as a royal mark of respect to Buddha. Today the swords are blunt or made of wood, but nevertheless injuries still occur. The triple "Wai" uttered during the opening ceremony is intended as a request for a royal pardon should injury be caused.

"Krabee" means small weapons, which can be fixed to the elbow or held in one hand, such as knives, sabres, cudgels, short-swords and shield, or two swords, one in each hand. In "Krabong" lances, spears, longstaffs or pikes are used, all of which require two hands to hold and wield them. The rules vary according to the equipment used.

Usually the tourist will have the chance to watch a performance such as used to be held in the palaces as a "Royal Command Performance". The two opponents will each have two swords. This type of duel is traditionally acompanied by music, from the initial "adagio" to the "crescendo fortissimo" as the fight nears its climax.

This duelling sport obliges the participants to defend themselves by means of technical skill, lightning reactions and attacking moves. Women participate almost as much as men and are quite often the winners.

Muay Thai (Thai boxing)

Legend has it that King Naresuan was able to escape from captivity by the Burmese in 1560 only because he was the best wrestler. This event is still recalled in Thai boxing, which has now become a national sport. Originally it was a form of self-defence which was taught even by the monks in the monasteries.

The rules of Thai boxing can scarcely be compared with the noble art of self-defence as we know it in the West, although "kick-boxing" is in fact now rapidly becoming established here too. The boxer punches and kicks any area of the body which his opponent may offer to him. Stomach and kidney regions are the main targets. Only in recent years have scratching, strangling, biting and spitting been prohibited. When an important contest is being staged in the Bangkok Lumphini Boxing Stadium on a Saturday night the whole nation sits glued to television sets, and tickets are usually sold out well in advance.

Thailand in Quotations

Inscription on the stone tablet kept in the National Museum of Bangkok about the inaugural declaration of King Ramkhamhaeng

Ramkhamhaeng
King of Thailand
(1256?–1317)

May the Land of Sukhotai flourish and thrive. There are fish in the water and rice in the fields. The Lord of the Kingdom raises no taxes on his subjects when they are using the roads on which they drive their cattle to market. They ride their horses; whoever would trade with elephants may do so, whoever would trade with horses may do so; whoever would trade with gold and silver may do so. When a simple man dies, or a man of rank, then his whole possessions, his elephants, wives, children, corn store and rice, his servants and his betel nuts fall to his son. When the king's subjects quarrel, then the king will judge the case in order to get to the basic cause of the dispute, and he will decide in a just manner. He suffers no thieves and rewards no receivers. When he sees the riches of somebody he will not be angry. When someone comes to him riding on an elephant in order to place his land under the protection of the king then he will help him; he will treat him munificently and will care for him and his household. When someone comes to him without elephants and horses, without a noble retinue and without gold and silver, then he will give him something so that he may set up a household. When he takes prisoners of war then he will not have them killed or beaten. Over there at the gate he has had a bell hung up. When a citizen of his country has cause for complaint, either of body or spirit, then he goes there and rings the bell. King Ramkhamhaeng, the ruler of the kingdom will hear the call of the bell and will examine the matter brought by the citizen so that he may come to a just decision for the good of his beloved people. For this the people of Sukhotai praise him.

About foreigners

Rama III
Phra Nang Klao
King of Thailand
(1788–1851)

There will be no more wars against the Burmese and Vietnamese, difficulties only with the "Farang" (= Europeans). Be careful, do not fall into their trap! What they have discovered and done is important for us and we should learn from them and copy them. But we should never entirely trust them.

Anna Harriett
Leonowens
English teacher
and tutor at the
court of King
Rama IV
(1802–7)

"I have 67 children", said His Majesty to me as we entered the audience hall. "You are to teach them and as far as possible also some of my wives insofar as they want to learn English. But you must also help me as I have a great deal of correspondence. Besides, I have great difficulty in reading and writing letters in French although I like the language. You must however promise to teach me also the gloomy, melancholy verbs . . . It will be a pleasure for us that you should live in this palace with our family." I replied that this would be quite impossible for me that, on the one hand, I should master the national language, and on the other be locked inside the gates of the palace every evening. "I should feel like an unfortunate prisoner." "Where are you going then this evening?", he asked furtively. "Without a definite destination I should at any rate feel very foreign here", I replied. "Then it would be useless to have the gates opened", he countered. I feared, however, that I did not wish to live in the palace. "Please remember, Your Majesty, you promised that I should have a residence outside the palace." He looked at me and an angry redness spread over his face. "I don't remember having made such a promise. You are an employee and as such welcome in our palace and I advise you to obey this order." The last four words he almost screamed. I ventured one last contradiction, but he roared me down: "You will live in the palace! I will give you female slaves as your servants." . . . With tear-filled eyes I bowed to him and noticed the astonished look of the Prime Minister's sister. When the king had gone she said, shaking her head repeatedly "My di! My di!" which means as much as "bad" . . . Later the king regretted his self-opinionated decision and accepted my wish.

Duke of Phentièvres "Voyage autour du monde" (*c.* 1849)

In the Grand Palace troops of fifteen to twenty women surprised by this unexpected visit immediately threw themselves down onto the colourful mats which covered the floor; lying on their knees and elbows they seemed very frightened; on seeing us others, probably about 160 in number, fled to the steps, balconies and recesses; others again disappeared like lightning among the shady avenues of the gardens, and behind the cracks of the not quite closed doors curious black sparkling eyes could be seen. Some of them, old matrons with wrinkled skin and withered charms moved aside; others, delicate chocolate-coloured nymphs, young languid sultanas wearing only a narrow band around their upper bodies, short blue skirts and diamonds adorning their necks, arms and legs huddled together in surprise.

First the king headed towards a group of older queens and taking one by the hand he pulled her shaking with fear towards us. Holding her with his right hand he reached for one of our hands with his left which he placed in her hand . . . "Good woman", said the king as he dismissed her after this forced handshake, "she gave me three children." Then he went to fetch another equally ugly one; the same handshake with Madame No . . . "Very good woman", continued the king, "she gave me ten children . . . "

Carl Bock Norwegian Explorer "The Kingdom of the White Elephants" (1885)

Describing a visit to a Karen village
After a tiring time we arrived at about 4 o'clock on a plateau which was fringed by forests and tall grass, a wilderness where some 800 feet above sea level, the Karen village lay. Close by was a village, inhabited by people from Laos, consisting of about half a dozen houses where we intended to set up camp for the night. We were all rather tired since we had been on the move since 4 o'clock in the morning and the route was largely uphill. Entering the Karen village we came first to a single hut in the forest which was built on piles. My leader asked me to go up to it which I did on a rickety ladder. I found myself among three women and two young men . . . Like the Dyak men who have deep incisions in the lobes of their ears in which round ornaments of wood were fixed, these men had bamboo about 4in. long and an inch in diameter in the lobes of their ears. Both men and women had necklaces of glass beads and in addition chains of small round Siamese coins (quarter ticals) . . . Another seven or eight minutes' walk through rice fields brought us to the actual village where we immediately went to the hut of the village chieftain. But even before I had reached the little balcony the chieftain jumped up and fetched a new mat for me to sit on, while his wife and his daughter came out of the hut into which they had withdrawn and at first looked me up and down, then with the greatest nonchalance smiled at me. Their strange gipsy-like features formed a striking contrast to their generally ugly faces. I wondered how the Karen could have chosen this man to be their leader. His right eye was blind with a great grey cataract round the pupil and iris, his face was horribly pockmarked. In addition, looked at closely, he was terribly dirty; his clothes consisted of a loin cloth and an even dirtier jacket which at one time must have been white.

Describing the Thai theatre
When the Siamese become tired of games they visit the nearest theatre . . . (where) normally only girls appear on the stage . . . Most of the performance consists of entwining fingers, hands and arms in such a way that the limbs appear to be dislocated. In Siam the limb movements and gyrations are the same as those seen in Java, but the

clothes worn are different. The young ladies of the "Lakon" wear gilt-embroidered, tight-fitting jackets with epaulettes rather like horns which, with a little imagination, can resemble wings; they wear false finger-nails extending some 12 or 15cm beyond the tips of their fingers and bent over at the end like the horns of long-horned cattle . . . The best theatre in Bangkok is the Phra Mahin and . . . I attended a performance there. The maidens were all attired in Scottish costume, but on their heads they wore a crown in the shape of a Phra Chedi . . . The Siamese are great music-lovers and enjoy European brass instruments as well as their native ones. Every man of rank has at least one band of musicians, two if possible – one playing solely European instruments . . . In (some) cases the conductors are German or Italian, but the players are all Siamese.

Joseph Conrad
(1857–1924)
"Shadowline"

About Bangkok

Early one morning we passed the sandbank (south of Packnam) and as the sun rose shining over the flat plain we streamed upstream along numerous curves in the river, passing under the shadow of the large golden pagoda and reached the outskirts of the city.

There it lay, spread out on both banks of the river, this oriental capital, which has never had to bow to a white conqueror; an extensive, wide area of brown bamboo houses, a mass of interwoven mats and leaves – architecture in the style of a vegetable garden growing out of the brown muddy earth. An almost incredible thought: in this sprawling mass of human shelters there is probably not even a half pound of nails. On his visit to Europe King Chulalongkorn first set foot in Venice and it is this very city which resembles Bangkok the most. For Bangkok is also a city of canals. On both banks of the yellow waters of the Menam, which is as wide as the Rhine at Mainz as it surges towards the Gulf of Siam, an intricate labyrinth of canals criss-crosses the fifteen square miles of lowland on which, circled by white walls beset with towers, Bangkok lies. Yes, it is as if there are, so to speak, two cities: one on top of the other; first, the city of the river and canals with the thousands and thousands of floating houses and where the volume of small and large craft is so dense that it is only with difficulty and thanks to the skill of the half-naked local oarsmen that you can get through. A storey higher on the mainland towers a second city of stone and wooden houses . . .

It is all flat alluvial land, the work of the great Menam, which here, like the Nile in Egypt, waters the land and occasionally floods large areas. So the people who live here have become a kind of amphibians. Those who live on the mainland spend half their lives on or in the water, those who live in the water spend all their lives there . . .

Rama IX
(Bhumibol)
King of Thailand
(b. 1927)

Speech on the opening of railway line

The construction of a railway network not only has the greatest influence on a country's development but is at the same time the most impressive proof of such development. To unite the different regions of a country the railway requires a capable administration for which clear oversight and vision are essential. In creating a means of transport that is both fast and comfortable it brings real investment for the country and manufacturing. Wherever it operates it takes with it enlightenment and encourages a sense of national identity which is such an important element for the well-being of the country.

On the office of a ruler

I have never liked "history" and I would like to add that I have never had the ambition to be a "great" king who "goes down in history". It has been proven that the reigns of such kings were always times of war . . . That is not for me. I hope that as long as I am on the throne my people may live happily and peacefully, without war.

From a speech on his constitutional role as "defender of all faiths"
Every faith has its philosophical and religious principles. Philosophy is a world of ideas and imagination which has to do with the origin and progress of the world and with our own happiness. Every religion has its own path to the goal which may be summarised by concepts such as fortune, heaven or success . . . and for every religion it is an ideal for everyone to help each other to reach this "peak" in the same manner. Along this path we must beware of arguing over what is the best route just because we have different ideas about what is right. Religious disputes could be described as the route to hell. All religions teach love and compassion for others and advocate respect for the convictions of others instead of threats and violence.

MYANMAR (BURMA)
Mae Sai
** Fang
** Chiang Saen
** Chiang Rai
* Phayao
R3
LAOS
VIETNAM
** Chiang Mai
** Lamphun
** Lampang
R2
** Si Satchanalai
* Nakhon Phanom
* Udon Thani
** Ban Chiang
R1
** Sukhothai
** Phitsanulok
* Khon Kaen
** Kamphaeng Phet
Amnat Charoen
* Nakhon Sawan
** Ubon Ratchathani
Chainat
** Nakhon Ratchasima
** Phimai
** Singburi
** Lopburi
** Ayutthaya
** Bang Pa In
** Saraburi
** Prakhon Chai
** Kanchanaburi
R5
R6
** BANGKOK
** Nakhon Pathom
R4
CAMBODIA
MYANMAR (BURMA)
** Phetchaburi
* Pattaya
** Chanthaburi
* Hua Hin
R7
* Sattahip
** Trat
** Rayong
* Prachuap Khiri Khan
Gulf of Thailand
* Chumphon
VIETNAM
Recommended Route (No.)
Places of interest on the route
Line of the route
* especially worth attention
** outstanding
** Surat Thani
** Phangnga
** Nakhon Si Thammarat
** Krabi
** Phuket
South China Sea
Indian Ocean
MALAYSIA
200 km
©Baedeker

Recommended Routes

The following suggested routes are intended to inspire the traveller to discover Thailand while still allowing scope for individual planning.

The routes have been selected to include the main towns, important religious buildings and places of interest so as to provide an insight into Thailand's great past. Not all the places described can be reached without making a detour; some can be omitted to simplify the tour, others can be added. The suggested routes can be easily followed on the map which accompanies this guide, thereby facilitating more detailed planning.

Places and regions listed in the A to Z section are printed in bold type.

Most of the towns, places, islands, regions, nature parks, rivers, etc. and sights mentioned can be found in the index at the end of this guide, so they can be easily located.

The distances in brackets following the titles of the routes are approximate and relate to direct routes. Distances which can be covered in one day are given in the margins. Distances for the longer recommended alternatives or detours are also given.

1. Tour of North-East Thailand

(8 to 9 days; about 2100 or 2600km/1300 to 1600 miles)

This route leads through areas of North-East Thailand which are not yet fully geared to tourism; as a result of this the accommodation on offer will not normally measure up to that available in towns more often visited by tourists. It is not advisable to drink the water, even in hotels; bottled water is safest.

Day 1
Bangkok to Nakhon Ratchasima
(260km/160 miles)

From Bangkok take Highway 1 north past the junction to **Ayutthaya** and on to **Saraburi**, then Highway 2 to **Nakhon Ratchasima**. The first part of this route passes through agricultural areas, mainly paddy-fields, followed by rather barren countryside typical of the north-east.

7km/4 miles this side of Saraburi stands Wat Phra Buddhachai ("Temple in the Shadow of Buddha").

Detour
Wat Phra Buddhabat
(32km/20 miles)

From Saraburi it is worth making a detour to Wat Phra Buddhabat, some 32km/20 miles north along Highway 1. This famous temple is the only one in Thailand with a "genuine" Buddha footprint.

About halfway to Wat Phra Buddhabat lies the cave-temple of Wat Tham Si Wilai with its imposing vault.

Day 2
Nakhon Ratchasima to Khon Kaen
(210km/130 miles)

Look around **Nakhon Ratchasima** early next morning before continuing to Khon Kaen. Although the journey on the second day may offer little in the way of sights – apart from an important detour to **Phimai** – there is nevertheless much to delight the observant traveller.

From Nakhon Ratchasima take Highway 2 north-east; 4km/2½ miles outside the town stands the Khmer temple Wat Prasat Phanom Wan. The tour then continues through villages and larger towns typical of Thailand.

Detour
Phimai
(10km/6 miles)

After 36km/22 miles turn right off Highway 2 to the very interesting Khmer temple complex of **Phimai**, which was restored a few years ago at considerable expense.

Khon Kaen has no sights of outstanding merit, but it is worth visiting on the following morning for two reasons: first, the National Museum has a number of interesting artefacts from early Thai history, including a grave opened up in Ban Chiang and some pottery, and secondly the visitor will be able to relax somewhat and prepare for the longish drive to Ban Chiang on the fourth day.

Day 3
Khon Kaen–
Udon Thani
(130km/80 miles)

The short trip from Khon Kaen to **Udon Thani** (Highway 2 north) provides an opportunity to see the countryside and stop in one or other of the little towns and villages and visit the mainly simple but pretty temples or perhaps a market.

Day 4
Udon Thanai–
Nakhon Phanom
(265km/165 miles)

In order to have enough time to visit Ban Chiang, leave Udon Thani early in the morning, taking Highway 22 eastwards. **Ban Chiang**, where the sensational find of pottery and bronze implements was made in 1967, is 46km/28½ miles from Udon Thani. The site and the National Museum about 1km/½ mile from it are just off Highway 22 (signs at 6km/4 miles).

Detour
Khmer shrine
(12km/7½ miles)

Shortly before reaching the village of Ban That Naweng (about 70km/44 miles from Udon Thani) there is an experimental rice-growing station; from here an unmade-up road leads to an interesting Khmer shrine with some very artistically sculptured door lintels.

Continuing along Highway 22, which turns north-east just before reaching Sakhon Nakhon and the Nong Han reservoir, the traveller will arrive by evening in **Nakhon Phanom**, on the River Mekong which here forms the frontier with Laos.

Day 5
Nakhon Phanom–
Ubon Ratchathani
(270km/168 miles)

From Nakhon Phanom travel south along Highway 212 and after about 30km/19 miles turn off right near Renu Nakhon. A few miles on lies the little village of Ban Renu with the temple of Wat Phra Renu built in the Laotian style.

Semmas (boundary stones) outside the National Museum of Khon Kaen

A further 15km/9 miles along the 212 lies the little township of That Phanom with the Phra That Phanom, another Buddhist shrine built in the Laotian style. There is a lively market on the opposite river bank.

Some 42km/26 miles further on, in Mukdahan, are two temples built by Vietnamese refugees.

Highway 212, which hugged the River Mekong between Nakhon Phanom and Mukdahan, now turns away from the river. The only other place of interest during the remainder of the day's journey to Ubon Ratchathani is Wat Phra Mongkol at **Amnat Charoen**, with its colossal figure of Buddha amid shady trees.

Day 6
Ubon Ratchathani and surroundings

The provincial capital of **Ubon Ratchathani**, with its lively market and several temples, is at its most interesting in the early morning. The surrounding countryside is so delightful that it is worth spending a whole day there, returning in the evening to the "Royal City of Lotus Blossoms", which is what the name means in English.

Day excursion from Ubon Ratchathani (62km/39 miles)

Take the 217 eastwards and change to the 2222 beyond Phibun Mangsahan. After 43km/27 miles the visitor will see Wat Phokhaokaeo, a very pretty temple in red brick. Continuing to Pa Thom, after 7km/4½ miles will be seen the Sao Chaliang hills, a national monument. The rock paintings at Pha Tham, a further 12km/7 miles away, are of importance. From here there is a superb view across the Mekong into Cambodia.

Additional day
Khao Phra Viharn (90km/56 miles)

Those who are interested should consider making an additional day excursion from Ubon Ratchathani to see the Khmer temple of Khao Phra Viharn, which has again been open to visitors from Thailand only (see A to Z, **Si Saket**). Although it is true that the route back to Bangkok later will pass quite close to the temple time then will not really allow a visit (however, there is acceptable accommodation to be found in Surin if desired). The temple lies to the south-west along the 2178, which joins Highway 221 near Kantharalak.

Temple of teak wood in Ubon Ratchathani

Days 7 and 8
Ubon Ratchathani –Nakhon Ratchasima (435km/270 miles)

On the penultimate and very long stage of the tour there are two important sights to visit. To allow sufficient time to see them properly an early start should be made. Drive south-east from Ubon Ratchathani on Highway 24 which then swings west at Det Udom. It is a further 260km/162 miles to **Phrakon Chai** in the province of Buriram.

About 14km/9 miles south of Prakhon Chai lies the little town of Ban Tako, where a board points the way to Wat Prasat Phanom Rung on a hill 158m/519ft above sea-level. Also worth a visit is Wat Prasat Muang Tam, in a valley 8km/5 miles further south. The main shrine is particularly imposing.

Return to Highway 24 and drive 130km/81 miles to Nakhon Ratchasima, which was visited in the course of the Day 2 stage of this tour.

Days 8 and 9
Nakhon Ratchasima –Bangkok (259km/161 miles)

Return to **Bangkok**. A visit can be made to the ruined city of **Ayutthaya,** which will be reached by the early afternoon. From there it is about 60km/37 miles to Bangkok.

2. From Bangkok to Chiang Mai (7 days; about 1000km/620 miles)

This highly recommended route is aimed primarily at those with a keen interest in the history of Thailand. Along the road between Bangkok and Chiang Mai lie the former royal cities of Ayutthaya, Lopburi and Sukhothai, as well as the interesting temple complexes at Kamphaeng Phet. In order to leave ample time for visiting these places none of the individual daily stages is more than about 200km/125 miles long.

It is recommended that the return journey fron Chiang Mai to Bangkok should be by air. Some car rental firms allow the hirer to hand the car back in Chiang Mai.

Day 1
Bangkok–Ayutthaya–Lopburi (174km/108 miles)

Leave Bangkok early in the morning and travel north along Highway 1 and then the 32 for 76km/47 miles to **Ayutthaya**, with its unique ruined city. Be sure to allow plenty of time to visit.

From Ayutthaya take the well made-up Highway 32 (turn east after about 50km/30 miles) to **Lopburi** (98km/61 miles). If time then does not permit visits to the Royal Palace and other sights, save those for the next afternoon when the only item on the programme for the trip to Nakhon Sawan is a temple in Chainat.

Alternative route

Instead of going direct from Ayutthaya to Lopburi the visitor can come back in a south-easterly direction along Highway 1 via **Saraburi** and through the Khao Sam Lan Nature Park to Wat Phra Buddhabat. Proceed from there to Lopburi (17km/10½ miles).

Day 2
Lopburi–Nakhon Sawan (149km/93 miles)

From Lopburi drive to **Singburi** and thence along the 311 to **Chainat** (85km/53 miles), where a short visit to Wat Thammamun with its statue of the Buddha dating from the Ayutthaya era will be found worthwhile. The route then continues along Highway 311 via Uthai Thani to the day's destination, **Nakhon Sawan**. A visit should be made to Wat Chomkiri Nagaproth on a hill above the Menam Chao Phraya, which here forms the two rivers Menam Ping and Menam Nan. The town itself lies on an intensively cultivated plain below an impressive chain of hills.

Day 3
Nakhon Sawan–Phitsanulok (129km/80 miles)

From Nakhon Sawan Highway 117 continues almost dead straight northwards to **Phitsanulok**. This stage of the tour is kept short in order to leave visitors the afternoon free to visit Wat Phra Si Ratana Mahathat with its uniquely beautiful Buddha statue of Phra Buddha Jinarat.

Day 4
Phitsanulok–
Kamphaeng Phet–
Sukhotai
(180km/112 miles)

Today's stage may seem rather odd at first, but was so designed because of the rather poor standard of accommodation available in Kamphaeng Phet. From Phitsanulok take the number 12 road to Sukhothai and then the 101 to **Kamphaeng Phet** (103km/64 miles, about 2 hours). Here the two neighbouring temples of Wat Phra Kaeo and Wat Phra That are well worth a visit. Aim to set off about noon on the 77km/48 mile return journey to Sukhothai so as to arrive in good time to see around it.

Day 5
Sukhothai–
Si Satchanalai–
Lampang
(210km/130 miles)

Take Highway 101 to Sawankhalok and then on to **Si Satchanalai**, a journey of 55km/34 miles. Visit Wat Chang Lom with its massive chedi, followed perhaps by one to Wat Chedi Chet Theow with its 32 stupas containing the ashes of members of the royal families.

From Si Satchanalai take the 101 and then just before Den Chai turn off on to the 11; it is then some 152km/95 miles to Lampang.

Day 6
Lampang–
Chiang Mai
(92km/57 miles)

Spend the morning visiting the many temples in **Lampang**. Outside the town will be found Wat Phra Kaeo Don Tao; before being moved to Wat Phra Kaeo in Bangkok, the famous Jade Buddha, to Thai Buddhists the most important of holy relics, was housed here for 32 years. 18km/11 miles south of the town along Highway 1 stands Wat Phra That Lampang, which is also well worth a visit.

Take Highway 11 through **Lamphun** (to be visited on Day 7) to **Chiang Mai**.

Day 7
Lamphun and
Chiang Mai

To do justice to **Lamphun** with Wat Phra Haripunchai and **Chiang Mai**, the "Rose of the North" without being rushed in any way will take up most of this final day.

3. From Chiang Mai into the "Golden Triangle"

(3 days: about 1030km/640 miles)

This route passes through the unique countryside of North Thailand, with its thick jungle and high mountains, as far as Mae Sai, Thailand's northernmost town. Only the native inhabitants are allowed to cross the border into Myanmar (formerly Burma).

Day 1
Chiang Mai–
Fang–
Chiang Rai
(about 230km/
143 miles)

In preference to the "Direttissima", Highway 118, from **Chiang Mai**, it is better to take Highway 107, because this road passes through some most delightful countryside. After 18km/11 miles turn left in the little town of Mae Rim onto the 1096. 11km/7 miles along this road there is an elephant camp, where young elephants are trained to lift timber and perform other tasks; there are some interesting displays at 9am every day. Return to Highway 107 and continue through the charming countryside. If time permits the opportunity should be taken to visit the Caves of Chiang Dao, which are 61km/38 miles from Mae Rim. Near **Fang** (155km/96 miles) the hot springs at Ban Pin, about 10km/6 miles outside the town, are also worth a visit. From Fang take roads 109/118/1 to **Chiang Rai**.

Day 2
Chiang Rai–
Mae Sai–
Chiang Saen
(about 145km/
90 miles)

The busy little town of Mae Sai, 63km/39 miles from Chiang Rai, is 1010km/628 miles from Bangkok, making it the northernmost town in Thailand and the border town with Myanmar (Burma). This border checkpoint is the only real "sight" here apart from the market held daily in the town centre, but the latter usually closes as early as 9am.

Return along the 110 and then turn left at Mae Chan and drive a further 70km/43 miles to reach **Chiang Saen**, known for its unique building styles. Beautifully situated among trees lies Wat Pa Sak; also highly recommended is a visit to Wat Chedi Luang with its 58m/190ft high chedi, which was once nearly 90m/295ft in height. On a hill outside the town stands Wat Phra That Chom Kitti with its lopsided chedi. From there it is only a short distance to a viewing point which

Training working elephants near Mae Rim

has been described – poetically rather than factually – as the "Golden Triangle". The confluence of the Menam Ping and the Mekong is worth seeing.

Day 3
Chiang Saen–Phayao–Chiang Mai (about 345km/214 miles)

This final stage is about 345km/214 miles long and therefore somewhat demanding. It is possible to break it up by staying overnight in Chiang Rai.

From Chiang Saen first take the road back to Mae Chan and Chiang Rai, then follow Highway 1, a good road which leads directly to **Phayao**, a journey of 162km/100 miles. The town lies by a lake some 24sq.km/9sq. miles in area, and on the edge of which stands Wat Si Kom Kam.

From Phayao Highway 120 winds through some fascinating and unique scenery past Wang Nua to **Chiang Mai** (182km/113 miles). This journey is particularly delightful during the rainy season, when everything is in full bloom.

4. From Bangkok to Phuket (7 days: about 1250km/776 miles)

This route leads along the coast of the Gulf of Thailand, on the only road which links Bangkok with Southern Thailand. In view of the distance it is best to fly back to Bangkok; the hired car can be handed over in Phuket. An interesting alternative is to do this tour by rail, which will be found far less demanding than going by road.

Day 1
Bangkok–Hua Hin (232km/144 miles)

Leave Bangkok on Highway 4, the early sections of which are quite good but later stretches are rather demanding of the driver's skills. Although the scenery is impressive there are no places of much interest to visit until Phetchaburi is reached, a journey of 170km/106 miles.

In **Phetchaburi** the climb up to Phra Nakhon Khiri, King Mongkut's summer palace built on a hill, should not be missed. The 62km/39 miles from Petchaburi to **Hua Hin**, the little town where King Bhumibol holidays during the hot season, can be covered comfortably in about one and a half hours. In Hua Hin there are plenty of hotels which – time permitting – are ideal for a short or even longish seaside holiday.

Day 2
Hua Hin–Prachuap Khiri Khan (92km/57 miles)

Prachuap Khiri Khan, 92km/57 miles from Hua Hin, is situated near where Thailand is at its narrowest. The backdrop on the left formed by the mountains in Sam Roi Yot ("300 Mountain Peaks") National Park is most impressive. There is not much to see in Prachuap Khiri Khan itself, but there are some caves and temples to be found in the vicinity.

Day 3
Prachuap Khiri Khan–Chumphon (183km/114 miles)

The journey to Chumphon passes through some ever-changing countryside and Highway 4 never strays more than a few miles from the Gulf of Thailand. There are very few sights worth stopping for en route, and the same applies to **Chumphon** itself, apart from the little fishing port of Paknam about 10km/6 miles east of the town.

Day 4
Chumphon–Surat Thani (193km/120 miles)

From Chumphon continue further south along the Gulf of Thailand on Highway 41. A detour to one of the fishing villages, where visitors are always made very welcome, can be recommended. This stretch can be covered in about four hours, leaving enough time to look around **Surat Thani**.

Day 5
Surat Thani–Nakhon Si Thammarat (143km/89 miles)

Two roads lead from Surat Thani to Nakhon Si Thammarat. Apart from beautiful countryside with numerous rubber plantations Highway 41 has little to offer in the way of sights, so the 401 is to be preferred; from Sichon onwards it hugs the coastline. As the distance to be covered is relatively short there should be time to look round the town of **Nakhon Si Thammarat**, once an important port and trading centre.

Day 6
Nakhon Si Thammarat–Krabi (233km/145 miles)

The 401 ends a few miles past Ron Phibun; from here drive west along the 41 to Thung Song and then south again on the 403, which joins Highway 4 (turn right) just before reaching Huai Yot. Our destination, **Krabi**, boasts some memorable, exotic coastal landscape and magnificent beaches.

At one time the whole of the south was covered in jungle forest; today there are rows and rows of rubber-trees. The visitor will also see a number of tin-mines which ceased to be worked some years ago and are now just ugly scars on an otherwise unspoiled landscape.

Day 7
Krabi–Phuket (176km/109 miles)

Leaving Krabi on the 4034 westwards it is only a few miles to the 75 million year-old "Shell Cemetery" of Susan Hoi. Return to Highway 4 and drive past the Than Bok Koroni Nature Park (which is worth a visit) to **Phangnga**. A day excursion from Phuket through the Bay of Phangnga with its famous "James Bond Rocks" can be recommended; such excursions are organised by travel agents or hotels and usually include a visit to Koh Panyi, a Moslem fishing village built on piles.

Near the village of Ban Koke Loi turn left onto the 402 and cross the Sarasin Bridge to the island of **Phuket**.

5. From Bangkok to Kanchanaburi (day excursion: about 300km/186 miles)

The scenery in the province of Kanchanaburi is particularly delightful. Easily reached by Highway 4 from Bangkok, it is a favourite with the people of Bangkok for outings at weekends and on public holidays, so to avoid the crowds it is best to go during the week.

Nakhon Pathom

Take Highway 4 from Bangkok and follow the signs to **Nakhon Pathom**, a distance of 54km/34 miles. There will be found the Phra Pathom Chedi, the tallest Buddhist building in Thailand.

Anyone wishing to make the rail journey from Kanchanaburi to Nam Tok as described below should postpone the visit to Nakhon Pathom until the return.

Kanchanaburi

It is a further 66km/41 miles along the well-made up 323 to **Kanchanaburi**, made famous by the "Bridge over the River Kwai". After perhaps making the optional rail journey described below, visit the YEATH War Museum on the bank of the Mekong, with its numerous exhibits and original documents illustrating the building of the infamous bridge during the Second World War. The bridge across the Menam Kwae lies about 5km/3 miles west of the town centre.

Rail journey

It is a moving experience to make the two-hour journey on the "Death Railroad" to the Nam Tok terminus, where the train stops for a few minutes before returning. Anyone going by car to Nam Tok via the 323 will have time for the rewarding two-hour walk to the Erawan Waterfall. The waterfall can also be reached by taking the 3199 (a good road) from Kanchanaburi.

Staying the night

In and around Kanchanaburi there is plenty of overnight accommodation available, including bungalows in Erawan National Park which must be reserved in advance in Bangkok (see Practical Information, Hotels).

6. From Bangkok to Ayutthaya and Bang Pa In

(day excursion: about 170km/106 miles)

Bang Pa In (61km/38 miles)

From Bangkok take Highway 1 in the direction of the airport, turn left after 52km/32 miles and follow the signs to **Bang Pa In**. The former royal summer residence is now open to the public.

Ayutthaya (34km/21 miles)

From Bang Pa In return to Highway 1 and follow it for 34km/21 miles to **Ayutthaya**. Until it was destroyed by the Burmese this was the capital of the Kingdom of Siam and one of the world's most beautiful cities. Today it is just a giant expanse of rubble; however, there are some temples which have been reconstructed in whole or in part which are well worth a visit.

The return journey to Bangkok is along the same route as was used for the outward journey.

7. From Pattaya to Trat

(one or more days: about 380–550km/240–340 miles)

This excursion, the length of which can be varied at will by staying overnight on the islands of Koh Samet or Koh Chang, is recommended for all those seeking a change from a seaside holiday in Pattaya. For a one-day excursion the visitor should content himself with going to Chanthaburi and back.

Sattahip

From Pattaya Highway 3 leads south to the little town of **Sattahip**, 32km/20 miles away, with little of interest.

Rayong/Ban Phe

Continuing on Highway 3, it is a further 56km/35 miles to the little town of **Rayong**, known for making fish into "nam pla", a fish sauce very popular in Thailand. In the village of Ban Phe (14km/9 miles) turn right towards the sea and drive to the harbour; from here ships sail several times a day to the island of Koh Samet, where there is ample overnight accommodation available, especially in bungalows.

On the right, just before reaching Klaeng (30km/19 miles from Ban Phe) lies Wat Sukpriwoon, a pretty temple with richly-carved tympana showing the Hindu god Indra riding on an elephant.

Chanthaburi

The town of **Chanthaburi**, 100km/62 miles from Ban Phe, is known for the mining of precious stones in the vicinity; some of the mines are open to visitors. In the town itself there is a pretty park with an equestrian statue of King Taksin. Well worth a visit are the largest Christian church in Thailand, that of Notre Dame built in the Gothic style, and the old fortifications around Chanthaburi.

Trat/Koh Chang

From Chanthaburi it is a 70km/43 mile drive to **Trat**, and from there a further 17km/10½ miles to Laem Ngob, from where visitors can cross to the relatively unspoiled island of Koh Chang, with some simple bungalow complexes.

It is possible that political uncertainties vis-à-vis Cambodia may stand in the way of the journey to Trat and further beyond.

To return to Pattaya take the 36 road, which is better constructed than the coastal road via Sattahip.

Figure of Buddha in the Wat Phra Buddha Mongkol near Amnat Charoen ▶

Thailand from A to Z

Amnat Charoen F 8

Region: North-east Thailand
Province: Ubon Ratchathani
Altitude: 213m/700ft
Population: 15,000

อำนาจเจริญ

Location

Although of no great historical or art historical interest, the busy little town of Amnat Charoen in north-eastern Thailand – between Mukdahan and Ubon Ratchathani, about 50km/31 miles from the Laos border – is the site of an important Buddhist shrine, Wat Phra Buddha Mongkol.

Access

By car: from Ubon Ratchathani (Highway 212; 75km/47 miles) or Yasothon (Highway 202; 53km/33 miles).
By bus: from Ubon Ratchathani, Sakhon Nakhon or Surin.

Wat Phra Buddha Mongkol

Wat Phra Buddha Mongkol is situated south-west of the town, at Ban Buddha Mongkol, a small village to which the temple has given its name. Shady trees surround the wat's 16m/52ft-high figure of the Buddha on its 5m/16ft base. The statue, clad in a mosaic of thousands of little pieces of glass, is of recent origin.

In February each year Wat Phra Buddha Mongkol is the scene of a major religious festival attracting great numbers of pilgrims from far and near.

Ancient City

See Samut Prakan

Ang Thong G 4

Region: Central Thailand
Province: Ang Thong
Altitude: 10m/33ft
Population: 12,000

อ่างทอง

Location

The provincial capital of Ang Thong – not to be confused with the archipelago of that name in southern Thailand, now a national marine park (see Surat Thani) – lies on the Menam Chao Phraya in the middle of Thailand's broad central plain, some 33km/20 miles from Ayutthaya. Agriculture (especially rice cultivation) dominates the countryside around. Although there are no sights to speak of in Ang Thong itself there are several interesting temples to visit in the vicinity.

Access

By car: from Ayutthaya (Highway 309 towards Singburi).
By bus: from Bangkok (Northern Bus Terminal; several departures daily) or Ayutthaya.
By rail: the nearest stations are at Ayutthaya, Suphanburi and Saraburi (several trains a day from Bangkok Hualampong).

Wiharn of the Wat Chai Yo Vora Wihara

Surroundings

Wat Pa Mok

Located about 13km/8 miles from Ang Thong on the far side of the Menam Chao Phraya, Wat Pa Mok has two wiharns, one containing a 22m/72ft-long late 14th c. reclining figure of a Buddha in the U Thong style, the other some noteworthy and well-preserved remnants of wall paintings dating from the early Ayutthaya period.

Wat Khun Inta Phra Mun

Three more temples are found along the road to Suphanburi (Highway 3195). The recently built Wat Khun Inta Phra Mun, a short distance off the 3195 about 11km/7 miles from Ang Thong, boasts a massive 50m/164ft-long reclining Buddha in the Ayutthaya style. This huge sculpture is almost certainly one of the biggest of its kind in Thailand and much venerated by the people. The remains of an old wat are to be found on a hillside near by.

Wat Kien

Although itself modern Wat Kien incorporates fresco-covered walls formerly belonging to its predecessor. The paintings depict battles against the Burmese, an unusual subject for art in Thailand despite the importance of such clashes for the country's history.

Wat Luang Suntararam

Wat Luang Suntararam, near the village of Ban Talat San Djao about 9km/5½ miles north of Ang Thong, has a bot embellished with a fine stucco relief from the Ayutthaya period.

Wat Chai Yo Vora Vihara

The triple-tiered roof and beautifully carved gable of the wiharn of Wat Chai Yo Vora Vihara (Ayutthaya period) adorn the banks of the Menam Chao Phraya some 16km/10 miles north of Ang Thong. Inside the wiharn is an enormous seated figure of the Buddha, again of recent origin.

Ayutthaya (Phra Nakhon Si Ayutthaya) G 4

Region: Central Thailand
Province: Ayutthaya
Altitude: 4m/13ft. Population: 63,000

พระนครศรีอยุธยา

Location

The old Thai capital of Ayutthaya, today one of the most impressive ruined cities in Asia, stands on the wide and fertile plain of the Menam Chao Phraya at a point where the river forms a natural loop. Indeed the city is completely encircled by rivers, the Menam to the south and west, the Lopburi to the north and the Pasak to the east. A man-made canal also links the Lopburi and the Menam, the effect being to create a most favourably situated island.

Access

By car: Highway 1 from Bangkok. After 86km/53 miles turn left onto Highway 32 at Wang Noi (signposted).

By bus: from Bangkok (Northern Bus Terminal). Departures at 40 minute intervals from 5am–7pm. All the larger Bangkok travel agencies arrange sightseeing tours (day trips).

By rail: from Bangkok Hualampong (1¼ hours).

By boat: the excursion on the Menam Chao Phraya can be quite delightful. There is no public boat service but tourists can join an organised tour aboard, for example, the "Oriental Queen" river boat, which leaves from the pier of the Oriental Hotel at 8am. Visitors normally go one way by bus, the other by boat.

Sightseeing

Those with a real interest in Thai history should allow at least two days for sightseeing and include visits to Lopburi and Sukhothai (see entries), two other "royal" cities in central Thailand closely linked historically with the old capital.

Organised tours usually allow visitors only an hour or so in Ayutthaya. They also tend to arrive in the heat of the day, which means not seeing the ancient ruined city at dawn or dusk when it is at its most magical.

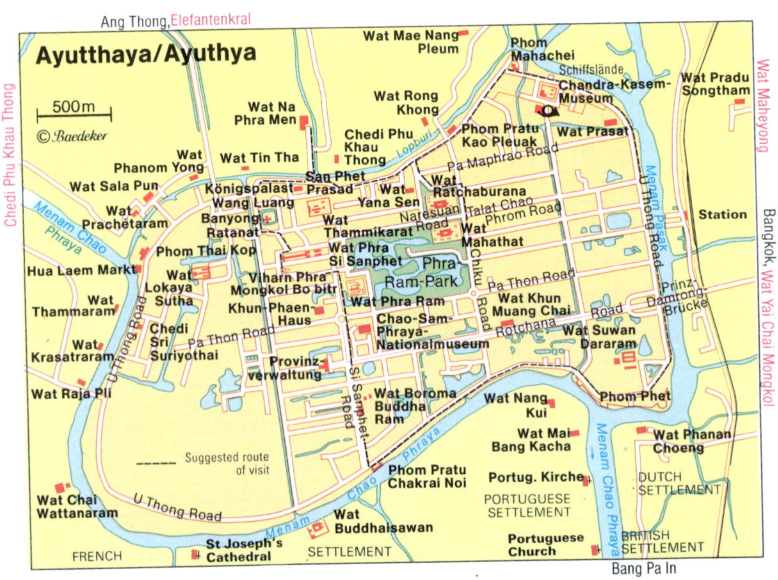

A mutilated statue of Buddha in Ayutthaya

History

For more than 400 years, between 1350 and 1767, Ayutthaya was the capital of the Kingdom of Siam; Western visitors waxed lyrical about the city, describing it as the most beautiful place they had ever seen. It began as a small outpost of the Khmer kingdom, being founded in the 11th c. on a site north-east of the present railway near Wat Khudi Dao. In the 13th c., after the Thais had conquered and cultivated the Menam plain, Ayutthaya and Lopburi became part of the principality of U Thong, a vassal state of Sukhothai. In 1347 disasterous plagues afflicted the country, reducing the population by more than half and forcing Prince U Thong to flee his capital. Ayutthaya, encircled by rivers and with an easily defended nucleus favourably situated beside the Menam, was chosen to replace it. Division of the Siamese kingdom into several new principalities following the death of Ramkhamhaeng led U Thong to distance himself politically from the rulers in Sukhothai. In 1350 he threw off their yoke altogether and, as King Somdet Phra Rama Thobodi (though history books usually refer to him as U Thong), established an independent state named after his new capital.

The designation "Rama Thibodi" reflects the god-like status of the kings of Thailand at that time. U Thong regarded himself as the reincarnation of the god Vishnu and of Rama, hero of the Indian epic "Ramayama". At his coronation he had his superhuman status and divine omnipotence authenticated by eight Brahmans from the holy Indian city of Benares.

Ayutthaya's subsequent history was carved out under no fewer than 33 kings. It developed into a flourishing cultural and commercial centre and many European trading companies established posts there. Traces of the latter can still be seen, including the foundations of a large Dutch warehouse as well as the recently restored French St Joseph's Cathedral.

There were four customs posts, the largest being on the east bank of the Chao Phraya south of the city. Warships and the royal barges were moored on the north bank of the Lopburi near Wat Tin Tha, opposite the Royal Palace. U Thong surrounded the city with an earth wall and stockades, only replaced by a more substantial wall of plastered brickwork in 1549. In 1580 the fortifications on the north side of the city were moved closer to the river where some remains can still be seen adjoining Pa Maphrao Road.

Of the six large forts built into the walls only some fragments of Fort Phom Phet, situated where the Pasak joins the Chao Phraya, have survived. After the destruction of Ayutthaya stones from the remaining forts, like those of other fortifications, were used in the construction of Bangkok's city walls.

The sacking of Ayutthaya in 1767 was a mark of the temporary decline of the Siamese monarchy. Rival members of the royal house, a number of princes among them, became embroiled in power struggles and intrigue. King Ekatot, the last reigning monarch of the Ayutthaya dynasty and also the weakest, was unable to impose his authority. When the Burmese laid siege yet again to the city, though apparently with little hope of taking it, one of the rival factions opened a gate and let the enemy in. The Burmese held the city for the next fifteen years, the Thais finally recovering it only after some bloody battles. In the meantime the invaders vandalised the country. No temple escaped their ravages, most, together with Wang Luang (the royal palace) being razed to the ground. The fall of Ayutthaya was accompanied by the destruction of thousands of statues of the Buddha, rendered worthless to believers by having their heads smashed off – Buddhists hold that the spirit dwells in the head. Several of these decapitated figures can still be seen amid the ruins.

Ayutthaya today is a vast collection of temple and palace remains which initially excited little interest from archaeologists. Since 1956 however, the foundations of a number of temples have been excavated to give an idea of their original size, and there has also been some reconstruction. So far about a hundred buildings and ruins have been designated national monuments by the Department of Fine Arts, more being added to the list as further reconstruction and restoration work proceeds with the help of UNESCO.

Sights

Note

At one time there were three royal palaces, 375 temples, 29 forts and 94 gates on Ayutthaya island alone. The major places of interest can be visited, and an idea obtained of the size and splendour of the city as it once was, by following the route outlined below, starting and finishing at the Prince Damrong Bridge near the railway station. The tour takes in ten temple sites, two museums, two palaces and a variety of other interesting buildings; it needs at least half a day to do it justice, more if both the museums are to be visited. Those who prefer to drive rather than walk can follow the route by taxi, asking the driver to stop at the various sights.

The Prince Damrong Bridge was erected in memory of Prince Damrong Rajanubhab, to whom is owed much of our knowledge of the history of art in Thailand. Having crossed the bridge, continue to U Thong Road which makes a complete circuit of the old city, turning left along it for some 700m/770yd.

Wat Suwan Dararam

Here, framed by three small lakes, stands Wat Suwan Dararam. Built around 1700 by the grandfather of Rama I it was extended by the rulers of the Chakri dynasty who also carried out a considerable amount of restoration work and decorated the temple with numerous paintings. Notice how the foundations incline towards the centre. Wat Suwan Dararam also has the distinction of being the only temple on Ayutthaya island still inhabited by monks.

Particularly noteworthy are the large bot with portico, the wood carvings on the gable, the internal frescos from the Early Bangkok period, the beautiful coffered ceiling and a statue of Buddha in the Ayutthaya style. The wiharn, built by Rama II (1809–24), was decorated in 1931 with modern murals depicting scenes from Thai history.

Fort Phom Phet

On leaving the temple compound the remains of Phom Phet, the only fort of which anything now survives, can be seen opposite, on the banks of the Menam River. Next continue round U Thong Road as far as Fort Phom Pratu

Chakrai Noi (about 30 minutes' walk). Here turn north off the ring road; some 400m/440yd or so along Si Sanphet Road lies Wat Boroma Buddha Ram.

Wat Boroma Buddha Ram

Wat Boroma Buddha Ram, of which only the walls remain, was built in 1683 during the reign of King Narai. In about 1740 the three doors into the bot were embellished with wooden panels inlaid with mother-of-pearl. Following the sacking of Ayutthaya these exquisite works of art were moved to Bangkok, one being installed in Wat Benchama bo bitr (the Marble Temple) and another in Wat Phra Kaeo in the Grand Palace. The third was made into a bookcase which is now in the National Museum in the capital.

★Chao Sam Phraya National Museum

Further along on the right, past the Ayutthaya provincial government offices, the Chao Sam Phraya National Museum was founded by King Bhumibol in 1961 (open: Wed.–Sun. 9am–4pm; admission fee). It houses some valuable and interesting items in the Lopburi, U Thong, Ayutthaya, Dvaravati and Sukhothai styles including finds from Ayutthaya, sculptures in bronze and stone, terracotta and lacquer work, ceramics, wood-carvings, votive panels and gold jewellery set with precious stones. Outstanding among the many earlier works of art are a seated Buddha (Dvaravati, 11–12th. c.) and a huge bust of the Buddha in the U Thong style.

Sanaam Luang Wiharn Phra Mongkol Bo bitr

Bear to the left on leaving the Museum from where it is only a short walk to Sanaam Luang (also known as Phra Men Ground); in the western corner stands the Wiharn Phra Mongkol Bo bitr. This was re-erected in 1956 by Thailand's then Prime Minister Pibulsonggram, in a style identical to the original – the latter having been burned down during the sacking of Ayutthaya and eventually collapsing. Rebuilding the wiharn made it possible to return the much revered and historically important bronze statue of the Buddha, one of the largest in Thailand, to its rightful place, where it had stood since 1603. Although little is known of the statue's early history the combination of U Thong and Sukhothai elements suggest the figure was probably cast in the reign of King Boroma Trailokanat (1448–88). It was he who introduced the Sukhothai style into the design of Buddhas and chedis in Ayutthaya, superceding the Khmer style which had been in vogue until then. Although over the years the statue has been several times restored, it remains little changed in appearance. Some years ago hundreds of small figures were discovered inside it. The artistically inferior ornamentation on the base was added in 1931.

Wat Phra Ram

Bordered by a pond the nearby Wat Phra Ram with its imposing Elephant Gates was begun by King Ramesuen in 1369. Since then it has been restored and enlarged many times. Of particular interest are the gallery adorned with nagas and garudas and the numerous shattered statues of the Buddha on the wat's wide terrace.

Khun Phaen House

On the opposite side of the road Khun Phaen House is built on an artificial island where a prison once stood. The traditional Thai house, one of the very few remaining, was constructed in 1940 from material salvaged from other old dwellings. It is not unlike Jim Thompson's House in Bangkok.

★★Wat Phra Si Sanphet

Continuing along Si Sanphet Road as far as Naresuan Road, turn left to Wat Phra Si Sanphet, the loveliest and historically most important temple in old Ayutthaya. Its three large chedis and numerous smaller ones on a long terrace make this wat – also known as the King's Temple – one of the most impressive sights in the ruined city.

Two of the large chedis, the eastern and central ones, were built in 1492 by King Rama Thibodi II to house the ashes of his father and elder brother. His own ashes are interred in the third chedi, built in 1530 by his son and successor on the throne, King Boromaraja IV. All three chedis were opened up and plundered by the Burmese who nevertheless failed to find the hundreds of small statues of the Buddha in bronze, crystal, silver, lead and

Chedis in the Wat Phra Si Sanphet

gold now on display in the National Museum in Bangkok. The building on the west side of the terrace, once crowned by a chedi, has numerous entrances with small prangs. Like the smaller chedis and chapels around it these probably contain the ashes of other members of the royal family. Between the chedis are what were presumably mondhops while in front of the terrace, roughly in the centre of the temple compound, are pillars and walls, the remains of the great wiharn which once housed a 16m/ 52ft-high figure of Buddha encased in gold. The statue itself, damaged and stripped of its gold by the Burmese, was removed by King Rama I to one of the large chedis of Wat Pho in Bangkok. Other smaller Buddha figures were also taken to the capital to be placed in Wat Buddhaisawan (now part of the National Museum in Bangkok) and the western wiharn of Wat Pho.

Royal Palaces

Leaving the Royal Wat – note the memorial to King U Thong opposite – take the turning on the left to Wang Luang palace, also sometimes referred to as "the Old Palace" to distinguish it from the Chandra Kasem Palace which was built later. A third palace, Klang Suan Luang, once stood close to the city's western wall in the vicinity of Queen Suriyochai's chedi. Of this latter palace nothing now remains.

The walls of Wang Luang extend right up to the Lopburi River. Apart from these and the well-restored foundations, there is little to be seen, the Burmese having been very thorough in their destruction of this part of Ayutthaya. For the same reason little survives from the once numerous old Thai houses. Even so a fairly good idea of the original extent of the palace complex, which also incorporated Wat Si Sanphet, can be obtained. Perhaps the best way to visualise this section of the old city is to compare it to the Great Palace in Bangkok which was actually modelled on Ayutthaya's Wang Luang though built in different styles. The oldest building in the complex was erected by U Thong in 1350, the year in which Ayutthaya became his new capital.

Sanphet Praset Palace

In 1448, under King Boromaraja II, Sanphet Prasat Palace was added. Situated opposite Wang Luang the remains of some tall pillars are still visible.

Wiharn Somdet

Wiharn Somdet was built in 1643 during the reign of King Prasat Thong. Records show it to have had two fairly large tower-like porticoes front and rear, with a further two smaller ones at the sides. It was also the first building in Ayutthaya to be panelled in gold, as a result of which it was popularly known as the "Golden Palace".

Chakravat Phaichayon Building

Prasat Thong was also responsible for the construction in 1632 of the Chakravat Phaichayon Building from where royal processions and military parades started out.

Banyong Ratanat Building

The Banyong Ratanat Building, begun around 1688 under Prasat Thong's son Narai and completed by King Petraja, is situated on an artificial island in the west of the complex. It was used by Petraja as his residence throughout his reign (1688–1702).

Trimuk Building

King Chulalongkorn rebuilt the Trimuk Building, an open pavilion standing on a broad terrace, in 1907. It has been the venue for many a ceremony held in honour of former rulers of Ayutthaya by a succession of kings, including the present King Bhumibol. An earlier building of unknown age on the site was burned down in 1427.

Suriyat Amarindra Building

This building, of which only a high wall remains, was erected by King Narai in the latter part of the 17th c. The royal white elephants used to be stabled near by.

Wat Thammikarat

Passing the overgrown ruins of Wat Thammikarat – an extremely large temple of which there remain sections of the terrace, the pillars of the portico and a chedi with a crooked spire – rejoin U Thong Road from where a small bridge crosses the Lopburi to Wat Na Phra Men on the opposite bank. The temple is well worth a visit.

Wat Na Phra Men

Wat Na Phra Men is one of the very few temples to have escaped destruction by the Burmese. It is not known when the temple was built, existing records showing merely that it was restored under King Boromakot (1732–58) and again during the Early Bangkok period. The bot is a large, imposing building with beautiful wood-carvings on the gable and door panels. The triple-tiered roof and large portico, the latter flanked by two graceful little porches, are fine examples of Thai artistry. Inside the bot two rows of octagonal columns supporting the richly carved ceiling add to the impression of height. Most unusually the large figure of Buddha appears in royal garb.

The small but beautifully proportioned wiharn houses a stone Buddha seated in European style, one of the best-preserved statues from the Dvaravati era (6th–10th/11th c.). An inscription in the wiharn claims, almost certainly incorrectly, that the statue came originally from Wat Phra Mahathat in Ayutthaya. Most of the evidence points, on the contrary, to this particular Buddha having stood, together with three others identical to it, in Nakhon Pathom's Wat Phra Men, where its richly ornamented stone base has been found. Parts of the base are displayed in the National Museum in Bangkok.

Wat Yana Sen

Recrossing the bridge and once more turning left, follow the road alongside the Lopburi River for about 800m/875yd to Wat Yana Sen, a temple with a tall chedi embellished with niches. Its fine, well-balanced structure is typical of the Ayutthaya style.

From Wat Yana Sen can be seen two of the most important ruined temples in Ayutthaya, Wat Ratchaburana and Wat Mahathat.

Statue of King U Thong

Buddha and prang in Wat Ratchaburana

★Wat Ratchaburana

Wat Ratchaburana was erected by King Boromracha II (1424–48) in memory of his elder brothers Ay and Yi, killed in a duel over the succession to the throne. Columns and walls of the wiharn still stand, as do some ruined chedis around the prang and also parts of the surrounding walls complete with lancet gateways. The large prang with its fine figured stucco-work portraying, e.g. nagas supporting garudas, is exceptionally well preserved.

The two crypts in the lower part of the prang contain some exceedingly interesting wall-paintings, probably the work of Chinese artists who settled in Ayutthaya and had the skill to harmonise such different styles as those of the Khmer and Burmese on the one hand and of Lopburi and Sukhothai on the other. While excavating in the prang between 1956 and 1958 archaeologists discovered more than 100,000 votive tablets, known in Thai as "phra phim". These were later sold and the proceeds used to build the Chao Sam Phraya National Museum. Such tablets, generally moulded in clay, were carried by pilgrims and usually bore pictures of holy places or simply of the Buddha. Various works of art were also uncovered in the prang; these included arm-bands with intaglio decoration, gold filigree headdresses and one in solid gold inlaid with precious stones, a five-part service used for betel nuts, two spittoons, and gold coins with Arabic lettering. Most of the finds are on display in the Chandra Kasem National Museum.

The prang itself is also of historical interest in that it combines the Indian (Ceylonese) and Burmese styles, merging them into a novel architectural form. Some of the stucco work at the top is well preserved. The square platform had a small chedi at each corner. Two more chedis at the crossroads house the ashes of the royal brothers while a third commemorates Queen Si Suriyothai who, during a battle with the Burmese in about 1550, dressed as a man and rode into the fray on a white elephant to save her husband's life, losing her own in the process. Near this chedi, on the site of the now completely destroyed Wat Lokaya Sutha, a giant reclining figure of the Buddha can be seen.

★Wat Mahathat

Immediately across the road from Wat Ratchaburana stands Wat Mahathat which tradition claims was erected in 1384 by King Ramesuen. He is also said to have built the central prang to house a relic of the Buddha. This however is considered doubtful; according to a more reliable source the first buildings on the site, including the above-mentioned prang, were actually constructed by King Boromaraja I (1370–88). The prang, 46m/150ft high, is one of the old city's most impressive edifices. In about 1625 the top portion broke off, being rebuilt in 1633 some 4m/13ft higher than before. Later it collapsed again and only the corners survived. In 1956 a secret chamber was uncovered in the ruins; among the treasures found inside were gold jewellery, a gold casket containing a relic of the Buddha, and fine tableware. Scattered around the temple are some important remains of variously shaped prangs and chedis, in particular an octagonal chedi with a truncated spire in the Ceylonese style. Near by, the head of a still much revered statue of the Buddha lies on the ground.

Chandra Kasem Museum

U Thong Road now follows the Lopburi as far as the Chandra Kasem Museum, well worth a prolonged visit (open: Wed.–Sun. 9am–4pm; admission fee). The exhibits include statues of Buddha and Bodhisattva, gold and decorative work, carvings, tympana, and various domestic and religious objects dating from the 13th to the 17th centuries. The museum is housed in a palace which was rebuilt by King Mongkut (Rama IV); originally occupied by the heir to the throne it was later used as a residence for royalty visiting Ayutthaya. While the items on display scarcely do justice to the power and magnificence of the early Thai kings, they do offer an insight into the lives of the city's inhabitants.

Passing Fort Phom Mahachei and then the landing-stage, U Thong Road continues round via the comparatively uninteresting Wat Prasat back to the start of the tour

Chedi of the Wat Yai Chai Mongkol

Other places of interest

St Joseph's

Anyone with time to spare who wishes to delve more deeply into Ayutthaya's history should include a visit to the French St Joseph's Cathedral on the south bank of the Chao Phraya. Restored only a short while ago the cathedral is a fitting monument to the large group of French settlers who left their country to live in Siam.

Several more wats are also located outside the walls of the old city. Much the best way to visit them is by boat along the Menam; departing from the landing-stage the trip takes about two hours.

★Wat Yai Chai Mongkol

On the eastern outskirts of Ayutthaya (cross the Pasak River and take the Bangkok road, turning right about 300m/330yd beyond the railway) stands the exceptionally interesting Wat Yai Chai Mongkol, its massive chedi rising from a square base surrounded by four smaller chedis. The wat, built in 1357 under King U Thong, was assigned to monks of a particularly strict order trained in Ceylon, members of which still live there. In front of the chedi are the stumps of columns which once supported the roof of the temple.

Elephant compound

Also worth visiting is the elephant compound, about 3km/2 miles north of the city. This is a square enclosure constructed in its present form by King Rama I. It was used for catching, taming and exhibiting elephants and is the only such compound still in existence.

Ban Chiang D 7

Region: North-east Thailand. Province: Udon Thani
Altitude: 138m/450ft. Population: 2500

เชียง

★★Archaeological finds

Before 1967 Ban Chiang was virtually unknown, a tiny village of a few hundred people who suddenly found themselves invaded by an army of archaeologists from all over the world. They came as a result of a sensational discovery which showed the area to have been inhabited at least as long ago as 3800 B.C. – i.e. during the Neolithic period in Europe. Previously it was thought to have been first settled by migrants from Laos less than 200 years ago.

Location and access

Ban Chiang is situated 6km/4 miles north of Highway 22 barely an hour's drive from Udon Thani (50km/31 miles).

By bus: services run between Udon Thani and Sakhon Nakhon (Ban Pu bus station).
Nearest airport: Udon Thani (one flight a day from Bangkok).

History

Farmers working the fields around the village had for many years been unearthing pottery chards, iron and bronze tools and, occasionally, bones. These finds had failed to attract wider interest until, almost by chance, an American called Steve Young heard about them. After visiting Ban Chiang on his own initiative, he alerted scientists in Bangkok to the existence of the site. Thermoluminescence dating subsequently showed the chards to be up to 5800 years old.

As well as pottery, systematic excavation of the site, initiated and directed by the American archaeologist Chester F. Gorman, also uncovered tools in a variety materials including bronze. These were evidently produced at a time roughly corresponding to the Bronze Age in Mesopotamia (the area between the Tigris and the Euphrates) which, beginning around 2000 B.C., pre-dated the Bronze Age in northern Europe. The reason why this caused such excitement among archaeologists was that, prior to the discovery at Ban Chiang, the Bronze Age was assumed to have originated in Mesopotamia.

Pottery

With its painted decoration applied in swirls and bands the pottery from Ban Chiang, probably grave-goods rather than items of everyday use,

A male skeleton, found at Ban Chiang . . .

. . . and pottery fragments almost 5800 years old

displays a degree of artistry hitherto unmatched in south-east Asia. Stylised plants and animals, at first appearing on simple, round-bellied vases but later also on more elegantly-shaped earthenware vessels, testify to a people with a highly developed culture. Fingers were probably used for painting, the pigments being derived from plants.

Manufacture of the earthenware pots evidently continued through three clearly identifiable periods, the first of which had four phases. Those from the earliest phase (*c.* 3600–2500 B.C.) of the first period were black with bands of decoration enclosed between lines. In the second phase (*c.* 2500–2000 B.C.) the pots were painted with a heavy pattern while in the third phase decorative bands were etched into the clay surface complementing the colouring. In the final phase of this first (Ban Chiang) period (*c.* 2000–1000 B.C.) stylised drawings of people and animals made their appearance in addition to the typical swirls and bands.

The middle period (*c.* 1000–300 B.C.) was characterised by pottery of the utmost simplicity left virtually undecorated by craftsmen evidently concentrating almost exclusively on shape.

The pinnacle of artistic achievement was reached in the third period (*c.* 300 B.C.–A.D. 200); most of the items now exhibited in the museums date from this time. The clay, fired naturally, was painted with red pigment, the patterns showing considerable inventiveness as well as an extraordinary feeling for the harmony of shape, pattern and colour. Shortly after this (about A.D. 400) Ban Chiang appears to have been abandoned by its inhabitants; at any rate no finds of more recent origin have as yet been made.

★Ban Chiang National Museum

A number of restored and reconstructed pots are on display in the small museum in Ban Chiang (open: Wed.–Sun. 9am–noon and 1–4pm; admission fee). The story of the excavations is also told, with the aid of dioramas and commentary in English as well as Thai. An interesting book on the history of Ban Chiang is available at the cash desk.

Original site

About a kilometre from the museum a burial area has been excavated and left in its exposed state, as too has a male human skeleton.

Next to it is a reconstruction of a "dig", with pottery from this and other sites around Ban Chiang. More pottery was taken to Bangkok where it can be seen in the Suan Pakkard Palace.

Astonishingly authentic-looking imitations are sold by villagers in Ban Chiang's main street.

Bangkok (Krung Thep · Phra Nakhon) H 4

กรุงเทพ

Region: Central Thailand
Province: Bangkok (City-state)
Altitude: 3m/10ft. Population: approx. 6 million

N.B.

This section is abbreviated, only the city's principal sights being described. Fuller information is contained in the Baedeker AA Guide to Bangkok.

Location

Bangkok (13°44′N 100°30′E), the economic and cultural as well as the administrative capital of Thailand, is situated on the fertile delta of the Menam Chao Phraya river at the junction of the country's four major regions, North West (Pak Nya), North East (Isaan), South East (Pak Dai Towan Org) and South West (Pak Dai) Thailand.

Capital city

With Dom Muang, south-east Asia's largest international airport, sited just outside the city, Bangkok is the point of arrival for the great majority of visitors to Thailand. The name Bangkok, probably a corruption of "Ban Makok" meaning "village of olives", is seldom used by the Thais themselves. The capital's official name is "Krung Thep Mahanakorn Amorn Rattanakosin Mahintara Mahadirok Popnoparat Ratchathani Burirom

Nonthaburi
Bangkok Centre
500 m
Chatuchak-Week-end market
Victory Monument
Siam Square
Lumphini Park
DUSIT
PHRA NAKHON
POMPRAP
YOMMARAT
BANGKOK YAI
SAMPANTHAWONG
KHLONG SAN
WONGWIEN YAI
Mae Nam Chao Phraya / Menam
Krung Thon Bridge
St. Francis Xavier Church and Convent
Tha Thewes (flower market)
National Library
National Assembly
Dusit-Zoo
Suan Amphorn
Chitralada-Palace
Chulalongkorn-Equestrian statue
Wat Benchama-bo-bitr
Bank of Thailand
Wat Indrawihan
Parlament
Santitham
Regierungs-gebäude
Ratchadamnoen-stadium
TAT
Turf
Rajatrinnamai
FAO
UNICEF
Nationalgalerie
Wat Bovornives
SEATO
Democracy Monument
Thonburi Station
Thammasat-Universitat
National-Theatre
National-museum
Sanaam
Luang
Wat Mahathat
Silpakorn-University
Chalerm-Thai Theatre
Goldener Hügel
Wat Rachanada
Wat Sakhet
Phukhao Thong
Sao Ching Chah
Lak Muang
Paris-Theater
Wat Phra Kaeo
Wat Rajapardit
Grand Palace
Wat Suthat
Wat Rat-bo-bitr
Wang Saranlom
Wat Pho
Mano Yon
Wat Tepsirin
National-stadium
Nakhon Kasem
Wat Arun
Pak Khlong Talat
Chinatown
Krung Kasem
Main Station
Hualampong
Chulalongkorn-stadium
Wat Kanrayanimit
Santa Cruz
Monastery
Memorial Bridge
Phra Pokklao Bridge
Wat Traimitr
Samyan Rama
Wat Phrathumkhongka
Rama-Theatre
Wat Sangkhachai
Phrachao-Taksin-Equestrian statue
Main Post Office
Bahnhof Wongwien Yai
Oriental Hotel
German-Thai Chamber of Trade
Bang Rak Markt
Sathorn Bridge (Taksin)
St. Louis Church
©Baedeker

Traffic in Bangkok

Udommahasthan Amornpiman Awathansathit", usually shortened, for obvious reasons, to "Krung Thep" (City of Angels). Alternatively the city is known as "Phra Nakhon" (the Heavenly Capital). Bangkok is the only city in Thailand which enjoys full provincial status in its own right.

History

When the old Siamese capital of Ayutthaya was sacked by the Burmese in 1767, General Phya Taksin, together with about 10,000 troops, made his escape to Chonburi by way of Bangkok. After launching a number of successful counter-attacks he finally drove the Burmese from the country and, in 1772, had himself declared king. One of his first official acts was to make Thonburi (now a district of Bangkok) the new capital of Siam. Bangkok at the time appeared, in the words of Europeans passing through on their way to Ayutthaya, a "small place with two forts". In fact the village was already a strategically situated trading post of some consequence, but one to which Europeans as yet attached little importance. In 1782 Bangkok itself became the kingdom's capital, seat of the royal house and of government and parliament. It was Rama I (1782–1809), founder of the still-ruling Chakri dynasty, who, in the early years of his reign, moved his royal residence from Thonburi to the opposite bank of the Menam Chao Phraya. In so doing he set the scene for the transformation of Bangkok from erstwhile village to metropolis. Monasteries and temples were built and leading business-houses established themselves on the banks of the Menam, quickly turning the city into a centre of international trade.

Bangkok experienced a particular heyday during the reign of King Chulalongkorn (Rama V; 1868–1910); it was he who built the first wide streets, and also a 10km/6½ mile-long tramway. Under his successors the city expanded in uncontrolled leaps and bounds, the lack of planning being all too evident today.

Now merged, Thonburi and Bangkok form a melting pot of more than six million people, who inhabit an area of only 650sq.km/250sq. miles. "Greater Bangkok" has a population of nearly nine million.

Sights

N.B.

Bangkok has over 400 temples the most notable of which are described below together with other major sights. The design of many of the wats was influenced by buildings in other parts of Thailand; for the visitor this means an insight into differing styles of temple architecture, not simply the Bangkok (or Rattanakosin) style.

★★Grand Palace Precinct

Location
Na Phra Lan Road
Main entrance Wiseedtschairi Gate

Opening times
daily 8.30–11.30am, 1–3pm (pavilions closed Sat., Sun.)

Entry charge

Suitable clothing should be worn!

The tour of Bangkok's Grand Palace and the sight of the Holy of Holies within – the Jade Buddha (also known as the Emerald Buddha) in Wat Phra Kaeo – are among the highlights of any visit to Thailand. Each of the buildings making up the 218,400sq.m/261,200sq.yd palace complex evinces not only the ethos of a period but, above all, the spirit of the monarch ruling at the time.

The whole of the holy precinct still preserves the pure undefiled style deriving from the time of its inception, notwithstanding many alterations and refurbishments – the last of these in 1984. When undertaking this restoration work, which has largely been carried out by students of the Bangkok Academy of Art, the utmost emphasis has been placed on being true to the original details, notably regarding the extensive murals which have been adversely affected over the passing of the years, not least by the high levels of air pollution to be found in Bangkok.

The palace is entered via the main or Wiseedtschairi Gate ("Gate of Wonderful Victory"), beyond which a wide roadway leads through the outer courtyard. On either side are modern buildings housing government offices. Anyone whose mode of dress is considered improper by the guards on duty will be asked to don a sarong, issued free of charge (although on production of some form of security, such as one's passport).

After obtaining an entrance ticket (the ticket office is at the start of the access roadway to the actual palace precinct), the visitor goes past a building standing slightly back, in which the Museum of Royal Regalia and Coins is housed. On display on the first floor are carved wooden furniture and interior furnishings of considerable interest (extra admission charge).

Wat Phra Kaeo
(Temple of the Emerald Buddha)

Photography forbidden

The inner sacred precinct, in the middle of which stands the Wat Phra Kaeo, is reached by a gate which is guarded over by two imposing demon figures. These, the gift of Chinese merchants, strike a discordant note and hardly match the graceful style of the typical Thai architecture to be found in the rest of the temple complex. Once inside, beside the gate, the first of a cycle of murals recounting the epic of "Ramakien" can be seen painted on the precinct wall. A commentary in verses composed by King Chulalonghorn (Rama V) is inscribed on a series of marble plaques nearby.

Turning to the left, the visitor can now see the gold-tiled chedi, Phra Si Ratana, which rises up from a circular base on five levels. Inside it contains a relic which, according to tradition, is a bone or hair of the enlightened Buddha. The needle-shaped spire of the chedi is typical of the way the Thais developed the style of the Indian pagoda.

Phra Mondhop

Behind Phra Sri Ratana is the Phra Mondhop, a building decorated liberally with tiny glass mosaics, which is impressive not least because of its delicate grace. Adorning its four corners are 14th c. figures in the Borobodur style. Inside is a black lacquered bookcase, beautifully inlaid with mother-of-pearl, containing the "Tripitaka" (Triple Basket), the sacred scriptures. The floor of the mondhop is of pure silver.

Angkor Wat (model)

The stone model of Angkor Wat, standing on the terrace, dates from the reign of Rama IV, when what is now Cambodia was a vassal state of Siam. Although diminutive compared with the original, and in a setting far removed from the latter's jungle site, the model is a history lesson in itself and for that reason much visited.

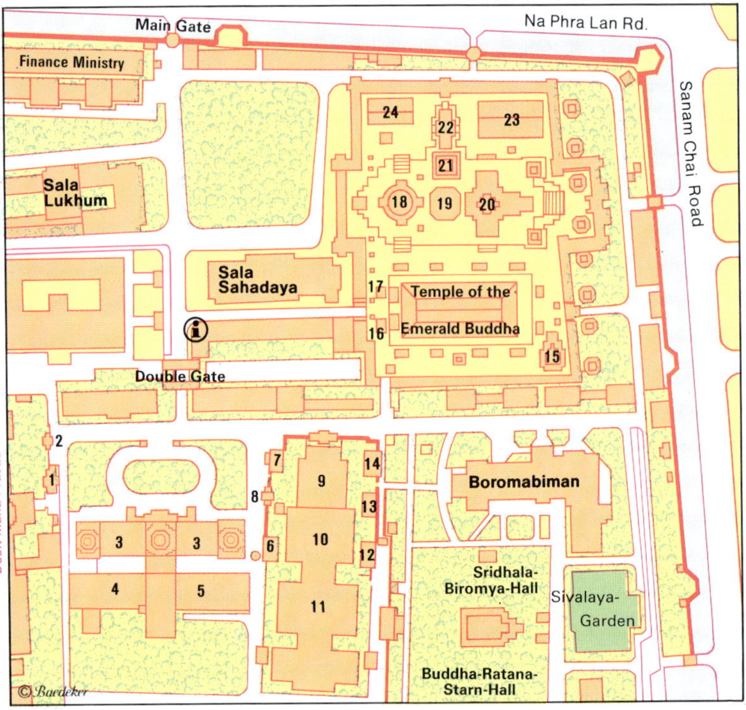

Grand Palace
Phra Borom Maha Rajawang

Temple of the Emerald Buddha
Wat Phra Kaeo

1 Royal Council
2 Amporn Phimok Prasad
3 Chakri Maha Prasad
4 Somut-Devaaraj-Ubbat Hall
5 Moonstarn-Baromasna Hall
6 Hor Phra Dhart Monthien
7 Dusida-Bhiromya Hall
8 Snamchandr Hall
9 Amarindra-Vinichai Hall
10 Paisal-Taksin Hall
11 Chakrabardi Biman
12 Hor Phrasulalaya Biman
13 Rajruedi Hall
14 Hor Satrakom
15 Hor Kanthararasdr
16 Hor Rajbongsanusorn
17 Hor Rajkornmanusorn
18 Phra Sri Ratana Chedi
19 Phra Mondhop
20 Prasad Phra Debidorn
21 Model of Angor Wat
22 Phra Viharn Yod
23 Hor Monthien Dharma
24 Hor Phra Naga

Phra Viharn Yot

Phra Viharn Yot, to the left of the terrace, has the distinction of housing the most ancient of all the treasures in the sacred precinct, a stone which served as a throne for Ramkhamhaeng, the 13th c. founder of Thailand. It was uncovered by King Mongkut (Rama IV) during his years of wandering as a monk and it was he who brought it to Bangkok.

Prasat Phra Debidorn (Pantheon)

The third building on the wide terrace is the Prasat Phra Debidorn, also called the Pantheon. The interior, which is only open to the general public on one day each year, Chakri Day (6th April), contains lifesize statues of the first eight kings of the Chakri dynasty (the present monarch King Bhumibol is the ninth member of this dynastic line).

Bot

Leaving the terrace, the visitor arrives at the Temple of the Emerald Buddha, Holy of Holies in Wat Phra Kaeo. Entry to the bot is through one of

The Great Chakri Palace

the side portals, the centre one being reserved exclusively for the king. Inside the bot the small but exquisite statue of the Buddha, only 75cm/29½in. high, rests on a tall plinth beneath a nine-tiered canopy. According to tradition the nephrite figure was carved in Patalibutr in India – though other sources claim it to be from Burma, the work of an unknown artist. It first came to light in 1434 in Chiang Rai, northern Thailand, having arrived there by way of Ceylon and Cambodia. At the time of its discovery the statue was encased in plaster. While in the process of being transported, the casing was damaged and split open, revealing the nephrite figure within. After many travels had taken it to, among other places, Luang Prabang, Vientiane and Thornburi, the Emerald Buddha was brought to Bangkok in 1778 and installed in Wat Phra Kaeo where it has remained ever since. Three times a year, at the start of each season, a special ceremony is held in which the Buddha's robes are changed by no less a person than the king himself. The beauty of the statue is most easily appreciated in the rainy season (May to October), being almost completely hidden during the cold season (November to February) beneath a covering of gold mesh.

The superb murals in the bot merit particular attention despite the fact that, owing to restoration necessitated by deterioration over the years, they are no longer in their original state. Above the entrance are scenes from the life of Buddha while, on the opposite side, the universe is portrayed in the symbolism of Buddhist astrology. Episodes from the "Ramakien" in pictures and in verse decorate the doors and window-shutters.

After leaving the temple it is well worth taking a walk round the delightful gardens with their graceful gilded statues known as "kinnaris" (bird-maidens). Also of interest are the demon figures, which provide the support for a tiered chedi.

Wat Phra Kaeo comes to life and is at its most interesting at weekends; however visitors should take care to avoid disturbing worshippers.

Between the bot of Wat Phra Kaeo and the covered walk which forms the boundary with the rest of the palace precinct, there are small pavilions

The central chedi in the Wat Phra Kaeo

which in earlier times were used by the king when he was preparing to undertake ceremonial duties in the bot. Today they provide welcome shade on hot days.

The murals in the covered way have been restored with much loving care for detail. They depict episodes from the "Ramakien" and also from Thai history.

Boromabiman Hall

Boromabiman Hall is the official name for the building overlooking the lawns where the king's annual garden party used to be held. Frescos inside depict the four Indian gods – Indra, Yahuma, Varuna and Agni – as guardians of the universe. Inscribed on plaques beneath are the ten royal virtues: liberality, propriety, readiness to make sacrifices, clemency, modesty, conscientiousness, freedom from anger, freedom from suspicion, patience and right dealing. Ever since the time of Rama VI all the Crown Princes, including King Bhumibol, have grown up here. Nowadays the building is only used occasionally, in particular to accommodate visiting Heads of State or high-ranking Buddhist dignitaries.

Mahamontien and Amarindra Vinichal room

To the west of the Chakri Palace is a large complex of buildings in three sections, the whole being known as the Mahamontien ("High Residence"). The front part of the building, which is open to visitors, comprises a single hall known as Amarindra Vinichai, meaning "Divine Decision", where King Rama I received homage seated on a large wide throne. The hall continues to be used for state occasions although King Bhumibol (crowned here on May 5th 1950) prefers to sit European-style on another throne placed in front of the great throne. Each year, on the anniversary of his coronation, the King holds an investiture here, bestowing honours and awards not only on fellow Heads of State and high-ranking dignitaries and officials in the public service, but also on deserving men and women from every walk of life – especially those who have distinguished themselves by their contribution to social work.

On leaving Amarindra Vinichai visitors turn right and walk around the peristyle in front of it, from where in former days royal proclamations were read out. The red and gold posts were used for tethering the royal elephants.

Great Chakri Palace

The Great Chakri Palace lies amid well-tended lawns. In the days when the kings and queens of Thailand resided here, the king would occupy the east wing and his consort the west (no entry to the public). Today, King Bhumibol having moved into the Chitralada Residence, it is used for official occasions such as the reception of foreign ambassadors and delegations. Though designed by an English architect in Italian Renaissance style, at King Rama V's insistence the palace was embellished with typically Siamese stepped roofs and mondhops. The tallest of the mondhops, above the central section, houses an urn containing the ashes of all the earlier Chakri kings. As well as being notable for the richness of their interiors, all the rooms in the palace are treasure-houses of valuable paintings, among them portraits of every Thai king. The incongruity of the exterior of the building cannot however be disguised; only when seen from the air does it harmonise with its surroundings. Royal proclamations were at one time read out from the balcony on the front; the oval picture in the centre depicts Rama V, the founder of the palace.

Dusit Maha Prasat

West of the Great Chakri Palace stands the Dusit Maha Prasat, a graceful edifice with four-fold overlapping roofs clad in red and green glazed tiles. It was built by Rama I in 1789. The groundplan of the building is such that the roofs intersect one another above gold ornamented gables, then rise step-like to a gilded mondhop culminating in a chedi-like spire. Forming a base for the mondhop as well as a harmonious feature at the point where the roofs converge are four garudas, mythical birds which served the god Vishnu as steeds and which are represented on the Thai royal coat of arms.

The single large inner hall, which is open to visitors, was originally Rama I's Audience Chamber. Here the king received his guests, seated, not on the large throne seen there today, but higher up, on a niche-like throne set in the wall of the south wing. The murals were painted in a later period, when the chamber became used for the lying-in-state of deceased monarchs. The richly ornamented couch and a number of other individual pieces of furniture do however date from Rama I's time, as do the beams in the walls and ceilings, laboriously transported over great distances from the north of Thailand.

Amphorn Phimok Prasat

The delicate wooden pavilion seen ahead on leaving the Dusit Maha Prasat is the Amphorn Phimok Prasat, used by Rama I as a robing chamber. Having "progressed" here in his litter, the king would change before entering the audience room. Drapes interlaced with gold thread were let down between the pillars behind which the king donned his ceremonial robes.

★★Wat Arun (Temple of the Dawn)

Location
On the west bank of the Menam Chao Phraya in Thonburi

Opening times
8am–5pm

Admission fee

When, having fallen to the Burmese, Ayutthaya was reduced to rubble and ashes, General Taksin and the remaining survivors vowed to march "until the sun rose again", and there to build a temple. Wat Arun, the Temple of the Dawn, stands on the spot to which they came and where later the new king built his royal palace and with it a private chapel.

The wat, with its 79m/259ft-high central prang surrounded by four smaller ones, has become a symbol of Bangkok despite the fact that it adorns the Thonburi embankment on the far side of the river. The plastered brick exterior is decorated with countless fragments of porcelain. It is

The Wat Arun, the landmark of Bangkok

possible to climb up the prang, the effort being rewarded by an excellent view of Bangkok. Seen from the Bangkok side of the Menam Chao Phraya, sunset over Wat Arun is an unforgettable experience.

★★Wat Benchama bo bitr (Marble Temple)

Location
In Dusit, on the corner of Si Ayutthaya Road and Nakhon Pathom Road (opposite Dusit Zoo)

Opening times
daily 8am–5pm

Admission fee

Benchamabophit, popularly called the Marble Temple, is one of the loveliest wats in Bangkok. It was erected in about 1899 by King Rama V (Chulalongkorn), the snow-white marble being shipped to Thailand from Tuscany in Italy. Thais also refer to the wat as "The Wat of the Fifth King", Rama V, crowned soon after his 20th birthday, having spent part of 1873 as a "bikkhu" (monk) in the old monastery immediately south of the temple.

Most unusually the compound is entered neither through a gate in a wall nor a wiharn, being separated from the street only by ornamental railings and an expanse of lawn. The boundary on the south side, between the temple and the monks' quarters, is also unusual, taking the form of a moat.

Exterior

The temple has a triple-tiered roof of Chinese glazed tiles. The little pavilions, matching the temple in colour and style, the red and gold curved bridges, and the green of the many trees, all play their part in creating a modern building perfectly in keeping with Thai tradition and style. King Chulalongkorn took a personal interest in many of the details while his half-brother Prince Naris, the accomplished architect, was on site for almost the entire period of construction.

Bot

The bot is cruciform in plan, its shape being enhanced by simple marble columns. At the rear is a courtyard, paved in squares of marble, around which runs a covered gallery with more than 50 statues of the Buddha. The

Bot of the Wat Benchama bo bitr

courtyard, the epitome of harmony and symmetry, accentuates the sweep of the triple-tiered roofs and gold ornamental nagas on the gable-ends while the exuberant ornateness of the older temple buildings in no way detracts from its dignity. Portrayed on two of the four elaborately carved gables, which also illustrate the origins of Buddhism, are the Hindu god Vishnu astride Garuda (east gable) and the three-headed white elephant Erawan (north gable).

A pair of lions in white marble, seated in the Burmese style, guard the main entrance to the bot; the building, though, is usually entered via the courtyard at the rear. The golden Buddha on the main altar is a full-size copy, made on the instructions of King Chulalongkorn, of the much revered Phra Buddha Jinarat ("Victorious King") from Wat Phra Si Ratana Mahathat in Phitsanulok. The Buddha figures around the courtyard illustrate every aspect of the evolution of Buddhist religious art. At the feet of each is a marble plaque recording its period and provenance, including whether it is original or a copy.

Festival of Visakha Bucha

The best time of all to visit the Marble Temple is during the Festival of Visakha Bucha in mid May, when pilgrims dance three times around the bot holding thousands of flickering candles.

★Vimarnmek Palace

Opening times
Daily
9.30am–4pm

Admission fee

Photography prohibited

Open once again to visitors following major restoration, Vimarnmek Palace is located at the rear of the park which surrounds the National Assembly (west of Dusit Zoo).

The four-storey teak building houses the extensive royal art collection of furniture, paintings, jewellery, etc., much of it acquired by King Rama V.

★★Wat Pho (Wat Chetuphon; Temple of the Reclining Buddha)

Location
Chetuphon Road, south of the Grand Palace

Opening times
daily
8am–5pm

Admission fee

Situated immediately south of the Grand Palace precinct, Wat Pho (or Wat Chetuphon), built by King Rama I, is the oldest and also the largest temple in Bangkok. In the 16th c. the site is said to have been occupied by a small residence belonging to a prince of Ayutthaya, with a wat called the "Temple of the Sacred Bhodi-Tree" (hence "pho", i.e. bhodi).

Wat Pho was renowned as a place of healing even in the olden days and famous for its pharmacy established at the time of Rama III. The same king turned the wat into Thailand's first "university", a seat of learning to which all had access. Today Wat Pho boasts a widely respected school which teaches the art of foot reflex massage.

Prangs and chedis

Among the 91 prangs and chedis adorning the courtyard around the bot, two of the larger ones deserve special mention. One is the green chedi, erected by Rama I over the remains of a statue of Buddha desecrated by the Burmese in Ayutthaya in 1767. The other is the blue-tiled chedi, finest of them all, built by Rama IV (Mongkut) in memory of Queen Suriyochai who, in order to save her husband's life, sacrificed her own.

The lions at the entrance to the bot are Burmese in design. Note too the marble bas-reliefs from Ayutthaya depicting scenes from the "Ramakien". The lofty, rectangular interior, divided into three by teak columns, is immensely impressive, with the red and gold of the ceiling reflected in the marble floor.

Temple of the Reclining Buddha

The Temple of the Reclining Buddha (as it is known in English) occupies the north-west corner of the compound. Inside the specially constructed wiharn lies an enormous reclining figure of the Buddha, 45m/148ft long and 15m/48ft high. Because the wiharn is narrow, it is quite impossible to take in the statue as a whole, attention having to be focused more on its detail, e.g. the finely curved lines of the face. The soles of the feet, inlaid

Exterior of the Wat Pho

with a myriad of precious stones, are particularly interesting, being decorated with the 108 signs of true faith. Also noteworthy are the long earlobes signifying noble birth and the lotus-bud configuration of the hand, a recurring symbol of purity and beauty.

The main entrance to Wat Pho is on Chetuphon Road, on the opposite side of which are the monks' living quarters. Although open to the public, only those with a serious interest in Buddhism are likely to find the visit rewarding. Anyone who does venture in is assured of a willing audience and eager interlocuters – at any time of the day or night.

★Giant Swing · Wat Suthat

Location
Sao Chingcha Sq.
In the eastern part of Old Bangkok

In the centre of the busy square in front of Wat Suthat stands one of Bangkok's most eye-catching sights, the 27m/88ft-high teak frame of the so-called Giant Swing. This used to be the focus of a religious ceremony held every year in December after the rice harvest. Teams of three took turns to balance on a dangerously narrow board and be swung 25m/82ft or more off the ground "up to Heaven", at which point they would attempt to catch a bag of silver coins in their teeth. Following a number of fatal accidents, the contest was banned by King Rama VII in 1932.

Ceremony

The ceremony was Indo-Brahman in origin, based on the legend of the god Shiva who was sent by Brahma to visit Earth. Brahma bade Shiva first test the firmness of Earth by putting down his right foot, crossing his left leg over his right knee, and waiting to see what came to pass. Shiva did as he was told, and nothing happened. Brahma then ordered Shiva to test whether, as prophesied, the mountains would fall into the sea when the nagas (water snakes) abandoned their mountain homes and returned to the ocean. Shiva again obeyed, whistling the nagas down from the mountains to the east and to the west into the billowing waves, waiting once more to see what would happen. The mountains did not fall into the sea, the nagas swimming happily in their new element where they have remained ever since. Each year thereafter, on the fifth day of the new moon in the second moon month (mid December), Shiva honoured Earth with a visit lasting ten days.

Naturally enough the god required an offering. His visit moreover coincided with the rice harvest (there was only one rice crop a year in those days), so Shiva had to be thanked and his blessing sought for the following year's crop. Four elements were deemed crucial to this: Sun, Moon, Earth and – most important of all – Water, carved symbols of which were kept in the little Hindu temple inside Wat Suthat (the temple can still be seen). These would then be taken out for the ceremony and put on display. At the same time the "Minister for Rice", the highest official in what was then an agrarian society, accompanied by hundreds of Brahman Court Astrologers, would go in procession around the city walls and then to the temple precinct where, at the Giant Swing, the remainder of the ceremony took place. Shiva's representative would test the solidity of Earth just as the god had done, placing his right foot on the ground near the Swing and crossing his left leg over his right knee, remaining in that position to witness the rest of the "trial". The mountains, symbolised by the upright frame of the Giant Swing, would again not fall into the sea even though the nagas, represented by the contestants in tall pointed hats, be swung back into their new element.

While the success of the harvests may have shown Shiva to be generally pleased with the spectacle, his earthly representative must have found the ceremony extremely tiring and provision of the silver offering expensive. Whatever the reason, Rama IV eventually decreed that the ceremony be carried out by a different dignitary each year. And while the "trials" are unlikely always to have gone to plan – the bag of silver perhaps eluding capture between the teeth and dropping to the ground or, worse still, one of the nagas on the swing or the left foot of Shiva's representative touching

Square of the Giant Swing with Wat Suthat

the ground – Thai chroniclers have drawn a discreet veil over any such mishaps.

The festival continues to be celebrated within the temple precinct, but inside the temple and with only 20 astrologers. First, before sunrise, Buddhist monks are made gifts of suitable offerings; afterwards the four elements – Sun, Moon, Earth and Water, symbolised by little statues – are placed inside a golden goose known as Hinsa which is then perched on a miniature swing to be ridden up to Heaven by the god Brahma.

★ **Wat Suthat**

Opening times
temple precinct: daily 9am–5pm
wiharn: weekends and public holidays only

Wat Suthat, adjacent to the Great Swing, is one of the oldest and most beautiful of Bangkok's Buddhist temples. Three kings had a hand in its construction: it was begun soon after his coronation in 1782 by Rama I, founder of the Chakri dynasty, continued by Rama II, and completed, ten years later by Rama III. Apart from its delightful architecture the temple boasts some exceptionally interesting wall-paintings. The compound as a whole covers an area of 40,800sq.m/49,000sq.yd. It is rectangular in plan (being roughly half as long again as it is wide) with a perimeter wall 949m/1038yd in length. The area is divided between the temple complex itself and the monk's living quarters.

Wiharn

From an architectural point of view the wiharn of Wat Suthat is of considerably more interest than the bot, as well as having a finer interior. On each side of the almost square building, six pillars with gilded lotus-blossom capitals support the richly decorated gable roof; two of the sides are embellished with superb porches. The massive doorways through which the visitor enters are famous for their carvings, while the shutters of the windows include one carved by Rama III himself. Pillars divide the 30m/98ft-high interior into three aisles.

The wiharn was built specially to house the 13th c. Phra Buddha Shakyamuni, which Rama I brought by river to Bangkok from Sukhothai. On its arrival in his new capital the king declared seven days of festivities, the bronze statue being paraded through the streets on the way to its chosen resting place. Rama himself walked barefoot in the procession, becoming so exhausted, it is said, that he staggered into the temple.

The statue shows Buddha in the pose known as "pang mara vichaya" (victory over mara). The bronze torso is gold-plated and rests on an ornate stepped podium the lower part of which contains the ashes of Rama VIII (Ananda Mahidol), half-brother of the present King Bhumibol.

Since it was first built, Wat Suthat has been known by several different names. Rama I originally christened it Wat Mahasuthavat; but it soon became popularly known as Wat Phra Yai (The Great Temple) on account of the imposing Buddha.

Pagodas

The wiharn is surrounded by a balustrade adorned with 28 Chinese pagodas, as well as with superb bronze horses and Chinese warrior figures. As is the tradition, rows of gilded Buddhas line the gallery around the inner court.

Wall-paintings

The wall-paintings underwent thorough and very costly restoration in the late 1980s, much of the finance being provided by the West German goverment in celebration of the city's bicentenary in 1982. Bat droppings were found to have been the principal cause of deterioration. The murals, covering an area of 2565sq.m/27,450sq.ft, are perhaps the most extensive and important of their kind in Thailand. Almost 50% were damaged, 10% irreparably so.

Most of the old Thai wall-paintings still preserved portray the life of the Buddha Gautama. Those in the wiharn of Wat Suthat however are different, depicting instead the preceding 24 Buddhas and three contemporaries. This came about as a result of the slates used by the artists, which were in Pali script and designated the order of each individual section of the painting. The name of the artist is not known, nor is the exact date. Experts believe the murals derive from a transitional period, being markedly dissimilar in style to the work of classical Thai painters and showing an obvious Western influence. They are assumed to have been commissioned at least in part by Rama II (1809–24) but may have been completed under Rama III, towards the end of his reign (1824–51).

Statue of King Ananda

A factor in the West German government's decision to help finance the restoration of the paintings was Rama VIII's special association with Germany. His father Rama VII trained there as a naval officer and Ananda himself (Rama VIII) was born in Heidelberg. A statue unveiled in his memory on November 2nd 1974 stands in a corner near the main entrance.

★★Wat Traimitr (Temple of the Golden Buddha)

Location
In Chinatown, junction of Yaowarat Road and Charoen Krung Road

Opening times
Daily 9am–5pm

Admission fee

Wat Traimitr owes its fame and its attraction to an accident, prior to which it was just one of the many hundreds of very ordinary temples scattered throughout Bangkok.

During the 1950s the land around it was purchased by the East Asiatic Company, a condition of the sale being the removal of a plaster statue of Buddha. The statue proved too heavy for the crane being used to lift it; the cable parted and the figure was dropped, being left overnight where it fell. This happened to be in the rainy season, and when next morning some monks walked past, they noticed a glint of gold shining through in one place. The plaster was removed, revealing a 3.5m/11½ft Buddha cast from 5½ tonnes of solid gold. All attempts to trace the origin of this priceless statue have so far failed. It is assumed however to date from the Sukhothai period, when marauding invaders threatened the country and its treasures, and it became common practice to conceal valuable Buddha figures such as this beneath a coating of plaster. Nor is it known how the statue came to Bangkok.

The Golden Buddha can be seen on the upper floor of a two-storey building access to which is by an external staircase next to the bot.

Opposite lie the precinct of another (less interesting) temple and the yard of a private school.

Chitralada Palace (royal residence)

Location
In Dusit, bounded by Rama V Road, Rajawithi Road, Sawankhalok Road and Si Ayutthaya Road

No admission

Once King Chulalongkorn's summer residence, Chitralada Palace stands in about 1sq.km/250 acres of grounds incorporating several artificial lakes. At each corner of the park is a fountain adorned with Late Baroque figures drawn from mythology, evidence of the cultivated taste of Thailand's rulers.

Chitralada is hardly a typical royal residence; visitors, were they to be granted access, would be reminded more of an agricultural research station. The palace indeed doubles as a sort of experimental farm, aimed primarily at boosting the income of rice-growers in the north by providing fish-breeding stock. The royal fish ponds are therefore much more than just a hobby. There is also a beef-rearing unit and an experimental dairy.

As befits their status, the famous royal "white" elephants (see Flora and Fauna) also have their quarters at the palace, where they are taken after first spending some time in Dusit Zoo. King Bhumibol now owns more albino elephants than any of his predecessors; never before have so many been presented to a monarch in the course of his reign.

The moat around the grounds made headlines during the unrest in 1973 when student demonstrators sought, and found, refuge inside the palace railings.

★Klongs (canals)

Bangkok no longer has an authentic floating market. Most of the canals (klongs) cutting through the city were either drained and filled because of the risk of cholera they posed, or converted into badly needed roads. Only in Thonburi do one or two vendors still set up shop on the klongs in the early mornings. Even so, a boat trip along the waterways remains an absorbing experience, best embarked upon from the landing-stage near the Oriental Hotel. Here, especially in the morning, a multitude of craft wait to ferry sightseers across the Menam Chao Phraya and through the tangled web of little and not so little canals. The time to go if at all possible is in the morning or the late afternoon when life along the klongs is at its most colourful and varied.

In order to see the kind of floating market which still existed in Bangkok up to a few years ago, it is now necessary to make the journey to Damnoen Saduak (see Ratchaburi).

Lak Muang

Location
opposite the south-eastern end of Sanaam Luang, near the Ministry of Defence

Opening times
daily

Admission free

Built around the stone which marks the city's foundation, this small shrine is the point from which all distances are measured. Here too, according to popular belief, dwell the guardian spirits of Bangkok, the real "masters" of the city. No matter what the hour of day or night a throng of people armed with flowers and joss-sticks is always gathered around the gilded lingam, the phallic symbol in the centre of the shrine, hoping to be granted good fortune in their various earthly ventures. They buy caged birds which they then release, not just to please the guardian spirits but also to smooth their own passage into Nirvana.

The area around Lak Muang swarms with people too – making their offerings at altars set up outside the shrine, or washing with holy lotus blossom water scooped from large pots placed near by. In one corner, day-time perfomances of Thai theatre are guaranteed an enthusiastic audience.

★★Jim Thompson's Houses

Location
2 Soi Kasem San, off Rama I Road

Opening times
Mon.–Sat. 9am–4.30pm

Admission fee

The story of the American-born James ("Jim") Thompson (see Famous People) reads like an adventure novel. Having made Thai silk famous throughout the world he suddenly disappeared without trace, at the peak of his business career, in 1967 while taking a short break in Malaysia.

The extraordinarily beautiful old Thai houses which Thompson found near Ayutthaya and brought by river to Bangkok have not vanished however. Now owned by a charitable trust, they are used to display the splendid art collection the American had built up. All the proceeds of admission go to various charitable institutions in Thailand.

The seven wooden houses – which every visitor should try to see – are now almost unique in the country and contain treasures representing every period of Thai art. They are picturesquely situated in Soi Kasem San, in a pretty garden by the side of a klong on the opposite bank of which the silk weavers once worked.

Once inside, the cultured taste of the former owner is everywhere apparent. As well as old pictures in Thai silk, and Buddha figures from nearly every major epoch, there are numerous everyday items and many other works of art. Note in particular the sideboard, once part of a Chinese altar, and the miniature palace which children of some rich family would have used for keeping pets. A Buddhist by conviction, Jim Thompson moved into his house only when temple astrologers deemed the moment auspicious. Even so, he was granted but a short time in it. Just seven years later he left Bangkok never to return.

★★Markets

General

Every day between sunrise and sunset, and in some cases long into the night, numerous markets are held in Bangkok and on its outskirts. Between them they supply most of the inhabitants' daily needs in the way of fresh vegetables, livestock (e.g. chickens and fish), clothing, textiles and other goods. Especially on Fridays and Saturdays when housewives shop for the

Jim Thomson's House, a unique monument of Thai culture

Market life in Bangkok . . .

. . . varied and colourful

weekend, these daily markets are every bit as colourful, bustling and full of interest and atmosphere as the big weekend market (see below).

Only a few of the markets can be mentioned here, but the others can be easily found.

Chatuchak (weekend market)

For some years now Bangkok's big weekend market has been held at Chatuchak on the northern edge of the city, having moved from its old site on Sanaam Luang, near the Grand Palace. It nevertheless remains a huge attraction, not least for many thousands of tourists. The variety of goods on offer seems almost endless, and as well as the numerous stalls there are restaurants and snack vendors. As early as the Friday evening locals start arriving from far and wide by bus, car or train. Be careful when buying "antiques"; most are simply clever reproductions.

Klong Toey

Klong Toey market is one of the cheapest in Bangkok, being situated away from the city centre and catering more for the needs of the poorer inhabitants. The traders display their wares in a somewhat haphazard fashion, fish being sold alongside clothing for example, but there is always a wide range of goods to choose from. Be warned though: some of the smells can be rather overpowering.

Nakhom Kasem (Thieves' Market)

Notorious many years ago for the dubious origin of its merchandise, the "Thieves' Market" in the centre of Chinatown still rather relishes its earlier bad reputation. The market should certainly be visited, if only for the unparalleled variety of goods on sale. Among the innumerable reproductions collectors with patience and a keen eye still have a chance of discovering a genuine antique, worth far more than its asking price. Nakhom Kasem is at its busiest in the evenings.

Tha Thewes (flower market)

Every type of flower grown in Thailand is found on sale in Tha Thewes market. From early in the morning often until late at night, scores of children lovingly and dexterously weave the garlands for which the country is famous, selling them to tourists, taxi-drivers and even locals for just a few bahts. In this way they make a contribution to the household budget from a very early age. Tha Thewes is one of the few markets actually on the Menam Chao Phraya embankment. Orchids in rare abundance, jasmine, hibiscus and lotus blossom are a joy to the senses, their scent drifting over the marketplace, while a multitude of garden and tropical forest plants combine in a verdantly luxuriant display.

Bangrak

Mutton is still sold "on the hoof" at Bangrak market (between Sathorn Tai Road and Silom Road) though trading takes place very early in the morning. The market is also well worth visiting later in the day however. Most of the fruit and vegetables are snapped up by the larger Bangkok hotels, taking advantage of the wide range of fresh produce available. This is a general market catering for all the Thais' daily needs.

Silom Road (night market)

Every evening Silom Road is transformed into a big street-market, with a huge variety of merchandise and a large number of open-air restaurants and snack vendors whose food can be safely sampled without the least qualms.

Patpong Road (night market)

With Patpong Road, hub of Bangkok's nightlife, being closed to traffic in the evenings, several dozen street traders now set up stalls there. Beware though of pickpockets, they are very active – as indeed they are in all the markets.

★★National Museum

Location
4 Na Prathat Road, on the west side of Sanaam Luang (Royal Square)

Opening times
Wed.–Sun.
9am–4pm

Admission fee

Photography prohibited

Bangkok's National Museum provides a splendidly comprehensive introduction to the history of Thailand, at least half a day being required to do it anything like justice. The extraordinary size of the collection is explained by the fact that, until the mid seventies, this was Thailand's only museum.

Since then the Thai Department of Fine Arts has established additional branches thoughout the country. The Department's policy is for archaeological and art historic finds to be put on display as near as possible to their place of origin, so there are plans for even more museums in the future.

An excellent catalogue is available at the entrance. There are guided tours in English and virtually all exhibits are labelled in English as well as in Thai.

Wang Na Palace

The old Wang Na Palace built by Rama I remains essentially as it was, as does the original nucleus of the collection made up of King Chulalongkorn's bequest and household effects from Wang Na: regalia, religious and ceremonial artefacts, ceramics, games, weaponry, musical instruments, the Viceroy's throne, etc., etc.

Collections

The older buildings in the museum contain some particularly interesting exhibits. They include a collection of presentation gifts to the king, a collection of curiosities, the royal barges and state coaches and hearses, etc. Principal attraction in the new wings is the fine collection of Buddha figures, arranged according to period.

Wat Buddhaisawan

Apart from the blue mosaic gable wall which was added later, this typical Thai temple dates from 1795. It was specially built to house its greatest treasure, a statue of Buddha enthroned beneath a canopy. Once a year, at the time of the Songkhram festival (the old Thai New Year) in April, this much venerated image is carried in solemn procession through the streets of Bangkok. Tradition has it that the figure came originally from Ceylon; historians on the other hand, influenced by its style, believe it is most likely to have been carved in Sukhothai around 1250. Like the famous Emerald

Cooking on the Silom Road in Bangkok

Buddha in Wat Phra Kaeo (see Grand Palace precinct), the statue is probably much-travelled, having almost certainly found its way to a number of different south-east Asian countries at various times. It was brought from Chiang Mai to Bangkok by King Rama I in 1795.

For some visitors the murals decorating the walls of the bot are of even greater interest than the statue of Buddha. Unlike those in Wat Phra Kaeo they are completely original and therefore almost 200 years old. Executed in tempera colours using mineral and earth pigments, the paintings, eschewing perspective, depict episodes from Buddha's earthly existence. The figures are portrayed in period dress.

"The Red House"

The Tamnak Daeng, or "Red House", was constructed towards the end of the 18th c. by Rama I for one of his elder sisters. It acquired its colour, and so too its name, from a plant pigment applied to the teak of which it is built. The house originally stood elsewhere, subsequently being moved to the National Museum. Inside, the bedroom in particular, with its carved and gilded bed, dressing-table and towel-rack, vividly evokes the life-style of a member of the royal family at the time. Note too the richly ornate lacquered wooden chest in which silken robes would have been kept.

It is not possible here to do more than simply draw attention to the National Museum's extensive and extremely valuable collection of Buddha figures from all the different periods. Special mention should, however, be made of the Dvaravati sculptures from Nakhon Pathom and statues in the Srivijaya and Lopburi styles (both South Wing, upper floor) as well as those from Sukhothai (North Wing, upper floor).

Bang Pa In — G 4

บางปะอิน

Region: Central Thailand
Province: Ayutthaya
Altitude: 4m/13ft. Population: 12,000

Location and history

Bang Pa In is situated on a natural island in the Menam Chao Phraya, about 60km/37 miles north of Bangkok. Now popular with people from the capital, long ago the kings of Ayutthaya made it their summer residence. Originally it was the family home of King Prasat Thong's mother, the king himself being born there. Following his accession to the throne in 1629, Prasat Thong erected the Buddhist temple of Wat Chumphol Nikayaram. He also enlarged the 1.6sq.km/400 acre lake, building beside it a small palace where he and his successors spent the hot summer months. When, under King Taksin, the more distant Thonburi became capital, Bang Pa In was to all intents and purposes abandoned, falling into ruin and disrepair. With the introduction of steamboats on the Menam Chao Phraya, making travel so much easier even for the sovereign, Bang Pa was "rediscovered" by King Mongkut. He replaced the old palace with a new one. Later enlarged by his successors this, together with some other buildings, has recently been thoroughly restored. Since Rama VIII's accession to the throne, the royal family's summer residence has been a palace by the sea at Hua Hin. However, Bang Pa In is still favoured today by King Bhumibol for state receptions. Most of the buildings, set in a delightfully laid-out park with several lily ponds, date from the reign of King Chulalongkorn.

Access

By car: from Bangkok via Highway 1, branching off left after 52km/32 miles (signposted).

By bus: from Bangkok's Northern Bus Terminal: departures daily at 40 minute intervals from 4.30am. Most Bangkok travel agencies arrange excursions to Bang Pa In.

By rail: Bangkok–Ayutthaya line (about 20 trains a day from Bangkok Hualampong; journey time 1½ hours).

By boat: along the Menam Chao Phraya. An ideal way to see Ba Pang In is to go one way aboard the "Oriental Queen" or "Ayutthaya Princess" and the other way by bus. Day trips can be booked at Bangkok travel agencies.

★★Palace precinct

Opening times
daily
8.30am–3.30pm

Admission fee

The palace precinct is enclosed within a high wall, around which massive towers are positioned at intervals. In fact Bang Pa In comprises two separate palace complexes, an outer and an inner. At one time the inner was barred to all but the royal couple and male courtiers.

Phra Thinang Aisawan Tippaya Pavilion

Set in the middle of a lake, the Bangkok-style Phra Thinang Aisawan Tippaya Pavilion, most delightful of all the buildings, was erected by King Chulalongkorn in 1876. Although not original, being a faithful copy of the Phra Thinang Aphonphimok Prasat Pavilion built by King Mongkut in the grounds of the Grand Palace in Bangkok, the graceful edifice is nevertheless among the purest examples of Thai architecture to be seen, and for that reason has frequently served as the model for the Thai exhibition pavilion at world fairs. Constructed in the first instance entirely of wood, the floor and supports were replaced in 1920 by reinforced concrete. In the centre of the pavilion stands a cast-iron, life-size statue of King Chulalongkorn by an unknown sculptor.

Phra Thinang Warophat Phiman

North of the landing-stage the Phra Thinang Warophat Phiman Hall, a mixture of Italian Renaissance and Victorian styles, was used as a royal audience chamber. Inside are a throne with a baldachin and, on the opposite wall, an oil-painting of King Chulalongkorn in his robes of state. Decorating the remaining walls are illustrations from the tales of "Inao", "Phra Aphaimani" and the "Ramakien". A covered bridge links the hall to a circular building opening onto a broad terrace from which wide stone steps lead down into the lake. All have been restored in recent years.

Uthayan Phumi Sathian Palace

Only a tall brick hexagonal Neo-Gothic tower now remains of the former Uthayan Phumi Sathian Palace, King Chulalongkorn's residence during the rainy season. The rest, built of wood, was destroyed by fire in 1938.

Phra Thinang Aisawan Tippaya Pavilion in Bang Pa In

Vehat Chamrun Palace

The Chinese-style Vehat Chamrun Palace at the north end of the precinct was built in 1889 at the expense of wealthy Chinese merchants hoping to curry favour with King Chulalongkorn. The brightly coloured roof tiles, roof ornamentation, wood carvings and most of the interior furnishings were either brought from China or made by Chinese craftsmen. Because it had glazed windows the palace was used by Chulalongkorn during periods of heavy rain. Inside, the magnificently carved furniture is particularly noteworthy, especially the sovereign's very ornate bed, King Vajiravudh's carved Chinese writing table, and the bookcase in the study containing old Chinese manuscripts from various different periods.

Royal observatory

The tower standing on a small island between the two palaces was built by King Mongkut, a keen amateur astronomer, for use as an observatory. A stone staircase leads up to a platform from where there is a fine view of the surrounding countryside.

Statue of Queen Sumantha

Among the monuments with which King Chulalongkorn embellished the park is a memorial to his first wife Sumantha Kumaritana who, together with her three children, drowned when their boat capsized on the Menam Chao Phraya. The Queen's attendants dared not go to her aid because of a century old law which made touching a member of the royal family an offence punishable by death. Following the tragedy Chulalongkorn abolished the law; it had been first introduced by King Rama Thibodi who believed himself a reincarnation of Vishnu.

Other places of interest

Also deserving mention are the open-air theatre, a small wooden pavilion near the Uthayan Phumi Sathian, and a prang beneath a large bodhi tree on the edge of the lake. The latter was erected by King Chulalongkorn, replacing a shrine dedicated to King Prasat Thong. Inside it stands a statue of Prasat Thong.

Royal Observatory in Bang Pa In

Wat Chumphol Nikayaram

Outside the palace grounds, Wat Chumphol Nikayaram, on the nearer side of the island not far from the railway station, was built by King Prasat Thong and several times restored and altered under his successors. The walls are decorated with murals from the reign of King Mongkut portraying scenes from the life of Buddha. The two beautifully proportioned polygonal chedis are from the same era.

Wat Niwet Thamapravat

Wat Niwet Thamapravat lies south of the royal residence, on an island in the Menam Chao Phraya. It was a gift from King Chulalongkorn to the monks of the Dhramayutika sect. The bot contains a large statue of Buddha by Prince Pradi Vrakarn, court sculptor to Kings Mongkut and Chulalongkorn.

Bang Saen H 4

บางแสน

Region: South-east Thailand
Province: Chonburi
Altitude: 2m/6½ft. Population: 30,000

Location

The beach resort of Bang Saen is situated on the Gulf of Thailand south-east of Bangkok. Highway 3, the main road link between the capital and the south-eastern part of the country, passes east of the town.

Access

By car: from Bangkok via Highways 3 or 34 (104km/65 miles).
By bus: buses from Bangkok's Eastern Bus Terminal to Pattaya or Chanthaburi stop at Bang Saen. Travel agencies offer day excursions to the beach.

Ocean World Leisure Park

Bang Saen is always overcrowded at weekends when people from nearby Bangkok come in their thousands to relax on the sandy but desperately

Monastic quarters in the Ship Temple of Luk Sam Po

overcrowded beaches (and all the accommodation is taken up). "Ocean World", an American-style leisure park complete with swimming pools, opened on the promenade a few years ago.

Bang Saen Aquarium

Bangkok Education College's interesting Scientific Marine Centre (in the inner courtyard of the College) exhibits numerous species of fish found in the Gulf of Thailand.

Luk Sam Po Fishermen's shrine

The ship-like Luk Sam Po Chinese temple (north of the town, best reached by the coast road) was built as a memorial to the victims of a disaster which took place when a ship carrying Chinese immigrants sank off the Thai coast in a heavy storm. The sole survivor not only built the temple but also founded a religious order with very strict rules – which probably accounts for its failure for a number of years now to attract novice monks.

Grouped around the central pagoda are some "ship's cabins", little houses which continue to be occupied by one or two monks and nuns. Note also the monks' quarters outside the temple complex itself, built in the form of small fishing boats.

The monastery possesses two small-scale reproductions of the chedi at Nakhon Pathom, the most revered chedi in Thailand. Buddhists come from all over the world to visit Luk Sam Po, but ordinary visitors are made welcome too.

Golf course

Very pleasantly situated on a rocky hill Bang Saen's modern 18-hole golf course is considered one of Thailand's most beautiful (see Practical Information, Sport).

Surroundings

Among places of interest further afield are a freshwater lake (dam) and a small temple with a square, tiled tower.

Buriram G 7

Region: North-east Thailand
Province: Buriram
Altitude: 65m/213ft. Population: 30,000

บุรีรัมย์

Location

Buriram, originally an early Khmer settlement and now principal town of Buriram province, lies on the southern edge of the Khorat plateau 265km/165 miles from Bangkok. This part of the country on the periphery of the north-eastern region – Thailand's "poorhouse" – is characterised by sparse vegetation, merging into mixed forest as the uplands are approached. From Buriram (reasonable hotels) two in part well-preserved and important temples can be reached – Prasat Phanom Rung and Prasat Muang Tam (see Prakhon Chai for both).

Access

By car: from Bangkok via Highway 1 as far as Saraburi, then Highways 2 (to Nakhon Ratchasima) and 226.
Bus: from Bangkok Northern Bus Terminal (also night-time service).
By rail: Bangkok–Ubon Ratchathani line.

History

From the 8th c. onwards the Khmer peoples gradually moved closer and closer to what is now Thailand, one group settling early on in the Malay penisula, another advancing west towards the Menam basin. That the Khmer developed their own distinctive culture has been clearly demonstrated by the wealth of archaeological finds from the late Mons Dvaravati period (*c.* 10th c.). From around the turn of the millennium until the end of the 12th c. the Menam basin and eastern Thailand in particular came under Khmer rule, administered by a viceroy from Lopburi. Exactly why the Khmer built several temple complexes at Buriram remains a mystery; perhaps the reason was simply geographical, the area lying on the direct route between Angkor Wat and Phimai.

Wat Utai Maggaram

Some rare early examples of Khmer art were uncovered near the small village of Lam Plai Mat about 30km/19 miles west of Buriram. One such find, dating from the 7th c., was a one metre tall stone Buddha in meditative pose, clearly revealing in its posture, facial expression and abundance of detail, the influence of the Indian Amaravati style (*c.* 2nd c. A.D.). This statue, well worth seeing, is now in Wat Utai Maggaram near Huai Thalaeng (Nakhon Ratchasima province). Another of the finds was a truly wonderful 8th c. bronze statue of Buddha, this time standing in the pose of a teacher. Now in the National Museum in Bangkok, the 110cm/43in. figure, the largest yet discovered from the Dvaravati period, demonstrates Khmer mastery of the technology of bronze casting.

Chainat F 4

Region: Central Thailand
Province: Chainat
Altitude: 55m/180ft. Population: 28,000

ชัยนาท

Location

Chainat, situated on the Menam Chao Phraya between Singburi and Uthai Thani in the northern part of Thailand's central plain, has been an important trade and distribution centre since time immemorial. Although lacking in "sights" as such, the town is very typical of its area, being surrounded by rice fields criss-crossed by a network of natural and man-made waterways.

Access

By car: from Lopburi by Highways 1 (151km/94 miles) or 311 (via Singburi; about 80km/50 miles).
By bus: from Bangkok Northern Bus Terminal.
By rail: Bangkok–Chiang Mai line; nearest railway station at Takhli (18km/11 miles).

Chainat

Dam

Completed in 1957 the dam south of Chainat was Thailand's first. By feeding a network of canals it regulates the water supply to the rice fields of the Menam plain where the main crop is water-rice.

Wat Boromathat

Above the dam stands Wat Boromathat, its chedi dating from the U Thong period (12th–15th c.) but showing unmistakable signs of Srivijaya influence. Note the seated Buddha figures in the four niches.

Temple museum

The museum next to the wat has an interesting collection of Buddhas, all of them found in this particular area by a local monk. The figures illustrate a variety and sometimes mixture of styles. One stone tablet is decorated with a seated Buddha and the "Wheel of the Law" (Dvaravati style, 9th/10th c.).

Wat Thammamun

Wat Thammamun, on the left bank of the Menam north of the town, boasts not only a seated Buddha figure in the Ayutthaya style but also a footprint of the Buddha (in the wiharn).

Wat Pak Klong Mak

Yet another wat, Wat Pak Klong Mak, is found a little further to the north, where the Klong Makham joins the Menam Chao Phraya. The interior is decorated with ffescos of Thailand's highly esteemed Prince Chumphon who grew up in the monastery.

Sanburi

See entry

Chaiya M 3

ไชยยา

Region: South Thailand
Province: Surat Thani
Altitude: 5m/16ft. Population: 22,000

Location

The town of Chaiya, once a thriving centre of trade, lies on the Malay peninsula just below the Kra isthmus. It has an interesting history and is well worth visiting, especially as part of a round trip including Surat Thani, Ranong, Nakhon Si Thammarat and Phangnga province (which has lovely scenery).

Access

By car: from Chumphon, following Highway 41 along the coast then turning off onto the 4112 at Tha Chana or continuing to Pala Ram from where a small road leads to Chaiya (150km/93 miles).
By rail: Bangkok–South Thailand line.
Nearest airport: Surat Thani (up to four flights a day from Bangkok).

History

Archaeological finds typically Gupta (4th–6th c.) in style indicate that Indian traders from Madras were visiting this town on the east coast of Thailand as early as the 5th c. (and probably even earlier). Chaiya in fact was one of the principal trading cities of the Srivijaya empire (8th–13th c.) which encompassed the greater part of the Indonesian archipelago (Sumatra, Java, Malaysia) and the southern part of Thailand roughly as far up as present-day Hua Hin (60km/37 miles north of Petchaburi). Although much of the town's history remains obscure, many historians now believe Chaiya to have been the capital of the empire, not Palembang in Sumatra as was previously thought. This is supported by the large number of archaeological finds from Chaiya (far in excess of those made at Palembang). Further testimony is provided by various stone inscriptions.

Of Chaiya's former prominence and splendour and its role in Indo-Asiatic maritime trade, few vestiges now remain. With its maritime links severed, the town lies almost forgotten, though archaeologists continue to unearth more and more evidence of its earlier highly developed culture. Of the pinnacle of architectural achievement reached in the Srivijaya period,

Chaiya's Wat Phra Mahathat provides the last truly well-preserved example. Others have survived, in Nakhon Si Thammarat especially, but all have fallen partly into ruin.

Sights

Wat Kaeo

Among the buildings to have survived from the Srivijaya period is a dilapidated stupa at Wat Kaeo, situated not far from Chaiya railway station. A seated Buddha and two smaller statues can still be seen in the base. The wiharn of nearby Wat Ratana Waram also contains a large seated Buddha while, scattered around, are several sandstone stelae and another statue of Buddha, this time standing.

★★Wat Phra Mahathat

Wat Phra Mahathat, a short distance out of the town on the road (4011) leading west from the railway station, is one of the most highly venerated temples in southern Thailand. Though twice restored (in 1901 and again in 1930), the 8th–9th c. central stupa, the oldest part of the wall-encircled temple complex, appears very much in its original form. It is a fine example of Srivijaya architecture with a strong Javanese influence (compare, for instance, the Borobodur temple complex in Java). The temple, as in Borobodur, is supported on a square base with sills around it, the walls being embellished with small blind porches and several little stupas crowning the triple-tiered roof. Although probably of later date, the chedi is also of considerable interest. Near by is a small museum containing copies of the statues found in Chaiya, some of which are quite exceptional (the originals being in the National Museum in Bangkok). Also on display in the museum is the famous bronze statue known as the "Grahi Buddha". While the Buddha figure itself shows clear Mons influence, the naga is just as clearly Khmer in style. Historians attribute the work either to two different periods or two different sculptors, suggesting it is possibly transitional in origin.

Wat Suan Mok (meditation centre)

Wat Suan Mok, a modern Buddhist meditation centre situated on a small hill a few kilometres further west, attracts many devotees. Bas-reliefs depicting episodes in Buddha's life adorn the exterior. Inside are paintings illustrating the history of Buddhism and also e.g. Aesop's Fables. One wall was inspired by the aphorisms of the American Buddhist Emanuel Sherman who came to Thailand having first spent some time in Japan.

Ban Pou Ma Riang (fishing village)

East of Chaiya lies the idyllic little fishing village of Ban Pu Ma Riang, built entirely on piles and famous for its silk.

Chaiyaphum (Jayabhumi) F 6

ชัยภูมิ

Region: North-east Thailand
Province: Chaiyaphum
Altitude: 186m/610ft. Population: 26,000

Location

The Khmer kings, and the officials charged with administering their vast empire, used to stop at Chaiyaphum (also called Jayabhumi) on the long journey from Angkor Wat to Si Thep, one of the Khmer kingdom's principal cities. Neither the town, which is now a provincial capital, nor its surroundings are particularly attractive, but two major religious sites lie near by.

Access

By car: from Nakhon Ratchasima by Highway 2 (north-eastwards), branching north-west onto Highway 202 for Chaiyaphum after 77km/48 miles.
By rail: nearest railway station Bamnet Narong (Kaeng Khoi–Bua Yai branch line); about 57km/35 miles.

★Wat Prang Ku

Wat Prang Ku, about 2km/1¼ miles from Chaiyaphum, was built at the time of King Jayavarman VII (1181–1201). The reasonably well-preserved temple has some fine sculptures on the gabling as well as on the lintels above the doors. Inside are three Buddha figures, two being seated, one in the

Dvaravati the other in the Ayutthaya style, and the third standing, also in the Ayutthaya style. A second building, this time dilapidated, has a well-preserved door lintel with decoration drawn from Hindu mythology.

★Buddha's Hill

"Buddha's Hill" is located about 30km/18½ miles from Chaiyaphum (follow the 201 north for about 13km/8 miles, turning left onto a track for a further 17km/10½ miles). Here, carved from one of the area's many sandstone boulders are seven Dvaravati-style Buddha figures. These, but more particularly the 2m/6½ft-high seated Buddha adorning another boulder near by, are the object of an annual pilgrimage to the site.

Chaliang

See Si Satchanalai

Chanthaburi J 6

Region: East Thailand
Province: Chanthaburi
Altitude: 37m/121ft. Population: 47,000

จันทบุรี

Location

Chanthaburi, a prosperous, lively, rapidly expanding town in south-east Thailand, basks in the lush green of the Menam Chanthaburi flood plain, 11km/7 miles from where the river enters the Gulf. It is set against a backcloth of mountains (the highest being Khao Sai Dhao, 1633m/5360ft) which mark the transition to the Thai–Kampuchean border country. Blessed with a mild climate the region is known as the "orchard of Thailand", oranges, pineapples, mangoes and the rather unpleasant smelling durian thriving on its vast plantations. Chanthaburi is also special from the point of view of the Thai jewellery trade, the surrounding area being dotted with mines yielding rubies, sapphires and other precious stones.

Access

By car: from Bangkok via Highways 3 or 344 (245km/152 miles); from Pattaya via Highways 3 or 36 (200km/124 miles).

By bus: from Bangkok Eastern Bus Terminal (a good 6 hour drive) or Pattaya (about 3 hours). Ordinary buses stop a little short of the town, passengers completing the journey by shared taxi; air-conditioned buses are allowed right into the centre.

History

Chanthaburi is thought to be very ancient, a belief confirmed by inscriptions dating back at least to the time of the Khmer (9th c.) for whom the town served as a port and trading post. In the 14th c. it became part of the kingdom of Ayutthaya. After the sacking of Ayutthaya by the Burmese in 1767, the governor of Chanthaburi tried to break free from the new kingdom centred on Thonburi. He was defeated and executed by King Taksin. From 1893 to 1905 the town was occupied by French troops. Today, partly because of its proximity to the "green frontier" with Kampuchea, many of Chanthaburi's inhabitants are of Chinese or Vietnamese origin. There are also large numbers of Vietnamese Christians whose forbears fled from religious persecution in Annam.

Sights

Gemstone mines

Being the hub of Thailand's gem industry, a day trip to Chanthaburi for example from Pattaya, is certain to recommend itself to anyone with an interest in precious stones. Not for that reason alone however, there being much of cultural interest too (though, with one jeweller's shop after another, visitors might be forgiven for supposing that the entire population makes its living from the jewellery trade). There are excursions to the nearby mines at Bo Rai in the neighbouring province of Trat (reached by road via the 3249), where rubies, sapphires, zircons and many other kinds

Equestrian statue of King Taksin

of gemstone are extracted from open-cast workings. At some of the mines visitors are allowed to search for stones themselves and can keep any they find.

Monument to Sunthorn Phu

A monument to the great poet Sunthorn Phu (1786–1855) adorns a small lake beside the road running north into the town. He used to journey regularly between Bangkok and the temple at Klaeng where his father was abbot.

Equestrian statue of King Taksin

Another monument, an equestrian statue of King Taksin (Phra Chao Taksin Monument), embellishes Chanthaburi's attractive city centre park – where there are also a number of pleasant restaurants offering respite for tired legs.

★Cathédrale de Notre-Dame

The French Cathédrale de Notre-Dame (also known as the Church of the Immaculate Conception) was built in 1898 by Vietnamese refugees. It is Thailand's largest Roman-Catholic church and serves Chanthaburi's Christian community, now about 5,000 strong. The girls' school run by nuns produces attractive wickerwork.

Relics from the colonial period

Other relics of the French colonial period include a square brick building on the outskirts of the town, believed to be an old customs house, and what is now the town's library in the marketplace, at one time used as a prison.

Surroundings

Khai Nern Wong (fort)

Near Khai Nern Wong ("Camp on a Small Hill"), some 5km/3 miles south of Chanthaburi, lie the remnants of a fort constructed in about 1834 by King Rama III. Apart from one or two shattered cannon of British and French origin, there is little of a military nature to be seen. Within the partly overgrown walls stands Wat Yottanimit, also built by Rama III, incorporating a well-preserved 11th c. Khmer prang, the walls around which are topped by four (crumbling) chedis. The shrine is modern, erected in 1977 on the foundations of its predecessor.

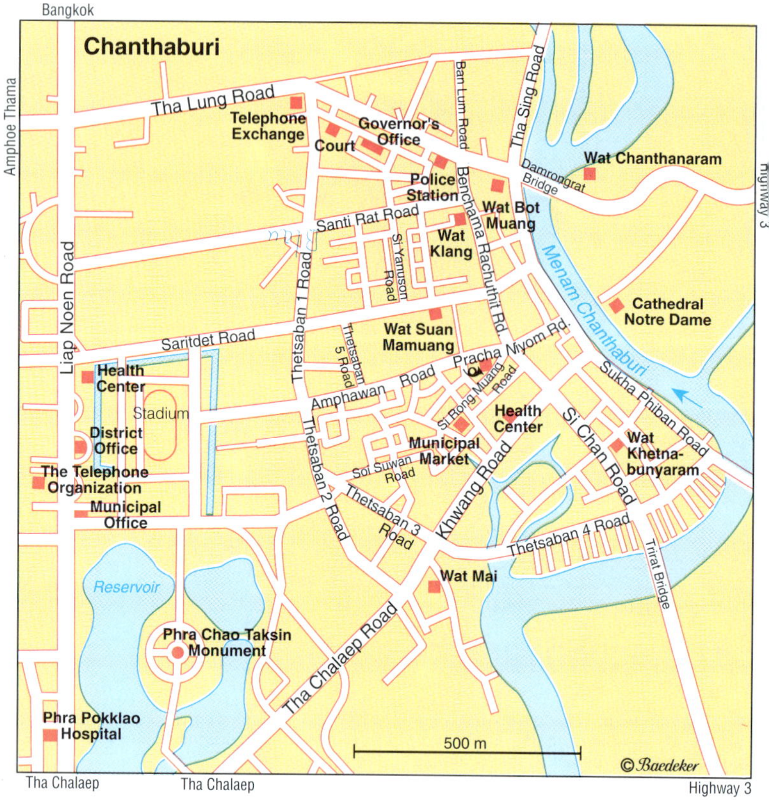

Harbour	Chanthaburi's harbour, some 11km/7 miles distant, no longer really contributes to the town's economy. The fishing village, built on piles and in a truly delightful setting, makes a pleasant excursion however, with boat trips to the islands off-shore.
Ban Kacha Mine	The nearest gem mine to Chanthaburi (visitors welcome) is located 4km/2½ miles away, near the small village of Ban Kacha. The temple on the nearby Phu Khao Phloi Waen ("Hill of Precious Stones") is another which boasts a footprint of the Buddha.
Waterfalls	About 28km/17 miles south-east of Chanthaburi, Nam Tok Krating ("Waterfall of the Bull") cascades 400m/1313ft over rather curious rock formations. Another waterfall, Nam Tok Soi Dao, with a thermal spring close by, can be reached via Highway 317, passing through some superb tropical scenery on the way. The big favourite with local people however is the Nam Tok Praew waterfall (about 13km/8miles south of Chanthaburi) where there is a pool suitable for swimming. This whole area is now a National Park (Khao Sor Bab National Park). Minibuses make regular runs from Chanthaburi town centre.
Wat Tong Tua (Khmer temple)	En route to Nam Tok Praew, the Khmer ruins at Wat Tong Tua can be visited. The phaniat, a solid structure surrounded by a 4m/13ft wall may have been

A cannon in the Fortress of Khai Nern Wong

an elephant-house. Also of interest are the 17th c. stone sculptures on display in the monastery and, near the access to the waterfall, the plain white chedi containing the ashes of Queen Sumantha, drowned when her boat capsized near Bang Pa In (see entry).

Laem Singh (fishing village)

Further along Highway 3, a turn-off to the right at the 348 kilometre mark leads to Laem Singh, another small fishing village – dried shrimps a speciality! The village presumably took its name from Koh Singh Island (from the Old Indian for "lion"), shaped something like a lion and facing it off shore.

Chiang Dao **B 2**

เชียงดาว

Region: North Thailand
Province: Chiang Mai. Altitude: 1000m/3282ft

Location

The tiny market town of Chiang Dao lies above the Menam Ping gorge on the green slopes of Doi Chiang Dao mountain. Limestone peaks reaching a height of 2186m/7174ft make an impressive backdrop.

Access

By car: from Chiang Mai via Highway 107 (72km/45 miles); magnificent, densely wooded mountain scenery.
By bus: from Chiang Mai (several buses a day).

★★**Scenery**

Agricultural development centre

Although the scenery around Chiang Dao is one of northern Thailand's greatest attractions, Chiang Dao itself, hardly more than a village, has little in the way of sights. Its principal feature is the nearby agricultural development centre run by the Thai government. As well as researching into tea and coffee cultivation, the centre provides an advisory service for local communities. One of the aims is to enable the mountain folk to switch to crops other than opium, grown here for centuries. Agricultural advisers go out into the Meo, Lisu and Karen villages, lending support to rice-growing, arable farming and cattle rearing.

★Chiang Dao Cave

The sacred Chiang Dao Cave, part of a network extending 14km/8½ miles underground, lies about 6km/4 miles along the track leading north from the village. Inside the cave, shafts of sunlight filtering through crevices in the rock bathe the statues of Buddha – the largest being carved from white marble – in a mysterious light. Near the entrance are a large white chedi surmounted by numerous little towers, and a spring-fed pond, home to the temple fish.

Trinity Village (leper colony)

The road winding its way north to the village of Fang (see entry) passes, at the 78 kilometre mark, the entrance to Trinity Village, a leper colony.

Chiang Mai C 2

Region: North Thailand
Province: Chiang Mai
Altitude: 310m/1017ft. Population: 160,000

เชียงใหม่

★★Location

Chiang Mai, Thailand's second largest city, is also unquestionably the most beautiful, its location earning it the soubriquet of "Pearl (or Rose) of the North". It sits at the foot of Doi Pui (1685m/5530ft), one of the highest mountains in the Indo-Chinese range, in a sheltered, mountain-ringed and fertile basin irrigated by water from the Menam Ping.

At one time splendid capital of the independent kingdom of Lan Na ("Kingdom of the Thousand Rice-fields"), Chiang Mai today takes pride in being the "northern capital" of Thailand. It has long since ceased to be simply the "City of Golden Temples" – as it was christened by the first European visitors. Austere modern concrete buildings and an efficient road network, together with many of the usual trappings of late 20th c. life, mean that old teak houses with tropically luxuriant front gardens have become something of a rarity. Bangkok's nouveaux riches consider it particularly smart to have a second home in Chiang Mai. Consequently more and more of the countryside is being developed and traditions evolved over centuries here in northern Thailand are being eroded. The resulting cultural contrasts could hardly be greater. Just a few kilometres from this university city, mountain peoples such as the Meo, Akha and Lisu continue in their age-old ways.

Chiang Mai is also the Mecca of the Thai craft industry, exporting elaborate wood carvings, brightly painted sunshades, batiks, silk fabrics and fine silverware to the tourist centres of the south as well as to all parts of the world. Less well known is Chiang Mai's role as the Thai centre for jade, this much prized mineral being brought in (often illegally) from Myanmar (Burma).

★Doi Inthanon National Park

Adding to its appeal, the countryside around the city is a nature lover's dream. About 60km/37 miles south-west lies the Doi Inthanon National Park (see Chom Thong), one of Thailand's finest conservation areas, its rugged gorges, picturesque waterfalls and impenetrable jungle being much more than simply tourist attractions.

Access

By car: from Bangkok via Highways 1 or 32 to Chainat, then 1 (to Lampang) and 11 (about 696km/432 miles).

By bus: air-conditioned bus from Bangkok's Northern Bus Terminal (journey time twelve hours).

By rail: from Bangkok Hualampong (751km/466 miles). Comfortable sleepers are available on overnight trains.

By air: about 700km/435 miles from Bangkok (several flights daily, flying time about an hour).

A restored part of the town wall around Chiang Mai

Suggested tours

While many operators include a stop in Chiang Mai as part of a tour of northern Thailand, the one or two days usually allowed are not nearly long enough. Just the city itself and the fascinating countryside in the vicinity merit a more extended stay. Added to that, Chiang Mai makes an excellent centre for exploring a host of interesting places near by and further afield, such as Lamphun, Mae Hong Son, Chiang Dao, Phrae, Fang (see entries), Mae Sai (see Chiang Rai, Surroundings) and Chom Thong (see entry), all within easy reach by car, bus or train. Local tour operators also arrange trips to the Thai part of the notorious "Golden Triangle", from which much of the world's opium is smuggled.

History

The original inhabitants of the region were almost certainly the Lawa tribe, now found only in small groups in Burma. They were either driven out or assimilated by the Mon who, in the 6th to 8th centuries, spread right across the whole of what is now Thailand. The centre of Mon power was Lamphun, still known at that time – as was the Mon kingdom itself – as Haripunchai (Haripunjaya). From the 7th c. onwards Thai tribes began filtering into northern areas, coming up against not only the Mon but also the Khmer, whose empire attained the height of its influence between about 1000 and 1250. In the 11th c. northern Thailand came under the sway of the Burmese King Annarudha of Pagan whose hegemony extended as far as present-day Cambodia. After his death the more easterly of these lands broke up into numerous small principalities ruled by the first of the Thai princes.

More Thai tribes had meanwhile migrated across the Mekong into north-east Thailand. Dominant force among the Thai rulers was Mengrai, born in 1239 in Chiang Saen. He founded the city of Chiang Rai and in 1281 conquered the Mon kingdom of Haripunchai.

Mengrai was evidently unimpressed by the former Mon capital Lamphun, constantly subject, among other things, to flooding. Together with King Ramkhamhaeng of Sukhothai and King Ngam Muang of Phayao he

The Three Kings Monument in Chiang Mai

surveyed the country around Doi Suthep in search of a site for a new capital, selecting one just 27km/18 miles away. Here Chiang Mai was founded. According to tradition 90,000 men were set to work constructing a ring wall around the city. Within the space of four years a splendid new capital had arisen, Mengrai living there until his death in 1317.

Chiang Mai's status as capital of an important kingdom lasted barely a century and a half, the influence of the Mengrai dynasty steadily waning following the founding of Ayutthaya in 1350. Once Ayutthaya had annexed neighbouring Sukhothai, it appeared only a question of time before Lan Na succumbed as well. But Chiang Mai's rulers proved strong enough to resist, even after the death of the last of the Mengrai dynasty in 1444. It was thus to the Burmese that Chiang Mai finally fell in 1556, bringing the kingdom of Lan Na under a rule which lasted for more than 200 years.

King Taksin, first Thai monarch of the Bangkok period, precursor of the Chakri dynasty and founder of a unified Thai state, drove the Burmese from Chiang Mai in 1767, installing the Prince of Lampang's son, Chao Kawila, as ruler of Chiang Mai. However the inhabitants, wearied by centuries of Burmese oppression, abandoned the city. For more than two decades it remained almost deserted, resettlement beginning only after 1796.

In 1873 Chiang Mai came under Siamese rule, administered by a governor appointed by Bangkok. The descendants of Prince Chao Kawila still live in the city and are held in great esteem, being formally honoured every year.

Chiang Mai features importantly in the history of Siamese art, developing a style of its own (Chiang Mai style) the heyday of which was from 1300 to 1550. The style originated in Chiang Saen (and hence is also called the "later Chiang Saen style"), incorporating elements from the Mon tribes, the Burmese and the neighbouring kingdom of Sukhothai. In this way Chiang Mai's temples came to unite several different traditions, giving them a degree of colour, brightness and grace unique in Thailand.

Sights

N.B.

Chiang Mai has nearly 200 temples, nearly all of which warrant a visit by anyone interested in art history. This is true even of the more recently built ones, the artistry and sensitivity to form shown by modern Thai craftsmen being in no way inferior to those of earlier centuries. Only the most important and beautiful can be mentioned here, the selection nevertheless illustrating well the rich art historical and religious heritage of Thailand's northern capital.

The gates

The old walled city is no longer the heart of Chiang Mai today, the new town centre being situated just to the east, closer to the Menam Ping. Four of the five original city gates – Tha Phae (east), Suan Dok ("Flower Garden", west), Chang Phuak ("White Elephant", north) and San Poong (south-west) – have been rebuilt from designs based on old models.

Night market

Location
Tha Phae Road/
Chang Klan Road

Every evening Tha Phae Road and Chang Klan Road, between the east gate and the Menam Ping, are transformed into a huge street market with a multitude of stalls selling food, fabrics and typical local products (mainly from the hill tribes). There are also numerous small, mostly open-air, restaurants from which the colourful atmosphere can be imbibed.

★Wat Chiang Man

Location
Ratchaphakinai
Road

Wat Chiang Man, the oldest of Chiang Mai's monasteries, was built by King Mengrai in 1296 even before the city itself was founded. The king probably lived here while his palace was being completed.

Wiharn

Although restored many times over the years the wiharn still retains its original appearance. The double-tiered roof, embellished with darting nagas, falls low in a slight curve towards the ground. Note the elaborately carved gables above the main entrance, the latter flanked by two lions. A tablet with an inscription in Thai marks the spot where King Mengrai is said to have died in 1317.

The interior of the wiharn, divided by teak columns into three aisles, contains two Buddha images of particular note, the first being a large

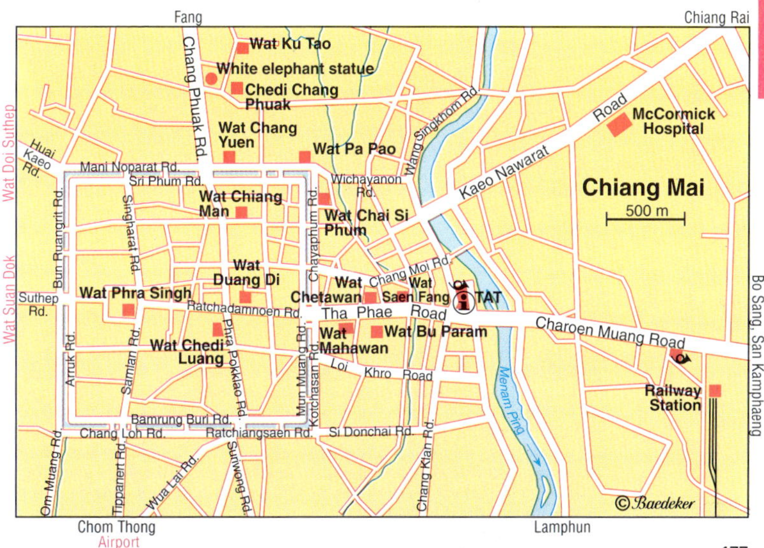

gilded statue and the second a replica bas-relief of the sacred Buddha Sila – the original of which, held in safe-keeping by the abbot, is brought out only once a year for a special ceremony. Believed to date from the 8th c., and Indian in style, it is credited with rain-making powers.

Crystal Buddha

Also kept under lock and key by the abbot is the Phra Sal Tang Kamani, the rock crystal figure on a gold base known as the Crystal Buddha. It was probably presented to Chama Thevi, Queen of Haripunchai, in 663, and was carried off by King Mengrai after the fall of Haripunchai in 1281. Wat Chiang Man boasts in addition a chedi supported on a base of fifteen stone elephants, the upper section being clad in gilded copper. There is a small bot, and a modern sala.

★★Wat Phra Singh

Location
Ratchadamnoen Road

Chiang Mai's largest and most important temple, Wat Phra Singh, stands at what was the centre of the old city, the main thoroughfare, Ratchadamnoen Road, leading directly to the precinct. It was built in 1345 by King Pa Yo whose father's ashes are preserved in the big chedi behind the wiharn.

Wiharn

The wiharn, built in 1518, has superb wood carvings on both gable ends, these however being of later origin. The exquisite little 14th c. library, in front of the wiharn to the right, is with justice regarded as a jewel of Thai architecture. Fine stucco-work, intricately patterned and also with figures, decorates the white lower section, the red and gold woodwork surmounting it being ornately carved and further embellished with inlay.

Bot

The small bot next to the chedi was constructed about 1600 and therefore during the period of Burmese occupation (which presumably accounts also for the numerous lions, typical of Burmese temple architecture, which guard the entrance to the wat). The well-preserved frescos with their lively pictures date from the 19th c. They tell the story of Princess Phra Sang Tong (born in a golden shell), while at the same time depicting the everyday lives of royalty and the household of a palace. The garments and the postures again suggest Burmese influence.

Phra Singh Buddha

The wat's most sacred shrine is a small, well-proportioned building beyond the bot, called the Phra Wiharn Lai Kam. It was erected during the reign of King San Muang Ma (1385–1401) to house the famous, now sadly headless, Sukhothai-style figure known as the Phra Singh Buddha. According to tradition the Buddha, in the familiar "calling the earth to witness" pose, came to Thailand from Ceylon, finding its way first to Ayutthaya and then to Kamphaeng Phet, Chiang Rai, Luang Prabang and back again to Ayutthaya before, in 1767, arriving in Chiang Mai where it has been ever since. There is some doubt however as to its authenticity. Both Nakhon Si Thammarat and the National Museum in Bangkok possess identical figures and, with the experts not yet able to rule authoritatively on the matter, all three lay claim to be the original.

Also of interest are two other figures, this time dating from the end of the 15th c. Both are bronze, one large, the other inlaid with precious stones; both again show the Enlightened One in the "calling the earth to witness" pose.

★Wat Chedi Luang

Location
Phra Pokklao Road

The ruined but nevertheless impressive brick chedi, oldest of the buildings in the spacious precinct of Wat Chedi Luang, collapsed during an earthquake in 1545. The massive base – unusually constructed in a combination of brick and laterite – gives only an inkling of the chedi's once towering height (90m/295ft). Its story began in 1401 with the erection of a small chedi in memory of San Muang Ma, who died in that year. This was later enlarged, first by his widow and then again by King Tiloka his grandson (the pagoda at Bodhgaya in India being taken as a model). Fine elephant heads and carvings of Buddha can still be seen in the niches. The famous

The Phra Wiharn Lai Kam in the Wat Phra Singh

Emerald Buddha (now in Wat Phra Kaeo in Bangkok) is reputed to have stood at one time in the niche on the east side.

Wiharn

Guarding the entrance to the large wiharn with its triple-tiered roof and highly ornate gables, are two magnificent rhinoceros-nosed serpents, their scales made out of brightly glazed tiles. They are quite the most splendid to be seen in Thailand. As well as a number of small statues and some elaborately carved elephant tusks, the wiharn contains three bronze statues of Buddha cast in 1440.

Chedis

Most of the finely-proportioned chedis in the outer court house cremation urns.

Lak Muang

Beneath a huge gum tree on the left of the entrance to the precinct stands a delightful little temple, the Lak Muang. Built in 1940 on the site of an earlier wooden building, the shrine is the abode of Chiang Mai's guardian spirit (Lak Muang). According to tradition, if the great tree should fall, disaster will overtake the city.

Other sights

★Wat Prachao Mengrai

Founded in 1288, Wat Prachao Mengrai (in Ratchamankha Road, opposite Wat Chedi Luang) was renamed in 1953, having previously been known as Wat Kan Kawd. The wat's chief treasure, housed in a small sanctum of its own, is a 4.5m/15ft-high statue of Buddha cast in 1320 and said to be a likeness of King Mengrai, founder of Chiang Mai. Also of interest are a Buddha image from Chiang Saen and a lovely reading desk, both in the wiharn.

Wat Chetawan

Situated a few hundred metres outside the city's east gate, Wat Chetawan is noteworthy for its three impressive, heavily articulated chedis, two decorated with fabulous beasts from Hindu mythology and all three inlaid with gold and coloured tiles which sparkle in the sun. Keep a look out also for the superb wood carvings on the wiharn.

The collapsed prang of the Wat Chedi Luang

Wat Mahawan

Wat Mahawan, almost directly opposite, on the other side of Tha Phae Road, boasts a very beautifully articulated chedi in the Burmese style topped by a gilded spire. Huge statues of lions adorn the four corners of the enclosure. Both the wiharn and the small chapel are ornately carved, reliefs on the doors depicting scenes from Buddha's life.

Wat Saen Fang

A little further along Tha Phae Road is the unpretentious entrance leading to the delightful Wat Saen Fang. A narrow alley flanked by two serpents opens into a picturesque precinct with a beautifully-kept garden, lovely chedi in the Burmese style and a wiharn with richly gilded carving on the façades.

★★Wat Pha Pong

The magnificent Wat Pha Pong (at the intersection of Suthep Road and Thipanet Road) is entered through finely articulated gates. Several chedis encircle a pretty pavilion, with steps leading up to a chapel inside. The façade of the square building, adorned with round-arched windows and pilasters, shows Chinese as well as Burmese influence. In addition to its statues of Buddha, the three-aisled interior is decorated with murals.

Chedi Chang Phuak

In the north of the city (at the end of Rattanakosin Road, 300m/330yd from Chang Phuak bus station) stand the ruined Chedi Chang Phuak and Wat Ku Tao, the latter having a rather unusual chedi built in 1613. The upper section above the square, tiered base consists of a series of interlocked spheres diminishing in size (and probably symbolising alms bowls).

Each is embellished with niches and clad in colourful glazed tiles laid in geometric patterns, the whole being crowned with a delicate spire. This curious and most unusual stupa is believed to contain the ashes of the Burmese Prince Tarawadi. Some ancient carvings survive on the gable of the wiharn. The bot is a 20th c. addition.

Elephant monument

In Chang Phuak Road near the city's north (White Elephant) gate, a plain monument erected by King Saen Muang at the end of the 13th c. commemorates two loyal comrades in arms who saved his life when the elephant carrying him into battle during the war with Ayutthaya was killed. The two were afterwards ennobled. The White Elephant Gate takes its name from the monument.

Chedi

Near the monument, a rusty water-tank and radio mast stand sentinel over the ruins of a collapsed 15th c. chedi, originally in the Lan Na style. Note the fragments of reliefs surviving on the central part.

★★Wat Suan Dok

In Suthep Road west of the city stands the famous Wat Suan Dok ("dok" means flower garden). The story of its foundation, closely linked with that of Wat Doi Suthep (see Surroundings), is woven around with legend. The big, bell-shaped, snow-white, central chedi, Ceylonese in style, houses one half of a miraculous relic only the size of a pea. The relic was found by a monk called Sumana, concealed in a receptacle hidden away inside a series of silver and coral "chinese boxes" contained in a bronze casket. It came into the hands of King Kuna of Chiang Mai (1355–85) who had the chedi built to house it. In 1383 the relic miraculously divided itself into two pieces, each growing back to the original size. Wat Doi Suthep was therefore built to house the second piece.

The variously shaped, glistening white chedis in the courtyard contain the ashes of members of the royal family.

The bot in Wat Suan Dok is graced by an exceptionally fine, 6m/19½ft-high Buddha in the Chiang Mai style (cast in about 1550). The wiharn, built as an open hall in 1932, is the largest religious assembly room in northern Thailand. The interior has richly ornamented columns and ceilings, two Buddhas standing back-to-back, and various other painted images of the Enlightened One. Note also the palace-shaped reliquary

Royal Chedis in the Wat Suan Dok

containing the ashes of Phra Si Wichai, the monk at whose instigation the wiharn was built.

Wat Umong

Wat Umong, situated west of Wat Suan Dok in forested surroundings just off and a little further along Suthep Road, was founded by King Mengrai for the benefit of a much revered phra (monk). Later, King Kuna (1355–85) added an underground chamber for use by another phra, where the latter could devote himself to meditation completely undisturbed. Remains of frescos can still be seen on the walls of the vault. The monastery, belonging to a strict Ceylonese Buddhist order, has served ever since as a refuge for monks living in retreat – recognisable by their dark robes.

Part of the temple complex functions by contrast as a meeting-place for people of all nationalities interested in Buddhism (courses in meditation are available by arrangement, see Practical Information, Meditation). The original chedi, built when the wat was founded, has collapsed. The other buildings, which include a Pali school, monks' quarters and library, are of recent date.

Outlying districts

N.B.

Of all Chiang Mai's temples, Wat Doi Suthep (or Wat Phra That Doi Suthep, see Surroundings) is perhaps the most magnificent. On the way to see it, leaving the city by Huai Kaeo Road in the north-west corner, Wat Chet Yot and several other places of interest such as Chiang Mai zoo can also be visited.

★Wat Chet Yot

Wat Chet Yot, sometimes called Mahabodharama or Photharama Wiharn, is located north-west of the city close to the Super Highway. Founded by King Tiloka in 1454 it was, for a hundred years or so, the most splendid temple precinct in the whole of Lan Na. Afterwards, having been ravaged by the Burmese, it was abandoned to the jungle, its fortunes reviving only in the 1950s when it was considered worth restoring. Tiloka's successors altered and enlarged it several times, leaving it lacking in any clearly discernible style.

The Wat Chet Yot, based on a celebrated predecessor

Completed in 1455 the chedi with the seven spires from which the temple takes its name was modelled (though not entirely faithfully) on the Mahabodhi Temple in Buddh Gaya, the small Indian town where Buddha attained enlightenment. Many details, e.g. the decoration on the doors, reflect the Indian original. The tall central spire houses a stucco figure of Buddha, and there is a prayer room beneath. Despite centuries of neglect the surprisingly well-preserved stucco-work adorning the walls (depicting deities in various poses) is quite exceptional, the detail in particular being finely executed. Tiloka's ashes are interred in a somewhat smaller square brick stupa erected by his grandson in 1486. In 1477 Wat Chet Yot witnessed a gathering of the Buddhist Council which Tiloka summoned to celebrate the bimillennium of Buddhism. This great event was probably the principal reason for building the temple.

★★Chiang Mai National Museum

Opened in 1972, Chiang Mai National Museum (a little further north along the Super Highway; open: Wed.–Sat. 9am–4pm; admission fee) has many fine sculptures in the Chiang Mai, Dvaravati, Lopburi, U Thong and Sukhothai styles (mainly the former), also terracottas from Haripunchai. The footprint of Buddha with mother-of-pearl intarsia also deserves mention. The upper floor houses a collection of tools and other artefacts used by the hill tribes.

University/ Tribal Research Centre and Museum

Chiang Mai University, opened in 1965, is also situated north-west of the city on the way to Wat Doi Suthep. The university's Tribal Research Centre and Museum is dedicated to the study of the hill tribes, and to ensuring their survival and that of their culture (open: Mon.–Fri. 8.30am–4.30pm). The museum provides an interesting insight into the lives of the hill peoples. Examples of their craftwork are also on display.

Botanic garden and zoo

The botanic garden, beyond the university, contains a wealth of exotic plants including orchids. The neighbouring zoo, Thailand's largest, is well worth a visit, concentrating on native south Asian animals and rare species of birds and butterflies. (The zoo is open daily from 8am–5pm.)

Craft villages

Being the centre of the Thai arts and crafts industry, handwork can not only be bought in Chiang Mai but also seen in the making. The visitor intending to buy a more valuable article is advised to visit the showrooms in the late afternoon when the coaches belonging to the main tour operators have been and gone and it is possible to look around for the desired purchase in relative peace.

Silversmiths for example are found concentrated in and to the east of Chom Thong Road (in the southern part of the city), producing silver and silver alloy bowls, dishes and jewellery. In the Ban Khoen district, a little further east, lacquer-ware is made (boxes, dishes and trays). Black lacquer, applied in several layers, is polished with ash or lime. Decorative patterns are then etched into the surface and picked out in paint, either coloured or gold.

Teak carvers ply their trade from workshops mainly located in Wulai Road and Ratchangsaen Road, the fruits of their labours being exported all over the world. With the felling of tropical hardwoods banned in Thailand, teak now has to be imported from Myanmar (Burma).

It is not often that tourists have the opportunity to watch bronze being cast. The place to go to in Chiang Mai is Chang Loh Road. Finished products include bells (without clappers, their clear tones being produced by small tin discs suspended on a thread) and the solid bronze cutlery sold in virtually every shop in the country.

The "Potters' Village" is on the north side of the city near the White Elephant Gate. Many families work in this particular trade, the pots being put out in front of the houses to dry (as well as to sell).

There are more craft villages at Bo Sang and San Kaemphaeng (see Surroundings, Other Sights).

Prettily decorated sunshades made of rice-paper . . .

. . . are popular souvenirs from Chiang Mai

A teak-carver at work

★★Wat Buakkhrok Luang

The San Khamphaeng road, along which many crafts have retail outlets, also leads to Wat Buakkhrok, one of Chiang Mai's loveliest but least known temples. The wat has a wonderful teak wiharn in the Lan Na style (late 13th c.). Divided into three aisles by rows of teak columns, it houses a fine statue of Buddha in the Chiang Saen-style; the old murals and the carved doors are also superb. To the left of the wiharn stands a beautiful bot. Up until 1988, when it was destroyed in a storm, there was a replica of this temple in Phayao (see entry).

"Old Chiang Mai Cultural Centre"

Despite its name the "Old Chiang Mai Cultural Centre" (on Highway 108, south) has absolutely nothing to do with the history of Chiang Mai, being the brain-child of an enterprising businessman. It is a reconstruction of a hill tribe village, members of various tribes (Karen, Lisu, Akha, Yao) living in traditional huts, wearing traditional dress and working with traditional tools. Handcrafted items such as jewellery and fabrics are sold in the village shops. Khan Toke dinners (as they are called), i.e. meals composed of typical North Thailand dishes, are served in the evening, accompanied by traditional tribal dancing. Many of the tours arranged by travel agencies include a visit to the Centre.

Surroundings

★★Wat Doi Suthep

Access
20km/12½miles north-west of Chiang Mai (via Huai Kaeo Road)

Wat Doi Suthep (altitude 1053m/3456ft) lies amid delightful scenery below the summit of Doi Pui (1685m/5530ft). Access from Chiang Mai is by road – car or bus – along the winding 1004. A rewarding detour on foot from the car park (bus terminal) leads to the attractively situated Nam Tok Huai waterfall. At the point where the road begins to rise sharply to the temple, a monument commemorates Phra Si Wichai, the monk on whose initiative in 1934 the first road was built. He raised the money among the people of Chiang Mai, and they helped construct it.

Wat Buakkhrok Luang: Wiharn . . .

. . . with artistically carved doors

The final lap is completed either on foot or by the little rack-railway. A huge staircase of 306 steps, adorned with copper plaques engraved with the names of donors, and flanked by balustrades in the shape of two seven-headed nagas writhing upwards, climbs to the temple's spacious terrace. From here the views over the city and the surrounding countryside are magnificent.

Legend

The wat is named after a devout monk called Vasuthep, believed to have been a hermit living on the site. According to legend, when the sacred relic in Wat Suan Dok miraculously split in two, King Kuna resolved to build a shrine to house the second fragment. The monk Sumana, who had discovered the relic in the first place, advised him to place the tiny object in an altar secured to the back of a white elephant, letting the animal roam free. Making its way up the mountain, the elephant lay down at the very place where Vasuthep lived and when the relic was taken from the altar, the animal died. So Kuna erected his temple on that precise spot and built a little chedi over the place where the elephant was buried (near the forestry office bungalow).

Statue of the Earth goddess Thorani

To the right of the platform at the foot of the great, naga-embellished staircase, stands a statue of the Earth goddess Thorani (symbol of the Earth's creative power) wringing water from her hair. Brahmanical tradition tells how Mara ("the evil one") and his demons led the meditating Buddha into temptation, whereupon Thorani appeared and, wringing water from her hair, washed the demon army away.

Temple precinct

The entrance to the temple precinct proper is guarded by statues of two demons with, at the side, little open spirit houses. Generally only two of the six gates leading to the gallery and the chedis are open. The gallery itself is

Chedi in the Wat Doi Suthep ▶

adorned with statues of Buddha in the Chiang Mai and Sukhothai styles; note also the recent paintings decorating the walls, depicting scenes from Buddha's life. Incorporated into the gallery are two wiharns, one opposite the other, both façades being embellished with superb carvings.

Wiharn

Wat Doi Suthep's central shrine contains a much revered seated Buddha.

Chedi

Every eye is irresistably drawn however to the glittering gold chedi, 20m/66ft high and crowned with a five-tier, tapering roundel. The entire chedi is sheathed in ornate gilded copper. At each of the four corners of the railing around it stands a small, elaborately sculpted altar and graceful filigree canopy in copper gilt.

On the north side of the precinct, outside the perimeter gallery, there is a delightful, richly decorated little chapel of recent date. In the courtyard hangs a large bronze bell surrounded by three smaller ones. Note also the little altar which carried the relic on the elephant's back, and the bust of the hermit Vasuthep.

Temple museum

Wat Doi Suthep's little museum, newly opened, contains some valuable exhibits including coins and stamps.

★Summer Palace

To reach Phu Ping, one of the royal family's summer palaces, continue along the road beyond the temple. The Bangkok-style building, in colourful gardens, lies a short way up the mountain. (Visitors are admitted only when no member of the royal family is in residence, and must be suitably dressed.)

Other sights

★★Doi Pui National Park

The superb panorama over jungle-clad hillsides and gorges is a splendid reward for a three hour hike through impressive scenery to the summit of Doi Pui. The path leads past a Meo village which, being popular with tourists, has become very commercialised (for example the villagers insist on payment for allowing themselves to be photographed). Nothing, though, can detract from their wonderfully colourful tribal dress and highly decorative silver jewellery, all of which is captivating.

Bo Sang

Almost the entire population of Bo Sang, the "Umbrella Village", about 8km/5 miles east of Chiang Mai, occupy themselves in making parasols and umbrellas. The bamboo frames are covered either with varnished paper manufactured from the rind of the tonsa tree or with silk. This is then lacquered and afterwards painted with patterns, flowers or landscapes. Even the children try their hand at complicated designs.

San Kamphaeng

In the 15th c. San Kamphaeng (east of Chiang Mai; leave by Charoen Muang Road) was famous for its ceramics – the ruins of the old potters' village can still be seen to the east of the present town. As far as pottery is concerned Chiang Mai has now taken over, without yet equalling, it should be said, the skill and artistry of those early craftsmen. San Kamphaeng remains well known but its reputation today is for hand-woven silks and cotton fabrics (some producers having displays illustrating the processes of silk manufacture).

San Kamphaeng also boasts an interesting old temple, Wat Sai Mon, several features of which are Burmese in style. The interior of the three-aisled wiharn is embellished with gold-on-red ornamented teak columns and elaborately worked furnishings.

Nong Wua Park

Nong Wua Park, situated 17km/10½ miles east of Chiang Mai, is a popular place for weekend outings. Reclaimed from previously swampy ground the park has a small lake covered in lotus blooms. There are restaurants and refreshment stalls.

Mae Rim elephant camp

Working elephants can be seen being trained at the elephant camp near Mae Rim (20km/12½ miles north of Chiang Mai; the camp itself is another

A morning bath for elephants

7km/4 miles beyond the village). Demonstrations take place daily and all Chiang Mai travel agencies arrange excursions.

With the Thai government having introduced, for reasons of conservation, a total ban on the felling of tropical hardwoods, the supply of trained working elephants now far exceeds demand. Several hundred "unemployed" elephants consequently rely for their subsistence on an allowance from the State. This is supplemented by income from tourists eager to learn more about training and caring for these endearing pachyderms, animals which have always had such an important part to play in Thailand's history. Visiting VIPs are sometimes treated to an "elephant spectacular" arranged by King Bhumibol, as many as 40 to 50 of the creatures being gathered together from the surrounding area.

Tours of the Doi Inthanon National Park leave from Mae Rim. They last from one to several days and use elephants for transport.

Huai Theung Thao dam

Another favourite outing among local people is to the Huai Thueng Thao dam (40km/25 miles from Chiang Mai). It offers windsurfing and boat rental.

Chiang Rai B 3

เชียงราย

Region: North Thailand
Province: Chiang Rai
Altitude: 380m/1247ft
Population: 44,000

Location

Chiang Rai, known as the "Crown of the North" on account of its being founded by King Mengrai – a somewhat unbejewelled crown, it has to be said, compared with Chiang Mai – is another gateway to the Golden

Triangle from where approximately a third of all the world's illegally traded (raw) opium originates (about 300 tonnes a year). Standing on the right bank of the Menam Kok, the town is well worth visiting for its extraordinarily beautiful scenery and makes a convenient centre from which to explore the country close by and further afield. Its good transport links with Chiang Mai, Chiang Saen and the rather more distant Lampang mean that a number of interesting northern Thailand towns are easily accessible. Also, the neighbouring highlands are populated by hill tribes such as the Akha, Lisu and Meo, still largely untainted by "civilisation". Colourfully attired hill tribesmen and women are a feature of local markets where they come to sell their wares.

Access

By car: from Lampang, Highway 1 (240km/149 miles); from Chiang Mai, Highway 107 to just before Fang, then Highways 109 and 1 (268km/166 miles).
By bus: from Chiang Mai and Bangkok (Northern Bus Terminal), several departures daily.
By air: from Bangkok and Chiang Mai (up to six flights a day).
By rail: nearest station Chiang Mai (180km/112 miles).

History

The town is older than Chiang Mai, having been founded by Mengrai in 1262 as the capital of his kingdom of Lan Na. Favourably sited on the Menam Kok, a tributary of the Mekong River, it had first been settled centuries before by the Lawa and the Mon. Chiang Rai was held by the Burmese for many years, coming under Siamese rule only in 1786 (four years after Bangkok became capital). Whilst little is known of its history in earlier times, Chiang Rai's fortunes have latterly been closely linked with those of Chiang Mai and Chiang Saen (60km/37 miles away).

Sights

King Mengrai Statue

On the way into the town from the north-east there is a monument to its founder Mengrai (or Meng Rai; 1239–1317).

★★Wat Phra Kaeo Don Tao

It was at Chiang Rai that the famous Emerald Buddha (now in Wat Phra Kaeo in the Grand Palace in Bangkok) first came to light, having remained hidden away for many years in Wat Phra Kaeo Don Tao. In 1434 lightning struck a chedi in the wat, investigation of which uncovered a small, rather undistinguished-looking stucco figure. Concealed beneath the plaster was the 75cm/29½in. green jade or nephrite Buddha. The discovery quickly drew the attention of the king of Lan Na, who resolved that the Emerald Buddha should grace his capital Chiang Mai. But on the way there, at a fork in the road, the elephant carrying it refused to continue towards Chiang Mai, turning aside instead for neighbouring Lampang. The king interpreted this as a sign and, until 1468, the Buddha remained, albeit temporarily, in Wat Phra That Lampang Luang. Eventually it was taken to Chiang Mai from where, after long-drawn out and circuitous travels, it found its way to Bangkok.

Wat Phra Kaeo Don Tao is of interest for its carvings and painted wooden façade. The wat dates back to the 15th c., as does nearby Wat Phra Singh. Both have been restored a number of times, thus altering their appearance.

Wat Ming Muang

Wat Ming Muang has an elaborately carved gable and several Chiang Saen-style (11th–16th c.) Buddha figures.

Wat Chet Yot

Wat Chet Yot is worth visiting for its beautifully proportioned wiharn and a chedi with seven little towers on a square base.

Monument to King Mengrai

Mae Sai: frontier with Myanmar (Burma)

Wiharn of the Wat Phra Kaeo Don Tao

Buddhist believers in the Wat Phra That Doi Thung

Surroundings

Mae Lo dam

Lovely surroundings make the Mae Lo dam (south on Highway 1, then Highway 109 towards Fang) a favourite spot among local people.

★Wat Phra That Doi Thung

Wat Phra That Doi Thung, a major place of pilgrimage, is situated just below the 1330m/4365ft-high summit of Doi Thung. At the beginning of March tens of thousands converge on the wat by car, bus, motorbike or on foot, making their way up the steep 17km/10½ mile road which branches off Highway 110 near the village of Ban Huai Krai. The summit offers a superb all-round panorama over the north Thai countryside and it is well worth the trouble of driving there just to see the view. The temple buildings are less interesting, being mainly of recent origin.

Mae Sai

Highway 110 heads north to Mae Sai (25km/15½ miles), the most northerly point in Thailand. This little frontier post with its busy markets once lay on a major trade route leading to China.

Mae Chan

Near to the Burmese border at the village of Mae Chan, agriculturalists from the Mae Chan Community Station assist the hill tribes, helping them switch to crops other than opium.

Ko Saen Chai (Akha village)

The unsurfaced track continuing beyond the bus station leads to an Akha village called Ko Saen Chai, at the entry to which stand swings used in age-old fertility rites. The huts, built on piles and with low-hanging roofs, are each the home of an extended family. Men and women live segregated.

Most hill tribes have their own language and believe in some form of animism (see Population) which invests every common object with spirits, good or evil. Water, for example, is held to be the abode of evil spirits – a reason therefore for washing as little as possible.

Since 1976 the Thai government has encouraged the assimilation of the hill tribes, but with only partial success. The Akha, dwelling in the mountains around Chiang Rai, have preserved their cultural identity more perhaps than most. They still adhere to their old traditions, including those embodied in skilled craftmanship practised over many centuries. The government-run Thai Hillcraft Foundation, responsible for marketing the products (mainly silverware, embroidery and woven fabrics), has offices in Chiang Rai.

Generally speaking, any visit to the hill tribes should be in the company of a local guide with a knowledge of the language. Communication difficuties can lead to misunderstanding and the possibility of an unpleasant incident. It goes without saying that, here more than anywhere, tourists should exercise restraint (especially as regards photography).

Chiang Saen A 4

Region: North Thailand
Province: Chiang Rai
Altitude: 455m/1493ft. Population: 16,000

เชียงแสน

Location

Chiang Saen is a small town in the jungle and upland country at the northernmost tip of Thailand. It stands on a big loop of the majestic Mekong, which in places further south forms the border between Thailand and Laos, with the Laotian hills on the other side of the river.

Access

Chiang Saen can be visited as part of a tour around the Chiang Rai district based on Chiang Mai (regular daily bus services from Chiang Mai, which also has the nearest railway station).
By car: Highway 110 from Chiang Rai to Mae Chan and then on 1016 (58km/36 miles).

History

Once the capital of the Chiang Saen Kingdom, probably the first Thai kingdom in present-day Thailand, the place then faded into obscurity, despite having acquired a certain fame for its Chiang Saen style (see Art and Culture). Finds of prehistoric tools have confirmed the theory that the area was already inhabited in palaeolithic times. A settlement in its own right over two thousand years ago, Chiang Saen had its heyday in the 10th–13th c. and under the rule of King Saen Phu. In 1238 it was the birthplace of King Mengrai who established his capital in Chiang Rai in 1261 and in Chiang Mai in 1297. Numerous wars with the Burmese and the King of Ayutthaya left their mark, and from the mid 16th c. to the late 18th c. Chiang Saen was under Burmese rule. King Rama I, the first king of the Chakri dynasty, had it razed to the ground so that it would no longer provide a target for enemy attack, and the town only came to life again under King Rama V (Chulalongkorn).

Sights

Town wall

The course of the 8km/5 mile-long wall that once encircled the town can still be traced from the ruins and ditches buried under grass and trees. Parts of the wall have recently been restored leaving the rest as grassy mounds. The Chiang Saen of today covers only a small section of the area once within the walls. Numerous remnants of temples, some of them very old and not all as yet accurately dated, serve as reminders of the town's past importance.

Wat Ku Tao

The sadly dilapidated ruins of Wat Ku Tao are on the right-hand side of the road coming from Chiang Rai, just before it crosses the Menam Kam River.

Wat Pa Sak

Wat Pa Sak, also outside the town wall, was begun in 1295 under King Saen Phu and got its name from the 300 teak (i.e. sak) trunks that originally

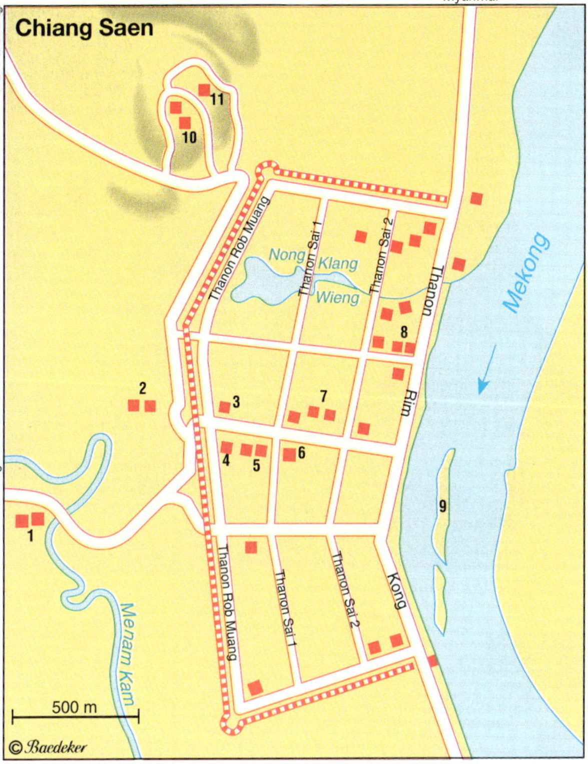

1 Wat Ku Tao
2 Wat Pa Sak
3 Wat Mahathat
4 Museum
5 Wat Chedi Luang
6 Wat Phra Buat
7 Wat Phra Chao Lan Thong
8 Wat Pa Kao Pan
9 Ruins of Koh Don Taen
10 Wat Phra That Chom Kitti
11 Wat Chom Chang

surrounded it. It still has a fine pyramidal chedi, said to hold a relic of Buddha brought here from Pataliputra the year it was founded. Twelve large and 16 smaller niches contain finely worked Sukhothai Buddhas, some of them very well preserved, and revealing on closer examination signs of Srivijaya and Dvaravati influences as well. Wat Pa Sak is one of the few remaining examples of the fine art of applying stucco and terracotta. It is worth noting the 14th c. decorative detail in the ornamental banding and the rich ornamentation of the middle section which carries on up into the spire.

★Wat Chedi Luang

Wat Chedi Luang, within the walls by the west gate, dates from the 13th c. and parts of the original bronze-clad spire can still be seen on the 60m/197ft-high, bell-shaped 16th c. chedi, now covered in grass.

★National Museum

The National Museum, just before the entry to Wat Chedi Luang (open: Wed.–Sun. 9am–4pm; admission fee), has several fine pieces in the Chiang Saen style, including Buddhas, amulets, silver and stucco work, stelae and a demon mask. The recently discovered stone reliefs brought here for safekeeping from Wat Sang Kha Kaew Don Tun are particularly worth

Wat Pa Sak: temple of the 300 trunks of teak

The viewpoint known as the "Golden Triangle"

seeing. Judging from the hair styles and apparel of the figures they probably date from about 300 years ago rather than from when the monastery was founded.

Other wats

Wat Phra Buat nowadays is a striking mass of ruins, but one of the collapsed chedis still bears the remains of a fine figure of Buddha. Only one chedi is left from Wat Phra Chao Lan Thong. Wat Pa Kao Pan, in a lovely setting on the bank of the Mekong, is more recent but contains an old chedi.

★★Wat Phra That Chom Kitti

The 10th c. Wat Phra That Chom Kitti, with its round chedi, stands on a hill outside Chiang Saen with a good view over the town and the border country of the golden triangle. The spire of the crooked chedi is covered in bronze, and also has a Buddha relief. Extremely well preserved Lopburi-style Buddhas can be seen in the niches on each side.

A broad flight of 393 steps leads down to the town from Wat Chom Chang's smaller brick chedi opposite.

Wat Phra That Pu Khao

What is left of Wat Phra That Pu Khao stands on a hill above the Golden Triangle Hotel, with a magnificent view over the point where the Mae Sai flows into the Mekong River.

"Golden Triangle" (viewpoint)

Sop Ruak, north-west of Chiang Saen and about 11km/7 miles further up the Mekong, is the official viewpoint at the centre of the Golden Triangle, looking out over where the Mae Sai River joins the Mekong, and the meeting place of the borders of the three countries that form the triangle, Myanmar (Burma), Thailand and Laos.

The roadside here is full of souvenir stalls, some of them selling pretty pieces from neighbouring Burma. The trickle of border traffic between Thailand and Laos – officially for nationals only – can be a fascinating spectacle.

Slate chedi in the Wat Phra That Chom Kitti

Baedeker Special

No Money on Khun Sha's Head

From time to time Khun Sha lets it be known what he thinks of the Thai government: absolutely nothing. Then he will grant an audience to a few selected journalists from famous newspapers, somewhere near the **Golden Triangle** in the dense jungle which forms the border region between the kingdom of Thailand and the Socialist Republic of Myanmar, formerly Burma. At the very idea of the government putting a sum of money on his head, Khun Sha laughs and expresses with total conviction the certainty that no member of his secret army would dare to betray him to his arch-enemy.

The latter sits a good thousand kilometres to the south in faraway Bangkok, in a grey building protected by barbed wire, and is called the National Drugs Police. Here there are not only Thai drugs prosecution officers working, but also policemen from the United States and other foreign countries. Once in a while this multinational force is successful in making what can be termed a spectacular seizure of perhaps several kilograms of raw opium. Yet amounts at least twice or three times as large as any of their hauls regularly cross over Thai borders undiscovered and find their way to all five continents of the globe. Even though drug couriers and traffickers face the death penalty in Thailand, many people accept this risk, as the lieutenants in the drugs police are only too aware, because of the fantastic amount of money that can be made.

Viewpoint: The Golden Triangle

Khun Sha's territory is the infamous "Golden Triangle", the border region which runs between Thailand, Laos and Burma. Some 300 tons of high-quality drugs are produced here every year. Hidden away high up in the mountains in this no-man's-land the fields of poppies flutter gently in the breeze. Just as well camouflaged are the many tiny opium kitchens, which are often situated partly underground in order to minimise the risk of detection. Khun Sha's men know exactly how to bend the peasants in the mountains to their will: they simply pay them that much more for the opium poppies than the Thai government is in a position to pay them for alternative crops.

The story is, however, much more complicated than that and it would be an over-simplification just to see it in terms of the opium trade. Khun Sha sees himself as a "wanderer between the worlds"; he and his warriors, all of them armed to the teeth, feel persecuted both by the Thai and Burmese governments. That is why for years Khun Sha has called on the government in Rangoon to grant independence to the Shan state, which was conquered by the British in the 19th c. and then later annexed by Burma. Then, as he declared again only just recently, he would see to it that the opium poppy was no longer grown for commercial profit.

The government of Myanmar(Burma) has always refused even to consider these demands and continues to maintain this stance. Hence Khun Sha continues to wage his war against them – and the profits from the drug trade are used to finance this war. His secret army is better equipped than that of his opponents.

Nevertheless, there are some signs that a victory is gradually being won against Khun Sha. First of all, the mother of the present Thai king devoted herself tirelessly over many years to securing the social integration of the mountain peoples of Thailand; institutions founded by her give their members instruction in other forms of agriculture and help them to sell their produce in the markets of northern Thailand.

★Boat trip on the Mekong

The three-hour journey on the Mekong to Chiang Khong can prove quite an adventure, but check beforehand with TAT on the dangers it could involve. The trip covers a 20km/12 mile stretch of the river, with many rapids, as it cuts its way through the mountain gorges and jungles.

Ban Houei Sai (Laos)

About 60km/37 miles from Chiang Saen, Ban Houei Sai is a lively frontier town in Laos across the Mekong from Chiang Khong. The fortifications left by the French include Fort Carnot, now used as offices by the Laotian government. The papers needed to make the ferry trip across the Mekong can be obtained from the Consulate in Bangkok, but be sure also to get a second visa for the return trip to Thailand to avoid having to wait.

Chom Thong C 2

จอมทอง

Region: North Thailand
Province: Chiang Mai
Altitude: 520m/1707ft. Population: 6000

Location

The little town of Chom Thong in north-west Thailand lies in the broad plain of the Menam Ping, hemmed in to the south by jungle covered mountains, not far from Thailand's highest peak, Doi Inthanon (2959m/9711ft). Its main claim to fame is its Wat Phra That Si Chom Thong.

Access

By car: Highway 108 from Chiang Mai (56km/35 miles).
By bus: daily services out of Chiang Mai.

Sights

★★Wat Phra That Si Chom Thong

The oldest part of the 15th c. Wat Phra That Si Chom Tong is the Burmese-style chedi, built in 1451 and said to contain a relic of the Buddha. The cruciform wiharn was built around 1550 in the reign of King Muang Keo, and has beautiful gilded wood carving along the gables, eaves and portals, as well as on the teak columns and beams in the interior, making it an outstanding work of art. Inside there is also a Burmese-style altar, its rich decoration including two ornately worked elephant tusks, and a number of Buddha figures. The seated bronze Buddha is the object of particular veneration.

Nam Tok Mae Klang (waterfall)

A little road behind the wat leads to the Mae Klang waterfall, 9km/6 miles away, where a path takes the visitor on to the rocks by the 100m/328ft-high cascade (swimming is dangerous!). Also worth seeing is Borichinda cave, another hour and a half on foot.

★★Doi Inthanon (mountain)

A trip to Doi Inthanon, 55km/34 miles from Chom Thong and Thailand's highest peak (2595m/9711ft), is one of the most scenic excursions in this supremely scenic part of the country. The mountain lies at the heart of the Doi Inthanon National Park, part of the granite massif (see Facts and Figures, Topography) which forms the southern foothills of Myanmar's Shan Mountains.

Travel agents offer three to five day treks on foot or by pony, staying overnight in Wildlife Association camping areas. It is also possible to hire local minibuses, and there are some bungalows by the National Park headquarters (just past the Hmong village Khun Klang).

Other excursions

Highway 108 carries on to Hot, passing along the narrow valley of the Menam Ping between rugged rock walls draped with vegetation. Yanhee Reservoir, in a magnificent mountain setting, has boats for rental, and swimming and fishing. A Karen village, built on poles, stands close to the lake and there are other Karen villages on the road to Mae Sariang, 105km/65 miles from Chom Thong.

★★Ob Luang Gorge

Another natural beauty spot en route to Mae Sariang is the Ob Luang Gorge where the Menam Chaem forces its way through a 30m/98ft-high massif. A view of the gorge below can be had from a bridge between the cliffs.

Chonburi (Cholburi) H 4/5

Region: East Thailand
Province: Chonburi
Altitude: 3m/10ft. Population: 52,000

ชลบุรี

Location

Chonburi, the capital of Chonburi Province (population 840,000), was founded by an Ayutthaya king in the 14th c. and is currently a large and lively township of fishermen, merchants and traders on the approach to Bangkok. The harbour is too shallow for large-scale commerce but this is probably also why it has remained a busy little fishing port, where the fishermen still put out to sea in their boats at dusk. Thailand's largest oyster beds are situated south of the town. The main local crops are sugar cane and manioc. This is chopped up and laid out to dry, giving off a pungent aroma, to make tapioca for baking and thickening. Thailand's tapioca is one of its most important agricultural products and is exported to a great many countries.

Access

By car: Highway 3 from Bangkok (96km/60 miles).
By bus: from Bangkok's Eastern Bus Terminal.

Sights

★Wat Sam Yot

Wat Sam Yot stands on a hill, with a good view over Chonburi, near the town centre, and has a 34m/112ft-high statue of the Buddha at the moment of enlightenment.

Chonburi has many temples, with plenty of decoration but little artistic significance, and only the two oldest – Wat Intharam and Wat Dhama Nimitr – are known by their own names.

Wat Intharam

Wat Intharam, near the old market in the centre of town, dates from the late Ayutthaya period and was built under King Taksin, whose statue stands by the entrance. The temple underwent restoration several times in the Ratta-

A huge figure of Buddha in the Wat Sam Yot

nakosin (Bangkok) period and has almost completely lost its original appearance, although it is still worth looking at the stucco figures on the roof and the china mosaics on the window arches. The interior of the bot has some very fine frescos, in early Bangkok style, of divinities and scenes from the life of the Buddha, as well as a great number of statues of Buddha, some of them quite rare. The courtyard of the wat is where the festivities take place that mark the great Chonburi buffalo races held every October, attracting thousands of visitors to the town.

Wat Dhama Nimitr

It is worth also paying a brief visit to the nearby Wat Dhama Nimitr, where the wiharn holds a giant statue of Buddha in a boat. According to legend, Buddha sailed in a boat to the Indian city of Pai Salee and through his compassion and fellow-feeling cured many of its people of cholera.

Surroundings

Ang Sila

Ang Sila, a little place 7km/4 miles south of Chonburi, gets its name, meaning stone basin, from a group of rocks stretching out into the sea. It is famous for its stone cooking utensils, including various sizes of mortar. South beyond Ang Sila lies the Chinese temple of Luk Sam Po, built like a ship (see Bang Saen).

Khao Khiao (wildlife park)

Within the 145sq.km/56sq. miles of the Khao Khiao nature park close to Chonburi visitors can see over 130 protected species, including butterflies, monkeys and even leopards, and an aviary of particularly rare birds.

Chumphon L 3

Region: South Thailand
Province: Chumphon
Altitude: 6m/20ft. Population: 17,000

Location

Chumphon Town, the capital of a province that has a population of about 356,000, appears to be one of those busy places largely untouched by tourism with no important sights of any great interest. Yet the country around it does have a great deal to offer, with open grasslands to the north, a nearby coastline extending for 220km/137 miles, fringed by offshore reefs and islands, dense rainforests in the hinterland, and mountains riddled with caves and caverns. Chumphon is also of particular interest in the geographical sense since it is the eastern point of the Kra Isthmus, the narrowest part of the Malay Peninsula, and only about 40km/25 miles from Kraburi on the Indian Ocean to the west. The area is also famous for the nests of its swiftlets, which are collected to make the Chinese delicacy of bird's nest soup. In 1989 the whole of the province was devastated by floods.

Access

By car: Highway 4 (460km/286 miles from Bangkok).
By bus: from Prachuap Khiri Khan or Surat Thani and Ranong.
By rail: on the line from Bangkok to Southern Thailand (8-hour, 485km/301 mile journey from Bangkok).

Fishing harbour

At the foot of a wooded hill 10km/6 miles south-east of the town is the fishing port of Pak Nam, busy morning and evening with the coming and going of boats. It is worth taking a walk down along the coast, with views over the sea and the high rocky islands, to a shrine erected in memory of Prince Chumphon, after whom the town was named.

From the harbour boats go on trips to islands such as Ko Raet, Koh Mattra, Koh Lawa, Koh Maphrao and Koh Talu, with the caves where the edible-nest swiftlets build their nests during the breeding season from March to August. These nests are taken by collectors and sold to the restaurants. Koh Tao, 8km/5 miles from Chumphon, is also worth visiting (attractive bungalow resorts).

An idyllic beach in southern Thailand

Fish market

Beaches

Paradonpap beach, 16km/10 miles south of Chumphon at the mouth of the Pak Nam Chumphon, has some good fish restaurants. On Ri Beach, 5km/3 miles further on, and very crowded at weekends and holidays, the torpedo boat HMS "Chumphon" is on show as a reminder of the battles that took place here in the 19th c. between Thailand and Burma. The nearby Prince Chumphon Shrine is dedicated to the Prince who was the founder of the Thai Navy. The Mo Phon Traditional Herb Garden grows many healing herbs on an experimental basis for the Thai government. There is also a fine beach at Thung Wua Laen, 17km/11 miles north of Chumphon towards Bang Saphan.

★Khao Kriap Cave

On Highway 409 18km/11 miles south of Chumphon, the Khao Kriap Cave, reached by 300m/328yd of track and at the foot of the Khao Kriap mountain, boasts a stalagmite 20m/66ft high.

Damnoen Saduak

See Ratchaburi

Fang B 3

Region: North Thailand
Province: Chiang Mai
Altitude: 655m/2150ft. Population: 12,000

ฝาง

Location

Set amid the grandeur of north-western Thailand's jungle scenery and the foothills of the Himalayas, Fang is a small but thriving place 24km/15 miles from the border crossing to Burma, now Myanmar. The political situation in the neighbouring country means this crossing point can no longer be used. The only way to get to Myanmar is by air to Rangoon from Bangkok.

Access

By car: Highway 107 from Chiang Mai (124km/77 miles) and Highway 1/109 from Chiang Rai (65km/40 miles).
By bus: several services daily from Chiang Mai or Chiang Rai.

History and Importance

Fang nowadays has little to show for the important position it once held during the Lan Na Kingdom as a trading centre and point of strategic significance. Its fascination lies in its role as a meeting place for the peoples of the surrounding hill tribes, the Akha, Lisu and Meo, who come here to sell their market produce. The city also has the dubious distinction of being the gateway to the notorious "Golden Triangle" where the bulk of the world's opium is grown for the heroin trade. The frontier is guarded by former soldiers from Chiang Kai-shek's Kuomintang forces, some of whom were allowed to settle here by the Thai government after they fled from the Chinese Communists in 1949.

Nearby Chai Prakan, founded around 900 and thus one of the earliest settlements in present-day Thailand, was an important base for earlier Thai tribes in their resistance to the south-west expansion of the Khmer Kingdom.

Fang itself was founded in 1268 by King Mengrai, and from here the Thais embarked on their gradual capture of the Mon Kingdom. It later developed into an important trading centre, and for a long time its people held out against conquest by the Burmese, only capitulating in 1732 after a lengthy siege (Chiang Mai had already fallen in 1556). The Thais managed to wrest the town from its captors in the late 18th c., and since the end of the 19th c. Fang has been part of the Province of Chiang Mai, and hence the Kingdom of Thailand. The oil that was discovered around here in the 1950s proved to be of little value, and the dream of "black gold" vanished as swiftly as it had arrived.

A hot spring near Fang

Fortifications

Apart from a few earthwalls, little remains of the fortifications thrown up by King Mengrai. The deep well in the centre of the town is where King Udom Sin and his queen are said to have hurled themselves rather than fall into the hands of the Burmese.

Experimental Farm and teaching station

The Tribal Welfare Committee's experimental farm and teaching station north of Fang is worth a visit (take the road to Tha Thon, turn left just before Ban Mae Ai, and follow the road to Doi Pha Hom Pok, Thailand's second highest peak, for about 15km/9 miles). Here the government in Bangkok is putting considerable resources into trying to ween the hill tribes from smuggling and cultivating opium by teaching them how to grow alternative crops such as fruit, vegetables, grain, tea and coffee.

Hot Springs

The village of Ban Pin about 10km/6 miles from Fang has around 50 hot sulphurous springs, some of which are permanently active. Take Highway 1089 north towards Ban Pin then follow the Hot Springs signs.

★★River trip on the Menam Kok

From Tha Thon, the border town about 22km/14 miles from Fang, it is possible to make the spectacular and potentially dangerous trip on a tour boat to Chiang Rai, travelling downriver between rocky cliffs and riding the Menam Kok rapids. It is advisable to check beforehand with local experts or the YMCA tourist information services in Chiang Rai on whether the political situation is such that these trips can go ahead, and what security precautions are necessary. (An armed guard should be demanded before undertaking this trip.)

Hill-tribe villages

Anyone wanting to undertake a trek in the mountains around Fang should take on a local guide and have a vehicle suitable for overland travel. The people of the Lisu, Haw, Meo, Akha and Yao hill tribes who live here still pursue their centuries old way of life and speak their own languages in what may appear to the visitor to be archaic conditions but are very much part of their culture. It is hoped, however, that modern farming methods will help eliminate the "slash-and-burn" agriculture that is the real obstacle to a more settled existence.

Hat Yai P 4

หัวหิน

Region: South Thailand
Province: Songkhla
Altitude: 12m/39ft. Population: 120,000

Location

The city of Hat Yai, 900km/560 miles south of Bangkok, plays an important role in the commerce of southern Thailand since it lies on the main trading route between Thailand and Malaysia/Singapore. It is also famous for its batiks and beautifully woven silks and woollen textiles, and is the location of the national Rubber Research Centre, where peasant farmers are taught growing techniques for rubber production.

Known as the Gate to Malaysia – the nearest frontier crossing is 52km/32 miles to the south – Hat Yai is an important rail junction at the point where the two lines from Malaysia to Bangkok meet. Although the city has virtually no sights of its own to offer it is a good starting point for trips to the islands in the Andaman Sea (see Satun).

Access

For many years the railway line built in the early part of the century was the only link between Bangkok and the south of the country. With the advent of air travel, however, Hat Yai airport is increasingly coming into its own, and now has twice daily flights from the capital. Another very pleasant way to travel is to take the train from Bangkok–Hualampong for the 19-hour journey through 945km/587 miles of a constantly changing landscape (trains leave Bangkok four times daily).

By bus: buses leave from the Southern Bus Terminal in Bangkok.

Nam Tok Nga Chang (waterfall)

It is worth paying a visit to Nam Tok Nga Chang, the "elephant's tusk" waterfall 20km/12 miles north of the city, although this can run dry in the height of the summer.

Koh Tarutao

See Satun

Hua Hin J 3

ก็ยหๅ๒เห

Region: West Thailand
Province: Prachuap Khiri Khan
Altitude: 3m/10ft. Population: 57,000

Location

Hua Hin (meaning stone head) is a popular beach resort on the Gulf of Thailand 232km/144 miles south of Bangkok, and, since the Royal Family stopped going to Bang Pa In, is where King Bhumibol has his summer palace. Apart from its other main attraction – a 3km/2 mile stretch of fine white sand – Hua Hin has little else of importance, but would certainly suit anyone who wanted to get away from the noise and bustle of Pattaya on the other side of the Gulf. There are a number of quiet hotels and bungalow complexes ranged along the coast that are particularly good for a family holiday.

Access

By car: Highway 4 or 35 from Bangkok via Samut Songkhram.
By bus: from Bangkok Southern Bus Terminal (about 6 hours).
By rail: on the main line from Bangkok down the Malay Peninsula (229km/142 miles from Bangkok, about 4 hours 30 minutes).

History

The rise of Hua Hin up to 1910 is closely linked with the building of the railway line down to the south of the country. Until then an insignificant little township, it was discovered by Bangkok's "top ten thousand" with chief among them the son of King Chulalongkorn, Prince Nares, who was the first to build a summer palace here (Saen Samran House). This was later to be extended with parks and bungalows by successive princes and princesses. Although visitors can tour the rooms and gardens of King Rama VII's palace they are not allowed into King Phumibol's palace, which is by the west entrance.

Sights

★Fish market

Hua Hin has Thailand's second largest fishing fleet and the bustling fish market in the north of the town is well worth a visit, especially in the morning when the big catches of fish are being landed.

★Royal Palace

Looking like a European pleasure palace, the royal residence of Klai Klangwan ("far from all cares") was built by Rama VII and completed in 1910. Recently renovated, it stands in magnificent grounds extending down to the sea. The rock which looks like a head at the southern end of the sandy beach gave Hua Hin its name.

The King's Summer Palace

The present summer palace of King Bhumibol and Queen Sirikit close by is not open to the public, but if the monarch is staying at Hua Hin visitors may be lucky enough to catch a glimpse of him out sailing.

★Wat Khao Lad

Wat Khao Lad, 20 minutes from Hua Hin by bus, is perched on a nearby rock and anyone who clambers up the steep flight of steps to it will be rewarded with a lovely view of the sea, the mountains in the east and the village of Khao Takiap.

Railway Hotel

The elegant Railway Hotel in the centre of Hua Hin is another place worth seeing. At one time the quarters for the employees of Thailand's State Railway, the Hotel Sofitel Central Hua Hin, as it is now called, has kept its original 1923 ambience of the colonial-style grand hotel, despite extensive refurbishment.

The royal waiting room in Hua Hin Station

The rock-temple Wat Khao Lad

The daily night market on Dechanuchit Road, with all its street traders, is also worth a visit, and has many restaurants and stalls selling cooked food. ★Night Market

Hua Hin's little station is the end of the line for a restored steam locomotive of the kind that was used by the Royal Thai Railway, as it was then called, until 1975. Nowadays steam has given way to diesel and some stretches of line have even been electrified. There is a charming little royal waiting room as well. Station

Surroundings

Caves

The limestone hills around Hua Hin are riddled with caves and make a good morning or afternoon excursion. They include the temple cave of Tham Dao, as well as the caves of Tham Mai Lab, Tham Kai Lon and Tham Kai Far, where there are some Buddha figures that although of no great art historical interest are nevertheless fine pieces.

Khao Takiap Bay

Khao Takiap Bay about 6km/4 miles south of Huan Hin has beaches of particularly fine sand and some good fish restaurants.

One impressive sight is the gleaming white statue of Buddha on a hilltop, fronting a temple which is home to a large troop of free-ranging monkeys.

Kaeng Krachan National Park

Kaeng Krachan, about 40km/25 miles west of Hua Hin (signpost in the town centre), is Thailand's largest national park, and contains the Pala U waterfall, which is very popular with Thai visitors in the hot weather.

It is one of the country's loveliest national parks and as yet still relatively infrequently visited. The main entrance is on Highway 3175 which joins Highway 4 at Tha Yang. An entry permit is needed to get into the park. There are bungalows for overnight accommodation at the park offices, about 20km/12 miles before the park entrance.

Pranburi

The route to Pranburi, about 25km/16 miles from Hua Hin, passes several quiet bays which are good for swimming. South of Pranburi is the Khao

Waterfall in the Kaeng Krachan National Park

Sam Roi Yot ("three hundred peaks") National Park in the rugged limestone hills, part of the Tenasserim Mountains, which line the coast. These are full of ravines and caverns, some of which can be reached by the park's network of roads and trails.

Kalasin E 7

กาฬสินธุ์

Region: North-east Thailand
Province: Kalasin
Altitude: 88m/289ft. Population: 24,000

Location

The capital of the province of the same name, Kalasin, in north-east Thailand, makes a good base, with its hotels for anyone with a particular interest in Thai cultural and architectural history who wants to visit the well-preserved reminders of the country's rich past roundabout. The town itself has no sights of its own, apart, perhaps, from its markets and the glimpses they provide of life in the countryside.

Access

By car: Highways 209/213 from Khon Khaen (about 95km/60 miles), Highway 213 from Sakhon Nakhon (110km/68 miles).
By bus: from Khon Khaen and Sakhon Nakhon.

★★Ban Sema

Ban Sema, a village about 20km/12 miles west of Kalasin, near Yang Talat, is a particularly interesting place to see since in the 9th to 11th c. it was the site of the Dvaravati city of Muang Fa Daed. This was surrounded by two moats where important finds have been made of items from the period between the 6th and 13th c., one of great significance in the development of Thai art and culture. There is an interesting mix of local art and that of neighbouring peoples, including the Khmer, and this is most notable in the semas, the boundary stones denoting the consecrated part of a temple. Two particularly fine ones have beautifully carved bas-reliefs showing the Buddha being worshipped by the Royal couple (this is kept in one of the monastery buildings of the Wat Po Chai Semaran), or illustrating Buddha's return to his family (Museum of Khon Kaen, see entry). More of these boundary stones are on display in the courtyard of the wat.

Dvaravati Chedis

Among the ruins of several Dvaravati chedis north-west of the temple is one well-preserved chedi of an elegant design with some of the original stucco decoration on the base still intact. The central section was restored at a later date and given a spire which is unmistakably in the Ayutthaya style.

Dvaravati Reliefs

On the road between Yang Talat and Kalasin, at Ban Nong Wang Noeng, there are three gilded reliefs, up to 3.15m/10ft in length. Interesting examples of Dvaravati art, they date from the 8th to 10th c. and show the Buddha at his rest. One of them, Phra Puttharup Cheun Po, is the object of particular veneration.

Kamphaeng Phet — E 3

กำแพงเพชร

Region: North Thailand
Province: Kamphaeng Phet
Altitude: 47m/154ft. Population: 32,000

Location

The provincial capital of Kamphaeng Phet stands amidst the jungle landscape of northern Thailand's hill country on the Menam Ping. The faded glory of the historic ruins nearby testifies to the fact that this was the site of one of the most important cities in the Sukhothai kingdom. Close to the town is the beginning of the last of Thailand's teak forests, stretching from here well up into the north of the country. Since 1988, when disastrous landslides brought a government ban on the felling of tropical timber, teak is no longer floated from here down to Bangkok on the Menam Ping.

A visit to Kamphaeng Phet would form part of a tour tracing the history of Thailand, and it is a good base for trips to Sukhothai and Si Satchanalai, both once linked to the town by the Phra Ruang Highway, and to Tak and Phitsanulok. Itineraries of this kind are included by Bangkok travel companies in their programmes.

Access

By car: Highway 1 from Bangkok (360km/224 miles), Highways 117/115 from Phitsanulok (102km/63 miles), Highway 101 from Sukhothai (76km/47 miles).
By air: nearest airport Phitsanulok (daily flights from Bangkok).

History

The building of the town to serve as a front line of defence for the Sukhothai kingdom was ordered by King Liu Thai (1347–68). It was intended to replace Chakang Rao, of which little remains, on the other side of the river. Since the Sukhothai kingdom only lasted till 1376 Kamphaeng Phet's heyday was brief, but temple building continued in the 15th and 16th c. and was not halted until invasion by the Burmese in the late 16th c. when they plundered and destroyed parts of the city.

Sights

Chakang Rao

The ruins of what was once Chakang Rao lie on the southern approach to the town on Highway 1 before the bridge over the Menam Ping. Their distinguishing features are the laterite remains of the town's fort, Phom Thung Setti, and the four elegant restored chedis. The tall chedi on the left-hand side of the road, probably modelled on Burmese lines, full of niches, and crowned with a 20th c. Burmese-style wrought-iron canopy, stands in the precincts of what was Wat Boromathat, which has recently been fully restored. This was built in the early Bangkok period over three

Figure of Buddha in the Wat Phra That in Kamphaeng Phet

Sukhothai chedis. These can still be seen inside the wat, which is open to the public.

National Museum

On the other side of the bridge the new town is on the right and the walled precinct of the old town, still with parts of earth ramparts once 6m/20ft high, is on the left. Anyone who has not yet been to Sukhothai should first visit the museum quite close to the ruins (open: Wed.–Sun. 9am–noon and 1–3pm). This contains a large collection of finds from Kamphaeng Phet, many of them showing the harmony and elegance which characterised the style of the Sukhotai period. There are also bronzes and sculptures from all the Thai art periods, including many masterpieces such as a bronze sitting Buddha in the U Thong style, 13th c. bronzes, and examples of the Lopburi and Dvaravati style of work.

★Wat Phra That

The ruins of Wat Phra That, the town's second most important wat, are opposite the museum. The bell shape of the central chedi on a square base are indicative of Singhalese influence – the strict form of Buddhism still practised in Sri Lanka today was very prevalent in Thailand when the chedi was built. It is surrounded by columns and held a relic, the whereabouts of which is unknown. All that remains of the wiharn are the foundations and some parts of square pillars.

★★Wat Phra Kaeo

Wat Phra Kaeo next to the Wat Phra That stands in what was the precinct of the royal palace. The royal temple, as opposed to a monastery, it has a number of very striking Buddha figures, standing in solitary splendour amidst the ruins. The features of the colossal figure on the high terrace of the former bot in front of a collapsed bell-shaped chedi have been totally weathered away, and another enormous Buddha in the centre of the wiharn has suffered the same fate. The serried ranks of the smaller figures

◀ *A recumbent Buddha in the Wat Phra Kaeo*

A ruined chedi in the Wat Phra Kaeo of Kamphaeng Phet

around this statue have been eroded into Giacometti-like shapes, their head, limbs and body assuming abstract lines as the stucco has broken off to leave just the slender laterite torso. One reclining Buddha in particular is worth seeking out since the head has retained all the clarity and sensitivity of expression of the beautifully sculpted features. Around the base of the big bell-shaped chedi there are fragments of the original 32 lions and some of the 16 niches in the upper section still contain Buddhas. There is a brick footprint of Buddha at the end of the compound.

Lak Muang

North of Wat Phra Kaeo is the town pillar, the Lak Muang, highly revered by the local people, together with two elongated pools surrounding a third round pool.

Other Ruins

To get to the finest, and most important, ruins, which are outside the city wall in a delightful park, leave the old town by the Sapan Kom Gate and follow the "Arunyik Area" signs. Here in the forests to the north of the town there are the splendid monasteries built in the Sukhothai style with considerable Singhalese influences by monks who followed a strict form of Buddhism.

Wat Phra Meud/ Wat Phra Non

The first of the ruins are of Wat Pu Mud Nok, followed by the smaller Wat Phra Meud, then the much larger Wat Phra Non, the temple of the reclining Buddha. The first building is a large bot which still retains pillars and walls with the narrow perpendicular window openings typical of Sukhothai architecture. The square wiharn behind it has four rows of four massive pillars. These once sheltered a reclining Buddha, but now all that is left is part of its long base. The larger of the two chedis in the temple precinct stood behind the wiharn, and was bell-shaped supported by an octagonal plinth on a square base.

Wat Phra Si Iriyabot

The mondhop of Wat Si Iriyabot once held statues of Buddha in the four traditional poses – standing, sitting, walking and reclining – and hence its

Elephant sculptures at the Wat Chang in Kamphaeng Phet

name (si = four, iriyabot = poses). Only fragments are left of three of the figures, but the statue of the remaining colossal standing Buddha is held to be one of the finest in the classic Sukhothai style.

Wat Singh

The existing remains of the "lion temple" of Wat Singh give an indication of the grandeur of scale it once enjoyed.

Wat Chang Rob

The ruins of Wat Chang Rob are also worth seeing. On its own hilltop, it had a high bell-shaped chedi, of which only the foundations, decorated with some fine stucco work of running birds, remain. The chedi was supported by 68 elephants, and the top half of their bodies protrude from walls that are also decorated by stucco trees and ceramic demons. The only two lions that are intact now mark the entrance to Kamphaeng Phet's National Museum. Four steep steps lead up to the top part of the chedi.

Wat Chao Arwat Yai

The deep pool near Wat Chao Arwat Yai was formed by the quarrying of the stone to build the temple. Enclosed in a low double wall, decorated with small chedis at the entrance, the temple precinct still contains traces of a wiharn in the centre, with ruined chedis on both sides of the courtyard. One larger chedi, standing on a stepped base, is still intact but has lost its spire.

Kanchanaburi G/H 3

กาญจนบุรี

Region: West Thailand
Province: Kanchanaburi
Altitude: 30m/98ft. Population: 50,000

Location

Kanchanaburi Province, west of Bangkok, has long been a favourite recreational area thanks to its pleasant scenery and its nearness to the capital.

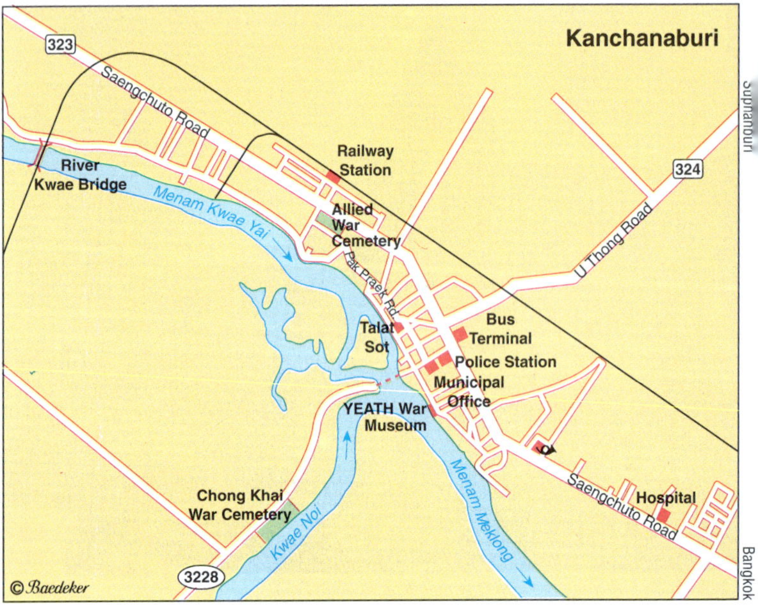

Excavations show that it was already settled in prehistoric times and that its rivers, flowing down from the mountains in the west, were part of an important trade route from Indo-China to Cambodia. It was through the Three Pagodas Pass close to the source of the Menam Kwae Noi that the Burmese armies were always launching their attacks, the last one taking place in 1767, when they fell upon Ayutthya and razed it to the ground. The town of Kanchanaburi, as provincial capital, was therefore strategically located as the point where the Siamese army could take on the enemy as the Kwae Yai, the River Kwai, joined with the Kwae Noi to become the Mae Klong, and then flow down through wild mountain gorges into a broad plain on the Gulf of Thailand.

Kanchanaburi was probably already an attractive place to settle since it had the kind of fertile soil which could be cultivated to grow sugar cane, tobacco, cotton, maize and manioc, although most of the farming here is now given over to rice. The many nearby sapphire and spinel mines also contributed to its importance.

The surrounding limestone hills, covered in rain forest and rising up to 1800m/5908ft, hold a great number of caverns and major waterfalls. The town itself, usually known just as "Kanburi", has little to offer apart from the usual lively street scenes, but is a good base for anyone seeking to get away from the hurly burly of Bangkok to relax in an idyllic setting.

Access

By car: Highway 4 from Bangkok or 338/4 to Nakhon Pathom, then 323 (130km/81 miles).

By rail: from Bangkok-Thonburi Station (also known as Bangkok Noi); also regular excursions by Thai Railways; information at Hualampong Central Station in Bangkok.

By bus: regular service from Bangkok Southern Bus Terminal. Many Bangkok travel companies include day-trips or excursions lasting several days in their programme.

History

The first systematic excavations were begun in the 1950s by Dr van Keekeren, one of the Dutch prisoners of war forced to work on the building of the bridge over the River Kwai (see below), who had stayed on after the end of the Second World War. The initial finds of prehistoric stone tools were made in Bo Phloi and Sai Yok, to the north and west of Kanchanaburi respectively. The implements found in two caves at Sai Yok and on the wooded banks of the Kwae Noi date back to palaeolithic times. Other discoveries included a complete Bronze Age burial. This took the same form as is still customary in Kanchanaburi today, with the face turned towards the north, the legs at an angle, and the upper torso weighted down with a stone, clearly to keep the spirit of the deceased held fast in the tomb so that it could not trouble the living.

★★Bridge on the River Kwai

Kanachanaburi's main claim to fame is the famous, not to say infamous Bridge on the River Kwai, popularised by Pierre Boulle's novel of 1956 and the epic film of the same name made in 1958, and actually filmed in Ceylon. See Baedeker Special pp. 216/217.

Mangkorn Thong Caves

The Mangkorn Thong caves are half an hour from Kanchanaburi (boat hire) by river on the Kwae Noi. Two brightly coloured dragons mark the foot of the steep flight of over 95 steps leading up to the Cave Temple of the Golden Dragon, the series of tunnels up to the mountain top, and a cavern with some fine stalactites.

Ban Kao (excavations)

Ban Kao on the Kwae Noi is one of the most important excavation sites in Kanchanaburi Province. The finds, including tools, skeletons, vessels, pottery and the Bronze Age burial already mentioned, are on display in Bangkok's National Museum, which also has statues in the Lopburi style (derived from the Khmer style, 7th–13th c.) found at the "Lion City" of Prasat Muang Singh, 34km/21 miles from Kanchanaburi.

Prasat Muan Singh Historical Park

Prasat Muang Singh was built as an outpost against the Burmese. The ruins of the city ramparts enclose a square compound 1000m/3282ft by 600m/1970ft with the well preserved shrine with its brick prang and four gopuram (tower gates) in the centre. A large number of inscriptions were found in the library in the inner courtyard.

Behind the little restaurant at the entrance to Muang Singh is a shelter where more recent discoveries are kept pending cataloguing. A small outdoor museum nearby has several well preserved statues and other artefacts on display.

Tham Keng Lawa caverns

Tham Keng Lawa is an exceptionally scenic system of caverns, full of stalactites and stalagmites, just a few minutes from the River Kwai Village Hotel, in a beautiful setting of jagged rocks, deep gorges, waterfalls and jungle-covered mountains.

Nam Tok Sai Yok Yai (waterfalls)

Anyone with a taste for adventure should make the river trip, passing between towering rock walls and riding the rapids, to the Sai Yok Yai waterfalls, half a mile from Nam Tok railway station, where a turbulent mountain stream cascades down into the Kwae Noi.

Three Pagodas Pass

From the Sai Yok Yai waterfalls a track leads through the jungle to the Three Pagodas Pass, one of the original terminals of the Death Railway. The area is inhabited by a number of hill tribes who eke out a meagre living from "slash-and-burn" agriculture. The pass gets its name from the three pagodas by the roadside, and leads up into the mountains on the Thai–Burmese border – the highest peak in the region is 1950m/6400ft. It is a favourite route for smugglers and exploration on foot in this wild place is certainly not to be recommended.

Bo Phloi Mines

Kanchanaburi Province owes part of its wealth to its mines and diggings. Some of these are still in operation today around Bo Phloi, a little place

Baedeker Special

The Death Railway to Burma

The spectacle is a daily occurrence – right down to the all-in price and the soft drinks and sandwiches served en route. After a morning departure from Bangkok and a journey of just under two hours, the engine-driver of the State Railway of Thailand (SRT) draws back the window of his heavy diesel locomotive just before the train starts to cross the unprepossessing steel construction which has achieved worldwide fame as the Bridge over the River Kwai (Kwae Noi). At the same moment dozens of camera shutters click in front of their owners' excited eyes, while, as like as not, some elderly tourist will be humming or whistling the first few bars of the "River Kwai March", which in the 1960s enjoyed worldwide fame and popularity.

Those men, however, who were involved in the actual building of this infamous bridge would have precious little cause to whistle a tune. Few constructions in the whole world can have been erected at the cost of so much human suffering. The men who built it were prisoners-of-war of the Japanese, deported to labour camps in defiance of all humanitarian laws. They numbered about 61,000 and they came from Great Britain, Australia, the United States and the Netherlands. In addition to them, it is estimated that there were a quarter of a million Asian prisoners or conscripted workers from Burma, Malaya, Thailand and Japan. Most of the prisoners were deported from Singapore to central Thailand after February 15th 1942, when Singapore was forced to surrender to the Japanese.

The place that today looks like a typical tourist centre with its hotels, restaurants and souvenir shops, was, at the time of the prisoner-of-war camp, the nearest thing to hell itself. Myriads of mosquitoes plagued the prisoners as they toiled away, sweat oozing from their pores in the suffocating heat. Many lost the battle against the weather and the insects, others died from sheer emaciation, from the brutal treatment which they received at the hands of their guards, or the bullets from their guns. Nor should those be forgotten who were killed by the bombing raids carried out by the Allied forces' planes. The story of their fate was brought to the attention of the whole world by Pierre Boule in 1956 in his novel, "The Bridge over the River Kwai". Later there was also a film version, shot, not in the original location, but in Ceylon.

The bridge was built over the tiny river Kwai Noi as part of a strategically important railway route which, it was envisaged, would cross the Three Pagodas Pass and link Thailand with neighbouring Burma in order to make secure the supplies of materials needed for the war. The railway line, the total length of which was 415km/260 miles, very quickly acquired the well-deserved appellation, "Death Railway". The construction work lasted for 13 months and as many as 300,000 prisoners-of-war were pressed into service.

What we see today is admittedly not the original construction. The "real" bridge was originally made predominantly of teakwood. About 100m/110yd further downstream there was even a temporary bridge, made just of bamboo, the remains of which are still visible in the dry season. It was not until the post-war years that concrete supports for the bridge were built and its construction replaced by the present steel one.

After crossing the bridge the train gradually picks up speed, only to slam on the brakes again a few kilometres further on. Another spine-chilling thrill awaits its passengers. The route now passes on to Nam Tok across a precarious section made of bamboo which cleaves to the rocks in almost daredevil fashion. Anyone reckless enough to look out of the window will be rewarded with a view into a yawning abyss; this is the valley which the River Kwae Noi has carved out for itself. Finally, along the side of the mountain, can be seen the tiny caves in which many of the

The Famous Bridge on the River Kwai

prisoners were forced to live. Some years later, the former Dutch prisoner of war, Dr. van Heekeren, who remained in Thailand at the end of the war and worked there as an archaeologist, discovered prehistoric tools and implements in these caves dating back to the Neolithic period.

Today the line terminates at Nam Tok. The track, which formerly continued deep into the heart of Burma, was dismantled after the war.

One further bit of history connected with the bridge over the Kwai is really only accessible to those who do not just limit themselves to an organised day-trip from Bangkok. On the banks of the Mae Klong in Kanchanaburi there is a small museum, whose name, the JEATH War Museum, owes its acronym to the initial letters of the five countries to which the prisoners of war belonged (Japan, England, Australia/America and Thailand). (Open: daily 8.30am–5pm; entry fee; no photography). The museum consists of three bamboo-atap long huts which are replicas of those used to house the hundreds of Allied prisoners of war. The huts contain old photographs, maps, paintings of camp life and surgical instruments improvised by the medics for operations on their wounded comrades.

The end of the war in Thailand did not spell freedom for most of the surviving prisoners of war; they were deported yet again by the Japanese – this time to the mines of Nagasaki. Right up to the end of World War Two many more thousands of prisoners perished after enduring unimaginable pain and suffering.

Visitors should also make the time to visit the smaller of the two military cemeteries, which can be reached by boat from the bridge. Here, amid lush green surroundings, are the graves of 1700 prisoners. A book of remembrance, containing the names of the fallen, is put on display at the entrance at certain times.

"City of the Lion": Prasat Muang Singh

48km/30 miles north of Kanchanaburi Town. Besides gold, silver, wolfram and tin, there is mining for such gemstones as sapphires, rubies, garnets, cornelian and amethyst. In fact jewellery and cut and uncut stones are cheaper in the Bo Thoi shops than anywhere else in Thailand.

Tham Than Lot/ Talad Yai Caves

About 95km/59 miles north of Kanchanaburi (Highway 3199 then left at Nong Preu), in Chaloem Rattanakosin National Park, there are two caves which are worth seeing. Than Lot, a large and lofty cavern with stalactites and stalagmites, was a site of prehistoric settlement, as the many finds made here testify.

The second cave, Talad Yai ("big cave"), about half a mile past the Nam Tok Trai Treung waterfall, has two resident hermits.

Other places to visit

Wat Kanchanaburi Khao

Other places worth visiting along the Kwae Yai valley include Wat Kanchanaburi Khao, a temple on the old site of Kanchanaburi Town, with a chedi and a prang from the Ayutthaya period, and Erawan Falls, 55km/34 miles from Kanchanaburi by road on Highway 3199 or about three hours by river.

Erawan Falls

The falls take the form of a series of cascades and pools over and among the rocks, and are supposed to be shaped like the divine Indra's three-headed elephant, hence their name.

The whole area has been declared the Khao Salop National Park. This extends over 2024sq.km/781sq. miles, and beyond it is Thung Yai, another National Park. Both parks are best visited during the week, since they attract large numbers of visitors from Bangkok at the weekend.

Pong Teuk (excavations)

The famous Pong Teuk excavations are east of Kanchanaburi on Highway 323 to Nakhon Pathom, presumably a very old trade route. Digging has uncovered the foundations of several buildings which were probably part of a temple precinct. A sensational find here in 1928 was a bronze Roman oil lamp, thought to have been cast in Alexandria, in Egypt, in the 2nd c. A.D.

The handle is shaped like a stylised palm leaf framed by dolphins and the lid is adorned with the head of a satyr, proof of the trade links that existed between South-east Asia and the Roman Empire.

Wat Dong Sak
Wat Pohra Taen Dong Rang

Reached by Highway 323 or 324, Wat Dong Sak is built of teak and is worth seeing for its 6th c. figure of Vishnu and extremely beautifully carved gable, while Wat Phra Taen Dong Rang is the place where, according to legend, Buddha lay down in a hollow to enter Nirvana. Not far from this temple is another hilltop shrine where the body of Buddha is said to have been cremated.

Khao Phra Wiharn (temple)

See Si Saket

Khao Yai National Park

See Pak Chong

Khon Kaen E 6

Region: North-east Thailand
Province: Khon Kaen
Altitude: 155m/509ft. Population: 120,000

ขอนแก่น

Location

The town of Khon Kaen about 380km/236 miles north-east of Bangkok is in the area where the relatively infertile limestone of the Khorat Plateau gives way to the green belt in the north. It is north-eastern Thailand's second most important centre for trade and administrative services after Nakhon Ratchasima, and has the only university in the region. Khon Kaen's economic progress owes much to the Friendship Highway (Highway 2), put in by the Americans as an important supply route for their troops stationed in north-eastern Thailand during the Vietnam War. Its main attraction is its famous museum, apart from which it has little else to offer.

Access

By car: Highways 1/2 from Bankgkok (440km/273 miles; from Nakhon Ratchasima 190km/118 miles); Route 12 from Phitsanulok (300km/186 miles).
By train: station on the Bangkok–Nakhon Ratchasima–Udon Thani line (7 hours and 450km/280 miles from Bangkok).
By air: daily flights from Bangkok.

★National Museum

Opening times
Wed.–Sun.
9am–noon,
1–4pm

Admission fee

The museum, on Lang Soon Ratchakarn Road on the northern edge of town, contains some of the sensational finds from Ban Chiang, including bronze and ceramic vessels decorated with various geometric patterns and flower and animal motifs. The pieces date from 4500 to 3500 B.C. but their precise origin is uncertain. One of the Ban Chiang burials is also on show. The ground floor holds a fine collection of Thai folk art as well as prehistoric artefacts, plus changing exhibitions.

The sandstone sema boundary markers on the ground floor (near the garden exit) and in the gardens depict scenes in relief from the life of Buddha such as his return home to his family after enlightenment. One relief shows his wife caressing Buddha's feet with her hair, while his son points to the sublime presence. Another shows a ceremony, possibly a wedding, while the God Indra can be seen in another. Some of the sema are from Muang Fa Daed (see Kalasin) and they are finely carved in the 8th to 10th c. Dvaravati style, mixed with traces of Khmer influence. There are also some interesting Dvaravati sculptures and Chian Saen bronzes.

East of the museum is an idyllic palm-fringed lake, with a little restaurant.

★Ubol Ratana Reservoir

A long lake, stretching for 80km/50 miles, Ubol Ratana holds the water used to irrigate the infertile soil of the surrounding area. 26km/16 miles north-west of Kon Khaen, it is named after the King's eldest daughter who renounced her right to the throne and went to live abroad.

Phu Kradung National Park

65km/40 miles west of Khon Kaen; see Loei.

Koh Chang (island)

See Trat

Koh Pha Ngan (island)

See Surat Thani

Koh Phi Phi (island)

See Krabi

Koh Samet (island)

See Rayong

Koh Samui (island)

See Surat Thani

Koh Similan (island)

See Phuket

Koh Tarutao (island)

See Hat Yai

Krabi N 2

Region: South Thailand. Province: Krabi
Altitude: 12m/39ft. Population: 17,000

กระบี่

Location

The port of Krabi in southern Thailand, on a line with the island of Phuket, stands on a tongue of land close to where the River Krabi enters the Andaman Sea. It is set against a scenic backdrop of bizarre karst formations, rising out of the tropical forest, while the landscape inland is dominated by mile upon mile of rubber plantations, with only the occasional patch of jungle. Palm-fringed white sand and shell beaches line the coast.

Access

By car: Highway 4 (210km/130 miles from Surat Thani, 230km/143 miles from Nakhon Si Thammarat, 870km/540 miles from Bangkok).
By bus: 13 hours from Bangkok Southern Bus Terminal. Buses also run from Phuket and Phangnga.
Nearest airport: Phuket (130km/81 miles).

Ban Thong Agricultural Station

En route to Krabi, about 22km/14 miles north-west of the town, Highway 4 passes Ban Thong Agricultural Station, a pilot farm for breeding new varieties of rubber, tea and coffee plants (open to visitors). Proof of the results can be seen in the rubber plantations stretching between here and the town. White mats of latex, made from the rubber sap that oozes into the cups on the trunks of the trees, are laid out to dry in front of the mostly wooden huts. Thailand's rubber plays a major part in its balance of trade and is exported to many countries throughout the world.

Hat Noparat Thara

The route (4033/4034/4202) bends right, south-east of Ban Thong Station, and presses on south between high rock walls then past scenic little villages to the beautiful beach of Hat Noparat Thara, which has fine white sand mixed with tiny seashells. At low tide it is possible to walk out to some of the little islands offshore.

★★Susan Hoi Shell Cemetery

One of the major sights of this region is the shell cemetery at Susan Hoi, 8km/5 miles further east on Route 4203/4204. Visible only at low tide, the giant slabs, 75 million years old, are the graveyard of fossilised freshwater snail shells. This is one of only three such sites in the world (there is another one in the USA).

★Koh Phi Phi (group of islands) O 2

Over the years the Phi Phi islands have been famous among backpackers as a remote tropical paradise. Like many other places in Thailand it was soon

Shell-cemetery of Susan Hoi, visible only at low tide

discovered by the more resourceful tour operators who first built little huts then followed up with reasonably comfortable bungalows. Now there are several hotels, discreetly fitting in with the island scenery so as not to detract from its unique charm.

Access

From Krabi (2 hours) and Phuket (1½ hours).

Phi Phi Don
Phi Phi Lay

Phi Phi Don is the only one of the islands that is inhabited. Although no one is allowed to stay on neighbouring Phi Phi Lay it is a popular outing for holidaymakers in search of peace and quiet. Both islands have wonderful scenery with truly exotic idyllic beaches of white sand, and crystal clear waters. Besides its attraction for the local fishermen Phi Phi Lay is also an important source of income as a place for collecting the nests of the edible-nest swiftlets from its numerous caverns and rocky hollows. Whole families compete for the franchise that allows them to risk their lives clambering up precarious-looking bamboo scaffolding, or liana ropes, to harvest the nests – a highly-prized ingredient in Chinese cooking, which can sell for as much as 2000 US dollars a kilo in Hong Kong, to where most of the Phi Phi Lay nests are exported. The edible part of the nest is the swiftlet saliva which binds it together. This is then separated out and cleaned to go into birds' nest soup.

★★Cave
Paintings

The so-called "Viking" cave paintings on the north side of Phi Phi Lay are still something of a puzzle to the experts since these paintings of sailing ships are unlikely to have been the work of those fierce northern seafarers. Countless other caves, some of which are venerated as holy, are impressive testimony to many thousands of years of natural processes.

★★Koh Lanta (group of islands) O 3

Location
and Access

The Koh Lanta islands are about 50km/30 miles south of Krabi in the Indian Ocean. Boats to Koh Lanta Noi leave from the pier at Ban Hua Hin (bus from Krabi), where small boats carry on to Ban Saladan, the largest settlement on Koh Lanta Yai (about 2 hours). Another option is to cross from Ban Bo Muang (about an hour) which is on the bus route from Krabi to Trang. There is no fixed timetable, the boats simply leave when they have enough passengers. Don't try and get to Koh Lanta in the rainy season, the crossing is too dangerous.

Tourism

A few years ago Koh Lanta Noi and Koh Lanta Yai, like the Phi Phi Islands, were still a paradise for the solitary globetrotter, but a number of bungalow complexes – with simple comforts and no electricity – have since been built on the west coast. The Thai government's plan to make Koh Lanta a nature reserve was thwarted by the resistance of its 18,000 or so inhabitants, mostly Muslims, who saw tourism as a welcome way of supplementing their living, sustained mostly by fishing and growing coconuts. For the islanders their rejection of the government plan was probably a mistake, since the expansion of tourism has meant that little of the land remains in local ownership. The two islands have no sights as such, but are a great place for anyone in search of rest and relaxation.

Lampang C 3

Region: North Thailand. Province: Lampang
Altitude: 242m/794ft. Population: 52,000

ลำปาง

Location

Lampang lies on the broad plain of the Menam Wang surrounded by the jungle and mountain scenery typical of northern Thailand. The provincial capital – it still feels like a township rather than a city – has grown in importance with the progress made in its economy in recent years. This is dominated by agriculture, and the fertile plain around Lampang is given over to great fields of rice, Maimaize and cotton.

Access

By car: Highway 1 from Tak (158km/98 miles), or from Chiang Mai/Lamphun (92km/57 miles); Highway 11 from Chiang Mai, through fascinating scenery. Distance from Bangkok: 600km/373 miles.
By rail: station on the Bangkok–Chiang Mai line (from Bangkok 642km/399 miles, about 13 hours).
By bus: five times a day from Northern Bus Terminal in Bangkok. Buses also run from the Chiang Mai Arcade station (2½ hours).
By air: twice a week from Bangkok and Phitsanulok.

History

The Lampang principality was founded by the Mon around the 7th c. and initially belonged to the Haripunchai kingdom before being annexed into the Khmer empire in the 11th c. King Mengrai finally brought Lampang into the Lan Na kingdom before it was seized in the 16th c. by the Burmese, who had already captured Chiang Mai and Lamphun. Clear signs of their occupation can still be seen today.

Sights

Apart from an octagonal tower which was part of the fortifications, nothing is left of the old city of Lampang. In order to get an idea of the original appearance of the famous Ho Kham, the gilded hall that was the governor's residence, it would be necessary to go to the Ancient City at Samut Prakan (see entry) and see the replica of it there. Some recent finds indicate that the earth still holds many secrets. One particularly interesting discovery was a number of stone reliefs in the Dvaravati style. These give some indication of the artistic quality of the buildings, but most of what can be seen in Lampang today dates from after the conquest by the Burmese, and their style has left its mark on all sides.

★★Wat Phra Kaeo Don Tao

Wat Phra Kaeo Don Tao, built in 1680 and one of Thailand's most revered temples, is very picturesquely situated on the Menam Wang. The little bot (*c.* 1800) in the centre, with its recently renovated central tower, is particularly worth seeing. An outstanding example of classic Burmese architecture, rich woodcarving frames the arched openings, the pillars are decorated with fine scrollwork and the imaginative and colourful relief on the magnificent coffer ceiling is inlaid with mother of pearl, enamel and

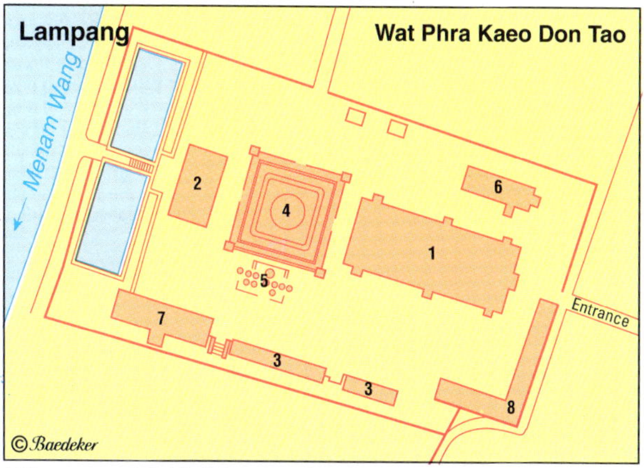

1 Viharn
2 Bot (Ubosot)
3 Buddha Galleries
4 Great Chedi
5 Stupas and Chedis
6 Monks' quarters
7 Buddha's footprint
8 Administration building

A concrete elephant

Two chedis in the Wat Phra Kaeo Don Tao

small pieces of glass, the colours and shapes working together with the building's proportions to form a harmonious whole. Another interesting feature is the copper Buddha. The adjoining stepped building from the later Bangkok period is distinguished by beautifully carved wood inlaid with blue ceramic tiles. The wiharn at a slight distance from the main buildings holds a Buddha in the Chiang Mai style, and there is some fine carving in a small museum near the entrance.

The clay elephant in the garden serves as a reminder of the events surrounding the famous emerald Buddha. Nowadays considered the "talisman" of the Thai kingdom, and the country's most venerated object, the Buddha, which is actually made of a type of jade, was discovered in Chiang Rai in 1434, although it was probably made in Burma. Sam Fang Kaen, the king of Chiang Mai at that time, is supposed to have ordered it to be brought to his palace in a procession, but the elephant chosen to carry it bolted and made straight for Lampang, where the statue spent the next 32 years in this wat. The Buddha eventually returned to Chiang Mai in 1468 then after further travels eventually arrived in Bangkok where it has since stood, much revered, in the "Temple of the Emerald Buddha", also called Wat Phra Kaeo.

Wat Si Rong Muang

Wat Si Rong Muang on the Takrao Noi Road is in the Burmese style and has finely carved gables and pillars.

★★Wat Chedi Sao

The 20 white chedis of Wat Chedi Sao are unique in Thailand, with their beautiful articulation crowned with a little golden canopy. Another well preserved example of the Burmese style, they stand amidst vast paddy fields in the north of the town.

Surroundings

★★Wat Phra That Lampang Luang

Wat Phra That Lampang, at Ko Kha about 18km/11 miles south-west of Lampang, is one of Thailand's most beautiful temples. The finest ornamentation probably dates from the time of Princess Chama Devi (*c.* 650–700), supposedly the founder of this temple complex. During its long

Wiharn of the Wat Chedi Sao

history this may well have been where the local people sought refuge from plundering invaders such as the Burmese, sheltering behind the thick walls which encompass the wat and give it its fortress-like appearance. Long flights of steps lead up to the entrances in the north and east, their balustrades in the serpentine form of a many-headed Naga, an unmistakable feature of Burmese architecture.

Atop a hill surrounded by ancient trees in the centre of the wat compound – the present buildings date from the 16th c. – stands a high chedi, sectioned by ledges, with a tapering gilded spire, the central part consisting of gold on copper. It is surrounded by a bronze balustrade with copper filigree canopies at each of the four corners. Legend has it that a hole in the balustrade was made by a canonball which killed the Burmese general who forced his way into the wat and captured it with his troops. The Thais are supposed to have crept into the compound through a drainage pipe, surprising the enemy while asleep and then killing them.

The chedi is flanked by two shrines. The decoration of the wiharn is particularly magnificent, with superb carvings of flowers, leaves and scrolling and a "wheel of the law" on the inner side of the portal, and imaginative sculpture on the pillars, façades and portals.

The wiharn contains two Buddhas in the Chiang Mai style and the open sala, which supports a stepped roof covered with glazed bricks, has an altar in the centre, richly embellished with reliefs in the Burmese style, surrounded by carved wooden "thongs", emblems hanging on poles. The ceramic tiles were not part of the original decor. Tucked away almost out of sight in a corner of the precinct is a teak temple which is actually Wat Phra That Lampang Luang's holy of holies. It houses a little Buddha, behind strong bars, which is supposed to have been carved from the same piece of jade as the Emerald Buddha, although it may only be a copy of the original, referred to earlier, which since 1778 has been in Bangkok.

A small temple museum nearby holds several precious objects, including red lacquered bookcases, Buddhas inlaid with gemstones, a head of

Buddha in the Chiang Mai style, wooden carvings with animal motifs and several "thongs". The figures of Buddha in the promenade along the inner wall are also worth seeing.

★Wat Mon Cham Sin

Wat Mon Cham Sin, on a small rise near Highway 1 to Chiang Mai, is also worth a visit for its three beautiful Burmese-style chedis, but above all for the striking views over the surrounding landscape.

Wat Phra That

Wat Phra That, 16km/10 miles north-east of Lampang, dates from the early days of the Lan Na kingdom (early 14th c.) and is in the Chiang Mai style. The large 17th/18th c. wiharn, with its three stepped roofs, looks like three houses pushed into one.

★★Landscape

The countryside north of Lampang is covered by dense almost untouched mountain forests, interspersed with deep ravines and towered over by rugged cliffs. The peak of Doi Khun Tan rises to 1348m/4423ft and there is a good view of it from the train and from Highway 11 to Chiang Mai.

Pratu Pa

Pratu Pa, the "gateway to the forest", is 50km/31 miles along Highway 1 to Chiang Rai where it narrows down to pass between the high cliffs on either side. The little temple is dedicated to the guardian spirit who resides there (there is another "Pratu" a couple of miles out of Lampang on the road to Chiang Mai).

Young Elephant Training Centre

A couple of miles further on there are signs to the Elephant Training Centre where young elephants are trained to become working animals. Public training sessions are held daily, between 7 and 11am but closed on Buddhist holidays.

★Tham Pu Thai Cave

After another 10km/6 miles Highway 1 passes the Tham Pua Thai cave, one of Thailand's largest and most interesting limestone caverns. Apart from the cave's stalactites and stalagmites nearby Nagao has no other sights.

"Pratu Pa", on the road to Chiang Mai

Ban Thung Kawaen Snake Market

Ban Thung Kawaen, a little place on Highway 11 about 16km/10 miles from Lampang in the direction of Chiang Mai, is notable for the daily snake market held in its centre. The snakes, some of them poisonous, are caught by children in the surrounding countryside; their sale is, strictly speaking, forbidden. Snakemeat, which has no particular flavour of its own and is therefore usually cooked in chicken broth, is mostly eaten by the Chinese Thais, who consider it something of a delicacy.

Lamphun C 2

Region: North Thailand
Province: Lamphun
Altitude: 295m/968ft. Population: 26,000

ลำพูน

Location

About 24km/15 miles south of Chiang Mai, Lamphun, on the right bank of a tributary of the Menam Ping, the Menam Kuang, is rather isolated, having been bypassed by the main road, so it still retains all the atmosphere typical of northern Thailand. This impression is particularly striking if instead of Highway 11 you take Highway 106, the older and more scenic road, lined by tall yang trees and with a whole host of interesting temples, ancient and modern, strung out along it like a string of pearls.

The people of Lamphun and the surrounding area make their living from farming and fruit-growing and from weaving the silks for which, along with its traditional silverwork, the town is famous.

The village of Pa Sang, about 10km/6 miles from Lamphun, is well known as a centre for hand-woven cotton.

Access

By car: south on Highway 11 or, much the prettier way, on 106 from Chiang Mai (about 26km/16 miles). Taxi from Chiang Mai.
By bus: several times a day from Chang Puak bus station in Chiang Mai.
By rail: on the Bangkok–Chiang Mai line (729km/453 miles from Bangkok).

History

Originally the centre of the Haripunchai kingdom, the city that was to become Lamphun retained its importance in the Lan Na kingdom, founded in the late 13th c. by King Mengrai and allied to the Mon empire. Modern times have done little to alter the venerable nature of the present-day city. Its people are also deemed to be the guardians of the north Thai dialect, virtually a language in its own right with many elements of the Mon tongue that was banned for a time under King Rama V but is now taught again in some schools.

According to legend this town of Haripunchai was first built for a relic of Buddha in Wat Phra That but soon took the form of a fortified city, founded and ruled over by the Mon princess Chama Devi (*c.* 650–700), brought here from Lopburi. As a principality Haripunchai lasted for about 600 years and only lost its independence with its conquest by King Mengrai (1281), when it was burnt to the ground. The first capital of the new Lan Na kingdom was at Kum Kam (now Saraphi), between Lamphun and Chiang Mai. (Important finds made in Saraphi around 1980 are currently being worked on for public access in the near future.)

Mengrai soon abandoned the new city, however, since it was constantly being flooded out by the Menam Ping, and the story tells us that the three kings of the three adjoining kingdoms – Mengrai, Ramkhamhaeng and Nareng Muang – chose the site for their new joint capital after climbing a mountain together to select it from the summit.

In 1369 King Kuna summoned the scholar monk Sumana here from Sukhothai to spread the teachings of Theravada Buddhism. These generally ran counter to those of Mahayana Buddhism, whose followers included the Mon peoples. Sumana also brought with him the relic which had so miraculously divided itself in two (see Chiang Mai, Wat Suan Dok) and King Kuna built Lamphun's Wat Phra Yun to house it – the relic stayed here until taken to Chiang Mai and Wat Suan Dok. In 1556 the Burmese captured

Snake-market in Lampang

the city as well as Chiang Mai, and both cities remained under foreign rule until 1775, when they were liberated by King Taksin. In 1873 they became part of the kingdom of Siam, under King Rama V, along with the whole of the former Lan Na kingdom. The city of Haripunchai became Lamphun, and today, like neighbouring Chiang Mai, it is the capital city of a province with a population of around 400,000.

Sights

There are about 50 temples in and around Lamphun. The most important ones are described below, but its greatest glory is Wat Phra That Haripunchai. It is also the most visited of all the temples, but there are others whose beautiful architecture makes them equally worth seeing.

★★Wat Phra That Haripunchai

Wat Phra That Haripunchai, a place of pilgrimage for the whole of Thailand, stands on the site of the former royal palace which lay outside the city wall, part of which is still visible. It is best viewed from the river end, as was originally intended. Here the visitor is greeted by two great lions, an unmistakable sign of the Burmese influence on the temple's architecture.

On the left, before reaching the actual temple complex, there is a smaller, plainer wiharn containing a reclining Buddha, 15m/49ft long.

The history of the wat dates back to 876 when the Mon king Atityaraj built a mondhop to hold a relic of the Buddha (a hair or a skull fragment). The chedi which took its place was modified and made taller over the centuries but its present height (58m/190ft) and appearance are roughly as they would have been in the 16th c. and fairly typical of the chedis of that period. The richly articulated base and upper part are covered in ornamental gilded copper plates with a nine-tier gold canopy on the tip of the spire. Once a year a ceremonial procession takes place when the chedi is washed down with holy water.

The Burmese-style tower east of the chedi holds the 13th c. temple gong, one of the largest in the world, with a diameter of about 2m/7ft. Almost all the present temple buildings are 20th c., including the wiharn, built in 1925

1 Lion statue
2 Great Viharn
3 Library
4 Gong
5 Great Chedi
6 Viharn
7 Open halls
8 Stepped Chedi
9 Old Museum
10 Monks' quarters
11 Bot
12 Kitten
13 School building
14 Administration
15 Drum

© Baedeker

but in the ancient style. Beautiful partly gilded carving embellishes the façades, doors and windows. Interesting features in the interior include a statue of Buddha in the Chiang Saen style, the lovely wooden ceiling and the richly decorated preaching stand. The wall paintings here and in the lobby have recently been restored.

The charming wooden library pavilion on the left side of the wiharn is also worth attention. Erected on the site of an older building in the 19th c. it has a top storey decorated with carving and inlay and a stepped roof. The old bookcases contain valuable palm-leaf manuscripts.

Past the large wiharn on the right there is an 8th c. brick chedi which once held 60 Buddha figures, 15 on each side. Only a few remain but on the square base, at the front of the chedi, there are three Buddhas in Chiang Saen style, one of which used to be shaded by a naga (the cobra's neck has been broken off). The inscriptions on these three statues are in the north Thai dialect which was banned from schools under King Rama V.

National Museum

At the rear of this large complex there is a little temple museum with some interesting figures of Buddha from various style periods, especially those in the Chiang Mai style with distinct Dvaravati features (open: Wed.–Sun. 9am–noon and 1–4pm). Other exhibits include several old engraved sema stones, bookcases, votive tablets, manuscripts, and some of the gold and silver vessels which were used for the ceremonial washing of the chedi. A number of other wiharns and monastery buildings, including an open pavilion with a fourfold footprint of Buddha, complete the complex.

In passing it is worth having a look at the typical northern Thai lacquerwork on the shutters of an otherwise plain building.

Surroundings

★Wat Kukut

Lamphun's second important temple, about half a mile out of town, is Wat Kukut, also known as Wat Chama Devi after the princess who first ruled Haripunchai. Her son, King Mahandayok, built the wat in the early 8th c. It is

Buddha figure in the Chiang-Saen style, with north-Thai inscription

Chedi in the Wat Kukut

worth visiting if only to see its two chedis which are magnificent examples of Mon architecture. The larger of the two, 21m/69ft high, holds Queen Chama Devi's ashes, and is the more important, even though lightning has robbed it of its spire. This is in fact how it acquired its present name – Ku in Thai means something like "chedi" and Kut stands for "with a broken-off spire". It rises from its mighty terraced plinth in five stories, with little chedis on the corners and three ornate niches at each level and on each side. These contain stucco Buddhas, 60 in all, and in various states of preservation, each originally with one hand raised in the gesture of dispelling fear, clearly showing the Khmer influence. Although most of them have their original bodies their heads have had to be renewed or restored in nearly every case.

The smaller chedi has kept the Mon style and also takes the form of a stepped pyramid with Buddhas in niches, accompanied by great demon figures.

★Wat Phra Yun

Another interesting temple, Wat Phra Yun, is about a mile north of Lamphun on the far bank of the Menam Kuang. It was built by King Kuna in 1369 for the scholar monk Sumana; in the early 16th c. a chedi was erected over the ruins of the mondhop that held the relic referred to earlier.

The figures of Buddha in the upper niches are mostly copies. A sandstone in the courtyard bears an inscription in Pali and Thai announcing the arrival of the holy Sumana.

The wiharn, containing three 16th c. standing Buddhas, the bot with beautiful gilded carving on the portal side, and the elegant library, all date from around 1900.

★Wat Saphoen

The distinguishing features of Wat Saphoen are the beautiful gilded carving on the gable, the massive teak pillars in the interior, and fine wooden timbered construction.

Children in the Karen village of Ban Kon Yang

★Wat San Kamphaeng

Fine carving also decorates Wat San Kamphaeng, and inside the wiharn the scene is set in red and gold. The chedi in the outer courtyard shows the Burmese influence.

Wat Phra Bat Takpha

One of the more modern temples, and highly venerated by the local people, Wat Phra Bat Takpha was built on a hill over a number of Buddha's footprints. The frescos inside its wiharn are by local artists.

Ban Kon Yang (Karen village)

The Karen village of Ban Kon Yang lies about 11km/7 miles beyond the village of Bang Hong, 40km/25 miles from Lamphun on Highway 106. Its inhabitants still wear their brightly coloured national dress and offer their handicrafts for sale.

Loei D 5

Region: North-east Thailand
Province: Loei
Altitude: 145m/176ft. Population: 18,000

เลย

Location

The township of Loei, the heart of one of Thailand's most beautiful provinces, lies on the northern end of the Dong Phaya Yen mountain chain, the watershed between the Menam Chao Phraya and the Mekong. About 50km/31 miles from the border with Laos, it has developed into a modest little regional capital, helped by cropping the local timber and fertile farming soil, but more especially by the mining of copper, manganese and other ores. Apart from the regular night market on Charoen Rat Road, however, Loei itself has nothing of interest, but the countryside around it is beautiful and unspoilt, especially in the Phu Kradung National Park.

Access

By car: Highway 1/21/203 from Bangkok (520km/323 miles), Highway 12 from Khon Khaen to Chum Phae, then 201 (209km/130 miles), 210/201 from Udon Thani (143km/89 miles).
By rail: nearest station Udon Thani.
By bus: from Bangkok Northern Terminal (10 hours) connections from Loei, Chum Phae and Udon Thani.

★★Phu Kradung National Park

Phu Kradung is the highest point in the province, and the National Park is on this high plateau at an altitude of between 227m/746ft and 1300m/4265ft. Founded in 1925 the park has precipitous cliffs, interesting and unusual flora and fauna, and pure, dry air, which also tends to be quite cool.

To get there take Highway 201 from Loei for 75km/47 miles then from the village of Ban Phuy Kradung it is another 7km/4 miles to the park entrance.

The park covers an area of about 350sq.km/135sq. miles and is criss-crossed by a good network of trails. It is best avoided at weekends and public holidays when it is crowded with people from Bangkok. During the rainy season (July to October) the park is generally closed.

The trek up to the plateau usually starts from Ban Si Than, and takes 4–5 hours. The trail between high rocks and through the dense jungle and bamboo thickets can be very steep in places, but there are steps, and railings for support, and eventually it emerges onto the plateau with its scattering of stone-pine groves. There is a wonderful view from the steep cliffs In March and April the rhododendrons and azaleas are in bloom, and there is a chance of a dip in one of the many pools and waterfalls.

In the forest live red deer and fallow deer, gibbons, wild boar and other forest animals – sometimes a bear, a panther, or even a tiger may be glimpsed. The park also has many species of birds (woodpeckers, peacocks and rare hornbills) and butterflies.

North-east of the park headquarters, which has some log cabins and tents, there is a relatively modern wat.

★Tham Erawan (elephant cave)

Tham Erawan, the elephant cave, lies 45km/28 miles before Loei, coming from Udon Thai. People probably lived there in prehistoric times. The climb

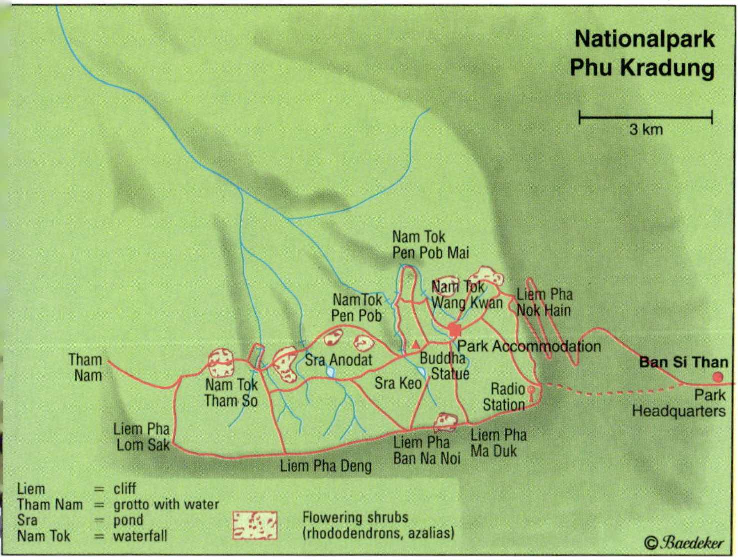

past a giant Erawan statue up to the cave, where light filters through holes and cracks into the lofty caverns, is quite difficult.

Chiang Khan

Chiang Khan, 53km/33 miles north of Loei, is on the banks of the Mekong, the frontier with Laos. Boats can be rented to travel down stream to the Kuang Kut rapids 4km/2½ miles to the south.

Lopburi G 4

Region: Central Thailand. Province: Lopburi
Altitude: 30m/98ft. Population: 46,000

ลพบุรี

Location

Lopburi, on the Menam Lopburi, is a city with a great and glorious past. On the northern rim of Thailand's central plain, it is the capital of a burgeoning province and its people live from growing rice, maize and cotton on the fertile river plain. Towering over the impressive scenery north of the town is Khao Wong Phra Chan, recognisable by the three jagged peaks that form its summit.

Access

By car: Highway 1 from Bangkok which makes a big loop, and one that is highly recommended, via Saraburi (see entry) and Wat Phra Buddhabat (about 153km/95 miles). The alternative is via Ayutthaya – Highway 32 to just before Singburi then 311 to the east.
By rail: about 2 hours on the Bangkok–Chiang Mai line (133km/83 miles from Bangkok).
By bus: regular service from Bangkok Northern Bus Terminal (3 hours).

History

Lopburi, or Lavo as it was then called, is supposed to have been founded in 468 by King Kalavarnadis of Taksila. Until about 950 it was the capital of the great Mon kingdom of Dvaravati, the name given it in the part Mon, part Sanskrit inscriptions on coins and stone tablets. This kingdom stretched north-east from the Menam plain to the Mekong and lasted until the 11th c.

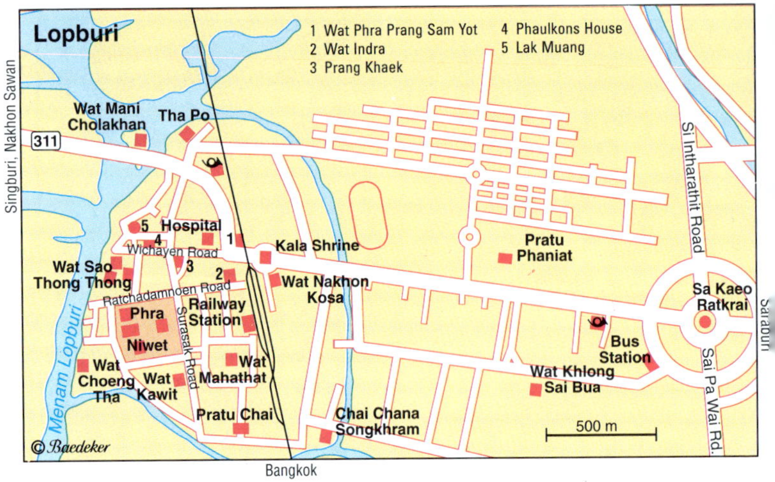

when the Khmer, under their king Suryavarman I (1002–50), captured large parts of what is now Thailand. Lopburi became a Khmer fortress and the seat of a provincial governor. The Khmer style that shaped art and architecture until the 15th c. became modified by contact with Dvaravati to form the Lopburi style, a blend of the two.

Following the end of Khmer rule the land in the southern Menam plain was occupied by the Thai king, Si Dharmatraipitok. The kings of Lopburi ruled the kingdom for about a hundred years then power was assumed by various different royal houses, including the Burmese King Annarudha and the Thai King U Thong who, when he moved his seat in 1350 from U Thong to Auyutthaya, installed his son, Prince Ramesuen, as Governor of Lopburi.

The city was of strategic importance in the fighting with the kings of Sukhothai. When this became a vassal state in 1376 and then part of Ayutthaya in 1438 Lopburi lost its importance, only regaining it when the city experienced a new heyday in the reign of King Narai (1656–88). Ten years after coming to the throne Narai chose to adopt Lopburi as his second capital alongside Ayutthaya. It was less prone to flooding but at the same time, with the river, had a guaranteed water supply for city and palace alike. When Ayutthaya, close to the Gulf of Thailand, was threatened by a Dutch naval blockade Narai moved temporarily to Lopburi and built a palace here (and in Phetchaburi, see entry), an interesting mixture of Thai and European styles.

As King, Narai also opened up towards Europe, establishing diplomatic relations with France. He received King Louis XIV's ambassador, the Chevalier de Chaumont, and it is to his reports that we owe much of what we know about Lopburi. The King also appointed the Greek ambassador, Constantine Phaulkon, to serve as his adviser (see Famous People). When the king died in 1688 his Minister of War Luang Sorasak, later King Petracha, seized the throne, murdering Phaulkon and many of his predecessor's other supporters, local traders and the French diplomats among them. Not liking Lopburi he returned to Ayutthaya, abandoning the palace to dilapidation and ruin. This lasted until the 19th c. when King Mongkut (1851–68) ordered the restoration of the only still relatively well preserved building in the palace precinct, the Chanthara Phisan pavilion, and erected new palace buildings, some of which can be seen today and have been made into interesting museums.

Kala temple in Lopburi

Sights

Monument to King Narai

The monument to King Narai (Sa Kaeo Ratkrai), the greatest king in Lopburi's history, stands in the middle of the first traffic intersection on Highway 1 into the town. Further on, in a road to the right, are remains of the city wall and an old gate, the Pratu Phaniat. The arena that once stood here was where King Narai showed Chevalier de Chaumont and the other French diplomats how elephants were trained.

Kala Shrine

At the third roundabout, just before the railway line, stands the ruin of the 10th c. Shrine of Kala, the Hindu god of death. The new temple from 1953 stands on the foundations of the old shrine – the massive substructure is all that is left of the once very high laterite prang – and contains images of the god. It is worth noting the relief on the lintel which shows Vishnu lying on a snake. The hordes of monkeys, for which the shrine is famous, scamper around it, in and out of the banyan tree roots and the streets nearby, seemingly oblivious of the traffic.

Wat Nakhon Kosa

At Wat Nakhon Kosa, along the street to the left before the Kala Shrine, there are still some remains of a fine Khmer brick prang, probably part of a Hindu shrine before it was made into a Buddhist wat in the Ayutthaya period. An Ayutthaya style chedi and the ruins of a wiharn are also worth looking at.

The ruins to the west are of Wat Indra, probably dating from the Ayutthaya period.

★★Wat Phra Prang Sam Yot

Wat Phra Prang Sam Yot in Wichayen Road – the "temple of the three towers" – is probably the town's finest ruin. A classic example of Lopburi architecture, it has three prangs, joined together, each on a cruciform base with doorways on each side and connected by what was once a covered walkway with a long brick building that was faced with stucco. Plenty of its remains are still visible, such as pieces of decoration and the grotesque faces on a corner of the base wall. Console vaulting appears in the rooms

Wat Phra Prang Sam Yot: Temple of the Three Towers

and the towers, and in the interior there are some fragments of old Buddhas and the well-preserved figure of a seated Buddha from the Sukhothai period. Originally it was presumably a Hindu temple, with the three prangs symbolising Vishnu, Shiva and Brahma, and only later converted to a Buddhist wat.

Wat Phra Si Ratana Mahathat

This large and impressive wat, on Nakala Road in the western part of town, was probably already an important shrine when the Khmer built it in the 12th c. A very tall slender laterite prang, in the Lopburi style, stands in the centre, decorated with beautiful stucco work. The main entrance to the prang is marked by a small lobby with a tower on top, and there are still signs of a gallery laid out as a quadrangle. Within this, leading to another gallery, stands the wiharn. It has bow windows, a very unusual stylistic feature showing that it was added by King Narai.

In the second courtyard and outside the second gallery there are a number of large and small chedis of different styles but mainly Ayutthaya, some of them with niches containing Buddha figures. The temple precinct has been remodelled several times, but mainly during the reign of the Ayutthaya kings.

★★Phra Narai Ratcha Niwet (King Narai's Palace)

Entrance
Surasak Road

Opening times
daily 8am–6pm

Admission fee

The main entrance to King Narai's Palace (as it came to be called at the time of the major renovations by King Rama IV in the 19th c.) is on Surasak Road, but it can also be entered from the side on the river. This would have had the landing stage where most kings would have arrived in Lopburi, since they tended to travel here by river. However, the tour that follows starts at the main entrance.

Tour

The palace precinct is divided up by walls, with gateways, into several courtyards. The most interesting features are to be found in the inner courtyard.

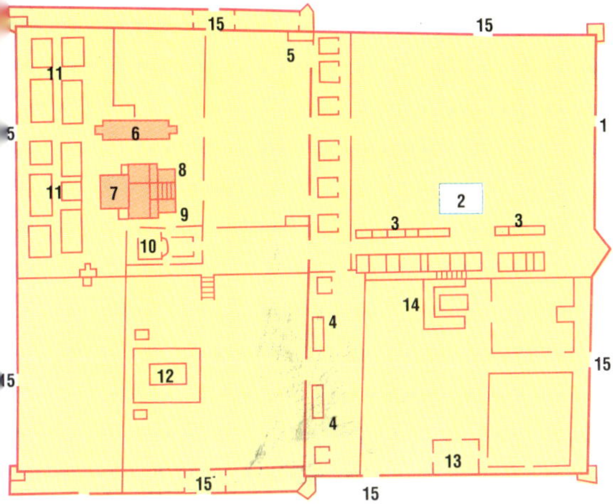

Lopburi

Phra Narai Ratcha Niwet

1 Main entrance
2 Water storage
3 Magazine
4 Stables for elephants and horses
5 Palace guard
6 Chanthara Phisan
7 Phiman Mongkut
8 Armoury
9 Reading room
10 Dusit Sawan Thanya Maha Prasat
11 "Harem"
12 Sutthasawan
13 Phra Chao Hao
14 Reception hall
15 Gates

The whole compound is enclosed in majestic walls topped by battlements. Large parts of the old complex are 17th c. and were designed and built by King Narai. The more modern buildings added later owe their appearance to King Mongkut who had many buildings demolished and put new ones in their place, apart, that is, from the Chanthara Phisan Pavilion which was in a relatively good state of preservation and therefore worth restoring.

Reception hall for foreign visitors

Starting the tour at the main entrance on Surasak Road, this gateway is where fate is supposed to have caught up with Constantine Phaulkon (see Famous People), whose residence is another of the sights of Lopburi. Lured to the palace on the pretext of being summoned to the presence of the dying king, the Greek adviser was grabbed by henchmen of Luang Sorasak, the Minister of War who had seized power, and subsequently beheaded.

En route to the next courtyard, also entered through a monumental gateway, there are several structures that are of interest. The traces of buildings can still be discerned to the right and left of the path. However what they were used for has never been clear, not even from the old documents, although it is reported that on his deathbed the King asked for some precious garments to be brought to him from one of these twelve halls, so they may have been treasure chambers.

Behind them to the right are the old brick water tanks which are fed by springs on a hill in the eastern part of the town. Italian and French engineers were commissioned to build a hydraulic system to pump the water to the palace, and it is supposed to have taken ten years' hard work to get it running properly. Beyond the water tanks, in a pleasant park setting, is the Phra Khlang Supharat which was the reception hall for foreign visitors.

Just before the second gate, on the left, are parts of the outer wall of the royal elephant stables. The statues on the grass beyond the portal are in the Dvaravati style and include items brought here from places outside Lopburi as well. A few ruins are all that remain of a pool and the armouries and magazines nearby.

Chanthara Phisan Pavilion
★National Museum

Opening times
Wed.–Sun.
8.30am–noon and 1–4.30pm

Admission fee

No photographs

In the second courtyard, on the right, the Chanthara Phisan Pavilion, restored by King Mongkut and now a national museum, was the residence of King Narai. Built in about 1665, it has a balcony on the front from which King Narai greeted his guests. The pavilion holds a throne, and the walls were covered with mirrors brought here by the Chevalier de Chaumont, the ambassador of Louis XIV of France. Originally just one big room, the pavilion was divided into two during the restoration by King Mongkut. The second room has a painting by an unknown artist showing the arrival of the French delegation. In the actual audience chamber are two magnificent wooden thrones and a number of beautifully carved gilded bookcases.

★Phra Thinang Visuthivinitchai

The building on the left of the Chanthara Phisan Pavilion is the three-storied Phra Thinang Visuthivinitchai, built by King Mongkut. The west wing was the Phiman Mongkut Pavilion; the top floor contained the king's apartments (large bedroom, study and gunroom) and the bottom floor rooms were for offices and giving audience. The pavilions now serve as museums displaying Dvaravati and Lopburi sculpture, votive tablets, arms, faïence and panelling (opening times as National Museum).

"Harem"

Behind the royal palace in a secluded courtyard were the living quarters of the King's many wives and children (part of this is now a museum of agricultural implements). Even during King Mongkut's time this part of the compound could only be entered by the chosen few; it was still absolutely forbidden to have contact with members of the royal family, a ban that lasted until its abolition by Rama V, King Chulalongkorn.

Royal Hall of Audience

On the left of the Phiman Mongkut Pavilion and surrounded by high walls are the ruins of the Dusit Sawan Thanya Maha Prasat, the royal hall of audience. Fragments indicate that the façade was European in appearance, with Gothic arches over the doors, for example, but the rear was Classical Thai. It was probably the tallest building in the whole of the palace compound and is reported as having a pyramid shaped roof, similar to the Dusit Maha Prasat in the Grand Palace in Bangkok. The interior must have been magnificent. The walls were covered with mirrors, a present from

Louis XIV, and according to Nicholas Gervais, a member of the French delegation, the hall was full of frescos, mosaic floors, Chinese crystal and porcelain and, at the end, had a throne 2m/6½ft tall, which the king reached by climbing a flight of marble steps.

Sutthasawan Hall

The foundations of the Sutthasawan Hall, where King Narais lived and, on July 11th 1688, died, are in the adjoining gardens. Some of the large laterite slabs were taken to Bangkok in the early 19th c. and used in the building of Wat Sakhet. According to Nicolas Gervais, the roof was covered with yellow glazed bricks and the roof-beams were richly ornated with gold. Around the building there were four pools where the king was wont to bathe, and if the sun was shining they would be shaded by an enormous baldachin. The king also had a little cave built by one of the pools.

In the south-east courtyard are another two private reception halls, including King Narai's well preserved Phra Chao Hao, with more pools and store rooms, stabling and the living quarters of the guard.

Other Sights

Wat Sao Thong Thong

Wat Sao Thong Thong, an early Ayutthaya temple, lies north of the palace near the river bank. In King Narai's time the wiharn, on a high plinth with long narrow lotus-blossom shaped windows and a stepped roof, was used as a Christian chapel and the large seated Buddha inside still carries the crucifix. The pillars are decorated with leafy capitals and there are Lopburi-style Buddhas in the wall niches. King Narai built the pavilions near the monastery buildings to house his foreign guests.

★Phaulkon's Palace (Chao Phaya Vichayen)

Opening times
daily 8am–6pm

Admission fee

Phaulkon's Palace is near the river on the Wichayen Road north of Wat Sao Thong Thong. A number of buildings had been erected for Chevalier de Chaumont. Phaulkon's palace is a large three-storey building in a mixture of European and Thai styles. The compound, surrounded by a 2m/6½ft-high wall, also had in it a kitchen (at the back on the left), stables (right) and baths, a church with a house for the Catholic priest, with a

Gate of the Royal Palace

Phaulkon's Palace

free-standing belfry, and a single-storey audience pavilion, all now in ruins. The three monumental gateways in the southern wall, which were once the entrance to the palace, have been well preserved and the central one now serves to gain admission to the very pleasant precinct.

Lak Muang

North-west of Phaulkon's Palace the Lak Muang stands guard over the city's foundation stone.

Fortifications

Fort Tha Po in the north-west, and Fort Chai Chana Songkhram and Pratu Chai in the south still remain from the massive fortifications that surrounded Lopburi. French engineers also built dams and sluice-gates in the north of the town for a large reservoir. King Narai built a pleasure palace, the Phra Thinang Yen Kraiso Sahavarat Pavilion, or the Yen Pavilion for short, on an island in the lake, now filled in. With imagination it is still possible to get some idea from the ruins of how beautiful it must have been.

Wat Mani Cholakhan

Right of Highway 311 to Chainat there is another fine chedi, full of niches, in the Ayutthaya style, which was once part of Wat Mani Cholakhan. Further along the road, at Ban Tha Klong, stands Wat Klai which has very fine stucco reliefs on the wiharn and bot and a seated Buddha in the Ayutthaya style.

Mae Hong Son B 1

Region: North Thailand
Province: Mae Hong Son
Altitude: 1500m/4923ft
Population: 15,000

แม่ฮ่องสอน

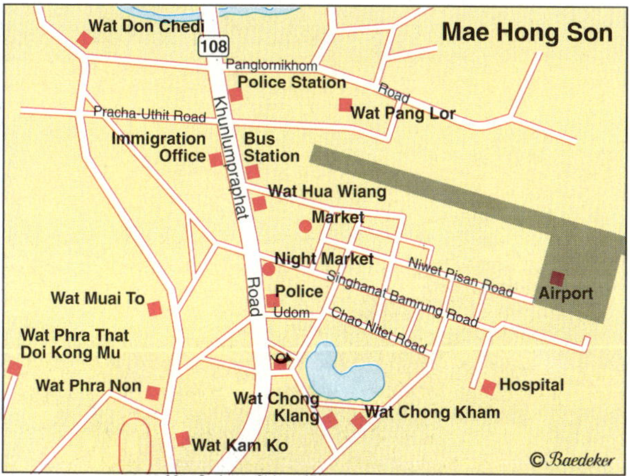

Mae Sariang, Chiang Mai

Location

The principal attraction of Mae Hong Son township, high in the mountains of northern Thailand on the Burmese border, lies in the rugged scenery and dense forests of its mist-shrouded valley, but it has another, more sinister claim to fame, which the Thai government would rather forget, and that is its proximity to the "Golden Triangle". As the authorities have increasingly clamped down on the opium-growing and drug-dealing in Chiang Rai's part of the "Golden Triangle" so the smugglers and dealers have turned to new routes in the mountainous frontier country behind Mae Hong Son.

Access

By car: Highway 107 north from Chiang Mai, turning onto Highway 1095 before Mae Taeng (130km/81 miles); Highway 108 from Mae Sarieng (about 170km/106 miles). Anyone who appreciates breathtaking scenery should follow the rather more difficult "horseshoe route", 380km/236 miles, from Chiang Mai via Hot and Mae Sarieng.
By bus: a 7–8 hour journey from Chiang Mai.
By air: 2 or 3 times a day from Chiang Mai (flights last about 30 min.).

Sights

★★Scenery

The mountain scenery around Mae Hong Son is among the most beautiful in Thailand, as already becomes evident on the way there. Mae Hong Son is a good base for trekking and rafting, whether for one or more days on an organised trip or as an individual.

Markets

The town is also a good place to see people from the hill tribes, especially when they come in for the daily market in the early morning between 5.30 and 8am. Meo, Karen, Lawa, Lisu and Lahu all sell their handicrafts there, along with locally-grown produce – fruit and vegetables, tobacco, betelnuts, etc.

★Wat Chong Kham
Wat Chong Klang

The two Burmese temples, Wat Chong Kham and Wat Chong Klang, stand next to one another by the little lake in the south of the town. The Wat Chong Klang wiharn holds over 30 statues, brought here from Burma around 1860. Opening times: Daily 8am–6pm. Admission fee.

★★Buat Luk Khaeo Festival

The Buat Luk Khaeo Festival, when young boys between 10 and 13 are ordained as novice monks ("nakh"), is celebrated here, where it is called Poy Sang Long, with more colourful ceremony than anywhere else in Thailand. It takes place in Wat Chong Kham at the beginning of April every year. Their youth means that the novices do not have to observe all the

Wat Chong Kham temple in Mae Hong Son

strictest ordinances, but the three-day ceremony traditionally begins with them having their heads shaved in the house of the richest lad on the first day. On the second day they receive presents then on the third day they set aside their ornate costumes of the first two days and receive the saffron habit of the monk. On the first day a sight particularly worth seeing is when the youngsters are borne on the shoulders of a swaying procession into the temple.

★★Wat Pra That Doi Kong Mu

It takes half an hour from the western edge of Mae Hong Son to climb the 250m/820ft Doi Kong Mu to the hilltop monastery of Wat Phra That Doi Kong Mu, with two Burmese chedis that can be seen lit up at night from down in the town. The ascent is quite an experience; in the middle of the forest, two enormous stone lions, in the Burmese style, guard the foot of the overgrown staircase covering the last few feet to the top. There are fine views over the town and the countryside.

Fish Cave (Tharn Pla)

The Fish Cave, on Highway 108, 17km/10½ miles north of the town, holds a pool – fed by a small river nearby – full of various kinds of exotic fish.

Shan Villages

For decades, although without much success so far, the Shan peoples have been fighting for their independence from Burma and from Thailand. They can still give visitors a hostile reception, so anyone going there should be accompanied by a local guide who is also known to be acceptable to the Shan.

Kuomintang Village

The village of the Kuomintang, here called the Mae Aw, is 20km/12 miles north-west of Mae Hong Son (Highway 108). The Chinese who live here are the direct descendants of General Chiang Kai-shek's Nationalist troops who after losing the war against Communist China fled to Burma, and then Thailand, where the government tolerated them, instead of following their leader to Formosa, now Taiwan. Many of the men work for the Thai police or as guards and officials along the Thai–Burmese border.

Two Pradong women

Pradong Village (longnecks)

The village of the Pradong is an hour and a half's travelling north-west of Mae Hong Son and only a couple of miles from the border with Myanmar. Little was known of this hill tribe until a few years ago when about 50 of them moved over the border into Thailand and made their presence known. It is not clear where they come from but their costume, traditions and habits indicate a northern Burmese origin.

From the age of four girls have golden rings put round their necks. Until they reach the age of 25 these are added at regular intervals and the number can reach 25.

Getting to see this "tourist attraction" is not cheap. The main reason for moving over the border was for the "longnecks" to be able to profit from Thailand's tourism, so as well as having to pay to get into the village it is necessary to pay to take their photograph as well.

Mae Rim

See Chiang Mai, Surroundings

Mae Sai

See Chiang Rai, Surroundings

Mae Sot

See Tak, Surroundings

Nakhon Nayok G 5

Region: East Thailand
Province: Nakhon Nayok
Altitude: 11m/36ft. Population: 18,000

นครนายก

Location

Nakhon Nayok is a provincial capital on the north-eastern edge of the great rice-growing plain of the Menam Chao Phraya which becomes densely forested hill country immediately behind the town. Its main attraction is Wang Takrai, a national park famed as one of the most beautiful in Thailand, and very popular with the people of Bangkok at weekends.

Access

By car: Highway 1 from Bangkok, then 305 just beyond the airport (110km/68 miles). Much prettier, if somewhat longer, variations are Highway 1 to Hin Kong (94km/58 miles) then Highway 33.
By bus: from Bangkok Northeastern Bus Terminal (137km/85 miles).

Wang Takrai National Park

To get to Wang Takrai Park from Nakhon Nayok take Highway 33 for 6km/4 miles then fork right and the park is in a hilly river valley 11km/7 miles further on. It covers an area of 80ha/198 acres and was laid out in 1955 by Prince Chumbot who is commemorated by a memorial on the river bank. When he died in 1959 his wife carried on his work and opened the park up to the public. She created a kind of botanical gardens full of native and imported trees and shrubs in a setting of lawns and parkland. There are bungalows for overnight accommodation.

Chao Pu Khun Dan (rock temple)

The way to the park passes the Chao Po Khun Dan rock temple, named after one of the close confidants of King Naresuen (1590–1605). Several gilded Buddhas stand under a rock wall. The gold was donated by the local people to show their gratitude to Chao Po Khun Dan, whom they believe is the guardian spirit of the mountains.

Nam Tok Nang Rong (waterfall)

The road to the left before the park entrance leads, after 5km/3 miles, to the Nam Tok Nang Rong waterfall, cascading over three rock ledges down into the valley. By climbing some stone steps it is possible to reach the rocks above the falls and watch this natural spectacle from there, although it is only worth seeing in the rainy season. Footpaths lead through the dense forest.

Nam Tok Sarika (waterfall)

Another waterfall worth visiting is Nam Tok Sarika, reached by Highways 3049/3050. The water crashes 70m/230ft down from the rocks onto the stone slabs in the valley below. Here, and at Nam Tok Nang Rong, there are a number of little restaurants.

Nakhon Pathom H 3

Region: West Thailand
Province: Nakhon Pathom
Altitude: 8m/26ft. Population: 63,000

นครปฐม

Location

The only indication that the city of Nakhon Pathom, about 50km/31 miles west of Bangkok, once stood on the Gulf of Thailand is the evidence in history books. In fact the rivers of the central plain accumulated so much silt and sand that the sea retreated those thirty odd miles, but despite its changed geographical setting Nakhon Pathom continues as a thriving trading city. It also holds within its walls the greatest Buddhist monument in Thailand and beyond, the Phra Pathom Chedi.

Access

By car: Highway 4 (Petchkasem Highway) from Bangkok (56km/35 miles).
By rail: an hour from Bangkok–Hualampong.

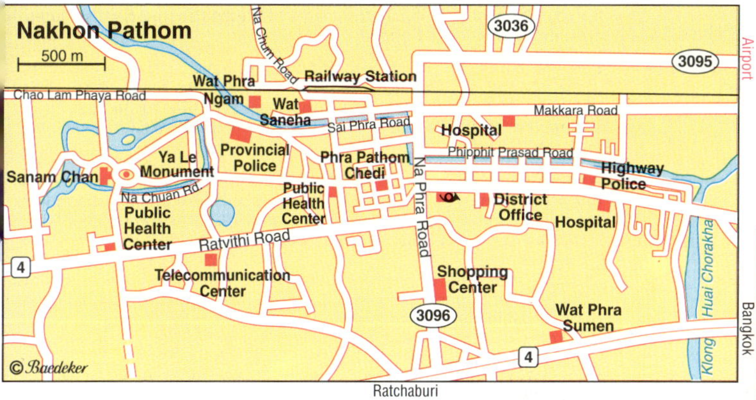

By bus: from Bangkok Southern Bus Terminal every 30 minutes from 5am. Tour operators offer day excursions, often linked with a visit to the floating market at Damnoen Saduak (see Ratchaburi) and the Rose Garden.

History

Although the earliest origins of Nakhon Pathom are shrouded in legend, the city is certainly one of the oldest on Thai soil. In the 3rd c. B.C. King Ashoka (273–231B.C.), who ruled over a great Indian empire, sent missionary monks to where the city stands today to preach the new doctrine of (Theravada) Buddhism. This must have been when the first chedi was built on the Phra Pathom site, but nothing is known of what it looked like.

Nakhon Pathom certainly existed after A.D. 675, when it was the centre of the city state of King Chaisiri (also Chaisi or Sirichai). Most of the population were Mon descendants, their culture very much influenced by the Indo-Buddhist Gupta style (as is borne out by finds of stone wheels of the law, Buddha figures, etc. from this period).

Nakhon Pathom followed U Thong as capital of the mighty Dvaravati kingdom. The wealth of the city is attested to by its entitlement to its own coinage; 7th/8th c. silver coins have the symbol of wealth on one side – a cow and calf, or a vase of flowers – and an inscription in Sanskrit on the other, reading "Sridvaravati Svarapunya" (credit of the Dvaravati King). Whether the Dvaravati Kingdom and its capital of Nakhon Pathom were conquered by the Burmese under King Annarudha is uncertain; historians tend to suppose it was destroyed either by King Suryavarman I (1002–50) or Jayavarman VII (1181–1218). The city then faded into oblivion, and most of its occupants left to found the new city of Nakhon Chaisi on the right bank of the Ta Chin river, where it still is today. The Phra Pathom Chedi was gradually swallowed up by the jungle. Its importance was not recognised again until Rama IV, King Mongkut, made a pilgrimage to the chedi during his time as a monk. When he came to the throne in 1851 he ordered its restoration. Since the old temple was in ruins he built a new chedi over the original Khmer dome-shaped shrine. This was actually finished by his successor, King Chulalongkorn, since part of the building collapsed during a storm.

Sights

Prang

At the western edge of the city, approaching on Highway 4 from Bangkok, there is a whitewashed prang on a square base. This is supposed to be the oldest Buddhist building in Thailand, older even than Phra Pathom Chedi. Close by archaeologists have discovered traces of the foundations and terrace of a sacred building, fragments of friezes decorated with figures, and several images of Buddha.

★★Phra Pathom Chedi

Opening times
daily 8am–5pm

Phra Pathom Chedi, "holiest and first among chedis", stands in the centre of the city and, at 118m/387ft, or 127m/417ft including the terraces, is the tallest Buddhist monument in the world, taller even than the famous Shwe Dagon, the Golden Pagoda in Rangoon (Myanmar; 99m/326ft, completed in 1773).

Legend

A figure in the wiharn on the north side of the precinct is supposed to be of King Phya Kong, who played a part in the legend surrounding the origin of the chedi. When an astrologer told him that one day his son would kill him he had his son put out into the forest where he was found by a woman who brought him up. As a young man the son, called Phya Pan, entered the service of the King of Ratchaburi, who was a vassal of the king of the neighbouring kingdom Nakhon Chaisi. Phya Pan's great wisdom and prudence brought him to the attention of the king, who adopted him. Phya Pan persuaded him to wage war against his feudal lord and during the ensuing battle killed his own father. As was the custom, after the victory he married the queen, his mother, but then learnt the story of his origins. The dagoba he built as an act of atonement was the predecessor of the Phra Pathom Chedi and is today concealed within it.

Precinct

The great chedi stands on a circular terrace in the middle of a square park, surrounded by a lattice-work wall, with the main entrance on the north side. The broad flight of steps leading up to the first terrace is edged by stone banisters inlaid with faïence and richly decorated with ornamentation and seven-headed nagas. The bot, one of the buildings on the terrace, holds a very fine Buddha of clear quartzite, overlaid with lacquer and gold leaf. This Dvaravati-style figure shows the Buddha seated in the European pose, "the Buddha of the future". There are three replicas of this statue, all of which used to belong to Nakhon Pathom's Wat Na Phra Men, of which only a few bricks are left. One copy now stands in the Wat Phra Men in Ayutthaya and the other two are in the National Museum in Bangkok.

On its circular base the massive dome (anda; 98m/322ft in diameter), shaped like a bell or a monk's begging bowl, stands on a series of tapering orange-glazed, curved cornices, and is topped by a square platform, symbolising the shrine standing on the top of the world. The conical spire is made up of a number of overlapping rings, the ceremonial canopy symbolising the solemn dignity of the Buddha. The colonnade round the base of the chedi is broken up by four wiharns at symmetrical intervals.

Phra Pathom Chedi

1 Upper terrace
2 Gallery
3 Viharn
4 Miniature mountain
5 Museum
6 Bot
7 Bell-towers
8 Chinese stove
9 Replica of the Khmer Prang
10 Model of the Nakhon Si Thammarat Chedi

100 m

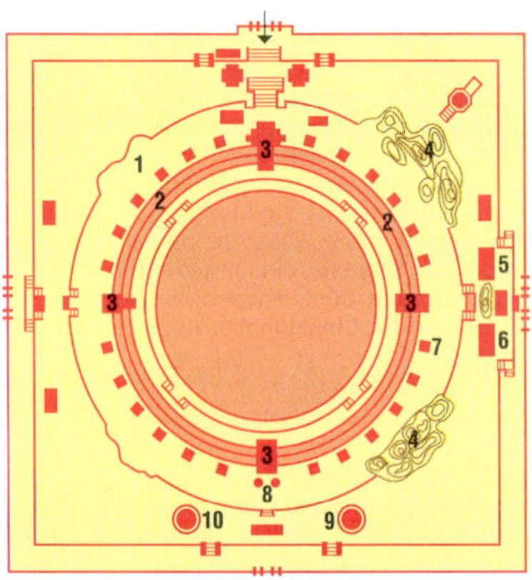

Buddhist figure outside the new Temple Museum

Temple museums

Opening times
Wed.–Sun.
9am–noon and
1–4pm

Admission fee

The old temple museum, containing Mon stucco and stone sculpture, is in the wiharn north of the east entrance. The new museum, the more interesting of the two, dates from 1979 and is by the south steps. On the outside there are stone wheels of the law from Nakhon Pathom's earliest days while displays inside include those of coins and everyday objects plus statues of Buddha (including some very fine ones in Mon style), stone and terracotta sculpture, the reconstruction of a bas relief of the Chulapradit Chedi, and an original bas relief from Wat Sai, south of Nakhon Pathom, showing the Buddha preaching before his first disciples.

Nearby is the model of the Khmer prang, the original monument over which King Mongkut erected the present chedi, and a replica of the famous chedi of Wat Mahathat at Nakhon Si Thammarat (see entry).

Where the stairs on the north side carry on to the top terrace it is worth noting the two salas in the Javanese style in the bottom part, before passing on to the double colonnade containing the four wiharns. The inner terrace, with 24 little towers holding bronze bells, is on the other side of the red lacquered gates. On the two terraces there are a number of Chinese stone figures, used as ballast for junks, two tall Chinese stoves, plant tubs and several salas. This is also a way to reach the monks' living quarters in the south-east of the temple compound.

Wiharns

The four wiharns consist of an open lobby and an inner room. The lobby of the northern wiharn has an 8m/26ft-high statue of a standing Buddha in the Sukhothai style, with the hands and feet of a stone figure found at Sawankhalok, Sukhothai, around 1915. The body was cast in bronze in Bangkok. The Phra Ruang Rojanarit, as the statue is called, is gilded and highly revered. An inscription on the wall of the wiharn says that the ashes of King Mongkut are interred in the plinth. The groups of figures on display in the wiharn depict the scene where two princesses show their reverence for the

◀ *Phra Pathom Chedi, the tallest Buddhist building in the world* newborn Siddharta (Buddha), and, one of the most important scenes from the life of the Buddha, how after forty days of fasting the beasts of the jungle brought him food. The southern wiharn has some beautiful stone carvings and, in a little niche in the wall, the figure of Phya Pan (6th/7th c., see Legend). The lobby of the western wiharn holds a 9m/30ft-long reclining Buddha, with another, smaller one in the inner room.

Temple Festival

Every year pilgrims from all over Thailand flock to Nakhon Pathom's grand temple festival in November. The chedi itself is lit up with fairy lights while classical dance drama, shadow plays and other entertainments take place on the terraces, and the great square at its foot is turned into an amusement park.

Other Sights

Sanam Chan Palace

In 1910, before he came to the throne, Rama VI built the Sanam Chan Palace in the north-west of the town. Standing in large grounds and connected by a broad avenue to the west gate of the Chedi, it has some interesting buildings in a mixture of Thai and European styles. The audience chamber has been kept in the Bangkok style. A little shrine contains the Hindu god Ganesha, with the head of an elephant and a human body with many arms. The curious-looking statue of a dog in front of the Chali Mongkol Asana, as the building is called, is probably meant to be Ya Le, the favourite dog of King Rama IV. These buildings now house provincial government offices.

Wat Phra Ngam

Wat Phra Ngam, west of Nakhon Pathom railway station, was built in the Bangkok style by King Chulalongkorn on the foundations of a Dvaravati temple.

Surroundings

Rose Garden

Opening times
daily 8am–6pm

Admission fee

The Rose Garden, 32km/20 miles south-west of Bangkok on the way to Nakhon Pathom, covers 20ha/49 acres, and its mainly Italian gardens are popular with golfers (18-hole golf course) and tired city-dwellers. There are restaurants on the Menam Chao Phraya serving western, Chinese and Thai food, and bungalow hotels, some with swimming pools and tennis courts. These need to be booked in good time, especially for Christmas and Easter.

The entertainment at 3 o'clock every afternoon gives visitors an opportunity to watch – and above all photograph – domestic and rural Thai ceremonies, elephants at work, traditional Thai dancing, sports and games, etc. and to follow this with an elephant ride.

Nakhon Phanom — D 8

นครพนม

Region: North-east Thailand
Province: Nakhon Phanom
Altitude: 138m/453ft. Population: 34,000

Location

The provincial capital Nakhon Phanom is in the extreme north-east of Thailand on the Mekong, and hence the frontier with Laos. On clear days the Laotian mountains beyond the town of Thakhek and the forests on the opposite bank of the river can be seen. During the Vietnam War, when there was an American base and radio interception station 12km/7 miles west of the town, Nakhon Phanom was a temporary haven for many thousands of refugees. Apart from a couple of busy markets, there is nothing to see in the town itself but its good hotels, some of which were established here to cater for the Americans, are a good base for trips to places in the surrounding area. Wat Phra That Phanom is famous for its annual Phansa festival week in January which attracts a great many pilgrims and stages events such as boat races and folk dances.

Access

By car: Highways 213/22 from Kalasin (98km/61 miles).
By bus: from Bangkok Northeastern Bus Terminal (727km/452 miles) and Kalasin.
By air: daily from Bangkok.

A performance in the Rose Garden

Surroundings

★★Wat Phra That Phanom

That Phanom, also on the Mekong, is about 76km/47 miles south of Nakhon Phanom. Its great attraction is the prang of the Wat Phra That Phanom on the west bank of the river and built around 900 although subsequently frequently restored. It contains a relic of the Buddha, reputed to be a collar-bone. The first building on this site, 8m/26ft high, was put up by five kings of the Si Gotapura kingdom eight years after the death of Buddha. Around 1614, during the Lan Chang period, the temple received new sides and a wall.

In 1690/92 the prang assumed something approaching its present form when the monk Phra Khru Luang Phonsamek raised its height to 47m/154ft and added various forms of decoration and the golden canopy on the spire. The sculpture and ornamental flowers on the sides date from the Siam period around 1901. The prang was restored by the Fine Arts Department in 1941 and left at its present height of 57m/187ft. The temple was closed in 1975 when heavy rains caused it to cave in, and the relic was temporarily housed elsewhere. The prang was removed and then rebuilt in its original form. On the day this was finished, in 1979, the canopied spire – 16kg of pure gold – was replaced as a sign of this highly revered Buddhist temple's completion, and the relic was returned to its original place.

Wonderful Khmer reliefs round the square base show scenes from Brahman mythology, homage to Buddha by the four keepers of the world, and the entry of the Enlightened One into Nirvana.

In front of the wat a Buddha sits on a stepped podium, shaded by a ceremonial canopy.

The other temple buildings are more modern and not as interesting. The cloister around the courtyard has some interesting frescos in the gateways, and its lovely flowers, shrubs and trees make it seem more like an immaculate garden.

Ban Renu (silk-weaving)

The village of Ban Renu, 7km/4 miles north-west of That Phanom, is famous for the weaving of silk fabrics, and its main street is lined with shops selling

That and Buddha figure in the Wat Phra That Phanom

beautiful silk woven in both classic and designer patterns. Wat Phra Renu has a very interesting stepped spire, covered all the way up with expressive, garishly painted reliefs, in a perceptively proportioned arrangement. The figurative representations of, for instance, Buddha in the traditional poses, or as a child on horseback and riding an elephant, lions, etc. appear sculpted, standing out against the artistic and intricate scrollwork, and indicate a modernity of approach alongside the traditional style.

Tha Rae (village)

Many of the villagers living in Tha Rae, about 10km/6 miles west of Nakhon Phanom on Route 22 to Sakhon Nakhon, are Vietnamese and Roman Catholic. Tha Rae is in fact the seat of a bishopric and has a seminary where young men can train for the priesthood.

Nakhon Ratchasima G 6

Region: North-east Thailand
Province: Nakhon Ratchasima
Altitude: 222m/729ft. Population: 110,000

Location

The town of Nakhon Ratchasima, once also called Khorat, lies 220km/137 miles north of Bangkok on the south-west edge of the Khorat Plateau. During recent decades it has become a centre of Thailand's most structurally-weak region; as railway lines from the north and the east meet here, Nakhon Ratchasima is of importance for the delivery of supplies to the north-east (which accounts for a third of Thailand's area). A good two-thirds of the region's population (approximately 2.2 million) live in the area around Nakhon Ratchasima, including many Laotians and Cambodians.

Reconstructed gate of Pratu Chumphon in Nakhon Ratchasima

Access

By car: from Bangkok Highway 1 as far as Saraburi, then Highway 2 ("Friendship Highway"; 265km/165 miles). From the Gulf of Thailand (at Chonburi) Highway 304 (260km/162 miles).
By rail: on the Bangkok–Ubon Ratchathani and Bangkok–Udon Thani lines.
By bus: from Bangkok Northeastern Bus Terminal.
By air: daily from Bangkok.

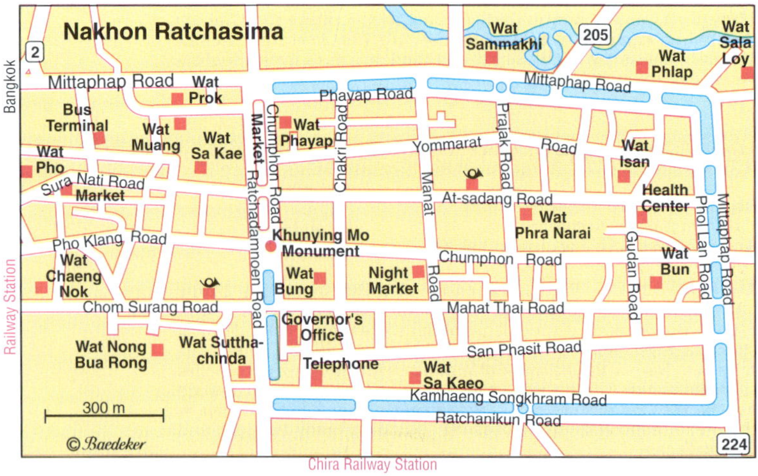

Witharn of the Wat Suthtachinda

History

The town is thought to have been founded at the end of the 13th c. as an outpost of the Thai principalities against the Khmer, when fortifications were built on the orders of King Narai (1656–88). Chronicles record an attack by Khmer troops in 1826 (Khunying Mo memorial in front of the western town gate).

Sights

Fortification sites

The wide moats and the reconstructed Pratu Chumphon gate give an impression of the size of the fortification sites. The bronze memorial to Thao Suranari, who is revered as a national heroine (Khunying Mo), stands on a terrace in front of the gate. When King Amu's Khmer troops invaded the town in 1826, the wife of the commander of the fort and other women staged a drinking session outside the town for the occupying forces and attacked the drunken soldiers. After a month they had finally driven the Khmer away.

★Wat Sutthachinda

Beautiful gardens surround Wat Sutthachinda. The small wiharn guarded by two bronze lions and the dainty bell tower are particularly charming. Of note are the wiharn's richly-decorated gable and the elaborately-carved windows on either side of the shrine. The well-proportioned wiharn contains three statues of Buddha, crowned with five-storeyed canopies. The largest of the statues shows the gestures of forgiveness, one of Buddha's five classical positions.

Maha-Wirawong National Museum

Opening times
Wed.–Sun.
9am–noon and
1–4pm

Admission fee

Next to the temple is a crematorium, where cremations are carried out according to Buddhist rites.

★Wat Phra Narai Mahathat

The extensive Wat Phra Narai Mahathat in Prajak Road lies near a large market (Mukkhamontri Road), which is worth seeing. Several sculptured sandstone slabs from Khmer temples stand here, as does a highly revered Vishnu figure in a small Hindu temple.

Silver Lake Park (leisure centre)

Silver Lake Park, a leisure park with a swimming pool and large water slides, is located on the edge of the town.

Surroundings

Silk production

Nakhon Ratchasima province is one of the most important centres of Thai silk production, both of thread and of materials. Silk production from the caterpillar onwards can be observed in the silk-weaving village of Pak Thong Chai, some 33km/20½ miles away (Highway 2 to the south-west, then Highway 304 in the direction of Kabinburi). Many mills offer tours through their production rooms and sell inexpensive silk articles in their showrooms. A number of smaller silk-weaving mills line the main road.

★Wat Prasat Hin Noen Ku

Old Khorat has an interesting Khmer temple, Wat Prasat Hin Noen Ku in present-day Muang Khorakhopura (about 37km/23 miles west of Nakhon Ratchasima; Highway 2 to Sung Noen, from there a further 7km/4 miles). Situated on a large square terrace, the construction, to which two more small buildings belong, possesses beautiful sculptures dating from the mid 10th c.

Wat Prasat Muang Khaek

Near Wat Prasat Hin Noen Ku can be found the ruins of Wat Prasat Muang Khaek with a prang and a porch. The wat is famous chiefly for the richly-articulated and finely-detailed sculptures on its door lintels, tympanums and pillars (mostly motifs from Brahman mythology). A number of elaborate 10th c. stone sculptures have been discovered in this temple.

★Wat Prasat Phanom Wan

Although the statues in old Wat Prasat Phanom Wan, approximately 14km/9 miles north-east of Nakhon Ratchasima (Highway 2, after 10km/6 miles turn off to the right, then continue for a further 4km/2½ miles to the village of Ban Kho), are revered by many believers and regular acts of worship take place there, the small, excellently-maintained Khmer temple appears still and almost deserted. The new monastery has partly incorporated foundations of the old one and the 11th c. shrine has been preserved. Details in the ornamentation indicate the 10th c., an older construction probably used to stand on this site. The surrounding rectangular wall, with a gallery on its inner side, had lavishly-decorated gates in the middle of

Ruins of the Wat Prasat Phanom Wan

each of its sides. Remaining ruins of a prang stand in the courtyard and many door lintels have also been retained. The shrine is a rectangular building with a grey sandstone Prang, to which porticoes were added on all four sides. A covered passageway, illuminated by a window, leads from the eastern portico to a 10m/33ft by 3m/10ft hall (Mandapa) with a stepped roof. The statues of Buddha, many of which are gold-plated, date from more recent times.

Muang Sema (area of debris)

An area of debris lies near the village of Muang Sema, 40km/25 miles west of Nakhon Ratchasima. An important Mon town, it is thought to have developed on this site between the 6th c. and the 11th c. The debris should be scientifically examined in the next few years, as the Thai tourism authorities have the money available for this.

Phimai
Prakhon Chai

The famous Khmer temple of Phimai (see entry) lies 56km/35 miles north-east of Nakhon Ratchasima. The town of Prakhon Chai (see entry), also well-known for its Khmer buildings, parts of which have been excellently preserved, can easily be reached on a day's excursion (130km/81 miles).

Nakhon Sawan F 4

Region: Central Thailand
Province: Nakhon Sawan
Altitude: 28m/92ft
Population: 107,000

นครสวรรค์

Location

Nakhon Sawan, once called Paknam Po, is located 240km/149 miles north of Bangkok on the confluence of the Menam Ping and the Menam Nan with the large Menam Chao Phraya, which irrigates the central plain and flows into the Gulf of Thailand. Always a flourishing town, Nakhon Sawan has been particularly concerned since 1989 with a ban on the felling of tropical trees, as the town was the terminus for the enormous rafts carrying wood from the north. However, the timber trade still plays a role in the town's life. Fields of jute, maize and peanuts characterise the scenery around Nakhon Sawan. The impressive Khao Pathawi mountain chain towers upwards in the west of the town.

Access

By car: from Bangkok Highways 1/32/1 (about 240km/149 miles).
By rail: on the Bangkok–Chiang Mai line.
By bus: from Bangkok Northern Bus Terminal.

★Wat Chomkiri Nagaproth

Today little can be seen of the old town of Nakhon Sawan. The wat on the nearby mountain on the opposite bank of the Menam Chao Phraya dates from the Sukhothai period. It contains a footprint of Buddha, which enjoys special adoration. Of greater importance is the Wat Chomkiri Nagaproth situated on a hill on the other side of the Menam Chao Phraya in the south of the town. The bot, surrounded by a double row of semas, was also built in the Sukhothai period. Inside is a beautiful statue of a seated Buddha in the Ayutthaya style, the throne borne by demons. Another statue of Buddha and a footprint can be found behind this statue. Within the wiharn are Buddha figures in the Ayutthaya style surrounding a main seated Buddha. A large, finely-chased bronze bell, cast around 1870, hangs in the courtyard between stone pillars.

Mosque

A mosque, built with donations from Pakistan, stands near the town centre. Visits are permitted when prayers are not in progress. The numerous markets held in the vicinity of the mosque are worth visiting.

Market in Nakhon Sawan

★Boeng Boraphet Lake

Nature-lovers should not miss Boeng Boraphet Lake to the east of the town. One of Thailand's largest lakes, it reaches its "true" size towards the end of the rainy season, measuring a considerable 20km/12½ miles in length. The lake is rich in fish and the home of many species of waterfowl. The area was declared a nature reserve years ago.

Phayuha Khiri (ivory carvers' village)

Phayuha Khiri, a village inhabited by numerous ivory carvers, lies 6km/4 miles south of Nakhon Sawan. The production of valuable art objects can be witnessed here. Today, however, artificial materials are used as African elephants are protected by the Washington protection of species agreement.

Nakhon Si Thammarat N 3

Region: South Thailand
Province: Nakhon Si Thammarat
Altitude: 13m/43ft. Population: 82,000

นครศรีธรรมราช

Location

The town of Nakhon Si Thammarat, rich in traditions, is located 780km/485 miles south of Bangkok on the Malaysian Peninsula, whose east coast lies only a few miles away. The mountains, covered with lush vegetation, climb gently from the fertile coastal plain to the 1835m/6020ft-high summit of the chalk massif Khao Luang. Fruit growing and mining brought wealth to the town, while the Niello technique, which attained the heights of perfection here, made it into a centre of the Thai craft industry. Its long past gives Nakhon Si Thammarat an air of venerable superiority.

Access

By car: from Bangkok Highways 35/4/41/401; from Surat Thani either south or first east along the coast.

By rail: From Bangkok–Hualampong two trains daily directly to and from Nakhon Si Thammarat (832km/517 miles, about fourteen hours); otherwise to Thung Song, then change.
By bus: From Krabi, Surat Thani and Bangkok (Southern Terminal).

History

The town once bore the Malaysian name of Ligor and has always been an important station on the trade route between Europe, Africa, India and China. During the first centuries A.D. Nakhon Si Thammarat is supposed to have been the chief town of a Tambralinga (Tampaling) principality, which survived until around 1360. It is certain that Nakhon Si Thammarat evolved in the 8th c. A.D. under the sovereignty of the Srivijaya kingdom, which encompassed Sumatra and large parts of the Malaysian Peninsula. A stone tablet from this time reports that around the year 775 the king of Srivijaya and Buddhist monks built a temple, in which the teachings of Mahayana-Buddhism would be disseminated. Towards the end of the 10th c. a prince of Tambralinga conquered the Mon kingdom of Lopburi, which already belonged to the Khmer empire, and declared himself king of Angkor Wat under the name of Suryavarman. In 1292 King Ramkhamhaeng of Sukhothal conquered Tambralinga; like the kingdom of Sukhothai it then became, in the second half of the 14th c., first a vassal state and subsequently part of the kingdom of Ayutthaya.

King Rama Thibodi II (1491–1529) permitted the Portuguese to found a trading settlement in Ligor in 1516. When Ayutthaya was destroyed by the Burmese in 1767, the Tambralinga principality became independent again for a short time, until King Taksin, the immediate predecessor of the present reigning Chakri dynasty, assimilated it into his newly-founded kingdom.

Nakhon Si Thammarat played an important role in art; a number of well-known artists, famous for the special quality of their depictions of Buddha (Nakhon Si Thammarat School), came from here.

Sights

Old Town

The town originally adjoined the sea (it now lies 26km/16 miles away), its main street following the coastline. It has now expanded across its northern border (fortification site) and the old town, containing the majority of the sights, has virtually become a suburb. Restored ruins of the town wall can be found in the centre of the old town.

Wat Maheyong

Follow Ratchadamnoen Road, with its beautiful wooden houses, southwards to reach the old town wall on the Wat Maheyong, within which stands a marvellous bronze Buddha in the Nakhon Si Thammarat style.

★Wat Sema Muang

Wat Sema Muang, also on the right-hand side of Ratchadamnoen Road, was founded in 775; the stone tablet previously referred to was discovered here. Remains of the construction are no longer in evidence. Only a few steps away stand two red-roofed Brahman temples from the Srivijaya period. The shrine on the right contains several Lingams (phallic symbols of the god Shiva).

★★Ho Phra Sihing

Ho Phra Sihing, a small chapel in the courtyard of the Thai-style prefecture (in the town centre, where Highway 4019 turns off to Thung Song), houses a famous figure, the Buddha Phra Sihing (Sukho style). In both the Bangkok National Museum and in Chiang Mai in Wat Phra Singh there are identical copies, whose authenticity is questioned. The original is thought to have come from China. Of note are the two Buddha figures dressed in gold and silver.

★★Wat Mahathat

Wat Mahathat in Ratchdamnoen Road, previously known as Wat Phra Boromathat until 1915, is Thailand's most famous temple and also one of its oldest. Recognisable from afar by its 74m/243ft-tall chedi, whose gold spire weighs 216kg/476lb, the exact date of the founding of this temple remains unknown (around the second half of the 10th c.). Extensive alterations, after which little of the old site remained, were carried out on the temple and its surroundings between 1157 and 1257.

Central Chedi of the Wat Mahathat

An entrance hall, roofed with bricks of coloured glass, surrounds the wat's extensive site. There are 156 small and medium-sized bell-shaped (stupas) chedis in the courtyard. The central chedi, whose foundations date from the year 757, is also surrounded by a covered gallery, decorated with 172 Buddha statues, most of which are in the Ayutthaya style.

The main shrine lies to the north in front of the chedi. A wide flight of steps, guarded by lions and yaks, leads from here to one of the chedi's terraces. Two chapels flank the stairs; the one on the left contains a Sukhothai-style statue of Buddha and stucco reliefs both in the Ayutthaya and the Srivijaya styles, while the right-hand one houses a Buddha statue in the Ayutthaya style and stucco reliefs on the altar. The small temple museum

1 Great Chedi
2 Viharn Kien Museum
3 Bholi Lanka Viharn
4 Phra Si Dharmasokaraj Viharn
5 Phra Ad Viharn
6 Royal Viharn
7 Dharma Sala Viharn
8 Tab Kaset Viharn
9 Phra Rabiang Viharn
10 Phra Thorani
11 Museum

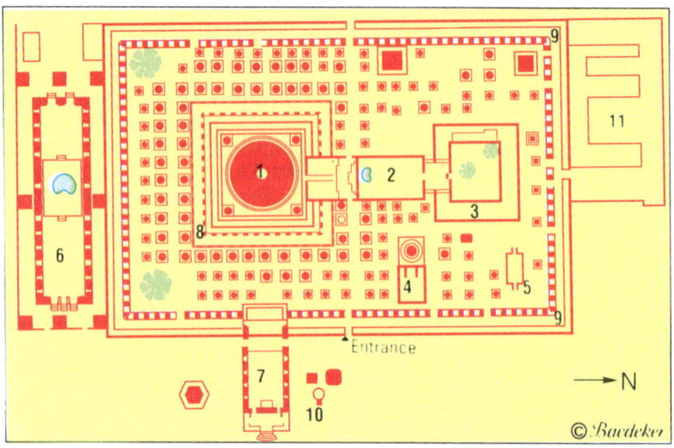

(Wiharn Kien; open: daily 8.30am–noon, 1–4.30pm) exhibits Chinese faïence and Sawankhalok as well as many craft objects. Of particular note are two valuable and extremely beautiful pieces of work, a seated Buddha in the Srivijaya style and a Dvaravati-style standing Buddha.

Wiharn Luang

Next to the Wat Mahathat, Wiharn Luang's very graceful interior and exterior pillars (typical of the Ayutthaya period) catch the eye. Monks live in Wat Na Phra Boromathat, diagonally opposite on the other side of the road.

★National Museum

Opening times
Wed.–Sun.
9am–noon
1.30–4pm

Admisision fee

No photography

Nakhon Si Thammarat's National Museum in the town's main road was opened in 1974 and is well worth visiting. It contains a large number of art objects both from the local area and from far afield in a variety of styles. Particular attention should be paid to three stone portraits in the Indian Pallava style (about 9th c.), depicting Vishnu with two adoring figures (a man and a woman). Neolithic finds (stone chains), eating and cooking implements from the third century and the magnificent tympanum of the Wat Sa Riang, built in 1769, are further attractions.

A unique 5th c. Vishnu figure is the oldest such figure ever to be found in south-east Asia. Agricultural and domestic tools can be seen in the museum's upper floor. Coaches and litters stand in the inner courtyard, while a neighbouring room displays particularly elaborately-decorated sticks, used to fend off snakes.

★Wat Phra Du

Wat Phra Du, another interesting temple, can be found in the extreme north of the city in a side street which turns off from Ratchadamnoen Road up at the railway station. The tomb of King Taksin is reputed to be located in a Chinese shrine. Contrary to historical tradition, he escaped execution in 1782 and is said to have spent his last years in a rocky grotto in the mountains near Nakhon Si Thammarat.

The craft industry

The Niello technique has enjoyed a long tradition in Nakhon Si Thammarat. It probably originated in China and first became native to Thailand in this town. Even now the most artistic pieces of work are said to come from Nakhon Si Thammarat. The Niello technique involves carving a drawing into a piece of metal (mostly silver) and filling it in with a melted black alloy. Many of the town's shops sell Niello tins, little boxes, ashtrays and pieces of jewellery.

Nang Theatre

Nang shadow play theatre originates from Indonesia and can only now be seen in south Thailand, predominantly in Nakhon Si Thammarat and especially on Buddhist holidays. Shadow pieces (often made from heavily tanned buffalo skin) can be bought in a number of shops.

★Animal Market

Try to visit the animal market held regularly near the bus station. Monkeys, elephants, snakes and, occasionally, wild cats are sold here.

Surroundings

The area surrounding Nakhon Si Thammarat is very charming and full of variety: vast rubber tree plantations dominate the region inland, while the coast offers some beautiful beaches. The mountains in front of the town contain numerous caves such as Taksin Grotto (Highway 4051 in the direction of Lan Saka). Located near to this grotto is Wat Khao Phun Phanom, a temple situated in the middle of grandiose jungle scenery, with several notable statues of Buddha and one of King Taksin. A visit to Phrom Lok Waterfall can be recommended (north-west, Highway 4061). Bathers can swim in its pool.

★Khao Luang National Park

Khao Luang mountain (1834m/6019ft), which has given its name to the surrounding national park, lies 30km/18½ miles west of the town (north of the road to Chawang). Opened in 1984, the park can be reached by driving to the village of Ban Ron and then following the signs. Particularly worth viewing is Nam Tok Karom, a waterfall whose cascades tumble over steps to a depth of approximately 40m/131ft. A path begins at Nam Tok Karom and crosses a fascinating, unspoilt landscape, passing a total of nineteen waterfalls.

National Museum of Nakhon Si Thammarat

Waterfall in the Khao Luang National Park

Naklua

See Pattaya, Surroundings.

Nan (Nang) C 4

Region: North Thailand
Province: Nan (Nang)
Altitude: 200m/656ft. Population: 22,000

น่าน

Location

Nan is situated near the border with the Menam Nan valley, one of the large tributaries of the Menam Chao Phraya, encircled by high mountain chains. The roughness of the terrain ensured the continued existence of a small kingdom up until this century. The town possesses important temple sites and the surrounding area will fill nature-lovers with enthusiasm. Nan's sweet oranges are famous, likewise the art objects made of reeds, which women and children make in their homes.

Access

By car: from Phrae Highway 101 (125km/78 miles); from Chiang Rai Highway 1 to Ngao, Highway 103 as far as Rong Khem, then 101.
By bus: from Bangkok, Chiang Mai, Lamphang, Phrae and Phayao.
By air: from Bangkok via Chiang Mai or Phitsanulok.

History

Traces of a settlement in the province of Nan date from about 1280. From the beginning of the 15th c. Nan was part of a kingdom, ruled by King Boroma Trailokanat (1448–88). For a time the kings of Nan were obliged to pay tribute to those of Chiang Mai, and for 200 years they were vassals of the Burmese, later the kings of Ayutthaya. However, the kings of Nan always held certain privileges. Nan was only annexed to the kingdom of Siam in 1931.

Sights

Town Wall

The Mon-style town walls, built in an oval, were constructed in 1857, after the Menam Nan had flooded several times and destroyed the old fortifications.

★★Wat Phumin

The architecture of the early Nan period contains features of both the Mon and the Chiang-Saen styles, while later Nan constructions feature the Sukhothai style. The town's famous temple, Wat Phumin, located south of the province's administrative buildings in Suriyaphong Road, dates from 1596 and contains elements of style from all periods. It has a cruciform ground plan and its three-stepped roofs are graduated upwards to the crossing, which is crowned by a gracious canopy. The four symmetrical entrances, approached by short, beautifully-curved, lion-guarded flights of steps, have richly-embellished, carved portals. Within the wat four Sukhothai-style, seated, bronze lions surround the cube-shaped altar. Pillars and artistically-strutted timberwork support a richly-decorated coffered ceiling. The wall frescos date from the 19th c. and depict, in vivid pictures painted in unusually bright colours, scenes from the country's history, particularly battles, and from the early life of Buddha (the "Jataka"). At the same time they portray the life-style of the population of northern Thailand.

★Elephant's Tusk

A 300-year-old elephant's tusk, one of Nan's chief attractions, is kept in one of the government buldings. Shorter and thicker than the usual tusk, its ivory colour has gradually turned blackish-yellow over time.

★Wat Cham Kang

Literally translated, the "temple carried by elephants" is located opposite the government buildings. Its beautiful 15th/16th c. chedi, whose pedestal is borne by 28 elephant sculptures, is typical.

The two shrines contain some marvellous Sukhothai-style statues of Buddha. The first has a walking Buddha and also one which is standing, with outstretched arms and open hands; the second a walking, golden Buddha. For centuries this Buddha was hidden beneath a thick layer of plaster; when it was decided to move it to another site, however, the plaster came off. Inscriptions on the pedestals of the first two figures mentioned reveal that King Ngua Pha Sum commissioned the completion of five statues in 1426; the two other life-size figures, perhaps the most beautiful in the series, stand in Wat Phaya Phun (see Surroundings).

Wat Suan Tan

Wat Suan Tan is situated at the northern end of Pakwang Road and was founded in 1456 by the wife of the first king of Nan. Its statue of a seated Buddha in the Sukhothai style with Chiang Mai style features and its 40m/131ft prang-like chedi are of note.

National Museum

Nan's small national museum (Pa Gong Road; open: Wed.–Sun. 9am–noon and 1–4pm; admisision fee) features some beautiful exhibition pieces representative of the different ethnic groups living in and around Nan.

Surroundings

★Wat Phra That Chao Meng

Wat Phra That Chao Meng, picturesquely located on a hill, is situated 3km/2 miles south-east of the town on the other side of the Menam Nan. It is said that Buddha himself visited this place and prophesied that relics would be found at the site and that a temple built to house them. Two wide paths, lined with nagas, lead up to the wat's entrances, which was founded in about 1300 and renovated in 1476. The 56m/184ft-high chedi is covered with gold-plated copper sheets, while its immediate surroundings are decorated with gold-plated copper canopies, small ornamental towers and statues of lions. The shape of the wiharn's roof is clearly Laotian in style.

★Wat Phaya Phun

Leave the town in a southerly direction to reach Wat Phaya Phun on the other side of Road 101. Standing on a hill, this wat's chedi has been built in the shape of a pointed, stepped pyramid with niches. It remains unclear whether it dates, like the Buddha statues, from the second half of the 14th c. (when, after years of Hinayana-Buddhism, Theravada-Buddhism was re-introduced and civilised Animismus was renounced) or from the 18th c.

Wat Phra That Khao Noi

Approximately 2km/1 mile further along the same road stands Wat Phra That Khao Noi, whose chedi is in the Chiang-Saen style. A far-reaching view of the plain and the town of Nan can be enjoyed from Noi mountain.

★★Scenery

At Sa, 24km/15 miles south of Nan, Highway 101 turns off on to Road 1026 leading to Ban Na Noi. Here there is a type of canyon with three groups of eerily towering rocks: Nom Chom, Sao Dip and Sao Nin.

★★Wat Bun Yeun

The small village of Sa is famed for its hand-woven silk and cotton featuring both modern and traditional patterns. Wat Bun Yeun, the village's temple, is an example of the best of the Laotian style; particularly noteworthy are the well-proportioned wiharn with its wonderfully carved door, on which a deity is depicted, and the Chiang-Saen-style chedi.

Narathiwat P 5

Region: South Thailand
Province: Narathiwat
Altitude: 3m/10ft. Population: 33,000

นราธิวาส

Location

Narathiwat lies 1148km/713 miles from Bangkok, but only 67km/42 miles from the Malaysian border. This fact accounts for the problems which characterise life in this town. Traces of the Malaysian way of life are evident everywhere, and a large number of the population speak the language of their neighbouring country. Alongside Buddhist temples muezzins call people to prayers, markets sell both pork and lamb. The population of the town have come to an arrangement, even if there are conflicts every now and then, with those who claim a connection with Malaysia. As well as Muslims, many Chinese live in Narathiwat, Thailand's most southerly province. The Thai royal family had a palace built for themselves here, at which they would stay on their yearly tour of southern Thailand (no visits).

Access

By car: from Songkhla Highway 408/43/42 (200km/124 miles).
By bus: from Pattani, Betong and Songkhla.
By rail: nearest station Songkhla.
By air: nearest airport Hat Yai (200km/124 miles).

History

It was not until this century that the southern provinces approached the rulers of Thailand to inform them that many of the local population felt more kinship with Thailand's neighbour than with Thailand itself. Cultural links, developed over centuries, did not weaken even after the drawing up of a border between Thailand and Malaysia in 1786 or as a result of the extensive economic help given by the Thai government. Certainly the Malaysian government had little interest in any union. Young people, in particular, are banding together into a separatist movement. Visitors will see little evidence of all this.

★ Townscape

The townscape is characterised by the onion domes of its mosques, its Malaysian-style houses and its brightly-dressed people. The markets and the lively fishing harbours are also very interesting.

Surroundings

★ Landscape

The marvellous, intensively-farmed land around Narathiwat deserves a visit. The vast coconut plantations, where trained monkeys are used as pickers, play an important role in the economy. The coast is rich in beautiful, fine sandy beaches with a number of estates of bungalows in the immediate vicinity.

A coconut picker at work

Nam Tok Bacho (waterfalls)

By driving approximately 25km/15½ miles to the north (Highway 42, turn off after 73km/45 miles) travellers will reach the beautiful Nam Tok Bacho waterfalls. Continuing a further 25km/15½ miles will bring them to Saiburi, the province's former principal town. Despite this earlier importance, Saiburi has few notable sights.

Excursion to Malaysia

A one-day excursion to the Malaysian town of Kota Baharu, about 62km/38½ miles away, proves rewarding. The border can be crossed easily at Sungai Kolok; visitors must ensure that they are in possession of a second visa to gain re-entry into Thailand. There are regular taxi and bus connections between Narathiwat and Kota Baharu.

Nong Khai D 6

Region: North-east Thailand. Province: Nong Khai
Altitude: 160m/525ft. Population: 27,000

Location

Visitors to Nong Khai are not attracted by its sights, such as temples and museums, but by its close proximity to the border with Laos and its main town of Vientiane (once called Viangchan). The view across the mighty Mekong, south-eastern Asia's largest river and the eighth-longest river in the world, is impressive.

Access

By car: from Udon Thani Highway 2 (53km/33 miles).
By rail: terminus of the Bangkok–south-west Thailand line.
By bus: from Bangkok Southern Terminal 3 times daily.
Nearest airport: Udon Thani (50km/31 miles; bus connections).

Mekong

The Mekong's water-level fluctuates considerably (up to 20m/66ft in the course of a year); during the rainy season it floods the fields, while during the dry season islands appear in the river bed.

Boats by the Mekong

★Wat Kaek

Wat Kaek stands on the Thai side of the Mekong and contains a large, apparently random collection of figures. This includes a monumental statue of a meditating Buddha (notice the portrayal with a richly-ornamented point on the head) and the sculpture of the four-armed Indian god Ganesha (the god of the arts), who is riding a rat.

Surroundings

Border crossing to Laos

Ferry boats to Laos can be found near the railway station; the real border crossing point for pedestrians is in the town centre. Officially only Thai and Laotian citizens are allowed to cross the border; however, at times, visitors' visas can be obtained from the Laotian embassy in Bangkok (see Practical Information, Diplomatic Representation). Those planning a longer stay after their return to Thailand should be in possession of a second entry visa (travellers can only obtain these in Bangkok or from the consulate in their own country before setting out), as upon return to Thailand only fourteen-day tourist visas are issued.

★Vientiane (Laos)

The crossing to Tha Deau in Laos only takes a few minutes. The town of Vientiane lies approximately another 20km/12½ miles away (taxis are the only possible way of travelling). Vientiane offers a number of sights, including the royal palace, Wat Phra Kaeo with its interesting and extensive museum, a triumphal arch and Wat That Luang with its famous pagoda. The town's many markets are also of interest.

Nonthaburi H 4

นนทบุรี

Region: Central Thailand
Province: Nonthaburi
Altitude: 18m/59ft. Population: 40,000 (town)

Location and Townscape

The town of Nonthaburi lies approximately 20km/12½ miles north of Bangkok on the banks of the Menam Chao Phraya. Numerous straight and winding watercourses and picturesque Klongs around the town flow towards the river where a considerable part of the town's daily life is played out. A number of attractive temples stand on the Klongs' banks, which are lined with lush vegetation and houses built on stilts.

Access

By car: from Bangkok along Samsen Road, which later crosses into Phibul Songkhram Road, along Menam Chao Phraya (approximately 20km/12½ miles).
By bus: from Thonburi Bus Station (several times daily).

The most beautiful approach from Bangkok is via the Menam Chao Phraya (boats depart Oriental Pier).

Wat Chaloem Phra Kiat

Wat Chaloem Phra Kiat, which, when viewed from Nonthaburi, stands a short distance upstream on the other side of the Menam, can be reached either by boat (to be rented in the town) or by regular ferries. The wat was constructed in the first half of the 19th c.; two high encircling walls – the first with battlements, the second characterised by small Chinese towers – surround the site. The richly-ornamented main temple and the chedi are remarkable for their pleasing proportions. Only the ruins of two further temples remain.

★Bang Yai (village)

Continue by boat and enter Klong Bong Yai on the left to reach the picturesque village of Bang Yai, surrounded by several Klongs. Sail further in a southerly direction to the village of Bang Kruai, passing a number of attractive, picturesquely-located, modern temples.

Wat Prang Luang

Wat Prang Luang, located on the right-hand bank behind Bang Yai, dates from the Ayutthaya period. An elegant prang has been maintained in very good condition.

★Wat Prasat

Wat Prasat, also in the Ayutthaya style, is situated some distance from the left bank of the Klong (built around 1700). The impressive main temple has

Thailand pottery is attractive and well-made

two colonnaded porticoes and is richly decorated with sculptures and wood carving. The frescos in the interior have bold brush strokes and are very vivid (typical characteristics of the first Bangkok period).

The ruins of two more temples will be encountered on the right bank and at Bang Kruai at Wat Chalo. Both date from the late Ayutthaya period.

Nonthaburi Prison

A unique place of interest is Nonthaburi Prison, which is still in use. Instruments of torture are displayed in a small museum belonging to the "Correctional Staff Division", affiliated to the prison, where prison officers are trained. During the Ayutthaya period these instruments were used by royal officials to extract confessions. Also of interest are a number of instruments employed in the execution of prisoners condemned to death. Of particular note is a rattan ball, with nails lining its interior. Criminals under sentence of death were put inside such a ball, after which elephants were allowed to play with their "football". With luck, visitors will encounter an English-speaking official able to explain the exhibits.

Surroundings

Pak Kret

Pak Kret lies about 8km/5 miles north of Nonthaburi near a bend in the Menam Chao Phraya. The entertaining boat trip from Nonthaburi to this old Mon settlement only takes 20 minutes. The area around Pak Kret and the settlement itself are still inhabited by Mons who, however, have become extensively assimilated by the Thai people. There is a long pottery tradition in Pak Kret. The objects produced, displayed and sold in the workshops along the river, stand out on account of their perfect shapes.

★★Wat Chim Phli

Graceful, white, rather faded Wat Chim Phli, built in the Mon style, stands at the southern tip of Pak Kret island, with boats berthed in front of it. A beautiful Buddha statue from the Ayutthaya period stands inside.

Boat trip along the Klongs

A boat trip along the many Klongs west of the Menam Chao Phraya approximately to Bang Bua Thong proves a very exotic experience.

Wat Chim Phli in Pak Kret

Pak Chong G 5

Region: Central Thailand
Province: Nakhon Ratchasima
Altitude: 459m/1492ft. Population: 15,000

ปากช่อง

Location and Sights

Pak Chong, a small town situated on the edge of the Khao Yai national park, is located approximately 200km/124 miles north-east of Bangkok. It lies at the foot of a range of mountains separating the Menam Plain from the Khorat Plateau. It is worth visiting the daily market where local people sell their wares. About 15km/9 miles east of Pak Chong, close to Highway 2, the beautiful Lam Takhong reservoir nestles in a wide valley. It supplies water to the population of Bangkok, as well as to the local area.

Access

By car: from Bangkok Highway 1 to Saraburi, then Highway 2.
By rail: on the Bangkok–Nakhon Ratchasima line.
By bus: from Bangkok Northern Bus Terminal (approximately four hours).

★★Khao Yai National Park (Map p. 268)

Buses depart from both Pak Chong and Bangkok for the national park. If travelling by car from Bangkok, turn off to the right shortly before Pak Chong on to Highway 2090 and follow the signs. Opened in 1962, the park covers an area of 2168sq.km/837sq. miles of land in the four provinces of Nakhon Nayok, Prachinburi, Saraburi and Nakhon Ratchasima. Hilly, jungle-like scenery with mountains rising to a height of 1350m/4429ft (still partially covered with original rain forest), picturesque waterfalls and idyllic lakes attract visitors to Thailand and Thais alike; because of this, the park should be avoided at weekends and on public holidays. The park offers comfortable accommodation – be sure to book well in advance through TAT in Bangkok.

The highest mountains, located in the southern section of the park, are Khao Laem (1328m/4358ft) and Khao Khiau (Green Mountain,

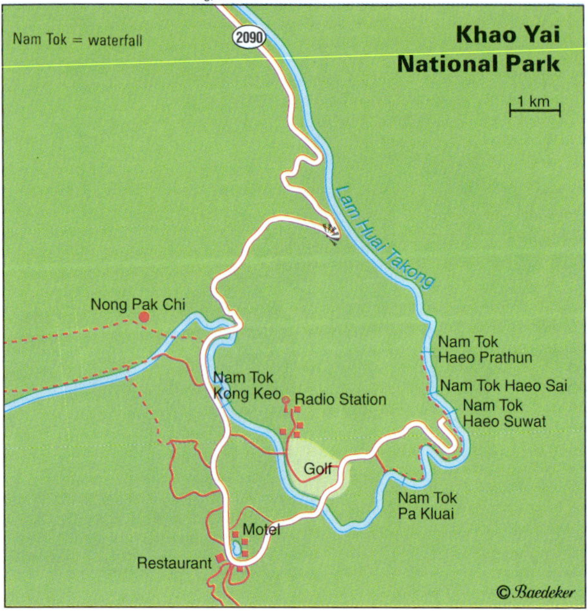

1350m/4429ft). Both can be climbed during a day tour, with the reward of marvellous views. The waterfalls Nam Tok Haeo Suwat, Nam Tok Pa Kluai (orchids waterfall, the rocks are surrounded by orchids) and Nam Tok Kong Keo are attractive. The eighteen-hole golf course occupies a beautiful location and meets international standards.

Numerous species of animals, including elephants, bears, tigers, tapirs, buffalo, wild pigs, fallow deer and monkeys, live in the park. The wild animals can be observed easily from Nong Pak Chi tower during morning and evening hours.

A modestly-priced plan has been produced by the park's administration, grading each of the park's total of twelve paths according to difficulty. Ask officials if the paths can be used.

Warning

Be careful of particularly "cheap" prices for taxi journeys from the park entrance; they are often only for one-way journeys. When in doubt it is advisable to rely on the tour operators in Pak Chong, Saraburi and Nakhon Ratchasima.

Pathum Thani **H 4**

ปทุมธานี

Region: Central Thailand
Province: Pathum Thani
Altitude: 7m/23ft. Population: 14,000

Location and Scenery

The area around Pathum Thani, the main town of the province located north of Bangkok, enjoys the typical landscape of the southern central plain, which is characterised by the wide delta of the Menam Chao Phraya.

Numerous Klongs and tributaries of Thailand's most important river facilitate intensive farming of the land.

Access

By car: from Bangkok Highway 1 (about 50km/31 miles).
By bus: connections from Bangkok Northern Bus Terminal.
By rail: on the Bangkok–Hualampong line to the north.
By boat: the distance is considerably less along the Menam Chao Phraya. Regular service boats depart from Oriental Pier.

History

Pathum Thani is a settlement founded by King Taksin (1768–82) for Burmese Mons, whose language is still spoken here today. The town gained its present name (meaning "Lotus Town") as a gesture of thanks to Ramas III, who was always presented with bouquets of lotus flowers by the inhabitants when he visited.

★Wat Pai Lom (stork's temple)

Wat Pai Lom, a temple on the other bank of the Menam Chao Phyra, provides the most interesting attraction here and is best reached either by rented boat (five minutes) or by river taxi from Bangkok. The wat itself is of no interest, but the temple grounds are home to hundreds of thousands of openbill storks (*anastomus oscitans*), whose numbers have increased more than eightfold in the last 30 years as a result of the protection they enjoy here (use of firearms and hunting are forbidden in the grounds of Thailand's temples).

Temple site

The site of Wat Pai Lom is thought to have been built during the Ayutthaya period, i.e. long before the founding of Bangkok. Its name means "Bamboo Temple" and was chosen either because the first temple buildings were made of bamboo or because of the dense bamboo forest, which once surrounded the temple grounds.

Storks

Storks live on snails, which they find in nearby rice fields during periods of flooding. They leave the temple in search of food in the morning and return

Storks in the Wat Pai Lom

in the afternoon. Bird excrement has over-fertilised the trees in which the storks nest, causing them to have lost their leaves.

It proves most interesting to observe the storks during the incubation period in March. Raised hides facilitate very close contact, only rarely possible. Photographs, nevertheless, should be taken using a telephoto lens, as storks are sometimes very easily startled.

The over-population of Wat Pai Lom has resulted in an interesting phenomenon, which has attracted ornithologists from all over the world. Storks are usually monogamous, but here they often take several "wives" who are likely to have to share a nest. Giant lizards also profit from the over-population: if the stork does not build its nest properly the eggs will fall to the ground and be rapidly consumed as delicacies.

Pattani P 5

ปัตตานี

Region: South Thailand
Province: Pattini
Altitude: 6m/20ft. Population: 36,000

Location

Pattini is one of Thailand's most southerly provinces, with the town itself located on the Gulf of Thailand some 1050km/652 miles from Bangkok. Most of its inhabitants are Moslem Malays, the majority of whom are trying to break away from Thailand, to which country they feel no cultural affinity. Following a close examination of the problems of the area's predominantly agricultural population by the government in Bangkok, ties to Thailand have strengthened. Pattini's hinterland comprises mountainous jungle and a coastal landscape rich in variety and full of charm.

Access

By car: from Songkhla Highway 408/42 (125km/78 miles); alternatively turn on to the coast road at Chana (100km/62 miles).
By rail: nearest station Khok Pho (23km/14 miles).
By bus: connections from Songkhla and Narathiwat.
By air: from Bangkok twice a week.
By boat: from Songkhla.

History

Since about the 8th c. Pattini has been a well-known trading centre; however, the harbour no longer plays an important role. In the 15th c. a relatively self-sufficient city-state evolved here which was ruled by princes, the Moslem Ratchas. They had to recognise the overlordship initially of the Srivijaya rulers and after them the sovereigns of Sukhothai and Ayutthaya. At the beginning of the 16th c. trade with Europe, India and China flourished, and the Portuguese and the Dutch established trading settlements here. In 1619 Dutch and English warships fought in the harbour, with the Dutch emerging victorious.

★Fishing Harbour

The numerous fishing boats in the harbour paint a colourful picture; it is particularly lively here early in the morning.

Buildings

Only ruins remain of the old Ratcha palace. The town's most impressive building is the mosque with its large onion dome (open: 9am–3.30pm). The Chinese temple dates from the second half of the 18th c.

★Bullfights

The town's population avidly follows bullfighting (where bulls fight each other). The Thai people's proverbial love of gambling plays an important role in this, with the bullfight itself almost a triviality.

Pattaya J 4

พัทยา

Region: South-east Thailand
Province: Chonburi
Altitude: 3m/10ft. Population: 50,000

Location

Pattaya is situated approximately 147km/91 miles south-east of Bangkok on the Gulf of Thailand. Blessed with sun, sea and sand, it is the largest and certainly most popular seaside resort in south-east Asia. Its development follows the line of the bay, the approximately 6km/4 mile-long, heavily-used coast road runs between the beach and the numerous hotels. The area south of the town with Jomtien Beach is tourist-oriented.

Access

By car: from Bangkok Highway 34/3 (147km/91 miles).
By rail: from Bangkok-Hualampong. From Pattaya station there is a shuttle service into the town and to the hotels.
By bus: from Bangkok East Terminal.

By air: nearest air route Bangkok-Don Muang.
The Royal Cliff Hotel offers guests a helicopter shuttle service (flight time from Don Muang 30 minutes).

History

For many years Pattaya led a peaceful, sleepy existence. Visitors from Bangkok would come here at weekends, but it was left to the US troops stationed at the air force base U Tapao at Sattahip during the Vietnam War to "discover" Pattaya. During the 1970s the small town developed very rapidly into a bathing and sex tourist resort; the building boom continued until very recently. The gap left by the withdrawal of US troops in the late 1970s was filled mainly by tour operators in Germany, Switzerland and Austria. A large-scale action programme has been initiated to "clean up" the resort's rather dubious reputation; in particular a war has been declared on prostitution. The quality of the sea water has been significantly improved, following the opening of a large sewage plant in 1992. On the other hand, water supplies in the dry season are still not very reliable.

Night-life

Sleepy by day, Pattaya's greatest attraction – both in a positive and a negative sense – is its night-life, famed worldwide and envied by its rivals. Countless bars, nightclubs, discothèques and other places of amusement are mostly crowded into the two main streets as well as the northern edge of the town. The pace of life continues to be a little slower at Jomtien Beach, south of the main resort, which for some years has been gradually developed into a "part" of Pattaya.

For those wishing to spend a peaceful beach holiday, the Royal Cliff Beach Resort, located on the edge of Pattaya, is recommended; otherwise search out resorts in southern Thailand, such as Phuket or Koh Samui.

Sport

All manner of watersports are popular in Pattaya, including surfing, diving, motorboat driving and parasailing (fairly expensive). Diving off the coast of Pattaya actually offers few attractions as the coral reefs have long since

In the amusement quarter of Pattaya

been plundered, although there are still a few attractive diving areas near the offshore islands. Almost every hotel has its own tennis courts, a number floodlit at night. Golf courses, some of which meet international standards, can be found at the Dusit Resort, and at the somewhat remote Siam Country Club and in Sattahip. In spring and in autumn motor racing takes place, motorsport fans can practise their skills on two go-kart tracks.

Surroundings

General Information

Pattaya itself has two more recent temple sites located to the south of the town on the summits of two hills. In one the small garden with Chinese figures is of note, while the other contains a huge statue of Buddha; neither is particularly attractive. Those not entirely satisfied by the *dolce vita* of a beach holiday can "escape" to the surroundings of Pattaya. Some offshore coral islands, such as Koh Lam, Koh Lin and Koh Khrok, have beautiful beaches, although no accommodation that can as yet be recommended. They can be reached by boat from the main beach in Pattaya. Many boat owners offer day trips to the islands.

"Mini Siam"

As in Ancient City (see Samut Prakan) the "Mini Siam" park on Sukhumvit Road (open: daily 7am–10pm) displays Thailand's most important attractions in miniature (scale 1:25). An evening visit should prove delightful as the 80 exhibits are then illuminated.

Pattaya Orphanage

Pattaya Orphanage is situated near the motorway to Bangkok. Run by a Redemptorist priest of Irish descent, it cares for the "by-products" of Pattaya's sex tourism. Visitors wishing to gain an impression of life behind the façade of a pleasure resort are heartily welcomed here at any time, provided that they have made an appointment.

★Nong Nooch Cultural Village

Nong Nooch (pronounced "nung nut") Village, approximately 15km/9 miles south-east of Pattaya, can be compared to the Rose Garden at Nakhon Pathom. The life of the agricultural population is portrayed in this 400ha/988 acre park, with Thai boxing, cockfights and an elephant show. The magnificent orchid garden is not just for flower-lovers to savour, and the zoo, housing animals typically found in the region, is not aimed solely

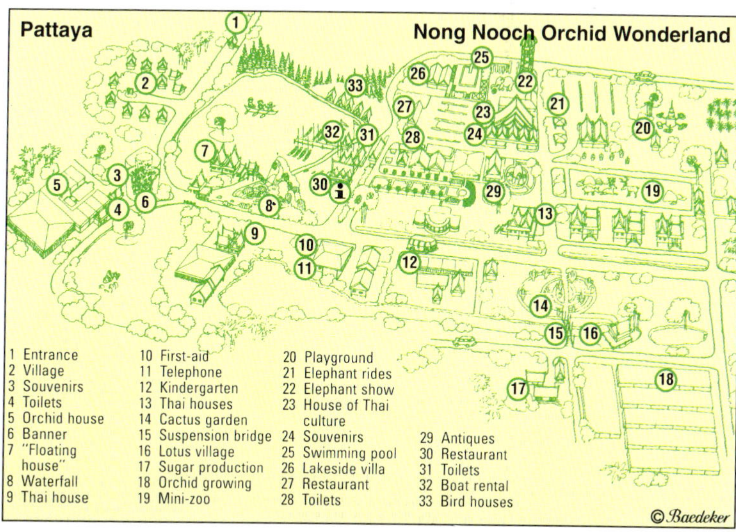

A little beach near Pattaya

at children. Outings to Nong Nooch depart from the office in Pattaya (opposite Nipa Lodge Hotel). Guests can also be collected from their hotels.

Wat Yansang-wararam

Shortly before the entrance to Nong Nooch a road turns off from Highway 3 to the recently-built Wat Yansangwararam. This temple was dedicated to King Bhumibol in 1988 to commemorate the 42nd year of his reign. To the right-hand side of the path leading to the temple there is a lake with attractive Chinese pavilions and other buildings. Wat Yansangwararam's shrine stands on a hill, reached by a flight of 299 steps lined with naga snakes. On the plain several buildings, including a round wiharn and monastic dwellings, are situated in a well-tended area of parkland.

Elephant Kraal

An elephant kraal is located 6km/4 miles from Pattaya. The pachyderms demonstrate their skills every day at 2.30pm (admission fee) accompanied by an English commentary. After the performances there is an opportunity to ride the elephants. Another elephant kraal can be found 5km/3 miles from Sukhumvit Road at Rodeo Ranch.

Pattaya Park (leisure centre)

Pattaya Park, with spacious pools and four giant water-slides, was opened several years ago and lies 8km/5 miles from Pattaya (take Cliff Road in a southerly direction and follow the signs). Pattaya Park contains several restaurants, as well as a complex of bungalows and a hotel.

Naklua

The little town of Naklua, about 12km/7½ miles away, should be visited either in the morning for its busy fish market or in the evening for its night market. A number of good restaurants can be found around the market. It is best to use a group taxi from Pattaya to travel there.

Excursions

Several other places, primarily Chanthaburi and Trat to the south-east, and Bang Saen and Chonburi (towards Bangkok) can easily be reached from Pattaya. The islands of Koh Samet (see Rayong), Koh Sichang (see Si

A market in Naklua

Racha) and Koh Chang (see Trat) are also of interest. A beach holiday in Pattaya should definitely include a visit to the capital Bangkok (one or several day visits, bookings at all travel agents).

Phangnga N 2

พังงา

Region: South Thailand
Province: Phangnga
Altitude: 6m/20ft. Population: 11,000

Location and Landscape

The town of Phangnga lies about 800km/497 miles south of Bangkok on the Malay Peninsula on the river of the same name, which comes down from mountains ranging in height up to 1000m/3282ft. The landscape around the Bay of Bengal is full of surprises: white mountain peaks stand out from the intensive greenery of the jungle, pretty villages cling to the mountain slopes, and a boat trip through the bays of Phangnga and Ao Luk, the northern parts of the large bay of Phuket, conveys one of the most marvellous natural experiences imaginable.

Access

By car: from Krabi and from Bangkok on Highway 4 (each about 85km/53 miles); from Surat Thani Highways 401/4040/4 (195km/121 miles).
By rail: nearest station Surat Thani.
By bus: from Bangkok Southern Bus Terminal (880km/547 miles, eighteen hours) and from Phuket Bus Terminal (2 hours).
By air: nearest airports Phuket and Surat Thani, several flights daily from Bangkok.

★Chinese Quarter

From the more low-lying Chinese quarter, where a number of old houses still stand, the rocky reefs which surround the town appear particularly steep; they stand out as sharp silhouettes against the sky.

Morning on the River Phangnga

Surroundings

★★Tham Reussi Grotto

The chalk mountains contain many grottoes, some with beautiful dripstones, which provide refuge for countless field-mice. One of the most famous caves is Tham Reussi, the "hermits' cave", close to the town (at the custom house). It comprises a labyrinth of strangely-shaped caves with dripstones. One particular stalagmite, with an almost human shape, is said by local people to look like a miracle-working hermit. It enjoys particular reverence and is covered each day with offerings, mainly little gold tiles. A small park with ponds has been laid out around the entrance to the cave.

★Wat Tham Pong Chang

From here a path leads through a tunnel for about 500m/1641ft to Wat Tham Pong Chang ("temple cave in the elephant's stomach") shrine, vaulted by Khao Chang, the mountain of the elephants (so named after its shape). Three statues of holy elephants stand inside.

★Tham Suwan Kutta (grotto)

A palm-lined path marks the entrance to the grotto temple Tham Suwan Kutta (approximately 13km/8 miles from Phangnga, Highway 4 in the direction of Khok Kloi, follow signposts). A number of various figures of Buddha are in the temple, while the cave behind the grotto contains several beautiful dripstone shapes.

Khok Kloi

Pretty Ban Khok Kloi lies 17km/10½ miles further on at the foot of the mountains. From here a bridge carries vehicles over to the island of Phuket (see entry).

★Ta Kuapa

The town of Ta Kuapa lies on the Bay of Bengal about 75km/47 miles north of Khok Kloi (120km/74½ miles from Phangnga). There are some very beautiful beaches in the vicinity of the town. In the first millennium B.C. Ta Kuapa was a destination for Indian traders who either settled on the coast of the Malay Peninsula or moved on from here to Cambodia and China. The area around Takua Pa has not yet been examined archaeologically. Three paintings of Pallava (late 9th c. B.C.) found here are displayed in the national

Tham Reussi, the "Hermit's Cave"

museum of Nakhon Si Thammarat; the remains of an old settlement have also been discovered.

Highway 401 leaves Takua Pa and passes through a valley to Surat Thani on the Gulf of Thailand.

★★Landscape

Highway 4 from Phangnga to Krabi (87km/54 miles) crosses a landscape of impressive jungle and cliffs.

Wat Kirivong

About 10km/6 miles behind Phangnga is the rock temple Wat Kirivong containing a statue of Buddha.

★★Than Bok Koroni National Park

The entrance to Than Bok Koroni National Park, one of the most beautiful national parks in Thailand, can be found at Ao Luk (42km/26 miles east of Phangnga). Magnificent vegetation, high rocky reefs and a river, which rises between the rocks from its underground course, characterise the scene. The towering cliffs of Ao Luk bay form a fantastic backdrop.

★★Phangnga Bay

Khao Khien cave paintings

Boat trips through Phangnga Bay depart the moorings at Klong Khao Thalu River (5km/3 miles along Highway 4 in the direction of Phuket, turn left at the signpost). The tour first passes through mangrove forests and after about 30 minutes reaches Phangnga Bay, where it heads for Khao Khien rock caves with their famous cave paintings. They depict, in brownish-red, ochre and black, crocodiles, fish, dolphins and other sea creatures surrounding humans, drawn very vividly as hunters. Another experience is to pass through the Tam Lod arch where stalactites hang down into the water.

★★Koh Panyi (Moslem village)

The Moslem village of Panyi, a settlement of buildings on stilts with about 1200 inhabitants, lies in the estuary of Phangnga River in front of the rocky island of Koh Panyi. The white and green mosque attracts the eye from a distance. Visitors are very welcome. Good fish restaurants and shopping.

Khao Ping Kan, known as the "James Bond Rock" ▶

The boat trip continues through grand scenery: weirdly-shaped, steep, densely-overgrown rocks, the imposing results of the effect of wind and weather over the course of millennia, rise up from the sea. Many have grottoes, which can also be visited, others small sandy beaches with crystal-clear water. Particularly beautiful islands for bathing are Koh Mak, Koh Chong Lat and Koh Klui.

★★Khao Ping Kan ("James Bond Rocks")

A unique sight is Khao Ping Kan Bay, which appeared in the James Bond film "The Man with the Golden Gun". After this film, whose outside scenes were partly filmed here, the steep chalk rocks towering up in the middle of the bay were commonly called "James Bond Rocks". The best view of the rocks and the bay is gained from a small path, which ascends steeply on the right of the beach at the place where the boats land. Numerous traders sell souvenirs on the beach and there are also some refreshment stalls.

Phatthalung O 4

พัทลุง

Region: South Thailand
Province: Phatthalung
Altitude: 32m/105ft. Population: 24,000

Location and Scenery

The town of Phatthalung lies approximately 100km/62 miles north of the Malaysian border amid scenery typical of southern Thailand. Its precincts are clearly defined by the southern foothills of the Tenasserim mountains, part of the backbone of the Malay peninsula. Phatthalung is separated from the Gulf of Thailand by a freshwater reservoir, with an area of approximately 1250sq.km/483sq. miles, which increasingly silts up. Visitors here discover an impressive landscape of dense jungle and steep cliffs, with varied flora and fauna; a number of the temples are good examples of

Children in southern Thailand

elaborate Thai architecture. Many of the people living in and around Phatthalung are Thai-Malay half-castes and Moslems.

Access

By car: from Nakhon Si Thammarat Highway 401 to Ron Phibun, then Highway 41 (about 120km/74½ miles). From Songkhla Highway 407 to Hat Yai, then 43/4 (140km/87 miles).
By rail: on the Bangkok–Malaysia line.
By bus: connections from Nakhon Si Thammarat, Hat Yai, Songkhla, Trang and Phuket.

★Wat Khuha Suwan

One of Phatthalung's most beautiful temples, Wat Khuha Suwan (Highway 4018 northwards in the direction of Khuan Khanum), lies at the foot of a steep, conically-shaped rock. The elaborately embellished tympanums and the decorations on the wiharn are noteworthy. Behind the wat a flight of steps leads to a grotto; numerous statues of reclining and seated Buddhas, some gold-plated, can be found in the large hall of rocks, which is illuminated by daylight. A bodhi tree, with copper leaves, rises above them. The smaller grotto nearby was once inhabited by hermits, who left several Buddha statues here. From a chedi up on the cliffs there is a marvellous view across the mountains, the town and Thale-Luang Lake.

★Wat Wang

Wat Wang, a palace temple, is situated approximately 8km/5 miles east of the town. The elegant chedi contains excellently-maintained frescos dating from the late 18th c. (early Bangkok period).

Ban Lam Pam (fishing village)

The fishing village of Ban Lam Pam lies about 7km/4 miles further east on the banks of Songkhla Lake, the northern part of which is called Thale Luang. A boat trip to Tham Malai Grotto (approximately fifteen minutes), which lies between two prominent cliffs on the Phatthalung plain, proves very beautiful. The cliffs are popularly called "mountain of the pierced heart" (the straight, towering cliff has a deep hole through it) and "mountain of the decapitated head"; according to legend they are two women turned to stone, who fought each other out of jealousy. There is a small shrine on the hill (entrance to the dripstone cave).

★Thale Noi Bird Sanctuary

Thale Noi Bird Sanctuary is located 34km/21miles north-east of Phatthalung. More than 220 species of birds live here in a natural environment (reeds, swamp, flooded pastureland and jungle).

Thermal Springs

Thermal springs can be found at Khao Chai Son, a village some 20km/12½ miles north of Phatthalung.

Excursions

See Songkhla; Trang.

Phayao B 3

Region: North Thailand
Province: Phayao
Altitude: 67m/220ft. Population: 26,000

พะเยา

Location

Phayao lies on the high ground of northern Thailand between Chiang Rai and Lampang on the east bank of an attractive lake, 6km/4 miles long and 4km/2 miles wide. Prominent mountains, some reaching a height of 1700m/5579ft, tower above the town and even on the journey here travellers will pass through fantastic scenery. Once the main town of a small sovereign kingdom at the time of the Lan Na kingdom, into which it became assimilated in 1338, today it is a small and almost unimportant town, although of interest historically. The town developed in the 11th c. on the foundations of a very old settlement, which had been protected by walls and moats and was entered via eight town gates. This town possibly existed already in the Bronze Age, covering an area of about 2sq.km/1sq. mile.

Remains of the Wat Ratcha Santhan in Phayao

Access

By car: from Lampang Highway 1 (145km/90 miles) or Chiang Rai Highway 1 (95km/59 miles). Alternatively from Lampang Highway 1035 northwards to Wang Nua, then the new Highway 1882 westwards, the magnificent scenery well repays the extra journey time.

Wat Ratcha Santhan

Of Wat Ratcha Santhan, a 12th c. teak temple, only sparse remains exist. This marvellous example of Thai temple architecture collapsed during a storm in 1988. In its place can now be found an almost plain construction, with only ruins remaining of the two rhinoceros-nosed snakes, which formerly flanked the steps to the entrance with heads held high. Closer inspection reveals wooden roof supports from the old temple, which were incorporated into the building of the new wiharn. A Sukhothai-style statue of Buddha can be found inside. The recently constructed temple earns praise for the beautiful carving on the tympanum. Interestingly, an almost identical building, Wat Buakkhrok Luang, stands in Chiang Mai (see entry).

★Wat Si Kom Kam

Wat Si Kom Kam, whose wiharn was constructed recently for the 16m/52ft-high massive statue of a standing Buddha, is located on the town's northern boundary. The elaborate gilded carving on the façade of the wiharn is remarkable.

Phetchabun E 5

Region: Central Thailand
Province: Phetchabun
Altitude: 152m/499ft. Population: 14,000

เพชรบูรณ์

Location

Phetchabun, the main town of the province of the same name situated in the northern part of central Thailand, lies in a narrow valley of the Menam

Pasak between high mountain chains overgrown with dense rain forest. (In the east of the town is the Dong Phaya Yen massif, the threshold to the catchment area of the Mekong.) It is the centre of an intensively-farmed area; rice, maize, cotton and tobacco thrive here. The scenery boasts marvellous beauty, but the town itself offers few special sights.

Access

By car: from Bangkok Highway 1, beyond Saraburi 21 (350km/217 miles).
By bus: from Bangkok Northern Bus Terminal.
By rail: nearest station at Taphan Hin (62km/39 miles).

★Tham Phra Grotto

On a mountain on the left-hand side of the road 22km/14 miles north of Phetchabun can be seen the statue of a seated Buddha. The entrance to Tham Phra Grotto, with its marvellous dripstone shapes, lies at the end of a path (signposted).

Economy

Large orange plantations extend for about 20km/12½ miles south of Phetchabun. In common with the cattle farm and the stud farm nearby they are privately owned, although visits are possible.

Thung Saleng National Park

About 80km/50 miles north-west of Phetchabun. See Phitsanulok, surroundings.

Phetchaburi (Phetburi) H 3

Region: West Thailand
Province: Phetchaburi
Altitude: 6m/20ft. Population: 46,000

สพรรณบุรี

Location and Townscape

Phetchaburi (town of diamonds), the main town of Phetchaburi province, is surrounded by impressive mountain chains and lies south-west of Bangkok, approximately 10km/6 miles from the mouth of the river of the same name in the Gulf of Thailand. Khao Khlang mountain with King Mongkut's palace towers above Phetchaburi and dominates the townscape. The temple sites in the valley bear witness to a great past; the Chinese quarter points to the fact that Phetchaburi was once a centre of overseas trade. There are some beautiful, quiet beaches only a few miles away.

Access

By car: from Bangkok Highway 4 (about 123km/76 miles), alternatively Highway 35.
By bus: from Bangkok Southern Bus Terminal.
By rail: on the Bangkok–south Thailand line.

History

The town of Phetchaburi was probably founded by the Mon people in the 8th c., although there was an important base here even earlier on the trade route from Europe via India to China. In the 11th/12th c. Khmer people seized the town and established a religious centre here. Around 1350 Phetchaburi became part of the Ayutthaya kingdom. In 1610 the town fell temporarily under the control of Japanese pirates whose leaders declared themselves independent princes. That, however, was not in accordance with the quite liberal-minded kings of Ayutthaya who had previously allowed numerous European trading companies to settle here. After several confrontations King Petraja drove the *farang* (foreigners) out of the kingdom; for the next 130 years Thailand was closed to all foreigners.

★★Phra Nakhon Khiri Royal Palace

Opening Times
Wed.–Sun.
9am–4pm

Entry fee

Phra Nakhon Khiri royal palace stands above the town on the 95m/312ft-high Khao Khlang mountain. Built by King Mongkut (Rama IV) in about 1860 in the European/Neo-Classical style, its architect was Thuam Bunnak who later acted as Minister of Defence. He had gathered impressions of

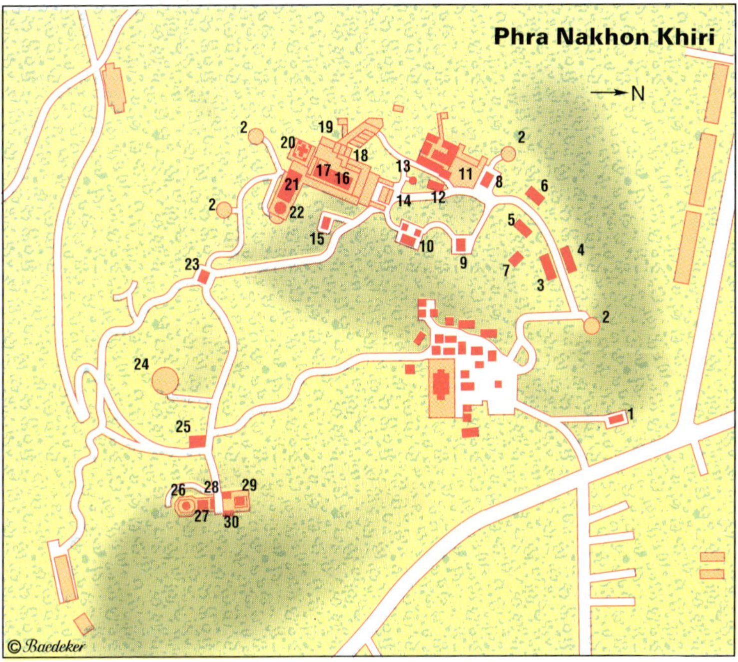

1 Sala Thasana Nakhathareuk
2 Fortification
3 Coach-house
4 Stables
5 Ratcha Wallaphakan
6 Sala Luk Khun
7 Public resting place
8 Sala Dan Na
9 Sala Yen Chai
10 Phiman-Phetmahet Halls
11 Phra Thinang Santhakarn Sathan Theatre
12 Sala Dan Klang
13 Wachara Phiban Fortress
14 Tim Dap Ongharak
15 Rong Sukathan
16 Phra Thinang Phetphum Phairot
17 Phra Thinang Pramot Mahaisawan
18 Royal kitchen
19 Storeroom
20 Phra Thinang Wechayan Wichien Prasat
21 Phra Thinang Ratchathamma Sapha
22 Chatchawan Wiangchai Observatory
23 Sala Dan Lang
24 Phra That Chom Phet
25 Chatuwet Paritaphat Pavilion
26 Chedi Phra Sutthasela
27 Consecration hall of the Wat Phra Kaeo
28 Belfry
29 Phra Prang Daeng
30 Pavilions

grand architecture during a European tour. King Mongkut himself cultivated the European way of life and was the first Thai ruler to learn a European language. His interests included mathematics, astronomy and political science. Like no other building in Thailand, this palace expresses the cosmopolitan way of life and thought of the Thai kings.

Site

Phra Nakhon Khiri was built on a hill with two summits, both attainable by paths. From the road which crosses the hill in the north visitors reach the palace grounds on the north-west summit either via a flight of steps flanked by nagas or on a small rack-railway, which operates during opening times. Remains of the fort, now inhabited by colonies of monkeys, and buildings used by royal guards are visible along the route. The site of the royal palace is open to the public if no members of the royal family are in residence. The extensive terraces offer a fine view of the valley and the small town of Phetchaburi.

Phra Thinang Phetphum Phairot

The foundation stone of Phra Thinang Phetphum Phairot, the site's largest building, was laid in July 1859. Constructed in the pure Neo-Classical style

The Royal Observatory in Phra Nakhon Khiri Palace

it first served as an audience chamber, later – as now, following fundamental renovation and partial reconstruction – as a residence for state guests. A large number of beautiful furnishings, including one of King Chulalongkorn's beds, are of note.

Phra Thinang Wichien Prasat

Phra Thinang Wichien Prasat, a very expressive building despite its simplicity, is a particularly magnificent example of Thai sacral architecture. On the roof four small, elaborately decorated towers surround a symbolic prang, whose base is encircled by a balustrade. Inside, beneath a seven-storeyed canopy, stands a statue of King Mongkut with a bust of the monarch in front of it. The bust was created by a French sculptor who modelled it initially on a photograph. King Mongkut was dissatisfied with the result and commissioned a Thai artist to cast another statue in bronze. This, however, followed the French example and so both pieces are displayed. King Mongkut died before the bronze statue was completed.

Observatory

The beautiful royal observatory (Chatchawan Wiangchai) has a glass roof and marvellous embellishments. Together with the buildings of the Phiman Phetmahet, the largest of which was used for the king's religious duties, it is worthy of attention.

Wat Phra Kaeo

An approximately 20 minute walk takes visitors from the north-west to the south-east summit. The most important building here is the Wat Phra Kaeo, which bears an amazing resemblance to the temple of the same name in the Grand Palace in Bangkok, on which it was modelled. From the time of the completion of the temple until King Mongkut's death a crystal statue of Buddha was displayed in the ordination hall, which has richly decorated tympanums and elaborately carved doors. The statue was returned to Bangkok and replaced by a copy. Chedi Phra Sutthasela (9m/30ft tall), partly built with material obtained from the island of Koh Sichang and

The Wat Phra Kaeo in the Royal Palace of Phra Nakhon Khiri

transported by ships via the Gulf of Thailand to Phetchaburi, stands behind the hall.

Three pavilions and a red sandstone prang are opposite the ordination hall. The main hill is occupied by a 40m/131ft-tall chedi, which King Mongkut had placed on the site of an older chedi.

Other Sights

Wat Mahathat

Wat Mahathat on the market place dates from the Ayutthaya period but was not completed until the 19th c. The scenery here is dominated by a tall Khmer-style prang, to which a gatehouse has been added, and the three smaller prangs grouped around it. Several beautiful statues of Buddha stand in the encircling gallery. The exterior of the large wiharn is decorated with stucco, while the interior has restored wall paintings and several statues of seated Buddhas, of which the very top one on the Ayutthaya-style altar is particularly noteworthy. Very beautiful stucco also embellishes the small building next to the wiharn in a separate courtyard.

★★Wat Yai Suwannaram

Of the many interesting temples in the town of Phetchaburi, Wat Yai Suwannaram to the east of the centre is one of the most beautiful. Dating from the 17th c., the oldest buildings are examples of the best Ayutthaya style. The wiharn contains murals, mainly horizontal friezes of gods praying to Buddha. The delicate colouring, the self-assured lines and careful attention to detail are striking. Also of note are a marvellous coffered ceiling and the figure of a seated Buddha. During the reign of King Chulalongkorn a gallery was laid out, which is decorated with sculptured lintels. There are two charming wooden libraries, one dating from the early days of the temple, the other from the end of the 19th c. The large sala with its beautifully ornamental decoration and its bold proportions also warrants attention.

Wat Phra Bat Chai

Wat Phra Bat Chai stands somewhat further to the north. Small and atmospheric, it has beautifully carved wooden doors.

Phetchaburi

Chinese Temple

A number of attractive Chinese temples in Phetchaburi's Chinese quarter are worth visiting.

Wat Kamphaeng Laeng

Already partly ruined, Wat Kamphaeng Laeng lies to the south-east of the town. It has a high Lopburi-style prang built from heavy laterite blocks (12th c.) and to which the door has been added. It is surrounded by three smaller prangs and some small buildings.

★Wat Ko Kaeo

Wat Ko Kaeo, called Wat Ko for short, is situated in the south of the town on the east bank of the river and was built at the beginning of the 18th c. It is famous chiefly for the marvellous paintings on the walls of the Bot. The very lively scenes depicting the life of Buddha stand out owing to their bold artistry and are particularly significant because they are triangularly framed, with the apex pointing downwards. The spaces form upward-pointing triangles, which imitate the form of the chedi; they are mostly filled with Jataka scenes (including more than 500 of the early life of Buddha). The wall painting behind the sacrificial altar shows Buddha's temptation by Mara and his victory over the temptor.

Surroundings

Tham Khao Luang Cave

Of the countless caves and grottoes found around Phetchaburi, Tham Khao Luang Cave, also a Buddhist place of worship, enjoys most fame (Highway 4 to the west, turn right on to Highway 3173, 3km/2 miles). It comprises several high and wide halls, with a number of Buddha figures in the entrance hall. Steep steps lead down into a very large hall filled with dripstones and countless statues of Buddha. The light entering the hall through holes and cracks in the vault conjures up a magical atmosphere.

★Khao Yoi (mountain)

After a further 18km/11 miles northwards on Highway 4 travellers will reach Khao Yoi, the "mountain of stalactites", with several dripstone caves. Some are used as shrines and are furnished with figures of Buddha.

A cave in the Khao Yoi mountain

Kang Krachan Reservoir

South of Phetchaburi a road turns off Highway 4 at Tha Yang and passes through cotton fields and sugar-cane plantations to the mountain-encircled Kang Krachan Reservoir. It irrigates the fields and also provides the water supply for Phetchaburi.

Phimai F 6

Region: North-east Thailand
Province: Nakhon Ratchasima
Altitude: 34m/112ft
Population: 15,000

พิมาย

Location

The town of Phimai, located 270km/168 miles north-east of Bangkok on the almost bare Khorat Plateau, was founded by the Khmers. The shrine is the largest and, without doubt, best preserved example in this area of Khmer art in Thailand. It was built only a few years after the important temple sites of Angkor Wat in Cambodia. Phimai's temple site is certainly considerably smaller than Angkor Wat, but, like its famous model, the most beautiful and purest Khmer style is evident in its design and its artistic quality.

Access

By car: from Nakhon Ratchasima Highway 2 to Talat Khae (44km/27 miles), then right along 206 (signpost; a total of 56km/35 miles).
By bus: from Bangkok Northeastern Bus Terminal and Nakhon Ratchasima.
By rail: nearest station Nakhon Ratchasima.
By air: nearest airport Nakhon Ratchasima (daily from Bangkok).

History

Discoveries of clay fragments and jewellery provide evidence that the area around Phimai had already been settled during the Neolithic age. In the 11th c. the Khmers had the town fortified and developed it into the centre of their empire. Like other towns in north Thailand, i.e. Buriram, Chaiyaphum and Lampang, Phimai lies on the route which linked Angkor to its provinces and which could be reconstructed from findings; the distance between Phimai and Angkor measured approximately 240km/149 miles. As the finds tell, Phimai was at that time a very important religious town.

In the 14th c., when the first ruler of Ayutthaya, King Rama Thibodi I (1350–69), conquered Angkor, Phimai lost importance as many of its impressive buildings collapsed. After Ayutthaya's destruction by the Burmese in 1767 and the fall of the empire, Phimai became the main town of a principality. This, however, was integrated into the new kingdom of Siam in 1768 after King Taksin's victory over Prince Phiphit of Phimai. The ruined town of Phimai was restored with considerable expenditure in the 1980s and opened to the public again as Phimai Historical Park.

Townscape

Present-day Phimai occupies only part of the former town, once protected by walls, ramparts and moats; it originally covered an area of 582sq.km/225sq. miles. Only ruins of the 4m/13ft-high sandstone walls remain and of the four pavilion-type town gates only the southern one, Pratu Chai (Victory Gate), still stands. The Khmer rulers would enter the town through this gate accompanied by their entourage, having come from Angkor. A shop-lined street led from here straight to the temple grounds.

Meru Boromathat hill rises by a parallel street on the right; the brick building in which King Boromathat's cremation is supposed to have taken place now consists solely of ruins. The cremation of Boromathat's wife probably occurred on a smaller hill opposite.

The town of Phimai occupies a strategically favourable position on an island; a canal, no longer in existence, was built between Menam Mun and Khlong Chakrai, one of its tributaries, which surround the largest part of the old town's precincts.

★★Ruined Town (Phimai Historical Park)

Opening times
Daily 9am–4.30pm

Entry Fee

The temple shrine, one of the few in Thailand to be fenced in and to be open only at fixed times as safeguards against pillaging, dates from the 11th/12th c. and was dedicated to Hindu gods and to Buddha. The temple site was constructed on the foundation walls of a very much older shrine. The appearance of this shrine remains unknown, as do its commissioners. The town and the shrine gained their names from the Buddha Vimaya. Next to the town's council building, only a few feet from the south gate, the remains of Khlang Ngoen can be seen. This pavilion was probably built during the reign of King Jayavarman (about 1200) and may well have been a royal inn or a hospital for the citizens of the town (sandstone blocks, used to crush herbs for medicinal purposes, were found here).

The temple site is entered through the well-maintained south gate in the second encircling wall. The outer courtyard was embellished at all four corners by large ponds; only ruins remain of their stone walls. They symbolised India's four holy rivers and contained rainwater, used to pour on the lingams (phallic symbols of the Hindu god Shiva) and other holy figures.

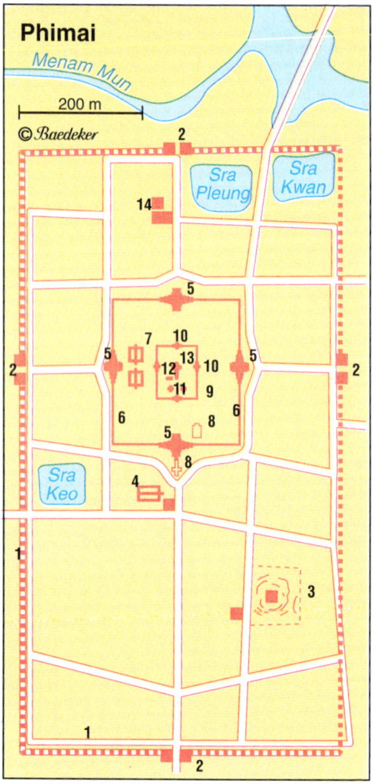

1 Third curtain wall
2 Town gates; South gate: Pratu Chai (Victory gate)
3 Meru Boromathat
4 Khlang Ngoen (treasury)
5 Portal buildings (Gopura)
6 Second curtain wall
7 Royal Palace
8 Terraces
9 First curtain wall (gallery)
10 Gate buildings
11 Shrines
12 Hindu shrine (library)
13 Principal shrine
14 Wat Doem

The two buldings constructed from laterite and sandstone close to the west gate were also built at the time of King Jayavarman VII and probably served as a library or provided accommodation for the Khmer kings. Remains of a terrace, on which a wooden building certainly once stood, can be seen on the right of the south gate. Some of the stone reliefs, no longer safe to be left in their original positions because of the danger of collapse, are displayed on it.

The 12th c. gallery's four gates, which point in all four directions of the compass, were laid out in the shape of a cross and stood, as did the porticos, on strong square pillars, which partially remain. On the left of the 5504sq.m/59,245sq.ft inner courtyard stands prang Hin Daeng, built

The "Thai Angkor": the temple precinct of Phimai

from red sandstone, a little further on a building (probably a treasure chamber or a library) designated as a Hindu shrine, and on the right Prang Meru Boromathat, constructed from laterite. An extraordinarily beautiful statue of King Jayavarman VII found in this prang is now displayed in Bangkok's National Museum.

Main Temple

The main shrine is crowned with a marvellous, richly articulated prang and has stepped porticos with elaborately sculptured superstructures and side doors on all four sides. The southern portico is joined to a long porch, lit internally by door openings on the sides and by a window with stone balustrades in the main entrance. A row of lotus buds adorns the roof.

Together with Angkor Wat, this complex, built from fine grey sandstone either at the end of the 11th c. or the beginning of the 12th c. by King Jayavarman VII and King Dharaindravarman I, constitutes the most beautiful example of Khmer architecture, exquisite in its proportions, moderate, but highly artistic in its ornamentation. The sanctuary's pyramid-shaped tower, crowned with a lotus bud, is borne by garudas and is covered with nagas as well as figures of gods and demons. The lintels (including those in the interior) are of high artistic quality and beauty, as are the tympanums on the porch and the prang. They depict scenes from the history of the Khmer empire and portraits of Buddha and the saints from Mahayana Buddhism. Nearby there are scenes from the Ramayana epos. Five-headed nagas border the tympanums on both sides; the ledges on the base and the pillars on the two sides are decorated with bas-reliefs.

The tower, which forms a false vault (i.e. with a stone inner vault) in the interior, once held the temple complex's most important statue of Buddha. This and other holy figures were sprinkled by priests during ceremonies, in which the town's population participated, with rainwater from the four ponds in the outer courtyard. The opening of the water pipe and the metal part underneath are still visible on the east side of the tower.

Relief ornamentation . . . *. . . on the principal sanctuary*

Remains of Wat Doem's encircling wall can be seen near the collapsed north gate in the outer courtyard. This also stood on the foundations of an earlier shrine.

★★Phimai National Museum

Opening Times
Wed.–Sun.
8.30am–4pm

Entry fee

No photography

A little jewel, Phimai's National Museum is to be found on the right in front of the bridge across the Menam Mun at the town's north-west exit. The exhibits are displayed in the open air and include, most importantly, marvellously sculptured lintels from local Khmer temples and portraits of Buddha, including one which shows Buddha underneath the unnatural shell of a seven-headed naga. The plinth forms the ringed body of the snake. This style is typical of Khmer sculpture.

★★Banyan tree

A road behind the bridge leads to the right to a reservoir and, after about a mile, to a botanical wonder, an enormous Banyan tree (*ficus indiaca*), whose canopy of leaves has a diameter of 85m/279ft and which, despite its network of aerial roots branching out in all directions, needs to be supported by concrete pillars. Its shade provides welcome shelter for whole families. The tree stands on an island, on whose banks are several restaurants.

Phitsanulok E 4

พิษณุโลก

Region: North Thailand
Province: Phitsanulok
Altitude: 50m/164ft
Population: 100,000

Location and Townscape

Phitsanulok is situated in the north of the central plain on Menam Nan, one of the main tributaries of Menam Chao Phraya, and is surrounded by rice fields. After fire destroyed most of the old town of Phitsanulok a new business and trading town was developed, where little trace can now be found of the former importance of the neighbouring town of Sukhothai. From the bridge across the Nan and the alleys leading alongside it a good impression can be gained of the lively atmosphere prevalent around the houses built on stilts and on the river.

It is worthwhile combining a visit to Phitsanulok with a "historical" tour of Sukhothai, Si Satchanalai and Kamphaeng Phet.

Access

By car: from Bangkok Highway 1/32/117, alternatively 11 (about 380km/236 miles). From Sukhothai Highway 12 (58km/36 miles).
By bus: from Bangkok Northern Bus Terminal.
By rail: on the Bangkok–Chiang Mai line.
By air: daily from Bangkok and Chiang Mai.

History

Around 1362 the Ayutthaya king Rama Thibodi (U Thong) conquered Phitsanulok, which was already at that time an important town in the Sukhothai kingdom. However, King Liu Thai soon regained it by peaceful means and made it his residence for the next seven years. From 1438 Phitsanulok was ruled by the crown prince of Ayutthaya as a viceroy and belonged, like the entire Sukhothai kingdom, to the Ayutthaya kingdom. The Burmese took the town in 1563. After the destruction of the Ayutthaya kingdom Phitsanulok became, for a short while, the main town of a small principality until, in 1770, King Taksin also annexed this to the developing kingdom of Siam. In 1955 Phitsanulok was almost completely destroyed by a devastating fire; a number of religious buildings have been reconstructed in a faceless modern style.

★★Wat Phra Si Ratana Mahathat

General Information

The most important construction in Phitsanulok stands near the bridge across the Nan on the edge of the old town. Wat Phra Si Ratana Mahathat can be recognised from a distance by its 36m/118ft-tall, Khmer-style prang, completed in 1482. The upper section of the prang is gold-plated. The wat was built at the end of the 15th c. by King Boroma Trailokanat (1448–88) as a symbol of his rule over the newly-acquired area. The temple has been restored several times, which has greatly altered its appearance.

Tour

The wiharn's steep roof is built of coloured glass bricks (Bangkok period) and is in three layers; the tympanums are decorated by gold-plated coffered carving. Slender pillars flank the portico, giving the entire building an appearance of striking ease. The Buddha statues on either side of the portico are marvellous examples of the Sukhothai and the Chiang Saen styles. The ebony doors with mother of pearl inlays date from 1756.

The wiharn is lit only by narrow openings in the low side walls. Its triple-aisled interior is one of Thailand's most beautiful sacral rooms. Dark blue, red and gold lend definite colour to the pillars, which end as lotus buds, and to the strutted entablature.

The wall paintings are more recent. The picture on the right depicts Buddha's enlightenment, the one on the left records the time in the life of the enlightened one, when he gave up all his worldly goods and dedicated himself totally to religion.

Phra Buddha Jinarat

The very eye-catching centrepiece is a statue of Phra Buddha Jinarat ("the victorious king"), a master work in the late Sukhothai style and cast in bronze aound 1350. It shows a seated Buddha in the gesture of invocation with a finely-chased aureole in front of a dark blue background, embellished with stylised gold flowers and hovering forms. Several copies of this statue have been made; one of the last, commissioned by King Chulalongkorn, can be found in Wat Benchamabo-bitr in Bangkok. According to

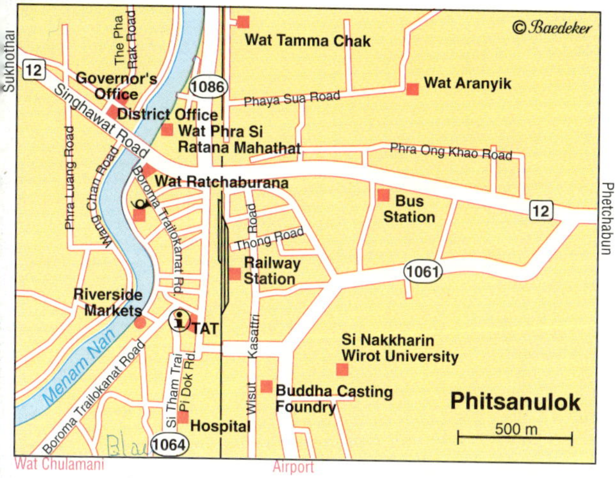

legend, at the time when Phitsanulok became the main town and the viceroy moved into it, this statue wept tears of blood. Not least because of this it is held in great esteem by local people.

Some of the statues of Buddha surrounding the central figure are very beautiful. The elaborately-carved teak pulpits are also of note. The larger one is used by a group of monks when singing Buddhist Pali texts, while texts in the Thai language are read out from the smaller one.

The terrace, from which the prang rises, borders the wiharn. Steps lead to the reliquary. The gallery around the prang is filled with numerous attractive statues of Buddha in the Sukhothai, U Thong and Chiang Mai/Chiang Saen styles, as well as wood carvings and Chinese and Thai ceramics. Other buildings, including the bot, adjoin the gallery.

By leaving the temple grounds via the main exit and walking round to the rear of them the giant statue of a standing Buddha and two other, modern statues of Buddha can be seen.

★Wat Ratchaburana

On the same river bank the new Wat Ratchaburana has been built on the ruins of an old temple opposite Wat Mahathat, on the other side of the street. Only an impressive chedi remains of the old wat.

An attractive bell tower and a shrine, whose carved wooden portal is inlaid with coloured stones and whose interior features interesting frescos (scenes from the Ramayana) completes the site.

Surroundings

★Wat Chulamani

The ruins of Wat Chulamani are to be found 5km/3 miles south of Phitsanulok. This shrine, clearly influenced by the Khmer style, stands on a three-stepped, richly-articulated brick plinth. The main portal, reached by a flight of steps, and the side portals, partly decorated with stucco, have been retained, together with a beautiful statue of Buddha. The recently-built small hall has little in common with the original building. The wat probably dates from the Lopburi period and was restored in the early Ayutthaya period under King Boroma Trailokanat (1448–88).

◀ *The "Phra Buddha Jinarat" statue in the Wat Phra Si Ratana Mahathat*

Temple precinct of the Wat Phra Si Ratana Mahathat

Wang Thong

Highway 12 leaves Phitsanulok in an easterly direction. After approximately 15km/9 miles the ruins of a chedi become visible on the summit of a hill: a marvellous view can be enjoyed from them. Behind the village of Wang Thong (20km/12½ miles east of Phitsanulok) the forestry commission has laid out a small park at the Menam Kok rapids.

Waterfalls

Of the waterfalls by the wayside or away from the road, Nam Tok Kaeng So Pa is particularly worth seeing. Follow the signpost about 52km/32 miles from Phitsanulok.

Nakhon Thai

A number of Burmese-style temple sites can be found in the small village of Nakhon Thai (once called Ban Yang), 31km/19 miles north of Highway 12 (turn off approximately 60km/37 miles from Phitsanulok).

Thung Saleng National Park

Thung Saleng Luang National Park, 1280sq.km/494sq. miles in size, lies about 65km/40 miles east of Phitsanulok. Highway 12 passes through a hilly landscape of mixed forest into the densely-overgrown jungle of the mountain heights, which separate the Menam Nan plain from that of the Menam Pasak. The national park is home to many species of animals, such as elephant, buffalo, wild boar, deer and the occasional tiger or panther, and rises to a height of 1500m/4923ft. Overnight accommodation is available in the guest house at the entrance to the park and in the selection of very comfortable bungalows. To the north of Highway 12 is a development centre for the inhabitants of the surrounding Meo villages.

Phrae C 4

Region: North Thailand
Province: Phrae
Altitude: 163m/535ft. Population: 24,000

แพร่

Location

Lively and rich Phrae, centre of the province of the same name and one of Thailand's oldest towns, lies approximately 550km/342 miles north of Bangkok in the fertile valley of Menam Yom, one of the tributaries of Menam Chao Phraya. Since the completion of the Yom dam, agriculture has been the most important factor in the region's economy. Tobacco (dried in large, brick-built ovens), sugar-cane, maize and peanuts are the main crops.

The numerous temple buildings are stylistically similar to those of Lamphun, as both towns once belonged to the Haripunchai kingdom. Traces of Burmese and Laotian occupation remain.

Access

By car: from Phitsanulok Highway 11 (180km/112 miles). From Lampang Highway 11/101 (85km/53 miles), from Nan Highway 101 (125km/78 miles).
By rail: nearest station Den Chai (23km/14 miles).
By air: daily from Bangkok and Chiang Mai.

Sights

Town wall

Phrae's old town wall has been almost completely retained or reconstructed. The town's most important sights are located within the wall.

★Wat Chom Sawan
★Wat Sa Bo Keo

Wat Chom Sawan, on the northern edge of the town, and Wat Sa Bo Keo, in Nam Khue Road, were both built in the Burmese style (the former at the beginning of this century). Both temples enjoy fine proportions, beautiful coffered ceilings, richly-decorated altars and large, marvellously-shaped chedis.

Wat Phra Bat Ming Muang Vora Vihara

The Laotian-style Bot, with its gracious pillars, and the charming library of Wat Phra Bat Ming Muang Vora Vihara in Charoen Muang Road are striking.

★Wat Si Chum

Wat Si Chum on Kham Saen Road encompasses a large complex, which includes three shrines, a beautiful 16th c. chedi and an attractive library. The shrine on the left houses a Laotian-style statue of Buddha, the central one contains another notable Buddha statue in the Sukhothai style.

Wat Luang

Situated on the western part of the town wall, Wat Luang's slender, Burmese-style chedi, its figure of a seated Buddha and the carving on the wiharn's beams are very beautiful.

★★Wat Phra Non

Particularly worth seeing is Wat Phra Non at the end of Wichaira Cha Road, which was named after the figure of a standing Buddha (18th c.). The figure is inside a building next to the wiharn, whose elegant proportions and richly-decorated gables also make it an attraction. The chedi dates from the 18th c.

Surroundings

Wat Phra That Cho Mae

Wat Phra That Cho Mae stands on a hill about 8km/5 miles south of the town (Highway 1022 in the direction of the airport). It is dominated by a 34m/112ft-tall chedi, clad with gold-plated copper tiles, and is famed for the figure of a seated Buddha, to which mainly women make pilgrimages to ask to be blessed with children. The proportions and decorations of the recently-built shrine are of interest.

Muang Pi (rock formation)

A group of unusually-shaped rocks in the north (Highway 101 in the direction of Nan, turn right after 9km/6 miles, turn off after 2.5km/1½ miles, straight on for 3km/2 miles) are known as Muang Pi (ghost village).

Wat Phra Luang

Turn right in the village of Sung Noen, 10km/6 miles north of Phrae, to find attractive Wat Phra Luang. The old 12th c. chedi resembles Lamphun's pyramid-shaped chedis, but is not so richly articulated. Statues of Buddha fill the niches on all four sides. Beautiful sculptures adorn the unique library building, whose entrances are reached via covered steps. The octagonal bell tower is also of interest. The modern wiharn is decorated with marvellous carving.

★Yom reservoir

The beauty of the mountainous landscape can be enjoyed on a journey to the idyllically-located Yom reservoir near to Song (28km/17 miles north of Phrae, Highway 101 to Rong Kwang, then 103). The reservoir supplies water to the inhabitants of the surrounding area.

Phuket (island) O 2

Region: South Thailand
Province: Phuket
Altitude: 2m/7ft.
Population: 174,745 (island) 55,000 (town)

ภูเก็ต

Location

Coconut palms and rubber trees grow on the hilly island of Phuket, located in the extreme south-west of Thailand (geographical location: approximately 8° north and 98° 20′ east) and famed for its long, white, sandy beaches lining the azure blue sea. Measuring 48.7km/30 miles long and 21.3km/13 miles wide, Phuket is Thailand's largest island. The Chinese and Portuguese-influenced houses of Phuket, the province's main town, continue to radiate charm.

Access

By car: from Bangkok Highway 4 to Ban Koke Loi, via 402 and Sarasin bridge to the island (860km/534 miles). From Surat Thani Highways 401/4 (290km/180 miles). From Nakhon Si Thammarat 401/403/4 (340km/211 miles).
By bus: from Bangkok Southern Bus Terminal air-conditioned buses (journey time approximately thirteen hours).
By air: both internal and charter flights fly to Phuket.

Climate

Phuket has an exceptional climate. The monsoon arrives here earlier than, for example, on the other side of the gulf. It does not rain constantly during

A house in Portuguese style in Phuket

Sarasin Bridge
Mai Khao Beach
402
268
Koh Pa Yu
Nai Yang Nat. Park
Nai Yang Beach
Koh Reat
450
Po Bay
Koh Nakha Yai
Talang
366
Khao Phra Thaeo
Koh Nakha Noi
Bang Thao Bay
Cape Son
Cape Yabu
4025
Surin Beach
2 Sisters Monument
Sapam Bay
Koh Rang Noi
Kamala Beach
Koh Rang Yai
Koh Maphrao Yai
Kathu
402
Cape Nga
Patong Beach
4029
4020
Koh Siray
Phuket
529
4022
4021
Makham Bay
Karon Beach
4023
Koh Taphao Noi
Koh Poo
Koh Taphao Yai
Kata Beach
4028
Chalong Bay
4024
Kata Noi Beach
Cape Phanwa
263
Koh Lon
Cape Ka
Nai Harn Beach
Rawai Beach
Koh Mai Thon
Cape Phromthep
Koh Bond
5 km
Koh Kaeo
Phuket
© Baedeker

the monsoon period but once or twice a day in sometimes heavy downpours: experts think that the subtropical character of the island is shown to its most beautiful advantage at this time. The months of December to March have the fewest rainy days (on average five a month). Throughout the year daily temperatures lie between 28°C/82°F and 32°C/90°F.

Warning

Strong underwater currents occur along the beaches particularly during the monsoon period (May–Oct.). Under certain circumstances these can be very dangerous. Take advice from local people.

History

Mons (Khmers) are thought to have been Phuket's first inhabitants: they came via the Bay of Bengal from Pagan in present-day Myanmar (Burma), named the island Iunsalen and founded three settlements: Thalang, Kathu and Phuket. The Mons were later joined by Indonesian nomads, "Chao Ley" or "Chao Nam" ("land/water people"); descendants of these people still live on Phuket ("sea gypsies"). King Ekatotsarot (1605–10) was the first to allow trade between Europeans and the native population. Soon after, French, Portuguese and Dutch established trading settlements: the English discovered the extensive tin deposits on Phuket.

The Burmese laid siege to Phuket for the first time in 1785; by the third siege, around 1800, the town had been destroyed. The sisters Chan and Muk led a resistance movement, which protected their home town of Thalang from capture by the Burmese: they pretended to the occupying forces that Thalang was full of soldiers because all the women had dressed up as military men. A bronze memorial situated between the airport and the town commemorates the two national heroines ("Two Sisters" or "Heroines' Monument", Highway 402).

At the beginning of the 19th c. countless Chinese immigrants streamed into Phuket, attracted by the rich mineral resources. They mixed with the native population and their presence is still evident today; about 50,000 of Phuket's inhabitants are "true" Chinese.

"Sea Gipsies", descendents of Indonesian nomads

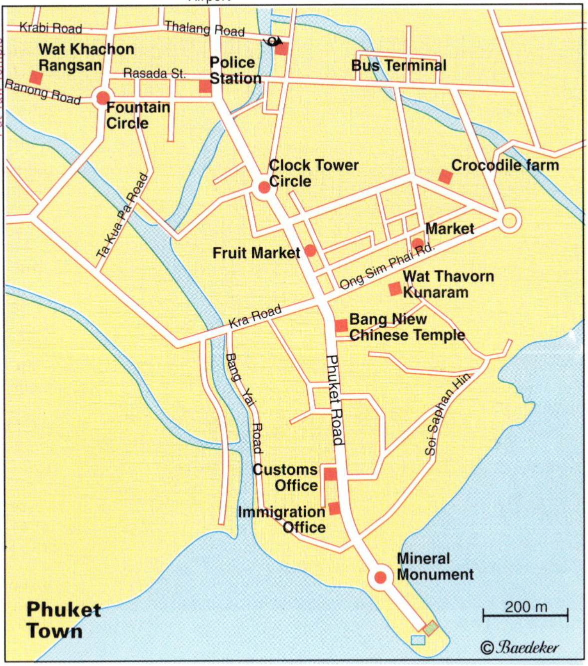

After King Rama V had annexed Phuket into his kingdom, the island officially joined the Kingdom of Siam, with Phuket declared the main town of the new province. About 170,000 people now live in the province. The town and the island's upswing are thanks to the systematic extraction of tin deposits. Most of the tin mines are now idle following the drastic fall in the price of tin during the 1980s. The appearance of many damage the otherwise unspoilt rural scenery and are supposed to be recultivated. In addition to tin, tungsten was also discovered on Phuket: raw rubber and copra (the cut and dried flesh of coconuts – the raw material used in the production of coconut oil) are important agricultural products.

Tourism

In little more than ten years – in 1980 Patong Beach was opened up to development – Phuket has changed from a lonely island with dreamy beaches to a playground of mass tourism with all the problems which come with it. The main resorts present the usual picture with hotel blocks, exotically-furnished restaurants, pleasure parlours and "chicken bars"; the airport is the "turnstile" of the south and, with 2.2 million passengers a year, Thailand's second largest. For the native population price increases have been vast, with only investors from Bangkok and abroad profiting from the boom. It is recognised that the influx of tourism must be checked and channelled: whether those responsible for ecology at TAT, in the province's government and in local trade will gain the upper hand against short-term economic interests remains to be seen.

Sights in Phuket town

Phuket, lying on the south-east coast of the island on a picturesque bay, was built in the mid-19th c. to replace the old town of Phalang, destroyed by the Burmese around 1800. The influence of Chinese immigrants is evident

Gate of the Put Yaw Chinese temple

At the "Vegetarian Festival": Chinese in a trance

Wiharn of the Wat Chalong, in pure Thai style

Townscape

in the two-storey, brick-covered houses decorated with wood carvings. Also typical are the arcaded passages, which allow walks to be taken protected from the rigours of the weather, and the ceiling-high displays in the shops to be admired. Around the town centre stand a number of houses with very beautiful gardens, built by rich Chinese and Malaysians, who made their fortunes from raw rubber and tin.

★Chinese Temple

The oldest and most beautiful Chinese temple on Phuket, Put Yaw in Ranong Road, documents the great influence of its Chinese-descended population. The main temple is dedicated to Kuan Yin, the goddess of grace.

Governor's Residence

The old governor's residence near Put Yaw Temple is the seat of the province's administration. Built in the 1920s in the colonial style, the stucco decoration and the capitals on the pillars in the entrance portal are remarkable. The residence was used in the US Vietnam war film "The Killing Fields" as the Cambodian governor's palace. Opposite stands a Portuguese-style building constructed in 1916 and now the province's law court.

Markets

Locals purchase their everyday requirements and stop for a chat at the lively market in Rasada Street (daily 5–11am). Further east in Rasada Street is the local bus station. Further interesting markets, held daily, are to be found in Ranong Road and Ong Sim Phai Road.

Festivals in Phuket

The inhabitants of Phuket know how to celebrate festivals. Songkhram Festival, the old Thai new year festival, is celebrated particularly loudly – and damply! Apart from their new year festival (Jan./Feb.), the Chinese celebrate the Vegetarian Festival during the first nine days of the ninth lunar month (usually mid Sept. or Oct.). A special spectacle can be seen each evening at this festival: entranced people run barefoot over hot coals or pierce their cheeks with lances, without injuring themselves.

Surroundings

★ Phuket Aquarium

By leaving Phuket in a southerly direction crossroads are reached from which Sakdidet Road (Highway 4023) turns off. Makham Bay (Ao Makham), the Marine Biology Research Centre investigating the life-style and conditions of the sea's fauna, where fish and other sea creatures are kept in enormous aquariums, is located at the end of this road (a further 6km/4 miles). (Open: daily 10am–4pm, entry fee.) A tour of the research station can be undertaken if an advance booking is made (tel. 391 126).

★ Wat Chalong

Wat Chalong, built in the pure Thai style, lies 6km/4 miles south-west of Phuket (Highway 4021). A gold-plated monument commemorates the abbot Luang Pho Chaem who worked as a non-medical practitioner in this temple in about 1880. Luang Pho Chaung, another monk honoured by the population, also lived in Wat Chalong.

Coconut Palm (botanical rarity)

A botanical rarity, a four-branched coconut palm, can be seen shortly before Rawai, 9km/5½ miles further south. The tree is more than 60 years old; after the first 20 years the trunk split in two, and after another 20 years two branches grew in turn out of the two trunks.

Ban Rawai

Vichit Road continues to the village of Rawai, which is inhabited by "sea gypsies". They belong to the Moken, a tribe whose roots are to be found, according to anthropologists, on the Andaman and Nikobar Islands. Some live by the sea while others lead a semi-nomadic life on the land. They believe in spirits and have maintained their own customs. Any attempts by the Thai government to integrate them have failed. The men of the village work mostly as fishermen and sometimes also as guides for sea trips.

The "sea gypsies" celebrate the Loy Rua Festival when twice a year sacrifices are made to the spirits, at the beginning and end of the fishing season.

Rawai itself has a small fishing harbour and a beach covered with coconut palms and swamp oaks. Boats can be rented here to sail to the offshore islands.

The beaches of Nai Harn (with the Phuket Yacht Club Hotel), Kata Noi, Kata, Karon, Karon Noi and, finally, the main beach, Patong Beach, lie south of Rawai Beach (Hat Rawai) and further north along the west coast.

Three Beaches View

By travelling along the branch road in front of Kata Noi Beach in a south-westerly direction, Three Beaches View, a viewpoint, is reached near the southern tip of the island of Phuket. From here, as the name suggests, a view across three of Phuket's most beautiful beaches can be enjoyed.

Patong Beach

The island of Phuket's longest beach – once also one of its most beautiful – is Patong Beach. As in Pattaya, multi-storeyed hotels abound here: peaceful beaches can only now be found away from this area. In the evening many visitors enjoy strolling along Patong Beach, with its shops, restaurants, night-clubs and bars.

★ Nam Tok Kathu (waterfall)

From the northern end of Patong Beach, Highway 4029 leads north-west to Kathu (5km/3 miles). Nam Tok waterfall, one of the island's most beautiful, lies a further 3km/2 miles north.

North of Patong other beaches along the west coast, which is very rugged in places, are Kamala, Surin (about 2km/1 mile north-east of an attractive mosque, Phuket's largest and open to the public apart from at prayer times) and Bang Thao Beach.

★ Wat Phra Thong

Wat Phra Thong at Thalang, away from Highway 402, owes its construction to the following legend: a boy was minding a water buffalo, which he tethered to a piece of metal protruding from the ground using a hemp-rope. Suddenly the boy died, but appeared to his father in a dream and told him about the piece of metal. The father began to dig and came upon a statue of Buddha cast in pure gold. The Buddha could not, however, be completely excavated and so a temple was built on the site in 1785. When the Burmese

"Three Beaches View" on the west coast

A beach on an island off Phuket

Built into the hillside: Phuket Yacht Club Hotel

conquered Thalang a second attempt was made to dig up the statue at which point it broke in two. One half disappeared, but the other still stands in the temple, where it can be viewed. The gables and windows of the temple buildings exhibit rich carving.

Hat Nai Yang National Park

Hat Nai Yang National Park covers the island's north-west coastal stretch. It lies about 30km/19 miles away from Phuket: take the road to the airport, then follow the signs. At night turtles still come on to the land here to lay their eggs.

Khao Phra Thaeo Game Reserve

Khao Phra Thaeo Game Reserve includes the hills which rise to a height of 445m/1460ft in the north-east of the island and is inhabited by buffalo, wild boar, elephants and monkeys as well as many species of tropical birds. Pleasant paths lead through the reserve. Information is available from TAT in Phuket.

★★Boat trips

A boat trip around the fantastic island world surrounding Phuket should not be missed. Particular mention must be made of Maphrao, Nakha Yai and Nakha Noi (on the east coast, pearl culture at the latter), Koh Bond, Koh Kaeo, Raja Noi and Raja Yai (off the southern tip) and the little Poo Island on the west coast off Hat Kata. Boats depart from Po Bay for a day excursion to Phangnga (see entry) with the famous "James Bond rocks". Two or more days are needed for a visit to Koh Phi Phi (see Krabi: trips from Phuket are also possible).

★★Koh Similan (island group) M 1

Location
95km/59 miles north-west of Phuket

The Koh Similan island group, composed of nine uninhabited islands, attracts diving enthusiasts. Tour operators and diving schools offer excursions to these still paradise-like islands, whose underwater world remains relatively intact. Those wishing to go there independently should travel

104km/65 miles north of Phuket to Thap Lamu and take a ferry from there. Boats sail daily from Patong Beach on Phuket to Koh Similan (journey time about 8 hours by regular boat or in 3½ hours as part of a tour operator's fast day trip). Some accommodation is available on the main island. Koh Similan was declared a national park some years ago but this has made no difference to the increase in tourism here, with all its negative side effects.

Prachinburi G 5

Region: East Thailand
Province: Prachinburi
Altitude: 9m/30ft
Population: 16,000

ปราจีนบุรี

Location

The town of Prachinburi, situated approximately 90km/56 miles north-east of Bangkok, was founded by the Mons, who also retained their importance during Khmer rule, and was a station on the old trade route leading from India via Burma to Cambodia and China. Finds verify that a settlement already existed here in prehistoric times. The town offers few sights: its charming appearance during the monsoon period is best experienced on a boat trip through the narrow canals. Menam Bang Pakong flows through the plain, which is bordered in the north by mountain chains.

Access

By car: from Bangkok Highway 1/305 to Nakhon Nayok, then Highway 33/319 (a total of 135km/84 miles).
By bus: from Bangkok Northern Bus Terminal.
By rail: on the Bangkok–Aranyaprathet (–Cambodia) line.

Surroundings

★Si Maha Phot

One of Thailand's most productive excavation sites is to be found at Si Maha Phot, 23km/14 miles south-east of the town. Numerous remains of 6th–7th c. Hindu temples (Dvaravati period) have been unearthed here. Many of the finds, including stumps of pillars, plinths, boundary stones, sculptures of lions and nagas, and a 2m/6½ft-tall sandstone lingam (phallus) are displayed near the dam. Laterite, found in abundance in this area, was used for the construction, which was decorated with stucco. The most beautiful pieces found include a stone statue of a standing Buddha, probably dating from the 8th c., several 7th/8th c. Vishnu sculptures (the Indian Gupta or post-Gupta influences are clearly recognisable) and a 1.7m/5½ft-tall stone sculpture of a seated Ganesha (6th/7th c.), one of the most marvellous Hindu sculptures ever found in Thailand, now exhibited in the National Museum in Bangkok. Similar rich finds were only uncovered at excavations in Nakhon Pathom and Lopburi.

★Dam

The nearby dam, built around 1200 by King Jayavarman to ensure the regular irrigation of this fertile area, is worth visiting. Remains of the laterite foundations, probably the ruins of a sluice, can be seen.

★Wat Ton Po

Continue from Prachinburi for a few miles on Road 3070 to reach old Wat Ton Po, the destination of numerous pilgrims. Its centre is composed of a fig tree with the large statue of a seated Buddha, around which an octagonal covered walk and two terraces are grouped. The scene imitates Buddha's enlightenment under a fig tree, from which the temple also gained its name.

Muang Phra Rot

Before reaching the former town of Muang Phra Rot, now an excavation site, a large pond is passed. Its laterite edging has Dvaravati-style animal pictures engraved into it. Muang Phra Rot was a town established by the Mons and protected by two earth walls with a ditch in between; their positions are still clearly evident. A leper colony was formerly housed in the town. Nearby are the ruins of several Hindu shrines; of note is the top of the roof of one which has the shape of an octagonal cupola, reminiscent of the Mamallapuramin temple in south-east India.

Prachuap Khiri Khan K 3

Region: West Thailand
Province: Prachuap Khiri Khan
Altitude: 3m/10ft. Population: 18,000

ประจวบคีรีขันธ์

Location and Landscape

The small town of Prachuap Khiri Khan, the main town of the province of the same name, lies next to the Gulf of Thailand, 280km/174 miles south-west of Bangkok, and is a jewel as yet widely untouched by tourism. The long curved coastline here boasts fine sandy beaches and is bordered in the north by a mountainous promontory and in the south by high rocky cliffs. The green mountains of the Tenasserim chain, which extends along the Malay peninsula, form an impressive backdrop. Thai national territory reaches its narrowest point here at Prachuap Khiri Khan (13km/8 miles). Prachuap Khiri Khan itself offers few sights, although the fishing harbour is of interest in the early morning. It is also worth visiting the typical Thai market in the town centre.

Access

By car: from Bangkok Highway 4 (280km/174 miles).
By train: on the Bangkok–Hualampong–Malaysia line (318km/198 miles; journey time approximately five hours).
By bus: from Bangkok Southern Bus Terminal (journey time about six hours).

History

For a few days at the end of 1941 this sleepy, uninteresting fishing village took centre stage in the war in Asia. One day after the Japanese attack on the US military base Pearl Harbor in Hawaii 2000 Japanese soldiers landed here in the early hours of December 8th and took over both the police station and the railway station. Thai troops were initially unable to drive back the invaders; the local civilian population fled into the surrounding

Fishing boats in the harbour of Prachuap Khiri Khan

mountains. Although the military authorities in Bangkok ordered the laying down of weapons and surrender, Thai soldiers, led by Lieutenant Pravas Xumsai, took up the fight. In the course of a 32-hour battle they managed to defeat the Japanese. There were 442 fatalities, including 400 Japanese. Every year, on December 8th, the Thai tourist board stages a sound and light show to demonstrate the fighting strength of the Thai army.

Kap Prachuap

The chalk massifs of three islands tower up near Kap Prachuap. Their sandy beaches are almost undisturbed and can be visited by boat from the harbour. The cave temple Tham Khao Kham Kradai, on a promontory in the north of the bay and particularly revered by the local people, can also be reached by boat.

Khao Chong Krachok (mirror mountain)

Khao Chong Krachok mountain towers above the town and is broken in two by a natural rock arch, through which the sky on the other side of the mountain can be seen (hence the name mirror mountain). The mountain is populated by colonies of wild monkeys (be careful – they are sometimes aggressive). A small monastery on the summit is reached by 398 steps and contains a Buddhist shrine. The summit also offers a marvellous view across the town and the coastal area.

Surroundings

★Nam Tok Huai Yang (waterfall and national park)

The cascades of the impressive Nam Tok Huai Yang waterfall drop 120m/394ft in the jungle near the Burmese border, 35km/22 miles from the town.

Myanmar border area

Nearby an old caravan route leads across Maw Daung Pass to Mergui in Myanmar, part of the road to Moulmein. Maw Daung mountain (1350m/4428ft) lies on Burmese national territory and is thus inaccessible. Smuggling between Thailand and Myanmar occurs here, particularly at night.

Further south the landscape of the plain is characterised by pineapple fields and coconut palm plantations, while to the west it is dominated by the typical chalk mountains with their jagged summits.

Bang Saphan

Bang Saphan, a small town 77km/48 miles south of Prachuap Khiri Khan (Highway 3169), boasts a gently-curving sandy beach more than 6km/4 miles long (south of the town, Highway 3374). It begins at Khao Mae Ramphung, a mountainous promontory covered with lush vegetation. Nearby is the charming island of Koh Thalu, best reached in a rented fishing boat.

Prakhon Chai G 7

ประโคนชัย

Region: North-east Thailand
Province: Buriram
Altitude: 179m/560ft. Population: 12,000

Location

Prakhon Chai, a small town about 280km/174 miles north-east of Bangkok, is the starting point for visiting two important ruined sites.

Surin, famous for its grand elephant festival held in the third week of November, is also nearby. Tourist offices in Bangkok, Nakhon Ratchasima and Surin include tours in their programmes.

Access

By car: from Bangkok Highway 1/2/24 (about 360km/224 miles).
By bus: from Bangkok Northern Bus Terminal (journey time about six hours).
By rail: nearest station at Buriram (45km/28 miles) on the Bangkok–Ubon Ratchathani line.

View of the precinct of the Wat Prasat Phanom Rung

Central sanctuary in the Wat Prasat Phanom Rung

Archaeological position

Evidence of earlier ages has only been secured and examined "for the state" during the last few decades. During this time, Prakhon Chai has rightly proved of particular interest to Thai archaeologists. However, while much still remains buried, much has also been plundered and sold abroad, including a bronze 7th/8th c. statue now in the Metropolitan Museum in New York. Even though important pieces, such as several 8th–10th c. Buddha statues, have been taken to the National Museum in Bangkok, the history of Thailand is no longer fully documented. As protection against a "cultural sell-out", trade in archaeological finds is threatened with heavy punishments.

Sights

General Information

Together with the ruined town of Phimai, Wat Prasat Phanom Rung, an important station and place of worship on the route between Angkor Wat, the main town of the empire in present-day Cambodia, and Phimai (see Buriram, history) is one of Thailand's most important Khmer buildings. The access road to the wat (signposted) turns off southwards from Highway 24 at the village of Ban Ta Ko approximately 18km/11 miles east of the junction of Highway 218 (from Buriram). If travelling by bus go from Buriram to Nang Rong, then to Ban Ta Ko station on Highway 24, from there use pick-up taxis. The wat lies on the summit of a 158m/519ft hill, from where there is a view across the plain in the north and the densely-wooded mountain slopes in the south.

Site

The severly geometric lay-out bears witness to a powerful desire of the Khmer architects to create a prestigious image. A 12m/39ft-wide flight of stone steps and a road lined with stone pillars leads from a U-shaped building called Rung Chang Puak (Stall of the White Elephant), some of whose walls are still standing, to another monumental flight of steps articulated by half-landings and ornamented with nagas (heads in the early Angkor Wat style). These steps and the right-hand corner of the wall, which surrounds the site, were probably not added until later, in the 12th c., under the Burmese king Suryavarman II. Note the sculptures at the entrance, which depict scenes from Hindu mythology.

On the inside of the encircling wall there are galleries which open on to the inner courtyard through cross-shaped gates and windows. The oldest buildings are three brick-built prangs, of which the ruins of two are still visible (early 10th c.). The two laterite constructions on either side of the main entrance were built at the end of the 12th c. The remains of a small sandstone prang with beautiful sculptures (in the south-west corner) were rebuilt into a chapel.

Shrine

The shrine in its present form, a sandstone prang on a square pedestal placed on to a smaller prang, probably dates from the 11th/12th c. Gopuram (door towers), marking the entrance to the holy area, were positioned on all four sides of the tower.

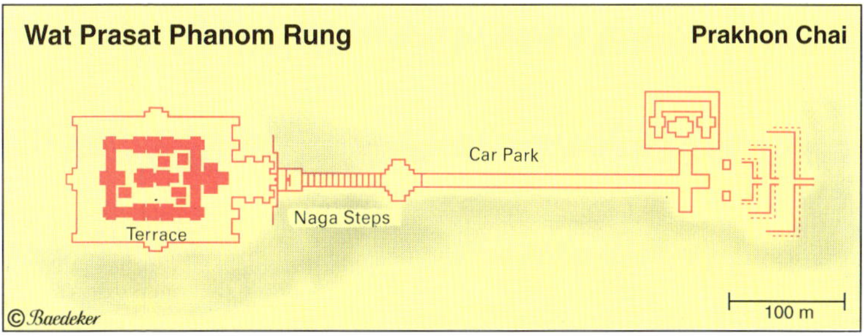

The east porch continues as a passage (Antarala) to an 8m/26ft by 10m/33ft hall (mandapa) open on its two narrower sides; on each of the longer sides are a portal and two windows. Of note are the sculptures (10th/11th c. figurative representations and ornamental decoration) on the tympanums, lintels, walls and pillars, which demonstrate the highest technical and artistic quality. The figurative representations depict scenes from Indian (Brahmin) mythology. Five hermits, one particularly emphasised, are portrayed above the shrine's eastern inner door. This depiction stems from a legend about a highly-respected man who retreated into the hermitage here: the first buildings of Prasat Phanom Rung were built for him.

Some early sculptures important to art history were found in the Prasat's grounds: the 53cm/21in.-tall stone torso of a woman, probably Uma, Shiva's wife, in the Khmer style of Koh Ker (first half of the 10th c.), and six new red sandstone blocks with reliefs (38cm/15in. by 47cm/18½in.), which each depict an Indian god of the points of the compass (in the Khmer style of Baphuon, 1010–80). There should have been a total of ten such blocks: eight for the points of the compass and one each for above and below. They probably stood in the open air and had an opening in the top in the shape of a lotus bud for donations. All named finds were taken to the nearby museum, a branch of the Department of Fine Arts in Bangkok, at Prasat Phanom Rung.

★Prasat Muang Tam

Access

Prasat Muang Tam lies only 8km/5 miles from Prasat Phanom Rung, but it is better to make a detour via Prakhon Chai. Take Highway 2075 from there southwards, following the signposts when leaving the town.

Location

Although partly ruined, Prasat Muang Tam remains imposing. It dates from the 10th/11th c. and is surrounded by four laterite walls (115m/377ft by 140m/459ft). For centuries it was overgrown by dense jungle and was only uncovered in the mid-20th c.

Entrance of the Prasat Muang Tam

The walls were interrupted by four gates (gopuram) in three parts, each placed centrally. The lintels have been partially retained and show finely-detailed lively sculptures with scenes from Brahmin mythology.

The outer courtyard presents a pleasant picture, with a little imagination the size of the former site can be realised. There is an large L-shaped pond in each corner, each surrounded by a naga with a tall headshell. Along with a few sandstone wall fragments, only the gates with their richly-decorated lintels remain of the galleries which once surrounded this courtyard.

Shrine

A 22sq.m/72sq.ft base in the prasat bears the main shrine: five brick-built prangs, arranged in two rows, of which only three remain. The main lintel has disintegrated down to the pedestal. Remarkable here are the particularly richly-ornamented lintels, some of which occupy their original positions, while others have fallen to the ground. One of the lintels shows Krishna (as a divine cowherd, one of Vishnu's many manifestations) standing on Kirtimukha's head: a rare portrayal, as Krishna is usually depicted with his beloved Radha.

Ranong M 2

ระนอง

Region: South Thailand
Province: Ranong
Altitude: 3m/10ft. Population: 22,000

Location

Ranong, about 450km/280 miles (as the crow flies) south-west of Bangkok, is, if approached from the north, the first Thai town on the Indian Ocean. The town owes its charm to its houses, Chinese-style with Portuguese influence, the nearby mountainous jungle, an interesting island world and its proximity to Myanmar (Burma). On the other side of the inlet, Victoria Point, the most southerly point of the Burmese mainland, can be seen.

Access

By car: from Bangkok Highway 4 (570km/354 miles). From Surat Thani Highway 401 to Takua Pa, then Highway 4.
By bus: from Surat Thani several times daily.
By rail: nearest station Chumphon (120km/74½ miles).
By air: nearest airport at Surat Thani.

Townscape

Like many Thai ports, it is worth visiting Ranong's harbour, particularly in the early hours of the morning when the fishing boats return. A stroll through the town along the main street is also interesting. The ground floors of the two-storey houses are arcaded passages. The old harbour in the wide mouth of the Ranong river has been replaced so that ships with large draughts can now be unloaded here.

Surroundings

★Koh Pha Yam (island)

A boat trip to Koh Pha Yam island proves interesting. With the help of Japanese businessmen a large pearl culture farm has been established on natural mussel beds (visits possible). The tour passes crocodile-inhabited mangrove swamps as well as numerous hilly, green islands.

Hot springs

Three hot springs lie approximately 2km/1 mile east of Ranong near the Janson Thara Hotel. The most productive spring supplies 500 litres/110 gallons of water, at a temperature of 70°C/158°F, per second. A small wat is dedicated to the spirit of the spring. A suspension bridge leads to a garden with a mineral water pool, in which bathing is permitted.

Tin mining

By continuing along the road leading to the hot springs, a tin mine is reached in the village of Hat Som Paen. Tin is still produced here using conventional methods. An idyllic scene is set by the village temple Wat Hat Som Paen, in whose pond swim sacred carp. Many of the open-cast tin mines passed on a journey south to the villages of Kapoe, Khuraburi and Takua Pa have been closed down.

Ranong island

From Paknam Ranong, the fishing port at the mouth of the Menam Kraburi river, an impressive boat trip takes visitors to Ranong island, where a number of houses on stilts have been built along the bank.

From Ranong to the north

Nam Tok Bunyaban waterfall lies near Highway 4, 18km/11 miles north of Ranong. A further 31km/19 miles along the deeply-indented inlet Menam Kraburi (also called Menam Pak Chan) brings travellers to Tham Phra Kayang grotto, which has many statues of Buddha and is well worth seeing. Kraburi, a town in the mountains, is reached after another 13km/8 miles.

From Kraburi Highway 4 leads via the narrowest point on the Malay peninsula, the Isthmus of Kra, to Chumphon: the distance here between the Bay of Bengal and the Gulf of Thailand measures only 60km/37 miles.

Ratchaburi (Ratburi) H 3

Region: West Thailand
Province: Ratchaburi
Altitude: 5m/16ft. Population: 50,000

ราชบุรี

Location

The town of Ratchaburi, about 80km/50 miles west of Bangkok, once joined the estuary of the Mae Klong in the Gulf of Thailand. Over the course of centuries the river built up so much mud that the sea is now 30km/19 miles away. Rice fields surround the town and border jagged chalk mountains in the west. Both during the Dvaravati kingdom, in the Lopburi epochs, and during the Sukhothai and Ayuttaya kingdom, Ratchaburi was an important trading town, a function which it still retains.

Access

By car: from Bangkok Highway 4 (100km/62 miles), or Highway 35 to Pak Tho, then Highway 4 (105km/65 miles).
By bus: from Bangkok Southern Bus Terminal several times daily.
By rail: station on the Bangkok–south Thailand line.

History

The area around Ratchaburi was already settled in the Bronze Age. Wat Mahathat in the town was built in the Dvaravati period, and Ku Bua, one of Thailand's most important excavation sites situated 12km/7½ miles away, obviously dates from the late Dvaravati perod. At that time Ratchaburi belonged to the Khmers' sphere of control, until Ramkhamhaeng, king of Sukhothai, annexed it to his kingdom. A stone inscription, completed by the king himself in 1292, tells of this. Following this Ratchaburi, together with the provinces of Suphan buri and Phetchaburi, was inherited by the founder of the Ayutthaya kingdom, King Rama Thibodi I (U Thong). In 1768 King Taksin, forerunner of the Chakri dynasty, drove out the Burmese occupiers and added the town to his newly-developing kingdom of Siam.

Wat Mahathat

Of the numerous ancient and modern wats to be found in Ratchaburi, Wat Mahathat, which probably gained its appearance in the Lopburi period, is the one most worth seeing. Older parts date from the 9th/10th c., while stucco decoration and murals were mainly added during the Ayutthaya period. The large prang, to which two smaller ones have been added, displays beautiful stucco ornamentation. The murals, dating from about 1500, inside the central prang denote a highpoint of Thai art and are some of the oldest ever retained. They depict pictures of Buddha on a yellow background in friezes arranged one on top of another. Their flowing lines and a certain naturalness of movement are striking. The bot houses several very attractive statues of Buddha in the Dvaravati style.

Surroundings

Khao Ngu (mountain)

The chalk mountain of Khao Ngu lies north-west of the town. Several cave shrines with sculptures from the early Dvaravati period are to be found here, including a bas-relief with a 2.50m/8ft-tall Buddha statue.

The floating market of Damnoen Saduak

★Ku Bua (excavations)

The foundations of a town with 40 shrines were discovered in 1961 at Ku Bua, 12km/7½ miles south-west of Ratchaburi. The rectangular site was 49sq.km/19sq. miles in size. Its water was supplied by a canal which crossed the length of the town. The town must have been a cultural centre during the Dvaravati period; the foundations of the Wiharn Wat Klong are easily recognisable. The terracotta ornamentation decorating the brick buildings, numerous figurative representations (including ceramic statues, among the most beautiful evidence of Dvaravati culture), stone tablets and wheels of the law are now displayed in the National Museum of Bangkok.

★★Damnoen Saduak Floating Market

Access

It is best either to drive to Damnoen Saduak floating market, about 5km/3 miles from Ratchaburi, or to travel by local bus from Bangkok (Southern Bus Terminal). There are taxi boats and public transport boats which depart from Damnoen Saduak's landing stage.

Travel offices in Bangkok offer tours here. To experience the market at its best visit it as early as possible in the morning – this will necessitate leaving Bangkok at about 5am. Use a rented car (preferably with a driver) or a local bus to arrive when the traders are by themselves. Private bus tours arrive from 9am at the latest. By noon the klong is empty of craft.

History

While the capital city Bangkok has barely retained one of the floating markets, which once gained it the nickname "Venice of the East", one remains in the province of Ratchaburi, with which the Thai tourist authorities are heavily involved. Damnoen Saduak market suggests the way of life found in Bangkok itself in the not too distant past. To be fair to the great crowds of tourists who visit it, the market, in existence since 1856, was moved in 1984 from its original site on Klong Ton Khem to Damnoen Saduak canal.

Floating markets were not only places to buy and sell everyday objects, they also fulfilled an important social function as a centre of communication. Traders would come to them from near and far. The system of

A "takeaway" on the floating market

canals is confusing, there are a total of 200 Klongs linked by small side canals. Brisk trade – including some classic bartering – is carried out on the narrow canals. Women row skilfully past roaring motor boats, their wobbly craft filled to the brim with all manner of goods. All the produce of agricultural Thailand is on offer here: fruit and vegetables, fish and meat. Less attractive are the many souvenir shops which sell the usual trinkets but at a higher price than elsewhere in Thailand.

Rayong J 5

ระยอง

Region: East Thailand
Province: Rayong
Altitude: 6m/20ft. Population: 29,000

Location

The lively typical provincial town of Rayong is situated about 140km/87 miles south-east from Bangkok on the Gulf of Thailand; apart from its scenic location there are no sights. The nearby town of Ban Phe is the starting point for trips to the off-shore islands such as Koh Samet. Beyond the town there are large areas cultivated with sugar cane, manioc and pineapple.

Access

By car: from Bangkok Highways 34/3/36 (180km/112 miles).
By bus: from Bangkok Eastern Bus Terminal (air-conditioned, about 4 hours).

Townscape

The fishing port lies in the oldest part of the town on the river estuary and is at its liveliest in the late afternoon. Rayong is famous for its fish sauce "nam pla", a Thai speciality, used instead of salt to spice many dishes. Other

Dried fish from Rayong is a popular speciality

A beach on Koh Samet

products of Rayong are "kapi", a shrimp paste, and dried fish, sold throughout the country.

The large wat in the centre of the town with a larger than life sized statue of Buddha is not of cultural interest but it is the focus of activity at weekends.

Beaches

There are beautiful sandy beaches along the coast between Pattaya and Rayong which are being opened up to tourists. These include the resorts of Suan Wang Kaeo to the east of Rayong and the beach at Tha Rua Klaeng.

★★Koh Samet (Island) J 5

General

With its magnificent beaches, crystal clear waters and luxuriant vegetation Koh Samet (also called Koh Kae Phisadan) was one of the first islands to attract tourists from all over the world. Declaring Koh Samet to be a national park in 1981 has done nothing to deter the stream of visitors. Today there are hundreds of bungalows and the beaches are not as clean as they once were. In May 1990 a ban on overnight visits was introduced to check the uncontrolled growth of tourism, but this is disregarded. Although the problems of rubbish, water shortage and built-up beaches have not been solved the ban was lifted two years later. At weekends whole groups of Thais, from as far away as Bangkok, come to have parties and the refuse they leave behind could be the last straw for this island, which until a few years ago, was unspoilt.

There is a risk of malaria on Koh Samet. It is necessary to use anti-mosquito cream every evening and sleep under the mosquito nets which are provided in the bungalows.

Access

From Rayong (minibuses from the clock tower) Highway 3 to Ban Phe; from there ferry (on request; last return trip daily 5pm). The nearest jetty on the island is near the small fishing village of Samet. In calm weather the boats sail round the western tip to the beaches and moor at temporary landing stages.

Sights

At its widest the island is 800m, only 200m at its narrowest point and 5km/3 miles long. From the beaches on the west side the wonderful sunset can be witnessed. There are two rocky beaches on the other side of the island. All beaches can be reached by well signposted footpaths and pickups.

Sakhon Nakhon D 8

Region: North-east Thailand
Province: Sakhon Nakhon
Altitude: 152m/499ft. Population: 30,000

สกลนคร

Location

From Sakhon Nakhon, a quiet almost sleepy town in the far north-east of Thailand (about 650km/403 miles from Bangkok) a lowland plain, well irrigated by Lake Nong Han, stretches to the Mekong; it is bordered in the south-west by densely wooded upland. Not many tourists are found here, only those who are interested in the rare but well preserved examples of Khmer art

Access

By car: from Khon Kaen Highways 209/213 (175km/108 miles). From Udon Thani Highway 22 (150km/93 miles).
By bus: from Bangkok Northeastern Terminal.

★Lake Nong Han

The northern edge of the town borders on Lake Nong Han, the largest inland lake in Thailand with a small port and well-stocked with fish. Close to the west bank is the decaying Khmer temple That Dum.

The new white prang of the Wat Cheung Chum in the town was erected on top of a 16th c. Khmer prang, its interior is still visible. The wiharn houses the statue of a seated Buddha.

★Wat Phra Cheung Chum

To the west of the town (near the rice research station on an unmade road, 12km/7 miles) stands the Wat Phra That Narai, an 11th c. temple in Baphuon style. Of particular interest are the beautifully carved lintels which are very well preserved depicting scenes from Brahman mythology (including the gods Vishnu and Krishna).

Surroundings

★Wat Phra That Narai

Highway 213 in the direction of Kalasin leads to Phu Phan national park, its spectacular mountains overgrown with monsoon forest.

Phu Phan national park

Samut Prakan H 4

Region: East Thailand
Province: Samut Prakan (Paknam)
Altitude: 3m/9ft. Population: 58,000

สมุทรปราการ

The provincial town of Samut Prakan, situated about 20km/12 miles south of Bangkok on the east bank of the Menam Chao Phraya near its estuary into the Gulf of Thailand, attracts many day trippers from Bangkok. It is reached by car or taxi on Highway 3; there are several daily bus connections from the Southern Bus Terminal in Bangkok. Apart from the old town centre and a small harbour there is not much to see.

Location and access

Sights

On the northern edge of the town on Highway 3 (Sukhumvit Highway) is the Shell Museum of Thailand with collections of different shells from all the world's oceans. Also on the Sukhumvit Highway the Marine Museum contains detailed replica models of ships and royal skiffs, sailors' uniforms and weapons (open: as for Shell Museum).

★Shell Museum

Opening times
daily 9am–4pm

Admission fee

To the south of the town (777 Taiban Road) the crocodile farm, the second largest establishment of its kind in the world, claims to be home to 40,000 crocodiles. The owner of this extensive site, which resembles an American theme park, began in 1950 with a few dozen animals; he claims his motivation is to save this threatened species from extinction. Making money is not purely incidental; the farm has a business which processes crocodile leather. The "Washington Biodiversity Agreement", which extends to reptiles, allows the export of crocodile leather if it is from farmed animals. Before purchasing shoes, bags or belts the goods should be examined to see that they carry an internationally valid certificate.

The tours are interesting and worthwhile. Together with the crocodiles (including the largest crocodile held in captivity in the world, 5.9m/19ft long and weighing 1.1 tonnes) are tigers, chimpanzees, snakes and elephants (rides available). The crocodile farm often features in one-day and half-day organised tours, often combined with a visit to Nakhon Pathom and the floating market at Damnoen Saduak (see Ratchaburi).

★Crocodile farm

Opening times
8am–6pm

Admission fee

Shows
Every hour from 9–11am and 2–4pm, with additional shows at 5pm at weekends

Muang Boran (Thai for "Ancient City"), one of the largest open air museums in the world, was financed by a rich citizen from Bangkok and cost more than 200 million $US. Over the ten years it took to develop the 80ha/197 acre site, designed in the shape of Thailand, some exhibits of original size were built together with 65 copies of the most beautiful and culturally significant buildings on a scale of 1:3, some of which are still only in ruins such as the Si Sanphet Prasat, the royal audience chamber of the old Ayutthaya. The visitor can drive along roads leading to the individual sights, most of which are located in their "correct" geographical positions. (Bicycles are also available for rental.)

★★Ancient City

Location
Sukhumvit Highway (at km 33)

Opening times
daily 8.30am–6pm

Admission fee

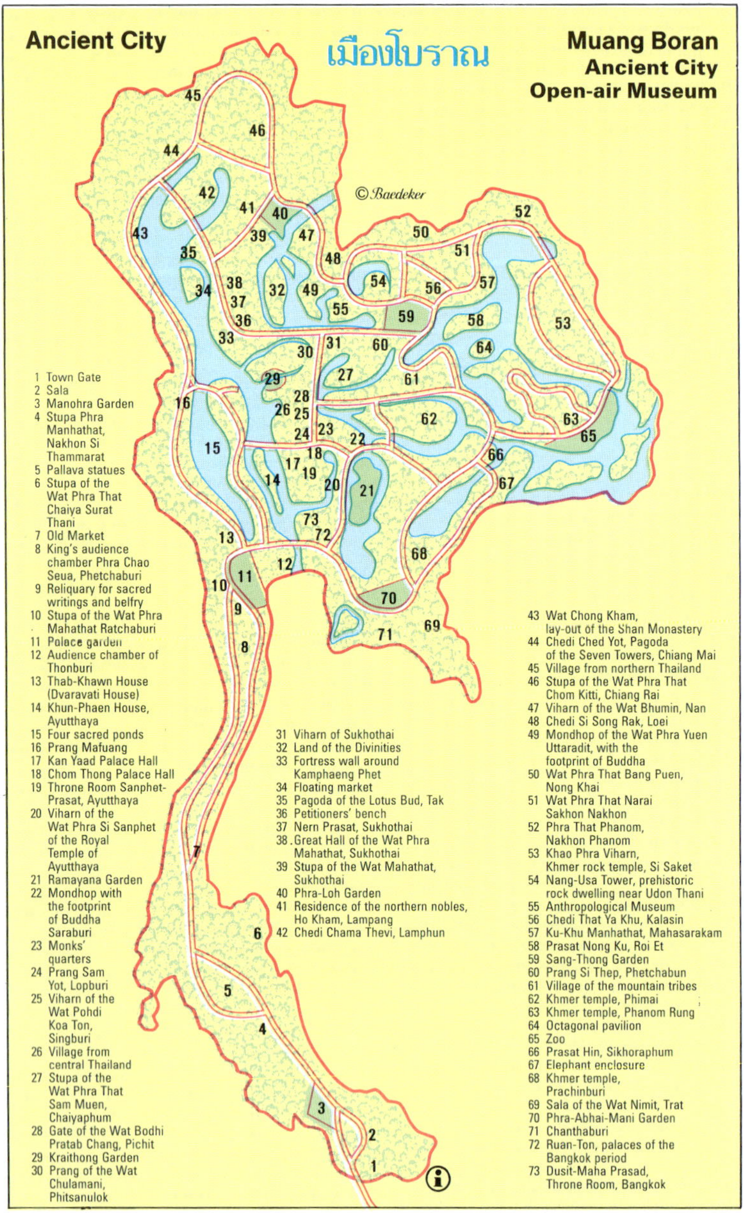
Ancient City
เมืองโบราณ
Muang Boran
Ancient City
Open-air Museum
© Baedeker
1 Town Gate
2 Sala
3 Manohra Garden
4 Stupa Phra Manhathat, Nakhon Si Thammarat
5 Pallava statues
6 Stupa of the Wat Phra That Chaiya Surat Thani
7 Old Market
8 King's audience chamber Phra Chao Seua, Phetchaburi
9 Reliquary for sacred writings and belfry
10 Stupa of the Wat Phra Mahathat Ratchaburi
11 Palace garden
12 Audience chamber of Thonburi
13 Thab-Khawn House (Dvaravati House)
14 Khun-Phaen House, Ayutthaya
15 Four sacred ponds
16 Prang Mafuang
17 Kan Yaad Palace Hall
18 Chom Thong Palace Hall
19 Throne Room Sanphet-Prasat, Ayutthaya
20 Viharn of the Wat Phra Si Sanphet of the Royal Temple of Ayutthaya
21 Ramayana Garden
22 Mondhop with the footprint of Buddha Saraburi
23 Monks' quarters
24 Prang Sam Yot, Lopburi
25 Viharn of the Wat Pohdi Koa Ton, Singburi
26 Village from central Thailand
27 Stupa of the Wat Phra That Sam Muen, Chaiyaphum
28 Gate of the Wat Bodhi Pratab Chang, Pichit
29 Kraithong Garden
30 Prang of the Wat Chulamani, Phitsanulok
31 Viharn of Sukhothai
32 Land of the Divinities
33 Fortress wall around Kamphaeng Phet
34 Floating market
35 Pagoda of the Lotus Bud, Tak
36 Petitioners' bench
37 Nern Prasat, Sukhothai
38 Great Hall of the Wat Phra Mahathat, Sukhothai
39 Stupa of the Wat Mahathat, Sukhothai
40 Phra-Loh Garden
41 Residence of the northern nobles, Ho Kham, Lampang
42 Chedi Chama Thevi, Lamphun
43 Wat Chong Kham, lay-out of the Shan Monastery
44 Chedi Ched Yot, Pagoda of the Seven Towers, Chiang Mai
45 Village from northern Thailand
46 Stupa of the Wat Phra That Chom Kitti, Chiang Rai
47 Viharn of the Wat Bhumin, Nan
48 Chedi Si Song Rak, Loei
49 Mondhop of the Wat Phra Yuen Uttaradit, with the footprint of Buddha
50 Wat Phra That Bang Puen, Nong Khai
51 Wat Phra That Narai Sakhon Nakhon
52 Phra That Phanom, Nakhon Phanom
53 Khao Phra Viharn, Khmer rock temple, Si Saket
54 Nang-Usa Tower, prehistoric rock dwelling near Udon Thani
55 Anthropological Museum
56 Chedi That Ya Khu, Kalasin
57 Ku-Khu Manhathat, Mahasarakam
58 Prasat Nong Ku, Roi Et
59 Sang-Thong Garden
60 Prang Si Thep, Phetchabun
61 Village of the mountain tribes
62 Khmer temple, Phimai
63 Khmer temple, Phanom Rung
64 Octagonal pavilion
65 Zoo
66 Prasat Hin, Sikhoraphum
67 Elephant enclosure
68 Khmer temple, Prachinburi
69 Sala of the Wat Nimit, Trat
70 Phra-Abhai-Mani Garden
71 Chanthaburi
72 Ruan-Ton, palaces of the Bangkok period
73 Dusit-Maha Prasad, Throne Room, Bangkok

Samut Prakan: in the crocodile farm

Reconstruction of the Si Sanphet Prasat in Ancient City

The reconstructed Great Hall of the Wat Phra Mahathat in Ancient City

★Anthropological Museum

The Anthropological Museum in the north of this extensive site contains exhibits covering over 1000 years of history and almost all regions of Thailand. It is housed in a group of farmsteads in Central Thailand style. The museum offers an insight into everyday life (e.g. musical instruments, pottery, implements for fishing and rice cultivation).

Ho Kham

The upper floor of the Ho Kham (Golden Hall) houses a collection of stone and bronze sculptures and ceramic, wood and mother-of-pearl works of art from Thailand's advanced civilisation. The prize exhibit is the most recent, a representation of about 70 episodes in the life of Buddha, handcarved from a single piece. The artist was 80 when he completed this work after ten years. The Ho Kham building is itself an original replica of the earlier governor's palace in Lampang, an example of Thailand's exceptional craftwork; the entire wooden building was constructed without a single nail.

Other buildings

Among the original buildings from different places reconstructed in Ancient City are, for example, some houses which stood by the canals of Bangkok and had to make room for road building in the Seventies. Some large scale buildings of temples and palaces, which today are either in ruins (the Throne Room Si Sanphet Prasat from Ayutthaya) or else have been completely altered in their appearance (such as the Duist Maha Prasat from the Grand Palace in Bangkok), have been reduced to one third of their original size but otherwise are an authentic reconstruction to the smallest detail. The Si Sanphet Prasat is remarkable for the high halls of its interior with their splendid wooden ceilings, gilded walls with mirror mosaics and stucco ornaments. In the Dusit Maha Prasat, a copy of the building in the Great Palace district of Bangkok, the frescos, which are true to the original, are particularly interesting, especially as very few have been preserved owing to the damage caused by the air pollution in Bangkok to paintings mostly from the early Bangkok period. They represent state ceremonies, religious festivals, military parades and court life at the time of Rama I (1782–1809). The carved doors and windows are particularly attractive.

Khao Phra Wiharn

In the north-east of the grounds ("No man's land" between Thailand and Cambodia) a 54m/177ft-high hill has been formed, on which the Khao Phra Wiharn stands, a temple, the original of which was the holy destination for both kings and pilgrims alike for 1000 years, and, following the peace agreement with Cambodia, is so once again. From a small river the visitor can scale four terraces – it is less strenuous in the morning when it is cooler – where there are stone ruins which used to be crowned by artistic gabled roofs in the Angkor-Wat style. Khao Phra Wiharn has an authentic reconstruction of such a roof. From the top of the "hill" there are good views of the whole site.

Gardens

There are seven gardens located throughout the site; areas of relaxation – surrounded by waterfalls, rocks and tropical flowers – representing the mythological world of Thailand. The "Garden of Gods", for example, has a bronze team of ten horses belonging to the Indian moon goddess Chandra, apparently flying over the waterfall. There is also the "Manohra Garden" depicting the beautiful girl with a bird's legs among her sisters.

Near the entrance is a Brahma shrine, the "Royal Stand", from which Queen Elizabeth II of England attended the consecration ceremony in February 1972. There is also an interesting elephant kraal and a small zoo in an attractively laid-out park for children. Here elephants, game, gibbons and many species of exotic birds roam around freely. The Floating Market in Ancient City has Thai wooden houses (partly reconstructed) built in the traditional style.

Samut Sakhon H 4

สมุทรสาคร

Region: West Thailand
Province: Samut Sakhon
Altitude: 5m/16ft. Population: 40,000

Location

The once important port of Samut Sakhon lies on the estuary of the river Tha Chin in the Gulf of Thailand. Today the port is overshadowed by Bangkok (about 35km/22 miles to the north-east) and is important only for fishing. To the north of Samut Sakhon the Klong Mahachai from Thonburi, which links the Menam Chao Phraya and the Menam Tha Chin, joins the Tha Chin.

Access

By car: from Bangkok Highways 4 or 35 (35km/22 miles).
By rail: station on the narrow guage Mae-Klong railway from Bangkok-Thonburi to Samut Songkhram.
By boat: charter boat from Menam Chao Phraya via Klong Mahachai from Bangkok (about 2 hours; very scenic).

★Harbour

The harbour is a hive of activity from morning until late at night. It is most interesting to see the fishing boats land their usually plentiful catches early in the morning. The jetty is in the centre of the town and close to the tall clock tower. Samut Sakhon is also renowned for its numerous excellent fish restaurants.

★Wat Yai Chom Prasat

A few kilometres north of the town the Wat Yai Chom Prasat stands on the bank of the Tha Chin. The entrance to the wiharn, built in Ayutthaya style has elaborately decorated doors. The wat is also accessible by boat (see above).

Wat Chom Long

It is worth taking a charter boat to the Wat Chom Long in the south which is situated directly on the estuary of the Tha Chin in the gulf; the trip takes in houses built on stilts where the fishermen's families live. The wat's extensive grounds are laid out attractively and the buildings are chiefly modern; there is a noteworthy wiharn from the Ayutthaya period.

Samut Songkhram H 4

Region: West Thailand
Province: Samut Songkhram
Altitude: 18m/59ft. Population: 36,000

สมุทรสงคราม

Location

Samut Songkhram lies 70km/43 miles south-west of Bangkok on the estuary of the Mae Klong, which flows from the Tenasserim mountains, which divide Thailand and Myanmar. It is mainly marshland to the west of the town broken up by huge salt-evaporation fields. To the north of the town fertile vegetable-growing areas are traversed by a dense network of canals; Damnoen Saduak (see Ratchaburi), one of the last floating markets in Thailand, is located in this network.

Access

By car: from Bangkok Highway 35 (72km/45 miles). Alternatively a rewarding detour via Nakhom Pathom (see Nakhom Pathom): Highway 4, 10km/6 miles past Nakhon Pathom on Highway 325 (96km/60 miles).
By bus: several times daily from Bangkok (Southern Bus Terminal).
By rail: Mae-Klong narrow gauge railway from Bangkok-Thonburi. Alight at Samut Sakhon, cross the Menam Tha Chin by ferry and continue the journey by the connecting train on the other bank.

Boat trip

The journey up the Mae Klong and through the canals by boat is through wonderful countryside which is partly cultivated and partly unspoilt. Some of the houses, which line the bank in places, are in the original Thai style.

Temples

There are interesting temples, all accessible by boat (see above), such as the wat in Ban Y San, to the east of the town on a hill, and the wat in Ampawa. Rama I, the first ruler of the Chakri dynasty, was born in Ampawa.

Damnoen Saduak

See Ratchaburi

Sanburi (Sankha Buri) F 4

Region: Central Thailand
Province: Chainat
Altitude: 55m/180ft. Population: 6000

สรรคบุรี

Location

Sanburi, also called Sankha Buri, on the bank of the Menam Noi only a few kilometres from Chainat (see Chainat), was a prosperous town known as Phraek during the Sukhothai and Ayutthaya periods. Today the small town is quiet and forgotten, only the ruins of some sacral buildings bearing witness to its past.

Access

By car: from Chainat Highway 340 (17km/11 miles). From Ayutthaya Highway 309 to Singburi, then Highway 3251 (110km/68 miles).

Sights

Fortifications

Some ruins of the town's fortifications still remain (walls and moats).

★Wat Song Pi Noi

The Wat Song Pi Noi in the south beyond the former town walls is probably of 15th c. origin. A chedi and a 14m/46ft-high brick prang are among the impressive ruins still to be seen with the remains of beautiful stucco decoration and interesting Buddha figures in three of the niches. Also of interest are a standing Buddha in a forceful poise with a wide face (late U-Thong style) and a stepping Buddha in the almost swinging position typical of Sukhothai style. The head is in late U-Thong style.

Wat Tanod Lai

From the Wat Tanod Lai, which can be reached in the same way as the Wat Song Pi Noi, are ruins of a 20m/66ft-high bell-shaped chedi.

The Wat Mahathat built in the Ayutthaya period is in an advanced state of decay. Remains of several chedis and prangs can be seen, a Buddha figure screened by a naga in a bot and in the open the large figure of a seated Buddha in Ayutthaya style. A small museum contains Buddha figures in different styles: the most beautiful are in the National Museum in Bangkok.

Wat Mahathat

The Wat Phra Kaeo is in the north of the town. Its relatively narrow soaring chedi in Sukhothai style stands on a massive square pedestal. On it is a rigidly formed square base and a richly sculptured part with niches. Upon this stands the lower part of the narrow bell, ornately decorated with ledges; it is finished by a ringed spire. The Buddha figures are high up in the niches.

★Wat Phra Kaeo

The small bot close by contains a seated Buddha in U-Thong style.

Saraburi G 4

Region: Central Thailand
Province: Saraburi
Altitude: 30m/98ft
Population: 49,000

สระบุรี

Location

Saraburi, provincial capital and important traffic junction, is situated 100km/62 miles north-east on the edge of the Central Plain. Here the endless expanse of rice fields gives way to delightful hills from which here and there soar craggy limestone rocks. In the vicinity are two holy places worshipped by Buddhists, the Wat Phra Buddhabat and the Wat Phra Buddhachai, whereas the Chinese pilgrims visit Hin Kong. The town itself has no sights.

Access

By car: from Bangkok Highway 1 (110km/68 miles).
By bus: from Bangkok (Northern Bus Terminal) several times daily.
By rail: station on the Bangkok-Ubon Ratchathani route.

Surroundings

★Wat Phra Buddhachai

5km/3 miles south of Saraburi near Highway 1 (turn right into Highway 3042) is the Wat Phra Buddhachai ("Temple to Buddha's Shadow"). The natural relief-like drawing of an almost vertical soaring monumental limestone rock is interpreted as the shadow of Buddha. A steep staircase hewn out of the rock leads to the wat, which is consecrated to the shadow. From here there is a magnificent view over a fascinating mountain landscape.

★Waterfalls

At the end of Highway 3042 paths lead right and left to the waterfalls Nam Tok Sam Lan and Nam Tok Bo Hin Dad.

★Chinese temple

4km/2 miles north of the small town of Hin Kong (Highway 1, about 8km/5 miles south of Phra Buddhachai) on a mountain slope are several Chinese temples, the destination of many Chinese pilgrims. There is a Chinese cemetery close by.

Wat Chanthaburi

Near Sao Hai, 8km/5 miles west of Saraburi, the 19th c. Wat Chanthaburi is worth a visit; its wiharn is decorated with original frescos.

★Phu Khai nature park

Approximately 16km/10 miles north of Saraburi lies the small nature park of Phu Khai which developed from a botanical garden. There are many tropical trees, bushes and magnificent blooms to admire. Plantations of teak around the edges of the park were planted on an initiative of the forestry ministry.

Bell-ringing . . .

. . . offerings in Wat Phra Buddhabat

★Wat Tham Si Wilai

The route to Phra Buddhabat (Highway 1 towards Lopburi) passes the cave temple Wat Tham Si Wilai with beautiful stalactite formations in the huge halls.

★★Wat Phra Buddhabat

Location
27km/17 miles north-west of Saraburi

The splendid Wat Phra Buddhabat (from "Buddhapada", Sanskrit for the symbolic presence of Buddha) is a jewel of Thai architecture and one of the holiest places in the country. The temple gets its name from a footprint belonging to Buddha which is worshipped here.

History and legend have become confused over the years. Around 1615 the Ayutthaya King Songtham (1610–28) sent Thai monks to Ceylon to pay homage to a footprint of Buddha. Singhalese monks, however, pointed out – according to Pali texts – that one of the five "genuine" footprints of Buddha to be found in the world was on Siamese territory. Shortly afterwards this place was discovered by a hunter: an injured stag showed him the way to a water-filled foot-shaped depression in the ground. On drinking the water he was cured of a bad skin disease from which he had suffered for years. This miracle was reported to the king who had a temple built here. It was destroyed in 1765 by the Burmese shortly before their invasion of Ayutthaya, the present buildings were built around 1800 by King Rama I on several hills.

Buildings

The mondhop with the legendary footprint is a richly decorated work in blue and gold. A high tripartite staircase with the body of a five-headed naga winding up its balustrade leads to the terrace bordered by white balustrades. Twenty narrow columns bear the ornate pyramid-shaped roof decorated with colourful glass mosaics which becomes a ringed spire ending with a delicate peak. Various large bronze bells hang on the terrace, gifts from pilgrims. The doors are beautifully inlaid with mother-of-pearl, the floor inside with the footprint heaped with votive gifts is covered by a mat of silver threads. The coffered ceiling is ornately decorated.

◄ *A temple with Buddha's footprint: Wat Phra Buddhabat near Saraburi*

In the temple grounds on the hillslope can be found a wiharn acting as a museum (votive gifts and temple relics), a small bot, a Chinese and Hindu temple and several chedis. From this height there is a fine view over temple roofs and chedi spires. At the base of the temple there is much activity, merchants selling wooden sticks with religious symbols (for striking the bells), amulets, cult objects, food and drink. Twice a year the Wat Phra Budhabat is the destination of several hundred pilgrims from near and far. One festival is in January together with a fair, the other takes place on fluctuating dates between March and October.

Sattahip J 4

Region: South-east Thailand. Province: Chonburi
Altitude: 7m/23ft. Population: 23,000

สัตหีบ

Location

Sattahip, former US airforce and navy base and today home to the Thai navy, is situated about 30km/19 miles south of Pattaya. This typical Thai small town has no notable sights. There are plans to expand the deep sea harbour thereby increasing its importance as an import and export centre. Jungle covered mountains, beautiful beaches and rocky headlands are characteristic of the countryside around Sattahip. In comparison with Pattaya it is relatively peaceful here; tourist development is, of course, beginning to creep in. The small fishing village of Ban Pala has fine sandy beaches nearby.

Access

By car: Highway 3 from Pattaya (30km/19 miles; from Bangkok 180km/112 miles).
By bus: Eastern Bus Terminal from Bangkok.

History

During the Vietnam war squadrons of B-52 bombers, among others, were stationed at the U Tapao airforce base. The base was not disbanded until the Eighties when the Thais cordially requested that the Americans withdraw. The airfield has since been used for both civil and military purposes; because of the importance of the south-east to tourism it is planned to expand it into an international airport.

Townscape

A wide promenade runs along the beach. The late afternoon is the best time to visit the fishing harbour and fish market when it is at is liveliest. The wat in the town centre is of no particular interest.

Harbour

The old naval base established around 1920 (its outline can be seen from the coast road) was modernised several years ago. The deep water allows large warships to dock and in the civilian harbour large cargo ships. Thailand has never been a great sea-faring nation, the Thais are more suited to inland and coastal waters.

★Bay of Chong Samae San

South-east of Sattahip on the extreme tip of a peninsula is the picturesque fishing harbour of Chong Samae San, called Chong for short. Boat trips depart from the bay sheltered by rocky promontories to beautiful fairytale islands with snow-white beaches. Some are privately owned, others belong to the naval base. Those which can be visited are Koh Ai Raet, Koh Samae San, Koh Chang Klua, Koh Nang, Koh Chan and Koh Chuang and Koh Rong Khon.

★Bang Sare

18km/11 miles north of Sattahip the new seaside resort of Bang Sare (beaches, bungalows, hotels) has developed over recent years near an idyllic fishing harbour (good restaurants). From here a visit to the rugged island of Koh Khram which has a beautiful bay on the north side is recommended. Further north towards Chanthaburi are the resorts of Sim Wong Village and Sonprasong Beach.

Satun P 4

Region: South Thailand
Province: Satun
Altitude: 6m/20ft. Population: 19,000

สตูล

Location

Satun is the most southerly town in Thailand on Lake Andaman, about 800km/500 miles from Bangkok as the crow flies. It is situated at the foot of the steeply rising Tenasserim mountain range on the estuary of the Menam Satun in an exotic countryside, almost devoid of humans, with dark green rain forest and soaring mountain chains. On the coast are idyllic beaches with crystal clear water and offshore islands with coral banks.

Access

By car: from Songkhla Highways 407/43 to Rattaphum, Highway 406 (155km/96 miles). From Trang Highway 404/4078 (135km/83 miles).
By bus: regular connections from the above towns.

★Townscape

Cut off from the world and close to the border this town has old world charm. The inhabitants earn their livelihood from fishing and trade with Malaysia. Two fishing harbours are the only source of activity in this otherwise quiet town.

Dusan reservoir

22km/13 miles north of the town, near Highway 406, is the beautifully situated Dusan reservoir. Soaring cliffs and surrounding parkland provide an impressive setting.

★★Koh Tarutao (Island)

National park

In 1974 the Koh Tarutao group of islands near the Malayan border was declared a national park; only a decade earlier pirates were terrorising the region. The island is one of the few remaining paradises of Thailand; however, it is feared that this archipelago of 51 islands, with Koh Tarutao being the main island, awaits the same fate as the island of Koh Samui – once popular with backpackers but now even planes land there. The almost exclusively indigenous population make the visitor very welcome. The rather arduous journey is rewarded by unspoilt beaches and luxuriant flora and fauna. As yet there is no tourist development.

Access

From Pak Bara harbour (65km/40 miles north of Satun; passenger boats twice daily during the season November–April). At weekends and during the Thai holiday period (May–June) early booking through travel agents is recommended.

★★Koh Ladang (group of islands)

An excursion to the Koh Ladang group of islands takes in natural scenery consisting of dense tropical vegetation, overgrown rocky islands, soaring limestone peaks and clear water with coral banks. Some of these islands are inhabited by "sea gypsies" (see Phuket, History).

Sikhoraphum

See Surin

Singburi G 4

Region: Central Thailand
Province: Singburi
Altitude: 21m/69ft. Population: 21,500

สิงห์บุรี

Location

Singburi, on the right bank of the Menam Chao Phraya, 120km/74 miles north of Bangkok in the middle of the Central Plain of Thailand with its endless rice fields, is the junction of several important roads. The town itself has no interesting sights.

Access

By car: from Ayutthaya Highways 309 or 32 (75km/47 miles). From Lopburi Highway 311 (25km/16 miles).
By bus: several times daily from Bangkok, Ayutthaya and Lopburi.

★★Wat Phra Nou Chak Si

5km/3 miles south-west of Singburi (2km/1 mile on Highway 309, then right along 3032) is the Wat Phra Nou Chak Si with a 40m/131ft-long statue of a recumbent Buddha, probably the largest in Thailand. Unfortunately the many attempts at restoration have damaged its artistic quality.

Ayutthaya-Prang

On a hill close by stands an ornately decorated prang in Ayutthaya style, the only remains of the Wat Phra That, the other buildings of which lie in ruins. Buddha statues occupy the three niches of the prang with another beautiful Buddha figure in the interior.

Bang Rachan

Highway 3032 leads to the fortified town of Bang Rachan. En route (32km/20 miles) are the partly restored ruins of the Khai Bang Rachan. The monks of the Wat Po Kao Ton, which has a new wiharn and some old chedis, played an important part in the war against the Burmese.

Lopburi

See entry

Si Racha H 4

Region: East Thailand
Province: Chonburi
Altitude: 3m/10ft. Population: 24,000

ศรีราชา

The Koh Loy Peninsula near Si Racha

Chedi of the Wat Asdangnimitr on Koh Sichang

Location

The up-and-coming town of Si Racha lies south-east of Bangkok between Chonburi and Pattaya on the Gulf of Thailand. Si Racha is renowned for its extremely hot chilli sauce which is produced here and sent all over the country. Numerous restaurants serve outstanding seafood. There are no sights of interest in the town but it is a popular destination for the population of Bangkok (best avoided at weekends and during the holiday period).

Access

Highway 34 (105km/65 miles) from Bangkok. It is best to travel by bus or hire car from Pattaya (34km/21 miles).

Surroundings

★Koh Loy (peninsula)

Evening is the best time to visit the picturesque peninsula of Koh Loy with its small monastery.

★Koh Sichang (group of islands)

There are boat trips from Si Racha to the offshore island of Koh Sichang, which actually consists of six rocky reefs (operates from the fishing harbour from 8.30am; last journey 3pm). On the island there is still a transshipment port which was important in the 19th c.; since the delta of the Menam Chao Phraya has been regularly dredged the cargo ships have been able to reach the capital. Nowadays Koh Sichang is just a fishing port which provides a livelihood for the population of about 2200.

Summer residence of King Rama V

The ruined summer residence of King Chulalongkom (Rama V) situated on the highest point of the island is worth a visit. As the island was occupied by the French in 1893 this palace was never completed. On the southern tip of the island a chedi remains from the Wat Asdangnimitr.

Temples

Other sights include two temples built on a steep slope. A yellow statue of Buddha makes one visible from afar; from the other, a Chinese temple, there is a good view of the island and the busy harbour which is worth the rather laborious climb up 500 steps.

Si Saket

F 8

Region: North-east Thailand
Province: Si Saket
Altitude: 172m/564ft. Population: 24,000

ศรีสะเกษ

Location

Si Saket, the chief town of the province with the same name, lies about 430km/267 miles north-east of Bangkok near the Menam Nun, which makes its way to the Mekong, in the southern part of North-east Thailand. The Cambodian border, which is marked by the impressive mountain chain Dong Rak, up to 755m/2477ft high in places, is about 70km/43 miles away. The rest of the region is famous for the legacy of its magnificent Khmer culture; the Khao Phra wiharn is, together with the temple grounds of Phimai and Prakhon Chai, the most important example of this highly developed sacral architecture.

Access

By car: from Surin Highway 226 (120km/74 miles; from Nakhon Ratchasima 270km/167 miles).
By rail: from Bangkok-Hualampong (515km/320 miles).
By bus: from Bangkok (570km/354 miles), Surin and Ubon Ratchathani.

Surroundings

Prasat Kamphaeng Noi

From the Prasat Kamphaeng Noi (Highway 2076, 8km/5 miles) there is a simple prang made of laterite. Within the well preserved walls there are fragments of beautifully sculptured door lintels and columns.

★Prasat Kamphaeng Yai

Some impressive ruins remain from the Prasat Kamphaeng Yai (Highway 2076 to junction with 226, then left). These include a monumental portal at the entrance, two brick buildings artistically sculptured in part, ruins of three prangs and the outer and almost completely preserved interior wall. Together with well preserved ledges, window and door lintels there is a relief of the god Shiva riding an elephant above a grotesque demonic face. The origin of a bronze figure (no arms), possibly representing Vishnu, is unknown.

★★Khao Phra Wiharn (rock temple)

Location
(Illus. p. 333)

The most sacred temple of the province of Si Saket, the Wat Khao Phra Wiharn, lies, according to a ruling of the International Court in Den Haag, in Cambodian territory, but because of its position on a rocky plateau can only be reached from Thailand. From Si Saket Highway 221 leads to Khao Phra Wiharn (about 100km/62 miles). See also Introduction, Recommended Routes.

General

Not until two decades after its discovery, during which time the rock temple was left to decay, did the Prime Minister Choonhavan and Hun Sen, leader of the Cambodian government, agree in July 1989 to reopen this unique cultural monument to the public.

Warning:
Essential to get up-to-date information from TAT about the border situation

The region has nevertheless remained so unstable that it is only occasionally possible to visit the temple. Even after an official peace agreement was reached between the Cambodian civil war factions in October 1991, there still continues to be sporadic military skirmishes between the government troops and the Khmer Rouge. Until the situation has significantly improved, it is absolutely imperative to seek up-to-the-minute advice from the tourist information service, e.g. in Ubon Ratchathani, as to whether a trip into the border area and to the temple is feasible. Anyone going there, when advised otherwise, could be risking their lives!

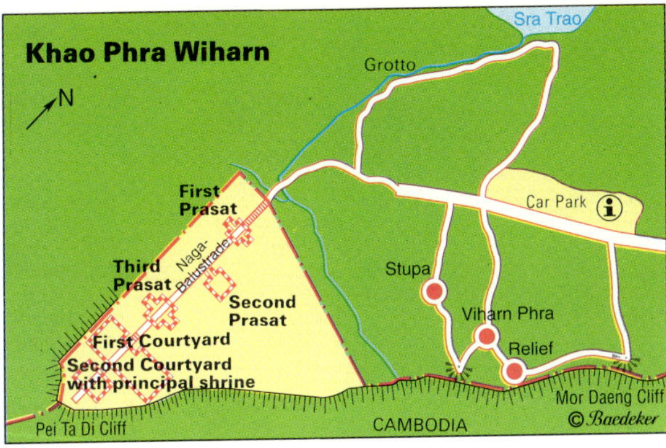

Legend of its origin

As with many of Thailand's temples there is a legend associated with its origin. A greedy couple who lived on the Mekong are said to have invented new kinds of fishing rods so as to become the richest fishing couple in the area. Pin, the couple's pretty daughter, was opposed to this and secretly gave the money to the poor. Her work did not go unnoticed and she won the heart of a prince who took her for his wife. To atone for the sins of the parents and show them the way to Nirvana Pin had the Khao Phra wiharn built.

Site

With a total length of over one kilometre the Khao Phra wiharn is one of the largest temple sites of the Khmer. Older than the temple city of Angkor Wat

The well-preserved gate to the Second Prasat

The richly ornamented tympanum on the First Prasat

it is thought to have been built under King Jayavarman II between the 11th and 13th c. based on an Indonesian model in honour of the Hindu god Shiva. Gate towers, called gopuram (singular gopura), form the entrance to the buildings of the temple on all four levels.

A partly preserved staircase decorated with nagas leads from the lowest level over several levels to the main temple. A pavilion (prasat) on the second level is laid out in the shape of a cross, as is another on the third. The ponds in which the holy water was collected have long since dried out and are overgrown with grass.

This sanctuary, which for the main part is in a state of ruin, was covered in dense jungle for many years and only recently exposed. A mondhop (mandapa) remains which is in Baphuon style as is most of the site. Only the foundations are visible from some of the buildings making it difficult to recognise the original size of the site. There are numerous stone Buddha images and several reliefs in varying states of preservation. Of interest are the pavilions with artistically finished door lintels and the remains of the outer walls.

Mor Daeng Cliff

Close by Mor Daeng Cliff (bas-reliefs in outstanding condition and rock drawings) provides wonderful views over the temple grounds and the neighbouring country.

Information

There is a miniature replica of the Khao Phra wiharn in the open-air museum near Samut Prakan (see Samut Prakan).

Si Satchanalai **D 3**

Region: North Thailand
Province: Sukhothai
Altitude: 68m/223ft. Population: 10,000

ศรีสัชนาลัย

The First Prasat of the Khao Phra Wiharn (see p. 330)

Location

Si Satchanalai, former twin town of the first Thai capital Sukhothai, lies in the extreme north of the Central Plain (420km/260 miles from Bangkok) on the right bank of Menam Yom, which makes its way through rocky green countryside here. The old town, somewhat off the tourist trail and less well known than Sukothai, is one of the most interesting seas of debris in Thailand. The magnificence of the young Thai empire found expression in buildings of high quality. The new town of Si Satchanalai, about 11km/9 miles from the ruins, and the modern Sawankhalok (18km/11 miles) were founded in the 19th c.

Access

By car: from Sukhothai route 101 (55km/34 miles).
By bus: regular connections from Sukhothai and Phitsanulok.
By rail: nearest station Sawankhalok (29km/18 miles).
By air: nearest airport Phitsanulok (114km/71 miles).

History

Si Satchanalai was founded around 1250, at the same time as Sukhothai, as a second seat of the Sukhothai empire (for the viceroy, usually the crown prince). Two Thai princes from the surrounding area had defeated the Khmer governor of Sukhothai in a bloody war; one of them pronounced himself king of Sukhothai, Si Satchanalai and the surrounding area. He was succeeded by his son and then King Ramkhamhaeng, one of the most powerful personalities in Thai history. In the 17th c. Si Satchanalai fell to the kingdom of Ayutthaya, was renamed Sawankhalok and declined in importance. In the 18th c., when the Burmese threatened to attack again, it was abandoned by its inhabitants.

Si Satchanalai Historical Park

Townscape

Si Satchanalai was laid out roughly in the shape of a right-angled triangle; parts of the once 5m/16ft-high wall from the 16th c. and the moat still remain. Two hills, once crowned with wats, dominate the surrounding region and offer good views of the ruins.

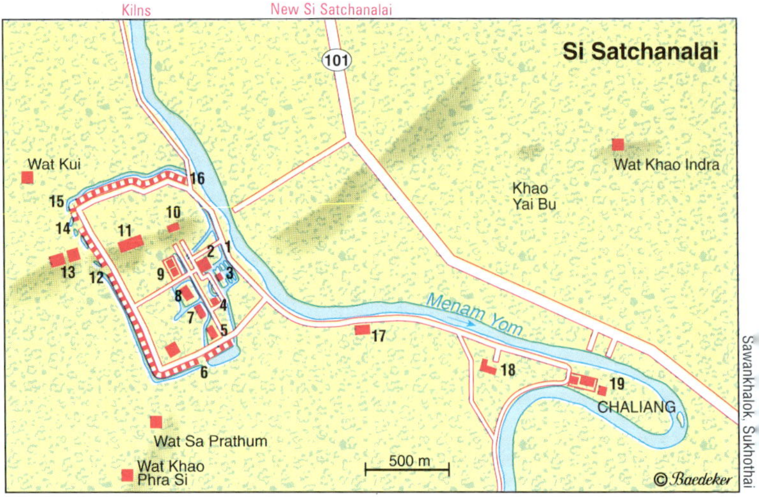

1 Entrance
2 Wat Utthayan Noi
3 Royal Palace
4 Lak Muang
5 Wat Nang Phraya
6 Pratu Ram Narong (gate)
7 Wat Utthayan Yai
8 Wat Chedi Chet Theo
9 Wat Chang Lom
10 Wat Khao Phnom Pleung
11 Wat Khao Suwan Khiri
12 Pratu Pi (gate)
13 Wat Chet Yot
14 Pratu Chana Songkhram (gate)
15 Pratu Chaya Preuk (gate)
16 Pratu Tao Mor (gate)
17 Wat Khok Sing Karam
18 Wat Chao Chan
19 Wat Mahathat

Wat Khao Phloeung

A colossal partly preserved staircase leads to the ruins of the Khao Wat Phnom Pleung (meaning "temple of holy fire") on the top of the eastern hill.

Wat Khao Suwan Kiri

On the other hill the remnants of the Wat Khao Suwan Kiri include a beautiful bell-shaped chedi with remains of stucco ornaments and a giant Buddha statue.

A third hill, Khao Yai, stands to the west of the town walls; only the ruins of a right-angled building with sculptures on the tympanum remain from the Chet Yot Wat, which once crowned it.

★★Wat Chang Lom

One of the most remarkable temples in old Si Satchanalai is the centrally located Chang Lom wat with its well preserved chedi of laterite and stucco. It was probably begun by King Ramkhamhaeng in 1285 and completed in 1291. The bell-shaped chedi, entwined with lotus leaves stands on two high square pedestals; the higher one is decorated with 20 niches which used to house 1.4m/4½ft-high Buddha statues. Some are still present and depict Buddha in a position of submission to Mara; on the lower pedestal 30 life size elephants have been sculptured, separated by candelabras, giving the impression that they are supporting the building. During excavations and restoration work columns with capitals were discovered behind these sculptures. It is assumed that the walls of the lower pedestal underwent alteration either in the Sukhothai period or in the Ayutthaya period.

★★Wat Chedi Chet Theo

The seven rows of 32 stupas in differing styles and forms of the Wat Chedi Chet Theo, which housed the ashes of members of the viceroys' families, present a magnificent picture. Particulary noteworthy is the central stupa in the shape of a lotus bud in Sukhothai style (as in the Wat Mahathat in Sukhothai) and some Srivijaya style stupas, which found their way into the Sukhothai empire when King Ramkhamhaeng conquered parts of southern Thailand in the 13th c. Many of the stupas which combine a

Elephant sculptures in Wat Chang Lom

A Buddha with a Naga snake

Chedi of the Wat Chang Lom

Stupas in the Wat Chedi Chet Theo

mixture of styles, erected chiefly by King Loei Thai (ruled 1347–*c.* 1370) around the mid-14th c., are distinctive for their elegant proportions. Fine stucco reliefs can still be seen; one for example, on the stupa in the middle of the northern row, of a beautiful meditating Buddha below a naga which shows the influence of the Srivijaya style. In a chedi in the north-west corner and in another behind the lotus bud stupa are remnants of wall paintings.

Wat Utthayan Yai

A chedi and the ruins of a temple remain from the Utthayan Yai Wat.

★Wat Nang Phaya

The Wat Nang Phaya, the "temple of the queen", has a bell-shaped chedi on a high square base and highly decorative stucco ornaments of plants surround the long narrow windows like fine carvings on an external wall of the ruined wiharn.

Old Royal Palace

Between these temples and the Menam Yom is the area of the former Royal Palace, of which only scarce remains survive apart from a few chedis. To the south of this district is the Lak-Muang shrine, which was built on the foundation stone of the town and is crowned with a lotus bud, surrounded by four Sukhothai style chedis.

Wat Khok Sing Karam

A tranquil path, about 2.5km/1 mile along the river leads to the town of Chaliang with its important Wat Phra Si Ratana Mahathat (see below). The path passes the 14th c. Wat Khok Sing Karam, of which several columns and chedis remain. There are interesting ruins of a bot enclosed by columns, which unusually was not built above a statue of Buddha but over a small chedi which has a Buddha statue in a niche.

Wat Chao Chan

A few hundred yards further stands the Wat Chao Chan, its laterite prang reconstructed with old stucco ruins. In one of the ruined temples are remains of a standing Buddha, in another those of a seated Buddha.

Ceramic ovens

In the north of Si Satchanalai are the remains of the ovens in which the Chinese-inspired famous Sawankhalok ceramics were fired (Highway 101 towards Neu-Si Satchanalai, then left and by boat across the Menam Yom; 4km/2 miles).

As early as the 13th c. the ceramics from the ovens of Ban Ko Noi (thought to be the oldest in Thailand) were known as "Chaliangware". The hard clay earth found here was well suited for the firing process. Chaliangware is relatively coarse and usually has a dark brown glaze. King Ramkhamhaeng saw this pottery on a visit to China and decided to introduce it in Thailand. He brought Chinese potters with him who settled around Sukhothai and Si Satchanalai.

Whereas Chaliangware was primarily functional, under Chinese guidance "Sawankhalokware" developed which was more completely finished with a delicate, silk glaze. It matched the quality of Chinese Seladon ceramics and became an important export of the Sukhothai empire to Indonesia, Japan, the Phillippines and Borneo. As well as jugs, teapots, bowls and crockery figures for toys and consecrated gifts to protective spirits were produced.

The Thais have retained the art of making ceramics over the centuries although style and shapes have not changed since the 15th c. Chiang Mai is a centre of modern ceramic production but the artistic perfection of the ceramics from Si Satchanalai, Sukhothai and Sawakhalok is no longer achieved.

Chaliang

★★Wat Phra Si Ratana Mahathat

Chaliang, situated about 2½km/1½ miles downstream on a bow of the Menam Yom, was an old Khmer town; the Phra That, a Khmer temple and predecessor of the Wat Phra Ratana Mahathat, was built where the bow is at its narrowest, and so was only accessible by land on one side. An inscription, commissioned in 1292 by King Ramkhamhaeng, states that in 1285 the king had relics excavated from the old Khmer prang (assumed to be the Wat Chang Lom) and removed to a new chedi in the Wat Chang Lom, built in six years for this purpose. Following their transfer he dedicated one month and six days to their worship.

The beautiful chedi, still standing today, with its ornately formed stepped base is of early 15th c. origin (early Ayutthaya style). It is possible, however, that this chedi constitutes the last ruins of the prang built by King Ramkhamhaeng.

The figure of the seated Buddha on the north side of the prang has been extensively restored. The lower floor was once surrounded by a covered gallery, from which parts of the wall and window slits remain. On the west side of the prang are the remains of a small temple with a bronze footprint of Buddha.

In a small niche close by can be seen an exquisite stone sculpture, which depicts Buddha shielded by a naga. The nine-headed snake is artistically decorated; the high relief of the stepping Buddha in a relaxed position is among the most beautiful carvings of the Sukhothai period. The stucco relief dates from the rule of King Ramkhamhaeng and is situated in the small temple to the east of the prang, where there is another standing Buddha.

Surrounding walls

The 1m/3ft-thick wall built from cylinders between 1285 to 1288 by King Ramkhamhaeng is noteworthy. Heavy roof-shaped laterite caps rest on the pillars; three higher pillars form the gates, the top part of the centre one is decorated with stucco figures and ornaments. Rather unusual are the large impressive faces in the four corners, possibly influenced by the formative style of the towers with faces in the temple at Angkor Thorn (now in Cambodia).

In the vicinity is a large chedi from the second half of the 14th c. clearly influenced by the Singhalese and erected by Mon monks. Right in the east of the site is a mondhop, called Phra Ruang and consecrated to the son of a snake goddess.

Si Thep F 5

Region: Central Thailand
Province: Phetchabun
Altitude: 128m/420ft. Population: 9000

ศรีเทพ

Location

A visit to this town in the Menam Pasak valley framed by jungle covered mountains is only for those seriously interested in the history of Thailand and who possess a vivid imagination. The archaeologists have only made a hesitant start in their excavations and the Department of Fine Arts is funding future work in the near future. The finest pieces from Si Thep are in the National Museum in Bangkok.

Access

By car: from Phetchabun Highway 21 south (132km/82 miles), from Saraburi also route 21 in the opposite direction (123km/76 miles).
By bus: connections from Saraburi and Phetchabun.

History

It is a matter of debate whether Si Thep enjoyed any importance before its function as a Khmer town. One of the earliest settlements in Thailand has been identified in the region around Si Thep. This theory has been reinforced by excavations which unearthed Brahman statues and reliefs. However, the discovery of some stone tablets bearing Khmer inscriptions indicated that Si Thep was an important town during the Khmer empire.

Layout

The oval wall surrounding the town built by the Mon, later to be made square by the Khmer, can only be distinguished with difficulty. The remains of prangs, town walls and five temple sites can be seen more or less clearly.

The stone statues found during excavations are among the oldest and finest Hindu depictions. They originate from the 6th–9th c., the time of the Dvaravati empire and display strong influences of Indian Gupta and post-Gupta art. These rare treasures have been in the National Museum in Bangkok for years where they are on display together with a plan of a ruined town. There is also an exceptionally fine Buddha statue with a Pali inscription on the pedestal.

None of the Khmer monuments appear to be more recent than early 11th c., suggesting that Si Thep was probably abandoned by the Khmer in that century.

Thamorat cave

Evidence of Buddhist art (wall carvings, date of origin unknown) can be found in the cave in the hill at Thamorat, to the west of Si Thep.

Songkhla O 4

Region: South Thailand
Province: Songkhla
Altitude: 4m/13ft. Population: 182,000

สงขลา

Location

Songkhla in the southernmost part of Thailand – 720km/447 miles from Bangkok as the crow flies – is among the most beautiful seaside resorts in Thailand and is unspoilt by tourism. The provincial capital (university and technical college) retains much of its original character. Songkhla, almost completely encircled by water, lies on a promomtory between the Gulf of Thailand and Lake Songkhla, the largest inland lake in Thailand, which has a narrow link to the Gulf here. Miles of white sandy beaches edged by casuarina trees stretch along the lake and the Gulf. The countryside between the sea and the land is of extraordinary beauty.

◄ *Buddha statue in the Wat Phra Si Ratana Mahathat in Chaliang*

The lake used to provide a livelihood for the numerous fisherman and their families but it has been overfished. A programme laid down by the government in 1991 is intended to replenish the fish stocks.

Access

By car: from Nakhon Si Thammarat Highways 401/41/4/43 to Hat Ya route 407 (220km/137 miles); or Highway 408 along the coast (160km/99 miles).
By bus: from Bangkok Southern Bus Terminal several times daily and from Hat Yai every 30 minutes until 7.30pm.
By air: nearest airport in Hat Yai; from Bangkok twice daily.

Port

Protected by a bay, this once significant port (known in former times by the Malay name Singora) is used increasingly for coastal traffic. Larger vessels berth between the islands Koh Nu and Koh Meo (Mouse and Cat Island).

Sights

★Townscape

The centre of the town has moved its location over the centuries. Remains of the fortifications of old Songkhla, which endured until the 17th c., can be seen near the present day village of Khao Hua Deang. They were constructed by a sultan who rebelled against Ayutthaya rule. On its recapture the town was destroyed and later rebuilt on the site of Laem Song. The present day town on the south side of the bay dates from the middle of the last century. Parts of the fort and town wall can still be seen (near the police station).

Many of the inhabitants of Songkhla and its surroundings are Malays or Chinese, a typical Chinese business quarter is on the Phatthalung Road.

Bullfights (bull versus bull) are popular and take place on Saturday and Sunday afternoons in the ring on the Rajchutid Road.

Governor's Palace National Museum

Built in 1878 the Governor's Palace (seat of the Na Songkhla family) is a wonderful Chinese style building with splendid carvings; nowadays it is a National Museum (open: Wed.–Sun. 9am–4pm; admission fee). There is another museum in the Matchimawat Wat (see below). Both house valuable bronze sculptures from the Srivijaya period, which bear a strong resemblance to early eastern and central Javanese art, ceramics from the Srivijaya and Ayutthaya periods together with everyday objects, including many curiosities (mostly discoveries from Sathing Phra).

★Wat Matchimawat

In the Wat Matchimawat (16th c.) there is a notable 2000 year old Buddha statue which was once decorated with a pure gold lotus crown. For security reasons the crown is kept in a safe and only put on the statue on religious holidays.

★Wat Klang

Although it is not particularly old the 19th c. Wat Klang is worth a visit. The Sala Reussi, a brick building and the bot guarded by Chinese lions are decorated inside with frescos which are among the least notable paintings of the Bangkok style and depict hermits practising yoga. The pedestal of the bot is finished with flat reliefs by a Chinese artist.

★View point

Two hills dominate the town; a park is laid out on the smaller one (Khao Noi). The higher one is crowned by a temple; from here there is a good view of Songkhla and the surrounding area.

★Beaches

Samila beach on the bay is popular with locals chiefly at weekends, whereas the beach on the Gulf coast is deserted. At the end of Samila beach lies the fishing village Ban Kao Seng, inhabited by Moslem fishermen. During the day their colourfully painted boats are drawn up on the beach.

Surroundings

★Wat Suwan Khiri

On the southern tip of the narrow strip of land opposite Songkhla stands the Wat Suwan Khiri, founded by the Na Songkhla family at the beginning of the 19th c. There is a fine chedi and Chinese bell tower together with the wiharn decorated with frescos.

For generations the Na Songkhla family provided the governor of Songkhla; the first progenitor being Chinese. It supports the efforts of the Thai government to integrate the southern provinces.

★Bay

A boat trip along the mountainous promontory north of Songkhla passes many picturesque fishing villages, built on stilts. Further north a soaring limestone ridge divides the inland lake into two parts, Thale Sap and Thale Luang. The brackish freshwaters harbour many sunda-gaviale (Siam crocodiles); terns make their nests in the rocks, the nests are a delicacy of Chinese cuisine. A possible destination of such a boat trip could be the island of Koh Yo with two temples.

★Sathing Phra

On the spit of land to the north of Songkhla there are interesting ruins of numerous places of worship from the Srivijaya empire. The most important is probably Sathing Phra, 30km/19 miles north of Songkhla right by the sea (easy access by bus or car, ferry across the inlet). The stupa has niches on three sides and is a fine example of Srivijaya style. The nearby temple houses a beautiful Buddha statue and interesting frescos. The stucco decoration on the trapezia is thought to originate from the Ayutthaya period. Excavations revealed numerous bronze sculptures from the 8th to the 12th c., which are kept in the National Museum in Bangkok and the Museum in Songkhla. Some display distinct Javanese influence, others are in the Khmer style.

Other ruins of Srivijaya temples, mostly stupas and Buddha figures, together with a cave temple (Tham Khao Pi) are to be found further north; these include the Wats Chedi Ngam, Khao Noi Chae Mae and Ko Mai. Additional places of interest include a coconut plantation where monkeys are trained to pick the nuts, and the Wat Khao Tum built on a rock.

Sukhothai D/E 3

Region: North Thailand
Province: Sukhothai
Altitude: 66m/216ft. Population: 26,000

สุโขทัย

Location

The ancient capital of Sukhothai, the historical and cultural centre of the Sukhothai period (*c.* mid 13th c.–mid 15th c.), is situated in the north of the Central Plain (a good 400km/248 miles north of Bangkok); this wide region, bordered by hills, is drained by the Menam Yom. The well-developed ruin site is situated 12km/7½ miles from the modern town of Sukhothai and is most conveniently reached by bus, taxi or rented car.

Access:

By car: From Bangkok Highways 1/32/117 to Phitsanulok, then Highway 12 (430km/267 miles).
By bus: from Bangkok Northern Bus Terminal (440km/273 miles), Sawankhalok, Phitsanulok.
By rail: nearest station Sawankhalok (38km/24 miles).
By air: nearest airport Phitsanulok (58km/36 miles).

History

For 140 years Sukhothai was the capital of an important empire. According to legend the town was founded around 500 A.D., one of its rulers is supposed to have been King Chao Aluna Khmara (also called Phra Ruang, "son of the twilight"), the result of a liaison between a human and a mythical Naya princess. Phra Ruang therefore took the name of the dynasty of the eight kings, which ruled the great empire. The first regent of this dynasty was Si Indratitja (*c.* 1235–79), who was able to shake off Khmer rule in 1238.

His empire essentially only consisted of the two towns Sukhothai and Si Satchanalai. If Si Indratitja was instrumental in the founding of an independent Thai culture then his grandson Ramkhamhaeng (1279–99) was much more so. His empire stretched as far as Vientiane in the north-east, Pegu in the west in present day Myanmar and to Nakhon Si Thammarat in the south (almost two-thirds of the existing country today). Events of this lively period (including the first diplomatic contact between a Thai ruler and neighbouring China) did not remain hidden from the world; an

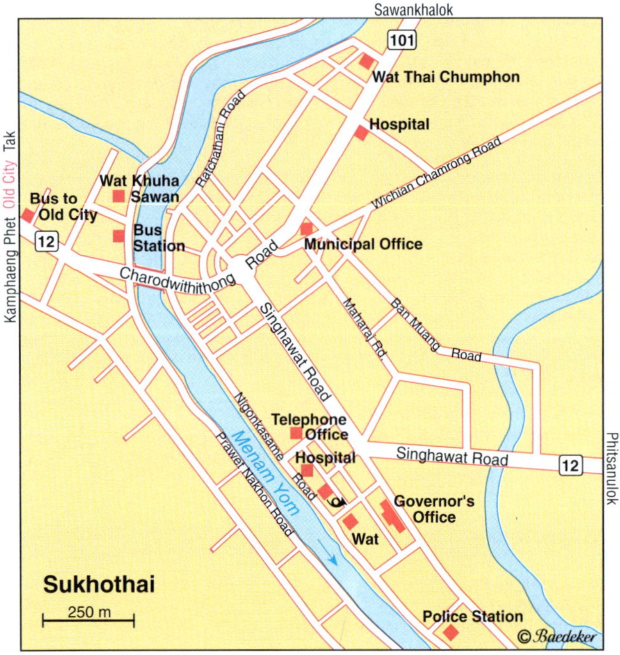

inscription in stone composed by Ramkhamhaeng, probably a form of inaugural speech, is preserved in the National Museum in Bangkok (see Introduction, Thailand in Quotations). The king invented the Thai alphabet and initiated porcelain and faience production based on a Chinese model.

Under Ramkhamhaeng's successor Loei Thai (1299–1347) most of the newly acquired territory was lost and his son Liu Thai (1347–68), who took the name Mahadharmaraya, did not succeed in restoring the former glory of the empire. The Ayutthaya king Boromaraja I conquered Sukhothai in 1378, in 1438 it finally became part of the Ayutthaya empire.

When the Burmese flattened Ayutthaya in 1767 the inhabitants of Sukhothai also left their town. However, just eleven years later Rama I, the first king of the Chakri dynasty which ruled Bangkok, founded the new town of Sukhothai on the left bank of the Menam Yom. It was largely destroyed by fire in 1968, all the houses in the town centre are recently built.

Sights in new Sukhothai

In new Sukhothai the buildings of the Wat Khuha Sawan on the western edge of the town originating from 1870 are especially noteworthy. In the bot are the colossal figure of a seated Buddha and several smaller ones in Sukhothai style, U-Thong and Ayutthaya style. The large Buddha in front of the bot is a recent addition.

Ruined city of Sukhothai

General

Following about 25 years of archaelogical works, supported by UNESCO, King Bhumibol opened up the ruined city of Sukhothai to the public; 193 temples were excavated and partly reconstructed. As many antiquities

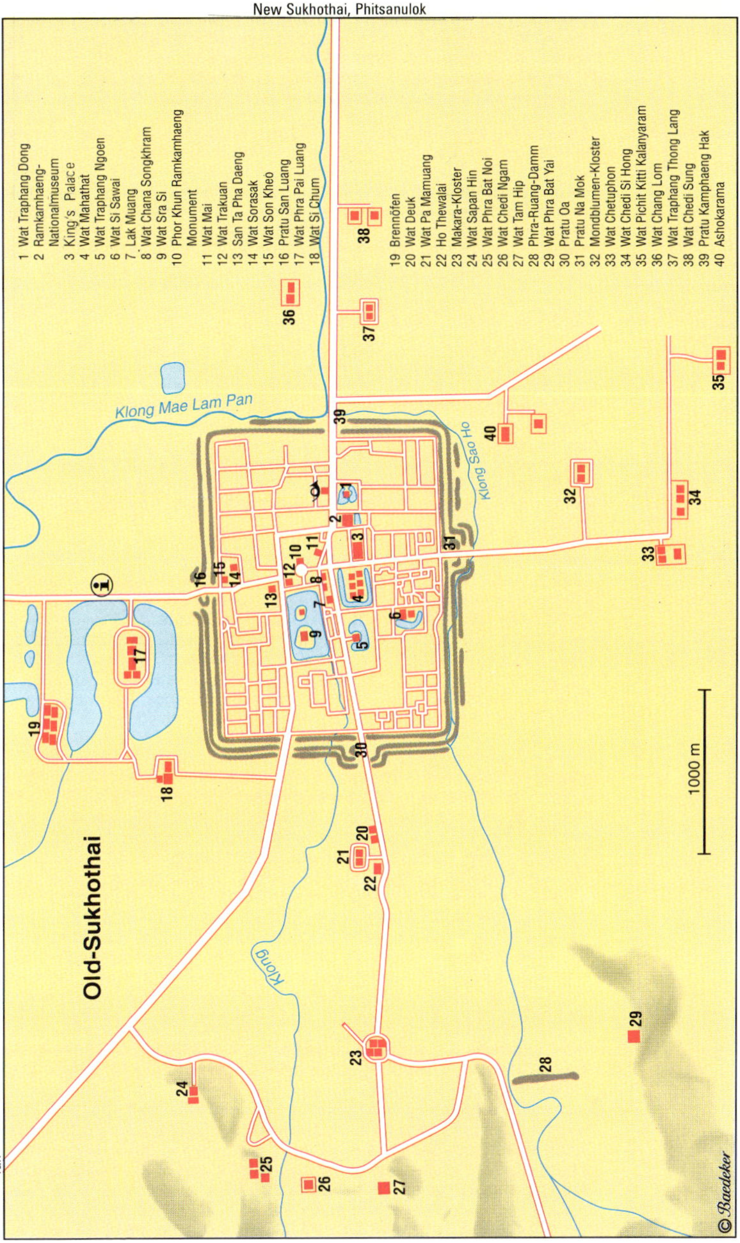
New Sukhothai, Phitsanulok
Tak
Old-Sukhothai
Klong Mae Lam Pan
Klong Sao Ho
Klong
1000 m
1 Wat Traphang Dong
2 Ramkamhaeng-Nationalmuseum
3 King's Palace
4 Wat Mahathat
5 Wat Traphang Ngoen
6 Wat Si Sawai
7 Lak Muang
8 Wat Chana Songkhram
9 Wat Sra Si
10 Phor Khun Ramkamhaeng Monument
11 Wat Mai
12 Wat Trakuan
13 San Ta Pha Daeng
14 Wat Sorasak
15 Wat Son Kheo
16 Pratu San Luang
17 Wat Phra Pai Luang
18 Wat Si Chum
19 Brennöfen
20 Wat Deuk
21 Wat Pa Mamuang
22 Ho Thewalai
23 Makara-Kloster
24 Wat Sapan Hin
25 Wat Phra Bat Noi
26 Wat Chedi Ngam
27 Wat Tam Hip
28 Phra-Ruang-Damm
29 Wat Phra Bat Yai
30 Pratu Oa
31 Pratu Na Mok
32 Mondblumen-Kloster
33 Wat Chetuphon
34 Wat Chedi Si Hong
35 Wat Pichit Kitti Kalanyaram
36 Wat Chang Lom
37 Wat Traphang Thong Lang
38 Wat Chedi Sung
39 Pratu Kamphaeng Hak
40 Ashokarama
© Baedeker

plundered from Sukhothai were finding their way to art collectors all over the world UNESCO stepped in to support the work in 1978. Nowadays the ruined city is closely guarded. (Open: daily 6am–6pm; admission fee.)

There is an information board in English in front of every building.

There is also an Information Centre; open: 9am–4pm.

Inside the walls

Old city centre

The old city centre was surrounded by three earth walls and two moats which formed a square of 1810m/5938ft×1400m/4593ft. Of the four entrance gates ("pratu"; Kamphaeng Hak in the east, Na Mok in the south, Oa in the west and San Luang in the north) three were secured by forts, the remains of which can still be seen. Apart from 21 wats four ponds have been uncovered: Thapang Thong, Thapang Ngoen, Thapang Trakuan and Thapang So. Temple sites were not only inside the walls but dispersed throughout the surrounding area.

★★Ramkhamhaeng Museum

Opened in 1964 the Ramkhamhaeng Museum (open: Wed.–Sun. 9am–noon and 1–4pm; admission fee; no photographs) contains numerous finds (especially statues, stucco work and ceramics) from Sukhothai, Si Satchanalai and Kamphaeng Phet, the three capitals of the empire. It provides a good over-view of the development of the Sukhothai style from its beginnings, where the Khmer influence was still dominant, to the final stage where the Ayutthaya style was prevalent. Particularly noteworthy are a stepping Buddha, the finest example of this type, a seated Buddha from the Wat Chang Lom in Si Satchanalai (both on the ground floor) and a seated bronze Buddha (upper floor). In the museum garden are other statues and a ceramic kiln. The admission fee includes a detailed brochure in English.

★★Wat Mahathat

The most splendid wat of the present ruined city was the Wat Mahathat near the earlier Royal Palace, a wooden building of which no trace remains. This wat alone covered an area of 40,000sq.m/47,840sq.yd and was surrounded by 185 chedis, six wiharns of varying size, a bot and eleven salas; a wall punctuated by gates encircled the area. The centre of the site is most impressive, a main chedi with both a wiharn and a bot. The towering finely constructed chedi in pure Sukhothai style terminates in the tip of a lotus bud. The middle section ressembles the Khmer prangs, the high square base is decorated by a procession of worshippers with 40 figures of about one metre high on each side. The niches of the four corner chapels show fine stucco work, rosettes, scenes from the life of Buddha, gods and demons in conflict; both niches and the pedestal ledge have Buddha figures.

Four Khmer prangs in the centre of each side describe the four points of the compass. On the east side a high staircase leads to the interior of the central chedi. The pillars of a small wiharn (14th c. Ayutthaya period; with the statue of a seated Buddha) and the massive bot (40×15m/131×49ft) are still standing. The rows of columns from the five-aisled bot in particular create an impressive picture. It once contained the gilded statue of the Phra Buddha Shakyamuni, which King Rama I had brought to the Wat Suthat in Bangkok at the end of the 18th c. Eight metre-high standing Buddhas are let in to the protective niches on both sides of the mondhops. Numerous crumbling chedis are located around this impressive group of ruins, in which the ashes of the deceased members of the royal family were interred.

Wat Si Sawai

Surrounded by a moat and two walls, the Wat Si Sawai, a Khmer-style temple built at the end of the 12th or beginning of the 13th c., before the capital Sukhothai was founded, first served the Hindu cult; following the addition of a bot and wiharn it became a Buddhist temple. Characteristic are the three brick prangs, each seven storeys high, covered with stone slabs and stucco. Buddha statues can still be seen in the trapezia of the upper storey. All three prangs encircle a cella; that of the higher central prang is above a gallery connected to the bot, whereas the other two are

Sukhothai: a well-tended park created on the site of the ruins ▶

The Wat Mahathat

only accessible from outside. Fragments of the relief, which originally decorated the walls of the prang, are on display in the Ramkhamhaeng Museum. The temple grounds also contain a chedi and two other temples on a square base.

★Wat Traphang Ngoen

To the west of the Wat Mahathat on an island covered with lotus blossoms in the Traphang Ngoen ("Silver Lake") are the outstandingly beautiful chedi of the Wat Traphang Ngoen and columns from a larger wiharn. In the niches of the chedi, which is an impressive sight against the mountains, are Buddha statues. It is crowned by a lotus bud.

Wat Chana Songkhram

The Wat Chana Songkhram with a bell-shaped chedi in Singhalese style and the bases of two temples which have disappeared stands on a raised platform. The crumbling small building to the south of this wat was built over the symbolic foundation stone of the town, the Lak Muang.

★★Wat Sra Si

The Wat Sra Si on a small island must have been quite magnificent; it has ten chedis influenced by the Ceylon-style. Six rows of columns and the beautiful statue of a seated Buddha in the pose of the Bhumispara-mudra remain from the large wiharn. The bot of the Wat Sra Si stands on an island in a pond covered with lotus flowers. The buildings of the wat on the bank, inhabited by monks, originate from a more recent period. The old laterite chedi in Singhalese style is decaying badly. In the mondhop is a stone footprint of Buddha, which was brought here from the Wat Phra Bat Yai; it is thought to have been discovered – according to an inscription – by King Liu Thai in 1359. In honour of this holy place the Loy Kratong festival (light festival) is celebrated here in November; the lake is transformed by thousands of tiny floating candles into a fascinating sea of light.

Wat Mai

Parts of the base of the wiharn, richly decorated with stucco, in the Wat Mai still remain, only the pedestal of the prang remains.

Prang of the Wat Chedi Sung

Elephant sculptures on the Wat Sorasak

Wat Trakuan

Several figures of Buddha in early Sukhothai style were found in the ruins of the Wat Trakuan, of which only a fine chedi and base of the wiharn can be seen; they display a rather unusual mixture of Ceylonese elements and Chiang-Saen style.

★★San Ta Pha Daeng

San Ta Pha Daeng, built end of the 12th/beginning of the 13th c., ranks among the most important Khmer ruins on Thai soil. The temple is on a 3m/10ft-high base and has four porticos. There are five wonderful stone fragments of male and female Hindu deities in Angkor Wat style.

★Wat Sorasak

The Wat Sorasak was constructed in 1412, towards the end of the Sukhothai empire. The decaying chedi in Singhalese style is supported by 25 elephants. The niches are occupied by statues depicting Buddha sitting in a "western" position with legs hanging down.

Wat Son Kheo

A beautiful chedi and the columns of a temple are what is left of Wat Son Kheo.

North of the walls

Leave the town centre through the Pratu San Luang gate to reach two important monuments and the ceramic kilns.

★Wat Phra Pai Luang

Surrounded by a moat Wat Phra Pai Luang is extensive and one of the oldest temples. It was probably one of the most important in this region and is thought to date from the end of the 12th or beginning of the 13th c. Of the three laterite prangs decorated with stucco the north one is still standing. On the gable of the false door Buddha and his followers are represented. Beautiful stucco work adorns the steps of the chedi and the base of the dilapidated eastern chedi. The outside wall, the foundations and ruins of four rows of columns still remain from the wiharn. In the mondhop statues were found depicting Buddha in the four basic positions. The Wat Phra Pai Luang was presumably the main wat of the old town at the time of

Prang of the Wat Phra Pai Luang

Buddha figure in the Wat Si Chum

the Khmer before it was moved further south to its present position in the ruined city.

★ Wat Si Chum

The mondhop of the Wat Si Chum, a huge, windowless cuboid construction (22×28×15m/72×91×49ft), stands on a 4.30m/14ft-high pedestal, the walls are 3m/9ft thick. There is access to the roof through an entrance in the southern wall. The ceiling of this walkway was once covered with artistically engraved stone plates (one is on display in the Ramkhamhaeng Museum in Sukhothai, the other in the National Museum in Bangkok) which illustrated in sweeping succession scenes from the life of Buddha. The illustrations are of outstanding beauty betraying the influence of Singhalese-Indian painters and having similarities with the temple walls of Polonaruwa on Sri Lanka.

In the interior of the mondhop is the colossal statue (14.70m/48ft high) of a seated Buddha, which was formerly gilded. It is probably the Phra Achana mentioned in an inscription by King Ramkhamhaeng in 1292. In front of the mondhop is a bot with an area of 21×12m/69×40ft, its 13 limonite columns covered in stucco work still standing. To the north of the mondhop are the ruins of a small wiharn and a brick building which contains a seated Buddha.

Ceramic kilns

The remnants of ceramic kilns are interesting; excavations has so far brought to light 49 of them (a model exists in the Ramkhamhaeng Museum). The ceramic and tile production began here around 1300 when King Ramkhamhaeng brought several hundred potters from China, and it lasted until the middle of the 15th c. when wars interrupted production.

West of the walls

Only a few of the ruins to the west of the town are worth a visit. Some of them are to undergo restoration in the near future.

Wat Pa Mamuang

In the Sukhothai period the Wat Pa Mamuang was a religious centre. Inscriptions in Pali, Khmer and Thai (today in the National Museum in Bangkok) provide information about its history. The base of the mondhop, the pedestals of several smaller chedis and the ruins of the bot can still be seen. Also from the Wat Tuk remains of the mondhop, wiharn and some chedis have been preserved.

Ho Thewalai

The Ho Thewalai stands on a platform which is reached by a staircase; eight columns of this Hindu temple can still be seen.

Wat Chang Rob

The pedestal of the chedi in the Wat Chang Rob is supported by 24 elephants. In the foreground – apart from some rubble – the laterite columns of a former wiharn still stand.

★Wat Sapan Hin

The Wat Sapan Hin lies on a hill at the edge of the Yom plain and offers a fine view of the mountains and Si Satchanalai. A paved path leads to the monastery giving it the name "temple of the stone bridge". In this wat King Ramkhamhaeng celebrated the Thot-Kathin festival annually in October, the end of the Buddhist fasting period. Tall stucco covered laterite columns once supported the wiharn. There is an impressive 12.5m/41ft-high statue of a standing Buddha in Sukhothai style leaning against a brick wall in the open, the right hand raised in a protective gesture. It is deeply revered by the population of the surrounding area.

Nearby is a statue of a seated Buddha also in Sukhothai style. Ruins of another temple and a chedi can also be found. Parts of this wat were restored in the 20th c.

★Wat Phra Bat Noi

The Wat Phra Bat Noi is also interesting ("wat to Buddha's footprint") with its unusual chedi (mixture of Thai and Khmer styles). The central part resting on a square basis has a niche on each side which is occupied by a smaller Buddha figure. The lower part of the apex has vertical ribbing,

Eroded by the ravages of time: Buddha statues in Sukhothai

which like the niches, is decorated with predominantly Hindu motifs. The footprint from the wiharn is in the Ramkhamhaeng Museum.

Wat Tham Hip

At the foot of the hill is the Wat Tham Hip. The chedi and wiharn, of which remains can be seen, are on different levels.

Wat Chedi Ngam

The bell-shaped chedi of the Wat Chedi Ngam rests on a richly decorated foundation. The base of the bell is decorated with a lotus frieze, on each side of the central part is a niche for a Buddha figure. About one metre below in front of the chedi are the laterite columns of the wiharn and four small stone chapels.

South of the walls

At the south gate Pratu Na Mok remains of the small fort can be seen. On the way to the Wat Chetuphon are the ruins of the Wat Kampang Lang with the foundations of a chedi and wiharn and the ruins of the Wat Ton Chan with a Singhalese style chedi.

★Wat Chetuphon

In the Wat Chetuphon there is a particularly beautiful example of sculpture in classical Sukhothai style, a stepping Buddha in stucco, the only one of four to be have been well preserved. The other three represent Buddha in sitting, standing and reclining positions. They occupy the external walls of the mondhop, a massive brick construction, which stood at the centre point of the temple grounds; only one wall of this remains. The chedi in the form of a mondhop contains the Buddha statue Phra Si Arijya Metrai ("Buddha of the future"). Part of the window frame from the wiharn has been preserved and appears to have been carved. An unusual feature at the Wat Chetuphon are the walls of slate which are sculptured like wood.

Wat Chedi Si Hong

In the Wat Chedi Si Hong the quality of the 14th c. sculpture on the laterite base of the foundation is remarkable; upright angel-like figures bear vases of flowers in the upper hand and symbolise prayer with the lower hand. Traces of Singhalese and Khmer art are visible in their clothing. Lions appear between the figures standing on the heads of elephants. Laterite columns from the wiharn and the pedestals of two chedis in the portico still stand.

★Wat Pichit Kitti Kalanyaram

Visible from afar is the high bell-shaped chedi of the Wat Pichit Kitti Kalanyaram from 1403. The square base has a 15m/49ft-long border. There are some beautifully carved moonstones here, which are common in Sri Lanka but rare in Thailand.

East of the walls

★★Wat Traphang Thong Lang

On the road to Sukhothai is the Wat Traphang Thong Lang with remarkable stucco relief on the side. The flat relief on the southern side is the best of its type in Sukhothai style; it shows Buddha, striding over steps, coming down from heaven Tavatimsa. Buddha, protected by two parasols, is accompanied by the Hindu goddeses Indra and Brahma together with worshippers. This is assumed to be the first (from the Sukhothai period) visual representation of the stepping Buddha. Another flat relief on the north side of the bot depicts, less artistically, Buddha taming the elephant Nalagiri, which his cousin Devadatta had set upon him. The relief on the west wall shows Buddha under a mango tree at the miracle of Sravasti. Painted interpretations of this kind are in Polonaruwa (Sri Lanka) and Pagan (Burma).

★Wat Chedi Sung

Somewhat further east the Wat Chedi Sung has a towering simple but effectively decorated chedi, a fine balance of strength and nobility. This stucco covered chedi from the late 14th c. ranges among the most beautiful sacral buildings of Sukhothai architecture. The high foundations on a square base has Srivijaya characteristics, whereas the narrow bell on an octagonal base has distinct Singhalese traits.

On both sides of the road to New Sukhothai are several complexes of old houses on stilts made of teak and linked by footbridges.

Suphanburi G 4

Region: West Thailand
Province: Suphanburi
Altitude: 73m/240ft. Population: 28,000

สุพรรณบุรี

Location

Surrounded by rice and sugar cane plantations, the modern commercial town of Suphanburi is situated about 90km/56 miles north-west of Bangkok in the Central Plain on the left bank of the Menam Tha Chin. Some ruins of the old town on the right bank, which was important during the Ayutthaya period, still remain.

Access

By car: from Bangkok first heading west on national Highway 4 or 338, then Highway 340 (98km/61 miles). From Ayutthaya Highway 3263 westwards (55km/34 miles).
By bus: from Bangkok Northern Bus Terminal.

Sights

Wat Phra Rup

Shortly after the bridge over the Tha Chin the Wat Phra Rup is on the left where a footprint carved in wood, said to have been washed ashore by the river, is highly revered.

★★Wat Palilei

The Wat Palilei on the bank of the Menam Tha Chin in old Suphanburi is from the U-Thong period, but underwent extensive alteration during the Ayutthaya period. It houses the colossal statue of a Buddha in Ayutthaya style. To the right and left of the road are fragments of some chedis, some of which are in an advanced state of decay.

Wat Phra Si Ratana Mahathat

The soaring prang of the Wat Phra Si Ratana Mahathat in the town centre is made of brick and decorated with stucco ornaments and in good repair. It is surrounded by ruins of prangs and chedis and fragments of Buddha statues.

Surroundings

Don Chedi

24km/15 miles north-west of Suphanburi is Don Chedi (Highway 322 to U Ya, then right); a bronze monument has been erected to commemorate a decisive battle of King Naresuan against the Burmese (1592). Seated on an elephant Naresuan killed the Burmese crown prince Min Chit Swa. The monument was designed by Prof. Silpa Bhirasi and cast in 1959 at the Silpakorn School of Art in Bangkok. The chedi, which was built by King Naresuan, has collapsed and been replaced by a modern monument.

Surat Thani M 3

Region: South Thailand
Province: Surat Thani
Altitude: 8m/26ft. Population: 46,000

สุราษฎร์ธานี

Location

Surat Thani lies on the Malayan peninsula in the fertile plain on the estuary of the Menam Ta Pi in the Gulf of Thailand. It was already inhabited during the Stone Age (numerous tools excavated) and in the first millennium the terminus of an important road from Ta Kuapa, which shortened the route to the South China Sea. Following the construction of good roads the town developed into an important trading place between Thailand and Malaysia; it is a centre for shipbuilding, fishing, mining and timber industry. There are no particular sights but the countryside with dense tropical rain-forest, mighty dolomite rocks and paradise-like islands is breathtakingly beautiful. The island of Koh Samui (see below) is an internationally famous tourist destination.

Access

By rail: from Bangkok-Hualampong (651km/404 miles, duration 12 hours; overnight train recommended, reservations necessary).

By car: from Bangkok Highway 4, from Chumphon Highway 41 (644km/400 miles). From Nakhon Si Thammarat Highway 401 (135km/84 miles).
By air: daily from Bangkok; also charter flights.
By ferry: express ferry between Bangkok and Surat Thani (duration about 15 hours), reservations from travel operators.

★Wat Dei Tamaram

One of the most noteworthy temples, even if it is modern, is the Wat Dei Tamaram on the Na Muang Road. It has a magnificent tall wiharn with richly decorated gables. Considerably older is a building in close proximity where the entrances are guarded by warlike demons. The activity around the temple site is interesting.

Port of Ban Dong

The port of Ban Dong (previously the name of the whole town) is a hub of activity, the markets are a colourful sight.

Surroundings

★★Countryside

The journey between Ta Kuapa on the other side of the peninsula on Lake Andamanen and Surat Thani is through some of the most beautiful scenery in Thailand. The dolomite rocks soar out of the tropical jungle up to heights of 1000m/3280ft.

★Wat Suan Mok

On the outskirts of Surat Thani is the Wat Suan Mok, a meeting place for Buddhists from all over the world. Meditation courses are held here but places must be booked in advance. Information is available from the World Fellowship of Buddhists in Bangkok (see Practical Information, Meditation).

★★Islands

There are about 60 islands off the coast of Surat Thani. Many have beautiful beaches and idyllic fishing villages, almost all of them offer a variety of scenery with rocky cliffs, dense vegetation and tranquil bays edged with white sand.

Wiharn of the Wat Dei Tamaram

The three largest islands are Koh Samui, Koh Pha Ngan (an archipelago which has been declared a national park) and Koh Phaului. Nature provides the islanders with everything they need to live: bamboo, wood and palm leaves to build houses, fish, coconuts and vegetables.

★★Koh Samui

Location

Together with 40 other unpopulated islands Koh Samui makes up the Ang-Thong Archipelago, a chain of islands north-east of Surat Thani. The best time to visit Koh Samui is between February and April, as in the following months the Gulf of Thailand is subject to heavy monsoon storms. The chief town of this 250sq.km/96sq. miles island is Nathon where there are fine beaches and some hotel and villa complexes. Other beaches with reasonable accommodation are Ao Maenam, Ao Bo Phut (with an enormous statue of Buddha), Ao Cherngmon, Chaweng Noi Beach and Chaweng Yai Beach (the two longest beaches on Koh Samui). Motorcycles and bicycles can be rented and are a good way of exploring the island.

Access

Since the construction of an airport on Koh Samui (despite the vehement but unsuccessful objections of conservationists) the island has become a magnet even for visitors seeking luxury hotels (seven flights daily from Bangkok; duration about 70 minutes).

By boat: bus from Surat Thani to Don Sak, from here boat to Koh Samui (about 3 hours in total, fare includes bus). Catamaran from Bangkok.

Fishing villages

There are picturesque fishing villages on Koh Samui together with coconut and durian plantations and – hidden in the dense jungle among the 600m/1968ft-high mountains – some waterfalls.

Wat Hin Ngu

Near the village of Ban Hua Thanon is the Wat Hin Ngu, built on stone cliffs. Once a year (around mid-March) a fair combined with a temple festival takes place in the temple grounds which attracts thousands of people from the surrounding area.

An airfield building on Koh Samui

Ban Chalok Lum
Ban Thong Nai Pan
627
Si Thanu Beach
Ban Madua Wan
Ban Hin Kong
Ban Nai Suan
Yang Beach
Koh Tae Nai
Ban Thong Sala
535
Koh Tae Nok
Ban Tai
Ban Khai
Koh Pha-Ngan
Laem Hat Rim
Laem Samrong
Koh Som
Ban Bang Po
Ban Mae Nam
Ban Plai Laem
Laem Yai
Ban Thong Phlu
Ban Bo Phut
464
218
Nathon
Ban Chaweng
Koh Matlang
Ban Chaweng Noi
Ban Li Pa Noi
630
Ban Chon Khram
635
Ban Sa Ket
Ban Lamai
Ban Taling Ngam
Laem Nan
Ban Hua Thanon
Ban Han
Ban Thong Tanot
Ban Thong Krut
Koh Samui
Laem Hin Kom
Laem Hua Sai
Koh Taen
Ban Koh Tan
Koh Mat Sum
5 km
© Baedeker

"Mama and Papa Rocks" on Lamai Beach

Laem Set (beach)

To the south of Ban Han lies Laem Set beach which has a beautiful coral garden off the coast and strange rock formations.

★Phang Ka Beach

The sunset is spectacular seen from Phang Ka beach to the north of Ban Thong Thanot.

Lamai Beach

There is a rock formation colourfully described as "Mother and Father Rocks" on Lamai Beach between Ban Hua Thanon and Ban Lamai, the busiest beach on Koh Samui.

Watersports

Koh Samui offers every kind of watersport: diving, snorkelling, windsurfing. It is advisable to check that the diving school belongs to one of the two international associations (see Practical Information, Sport), which regulates the safety standards of the equipment and quality of instruction.

★★Koh Pha Ngan

Location

The 19.4km/12 miles-long and 11.6km/7 miles-wide island of Koh Pha Ngan is situated about 16km/10 miles north of Koh Samui and for some years has served as an overflow resort when Koh Samui has been overcrowded. More than half of the island still consists of jungle dominated by the limestone mountains which descend to the beaches in places. The population of about 8000 is dependent primarily upon fishing for its livelihood with tourism increasingly becoming more than just a source of additional income. Koh Pha Ngan has excellent beaches but, apart from the beauty of the jungle, no particular sights. The chief town, Thong Sala, roughly in the middle of the south-west coast, has an adequate infrastructure (post office, telephones, exchange) and even a little night life.

Access

By ferry from (Surat Thani-) Don Sak, usually calling at Koh Samui. One boat leaves from Bo Phut Beach on Koh Samui at 9.30am, arriving at Chalok Lam, Koh Pha Ngan, 1½ hours later. Return boat to Koh Samui leaves at 2.30pm.

A beach on Koh Pha Ngan

★Wat Khao Tham

A visit to the meditation temple of Wat Khao Tham with a footprint of Buddha is worth a visit. The temple stands on a hilltop near Ban Tai.

Beaches

Among the beautiful beaches with good snorkelling are Thong Sala Beach, Ban Tai Beach, Yang Beach, Ban Khai Beach and Si Thanu Beach.

★Boat trips

The fascinating subtropical world and superb beaches of the other islands in the Ang-Thong archipelago and Marine Park can be reached by boat. Whilst numerous islands are still uninhabited there are already some bungalows on Koh Khanom and Koh Sichon. The "Blue Lagoon" on Thale Nai is worth a visit and the climb up the Utthayan hills (approx. 40 minutes, viewing platform) should not be missed. Daily boat trips to Ang-Thong Marine Park leaves Na Thon, Koh Samui, at 8.30am and returns at 5pm.

Surin G 7

สุรินทร์

Region: North-east Thailand
Province: Surin
Altitude: 145m/475ft. Population: 38,000

Location

The provincial town of Surin, situated in a broad plain of the Khorat Plateau in eastern Thailand, is the centre of the Thai silk and weaving industry, built partly on the foundations of an old Khmer settlement. Every November it is the setting for the Elephant Festival which attracts thousands of visitors. During this period Surin is bursting at its seams but for the rest of the year it is a quiet, peaceful town from where some important Khmer temples can be visited (good tourist infrastructure owing to the elephant festival).

Elephant festival in Surin

Access

By car: from Bangkok on Highways 1/2/24, from Prasat Highway 214 (460km/289 miles).
By bus: several times daily from Ubon Ratchathani.
By rail: station on the Bangkok–Ubon Ratchathani line (420km/261 miles, 6–8 hours). Special trains operate from Bangkok to Surin for the Elephant Festival (reservations through tour operators).

★★Elephant festival

The best elephant trainers and guides (mahouts) are supposed to come from the region around Surin. This is possibly the reason why the Thai tourist board organised the largest elephant round-up here. The spectacle lasts several days and is a huge national folk festival (individual travellers are advised to book hotel accommodation well in advance). Around 200 elephants are brought in from all over the country and are judged in front of stands for their skill, strength and obedience to their mahout. This is interspersed with dances performed by members of the many Thai tribes in original costumes. The festival takes place on the third weekend of November.

Surroundings

Prasat Pluang

The north-east of Thailand, especially the strip between the railway line to Ubon Ratchathani and the Cambodian border, is scattered with important Khmer ruins. Approximately 30km/19 miles south of the town near Prasat is the Prasat Pluang, an 11th c. Khmer temple. A square tower on a pedestal with artistically sculptured lintels and surrounded by water basins has been preserved.

Prasat Yai Ngao

From here Highway 24 heads east to Sangkha (51km/32 miles) and the Prasat Yai Ngao, which consists of two brick prangs decorated with sculptures (five-headed naga).

Prasat Phnum Pon

A few kilometres south of Sangkha at Ban Dom are the ruins of a very early Khmer temple, the Prasat Phnum Pon (7th c.). Lintels and columns display noteworthy sculpture (garlands, blossom and medallions decorated with leaves).

★★Prasat Ta Muen

To visit the most important Khmer temples of this regions requires certain scouting skills. The Prasat Ta Muen is situated south of Surin (on Highway 214) near the border with Cambodia at the town of Ban Ta Muang; it is advisable to enquire about security in advance at the TAT office in Surin (local guide). This 10th c. temple has several well preserved prangs.

★Sikoraphum

Sikoraphum, 32km/20 miles east of Surin, is also an old Khmer settlement, with fine – partly restored – temple grounds. The Wat Ra Ngeng (Prasat Hin Sikhoraphum) is 11th c. The main temple stands on a 25m/82ft-long terrace; the five tall prangs, which mark the corners and the centre, create an attractive picture with the trees in leaf. The magnificently carved lintels and door posts of the central prang have been preserved in the best Baphuon style (11th c.) and inside are two fine Buddha statues. The covered galleries along the sides of the site are in very good condition.

Wat Prasat Chang Pi

The same layout can be seen at the site of the Wat Prasat Chang Pi 12km/7 miles west of Sikoraphum, to the right of Highway 226 to Surin and the railway line.

Information

The most important Khmer temples, the Wat Prasat Phanom Rung and the Prasat Muang Tam (see Prakhon Chai), can easily be reached from Surin.

Tak (Dak) E 3

Region: North Thailand
Province: Tak
Altitude: 111m/364ft. Population: 21,000

Location

High mountains line the valley of the wide Menam Ping, one of the larger tributaries of the Menam Chao Phraya, near the idyllic provincial town of Tak, the "gateway to the north". The spectacular countryside is impressive and worth a detour from Sukhothai on the way to Chiang Mai. Owing to its proximity to Myanmar (Burma) the cultural influences are clearly apparent. However, it is still not possible to travel overland to Myanmar.

Access

From Sukhothai Highway 12 (80km/50 miles), from Kamphaeng Phet Highways 1/104 (60km/37 miles).
By bus: from Bangkok Northern Bus Terminal (420km/261 miles), Surin and Kamphaeng Phet.
By air: four times weekly from Bangkok.

Sights

Townscape

There are numerous wooden houses built in traditional Thai style in the picturesque old town. A monument, the Sala Somdet Phra Chao Maharat, is dedicated to the town's most famous son, King Taksin (1768–82), founder of the present day kingdom of Siam.

★Wat Sibunrung

Tak only has one temple worth visiting. The wiharn of the Wat Sibunrung has an artistically decorated trapezium, a fine chedi and a splendid Buddha statue in Sukhothai style.

Surroundings

★Lan Sang National park

Highway 105 heads westwards through mountainous jungle, past Lan Sang national park with its beautiful waterfalls and villages of the Meo, Lisu and Lahu tribes, to Mae Sot, the border town for Myanmar (98km/61 miles).

Mae Sot

Mae Sot is an attractive, lively town in the valley of the Menam Moei, which here forms the border with Myanmar. The temples of this small town are also in typical Burmese style; the most interesting lies about 5km/3 miles out of the town towards the Burmese border. Its wiharn contains four Buddha statues, one of which is of special interest: jewels cascade from its ears.

Yanhee dam

66km/41 miles north-west of Tak is the Yanhee dam, often referred to as the "King Bhumibol reservoir dam", with a 154m/505ft-high wall. Damming the Menam Ping was intended to prevent the floods which frequently affect this region and to provide irrigation for the fertile land. The electricity produced is transmitted as far as Bangkok. The reservoir is a paradise for watersport enthusiasts (there is a hotel here).

Ban Tak

Village life can be observed in the small town of Ban Tak, about 20km/12 miles north of Tak. This town on the banks of the Menam Ping with its houses built on stilts is particularly charming at sunset.

Trang — O 3

Region: South Thailand
Province: Trang
Altitude: 46m/151ft. Population: 58,000

ตรัง

Location

The provincial town of Trang on the river of the same name is in the south of the Malayan peninsula, only about 20km/12 miles from the Indian Ocean in an undulating upland area with extensive rubber plantations upon which the wealth of this busy town is based. Many Chinese and Malays live here giving it the typical southern Thai atmosphere. On the Phattalung road is a large park with pretty lotus ponds and tall trees and palms.

Access

By car: from Krabi and Phattalung Highway 4 (140km/87 miles and 55km/34 miles respectively). From Nakhon Si Thammarat Highways 403/4.
By rail: station on the branch line from Thung Song (on the stretch Bangkok–South Thailand) to Lake Andaman.
By bus: from Bangkok Southern Bus Terminal (940km/584 miles, duration 13 hours).
By air: from Bangkok (2 hours 10 mins.).

Surroundings

★Chinese temple

3km/2 miles north is a Chinese temple devoted to the god Kwan Tee Hun with a colourful fantastic decorated ceiling.

Khao Pina (cave temple)

Another 10km/6 miles further on a path turns off Highway 4 to the cave temple of Khao Pina, with Thai-Chinese works of folk art and beautiful stalactites.

Beaches

A row of beautiful beaches stretches along the Indian Ocean. Highways 4046/4162 (about 40km/25 miles) lead to the miles-long beach of Pak Meng with very fine sand. The island Koh Ngai can be visited from here (40 mins.).

Trat — J 6

Region: East Thailand
Province: Trat
Altitude: 6m/20ft. Population: 14,000

ตราด

Location

Trat is a bustling commercial town built on alluvial land on the Gulf of Thailand. It is the last town in the south-eastern tip of Thailand and is situated in close proximity to the Cambodian border. The main attractions are the islands off the coast including Koh Chang and the jewel mines of the surrounding area (see below).

Just beyond Trat the country of Thailand narrows to a 88km/54 miles-long strip of land with outstanding scenery. As a rule the journey on Highway 318 to Khlong Yai is unproblematic but further south-east there can be military check points on the road to the border town of Ban Lek (unstable area at times).

Access

By car: from Chanthaburi Highway 3 (75km/47 miles).
By bus: from Bangkok Eastern Terminal.

History

During the Seventies the province of Trat became internationally famous for the huge camps where Vietnamese and Cambodians fleeing from the Pol-Pot regime took refuge. Hundreds and thousands fled across the open sea, often in tiny fishing boats. From 1986 Thailand has refused to take in any more refugees and two of the camps which each housed 60,000 people have been torn down. Following the peace agreement between the warring factions of the Cambodian civil war in October 1991 the refugees are to be returned to their homeland.

Precious stones

The town, like Chanthaburi, is an important centre for precious stones. There are numerous mines around Chanthaburi and Trat where rubies, saphires and other precious stones are extracted by open-cast mining. It is possible to visit independently; in Pattaya, the usual departure point for a visit to Trat, travel agencies organise tours.

★★Koh Chang

General

After Phuket and Koh Samui, Koh Chang is the third largest island in Thailand. It is still relatively unspoilt; secluded beaches, fascinating jungle with waterfalls (Nam Tok Tham Mayom is especially beautiful) and an abundant variety of flora and fauna will no doubt change this. At present there is only basic accommodation. Access is from the small port of Laem Ngop (20km/12 miles from Trat; duration approx. 1 hour).

Points of interest

The largest settlement on Koh Chang is the pretty fishing village Klong Son where some of the houses are built on stilts. Among the magnificent beaches are Ao Sapparot ("Pineapple Bay"), Klong Phrao and Hat Sai Khao (all have exceptionally white sand). Beyond the beaches lie dense forests and the large coconut and rubber plantations provide the second most important source of income for the islanders after fishing. From the mountains, which reach heights of up to 800m/2624ft, there is a unique view over the island of Koh Chang.

Ubon Ratchathani (Ubol, Rubol) F 8

Region: North-east Thailand
Province: Ubon Ratchathani
Altitude: 125m/410ft. Population: 60,000

อุบลราชธานี

Location

The "Royal Town of the Lotus Blossom" lies on the Menam Mun in north-east Thailand, 75km/47 miles from the border with Laos. It only really began to develop during the last decade when the various programmes by the government in Bangkok to promote this poorest region of Thailand began to show the first signs of success. The airport has been expanded and is now one of Thailand's international airports. In the town itself there is little of interest apart from the annual Phansa festival which is held at the beginning of the Buddhist fasting period (end of July). The important temple, Wat Khao Phra Wiharn, on the border between Thailand and Cambodia (see Si Saket) can be reached from here.

Central stupa of the Wat Phra That Nongbua ▶

Ubon Ratchathani

Access

By car: from Bangkok Highways 1/2/24 (630km/391 miles).
By bus: from Bangkok Northeastern Bus Terminal (672km/417 miles, about 10 hours).
By rail: from Bangkok–Hualampong (575km/357 miles, 10–12 hours).
By air: from Bangkok (1½ hours).

Temple sites

The town's magnificent temple sites were almost exclusively built in recent times and are of little historical value. However, the Wat Si Ubonat Thalam with a beautiful wiharn in extensive grounds is worth seeing, as is the Wat Supattanaramworwihan, built by King Rama IV, which combines Khmer, Thai and European elements in three different styles of architecture.

★★Wat Phra That Nongbua

Another temple of interest is the Wat Phra That Nongbua near the Chayankun Road, its two stupas are modelled on those of the Indian temple of Bodhgaya. The central stupa is the tallest building in the town and is situated within an attractive park. On its base are stone reliefs carved in 1977 to commemorate the celebration of 2500 years of Buddhism.

Surroundings

Some very interesting sights of the region of Ubon Ratchathani are to be found to the east of the town (Highway 217).

★Wat Phokhaokaeo

After 43km/27 miles the road comes to the fine Wat Phokhaokaeo with buildings made from burnt-red clay bricks. From the wiharn (artistically carved doors and shutters) with a square foundation there are good views of the countryside.

★★Sao Chaliang (natural monument)

Past the entrance to the Kang Tana national park (Highway 217 to Phibun, 2222 to Khong Chiam, then north on 2134 and 212) just before Pa Tham is the natural monument Sao Chaliang. Wind and weather erosion have formed an imposing group of rocks which the locals believe is home to both good and evil spirits.

A natural formation: the rock group of Sao Chaliang

Rock-paintings of Pa Tham

One of the biggest surprises for historical research in Thailand was the discovery of the rock paintings at Pa Tham in 1987, although it was thought that an ethnic group of little historical importance had settled here. The paintings above the banks of the Mekong are the largest of their kind in Thailand. The 3000–4000 year old paintings, which are very well preserved and about 150m/492ft long, depict the everyday life of fishermen and hunters. The detail in which the everyday objects, animals and people are represented is remarkable.

★★Rock painting at Pa Tham

Access to the paintings is over a plateau where a path about 1km/½ mile long on the right hand side leads down along the rock wall. More paintings can be seen further along the path (about half an hour's walk). In places there is a very good view over the Mekong, the longest river in south-east Asia.

Lam Dom Noi dam is worth a detour because of its delightful setting. It was completed in 1971 and is also called the Sirindhorn dam after the second daughter of the Thai royal family. It is situated near the Laos border and access is via Highway 217 (from Ubon Ratchathani approx. 85km/53 miles).

★Lam Dom Noi (barrage dam)

Udon Thani (Udorn) D 6

Region: Northeast Thailand
Province: Udon Thani
Altitude: 186m/610ft. Population: 85,000

อุดรธานี

Location

Udon Thani is the last large town before the border with neighbouring Laos, about 560km/348 miles from Bangkok. It lies in the plain of the Menam Luang which flows into the Mekong, and in recent years has

In the market of Udon Thani

developed into a lively commercial and communications centre. The temples are of recent origin; not far to the east (46km/29 miles), however, is Ban Chiang (see Ban Chiang), which is of great archaeological interest.

Access

By car: from Nakhon Ratchasima Highway 2 (200km/124 miles).
By bus: from Bangkok Northeastern Bus Terminal (560km/348 miles).

Surroundings

★Wat Phra Buddhabat Ban Kok

65km/40 miles northwest of Udon Thani is the Wat Phra Buddhabat Ban Kok in a setting which is completely unique and untypical characterised by giant sandstone blocks cracked and moulded by erosion. The monks from this wat are helpful and willing guides through this unusual landscape.

The temple is picturesquely sited on the bare peak of the densely-wooded hill. It has one large and several small chedis as well as a more recently built wat based upon the Wat Phra That Phanom in Nakhon Phanom. The main attraction of the Wat Phra Buddhabat is the symbolic footprint of Buddha.

Archaeological finds suggest that there was an early settlement here (probably around 6000–5000 B.C.), with the rocks and caves providing shelter for the nomadic population. In the 9th c. the Khmer tribes are supposed to have settled here. Some of the rocks have names which refer to legends. Below some rocks are recent statues of Buddha; the walls are decorated with flat reliefs of seated and standing Buddhas from the Dvaravati period.

U Thong — G 3

อู่ทอง

Region: Central Thailand
Province: Suphanburi
Altitude: 186m/610ft. Population: 16,500

Location

U Thong is situated 135km/84 miles northwest of Bangkok on the edge of the Central Plain; in the north-west is the impressive backdrop of the Burmese mountains. It had its heyday as the first capital of the Dvaravati kingdom and cultural centre of the Khmer empire. An original artistic style, especially in the field of sculpture, developed.

Access

By car: from Bangkok Highways 4 and 338 to Nakhon Pathom, then 321/324 (100km/62 miles).
By bus: from Bangkok and Suphanburi.
By rail: nearest station Suphanburi (30km/19 miles).

History

The history of U Thong stretches back to the early Stone Age (finds of tools). According to a Chinese source U Thong was the capital of the Funan kingdom (1st–6th c.), the oldest continental empire of south-east Asia. When it split up the earlier vassal state of Dvaravati gained independence. It is more or less certain that U Thong was also the first capital of this kingdom, although in the 11th c. it came under the rule of the ever expanding Khmer. After renewed independence King U Thong transferred his residence in 1350 to Ayutthaya and assumed the name King Rama Thibodi I. (ruled 1350–69).

★Museum

Opening times
Wed.–Sun.
9am–4pm

Admission fee

The U Thong style (see Introduction, Art and Culture) found its most definitive expression in its sculpture (no single building has been preserved from the U Thong period). The U Thong Museum, opened in 1976, offers an overview of the three styles of the sculpture of this period. Other exhibits include stone tools (from the early Stone Age), reliefs in burnt clay (4–5th c.) influenced by Indian Amaravati art, terracotta figures and sculptures from the Dvaravati period (6–11th c.) and evidence of Srivijaya art. There is also a plan showing the assumed layout of the town; the foundations of various buildings can be seen scattered throughout the countryside. The fortified town was encircled by an oval wall 1600×830m/5249×2723ft.

Wat Si Sanphet

The site of the old town can be seen from the Wat Si Sanphet, a temple from more recent times on a hill.

Uttaradit D 4

Region: North Thailand
Province: Uttaradit
Altitude: 81m/266ft. Population: 32,000

อุตรดิตถ์

Location

Uttaradit, about 450km/280 miles north of Bangkok in the wide valley of the Menam Nan was rebuilt following the fire in 1967 which almost completely destroyed the old town. Since a huge reservoir was constructed approx. 45km/28 miles to the north-east of the town, the Pa Som barrage (also called the Sirikit dam after the queen), the economy of Uttaradit has flourished particularly owing to the profitable agriculture.

Access

From Phitsanulok Highways 12/11/1045 (130km/81 miles). From Sukhothai Highway 101 to Si Satchanalai then 102 (105km/65 miles).
By rail: station on the Bangkok–Chiang Mai line (from Bangkok–Hualampong, 485km/301 miles, duration about 8 hours).

Monument to Governor Dat Nak

A monument in front of the provincial administration building commemorates Governor Phraya Pichai Dat Nak, who repulsed an attack by the Burmese army in 1772.

Wat Tha Thanon

The Chinese style Wat Tha Thanon houses the statue of a Chiang-Saen style seated Buddha.

Wat Phra Boromathat near Uttaradit

Surroundings

★Wat Phra Boromathat

The Wat Phra Boromathat 5km/3 miles out of the town (on Highway 102) is very interesting. It has Laotian stylistic features and ornate carving on the trapezia of the projecting portals of the wiharn, wall paintings from the Ayutthaya period and a group of fine chedis from the Sukhothai period.

★Wat Phra Tan Sila Aat

Not far away is the Wat Phra Tan Sila Aat with one stone and four bronze footprints from Buddha; there are also several beautiful figures of Buddha in Sukhothai style. Next to it is an attractive Chinese temple with splendid teak timberwork.

★Wat Phra Yeun Phra Bat Yukon

Nearby there is another interesting temple, the Wat Phra Yeun Phra Bat Yukon with a charming mondhop and bronze Buddha statues in Sukhothai style.

★Wat Phra Fang

16km/10 miles south of the town situated on the left bank of the Menam Nan is the beautiful Wat Phra Fang from the Sukhothai period.

★Sirikit dam

Highway 1045 leads eastwards to the beautifully situated Sirikit reservoir with a 160m/525ft-high and 800m/2625ft-long wall, named after the wife of the king of Thailand. It was completed in 1973 and is the largest in Thailand. The lake covers an area of 22,000ha/54,362 acres; by means of an extensive network of canals it not only irrigates the surroundings to create a rich agricultural area but also provides energy for the population. On its banks are some houses on stilts belonging to the fishermen.

It is possible to drive up to the dam and around the reservoir. About halfway between the village of Tha Pla and the dam is a checkpoint where an admission fee is payable.

Wat Doi Suthep

See Chiang Mai, Surroundings

Wat Phra Tan Sila Aat near Uttaradit

Wat Khao Phra Wiharn

See Si Saket, Surroundings

Yala P 5

Region: South Thailand
Province: Yala
Altitude: 15m/49ft. Population: 52,000

ยะลา

Location

Yala is the busy capital of a densely populated flourishing province in the extreme south of Thailand not far from the Malaysian border. In the town the majority of the people are Chinese, in the province they are chiefly Malayans of the Moslem faith; the spoken language is Malayan.

Access

From Songkhla Highway 408 to Nathawi, then Highways 42/409 (128km/80 miles); alternatively take the coast road at Chana. From Pattani Highway 410 (43km/27 miles).

By bus: from Bangkok Southern Bus Terminal to Hat Yai (1000km/621 miles, 14 hours), connecting service from here.
By rail: station on the Bangkok–Malaysia line (from Bangkok–Hualampong 1055km/656 miles, about 20 hours; sleeper with air-conditioning).

★Wat Kuhaphimuk

Wat Kuhaphimuk, a rock temple about 1200 years old, lies on the edge of the town. There is a well proportioned modern wiharn in an attractive nearby park. In one of the caves in the limestone rocks above the park (about 10 minutes' walk) can be seen a 24m/79ft-long reclining Buddha which is worshipped by the people of the area.

Other interesting temples are the Chinese places of worship; there are also several mosques in the town.

Surroundings

★Caves

In the mountains around Yala numerous caves have been turned into temples. Of particular interest are the caves of Tham Koo Ha Pimsak (with a 25m/82ft-high Buddha) and the cave at Tham Silpa with fragments of 13th c. wall paintings (Srivijaya period). From Yala it is signposted on Highway 409 in the direction of Hat Yai.

★★Countryside south of Yala

Highway 410 heads south through highlands covered with dense tropical rainforest broken by the typical limestone mountains of southern Thailand. A winding road 133km/83 miles long (a short stop at the scenically situated Bang Lang reservoir and the hot springs about 20km/12 miles beyond the village of Ban Ayerweng is recommended) leads to the border town of Betong, which is inhabited by Chinese. After the Malayan border the road forks, one branch leads towards Singapore, the other to Butterworth on the Indian Ocean.

Yasathon F 8

Region: North-east Thailand
Province: Yasathon
Altitude: 31m/101ft. Population: 22,000

ยโสธร

Access

By car: from Bangkok Highways 1/2 to Ban Wat (near Phimai) then 207/202 (530km/330 miles). From Ubon Ratchathani Highway 23 (98km/61 miles).
By bus: connections from the above towns.
By air: nearest airport Khon Kaen (180km/112 miles).

Children bathing in the Sirikit reservoir

★★Rocket festival

Yasathon, one of the newest provincial capitals of Thailand, would not be worth a visit if it were not for a spectacle which takes place every second week in May attracting both visitors and locals alike. Towards the end of the dry season the giant folk festival "Bun Bang Fai" ("Service of the Bamboo Rockets") takes place, which is celebrated throughout the province of Yasathon for a week. The festival is intended to bring the attention of the rain god Phraya Thaen to the drought.

For weeks before the great event the population of Yasathon are busy making the rockets which consist mostly of bamboo canes driven by a mixture of saltpetre and charcoal up to 600m/1969ft high. The fuse is a piece of saffron-yellow material. A colourful procession accompanies the rockets to the firing point at the edge of the town. The men's faces are thickly coated with mud probably to fool Phraya Thaen: he is not to see that humans are behind this ploy. The governor himself gives the signal to start and if the rockets have not already exploded on the ground they soar towards the sky to the delight of the crowd. And sometimes it begins to rain the very next day. . . .

Wat Thung Sawan

The Wat Thung Sawan in the east is notable for its particular Khmer style of construction.

Wat Mahathat

The main temple and the splendid library (Ho Trai) are of architectural interest in the Wat Mahathat.

That Luk Khun Mae

7km/4 miles south of the town on Highway 23 is the That Luk Khun Mae which combines a mixture of Laotian and Khmer features.

Practical Information

Accommodation

See Hotels, Youth Hostels

Air Travel

In addition to the many airlines with scheduled services to and from south-east Asia (these include Royal Brunei, Thai Airways International, Singapore and other Asian airlines) there are also a number of UK charter companies with heavy involvement in the Thai tourist trade.

Airports

See Facts and Figures, Transport

Bangkok International Airport

Bangkok's International Airport is situated about 22km/14 miles north of the city. The journey to and from the city centre takes at least an hour, and two hours ideally need to be allowed. Current traffic conditions are best ascertained at the hotel reception.

Passengers travelling on international flights check in at the "International Airport", where the international airlines also have their reception desks. For internal flights within Thailand there is a separate terminal located a few hundred metres from the international terminal and a regular free bus shuttle service connects between the two.

Travellers on package tours are met on the airport arrival level by the representative of their travel company, who will arrange their connecting transport. Local couriers can be recognised by their badges, which have the name of their company and often even carry the name of the passenger whom they have come to meet.

For independent travellers there are various ways of making the journey into the centre of Bangkok. The Thai Limousine Service, a shuttle service belonging to Thai Airways, is very reliable. It has a desk in the arrival hall on the ground floor of the International Passenger Terminal (southern side).

Prices

While the official IATA tariffs give fares of between £700 and £1500 (1st class £3000) from Europe to Thailand, there is a wide range of special fares, details of which can be obtained from a travel agent. At the present time it is possible to book a fare of £600 with a reputable firm; overcapacity in the available hotel accommodation makes these deals very advantageous, and there is always the possibiity of last-minute special offers. It is as well not just to compare costs but also the flight times, which can vary from 10 to 24 hours. Stopovers, supplementary payments and charges and flexibility of dates for the return flight are all worth looking into. Cheap flights often means that the opportunity to switch to other airlines is not possible and may force the traveller to have to make unwelcome stopovers.

Internal flights

For internal flights within Thailand travellers can use Thai Airways International and Bangkok Airways (network of routes shown opposite). In addition there are the Yellowbird flights between Bangkok and Pattaya and Hua Hin using propeller-driven seaplanes.

Prices are very reasonable, with children paying reduced fares.

Thailand Discover Pass

Thai Airways International offers a "Thailand Discover Pass", which entitles the holder to 4–8 flights on on the Thai route network and is valid for

◀ *A "collective taxi" in north-eastern Thailand*

60 days (Prices between US $239 and $439). The pass should be obtained from Thai Airways International before departing for Thailand.

Smoking ban

Since 1989 there has been a complete ban on smoking on all flights with Thai International and Bangkok Airways.

Changing flight reservations

It is basically possible to change flight reservations, but attempts to do so can often come to grief, due to the fact that flights are booked up and frequently even overbooked at weekends and before the main public holidays. A reservation can only be changed without financial penalty if done by noon on the day before departure; after that a charge is levied. Bangkok Airways makes quite high charges (as much as 30% of the ticket price).

Airport charges

Every passenger has to pay an airport tax on departure – at present 200 baht. For internal flights the charge is 20 baht. Travellers on package deals will often find this charge has been met by their tour operator.

International offices of TAT

Most of the airports have a branch of the Thai tourist organisation (TAT) in their arrival halls, and here any enquiries can be dealt with and a list of hotels obtained.

Last minute calls

There are special telephone kiosks in both the arrival and departure halls of Bangkok International Airport where passengers can make last-minute local calls free of charge.

Check-in times

For internal flights the check-in time is one hour, while for international flights the passenger should check in at least two hours before the scheduled time of departure. After a certain time the airline reserves the right to reallocate the seat.

Flight change-over time

The change-over time between international flights is two hours, while for connecting flights within Thailand the same amount of time really needs to be allowed owing to the need to transfer between buildings.

Return flights

As a rule, return flights need to be confirmed at the office of the relevant airline 48 hours before departure. For charter passengers the local agent of their tour company will normally see to this (see Travel Agents), while passengers on scheduled services are themselves responsible.

Airlines

In Thailand

All international airlines which fly to Bangkok have offices there. They can handle all enquiries, bookings, reservations, cancellations, and confirmations.

Thai Airways International Ltd.

Head Office: 89 Vibhavadi Rangsit Road; tel. (02) 513–0121
485 Silom Road, Bangkok, tel. (02) 233–3810
215 Yaowaraj Road (Grand Central Tower), tel. (02) 223–9746–50
6 Larn Luang Road, tel. (02) 280–0070/80
296 Phyathai Road (in Asia Hotel), tel. (02) 215–2020/1
Airport office: tel. (02) 523–6121, 535–2081
Freight office: tel. (02) 234–3100–19
Office hours: Mon.–Fri. 8am–5pm

Sales and reservation offices of Thai Airways International

Chiang Mai

240 Prapokklao Road, tel. (053) 210–043, 211–044, 211–541

Chiang Rai

870 Phaholyothin Road, tel. (053) 711179

Hat Yai

190/6 Niphat Uthit 2 Road, tel. (074) 231–272, 232–392

Air Routes
Rail Routes
Mandalay
MYANMAR
(BURMA)
Pagan
Mae Hong Son
Chiang Rai
Chiang Mai
Nan
Phrae
Lampang
Nong Khai
Udon Thani
Loei
Sakon
Nakhon
Tak
Mae Sot
Phitsanulok
Khon Kaen
Ubon
Ratchathani
Nakhon
Ratchasima
Kanchanaburi
BANGKOK
Aranyaprathet
CAMBODIA
MYANMAR
(BURMA)
Hua Hin
Gulf of
Thailand
Phnom Penh
VIETNAM
Samui
Surat Thani
Nakhon Si Thammarat
South China Sea
Phuket
Trang
Thai Airways
Bangkok Airways
Railway
Indian
Ocean
Hat Yai
Pattani
Narathiwat
Kota Baharu
MALAYSIA
200 km
© Baedeker

A Jumbo of Thai Airways International

Khon Kaen	183/6 Maliwan Road, tel. (043) 236523
Lampang	314 Sanambin Road, tel. (054) 217078
Loei	191/1 Charoenrat Road, tel. (042) 812344
Mae Hong Son	71 Singhanathbamrung Road, tel. (053) 611297
Mae Sot	76/1 Prasat Withi Road, tel. (055) 531730
Nakhon Ratchasima	14 Manas Road, tel. (044) 257211/5
Nakhon Si Thammarat	1612 Rajadamnoen Road, tel. (075) 342491
Nan	34 Mahaphrom Road, tel. (054) 710377
Narathiwat	322–4 Phupha Phakdi Road, tel. (073) 511161
Nong Khai	453 Prachak Road, tel. (042) 411530
Pattani	9 Preeda Road, tel. (073) 349149
Pattaya	Royal Cliff Beach Hotel, tel. (038) 429–286/7
Phitsanulok	209/26–28 Boromtrailokanat Road, tel. (055) 258020
Phrae	42–44 Rasdamnoen Road, tel. (054) 511123
Phuket	78/1 Ranong Road, tel. (076) 211–195, 212–946, 216–678, 216–755
Sakhon Nakhon	1446/73 Yuvapatana Road, tel. (042) 712259/60

Songkhla
2 Soi 4 Saiburi Road, tel. (074) 311012

Surat Thani
3/27–28 Karoonrat Road, tel. (077) 272610, 273710, 273355

Tak
485 Taksin Road, tel. (055) 512164

Trang
199/2 Viseskul Road, tel. (075) 218066

Ubon Ratchathani
364 Chayanggoon Road, tel. (045) 244450, 254431, 255894

Udon Thani
60 Makkang Road, tel. (042) 246697

Bangkok Airways
Pacific Place Building, 140 Sukhumvit Road, Bangkok,
tel. (02) 253–4004–6, 229–3456

Other sales offices at
Koh Samui: tel. (077) 421–483
Phuket: tel. (076) 212–341
Rayong: tel. (038) 603–063

China Airlines
153 Rajadamri Road
Peninsula Plaza, 4th floor, Bangkok
Reservations: tel. (02) 253–4438
Airport office: tel (02) 535–2160

German Lufthansa
66 Sukhumvit Road 21
House Asoke Building, 18th floor, Bangkok,
tel. (02) 2642–2391
Reservations: tel. (02) 2642–400
Airport office: tel. (02) 535–2211, 535–2212
Freight office: tel. (02) 264–2420, 535–2216
Office hours: Mon.–Fri. 8am–5pm

Lauda Air
67–68 Surawongse Road, Wall Street Tower, 14th floor, Bangkok,
tel. (02) 233–544
Airport office: (02) 535–2635

Malaysian Airline System
898 Ploenchit Road (Ploenchit Tower), Bangkok
Reservations: tel. (02) 263–056571
Airport office: tel. (02) 531–2288

Swissair
1 Silom Road, Bangkok
Reservations: tel. (02) 233–2935–9
Airport office: tel. (02) 535–2371–2
Freight office: tel. (02) 531–0078–9
Office hours: Mon.–Fri. 8.30am–5pm

Singapore Airlines
2 Silom Road, Center Building, 12th floor, Bangkok
Reservations: tel. (02) 235–0005
Airport office: (02) 523–7299

Antiques

Import and export

Special regulations govern the export and import of antiques. Since 1961 (the date when systematic excavations began in Thailand), it has been forbidden to take figures of the Buddha and other deities out of the country. The ban includes the often very authentic copies which are to be found on sale everywhere. The manufacture and sale of these figures within Thailand is in fact legal – it is only their export which is against the law. There are exceptions to this, however, and further information can be obtained from

The export of Buddha figures is forbidden

the Director, Department of Fine Arts, Na Phra That Road (near the National Museum); tel. (02) 221 4817.

Miniature Buddha figures are exempt from the export ban, but only so long as they are clearly identifiable as copies and are no larger than 12cm/5in. Airport customs officials carry out spot checks on the baggage of travellers leaving the country.

Export licences are also required for all other kinds of antiques. Processing of an application normally takes about two weeks, as approval must be sought from the Ministry of Trade and the appropriate export duty determined. The regulations are specifically intended to prevent the export of any object important to the history of Thailand. It is the old royal towns of Ayutthaya and Sukhothai, especially, where the trade in archaeological finds flourishes, with children often offering the tourist fragments of pottery and coins. The visitor is expressly warned against making any attempt to take such objects out of the country. Offences are liable to be punished with high fines. If in doubt, to avoid problems, the visitor should seek advice from TAT, the Thai Tourist Authority (see Information). Shops approved by the TAT will undertake the necessary formalities if required.

Anyone bringing genuine antiques into Thailand which have been bought in neighbouring countries must be able to produce documentary proof of their origin. Similar documentation is required in the case of items purchased in Thailand but originating elsewhere – Myanmar (Burma) for example.

Authenticity

There are good reasons for initially questioning the authenticity of any antique. There are few actual originals in circulation and because of this the trade is subject to government control. Certificates of authenticity can also be obtained (for a fee) from the Department of Fine Arts in Bangkok.

"Genuine copies"

"Genuine copies" of objets d'art can be purchased in state-owned shops in Bangkok and Chiang Mai (addresses available from TAT).

Banks

See Currency

Beaches

The Gulf of Siam possesses a string of exceptionally fine beaches which epitomise what we generally understand by "tropical beaches". The best of the beaches are, however, also popular with the local population, which also values the facility they offer for cooling off on hot days. In particular, those beaches which are within two or three hours' drive of Bangkok tend to be overrun by people at weekends and during the summer holidays (May – July). Really idyllic beaches can be found just a few miles outside the main tourist centres. This is also true, with some reservations, of the area around Pattaya, where there are fine beaches both along the road to Sattahip and on the offshore islands.

With the exception of Phuket, the beaches in the south (Malayan Peninsula) have not yet been developed for tourists to any great extent. The beaches at Hua Hin and Cha Am, for instance, are beautiful and unspoilt; the beaches on islands such as Koh Samui, Koh Samet, Koh Phi Phi are especially worthy of mention. Although it cannot be claimed that they are any longer untouched, it is still possible to find small bays, set on their own, with crystal-clear water ideal for bathing.

Water pollution

Water pollution affects some beaches to a considerable extent – notably in Pattaya, where part of an enormous sewage plant, which has been planned for a number of years, is now in operation. Bathing there can be dangerous, and to be on the safe side, visitors should enquire at their hotel reception and, in case of doubt, content themselves with using the swimming-pool.

Two beaches on Koh Phi Phi

Underwater currents

Underwater currents represent a potentially life-threatening danger to the swimmer who does not take sufficient care. They cannot be detected from the shore and are especially prevalent in the monsoon period. The beaches most affected are those on the island of Phuket. On Thai beaches there are generally no life-savers or other organised emergency services.

Begging

The visitors will encounter beggars everywhere, but in particular at places and sights frequented by tourists. As well as old and sick men, they are often children, and it is best not to give them any money and thereby reinforce them in their wayward life-style. In Bangkok, Pattaya and Phuket, in particular, there are organised gangs which force children to go begging. It is better to offer to pay for these young beggars to get something to eat from one of the many hot food stalls.

Boat Charter

The Gulf of Siam and the Indian Ocean (Andaman Sea) coastline are ideal areas for sailing. "Island hopping" is especially popular, with anchoring possible almost anywhere and restrictions confined mainly to the groups of islands which have been declared national parks. Mention should be made of the islands of Koh Phi Phi, Koh Tarutao and Koh Similan as being particularly fine sailing areas, while on the east coast there are some attractive areas around Pattaya.

Maps

Reliable nautical maps, which give information about dangerous shallows and treacherous currents during the monsoon season, are indispensable. Responsible boat owners supply this sort of material when they rent out the boat.

Life-saving equipment

It is essential to check that life-saving equipment on board the boat is complete and ready for use.

Sailing pass

Those renting a boat independently are required to produce an internationally recognised sailing pass. It is nevertheless possible to rent a boat with a complete crew or, at the very least, a captain with specialised local knowledge.

The largest boat rental company in Thailand is the Thai Yachting Co. Ltd., 95 Rajdamri Road, 7th floor, Bangkok; tel. (02) 253 1733, 251 6755. Phuket office: B 1–2 Patong View Plaza, 94 Thaveewong Road; tel. (076) 321301–2, 321304–6.

In Pattaya the "Noble House" restaurant (roughly halfway along Beach Road) offers trips lasting one day and longer, on a luxurious converted junk.

Deep-sea fishing

See Fishing

Bookshops

Most of the larger hotels have shops ("drugstores") selling items for everyday use. These also stock books and periodicals.

The bookshops listed below stock English titles (and in some cases German and French titles too):

Asia Book, Soi 61, Sukhumvit Road

Bangkok Book Supermarket
330 Phaholyothin Road

Best Book, 76/29 Soi Langsuan Ploenchit Road

The Bookseller
81 Patpong Road (open till late evening)
travel guides, illustrated books

Chalermnit Bookshop
1–2 Arawan Arket and 137/8 Kesom Road
specialises in travel guides and art history

Duang Kamoi Bookstore ("DK")
Siam Square Soi 2 and at the "Alliance Française", Sathon Thai Road (near the German embassy

Elite Book House, 593/5 Sukhumvit Road

White Lotus Co. Ltd.
47 Sukhumvit (corner of Soi 16)
specialises in books of cultural interest including art, and illustrated books.

Periodicals

See Newspapers and Periodicals

Business Hours

Commercial business in Thailand is not bound by rigid rules imposed by a shop-opening law. The information which follows, therefore, applies primarily to public institutions and larger concerns.

Banks

Mon.–Fri. 8.30am–3.30pm, Sat. 8.30am–noon

Money changers

Mon.–Sat. 9am–8pm, Sun. mostly closed. Occasionally money changers run out of money to change and will then close. Major banks operate currency exchange centres in most tourist areas daily 7am–9pm.

Department stores

Daily 10am–8pm

Government offices

Mon.–Fri. 8.30am–noon and 1–4.30pm

Private offices

Mon.–Fri. 8am–5pm

Retail businesses

Mon.–Fri. 8am–9pm, Sat. 8am–noon

Shops

Mon.–Sat. 8am–9pm (some even longer)

Post offices

Mon.–Fri. 8am–4.30pm, Sat. 9am–1pm (telegrams accepted 24 hours). Bangkok Central Post Office Mon.–Fri. 8am–4.30pm, weekends and public holidays 9am–1pm.

Embassies

See Diplomatic Representation

Chemists

See entry

Camping

There are no properly organised campsites as such in Thailand, but "camping rough" is allowed; permission should be sought from the owner of the land. Camping in the national parks is only possible with prior permission from the park administration. The rangers sometimes rent out tents and other equipment and will allow visitors to use the sanitary blocks for a small charge.

Basically it is possible to camp on the islands in the south, but on Koh Samet, Koh Tarutao and Koh Chang, which are designated national parks, it is necessary to apply to the park officials first. Nevertheless, camping is not really advisable because of the dangers from snakes, and also the risk of robbery and theft. It is safer to rent bungalows, which are available at reasonable prices.

Car rental

Travelling by car in Thailand can be very enjoyable (see Introduction, Suggested Routes). It is best not to attempt to cover more than 300km/185 miles in one day, otherwise it is all too easy to miss much of the beautiful scenery and the many sights which are to be found hidden away off the main roads.

Driving is on the left and the typical Asian traffic conditions demand cool nerves and good driving technique. Without these, the visitor is probably best to hire a chauffeur. This is not as expensive as might be thought, and the drivers are very experienced. A rental car can normally be collected on the outskirts of Bangkok, which is advisable given the chaotic traffic conditions which exist in the centre of the capital. A minibus with chauffeur can be rented relatively cheaply and has the advantage that small groups of up to eight people can follow the itinerary of their wish.

Import of private cars

There is a considerable amount of correspondence involved in bringing one's own private car into Thailand by a sea route. A personal vehicle may be used in Thailand for a period of up to six months, after which it is liable to an import tax of up to 100% of its replacement value. The same applies if the owner wished to leave the country without the imported vehicle.

Driving licence

Visitors require an international driving licence and you must be over 21 to rent a car.

Car rental companies

All the well-known international car rental companies have branches in Bangkok and often in Chiang Mai, Phuket and Pattaya as well. Arrangements for renting a car from one of these firms can therefore be made before leaving Europe. In addition there are a large number of local car rental firms.

Prices are very reasonable, but it is strongly recommended to take out full comprehensive insurance. The general-purpose vehicles rented out by firms in Pattaya and Phuket are not generally insured, and in any case their roadworthiness can often leave a lot to be desired.

Equipment

Before taking over a vehicle make a point of examining its general state of roadworthiness (wear on tyres, oil level, existing damage to bodywork, etc.). Check also that it has air-conditioning and is covered by third party insurance (not compulsory in Thailand). If in doubt on any score it is best to go to one of the reputable car rental companies.

Avis
Bangkok

2/12 Wireless Road, tel. 255–5300/4
Dusit Thani Hotel: tel. 233–5256
Royal Princess Hotel: tel. 281–3088

Cha-Am/Hua Hin

Dusit Resort & Polo Club: tel. (032) 520–008
Royal Garden Resort: tel. (032) 511–881–4

Chiang Mai

Airport: tel. (053) 222–013
14/14 Huaikaeo Road: tel. (053) 221–316
Royal Princess Hotel: tel. (053) 281–033–36

Chaing Rai

Baan Boran Hotel: tel. (053) 716–678
Dusit Island Resort: tel. (053) 715–777–9
Delta Golden Triangle Hotel: tel. (053) 714–801–5

Hat Yai

Dusit J. B. Hotel: tel. (074) 234–300–6

Koh Samui

Imperial Samui Hotel: tel. (077) 421–391–4
Imperial Tongsai Bay Hotel: tel. (077) 421–451–56
Boat House Hotel: tel. (077) 421–460–1

Pattaya

Dusit Resort Hotel: tel. (038) 429–901–3
Royal Cliff Beach Resort: tel. (038) 421–421–30
Royal Garden Resort: tel. (038) 428–126–7

Phuket

Airport: tel. (076) 311–358, 327371
Dusit Laguna Hotel: tel. (076) 311–320–9
Le Meridien Hotel: tel. (076) 321–480–5
Holiday Inn Hotel: tel. (076) 321–020
Kata Beach: tel. (076) 381–530–3
Phuket Island Resort: tel. (076) 381–010–7
Phuket Arcadia: tel. (076) 381–038–44

Hertz
Bangkok

420 Sukhumvit Road: tel. (02) 711–0574–8
Opening times: Mon.–Sat. 8am–5pm

Chiang Mai

90–1 Sri Don Chai Road: tel. (053) 270–184–7
Chiang Mai Plaza Hotel: tel. (053) 270–036
Chiang Inn Hotel: tel. (9053) 270–070
Diamond Hotel: tel. (053) 270–080
Empress Hotel: tel. (053) 270–240
Holiday Inn Green Hills: tel. (053) 220–100–10
Mae Ping Hotel: tel. (053) 270–610

Hua Hin

Royal Garden Resort: tel. (032) 511881–4

Pattaya

Royal Garden Resort, 218 Beach Road, tel. (038) 428122, 428126

Phuket

Airport: (076) 327–230
20/5 Thepkrasattree Road: tel. (076) 217–190
Holiday Inn Phuket: tel. (076) 340–608
Pansea Hotel: tel. (076) 324–017
Patong Merlin Hotel: tel. (076) 340–038
Pearl Village Hotel: tel. (076) 324–021
Royal Park Travelodge: tel. (076) 324–021
Thavorn Palm Beach: tel. (076) 396–090

Motor-cycles

The renting of heavy motor-cycles is something that must be discouraged, partly because in the majority of cases they tend not to be completely roadworthy, but also because the difficulties imposed by the traffic conditions are frequently underestimated. The number of serious accidents, which often condemn their victims to a stay of many months in hospital, has dramatically risen in recent years.

Small motor-cycles, which can be rented all over Thailand, are, on the other hand, for the most part reliable. Even here, however, it is advisable to examine the vehicle closely before signing the rental contract.

Chemists

There are hundreds of chemist's shops in Bangkok and Chiang Mai as well as in tourist centres such as Pattaya and Phuket. Usually opening directly on to the street those marked "Pharmacy" or "Ram Kai Jaa" stock a large choice of almost all the medicines in common use in Europe. Virtually the only difference is that here in Thailand they are a fraction of the price. This is explained by the fact that, almost without exception, such remedies are dispensed on the spot from original recipes. They have the same effect though, and often even the same name.

The keen competition which exists between the chemist's shops means that they do not merely sell medicines. Often the customer will be offered traditional old Chinese homeopathic remedies, without which the chemist would not enjoy the confidence of his local clientele.

"British Dispensaries"

Exceptions to the rule are the "British Dispensaries", which sell proprietary medicines at fixed prices and often require a prescription for certain medicines.

Warning

To avoid any possibility of confusion when buying medicines it is a good idea to take along the original packaging. In the better chemist's shops (recognisable by the cleanliness of their premises) at least one of the staff is likely to speak English. Anyone needing a definite named medicine should not accept something merely "similar". If in doubt, phone the Bangkok branch of the appropriate European pharmaceutical company (see the Yellow Pages) and check the name by which the drug is known in Thailand.

Prescriptions

Prescriptions which can be used for the purchase of medicines are only given in exceptional circumstances when consulting a doctor. Private practices belonging to doctors trained in Europe or the United States normally employ their own pharmacists. Instead of a prescription patients are given a few days' supply of medicine in a small plastic bag. Be sure to inform the doctor of any known allergic reaction or intolerance to drugs.

Opening times

Mon.–Sat. 9am–5pm (6pm in smaller places, or until 9pm in large cities). On Sundays many are closed or only open until noon.

Church Services

Both Protestant and Catholic Churches are very active in Bangkok, and there are also regular services in Chiang Mai, Pattaya and Phuket.

Catholic services in Bangkok

Holy Redeemer Catholic Church
123/19 Soi Ruam Ruedee (behind the United States Embassy)
Tel. (02) 253 0353
Mass in English: Sun. 8.30am, 9.45am, 11am, 5.30pm

Protestant services in Bangkok

The Evangelical Church
10 Sukhumvit Road, at the end of Soi 10
Tel. (02) 251 9539 (services in English)

Catholic services in Chiang Mai

Chiang Mai First Church
10 Jarernrasd Road
Mass in English: Sun. 10am

Protestant services in Chiang Mai

Church of Christ
32/13 Huai Kaeo Road
Service: Sun. 9am (in English)

Catholic services in Pattaya

Roman Catholic Church (outside Pattaya near the Pattaya orphanage on the highway to Bangkok)
Mass in English: Sun. 9am

Protestant services in Pattaya

Pattaya Christ Church
182/1 Soi 13, Beach Road
Service: Sun. 10am (in English)

Our Lady of Assumptions
Soi Talingchan
Mass: first Friday in the month 7pm, Sun. 9am (in English)

Catholic services in Phuket

Christian Church
Chi Fa Road
Services: Sun. 10.30am, service with sermon Thur. 7.30pm (in English)

Protestant services in Phuket

Church of Christ
56 Talang Road
Service: Sun. 10am (in English)

Catholic Cathedral of Chanthaburi
(largest church in Thailand)
Mass: Sun. 10am (in English)

Catholic services in Chanthaburi

Clothing

Light airy cotton clothing is basically all a visitor will need during any of the three seasons which make up Thailand's year. A pullover or light cardigan is also recommended for evening wear during the period between November and February and for trips to the north of the country. It can also be appreciably cooler at times in the morning (see Introduction, Climate). It is important to wear light headwear as protection from the sun. Rather than open sandals it is better to wear light shoes with woven or perforated uppers.

Most tourists visiting Thailand take too much clothing with them. If anything is forgotten, it can always be purchased quite cheaply at one of the numerous markets which exist all over the country, or in the shops. There are also vast numbers of copies available of items of sportswear bearing the names of internationally renowned manufacturers. When looking for a garment here, it is best to insist on export quality, as only in this way can one be reasonably sure of getting something which is made of pure cotton.

Be sure not to forget to take suitable clothing for visiting a temple, as great importance is attached to correct dress in Thailand, particularly in Bangkok (see Thai Society and the Visitor). It is expected, for instance, for a man to wear long trousers (and, incidentally, a jacket when visiting a restaurant).

Craftwork

The various ethnic roots which make up Thailand can be clearly perceived in the country's craftwork. Much of the material though which is on offer in markets and souvenir shops is not typical of any particular population group, but is produced more for its appeal to tourists. It is important that visitors should refrain from buying products made of ivory (which are still available) or crocodile skin. In addition, pictures and boxes made using butterflies, which are often to be found on sale, are an important reason why certain species in Asia are threatened with extinction.

Central Thailand

Wood carvings of any kind (whether figures of dancers, salad servers) tend to come from the poorer parts of Thailand and tend to be produced in families, as they have been for generations. Since a ban on the felling of teak was brought in in Thailand, its use has been replaced more and more by other tropical woods, although the difference is often scarcely noticeable. Jugs, vases and plates made both of burnt earthenware and porcelain are produced in central Thailand, as the necessary raw materials are available here. Leather goods are also of good quality.

Northern Thailand

The northern part of the country is well-known for its pewter, wooden and woven goods (especially those made from the famous Thai silk). Other goods displaying real skill are silk paintings and embroidery. Around Chiang Mai there are numerous furniture manufacturers who produce artistically carved chairs, tables and cupboards. Export by ship can be arranged by the suppliers. Sunshades made of rice-paper and painted with peasant motifs can, with a little ingenuity, be turned into lampshades. Inhabitants of the mountain areas are skilled in making attractive dolls and puppets, which they are able to make look "antique" through an artificial ageing process. With brass cutlery it is important to check that individual items have been finished off carefully after the moulding process. Women from the Meo people in the mountains also produce beautiful woven goods (mainly from cotton) and silver jewellery.

Southern Thailand

Typical of the southern part of the country are shadow-play figures, which are carved out of hard-tanned buff leather and then painted. Sophisticated craftwork (e.g. chess pieces) using fish bones, which are crushed down and then heated up and formed into shapes while still liquid, is also particularly associated with southern Thailand.

Shopping

See entry

Currency

Currency

The unit of currency in Thailand is the baht, equivalent to 100 satang (also known colloquially as "dang").

Coins and banknotes

The smallest coin in circulation has a value of 25 satang, or 1 salung. There are also coins of 50 satang (= 2 salung), 1, 2, 5 and 10 baht.

Thai money

Thai banknotes are in denominations of 20 (green), 50 (blue), 100 (red), 500 baht (mauve) and 1000 baht. All banknotes are also inscribed in Arabic numerals.

Official exchange rate

The exchange rate available from banks is set by the Thai authorities and published in the daily papers. The same rate applies in the official exchange bureaux at Bangkok Airport and throughout the country. Somewhat more advantageous rates can often be secured from a "money changer". The rates offered by hotels on the other hand are generally less favourable, so recourse to this form of exchange should only be as a last resort.

Foreign currency regulations

There are no limits on the amount of foreign currency which can be brought into the country. The amount of Thai currency is limited to 50,000 baht per person on entering or leaving the country, unless special permission is obtained.

Traveller's cheques

It is best to take money in the form of traveller's cheques. As well as being more secure they usually enjoy an advantageous rate of exchange compared with cash, even after allowing for the 1% insurance fee on the value of the cheque. The insurance is of immediate assistance in the event of loss or theft (though it is essential to keep the cheques and confirmation of purchase separate). Whether to take sterling or dollar traveller's cheques is largely a matter of individual preference, although it is worth taking into account recent currency fluctuations and the likelihood of their continuance.

Passports must always be produced when changing traveller's cheques. As an additional safeguard the name of the visitor's hotel in Thailand is entered on the transaction form. Always ask for a receipt and always check the money against the receipt immediately it is handed over.

Eurocheques

The Thai Farmers Bank (branches throughout Thailand) will accept up to five Eurocheques a month. In practice, however, it is difficult to monitor the number cashed (an entry is sometimes made on the visa page of the visitor's passport). Eurocheque guarantee cards and passports must of course be produced.

Credit cards

All the usual credit cards (American Express, BankAmericard/Visa, MasterCard/Eurocard, Diners Card) are accepted throughout Thailand in hotels, restaurants, private shops, duty-free shops, banks, travel agencies and by the airline companies. There are also one or two cash dispensing machines where money can be withdrawn using a credit card and PIN number. As a rule only the international car rental companies will accept payment by credit card.

When making a payment by credit card always check immediately that the cardholder's copy of the transaction tallies with the original. For security reasons always destroy the carbon copy between the two papers personally.

If a credit card is lost or stolen the cardholder should immediately inform the company in question:

American Express, tel. 273 0033
Diners Club, tel. 233 5645, 238 3600
Visa/MasterCard/Eurocard, tel. 270 1259, 270 1801–10

Banks

The main Thai banks have substantial branch networks covering the whole of Thailand. In addition to the usual monetary transactions they can organise the teletransfer of funds from Europe. Some banks also provide mobile branches at the main tourist spots.

Bangkok Bank Ltd.
333 Silom Road, Bangkok; tel. (02) 234 3333

Krung Thai Bank
35 Sukhumvit Road, Bangkok; tel. (02) 255 2222

Thai Farmers Bank
400 Phaholyothin Road, Bangkok; tel. (02) 270 1122

Thai Military Bank
34 Phayathai Road, Bangkok; tel. (02) 246 0020

Opening times

See Business Hours

Cash Service

All the main Thai banks (Thai Farmers Bank, Siam Commercial Bank, etc.) offer their account holders the opportunity to make cash withdrawals either during bank opening hours or through cash dispensing machines. Anyone planning a longer stay in Thailand or intending to make several trips during the course of a year, would be advised to open an account in order to be able to deposit larger sums of money.

Customs Regulations

On entry

Ordinary personal effects including a camera and a movie or video camera can be taken into Thailand duty-free, as can up to 200 cigarettes or 250 grams of cigar or tobacco and 1 litre of wine or spirits. To avoid any problems arising on departure valuable items such as video cameras, portable computers, etc. should also be declared.

The importing of drugs and pornographic literature is strictly forbidden. Firearms and ammunition can be taken in only with permission from the Police Department. The import of harpoons for underwater hunting is forbidden.

Any valuable effects, e.g. photographic equipment, are best listed in writing (with their serial numbers). This list can then be handed to officials on arrival and departure and will considerably speed up customs clearance. In the event of the loss or theft of items on the list, however, there can be problems when showing it on leaving the country.

Diplomatic Representation

Embassies in Bangkok

United Kingdom

1031 Wireless Road; tel. 253 0191–9
Office hours: Mon. and Tues. 8am–1.30pm, Wed. 8am–2pm, Thur. and Fri. 2–4.30pm

United States of America

95 Wireless Road; tel. 252 5040–9
Office hours: 7.30–10am and 12.30–3pm

Canada

11/F Boonmitr Building, 138 Silom Road
Tel. 237 4126
Office hours: 9am–12.30pm

Australia

37 South Sathorn; tel. 287 2860
Office hours: 9.30am–noon and 2–3pm

New Zealand

93 Wireless Road; tel. 251 8165
Office hours: 8am–noon and 1.30–4pm

Thai Embassies abroad

United Kingdom

Royal Thai Embassy
30 Queen's Gate
London SW7; tel. (0171) 589 2857

Royal Thai Embassy
2300 Kalorama Road, NW
Washington D.C. 20008; tel. 483 7200–2

United States of America

Royal Thai Embassy
85 Range Road, Suite 704
Ottawa, Ontario K1N 8J6; tel. 237 1517, 237 0476

Canada

Royal Thai Embassy
111 Empire Circuit, Yarralumila
Canberra, A.C.T. 2600; tel. 731149, 732937

Australia

Royal Thai Embassy
2 Cook Street, P.O. Box 17–226
Karari, Wellington; tel 767864

New Zealand

Drinking Water

In the main tourist resorts in Thailand drinking water can be enjoyed without undue worry. A large number of hotels have their own water purification plant. If travelling in more out of the way rural areas it is a good idea to enquire at the hotel about the quality of the water. Anyone with a delicate constitution, who wants to be absolutely sure, should use the bottled "Polaris" drinking water which is always available. Any advice given by hotel staff should always be followed.

Drugs

Throughout south-east Asia the attitude of the authorities towards those dealing in, possessing and taking drugs has undergone a radical transformation, not least because of intense diplomatic pressure from Europe and America. In Thailand the police are more heavily engaged than ever before in combating drug-related crime and a highly effective drugs squad has been specially formed for this purpose. Police raids on bars associated with such crimes are possible at any time. Visitors should never let themselves be led astray by local people, as these are all too frequently police decoys.

In particular people should be warned against "magic mushrooms" which, although counting as "soft drugs", can when consumed lead to hallucinations and often cause severe physical and mental damage.

A further warning: Do not be talked into taking anything out of Thailand "for a friend". Unsuspecting travellers used as drug couriers have in many cases ended up as defendants in the law-courts.

Penalties

Possession of even the smallest quantity of a drug can result in many years of imprisonment – and Thai prisons bear little comparison with those in Europe. Thailand, moreover, retains and applies the death penalty for serious offences. Anyone foolish enough to become involved with drugs can expect little or no help from their country's consular representatives.

Electricity

The electricity supply in Thailand is adequate. On some of the islands diesel generators are used as a back-up.

Voltage

Thailand has 220 volt 50–cycle AC power as standard. The frequency can quite often fluctuate, so accumulators are used to extend the charging time. As simple plugs are generally fitted (no safety sockets), adaptors are unnecessary, even in country districts.

Batteries

Batteries for radios, etc. can be obtained at reasonable prices in most "drugstores" or in the shopping streets around the large hotels.

Emergencies

Tourist Assistance Center (TAC)

The Tourist Assistance Center (TAC) is a department of the Tourist Authority of Thailand (TAT). The Bangkok switchboard is manned by English-speaking officials between 8am and midnight and can be contacted by telephoning 281 5051 (preceded by 02 for Bangkok). In Pattaya: tel. 429 113. In Chiang Mai: Chiangmai–Lamphun Road (at the premises of the TAT office), tel. (053) 248604, 248697 (daily 6am–midnight).

Tourist Police

English-speaking officers of the tourist police can be reached on 195 or on one of the following numbers:

Bangkok	(02) 221–6206–10
Chiang Mai	(053) 248–607
Hat Yai	(074) 246–733
Kanchanaburi	(034) 512–795
Koh Samui	(077) 281–828
Pattaya	(038) 429–371
Phuket	(076) 211–036

Officers of the tourist police also operate motor-cycle patrols.

Crime Suppression Division

The Crime Suppression Division performs the functions of a crime detection agency and flying squad. It can be contacted day and night on the numbers 225 0085. As with other numbers that occur in the next few paragraphs, there may well be difficulties in making oneself understood as only a few officers have a reasonable command of English.

Metropolitan Mobile Police

The Metropolitan Mobile Police are the traffic police and flying squad for the whole Bangkok area and can be reached on the numbers 191, 123 or 246 1338.

Highway Patrol Division

The Highway Patrol Division can be contacted on tel. 281 6240, 281 6241 and 281 6250. Police patrols are generally quick to arrive on the scene of any incident, but reporting a crime and instituting court proceedings can often be difficult owing to the complicated nature of legal jurisdiction in Thailand. In the case of accidents it is best therefore to go to the TAT. Nevertheless, it is particularly important at night to call the Highway Patrol Division, so that statements can be taken down properly.

Fire brigade

There are fire departments in all towns, and in almost all places they can be reached on the number 199 (otherwise through the police).

Emergency doctor or ambulance

Ambulances and emergency doctors can be reached in Bangkok on the number 252 2171–5, via the police (tel. 123 or 191) or by telephoning the hospitals (see Medical Assistance).

Events

See Public Holidays and Festivals

Ferries

There are ferry connections throughout the year between the mainland and the many offshore islands. There are exceptions to this during the monsoon season (June–September) when there are often dangerous currents. Many ferries do not depart until there are sufficient passengers on board.

In addition there are a large number of local connecting services between the islands which do not operate to any fixed timetable. Enquiries about these should be made on the spot.

Prices and reservations

Prices are very low, but as a rule there are no reductions, e.g. for children. It is not possible to make reservations on local services.

Ferry connection	Frequency	Journey time
Bangkok–Pattaya (hydrofoil)	daily	3hrs
Hat Yai–Koh Tarutao	daily	2hrs
Koh Samui–Koh Ang Thong	daily	1hr 15mins
Koh Samui–Koh Phangan	daily	40mins
Krabi–Koh Lanta	daily (noon)	3hrs
Krabi–Koh Phi Phi	daily	1hr 15mins–3hrs
Laem Ngob–Koh Chang	daily (noon)	50mins
Pattaya–Koh Lam	daily	40mins
Pattaya–Koh Khrok	daily	1hr
Pattaya–Koh Sak	daily	1hr 30mins
Phuket–Koh Phi Phi	daily	1hr 45mins
Rayong(Ban Phe)–Koh Samet	daily	1hr 30mins
Si Racha–Koh Sichang	6 times daily	30mins
Surat Thani–Koh Samui	several times daily	2hrs 30mins–5hrs

Festivals

See Public Holidays and Festivals

Fishing

The coastline of Thailand extends for 1875km/1165 miles along the Gulf of Siam and 740km/460 miles along the Indian Ocean. The areas which have been developed for tourism, such as Pattaya on the south-east coast or Phuket on the south coast, offer ideal conditions for fishing. However, good catches are now hard to come by owing to the over-exploitation which has occurred in these once rich fishing-grounds over the past few decades.

Deep-sea fishing

There are many boat owners in Pattaya and Phuket as well as on the islands in the Gulf of Siam who offer deep-sea fishing trips – quite a few even offering a guaranteed catch. With the right amount of luck the fishermen can catch sharks, rays, tuna fish, swordfish, pollack, sea perch and mackerel, etc. The period January–May is particularly favourable. No special permits are needed for deep-sea fishing. A larger catch can be conserved after one's return if desired, though this can take a few days, sometimes even weeks.

Coastal fishing

There is no special permission or fishing permit needed for coastal fishing either. Opportunities are very limited, however, as the coastal areas are already overfished by the local fishermen. With a degree of patience, though, it is possible to catch pollack, sea bream, sole or moray from these waters. Along the rocky stretches of coastline, there is also a more or less abundant supply of molluscs such as cuttlefish, oysters, mussels and sea-snails, and crustaceans such as crayfish and lobsters.

Underwater fishing

See Sport (Diving)

Folklore

The visitor will need some degree of good fortune if he is to experience Thai popular theatre, classical Thai dancing or Chinese opera in their traditional forms. The most likely occasion will be one of the many traditional festivals (see Public Holidays and Festivals), as a festival without theatre and dancing is unthinkable to the Thais. In large hotels in the main tourist resorts there are all kinds of events, which will give the visitor an insight into the cultural heritage of the country. Excellent performances of classical theatre can be seen on certain days at the National Theatre in Bangkok. Early reservation is essential for these performances, or for rehearsals which are open to the public.

Food and Drink

The rich and varied cuisine of Thailand is closely related to those of the other south-east Asian countries. Indian, Chinese and Ceylonese dishes have been given a typical Thai character by the use of different spices. Thailand's receptiveness to foreign influences is evidenced by its adoption of Western recipes; in the tourist centres there are many restaurants which offer international cuisine and are quite prepared to serve quite specialised Western dishes.

Courses in Thai cooking

The renowned Oriental Hotel in Bangkok (see Hotels) arranges cooking seminars where the subtleties of Thai cooking are taught.

Customs

The Thai do not really follow the western custom of eating three meals a day. They patronise the many hot-food stalls at almost any time and eat six or seven times a day, but only a tiny portion at any one occasion. Breakfast in the European sense of the word is a rare occurrence – morning fare still being the traditional large dish of rice soup or vegetable soup.

People do not use a knife and fork for eating (these implements still being symbols of aggression), nor are chopsticks often employed. Instead the Thais cut up their food ready for eating with just a spoon, and generally this is also how it is served in restaurants. The golden rule is that a piece of meat and a small portion of rice should always combine to form a single mouthful. Some bars have a long-kept tradition of customers being fed by a waiter; some of these bars are still to be found in Bangkok.

Main ingredients

Classic Thai cooking employs ingredients which are essentially very simple but at the same time always absolutely fresh. The daily menu of the country people consists of fish, vegetables and rice; only on holidays is it normally enriched with pork or beef. Until just a few years ago fresh fish was only served on festive occasions in the northern part of the country. It was only when perch (*tilapia*) began to be farmed without any problems in the irrigation canals running through the rice fields that fish became within the average person's means there. Dried fish is a speciality from the south of Thailand and is enjoyed throughout the country as a delicious snack.

Spices

Thai cooking can be considered in the main to be moderately hot. The combining of many spices and herbs (e.g. curry, coconut milk, onions, chili, ginger, coriander, basil, mint, lemon balm, garlic) and the use of sweet, sweet-and-sour and highly seasoned sauces give Thai cooking its own special quality. Salt is hardly used at all; instead a fish sauce (*nam pla*) is added. Soups and main courses are normally served with a choice of spices and herbs so that people can season their food according to their own taste.

Fresh vegetables . . .

. . . and chilli pods

Be careful to use the tiny red and green peppers known as *nam prick* sparingly as they are very strong indeed!

Soups

Most soups are creamed and extremely tasty, as well as being very nutritious. As well as vegetable there are soups made from poultry, meat and fish (*bla joot*), often served with noodles. There is a well-known soup called *tom yam gung*, which is made of vegetables and meat in a strong beef stock. Soups are generally very highly seasoned; anyone preferring something milder should let the waiter know when ordering, by saying *mai sai prik*, which is Thai for "not hot, please".

Main courses

There are a great variety of typically Thai dishes to be sampled, all prepared with generous amounts of garlic and onion and garnished with different kinds of salad. Pork (*moo*) and beef dishes (*woo-a*), chicken (*gai*) and fish (*plah*), appear frequently on the menu in all sorts of guises. Steaks are also very popular. They are usually eaten with rice (*kao*), noodles (*ba-mee*) and chips (*mun fa-rung*). To order pork with fried rice for example, simply say *kao put moo*; if beef is preferred to pork *kao put woo-a*, and so on.

Meat

Meat is mainly roasted, grilled or fried. Classic meat dishes include: beef with rice noodles, roast beef with basil leaves, soya sprouts or bamboo shoots (*sen mee noo-a yang*), chicken curry with coconut and rice (*kaheng kow kee-ao wahn kai*).

Fish and shellfish

Fish and shellfish (lobster, spiny lobster and crab) are very reasonably priced, always fresh, and excellently prepared. Examples of fish dishes include sweet-and-sour fish curry (*kaheng som*) or steamed fish with hot tomato sauce (*pla nueng yah-eh-o makhooa tet*). Many restaurants display their seafood in cool-cabinets. The giant crabs, which are caught fresh in the bays of southern Thailand and cooked over a charcoal fire before being served with a variety of accompaniments, are exceptionally tasty.

Fish and crustaceans, always fresh

Vegetables

Vegetables such as beans, white cabbage, Chinese lettuce, turnips, aubergines and mushrooms are generally only lightly cooked or even served raw, thereby retaining most of their vitamins. They are often cooked in the wok, well-known for its importance in Chinese cooking. Fat is almost never used, steaming being the most important method employed.

Dessert

Desserts (*korng wahn*) usually take the form of little puddings, very sweet and very brightly coloured, or some form of rice dish. Small, dry, raisin cakes are also a favourite. The Thais are exceptionally good at preparing sweet rice dishes (*ka-nom*, etc.) and have mastered the art of ice-cream making from the Americans. Their ice-cream sundaes in particular, sometimes served in a hollowed-out pineapple, are superlative.

Fruit

Thais insist that food should appeal to the eye as well as to the palate. As is so often the case with a tradition, the Thai art of cutting fruit and vegetables is traced back to a legend. In one of King Rama II's poems the story is told of a queen who loses the king's favour to a rival. Banished from the palace she returns secretly as a kitchenmaid, revealing herself to her son by depicting incidents from her life at court in the vegetables she prepares for the soup. Recognising his mother the boy intercedes with the king on her behalf and she is at last restored to her rightful place. And so, it is said, this ancient Thai tradition was founded. Today hotel kitchens have staff who are masters in the art of sculpting fruit and vegetables.

Thailand is a veritable orchard, with many kinds of tropical fruits unknown to European visitors. Many restaurants can offer – depending on the season – fresh fruit. If buying fresh fruit at the market, do not forget to wash it thoroughly.

Fresh pineapples (*supparot*) are available from April to July, and there are no less than eleven different types to choose from – all rich in Vitamin C and low in calories. Some kinds are allowed to ferment before being eaten.

There are fifteen different types of banana which can be enjoyed throughout the year. Those sold in the evenings from grills on the street are

Pineapples (sapparot)

Bananas (kluey)

usually soaked in fresh coconut milk. Remember that the smaller the banana the sweeter the taste.

The subtle floury tasting flesh of the durian is considered a great delicacy by the Thais (available April to June), although it has been called "stinking fruit" by Europeans on account of its unpleasantly strong smell. Indeed guests are often asked by managements to refrain from bringing them back to their hotels.

Fa-rung fruit (guavas) are usually served with sugar or a pinch of salt. "Fa-rung" is the Thai word for a European and guavas are so called because they are considered outsiders among the country's fruit. They are available from September to January.

Jackfruit (*ka-noon*), large, round fruit weighing several kilograms, are sweet and aromatic. Ripening in August and September they are served sliced and chilled.

The milk of the coconut (*ma-prao-onn*) provides a healthy, refreshing drink while the flesh is eaten with a pointed spoon.

Langsats (langsard) are tasty berries, light-brown in colour, with a thin but tough skin which has to be peeled with a knife. Care is required when eating them because the sweet flesh hides a very bitter pip (June to September).

Limes, round and green, the cheap local version of the lemon, are found all through the year. The yellow lemons familiar to Europeans have to be imported and are very expensive.

Longans (*lam-yai*) come from the northern provinces and are rather expensive if bought in Bangkok (July–September) because they have to be transported a considerable distance and yet only keep for a few days.

Lychees (*hong Huay, gim yeng, ohia*) were also once a luxury, imported from China in cans. Nowadays they are grown in Thailand, mainly in the north. The three names refer to the different price categories, which in turn reflect varying degrees of vulnerability to pests. All taste virtually the same, however. They are fresh and ripe (with red skins) from May to August.

Stink fruit (durian)

Opening a coconut

Mangoes (*ma-moo-ung*) are second only to pineapples as the favourite fruit among tourists. They need to be completely ripe before eating, the skin yellow, not green. Then they are sweet, juicy and aromatic but will only keep for a limited time. They should be sliced through the middle, the pulp being scooped out with a spoon or eaten straight from the skin (March to June).

The purple-skinned mangosteen (*mung koot*) is on sale from June to November. It has white flesh and a sweet taste not unlike a lychee.

Thai oranges (*som*) are mostly green and thin-skinned; the yellow ones are particularly sweet (available all the year round).

Grapefruit (*som-oh*) are also found fresh throughout the year and are generally the delicious pink variety. The Thais enjoy them best with a pinch of salt.

Papayas (*ma-la-gor*) are the cheapest of all Thai fruit and can be bought on any market stall at any time of year. The hotels serve papaya halves for breakfast, sprinkled with lemon. Eaten to excess papayas are an effective laxative.

Rambutans (*ngor*) were christened "hairy" by the Americans on account of the spiky covering they have when they are fully ripe. Cut the skin with a knife and eat the juicy flesh, but avoid the stone (May to October).

Rose apples (*chom-poo*) are pear-shaped, with a rust-coloured waxy skin and spongy white flesh, both of which can be eaten. It has a slightly sharp taste and so is best eaten with sugar or a pinch of salt (January to March).

Drinks

Weak tea (*cha*) is served cold and in many restaurants is available free of charge. Hot tea (*cha rorn*) on the other hand has to be specially ordered.

Coffee tends to be served either hot with milk and sugar (very sweet) or iced and black (*oh-lee-ung*). Italian-style espresso coffee has also become widely available.

Fresh milk (*nom*), usually from Denmark, is sold in plastic cartons. Ask for *mai waan*, otherwise it will be sweetened. As Thai soft drinks tend to be

A "takeaway" on the floating market of Damnoen Saduak

very sweet and heavily coloured, Europeans generally prefer to drink pure orange and lemon juice (*num som or num ma-nao*), which should be ordered fresh (*sod*).

Large quantities of ice are usually added to drinks as a matter of course so the words *mai sai num kairng* ("without ice please") are more likely to be needed than *kor sai num kairng* ("with ice please"). Soda is generally understood as referring to mineral water.

Alcoholic drinks

In addition to the iced water available everywhere – sometimes the cause of stomach upsets – German-style lagers (Singha, Amarit, Kloster) are very popular. They are sold throughout the country in either small bottles (*koo-ut lek*) or large bottles (*koo-ut jai*). They are fairly expensive as hops are not grown in Thailand and have to be imported from abroad.

Mekong is a typical Thai drink: it is a spirit made from rice (28% proof) and is usually drunk with cola, soda or lemon.

Thai wine (*lao angnun*) is very sweet. Imported wines are generally overpriced and poorly stored, an exception being the Australian wines available in supermarkets.

Restaurants

See entry

Health Precautions

See entry

Frontier Crossings

Malaysia

The frontier crossing at Sungai Kolok is open daily 8am–6pm.

Myanmar (Burma)

The frontier crossing to Myanmar (formerly Burma) in Mae Sai is open to tourists as from January 1st 1993. A visa valid for one day can be issued at the border, but visas for longer stays have to be obtained at the embassy in Bangkok.

Cambodia

Cambodia can only be reached by air (airport Phnom Penh-Pochentong, e.g. via Moscow). However, it is very likely that a land crossing point will soon be opened, enabling foreign visitors to cross over into Cambodia and back again. It is also planned to open a Cambodian embassy in Bangkok. Travel agents in Bangkok are the best source of information regarding the current state of affairs.

Laos

The frontier crossing to Laos is at Nong Khai, but the nearest Laotian towns of any size with sights to see are Luang Prabang and Vientiane. There are no problems crossing over into Laos for travellers in possession of a valid visa.

Visas

See Travel Documents

Getting to Thailand

By air

Given the distances involved most visitors to Thailand arrive by air. Modern jet travel means that the long (about 10,000km/6215 miles) journey from Europe can be completed in as little as eleven hours (non-stop) and fifteen hours at most. From the USA and Canada flights operate across the Pacific. There are international airports by which visitors can enter Thailand, not only at Bangkok International, but also at Chiang Mai, Phuket, Surat Thani, Ubon Ratchathani and Hat Yai.

By car

Coming by car from Singapore or Malaysia it is necessary to use one of the three border crossings in the south of the country on the Thai–Malaysian border: in the provinces of Songkhla, Yala and Narathiwat (Sungai Kolok). Entering the country by car is only possible by one of these crossings (open until 6pm). The "Asian Highway" from the Bosphorus to Singapore is at present blocked through Myanmar (Burma), where the border crossings are closed.

By train

There are daily services from Singapore and Malaysia; the fares are low, the trains are comfortable and the timetables are consistently observed. The journey time from Singapore to Bangkok is 1½–2 days. Reservation in advance is necessary for first-class travel and also for couchettes and sleeping cars.

It is possible to travel from Singapore to Thailand on the luxury "Eastern and Oriental Express"; the journey can be broken at any of the larger stations in Malaysia and Thailand; bookings need to be made before departure from the Eastern and Oriental Express office in the visitor's own country. For further information see Rail and Bus.

By sea

Most round-the-world cruise liners put in to Bangkok, mooring in the river section of the harbour (generally between Piers 9 and 12), while at Pattaya, Sattahip or Phuket they dock outside the actual harbour and passengers are transported to land in small boats. At the quays and landing-stages there are always taxis waiting for any passengers who wish to travel independently. As the port at Bangkok is very large it is a good idea to make a note of the ship's exact landing-berth and have it written down in Thai letters.

By cargo-ship

One of the last adventures of our time is a sea voyage by cargo-ship from Europe to Thailand which takes about a month. Further connections by cargo-ship to Japan, Hong Kong and Singapore can also be made and arrangements for these can best be made on the spot.

Travel agents: See entry

Travel documents: See entry

Health Precautions

A holiday in the tropics requires certain preparations and also responsible behaviour when there, in order for the overall experience to be a positive one. The prospective visitor should consult their own doctor in good time before going on holiday in order to eliminate any unnecessary health risks (most important for pregnant women and children).

Inoculations

The Thai authorities do not require that European visitors should have any inoculations, unless they are coming into the country from another area where there is infection. In 1989 Thailand was declared free of cholera by the World Health Organisation (WHO). A satisfactory course of inoculation against tetanus and poliomyelitis should have been undergone and an inoculation certificate (which should contain details of possible allergies as well as a person's blood group) should be carried.

Visitors are also recommended to have a course of inoculation against Hepatitis A, which can be transmitted where there is unhygienic preparation of food and drinks. People who are susceptible should have themselves immunised before their departure with gamma globins. Those intending to spend a long period in the rural areas of northern Thailand should be vaccinated against Japanese encephalitis.

Malaria prophylaxis

There have recently been renewed occurrences of malaria in Thailand. In particular visitors to the northern areas of the country and those intending to spend some time outside the main tourist centres are urgently recommended to take a course of one of the various prophylactic or preventive medicines. There are special preparations for children.

First aid kit

Having a first aid kit is of far greater importance here than when travelling around Europe. On the one hand the risk of infection is higher, on the other there are many medicines which are used in the Asiatic areas under different names or are not available at all. Obviously visitors should take adequate supplies with them of medicines or drugs which they need to use on a regular basis (including contraceptives).

Any first aid kit should include the following: scissors, tweezers for removing splinters, cotton wool, two gauze bandages, a packet of dressing, two packets of instant bandages, adhesive plasters and tape, antiseptic solution, pain-killers, medicines for diarrhoea, constipation, travel sickness, circulation disorders, infections. As well as sun protection cream, an insect repellant, which can be applied to the skin, is also important.

During the flight

For the long flight to Thailand light comfortable clothing is recommended and experienced air-travellers swear by a pair of comfortable slippers. Inflatable cushions rather like a ruff, which support the head while sleeping, are also useful.

Acclimatisation

The visitor must allow the body the necessary time to adjust to a tropical climate. It is a good idea to avoid any strenuous activity during the first few days and not to expose oneself to full sunlight for too long. Use a sun cream with a high filter factor.

Where there is air-conditioning, avoid frequent changes of cool and warm (inside and outside) and turn the air-conditioning off when sleeping at night to avoid the risk of catching cold.

Food

Food bought at hot-food stalls is generally acceptable for Europeans to eat, although it is obviously important to check the cleanliness of the establishment as far as possible. Fruit should always be washed thoroughly before being eaten. As a rule visitors should refrain from consuming raw food, unpeeled fruit, ice-cream and open drinks to which large quantities of ice-cubes have been added. Caution is also advisable in the tropics with regard to alcohol consumption. The best protection against infection is to keep as clean as possible (wash hands frequently, shower and change clothes regularly).

Aids — The danger of becoming infected with Aids (HIV) is also very real in Thailand. Anyone sexually active should always use condoms, but as the disease is normally fatal, complete abstinence is the best advice when travelling in south-east Asia.

Chemists — See entry

Doctor — See Medical Assistance

Hospitals — See Medical Assistance

Help for the Disabled

Information — The Thai Tourist Office in London (see Information) provides information on request for disabled people planning a visit to Thailand.

Transport — Transport in Thailand is not very well equipped to deal with the needs of the disabled, but local tour operators are often able to arrange special programmes for individual needs.

Sightseeing — The most important sights, such as temples and museums, can generally be visited by travellers in wheelchairs. The Thais are a very helpful people.

Accommodation — Both those hotels belonging to the big international chains as well as the better category Thai-owned hotels are fully equipped for the needs of disabled visitors. It is not possible, however, to provide a list of accommodation specially designated "suitable for the disabled".

Hotels

The tourist boom of the last few years is most clearly evidenced in the number of new hotel buildings. Whereas just a few years ago there were only about 20,000 hotel beds, by 1992 the number had increased fourfold (about 75,000 beds). There is a choice of accommodation from the luxury category of hotel down to the most basic guest houses and youth hostels (see Youth Hostels).

When travelling outside the areas served by the normal tourist infrastructure it is necessary to accept certain limitations with regard to comfort and facilities. In compensation the service is generally that much more attentive. The price of rooms tends to be significantly lower than in the main tourist centres.

Cheap accommodation — Apart from hotels there are also guest houses and – particularly on the islands – reasonably comfortable bungalow complexes (e.g. with fans rather than air conditioning). In Bangkok there are also a large number of guest houses for back-packers where a night's accommodation can cost well under £10/$15.

Royal Orchid Program — Thai Airways International offers the "Royal Orchid Program", by which intermediate stops, or, indeed, even the traveller's whole itinerary, can be arranged at a guaranteed reduced rate. This needs to be booked before leaving Europe (see Air Travel).

Prices — The most expensive hotel rooms are to be found in Bangkok and the main tourist centres. A room in the legendary Oriental Hotel in Bangkok is about £800/$1200 whereas a simple guest house need only cost £4/$6. Outside the main centres a room will cost between £10/$15 and £40/$60. Out of season (March to October) it is possible to negotiate a lower price, even in the higher category establishments.

★★★★★	£100–200/$150–300
★★★★	£60–100/$90–150
★★★	£40–60/$60–90
★★	£25–40/$40–60
★	up to £25/$40

Reservations

While advance reservation is necessary during the main tourist season (November to the end of February), at other times it is almost always possible to find accommodation in whatever category is desired.

The Thai Hotel Association has a desk in the arrival hall at Bangkok International Airport. Besides finding where there are rooms available, they will also organise transfer to the hotel. Similar information desks are to be found at all the other airports in the country; they are always open when flights come in or are expected.

Other accommodation

Camping (see entry)
Youth Hostel (see entry)

In the following selective list of hotels the following terms are used which possibly require a short explanation:

Coffee shop = Simple restaurant where snacks, refreshments and simple meals are served.
Coffee shops are often open 24 hours.
Business center = Specially intended for businessmen. They offer the usual secretarial services as well as access to telecommunications facilities (telephone, fax, data transmission, etc.)

Selection of hotels

Abbreviations

r = number of rooms

Ayutthaya

★★

Ayutthaya Grand Hotel, 55/5 Rochana Road, tel. (035) 335–483; 122r, restaurant, coffee shop, bar, swimming pool.

★

U Thong Inn, 210 Mu 5, Rochana Road, tel. (035) 242–236–9, 242–618, fax 242–235; 96r, restaurant, coffee shop, bar, swimming pool, shops.

Bangkok

★★★★★

Airport Hotel, 33 Chert Wudhakat Road, Don Muang (opposite airport), tel. (02) 566–1020–1, fax 566–1941; 300r, restaurants, coffee shop, bar, night club, swimming pool, fitness room, shops.

Amari Boulevard, 17 Soi 7 Sukhumvit Road, tel. (02) 255–2930, fax 255–2950; 129r, coffee shop, bar, fitness room, business center, shop.

Central Plaza, 1695 Paholyothin Road (between airport and city centre); tel. (02) 541–1234, fax 541–1087; 607r, restaurants, coffee shop, bar, night club, swimming pool, hairdressing salon, fitness room, shopping arcade.

Dusit Thani Hotel, 946 Rama IV Road, tel. (02) 236–0450–9, fax 2365–6400; 533r, restaurants, coffee shop, bar, night club, swimming pool, fitness room, tennis court, hairdressing salon, business center, shopping arcade, travel agent, car rental desk.

Grand Hyatt Erawan, 494 Rajadamri Road, tel. (02) 254–1234, fax 253–5856; 400r, restaurants, coffee shop, bar, night club, swimming pool, fitness room, tennis court, hairdressing salon, business center, shopping arcade, travel agent.

Hilton International, 2 Witthayu Road, tel. (02) 253–0123, fax 253–6509; 400r, restaurants, coffee shop, bar, swimming pool, fitness room, tennis court, hairdressing salon, business center, shopping arcade, travel agent.

Imperial, 6 Witthayu Road, tel. (02) 254–0023–100, fax 253–3190; 370r, restaurants, coffee shop, bar, swimming pool, fitness room, tennis court, squash court, hairdressing salon, business center, shopping arcade, travel agent.

Indra Regent, Rajprarob Road, tel. (02) 251–1111, fax 253–3849; 439r, restaurants, coffee shop, bar, night club, swimming pool, fitness room, tennis court, hairdressing salon, business center, shopping arcade, travel agent.

Royal Orchid Sheraton, 2 Cptn. Bush Lane, tel. (02) 234–5599, fax 236–8320; 776r, restaurants, coffee shop, bar, night club, swimming pool, fitness room, tennis, hairdressing salon, business center, shops, travel agent.

Shangri La Hotel, 89 Soi Wat Suan Plu, tel. (02) 236–7777, fax 236–8570; 694r, restaurants, coffee shop, bar, night club, swimming pool, fitness room, tennis, hairdressing salon, business center, shopping arcade, travel agent, jetty.

Siam Intercontinental, 967 Rama I Road, tel. (02) 253–0355–7; 400r, speciality restaurants, coffee shops, bar, swimming pool in 12ha/30 acres of gardens, tennis court, practice golf course, jogging track, business center, shopping arcade, travel agent.

The Mansion Kempinski, Sukhumvit Road, Soi 11, tel. (02) 255–7200, fax 253–2329; 120r. Former apartment block in a central location with extremely large rooms (often ideal for business travellers), restaurant, bar, swimming pool, business center.

The Menam, 2074 New Road, tel. (02) 289–1148, fax 291–1048, 718r; situated directly on the Menam Chao Phraya with restaurants, bars, night club, swimming pool, fitness room, hairdressing salon, business center, shopping arcade, travel agent.

The Oriental, Oriental Avenue, tel. (02) 236–0400–39, fax 236–1937, 393r; legendary hotel directly on the Menam Chao Phraya with large terrace, speciality restaurants, bars, night club, swimming pool, fitness room, tennis court, hairdressing salon, luxury shopping arcade, business center, travel agent, jetty.

★★★★

Asia Hotel, 296 Phya Thai Road, tel. (02) 215–0801, fax 215–4360; 640r, restaurants, coffee shop, bar, night club, swimming pool, fitness room, hairdressing salon, shopping arcade.

Narai Hotel, 222 Silom Road, tel. (02) 237–0100–11, fax 236–7161; 500r, restaurant, coffee shop, bar, night club, swimming pool, fitness room, business center, shopping arcade, travel agent.

★★★

Plaza, 178 Surawongse Road, tel. 235–1760–79, fax 237–0746; 160r, coffee shop, swimming pool, shops, travel agent.

Rembrandt Hotel, 19 Sukhumvit Soi 18, tel. (02) 261–7100, fax 261–7017; 406r, new hotel in quiet, yet central location, restaurant/coffee shop, bars, swimming pool, hairdressing salon, business center, shopping arcade, travel agent.

★★

Collins International House (Y.M.C.A.), 27 Sathorn Thai Rd., tel. (02) 287–2727, fax 287–1996; 250r, young people's guest house specially suited to young travellers; restaurant, coffee shop, bar, swimming pool, fitness room, business center, shops.

New Trocadero, 343 Surawongse Road, tel. (02) 234–8920, fax 236–5526; 116r, restaurant, coffee shop, swimming pool, fitness room, hairdressing salon, shops.

★

Bangkok Youth Hostel, 25/2 Phitsanulok Road, tel. (02) 282–0950; 20r, restaurant, coffee shop and travel agent.

Sathorn Inn, 37 Soi Suksa-Vithaya, tel. (02) 234–4110, fax 235–3024; 90r, restaurant, coffee shop.

Ban Phe
★★

Ban Phe Cabana Resort, 120 Damrongrak, tel. (038) 280–1820; 60r, restaurant, coffee shop, swimming pool.

Buriram
★

Tepnakorn, 139 Jira Road, tel. (044) 613–400, fax 613–400; 30r, restaurant, coffee shop and night club.

Cha Am

★★★★★ Dusit Resort & Polo Club, tel. (032) 520–008, fax 520–296; 308r, restaurant, coffee shop, swimming pool.

★★★ The Regent Cha Ama Beach Resort, tel. (032) 471–480–91, fax 471–491–2; 650r, restaurant, coffee shop, swimming pool (particularly suitable for families with small children).

★★ Cha Am Lagoon Resort, on the road from Klong Khon to Cha Am, tel. (032) 471–326–7; 56r, restaurant, coffee shop, swimming pool.

Chaiyaphum

Lert Nimitra, 447 Niwetrat Road, tel. (044) 811–522–3, fax 822–335; 96r, restaurant.

Chanthaburi

★★ Caribou Highland Hotel, 14 Shavana-Utit, Wat Mai, tel. (039) 321–584, fax 321–584; 55r, restaurant.

Chiang Mai

★★★★★ Chiang Mai Orchid, 100 Huai Kaeo Road, tel. (053) 222–091, fax 221–625; 267r, restaurant, bar, discothèque, swimming pool.

★★★★ Chiang Mai Plaza, 22 Sridonchai Road, tel. (053) 270–040, fax 272–230; 444r, restaurants, coffee shop, bar, discothèque, swimming pool, central position near the night-time market.
Holiday Inn Green Hill, 24 Chiang Mai-Lampang Superhighway, tel. (053) 220–100, fax 221–602; 168r, restaurant, coffee shop, shops.

★★★ Royal Princess (Dusit Inn), 112 Chang Khlan Road, tel. (053) 281–033–6, fax 281–044; 198r, restaurant, coffee shop, shops.

★★ Rincome, 301 Huai Kaeo Road, tel. (053) 221–044, fax 221–915; 158r, restaurant, coffee shop, bar, swimming pool, tennis, hairdressing salon, shops, travel agent.
Mae Hong Son Resort, 50–52 Tha Pae Road, tel. (053) 249–006, fax 249–133; 34r, restaurant, coffee shop, bar, shops.

★ Anodard, 57 Ratchamanka Road, tel. (053) 270–755–9, fax 270–759; 160r, restaurant, coffee shop, swimming pool.

Chiang Rai

★★★★ Delta Golden Triangle Resort & Hotel, 222 Golden Triangle, Chiang Saen, tel. (053) 777–031, fax 777–005 (reservations in Bangkok: 260–7388); 73r, restaurant, coffee shop, bar, discothèque, swimming pool.
Dusit Island Resort, 1129 Kraisorasit Road, tel. (053) 715–777–9, fax 715–801 (reservations in Bangkok: 238–4790); 270r, coffee shop, bar, discothèque.
Le Meridien Baan Boran (in Golden Triangle), tel. (053) 716–678, fax 716–702 (reservations in Bangkok: 251–4707); 110r, restaurant, bar, swimming pool, hairdressing salon.

★★★ Rimkok Resort, Tathon Road, tel. (053) 716–445, fax 716–445 (reservations in Bangkok: 279–0102); 256r, restaurant, coffee shop, bar, swimming pool, shops.
Wiang Inn, 893 Phaholyothin Road, tel. (053) 711–543, fax 711–877 (reservations in Bangkok: 513–2926); 258r, restaurant, coffee shop, bar, discothèque, shops.

★★ Wang Come, 869/90 Pemawiphak Road, tel. (053) 711–800, fax 712–972 (reservations in Bangkok: 254–8773); 220r, restaurant, coffee shop, bar, swimming pool, hairdressing salon, shops.

Chumphon

★★ Pornsawan House, 110 Mu 4 Pharadon Phap Beach, tel. (077) 521–031–30; 75r, restaurant, swimming pool, tennis court.

★ Chumphon Cabana, Thung Wua Laen Beach, tel. (077) 501–990 (reservations in Bangkok: 224–1884); 40r, restaurant, shops.

Hotels

Hat Yai
★★

Asian Hat Yai, 55 Niphat–Uthit 3 Road, tel. (074) 245–455, fax 234–890 (reservations in Bangkok: 512–1690); 104r, restaurant, coffee shop, bar, hairdressing salon, travel agent.

President, 420 Petkasem Road, tel. (074) 244–477, fax 285–355; 110r, restaurant, coffee shop, bar, discothèque, swimming pool, hairdressing salon, shops, travel agent.

★

Amarin. 285 Niphat Uthit Road, tel. (074) 244–012; 140r, restaurant.

Hat Yai Ambassador, 23 Phadung Phakdi Road, tel. (074) 234–411–7; 170r, restaurant, coffee shop.

Hua Hin
★★★★★

Royal Garden Village, 45 Phetkasem Road, tel. (032) 512–412–5; 162r, restaurant, coffee shop, bar, swimming pool, tennis, shops.

★★★★

Club Aldiana (about 35km/22 miles from Hua Hin near Pranburi), tel. (032) 631–235 (reservations in Bangkok: 233–3871); 185r (hotel and bungalows), restaurant, coffee shop, bar, discothèque, swimming pool.

Royal Garden Resort, 107/1 Phetkasem Road, tel. (032) 511–881–4, fax 512–422; 222r, restaurant, coffee shop, bar, discothèque, swimming pool, tennis, shops, beautiful sandy beach, ideal for families with children.

Sofitel Central Hua Hin, 1 Damnoenkasem Road, tel. (032) 512–021–40 (reservations in Bangkok: 233–0974); 200r, restaurant, coffee shop, bar, discothèque, swimming pool, tennis, shops.

★★

Hua Hin Highland Resort, 4/15 Ban Samophrong, tel. (032) 211–2579; 13r (bungalows), restaurant, discothèque, swimming pool, tennis.

Kalasin
★

Suphak, 81/7 Saneha Road, tel. (043) 811–315; 52r, restaurant.

Kamphaeng Phet
★

Chakangrao, 123/1 Thesa Road, tel. (055) 711–315, fax 711–326 (reservations in Bangkok: 279–5322); 116r, restaurant, coffee shop, fitness room, tennis, hairdressing salon, travel agent.

Navarat, 2 Soi Prapan Thesa Road, tel. (055) 711–106, fax 711–961; 78r, restaurant, bar.

Kanchanaburi
★★★★

Sheraton River Kwai Resort, 9/1 Mu 3, tel. (034) 515–094–5; 256r, restaurant, swimming pool.

★★★

River Kwai Hotel, 284/3–16 Saeng Chuto Road, tel. (034) 511–184, fax 511–269; 127r, coffee shop, bar, swimming pool, hairdressing salon.

River Kwai Village Hotel, 72 Mu 4, Amphoe Soi Yak, tel. (034) 251–7552, fax 591–054 (reservations in Bangkok: 251–7828); 60r + 28 houseboats, coffee shop, swimming pool.

Khon Kaen
★★

Kaen Inn, 56 Klang Muang Road, tel. (043) 237–744, fax 239–457 (reservations in Bangkok: 247–1661–2); 163r, restaurant, coffee shop.

Kosa, 230–252 Si Chan Road, tel. (043) 225–014–8, fax 225–013; 92r, restaurant, bar, swimming pool.

Koh Chang
★

Bang Bao Beach Resort, tel. (039) 511–604; 10 bungalows, restaurant, bar.

Koh Phi Phi
★★★★

Phi Phi Palm Beach Resort, Laem Thong Bay, tel. (077) 76214–488 (reservations in Phuket: 076/214–654); 70 bungalows, restaurant, bar, coffee shop, swimming pool, own diving station.

Koh Samui
★★★★★

The Imperial Thong Sai Bay, Laem Ban Plai, tel. (077) 425–015–024, fax 421–462; 72r, restaurant, coffee shop, bar, swimming pool, tennis, shops.

Tong Sai Bay, Thong Takian Bay, tel. (077) 421–451–60, fax 421–462 (reservations in Bangkok: 254–0111); 80r, restaurant, swimming pool, tennis.

★★★★

Boat House Samui, Thong Takian Bay, tel. (077) 425–041, fax 425–462; 216r, restaurant, coffee shop, bar, swimming pool, shops.

Chaweng Blue Lagoon, Chaweng Beach, tel. (077) 422–401, fax 422–401 (reservations in Bangkok: 250–0360); 61r (including some huts in the Thai style), restaurant, coffee shop, bar, swimming pool, shops.

★★★

Chaba Samui, 19 Chaweng Beach, tel. (077) 421–380, fax 422–380; 16r, restaurant, bar, travel agent.

Coral Bay Resort, Chaweng Beach, tel. (077) 286–902, fax 286–902 (reservations in Bangkok: 233–7711); 42r, restaurant, coffee shop, bar, swimming pool, shops.

Palm Reef, Chaweng Beach, tel. (077) 281–000, fax 282–001 (reservations in Bangkok: 252–6045); 84r, restaurant, coffee shop, bar, swimming pool, travel agent.

★★

Samui Yacht Club, Tongtakien Beach, tel. (077) 421–400, fax 421 400 (reservations in Bangkok: 319–6631–2); 65r, restaurant, coffee shop, bar, swimming pool, fitness room.

Tropicana Beach Resort, Chaweng Noi Beach, tel. (077) 421–408, fax 421–408; 50 bungalows, restaurant, coffee shop, swimming pool.

★

Golden Sand Beach Resort, 124/2 Lamai Beach, tel. (077) 421–430, fax 421–430 (reservations in Bangkok: 252–4101); 40r, restaurant, coffee shop, bar, shops.

Sandy Resort, 177/1 Hat Bo–Phut, tel. (077) 425–353, fax 425–354 (reservations in Bangkok: 314–7420); 52r, restaurant, coffee shop, travel agent.

Krabi

★★★

Phra Nang Plantation Club, Khlong Muang Beach, tel. (075) 612–173–4, fax 612–174; 60r, restaurant, coffee shop, swimming pool, hairdressing salon.

Krabi Resort, 53–57 Phattana Road, Ao Nang, tel. (075) 612–161, fax 612–160 (reservations in Bangkok: 208–9165); 79r, restaurant, bar, swimming pool, tennis court, travel agent.

★★

Phra Nang Inn, Ao Phra Nang, tel. (075) 612–173–4, fax 612–174; 51r, restaurant, coffee shop, swimming pool, hairdressing salon.

Beach Terrace, Ao Nang, tel. (01) 722–0060, fax 722–0061; 34r, restaurant.

★

Thai, 7 Issara, tel. (075) 611–122, fax 612–556; 150r, restaurant.

Lampang

★★★

Thipchang Lampang, 54/22 Thakraw Noi Road, tel. (054) 2224–273, fax 225–362; 130r, coffee shop, bar, swimming pool.

★★

Lampang River Lodge, 330 Mu 11, tel. (054) 217–054; 120r, restaurant, coffee shop.

★

Asia Lampang, 299 Boonyawat Road, tel. (054) 227–844, fax 224–436; 73r, coffee shop, bar.

Loei

★

Phuluang, 55 Charoen Road, tel. (042) 811–532, fax 811–2558; 86r, restaurant, hairdressing salon.

Thai Udom, 112/1 Charoenrat Road, tel. (042) 811–763; 76r, coffee shop, hairdressing salon.

Mae Hong Son

★★

Holiday Inn, 114/5–7 Khunlumpraphat Road, tel. (053) 611–390, fax 611–524; 114r, restaurant, coffee shop, swimming pool, tennis, shops.

Bai Yok Chalet, 90 Khunlumpraphat Road, tel. (053) 611–486, fax 611–533; 40r, restaurant, coffee shop.

Mae Hong Son Resort, 24 Ban Huai Dua, tel. (053) 611–406, fax 251–135; 40r, restaurant, coffee shop, bar, shops, travel agent.

Mae Sot

★★

Mae Sot Hill Hotel, 100 Asia Road, tel. (055) 532–601–8 (reservations in Bangkok: 541–1071); 114r, restaurant, coffee shop.

Baedeker Special

Sabai, sabai!

Kurt Wachtveitl celebrated his 60th birthday in a manner befitting the man who for so many years has been the director of the legendary *Oriental Hotel.* According to insider reports, no fewer than 1000 guests turned up to pay their respects – among them members of the Thai royal family, who fully recognie the achievements of this man from the Allgauer Alps in Germany. For no fewer than nine years the *Oriental* in Bangkok enjoyed the reputation of being the world's no. 1 luxury hotel – an accolade which can be considered very much a personal triumph for Wachtveitl. Other hotels may have subsequently overtaken the *Oriental*; but for visitors to the Thai capital, there is no question that the most sought-after address is that of the hotel where such famous authors as Somerset Maugham and Joseph Conrad resided. And for those who can afford it there are the six VIP suites named after these and other eminent writers.

However, Bangkok can also boast a number of other hotels which, in terms of comfort and atmosphere, yield few if any points to the *Oriental.* Visitors, for example, wishing to escape the stresses of a bustling and chaotic capital city will probably find an oasis of peace and tranquillity in the *Siam Intercontinental* on the Rama I Road, with its 400 rooms grouped in a semi-circle around the swimming pool and its 12ha/30 acres of parkland, including a jogging track and practice golf course.

No less luxurious are the hotels to be found in the beach resorts lining the coast of the Gulf of Siam. As an antidote to the hectic night life of Pattaya, what better than the *Royal Cliff Beach Resort*, reputed to be the best beach hotel in South-East Asia, whose general manager, Alois X. Fassbind, is an equally illustrious name within the Thai hotel industry. Carefully distancing himself from the nearby resort's slightly dented reputation, he describes his group of four hotels on a single site as being "in the vicinity of Pattaya". The most opulent part of the *Royal Cliff* is the Royal Wing with its 86 suites, in which breakfast is prepared for visitors in their room by their own personal butler.

Further along the coast road in a south-easterly direction are the beach resorts of the future: for example, Rayong, just 200km/125 miles from Bangkok, where large numbers of luxury hotels and apartments have sprung up in the last few years. Visible over a considerable distance is the massive tower-block of the *P.M.Y. Beach Resort* with its 165 spacious bedrooms and a roof restaurant on the 19th floor.

On the opposite side of the Gulf of Siam visitors seeking somewhere quieter will find the much smaller resort of Hua Hin, which over the last few years has merged with the neighbouring village of Cha Am. Hua Hin is famous among Thais for being the favoured holiday resort of King Bhumibol, who chooses to spend the summer months here, where the cool sea breezes provide welcome relief from the prevailing heat. The most luxurious hotel here is the long-established *Sifitel Central Hua Hin*, the former Railway Hotel, which possesses its own beach of fine sand and is particularly suitable for families with small children.

In just the last ten years the number of hotel beds in Thailand has multiplied rapidly and there is no end in sight to the building boom. The erstwhile back-packer who has fond memories of the island of Koh Samui would scarcely believe his eyes if he were to visit the island today. A room with breakfast *en famille* for 35 baht? Forget it! The island now consists of row upon row of hotels and the tourist now being wooed is one seeking luxury accommodation and with the financial means to pay for it. In return he will be offered a full range of popular leisure facilities – in particular water-sports. No expense spared in the cause of the Thai dictum "Sabai, sabai!" which roughly translated means "to have a feeling of well-being".

The upmarket establishments on the island of Phuket include the *Phuket Yacht Club*, a high-quality luxury development of only 108 rooms, built into the cliffs, which overlooks terraces large enough to be able to dance on. Just a few kilometres away at Krabi lies the *Dusit Rayavadee*, which can only be reached by boat. Each bungalow here stands within its own grounds and is fitted out in the local style with heavy wooden furniture, as well as having every conceivable facility.

Leaving aside Pattaya, Phuket, Koh Samui and Hua Hin, by heading into the interior of the country the visitor is likely to find the sort of simple hotels originally

Hotel Royal Cliff in Pattaya

built merely to provide serviceable accommodation for people travelling on business. Now, with tourists going inland actively to seek out Thailand's rich cultural heritage, faded hotels of yesteryear are being refurbished and new ones built. The friendliness of the personnel in these establishments often more than makes up for any shortcomings in facilities and comfort.

One hotel with its own unique qualities is the *Hmong Hilltribe Lodge* high up in the mountains above Chiang Mai. To create this "hotel", Diethelm Travel, the leading travel operator in Thailand bought up a complete village belonging to the Hmong, one of the mountain peoples, but then left it more or less in its original condition. There is no electricity here, the evening buffet being served by torchlight. Even the means of access to the hotel is out of the ordinary: as there are no made-up roads, guests have to change to special vehicles able to negotiate the local terrain. Staying here is only possible by booking one of the special north Thailand tours arranged by Diethelm.

In Chiang Mai itself the *Dusit Inn* enjoys an excellent reputation, while the *Rincome Hotel*, pleasantly situated some distance away from the town centre, can also be recommended.

Even further north, in the world-famous "Golden Triangle", is the *Delta Golden Triangle Hotel*, situated right at the point where Thailand shares its borders with Laos and Myanmar (Burma).

The north-eastern corner of Thailand has only been opened up to tourism in the last few years; the quality and standard of comfort to be found in the hotels in this region, therefore, tend not to be comparable with those in other places, for example, the capital Bangkok. However, with more and more visitors eager to explore the historical and cultural riches which Thailand has to offer, it is only a matter of time before these areas are also able to provide a high standard of accommodation.

It would be a fallacy, however, to suggest that Thailand only caters for the well-off visitor. Guest houses offering cheap accommodation are in plentiful supply. The modest prices charged will often include a Thai breakfast and hospitality on an *en famille* basis.

Nakhon Phanom
★★
The Mae Nam Kong Grand View, 527 Sunthon Wichit Road, tel. (042) 513–564–73, fax 511–037; 114r, restaurant.

★
Nakhon Phanom, Aphiban Banchan Road, tel. (042) 511–455, fax 511–071; 79r, restaurant, coffee shop, discothèque, swimming pool, golf, shops.

Nakhon Ratchasima
★★★★
Golden Valley Resort, 188 Mu 5 Tharat Road, tel. (in Bangkok) 259–7382–5; 86r, restaurant, bar, swimming pool, fitness room, hairdressing salon, travel agent.

★★★
Juldis Khao Yai Resort, Thanarat Road (at kilometre 17), reservations only possible in Bangkok: tel. 235–2414–21, App. 71129; 56r, restaurant, coffee shop, bar, swimming pool, tennis court.

★★
Chomsurang, 2710/1–2 Mahadthai Road, tel. (044) 257–081–9; 168r, restaurant, coffee shop, swimming pool.

Nakhon Sawan
★★
Pimarn, 605/244 Asia Road, tel. (056) 222–473, fax 221–253; 140r, restaurant, coffee shop, bar, discothèque, swimming pool, hairdressing salon.

Nakhon Si Thammarat
★
Khanab Nam Diamond Cliff Resort, Nai Phlao Beach, tel. (075) 341–518; 25r, restaurant, swimming pool.

Nai Plao Bay Resort, 51/3 Mu 8, Tambon Khanom, tel. (075) 529–039; 20r, restaurant.

Nan
★
Thewarat, 466 Sumonthewarat Road, tel. (054) 710–094, 710–212; 165r, restaurant, coffee shop, bar, travel agent.

Narathiwat
★
Grand Garden, 104 Arif-Makkha Road, tel. (073) 611–868, fax 613–500; 129r, restaurant, coffee shop, discothèque, swimming pool, hairdressing salon.

Family, 18/1 Charoenmakkha Road, tel. (073) 611–200; 132r, restaurant, coffee shop, bar, swimming pool, hairdressing salon.

Pattani
★
My Gardens, 8/28 Charoenpradit Road, tel. (073) 348–933, fax 348–200; 135r, restaurant, coffee shop, discothèque, hairdressing salon.

Pattaya
★★★★★
Dusit Resort, 240 Pattaya Beach Road, tel. (038) 425–611–3, fax 428–239; 474r, restaurants, coffee shop, bar, discothèque, night club, swimming pool, fitness room, tennis court, hairdressing salon, business center, travel agent. The hotel is situated at the north end of Pattaya Bay.

Royal Cliff Beach Resort, Cliff Road, tel. (038) 250–421–30, fax 250–511 (reservations in Bangkok: 282–0999); 843r (+ 86 Royal Wing suites). Best beach hotel in South–East Asia, in fact four separate complexes within the same area of parkland: Royal Cliff Beach Hotel, Royal Cliff Terrace Building, Royal Cliff Grand and Royal Wing. Various speciality restaurants, coffee shop, bars, discothèque, night club, several swimming pools, own beach with water–sports facilities, business center, shopping arcade, travel agent, car rental service (AVIS).

★★★★
A-One · The Royal Cruise, 499 North Pattaya, tel. (038) 424–242, fax 424–242; 200r, restaurant, coffee shop, bar, swimming pool, fitness room, tennis, hairdressing salon. The hotel was built in the shape of a ship.

Ambassador Resort Jomtien, 21/10 Sukhumvit Road (at kilometre 155 south of Pattaya), tel. (038) 254–0444; 2500r. Claims to be the largest hotel in the world – at any event a mini-town in itself. Several restaurants, bars, night clubs, swimming pools, fitness room, hairdressing salon, travel agent, car rental service.

Royal Garden Resort, 218 Beach Road, tel. (038) 428–126–7; 300r, restaurant, coffee shop, bar, swimming pool; central position.

★★★
Asia Pattaya Hotel, Cliff Road, tel. (038) 428–602, fax 423–496 (reservations in Bangkok: 215–4360); restaurants, bar, discothèque, night club, swimming pool, fitness room, tennis court, 9–hole golf course, own beach, water–sports facilities, travel agent.

Montien Pattaya, 369 Mu 9, Pattaya Klang Road, tel. (038) 428–155, fax 423–155; 320r, restaurant, coffee shop, bar, swimming pool, fitness room, hairdressing salon, shops.

Wong Amat, Pattaya–Naklua Road, tel. (038) 426–990, fax 428–599; 207r, restaurant, coffee shop, bar, swimming pool, fitness room, tennis, hairdressing salon, shops.

Siam Bayview, Pattaya Second Road, tel. (038) 423–871–7, fax 423–829; 302r, restaurant, coffee shop, bar, discothèque, swimming pool, fitness room, tennis court, hairdressing salon, shops.

★★

Cosy Beach, 400 Mu 12, Cliff Road, tel. (038) 428–818, fax 422–818; 62r, restaurant, coffee shop.

★

Island View, Cliff Road, tel. (038) 250–813, fax 250–818 (reservations in Bangkok: 249–8491); 209r, restaurant, coffee shop, bar, swimming pool, tennis court, hairdressing salon, shops.

Koh Larn Island Resort, on the island of Koh Larn, tel. (038) 428–422; 60r, restaurant, coffee shop, water–sports facilities.

Regent Marina, Beach Road, North Pattaya, tel. 428–015, fax 423–296; 210r, restaurant, coffee shop, bar, swimming pool, golf course, shops.

Sea Breeze, 347 Jomtien Beach, tel. 231–056–9, fax 231–059; 105r, restaurant, coffee shop, bar, swimming pool, hairdressing salon, shops.

Phangnga

★★

Phang Nga Bay Resort (on the island of Koh Panyee), tel. (076) 411–201–70, fax 412–057 (reservations in Bangkok: 216–2882); 90r, restaurant, coffee shop, bar, swimming pool.

Phitsanulok

★

Amarintr Nakhon, 3/1 Chao Phraya Road, tel. (055) 258–588, fax 258–945 (reservations in Bangkok: tel. 235–7399); 130r, restaurant, coffee shop, bar, discothèque.

Pailyn Hotel, 38 Boromtrailokanat Road, tel. (055) 252–411–5, fax 258–983 (reservations in Bangkok: 215–7110); 240r, restaurant, coffee shop, bar, discothèque, fitness room, hairdressing salon, shops.

Rayong

★★★

Boat House Inn and Restaurant, 2/2 Mu 2, Kata Beach, tel. (076) 215–185, fax 381–561; 36r, restaurants, bar, swimming pool, hairdressing salon.

Club Andaman Beach Resort, 77/1 Thaweewongse Road, Patong Beach, tel. (076) 340–530, fax 340–527 (reservations in Bangkok: 270–1627); 128r, restaurants, coffee shop, bar, swimming pool, fitness room, tennis court, business center, travel agent.

Club Méditerranée, 7/3 Mu 2 Tambon Karon, Kata Beach, tel. (076) 214–830–1, fax 381–460 (reservations in Bangkok: 253–9780); 300r (bungalows), restaurants, coffee shop, bar, discothèque, swimming pool, fitness room, golf course.

Coral Beach, 104 Mu 4, Patong Beach, tel. (076) 340–106–12, fax 340–115 (reservations in Bangkok: 252–6087); 200r, restaurants, coffee shop, bar, night club, discothèque, swimming pool, fitness room, tennis court, hairdressing salon, shops.

Karon Beach Resort, 27 Rasada Road, tel. (076) 381–527–8, fax 381–529 (reservations in Bangkok: 214–4538); 80r, restaurant, coffee shop, bar, swimming pool, shops.

Le Meridien Phuket, 8/5 Mu 1, Karon Noi Beach, tel. (076) 321–480–5, fax 321–438 (reservations in Bangkok: 254–8147–50) 470r, restaurants, coffee shop, bar, night club, discothèque, swimming pool, fitness room, tennis court, hairdressing salon, shops.

The Phuket Yacht Club Hotel & Beach Resort, 23/3 Viset Road, Nai Harn Beach, tel. (076) 381–156–63, fax 381–164 (reservations in Bangkok: 254–4264–5); 108r, restaurants, coffee shop, bar, swimming pool, private beach, fitness room, tennis court, hairdressing salon, shops.

Rayong

★★★

Ban Pae Cabana, 205/7 Mu 3, Tambon Klaeng, tel. (038) 280–1820, fax 280–3648; 35r, restaurant, coffee shop, swimming pool.

Sukhothai
★★
Pailyn Hotel, Jarodvithithong Road, tel. (055) 613–311–5, fax 613–317; 238r, restaurant, coffee shop, swimming pool.

Surat Thani
★
Siam Thani, 180 Surat–Phunphin Road, tel. (077) 391–0280, fax 282–169 (reservations in Bangkok: 271–0924–5); 170r, restaurant, coffee shop, bar, swimming pool, tennis court, shops.

Surin
★
Tarin Hotel, tel. (044) 514–281–8, fax 511–580; 243r, restaurant/coffee shop, bar, discothèque, swimming pool.

Ubon Ratchathani
★
Pathumrat, 337 Chayangkool Road, tel. (045) 241–501, fax 243–792; 168r, restaurant, coffee shop, bar, discothèque, swimming pool.

Yasothon
★
Yot Nakhon, 141–143/1–3 Uthai–Ramrit Road, tel. (045) 711–112; 75r, restaurant, coffee shop.

Information

In Thailand

The Tourism Authority of Thailand (TAT) operates an information service from offices in Bangkok, at the international airports, and in the main resorts. As well as supplying useful brochures, etc. (either free or for a nominal charge) TAT offices will also try to help resolve any specific problems which visitors may encounter.

Tourism Authority of Thailand (TAT)
Head Office: 372 Bamrung Muang Road, Bangkok 10100
Tel. (02) 226 0060, 226 0072, 226 0085, 226 0098
Open: Mon.–Fri. 8.30am–4.30pm, Sat. 8.30–noon

Branches

All other branches are open Mon.–Fri. 8am–4.30pm.

Cha-Ama

500/1 Phetkasem Road; tel. (032) 471005

Chiang Mai

105/1 Chiang Mai-Lamphun Road; tel. (053) 213666

Chiang Rai

Singhaclai Road; tel. (053) 717 433

Hat Yai

1/1 Soi 2 Niphat Uthit 3 Road; tel. (074) 243747, 238518, 231055

Kanchanaburi

Saeng Chuto Road; tel. (034) 511200

Khon Kaen

Salaprachakhom, Klang Muang Road; tel. (043) 244498, 244499

Nakhon Ratchasima

2102–2014 Mittraphap Road; tel. (045) 243770, 243771

Nakhon Si Thammarat

1180 Ratchadamnoen Road; tel. (075) 356 356

Pattaya

382/1 Chaihat Road, Pattaya South; tel. (038) 428750, 429113

Phitsanulok

209/7–8 Surasi Trade Center, Boromtrailokanat Road; tel. (055) 252742, 2550743

Phuket

73–75 Phuket Road; tel. (076) 212213, 211036

Surat Thani

5 Talat Mai Road, Ban Don; tel. (077) 282 828

Ubon Ratchathani

264/1 Khuan Thani Road; tel. (053) 248604, 248607

"Yellow telephones"

In Bangkok telephones in conspicuous yellow kiosks have been installed at places frequented by tourists (e.g., the Grand Palace, Patpong Road and Don Muang Airport). Callers are connected with English-speaking staff at the TAT office immediately on lifting the receiver without the need to dial. This service, which operates between 8.30am and midnight, can also handle emergency calls. If these telephones are successful there are plans to install similar ones, connected to the nearest TAT branch, at important tourist locations throughout the whole country.

Travel documents

See entry

Insurance

Visitors are strongly advised to ensure that they have adequate holiday insurance, including cover against illness, accident, etc., loss or damage to luggage, loss of currency and jewellery and, particularly if a package holiday has been booked, cancellation insurance.

Arrangements can be made through a travel agent or an insurance company. Many companies operating package holidays now include insurance as part of the deal.

Language

Learning the Thai language is probably beyond the scope of the average visitor to Thailand (see Facts and Figures, Language). There are, however, some words which are fairly easy to pronounce or which will not be misunderstood even if given the wrong intonation. We should not underestimate the positive effect that, for instance, the customary greeting of *sa-wut-dee* or the courtesy phrase *mai pen rai* (it doesn't matter) will have on the person with whom we are seeking to make contact – making it clear that as *farang* (foreigners) we are keen to understand the country and embrace its culture.

Transliteration

A "European" method of writing down Thai words and names can vary considerably, depending on whether the transcriber attempts to follow a system of letters or sounds. The latter method will be affected by the target language of the transcriber, with a German speaker inevitably choosing a different transliteration from an English speaker. That is why even in Thailand it is possible to see many different versions of the names of people and towns, not to mention roads and buildings. The same is likely to be true of this guide-book, although an attempt has been made to make the transliteration as consistent as possible. Nevertheless, a visitor must be prepared for different spellings depending on where he is. Examples:
(Wut Phra) Khaeo (temple name): Kheo, Keo
Koh (island): Ko, Kho
Prasad (temple building): Prasat
Ratchadamnoen (street name): Rajadamnoen, Rachadamnern

Pronunciation

The most important thing first: "r" is almost always pronounced as "l"; e.g. "rai" will always be pronounced "lai".

Ph, th, ch are pronounced like p, t, k but followed by a definite breath; p, t, k are pronounced without this breath following and sound rather like b, d, g.

W is pronounced rather gently, like an English "wh".

Ae, oe indicate a vowel mutation. For an English "ch" sound there are various spellings: ch, j, tch (see above for Ratchadamnoen).

Form of address

The word *koon* is normally placed before any form of address, usually following the first name. *Koon nai* is used if an older lady is being addressed, *koon nuh* if it is a younger one. The word *koor* is followed by the courtesy word *kaa*, if a female person is speaking, *kaap* if a male person is speaking.

Phrases	yes	kaa(p)
	no	plao or mai chai
	please	chui
	thank you	korp koon ka
	(form of address)	koon
	hello	sa-wut-dee (at any time of day)
	What are you called?	Koon choi arai
	sorry	mai pen lai, ka
	Where is . . .?	Tee nai . . .?
	Can you help me?	Koon choo-ee koon dai mai?
	What's the time?	Kee mong, koon ka?
	Do you speak English?	koon poot pah-sah ung-grit bpen mai
	I do not understand	mai khao jai
	I do not speak Thai	poot pah-sah thai mai phen!
	How much is that?	ni rah-kha tao-rai?
	It is too expensive	mai pairng mahk mahk!
	The bill, please	khep dang! / check bin!
	May I take a photo?	Thai roob dai mai?
Transport	bus	rodmay
	bus station	satahnee rodmay
	railway	rod fai
	railway station	satahnee rod fai
	airport	sanahm bin
	boat / ship	rew-hah
	car	rod yon
	street	thanon
	side-street	soi
	What's the name of this street?	Thanon nee arai?
	left	sai
	right	khwa
	straight on	trong pai
	fast	leyo leyo
	slow	chah chah
Accommodation	hotel	rohng rairm
	room	hong
	Do you have a room free?	Khan mee hong wang mai?
Days of the week	Monday	wun jun
	Tuesday	wun ung-kahn
	Wednesday	wun poot
	Thursday	wun pa-reu-hut
	Friday	wun sook
	Saturday	wun sao
	Sunday	wun ah-tit
Food and drink	breakfast	ahan chow
	lunch	ahan klangwahn
	dinner	ahan yen

soup	soob/keng
salad	yahm
pork	moo
beef	woo-a
steak	satek
chicken	gai
fish	pla
lobster	kang
crab	booh
noodles	bah
rice	kow
dessert	khong wahn

Not too hot, please	mai sai prik
chili powder	prik bon
fish sauce (with spices)	nahm pla
salt	goo-a
sugar	nahm dahn

Times of day

morning	chao
midday	tiang
evening	yen
today	wun nee
yesterday	wahn nee
tomorrow	proong nee

Numbers

1	neung	11	sip-et
2	sorng	12	sip-sorng
3	sahm	13	sip-sahm
4	see	14	sip-see
5	hah	15	sip-hah
6	hok	16	sip-hok
7	jet	17	sip-jet
8	bpairt	18	sip-bpairt
9	gao	19	sip-gao
10	sip	20	yee-sip

21	yee-sip-et	50	hah-sip
22	yee-sip-sorng	100	roy neung
23	yee-sip-sahm	200	sorng roy
30	sahm-sip	300	sahm roy
31	sahm-sip et	500	hah roy
33	sahm-sip-sorng	1000	pun
40	see-sip	0	soong

Thai language courses

American University Alumni Association (AUA)
179 Ratchadamri Road; tel. 252 8170–3
Inlingua School of Languages
22 Ploenchit Road; tel. 254 7028
Nisa Thai Language School
27 Sathon Thai Road; tel. 286 9323

Libraries

There are several libraries in Bangkok where literature about Thailand, its history, culture and people, can be found. The universities of Bangkok and Chiang Mai also possess reference libraries with literature in English (open to tourists).

Bangkok

British Council Library, Siam Square; tel. (02) 252 6111
Open: Tues.–Fri. 10am–7pm, Sat. 10am–5pm

American University Alumni Association, 179 Ratchadamri Road; tel. (02) 252 8170
Open: Mon.–Fri. 8.30am–6pm, Sat. 9am–1pm

Alliance Française, 29 South Sathorn Road; tel. 213 2122
Open: Mon.–Fri. 8am–7.30pm, Sat. 8am–6pm

National Library of Thailand
Samsern Road (near Tha Thewes Market)
Open: Mon.–Sat. 9am–4.30pm

Chiang Mai

Alliance Française
138 Jarernprathet Road; tel. (053) 235277

British Council
198 Bumrungrad Road; tel. (053) 242103

Chiang Mai University
Huai Kaeo Road; tel. (053) 221699, ext. 4528

Lost Property

There are no official lost property offices in Thailand, even at railway and bus companies. Any articles lost and subsequently handed in can be collected from the Tourist Assistance Center (see Practical Information, Emergencies).

The level of honesty in Thailand is generally high – but as always of course there are exceptions.

Maps

As well as the map of Thailand included with this guide-book the following maps have proved their worth:

1 : 1 600 000

Thailand Highway Map (with town plans, useful telephone numbers and distance tables), produced by Highway Deparment Club / Department of Highways, Bangkok (available in Thailand)

1 : 1 500 000

Thailand World Travel Map (Bartholomew, Edinburgh)
Road map of Thailand (Freytag & Berndt, Vienna)
Road map of Thailand (Nelles Map)

1 : 1 000 000

Highway Map Thailand (official; 2 sheets)
Thailand Highway Map (Road Association of Thailand; road atlas, available in Thailand)

Various map publishers in Bangkok provide plans of parts of the country, towns and islands which are generally reasonably accurate.

"Nancy Chandler's Map"

The maps of Nancy Chandler, which are available in bookshops in the main tourist places, are beautifully drawn and provided with copious information, but as they are not drawn to scale their usefulness is limited.

Town plans

Up-to-date town plans can be obtained in Thailand at offices of TAT, the Tourism Authority of Thailand (see Information). Hotel reception desks in the large holiday resorts also provide simple town plans, generally with advertisements for shops, restaurants and places of entertainment.

Markets: Butcher . . .

. . . and lottery-ticket seller

Markets

There is probably nowhere else where typical Thai life can be better experienced than on the markets which are held every day all over the country. Generally they take place right in the middle of towns and villages. They not only provide the local population with goods of all kinds, but also serve as a place for communication and social intercourse.

Markets in Thailand are completely disorganised with the wares set out in totally haphazard fashion. Fish will be on sale next to toys, and living animals alongside plastic flowers and household goods. That, however, is what makes a Thai market so absorbing, with one's sense of smell sometimes having to take quite an onslaught.

Activity at the markets starts very early in the morning, generally before 6am. Traders often travel in the evening before and spend the night there, so as to be able to parade their goods to the very first customers. Usually trading is over by ten o'clock in the morning.

The Thai word for "market" is "talad", which is linked to the question "tee nai?" (where?), and every Thai will gladly show the visitor to the nearest market.

Massage

Traditional Thai massage has absolutely nothing to do with sex and prostitution; instead masseurs follow bona fide medical methods taught and applied all over the world. In Wat Pho, one of the oldest temple sites in Bangkok, there is a special school which instructs in the classical massage methods, a combination of "Western" massage and foot reflex-zone massage. The dexterity of the superbly trained masseurs and masseuses can reduce tension in a highly beneficial way; the Thai word for this is "sabai" – "pleasant feeling".

Where to go?

Massage is practised all over Thailand in steam-baths which are strictly segregated according to sex. Respectable masseurs (generally of the same sex as their client) will come to a hotel for a very small additional charge; this can be arranged by the hotel. Apart from that there are very few addresses which can be recommended. In Wat Pho in Bangkok (to the right of the main entrance) there are experienced masseurs available (half an hour costs 100 baht, an hour 150–200 baht). In Chiang Mai classic massage is offered in Wat Suan Dok or in the Chiang Mai Center for Traditional Massage (330 Sirimungklaian Road; tel. 221122, ext. 5422), where instruction in the skills is also provided.

Prostitution

What is more or less in effect open prostitution is known as "massage for tourists" and is available above all in the bars and "massage salons" of Bangkok and Pattaya.

Medical Assistance

Health care

Medical provision throughout the country can be described as adequate to good. The Thai health service operates on two levels: on the one hand there are modern well-equipped hospitals based on western models (especially in Bangkok and the areas which have been developed for tourism), on the other (in the country) a large number of small medical stations, generally served by just one doctor.

The doctors in Bangkok are exceptionally well trained, many having undertaken studies or professional training in Europe or the USA and able to speak English. In the country areas it cannot be assumed that health care staff will be able to speak English.

Finding a doctor

Both the hotels and the local representatives of the travel companies will arrange for a doctor to make a visit to a house or hotel in urgent cases. In the country, on the other hand, it is sometimes difficult to find a doctor. Here the first port of call should be the nearest police station which will obtain the services of a doctor or refer the visitor to the nearest hospital.

Emergency services

Emergency services in Thailand are, at least by Western standards, organised along very simple lines. As there are no rescue helicopters there is likely to be a lengthy waiting time in the event of an accident. However, in general the Thais can be relied upon to be helpful in such situations. If transport back to Europe is necessary, arrangements must be made in the home country; embassies will help with the organisation, although they cannot provide financial support.

Medical costs

The cost of medical treatment and medications must be borne by the patient. For this reason it is imperative that any traveller to Thailand should have travel insurance which covers such costs, including the considerable expense which emergency transport back to Europe can entail.

Snake bites

Serum against snake bites can be obtained in Bangkok on weekdays at the Pasteur Saovapha Institute on Saladaeng Road and on public holidays and weekends at Chulalongkom Hospital on Saladaeng Road. In the event of an accident with a snake in rural areas it is best to go straight to the nearest police station so that help can be obtained locally. There is no central emergency telephone number in such cases.

Hospitals

In Thailand there is at least one state-run hospital (S) in every provincial capital, and often a private clinic (P) as well, with doctors who will have completed at least some of their studies in Europe or the USA. In addition there are denominational hospitals (D) and certain charitable institutions

(C) which offer treatment. The following list includes the main hospitals in the important tourist centres.

Bangkok
Dialling code: 02

Bangkok Christian Hospital (D)
124 Silom Road
Tel. 233 6981–89, 24-hour ambulance service 233 6981

Bangkok General Hospital (P)
2 Soi Soonvijai 7, Petchburi Road
Tel. 318 0066, ambulance: 318 0066

St Louis Hospital (P)
215 South Sathorn Road
Tel. 212 0033–48 (24-hour ambulance service)

Bangkok Nursing Home (C)
(good maternity unit)
9 Convent Road
Tel. 233 2610–19

Bumrungrad Medical Center (P)
33 Soi Nana, Sukhumvit Road
Tel. 253 0250–69, 24-hour ambulance service 251 0415

Chulalongkorn University Hospital (S)
University hospital with special burns unit
Rama IV Road (near Dusit Thani Hotel)
Tel. 252 8381

Ramathibodi University Hospital (S)
University hospital
Rama VI Road
Tel. 246 0024, 2476 1073–99

Police General Hospital (S)
Accident hospital
Rajdamri Road (opposite Erawan Hotel)
Tel. 252 8111–20, 24-hour ambulance service 252 2171

Thai Red Cross Society (P)
1871 Rama IV Road
Tel. 252 7789, 251 6964
Specialists in snake bites (in conjunction with Chulalongkom Hospital) and inoculations for cholera, typhus, tetanus, polio, hepatitis B, encephalitis.

Chiang Mai
Dialling code: 053

Huai Kaeo Policlinic (P)
Huai Kaeo Road,
Tel. 223060
Consulting hours: Mon.–Fri. 5–8pm, Sat., Sun. 9am–5pm

Lanna Hospital (S)
Superhighway
Tel. 211037–41

Maharaj Hospital (D)
Suthep Road
Tel. 221122, 222082–85

McCormick Hospital and Policlinic (P)
Kaew Nawarat Road
Tel. 241311, 241107
Consulting hours: Mon.–Fri. 5–8pm and in emergency

Chiang Rai
Dialling
code: 053

Overbrook Hospital (P)
(opposite Chat House)
Tel. 311368

Phuket
Dialling
code: 076

Provincial Hospital (S)
Sanambin Road
Tel. 711300

Vachira Hospital (P)
Yaowarat Road
Tel. 211 114, 24-hour ambulance service 211 114

Mission Hospital (D)
4/1 Thepkasatree Road
Tel. 212 386, 211 173, 212 149

Phuket Ruam Phaet Hospital (S)
340 Phuket Road
Tel. 211 578, 212 666

Pattaya
Dialling
code: 038

Pattaya International Clinic (P)
(24-hour ambulance)
Soi 4, Beach Road
Tel. 428 374–5, 428 387

Pattayaland Dental Clinic (P)
325/61 Pattayaland soi 2
Tel. 428 928, 429 639 (Dr Visith)

Pattaya Memorial Hospital (S)
Pattaya 2 Road/Central Road
Tel. 429 422

Pattaya Nue Clinic (P)
129/1 Pattaya Klang Road
Tel. 428 876

Pattaya Rama Policlinic (P)
205/Pattaya 2nd Road
Tel. 429 662

In most of the clinics which feature above all areas of medicine are represented, from surgeons to dentists. In addition some have policlinics staffed day and night which provide an out-patients' service.

Outside the main tourist centres there are usually well-equipped out-patients' clinics, often with small medical stations with well-trained doctors attached to them. The addresses of these clinics can be obtained at the nearest police station or from local people.

Chemists — See entry

Health Precautions — See entry

Inoculations — See Health Precautions

Meditation

Meditation centres exist not only for Buddhists among the native population – visitors to the country are also welcome to attend them. It goes without saying, of course, that they should be fully prepared to get to grips with the teachings of Buddha.

Information about opportunities for meditation, as well as a list of monasteries which are open to foreigners, can be obtained at the World

Fellowship of Buddhists in Bangkok (33 Sukhumvit Road, between Soi 1 and Soi 3; open: Mon.–Fri. mornings). This organisations regularly offers evening sessions with practice in meditation and lectures by Buddhist monks. A further source of information is the Buddhist Promotion Center of Thailand in Bangkok (tel. 281 2139).

Meditation centres

Several of the meditation centres in Thailand have gained renown beyond the country's borders. These include the Wat Mahathat in Bangkok (one of the oldest Buddhistic universities in Thailand), the Wat Umong, the Wat Ram Poeng in Chiang Mai and the Wat Suan Mok in Surat Thani. In the Wat Mahathat people are advised to go to one of the mainly English-speaking monks in Section 5 who are geared to looking after the needs of Western visitors. In Surat Thani courses in meditation are offered each month; early application is essential. This, incidentally, is where instruction is given by the most famous monk (bikkhu) in the country, the Bikkhu Buddhadhasa, one of King Bhumibol's advisers, who is over 80 years old.

Motoring Assistance

Breakdowns

Thailand has no automobile clubs comparable to those found in Western countries and there are no emergency telephones on the roads. Drivers are consequently left to rely very much on such assistance as may be forthcoming from other road users. The best course of action for anyone whose vehicle breaks down on the road is to wave down another driver. It will not usually be long before someone stops and, apart from being very helpful, almost every Thai is of necessity something of a mechanic. If the fault cannot be rectified there and then, they are often ready to drive the motorist to the nearest garage to obtain the necessary spare part. Towing vehicles to the nearest garage is permitted.

At night the situation is much more problematic, particularly when at some distance from a town. Since robberies are not uncommon, especially on the poorly lit motorways, Thais are often reluctant to stop when they see someone waving for help in the dark. In that case the only thing to be done is to wait for the Highway Patrol (*dtum-roo-ut*).

Motor repairs

When renting a car a comprehensive list of garages which can be relied upon to carry out repairs is usually provided. All the major car manufacturers, European included, maintain service networks in Thailand and some even provide an emergency service. Most of the staff employed in these authorised repair workshops will be familiar with the English terms for the different motor accessories and spare parts.

Filling stations linked to international petroleum companies, such as Esso and Shell, often have a workshop attached where minor repairs can be effected on the spot.

Payment

When having repairs done the cost should be fixed in advance wherever possible and the progress of the work checked. Be sure to get a receipt (*bin*).

Useful words for motorists

engine	yon
brakes	haarm lor
tyres	yahng
headlights	fai
cold water	nahm yen yon
oil	mun
tool	kry-ung
check	dtroo-ut, or check
change	bplee-un
not working	see-a

A filling-station in southern Thailand

Filling stations

Fuel is readily available all over Thailand, with the major multi-national companies such as Shell, Esso, Elf, etc., all having filling stations. There are no self-service pumps. Signs on the pumps are usually in Thai so it is important to be able to explain what fuel or grade is required before filling up.

Thai words for fuel

diesel	pum num mun/sola
two-star petrol	tumma da
four-star petrol	priset or special

Fuel is mainly sold by the litre, use of the gallon measure nowadays being rare. The indicators on the pumps display the amount to be paid in whole baht only.

Fuel prices

Diesel is state subsidised and very cheap (about 6 baht a litre). Two-star and four-star petrol (international octane ratings are normal) cost about 8–10 baht a litre.

Museums

For over 150 years many of the artistic, cultural and historical treasures which had been rediscovered were brought to Bangkok and are today to be seen in the National Museum. In the 1970s the Department of Fine Arts decided on a new direction. It set up branches of the Bangkok National Museum in other parts of the country, so that important testimonies to the country's past could be kept and displayed near the place where they were discovered. Many of these small national museums have been integrated into some of the important temple sites.

The contents of many of these museums has not yet been systematically assembled, so that mere curiosities can easily find themselves next to outstanding works of art. There are still very few inscriptions or explanations in English. Sometimes, however, it is possible to meet a knowledgeable monk, particularly in museums which are attached to temples, who will be happy to show visitors around the exhibitions.

Details of museums can be found in the section Sights from A to Z under the relevant entry for the town or locality.

Visiting
Opening times

Most museums in Thailand are closed on Mondays and Tuesdays and on state and Buddhist holidays. They also charge for admission (normally a very small amount). In many museums it is forbidden to take photos and anyone not observing this rule is liable to have their film confiscated. There are usually information booklets in English available at the ticket offices, some of which are more comprehensive than others.

Bangkok

There are museums in Bangkok well worth visiting, which give a good overview of Thai history. These include the Thai Houses of Jim Thompson, which contain unique art treasures from the whole of south-east Asia, the Suan Pakkard Palace and of course the National Museum. The Kamthien House (131 Soi Asoke, Sukhumvit Road, open: Tues.–Sat. 9am–noon and 1–5pm) is also interesting, with its Thai houses over 200 years old, which were brought by the Siam Society from Chiang Mai to Bangkok. Objets d'art, tools and utensils from the whole of Thailand and further afield in south-east Asia can also be seen here.

National parks

There are 63 national parks in Thailand, scattered over the whole of the country. Many of these have only been set up in the last few years as the value of nature conservation has begun to be appreciated. Some of them, however, are maintained by private investors and are being turned into tourist attractions, which is unlikely to guarantee that they will remain unspoilt.

The national parks are primarily concerned with conserving the flora and fauna which is characteristic of a region, their role as a leisure facility being of only secondary importance. They are under the control of the Forestry Department and are managed by rangers. Simple maps showing paths and routes through the parks are available from the park offices for a small charge.

Rules of conduct

Information is given on the spot by the use of signs. Camping is only allowed at certain places. Information about this can be obtained from the park offices. Picking flowers, felling trees, hunting and fishing are forbidden and infringements are likely to be severely punished. Open fires are only permitted in designated places.

The following list features the finest of the national and nature parks. Reference to them is made in the A to Z section under the place-name given in the list.

Ang Thong	see Surat Thani
Ao Phangnga	see Phangnga
Boeng Boraphet	see Nakhon Sawan
Doi Inthanon	see Chiang Mai
Doi Pui	see Chiang Mai
Erawan (Khao Salop)	see Kanchanaburi
Hat Nai Yang	see Phuket
Kaeng Krachan	see Phetchaburi
Kaeng Tana	see Ubon Ratchathani
Khao Khiao	see Chonburi
Khao Sam Roi Yot	see Hua Hin
Khao Yai	see Pak Chong
Koh Phi Phi	see Krabi

National Parks
MYANMAR (BURMA)
LAOS
VIETNAM
CAMBODIA
MALAYSIA
Gulf of Thailand
South China Sea
Indian Ocean
Chiang Rai
Doi Luang
Nam Tok Mae Surin
Sri Lanna
Mae Yom
Chiang Mai
Doi Inthanon
Lampang
Wiang Kosai
Mae Ping
Nam Tok Chatrakhan
Udon Thani
Ramkamhaeng
Phu Kradung
Phu Phan
Thung Saleng
Nam Nao
Huai Thuat
Khlong Wang Chao
Phitsanulok
Khon Kaen
Mae Wong
Tat Ton
Nakhon Sawan
Sri Nakharin
Nakhon Ratchasima
Ubon Ratchathani
Phu Chong Na Yoi
Erawan
Khao Yai
Thap Lan
Sai Yok
Pang Sida
BANGKOK
Kaeng Krachan
Chanthaburi
Khao Sam Roi Yot
Koh Samet
Koh Chang
Laem Son
Ang Thong
Koh Surin
Khao Sok
Surat Thani
Khao Luang
Nakhon Si Thammarat
Koh Similan
Ao Phangnga
Hat Nai Yang
Koh Phi Phi
Khao Pu
Kho Lanta
Hat Chao Mai
Kho Phetra
Songkhla
Thale Ban
Tarutao
200 km
© Baedeker

Koh Samet	see Rayong
Koh Tarutao	see Satun
Lan Sang	see Tak
Phu Khai	see Saraburi
Phu Kradung	see Loei
Phu Phan	see Sakhon Nakhon
Thale Noi	see Phattalung
Thung Saleng Luang	see Phitsanulok
Thung Yai	see Kanchanaburi
Wang Takrai	see Nakhon Nayok

Newspapers and Periodicals

Local press

Three morning dailies, "The Bangkok Post", "The Nation" and the "Morning Post" are published in English, as is the evening paper "The Bangkok World". All three morning papers include coverage of world events as well as information about what's on in and around Bangkok. In the business section the current exchange rates are printed each day. As the newspapers are printed in Bangkok they are normally not available in other towns until noon at the earliest.

International press

British and other daily and weekly newspapers, periodicals and magazines are sold in drugstores in hotels and drugstores all over Thailand. They are fairly expensive, however, and often do not reach Thailand until several days after their publication.

Night Life

When reference is made to night life, generally it is the night-clubs along Patpong Road in Bangkok and those in Pattaya and Phuket which spring to mind. Yet there are also bars, night-clubs, discothèques and other places of amusement everywhere which do not have any connection with Thailand's reputation as a tourist haven for sex and promiscuity. Generally speaking the establishments advertising themselves as "pubs", "bars", "cocktail lounges" or "nightclubs" are the ones providing the sort of evening entertainment acceptable to the ordinary holidaymaker from the West. These night-spots are found mainly in the better class hotels and typically stay open until 1am. They are likely to offer dance music and jazz, while bars with piano music are also very popular.

Respectable night clubs are usually brightly lit and offer good food and live dance music with a strong Western American influence. They are usually open until 2pm, sometimes even later.

Night clubs of the more traditional kind are not difficult to find. The clientele of these clubs is predominantly Thai and the greater part of the club is usually kept in almost total darkness (waiters having to use torches). Young Thai girls, each wearing a numbered label, sit behind a glass or metal screen in a brightly-lit side room, waiting to be summoned as a dancing partner or to join a client at a table.

Coffee shops

The so-called coffee shops really come under the category of restaurants. They are quite often open right round the clock.

Massage parlours

Nobody should be under any illusions about the massage parlours of Bangkok, Pattaya and elsewhere; they have nothing to do with traditional massage and are simply a cover – not always very subtle – for prostitution.

Sex shows

Strip-tease and sex shows, pornographic films and videos abound, usually accommodated in back-street premises. The police prefer to turn a blind eye rather than try to curb this area of activity.

Opening Times

See Business Hours

Photography and Films

Thailand offers the visitor a wealth of things to photograph, so it is important to take all the necessary camera equipment, including films. These tend to be expensive in Thailand and there is no way of telling how long the shop has had them stored.

The optimum time of day for taking pictures is in the morning or afternoon (rather than the middle of the day when the sun is at its highest). A polarising filter is essential. Sea water and a salt-laden atmosphere are the worst enemies of any camera or lens, so take a supply of cleaning fluid and wipes from home. Always keep lenses covered when not in use.

Taboos

As a rule Thais enjoy having their photograph taken. If copies of the snaps are promised to the subject, the promise should unfailingly be kept. Otherwise there will be "loss of face", just about the worst thing that can happen to anyone as far as the Thais are concerned.

Visitors should accept certain taboos and respect the feelings of the population. It is quite easy to wound someone's feeling unintentionally, especially when taking photos. Monks for example are often ill at ease in the presence of a camera and any form of religious observance should be treated with suitable respect. Thais generally do not take kindly to seeing the objects of their worship doubling as stage props on holiday snaps. Clambering about on figures of Buddha, or for that matter on temple statues of any kind, is strictly forbidden and likely to result in a heavy fine.

Anyone who has the rare good fortune to meet the King and Queen, or to see them at some event, should bear in mind that no one is permitted to stand higher than the King. Intending photographers poised to take a shot from a good raised position will quickly be asked to get down – sometimes in none too gentle a tone. If infringing the rule cannot be avoided, e.g by those on a balcony or roof of a house, a symbolic gesture should be made by kneeling (see Thai Society and the Visitor).

Developing films

Slide films can be developed, if absolutely necessary, at Kodak branch in Bangkok (Phaholyothin Road, between the city and International Airport).

Airport baggage control

The X-ray equipment used for checking hand luggage at Thai airports is of German manufacture and unlikely to damage films. Should there be any doubt (particularly in the case of highly sensitive films) it is advisable to insist on a hand search being carried out instead.

Camera repairs

The following camera shops will undertake repairs:

T.K. Fotoshop, 164 Sukhumvit Road (near Soi 8), Bangkok
Apakom Shop, 44/7 Rama I. Road, Bangkok
A.V. Camera, 310/2 Silom Road, Bangkok

Police

See Emergencies

Post

By south-east Asian standards the Thai postal services are efficient and reliable. Letters, if sent by airmail (par avion), usually take about six days to reach Europe (or the USA). Unless properly marked with an airmail sticker post will go by surface mail, in which case it can take up to three months to arrive.

Post offices

The main post office in Bangkok is located in New Road (Charoen Krung) by the Oriental Hotel (see Business Hours). There are post office branches in all towns, often in the villages as well, and at all airports and in some of the large hotels.

All post offices offer poste restante services. A post office is easily recognised by the sign "Post and Telegraph Office".

Letter boxes
Hotel receptions

Letter boxes are red and in Bangkok have two openings, one for Bangkok addresses, the other for destinations outside the capital. All hotel receptions will accept mail for dispatch, sell stamps and forward mail where necessary.

Postal rates

At present postage is 8 baht for an air letter and 6·50 baht for a postcard. Registerd letters cost an extra 10 baht (any important letters should always be sent by registered mail).

Sending parcels and packets abroad

Any parcels and packets being sent abroad have to be made up in the presence of a customs official – go to the special Customs Window in the main post office. A packaging service selling all the necessary things for making up the parcel is available at the post office if required. Customs duty is not usually charged on gifts and personal items sent abroad.

The Post Office on Koh Samui

Telegrams

Most post offices will accept telegrams. Telegrams take about one day to reach Europe. There is no telegram service in the United Kingdom

Precious stones

In south-east Thailand in particular (see Chanthaburi) there are rich deposits of precious stones. Moreover the Thais are skilful goldsmiths and Thailand is after Italy the second largest producer of jewellery in the world. Stone cutters, goldsmiths and jewellery dealers from all over the world come to Bangkok in order to receive internationally recognised training at the Asian Institute of Gemmological Science.

Buying jewellery

The vast amounts of jewellery on offer can tempt the visitor to Thailand into buying something in a hurry. But it is advisable to be careful, particularly if one has no specialised knowledge. First of all check that the shop follows the strict code of practice laid down by the Tourist Authority of Thailand (recognisable by the TAT logo on the shop door) and then always insist on being given a certificate of authenticity which provides exact details of the jewellery being purchased (many dealers take a photo of the jewellery and affix it to the certificate). Only if these procedures are followed has the purchaser a chance of redress. The metal content of items of jewellery should be indicated by a hallmark. If precious stones have been cut the carat weight should also be given (the weight of all the stones should be added together).

On no account buy anything from a travelling salesman. Also never be taken in by spectacular sales demonstrations; the goods are always overpriced imitations and are virtually worthless.

Precious stones

Sapphires (in various colours), red rubies and emeralds, a green transparent variety of beryl, are all found in Thailand, less frequently, diamonds. It is possible to watch these stones actually being mined, for instance at Chanthaburi at the south-eastern tip of Thailand, and indeed this alone makes a trip to this remote region of the country worth undertaking. Prices of stones can be much more reasonable when buying at the actual mine rather than in Bangkok for example; however, to make such a purchase successfully demands a good deal of expertise.

Jade

Jade has been a popular raw material for jewellery making from earliest times. The actual jade market is in Hong Kong, but Chiang Mai is another centre for the processing of jade. There are two materials which can be called jade: "nephrite" is normally dark green (like the famous jade buddha in Wat Phra Kaeo in Bangkok), although it can also be light or medium green. Another yellowish or brown type of nephrite is called yellow jade which gets its colour from the long time it lies embedded in yellow Chinese loess soil. The jade which is available in Thailand is usually from Burma and is actually another mineral known as jadeite. Its colours range from whitish green through to green, brown, red, orange, yellow, mauve and black. The stones are often speckled and display veins of brighter colours.

Precious metal

Pure gold has 24 carat; 18 carat corresponds to a content of 18 parts gold to six parts of other metals such as copper or silver. In the case of silver the pure metal content should be at least 90%. Gold is more reasonably priced than in Europe, where the prices are usually calculated on a new basis every day, according to the stock exchange prices. Even the labour and manufacturing costs of an item of jewellery cost less. Warning: sometimes an amount for the gold content of an item is given which does not correspond to the internationally usual carat weight. In such cases it is necessary to ask for the "international weight".

Public Holidays

Holidays and festivals in Thailand are of a religious nature, commemorate important events in the history of the country or are connected with ceremonies at court. They are generally observed in a very unrestrained way. Shops, banks and municipal offices are closed. The dates of religious holidays are determined by the lunar calendar (exact dates can be obtained at the TAT), while national holidays are fixed.

Fixed public holidays

Dec. 31st/Jan. 1st

New Year's Eve and Day
The Western calendar's change of year is celebrated here with lively festivities. Visitors bring New Year gifts.

April 6th

Chakri Day
A national holiday commemorating Rama I, founder of the reigning Chakri dynasty, and all the other Chakri kings. This is the only day on which the general public can enter the pantheon of Wat Phra Kaeo in Bangkok to see the eight statues of the kings. Chakri Day also celebrates the founding of the capital Bangkok in 1782.

April 12th–14th

Songkhram Festival
This is the celebration of the traditional Thai new year which commences when the sun reaches the constellation of Aries, before the rice crop is sown. Offerings are made to monks and fish and birds are set free. Statues of Buddha are also symbolically "bathed", i.e. splashed copiously with water. In Bangkok there is a carnival-type procession, as indeed there has been in Pattaya now for many years. On the second day, and up to the end

Royal Parade

of the festival, there are "water fights" on the streets, with much throwing of water, especially by boys and girls (the water often being mixed with rice powder or even coal dust).

May 1st — Labour Day
In addition to the usual trade union rallies and the traditional offerings to monks, musical events and plays take place in Lumphini Park. These include the immensely popular "krabi", a type of comedy entertainment.

May 5th — Coronation Day
A national holiday on the anniversary of the coronation in 1959 of the reigning King Bhumibol and Queen Sirikit.

August 12th — The Queen's Birthday
Marked by Queen Sirikit's participating in various religious ceremonies and distributing gifts to monks at the Chidralada Palace and elsewhere.

October 23rd — King Chulalongkorn Day
Festival commemorating King Chulalongkorn (Rama V, grandfather of the present king) who died in 1910 and was held in great affection by his people. In Bangkok there is a parade of military cadets before the equestrian statue of King Chulalongkorn, in the square in front of the National Assembly building.

December 5th — The King's Birthday
The birthday of King Bhumibol (Rama IX, b. 1927) is celebrated with much pomp and splendour. A few days after the royal birthday the traditional sailing regatta takes place at Phuket with the King's Cup as prize.

December 8th — Prachuap Khiri Khan
The victory over the Japanese invaders is celebrated with a son-et-lumière display and a great popular festival.

December 10th — Constitution Day
The day on which Thais celebrate the introduction in 1932 of the country's first democratic constitution. Monks once again receive gifts.

Festivals with movable dates

January — Bangkok (Lumphini Park): Red Cross Day. Bazaars with hot-food stalls, displays, entertainment; traditionally attended by accredited ambassadors to Bangkok. The proceeds go to good causes.

Chaiyaphum and Surin: elephant festival

Late February/early March — Makha Bucha
This festival, which is one of the highest in Buddhism, celebrates the day when at full moon 1250 disciples gathered round to hear the teachings of Buddha. The faithful take part in evening processions around the various temples, bathed in the light of the full moon.

Saraburi
Around Wat Phra Buddhabat there is a great popular festival with folk music, traditional Thai dancing and drama and a large fair.

February — Nakhon Phanom: temple festival at That Phanom (folk music and dancing, boat races on the Mekong).

1st weekend in February — Chiang Mai: flower festival. Big procession with fantastic decorated floats. Displays with tropical flowers (incredible variety of orchids). Workshops on the theme of flowers, guided botany tours.

Chinese New Year This festival is celebrated mainly by the inhabitants of Bangkok's Chinatown where shops close for the day (some for the whole week!). All kinds of colourful entertainments take place.	Late February early March
Kite-flying season (especially beautiful on the Sanaam Luang in Bangkok).	End of February until middle of April
Mae Hong Son: Festival of Buat Luk Khaew (consecration of the beloved sons).	March
Pattaya: Pattaya Festival (originally Songkhram Festival) with water entertainments, automobile and motor-cycle races and a big popular festival.	April
Ploughing ceremony In Brahman rites grains of rice are blessed and scattered as lucky charms to farmers who come to Bangkok from all over the country. High ranking public figures in white and gold form a procession on the Sanaam Luang in Bangkok with the plough, symbol of a rich harvest, and pass before the king and his royal guard.	May
Visakha Bucha (a public holiday throughout Thailand) is the highest Buddhist festival, celebrating his birth, his Enlightenment and his entry into Nirvana. It is celebrated with candlelit processions and temple festivals.	Full moon in May
Yasothon: the rocket festival of Boon Bang Fai. During the festival home-made rockets are fired, to ask the rains to come. There is also popular theatre and folk dancing.	Middle of May
Chiang Rai: lychee festival Loei: the festival of Phi Ta Khon, which commemorates the return to the town of Prince Vessandom, the last incarnation of Buddha. The welcoming procession was so beautiful that even the spirits (phi) joined in the celebrations. In memory of this legend young men masquerade as spirits, carry a holy Buddha statue and make fun with the onlookers.	June
Asanrha Bucha Festival commemorating Buddha's first teachings delivered to five initial disciples. Ceremonies and processions again take place all over Thailand on the night of the full moon.	Full moon in July
Khao Pansa The beginning of the Buddhist period of fasting. Particularly attractive is the way the festival is celebrated in Ubon Ratchathani, where giant, beautifully carved wax candles are carried in a procession.	July
Surat Thani Festival of the twin plums (Rambutan).	August
Nakhon Pathom: harvest festival with flowers and fruit procession, cooking displays and many other entertainments.	September
Kamphaeng Phet: Khluai Khai (banana festival). The best bananas in Thailand come from here. The end of the harvest is marked by a large celebration.	
Phuket: vegetarian festival (end of September, early October): Thais of Chinese descent become vegetarians for a week with many restaurants adapting specially to this change of diet. There are processions and occult demonstrations (men in trances running across glowing charcoal).	
Chonburi: water-buffalo races.	October

One of the finest Thai festivals: the Loy Kratong Festival of Lights

Sakhon Nakhon: festival of the wax castle to mark the end of the Buddhistic rainy season seclusion. Miniatures of temples in beeswax are carried in a procession and boat races are organised.

Late October/ early November

Thot Kathin:
This is the end of the three-month Buddhistic period of fasting. During these days the country people celebrate the end of the rainy season and conclude the main rice harvest. Monks are given new robes and the King visits Wat Arun in Bangkok. Since their restoration he now uses the royal barges for spectacular parades on the Menam Chao Phraya. The magnificently colourful boat races in Phra Pa Daeng (opposite Paknam) and Phitsanulok are especially worth seeing.

November

Loy Kratong
One of the most beautiful of all Thai festivals. Thousands of little banana and lotus leaf rafts carrying lighted candles, incense sticks, lotus blossom and often a few coins are set adrift on the rivers and canals, a myriad of tiny lights flickering beneath the full moon. Although actually a Festival of Lights dedicated to Mae Kongka, Goddess of the Waterways, Thais also associate it with the story of a princess who, as evening fell, would send little boats with lighted candles floating across the Menam Chao Phraya to her beloved. Sukhothai (with fireworks and folk dancing) and Chiang Mai are particularly good places to witness the festival but it is worth seeing in Bangkok too. In Bang Sai (near Ayutthaya) the Thai longboat championships are held on the Chao Phraya.

Surin: Large elephant festival (Elephant Round-up) lasting several days.

Nakhon Pathom: pilgrimage to the oldest pagoda in Thailand. Large temple celebration with a fair and other entertainments.

Bangkok: Golden Mount Fair. About November 22nd bands of pilgrims make their way up to Wat Sakhet in order to pay their respects to relics of Buddha. There is a large bazaar.

Late November/ early December

Mae Sarieng: sunflower festival (end of November/beginning of December).

Kanchanaburi: River Kwai bridge week (end of November/beginning of December).

Khon Kaen: silk festival with the ritual of Phuk Sieo (ritual of friendship) (end of November).

Public Transport

Taxi

In Bangkok alone there are reckoned to be some 16,000 taxis, not including those drivers who moonlight. Taxis, however, also have an important role to play in the country. Many taxis possess a moderately effective air-conditioning system. 99% of taxis run on environmentally friendly liquid gas.

Simply hail a taxi from the kerb – at least half a dozen will invariably pull up. Taking advantage of the competition to bargain over the fare can result in a cheap ride. If the price demanded seems too high, simply hail another cab. Be sure, however, to choose one that is insured – look for the disc on the windscreen marked with the current year (the Buddhist year, remember, e.g. 1993 + 543 = 2536).

Taxis can be ordered by telephone. Bangkok is divided into four zones and their numbers can be found under "Taxi Service" in the "Yellow Pages" or obtained in the nearest hotel or restaurant.

Waiting rickshaw-drivers in the country

In recent years taxis have frequently been fitted with meters although these were quite often just a sham. Now new taxi meters are being introduced in Bangkok. These taxis are recognisable by their green and yellow colours and the sign "Taxi Meter" on the roof; they are licensed and adequately insured. At the present time there are 16 taxi ranks in Bangkok (mainly at the large hotels and shopping centres). The first 2km cost 35 baht, the 3rd km 5 baht, the 4th–6th km 4·50 baht, and from 7km each additional kilometre costs 3·50 baht (therefore less than normal taxis where the cost needs to be settled in advance). Every minute which is spent in a traffic jam, however, costs 1 baht.

Limousines

The majority of hotels have their own limousine service. The cars operate from the front of the hotel and can be hired by anyone. Limousines are expensive but they are well cared for, air-conditioned and are certain to be insured. The fares are fixed and bargaining is possible only for longer excursions.

Airport taxi

Thai Airways International runs its own taxi service catering for transfers to and from the airport. Reservations and bookings can be made at the airline's offices, at the airports, or in any of the larger hotels.

Shared taxis (pickups)

The so-called "pickups" operate mainly in resorts such as Pattaya, though they are also found in the north of the country. They are shared taxis which usually make regular runs along a particular route, taking anyone who catches the driver's attention in time. Fares can be extremely cheap. On request pickups will deliver holidaymakers right to their hotel (but agree on a price first)

Tuk-tuks or samlors

A ride in one of the innumerable open three-wheeled samlors, also known as tuk-tuks, costs about half as much as a taxi and is infinitely more interesting. Since bicycle rickshaws were abolished in the cities a number of years ago (although they are still to be found in the country), samlors have come to dominate Bangkok's streets. No matter how impossible it may seem to get through the traffic, the fearless tuk-tuk driver will always find a way (though the well-being of his passengers may not always appear paramount in the process). Tuk-tuks with their noisy two-stroke engines not only transport tourists on their sight-seeing but children to school and traders to market. In the evening whole families drive out in them. A tuk-tuk ride in Thailand is a never-to-be-forgotten experience and one that should definitely not be missed.

River boats

Boat traffic on the Menam Chao Phraya is as important today as it always has been, especially as a link between the "new" capital Bangkok and the one-time capital Thonburi on the opposite bank. Thousands of people ranging from school children to market traders use water transport every day. Altogether there are sixteen piers or landing-stages in Bangkok. The word for them is "taa", followed by the particular location (e.g. "Taa Orientään", Oriental Hotel Pier). Make sure the boatman knows your destination in good time as they only stop on request. The boats operate from 6am to 8pm.

River taxis

River taxis can be rented by the hour, the best place in Bangkok being the pier beside the Oriental Hotel. A trip on one of these river taxis through Thonburi's ancient klongs is particularly recommended (negotiate the price).

Buses

See Rail and Bus

Radio and Television

Radio

All the larger cities have their own radio stations and in general channels transmitted from Bangkok can also be picked up. The news is given on some channels in English. In Pattaya and on Phuket there are English-language local radio stations which broadcast light music and world news.

Television

Four television stations – one of them the official voice of the military – transmit nationwide. Some programmes are broadcast in English. Daily papers carry previews of the day's programmes (see Newspapers and Periodicals).

In many of the big hotels an information service (similar to video text) is provided on the closed-circuit TV system installed in every room.

Rail and Bus

Rail

Railway stations and distances from Bangkok (km/miles)

Northern Line: Bangkok – Bangkok International Airport (22/14) – Bang Pa In (58/36) – Ayutthaya (71/44) – Lopburi (133/83) – Ban Takhli (193/120) – Nakhon Sawan (246/153) – Taphan Hin (319/198) – Phichit (347/216) – Phitsanulok (389/242) – Uttaradit (485/301) – Sila At (488/303) – Den Chai (534/332) – Mae Mo (609/378) – Lampang (642/399) – Khun Tan (683/424) – Lamphun (729/453) – Chiang Mai (751/467).

South-eastern Line: Bangkok – Hua Takhe (31/19) – Chachoensao (61/38; branch line goes off here to Sattahip 196/122) – Prachinburi (122/76) – Kabinburi (161/100) – Aranyaprathet (255/158).

Eastern Line: Bangkok – Don Muang Airport (22/14) – Ayutthaya (71/44) – Ban Phachi – Saraburi – Kaeng Khoi (from here a branch line goes off north-east to Nong Khai) – Muak Lek (152/94) – Pak Chong (180/112) – Nakhon Ratchasima (264/164) – Thanon Chira – Lam Phai Mat – Buriram – Surin (420/261) – Sikhoraphum – Si Saket (515/320) – Ubon Ratchathani (575/357).

North-eastern Line: (Branch line from the Eastern Line at Nakhon Ratchasima): Bua Yai (346/215) – Ban Phai (408/254) – Khon Kaen (450/280) – Udon Thani (569/354) – Nong Khai (624/388).

Southern Line: Bangkok – Thonburi – Nakhon Pathom (64/40; branch line from here to River Kwai Bridge) – Ratchaburi (117/73) – Phetchaburi (167/104) – Hua Hin (229/142) – Prachuap Khiri Khan (318/198) – Chumphon (485/301) – Lang Suan – Surat Thani (651/405) – Thung Song (773/480) [Trang (845/525), Nakhon Si Thammarat (832/517)] – Phatthalung (862/536) – Hat Yai (945/587) – Yala (1055/656) – Sungai Kolok (1159/720; border crossing to Malaysia). At Hat Yai connection to Padang Besar, Butterworth and Kuala Lumpur, at Sungai Kolok for Singapore.

Sleeping-cars and couchettes

On all four railway lines the night trains have 1st and 2nd class sleeping and couchette cars (reserve in advance). Reservations for sleeping and couchette cars must be remade if there is a change of travel plans.

Tickets

Fares are very low, a rail ticket from Bangkok to Chiang Mai 1st class, for example, costing about £12 (supplement for a single compartment in a 1st sleeping-car about £7.50). Couchette cars cost half as much as sleeping-cars. Supplements also have to be paid when travelling on express and fast trains. Children from three to twelve years of age pay half price. Tickets can be bought at the earliest 90 days before the start of the journey. Breaking one's journey is not possible.

Special journeys

The Thai State Railways (SRT) run regular special excursions and also organise group trips by train.

Thailand Railway Pass

The Thailand Railway Pass entitles the holder to any number of train journeys throughout the whole of the rail network. It is valid for three weeks and costs about £45 2nd class. These special tickets are only obtainable at the main Hualampong station in Bangkok.

Rail and Bus

Information

At all stations there are information and reservation counters (open: Mon.–Fri. 8.30am–6pm, Sat., Sun. and holidays 8.30am–noon).

Buses

Buses are probably the most important means of transport in Thailand, both for short and long distances; they can reach even the most inaccessible places. Bus is the cheapest option when travelling through Thailand, and moreover the best way of experiencing the warmth and friendliness of the people. Besides the state-run bus companies, which cover the most important routes, there are also countless private operators.

As both routes and departure times can be altered from time to time, it is best to buy a current timetable when actually in Thailand. The only timetable that can be considered in any way binding is that issued for the state-run buses, as private companies tend to operate according to demand. Their buses will stop for people standing on the roadside who gain their attention by hailing them.

Service buses

Regular service buses (*rohtmay tamadah*) normally only have air-conditioning near the driver which only cools the front portion of the bus.

Air-conditioned buses (*rohtmay dew-en*) are much more comfortable but dearer, although generally faster.

Tickets

Tickets can either be bought at the bus terminals (see list below) or on the bus from the driver. Fares are very low (e.g. Bangkok – Chiang Mai, about 700km/435 miles, under £6).

Bangkok

Southern Bus Terminal (Dai), Nakhonchaisi Road
Aircon Buses: tel. (02) 435 1199; normal buses: tel. (02) 435 1199
Buses to Hua Hin, Nakhon Si Thammarat, Surat Thani, Phuket, etc.

Northern Bus Terminal (Nya), Phaholyothin Road
Aircon Buses: tel. (02) 271 2961; normal buses: tel. (02) 271 0101–5
Buses to Chiang Mai, Sukhothai, Phitsanulok, Ubon Ratchathani.

Eastern Bus Terminal (Ekamai), Sukhumvit Road
Aircon Buses and normal buses: tel. (02) 391 2504
Buses to Pattaya, Rayong (ferry to Koh Samet), Chanthaburi, etc.

Chiang Mai

Arcade Station, Kaeo Nawarat Road
Aircon Buses: tel. (056) 242 664
Long-distance routes: Bangkok, Chiang Rai, Lampang, Phrae, Nan, Sukhothai, Nakhon Ratchasima, etc.

Chuang Puak, Chotana Road
Aircon Buses: tel. (056) 221 586
Shorter routes: e.g. Fang, Hot, Lamphun, Thaton

Hua Hin

at the entrance to the town coming from Bangkok
Buses to Bangkok, Nakhon Si Thammarat, Phuket, Surat Thani, Trat, etc.

Nakhon Ratchasima

Bus Terminal 1, Burin Road
Buses to Bangkok, Pak Chong (Khao Yai National Park), Surin.

Bus Terminal 2 (on the northern edge of the town)
Buses to Chiang Mai, Sukhothai, Phitsanulok, Lampang, Lamphun, etc.

Nakhon Si Thammarat

About 1km/½ mile south of the station on Highway 4015 (from there shared taxis into the town centre)
Buses to Bangkok, Surat Thani, Phattalung, Songkhla, Phuket, etc.

Pattaya

Beach Road (between South and North Pattaya)
Buses to Bangkok, Rayong (ferry to Koh Samet), Chanthaburi, Laem Ngob (ferry to Koh Chang), Trat.

Phuket — Phuket Road
Buses to Bangkok, Surat Thani, Nakhon Si Thammarat, Sungai Kolok (border crossing to Malaysia), Krabi, Phangnga.

Surat Thani — Bus Terminal(at Ban Don Harbour)
Buses to Bangkok, Phuket, to the Koh Samui ferry, Ranong, Phangnga, Prachuap khiri Khan, Nakhon Si Thammarat.

Ubon Ratchathani — 4km/2 miles north of the town (shared taxis to the centre)
Buses to Bangkok, Mukdahan, Nakhon Phanom, Buriram, Surin.

Restaurants

The best cooking from all over the world can be sampled in the restaurants of Bangkok and the main tourist centres. Many restaurants, particularly those in the large hotels, employ foreign staff, both chefs and managers, who enthusiastically uphold the culinary traditions of their native land. Nevertheless, traditional Thai cooking is far from taking a back seat; freshly produced products delivered from the country are the basis of a cuisine which is characterised by its light, distinctively spiced dishes (see Food and Drink).

Menus — Menus in the main tourist resorts are printed in Thai and English; if that is not the case, the visitor must try asking the people at the next table, who may speak some English, or seek the advice of the waiter.

Hot-food stalls — During the day there is no need to visit a restaurant; instead one can do as the Thais do and eat at one of the countless hot-food stalls. On no account should the visitor neglect to sample the delights of one of these; there are numerous local specialities which can only be found here. At first glance they may seem to lack proper hygiene, with the result that many tourists pass them by, but the actual food is of impeccable quality.

Variety — The following list contains merely a selection of the excellent restaurants which exist and no one should be deterred from making their own discoveries.

Bangkok

Thai cuisine

Baan Thai, Soi 32, Sukhumvit Road
Ban Nunthida, 110/26 Soi Santinives Ladprao
Bangkapi Terrace (in the Ambassador hotel)
Cabbages & Condoms, 10 Sukhumvit Road, Soi 12
Lemongrass, 5/1 Sukhumvit Road, Soi 24
Sala Rim Nam, 531/1 Charoen Nakom Road (opposite the Oriental Hotel)
Seefah Restaurant, 47/19–22 Rajadamri Road
Silom Village, 286 Silom Road (with Thai music and classical dancing)
Talad Nam, 209 Silom Road
Tum Nak Thai, 131 Ratchadapisek Road (open-air restaurant)
Whole Earth Café, 93/3 Soi Lang Suan (incl. vegetarian cooking)

Seafood

Chinese Seafood, Wall Street Tower, Surawong Road
Chom Talay (in the Central Plaza Hotel)
Cosmopolitan, 10 Sukhumvit Road, Soi 24
Lord Jim's (in the Oriental Hotel)
Royal Seafood, 50 Soi Langsuan, Ploenchit
Savoey Seafood (in the Terrace River City Shopping Center)
Seafood Bangpoo Restaurant, 199/5 Sukhumvit Road
Seafood Restaurant, 1980 New Phetchburi Road
Seafood Market, 388 Sukhumvit Road (between Soi 16 and 18)

Restaurants

Chinese cuisine	Galaxy, 19 Rama 4 Golden Gate, 392/27–30 Siam Square 5 May Flower (in the Dusit Thani Hotel; Cantonese cooking) New Great Shanghai, 648–52 Sukhumvit Road New Shangri La Restaurant, 154/4–7 Silom Road
Japanese cuisine	Benkay (in the Hotel Royal Orchid Sheraton) Canton, 488/3–6 Henri Dunant Friendship Sukiyaki, 120/171 Rajprarop Genji (in the Hotel Hilton International) Kobe Steak House, 460 Siam Square 4 Shogun (in the Dusit Thani Hotel) Sincere Sukiyaki, 392/34–38 Siam Square 7
Indian cuisine	Café India, 460/8 Surawong Road Himali Cha-Cha, 1229/11 New Road
International cuisine	Avenue One (in the Hotel Siam Intercontinental) Cosmopolitan, 4–10 Sukhumvit Road 24 Le Bistrot, Soi Ruamrudee La Brasserie (in the Regent Hotel) La Rotonde (in the Narai Hotel, revolving restaurant) Le Chancelier, 70/1 Sukhumvit Road Le Vendôme (in the Ambassador Hotel)
French cuisine	Floating Restaurant, Supakarn Shopping Complex Jazzy Queen and Oriental Queen (both in the Oriental Hotel) Salaloy Floating (in the Menam Hotel) Thalay Thong (in the Hotel Siam Intercontinental) Wan Fah, 671/3 Charansanitwong Road
Italian cuisine	Don Giovanni (in the Central Plaza Hotel) Il Colosseo, 578–580 Ploenchit Lumphini L'Opera Pizzeria, 55 Sukhumvit Road, Soi 39 Paesano, 97/7 Soi Tonson, Ploenchit Road Pan Pan, 45 Soi Langsuan Ploenchit Ristorante Sorrento, 66 North Sathorn Road Trattoria da Roberto, Patpong Soi 2
German cuisine	Bei Otto, Sukhumvit Road, Soi 20 Bier-Kutsche, Sukhumvit Road, Soi 3 (beer garden) Beer House, 6 Sukhumvit Road, Soi 23 (near Soi Cowboy)

Chiang Mai

Thai cuisine	Baan Suan Restaurant, 51/3 Chiangmai-Sankamphaeng Road Bain Garden, 2/2 Wat Gate Road Chang Puak Garden, Superhighway (opposite the National Museum) Krua Poy Luang (in the Poy Luang Hotel), 146 Superhighway Lanna Him Ping Restaurant, 28/1 Wangsingcome Road Old Chiang Mai Cultural Center, 183/5 Wualai Road (dance performances) White Elephant, 1 Soi Wat Saenfang
Seafood	Kaithong, 67 Kotchasarn Road (speciality: python steak) White Orchid River Terrace (in the Diamond Hotel), Charoenprathat Road
Chinese cuisine	Romwa Garden, corner of Rajadamnoen Road White Orchid River Terrace (in the Diamond Hotel), Charoenprathat Road
International cuisine	Captain Hook's Bar & Restaurant, 4/1 Chaiyapoom Road Chalet Restaurant & Bar, 71 Charoen Prathet Road La Grillade (in the Chiang Inn Hotel) Oak Tree Restaurant, 77/9 Kotchasarn Road

Papillon (by the station)
White Elephant, 1 Soi Wat Saenfang

Bierstube, 33/6A Munmuang Road — German cuisine
Zum Wiener, 10/5 Bumrungrad Road

Pattaya

Thai cuisine

310 Noble House Restaurant, Pattaya Beach Road
Krua Talay, 345 Jomtien Beach
Sawasdee (in the Wong Amat Hotel), North Pattaya
Siam Shark Fins, Central Road, Pattaya City
Thai Market Restaurant (in the Royal Cliff Hotel), Cliff Road

Seafood

Lobster Pot, 228 Beach Road (South Pattaya)
Villa Sea Food, Soi 7, Pattaya Beach Road
Sea Food Market Restaurant (in the Royal Cliff Hotel), Cliff Road
Numerous seafood restaurants along Beach Road

International cuisine

Bayshore Grill & Steak House (in the Siam Bayshore Hotel)
Dolf Riks, Srinakhon Shopping Center (speciality: Indonesian rice dishes)
El Toro Steak House, Pattaya 2nd Road
Orient Express (in the Nipa Lodge Hotel) Beach Road

German cuisine

Alt Heidelberg, 273 Beach Road (South Pattaya)
Bavarian Beer House, Beach Road (South Pattaya)
Bierkutsche, Beach Road (South Pattaya)
Haus München, Beach Road

Italian cuisine

La Gritta (in the Orchid Lodge Hotel)
Pan Pan, Tapraya Road, Jomtien Beach

Phuket

Thai cuisine

Hayashi Thai House, Soi Hinkao, Patak Road (Karon Beach)
Kan Eang (Chalong Bay)
Khamwaan, 64/8 Rasada Center (Phuket)
Khao Rang Restaurant, Kao Rang Hillto (Phuket)
Krua Thai, 62/7 Rasada Road (Phuket)
Krua Thai, 99/61 Uthit Road (Patong Beach)

Seafood

Lobster & Prawn, 114/28–29 Kata Center (Kata Beach)
Lucky Seafood Garden, Phuket Road, Soi Saphan Hin (Phuket)
Mai Ngam, opposite the main post office (Phuket)
Male Seafood, Beach Road (Patong Beach)
Maxim Seafood & Supermarket (Karon Beach)
Phuket Seafood, 66/2 Phuket Road, Soi Saphan hin (Phuket)

Chinese cuisine

Khaw Yaam, 1–11 Thungkah Road (Phuket)
Pearl Chinese Restaurant (in the Pearl Hotel), Montree Road (Phuket)
Sabai Sabai, 89/7 Soi Post Office (Patong Beach)

International cuisine

Buffalo Steak House, 94/25–26 Soi Patong (Patong Beach)
Boat Restaurant (Kata Beach)
Doolie's Place, 2nd Road, Soi Bangla (Patong Beach)

Italian cuisine

Babylon Italian Restaurant & Pizzeria, 93/21 Bangla Road (Patong Beach)
Vecchia Venezia Italian Restaurant, Rat Uthit Road (Patong Beach)

German cuisine

Jägerstube (Patong Beach)

Road Transport

Left-hand driving Driving is on the left throughout Thailand. For those not used to this, particular care needs to be taken on roundabouts.

Road network Thailand has a well developed network of roads. Only the national roads, which link Bangkok with all parts of the country and are officially known as Highways (motorways), can be said to fulfil European standards. Apart from a few smaller rural and mountain roads, all roads are passable even during the rainy season (June–September).

Signposts Signposts are in Thai and English, so that finding one's way presents no real difficulties. The traffic signs are the standard international ones, with a few exceptions which are easily understood.

Speed limits In built-up areas the speed limit is 60km/h (37mph), while on country roads and motorways it is normally not permitted to exceed 100km/h (62mph). The speed limit is 100km/h (62mph) on Bangkok expressways. Hardly anyone keeps to these limits, however, and driving is generally as fast as the traffic will allow. In order to combat this there are a number of radar controls around Bangkok.

Traffic in Bangkok The roads in the Bangkok city centre which generally have more than two lanes are often hopelessly congested and overtaking tends to occur on whichever lane is less busy at any given moment. Buses assume total priority for themselves and bus-stops are quite likely to be right in the middle of the road.

In the midst of this traffic chaos it is essential to watch out for pedestrians. Often in a hurry, they can weave in and out of the lines of cars without paying any regard to the traffic around them. Traffic lights often seem to

Road numbers

Signposts with distances in kilometres

have the sole function of being bright lights, and the same can be said of indicator lights. At large intersections traffic policeman endeavour to exert some sort of control over the chaos – generally in vain.

Warning: On one-way streets there are often special bus lanes on which buses are allowed to travel in the opposite direction to the prevailing traffic. Therefore, when crossing a one-way street, look carefully in both directions!

On many single-lane residential streets (Soi) there are no pavements and therefore it is important to keep a special look out for children playing, old people and invalids, as well as sleeping dogs.

Visitors are strongly advised not to venture out into the Bangkok traffic maelstrom with a hired car. Even experienced drivers have problems with the chaotic traffic conditions, which are not comparable to any to be found in Europe. Anyone wishing to avoid stress or a possible accident should travel by taxi or bus (see Public Transport).

In the country

There is certainly much less traffic on the roads outside the capital though even here the utmost care is needed when driving. It is best to collect a hire car on the edge of Bangkok.

Animals roaming loose, children playing, traders, pedestrians or even people sleeping on the roadside are all frequent occurrences. It is necessary therefore to drive in a defensive way, however unnatural this may feel, and on no account to let oneself be tempted to imitate the driving habits of the local population.

All over Thailand there is an additional danger to motorists posed by the country buses which tend to race along the highways at night and often cause serious accidents. Yet another hazard is that of the trucks, often poorly-lit or not lit at all, which go back and forth at night between Bangkok and the provinces.

The number of night-time attacks on motorists has declined, but even so the careful driver should not leave his car in the dark without a good reason.

Security

The number of crimes, thefts and robberies is no greater in Thailand than anywhere else in the world and the country can claim to be one of the safest places in south-east Asia to travel in. The Thais are basically an honest race, although there are exceptions, as there are anywhere. It is also true that crimes against personal property are often the result of undue carelessness on the part of the victim: it needs to be borne in mind that the average visitor from the West is often carrying around with him more money in cash than the average hotel employee or similar worker earns in a year.

As a general rule the visitor – and this is really a question of sensitivity – should not flaunt his affluence. The best place for items of value is the hotel safe and it is best always to carry the minimum amount of money that one could foreseeably need.

In the hotel

Most hotels provide lockers or room-safes free of charge. Larger items of value (e.g. camera cases), if not actually being carried on one's person, should be deposited in the hotel reception, as normally no liability for articles stolen from one's room can be accepted.

The room-key should always be handed in at the reception.

Travel documents

It is essential to carry two photocopies of travel documents (e.g. passport with visa entries, airline tickets). These can be of considerable assistance in recovering such items in the event of loss.

Traveller's cheques

The documentation showing proof of purchase must be kept separate from the actual cheques; otherwise the insurance protection may be invalidated.

Shopping

Credit cards (see Currency)	When paying with credit cards never let the actual card out of your sight. Destroy the carbon between the two copies of the sales voucher yourself and also check that the total on the two copies is the same. Report any lost card to the issuer immediately.
Pickpockets	Always look out for pickpockets, particularly in places where there are large numbers of tourists. The best protection is to carry cash and other valuables in a money-belt or bag worn round the neck.
Warning	The visitor is likely to be "ripped-off" or find himself involved in disputes over exorbitant bills if he ventures into places associated with Thailand's traditional night-life. He should therefore on no account let himself be importuned by touts of any kind.
Emergencies	See entry
Embassies	See Diplomatic Representation
Credit card firms	See Currency

Shopping

Bangkok, and indeed all the tourist centres (whether in the north or the south) are a real shopper's paradise. Not everything though is cheap. Imported goods such as optical and electronic equipment are heavily taxed and therefore expensive. And of course there is the familiar trash offered to tourists the world over.

Painted porcelain vases from central Thailand

Most tour guides will take their guests to stone-cutting factories, textile shops, etc. when on a city sightseeing tour or round trip and obviously they receive commission on any sales made during the course of such a visit. Buying goods under these circumstances is therefore not always a wise thing to do.

When buying any kind of appliance check that it is in the original packaging, watch it being packed up (so that the original cannot be replaced with a copy) and insist on being given a guarantee card which should be free of charge and valid worldwide.

Bargaining

Bargaining over prices is practised everywhere in Thailand, except in specialist shops and department stores. All too often the price of an article is fixed according to the presumed thickness of the would-be purchaser's wallet. Providing the visitor carries on the bargaining in a polite way and turns it into a kind of sporting contest it is possible to buy something at a significantly lower price than the one that was originally quoted. The first step is to offer about half the price asked for and from there reach a compromise. But remember: always keep the transaction good-humoured and polite.

Thai silk

It is only since the American Jim Thompson, Thai by adoption (see Introduction, Famous People), created more tasteful designs and introduced high-quality production methods that Thai silk has acquired a worldwide reputation. Although not as fine as the Chinese variety it is stronger and more reasonably priced. Every tailor's shop stocks Thai silk and anyone not wanting a garment made to measure there and then (see Clothing) can buy material by the metre. Silks in pastel shades are usually the most popular since the patterns appeal more to Western tastes in fashion. The silks, which include a small amount of man-made fibre (10–20%), have the extra advantage of being easy-care.

Masses of imitation textiles . . .

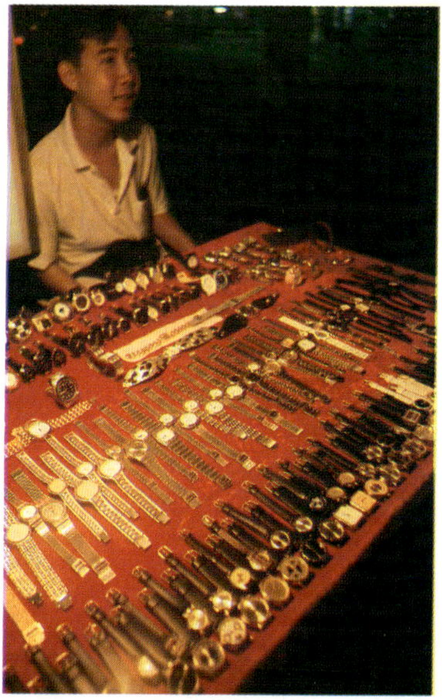

. . . and watches

Shopping

Textiles

Thailand is unquestionably the best country in south-east Asia for textiles. Many of the goods are produced specifically for the tourist trade. The imitations of products by internationally famous clothing manufacturers are undoubtedly attractive and cost a mere fraction of the originals. Be warned, however, that importing these garments into Europe in any quantity is forbidden, the originals being protected by trade legislation. Customs checks at UK airports can result in bulging tourist suitcases suddenly becoming half empty!

Carpets

Patterned hand-woven and hand-knotted carpets of Thai silk make very attractive souvenirs from Thailand. The vendor will arrange transport by sea or air to the UK.

Japanese watches

Authentic Japanese watches of well-known brands are cheaper in Thailand than in Europe. There are reliable dealers from whom they can safely be purchased (who will provide for example all the necessary guarantee and service registration forms). But beware, there are also thousands of cheap imitations, even of famous Swiss makes, which may well stop working before the end of the holiday. The manufacture of such imitations is banned in Thailand and from time to time Thai newspapers report a police raid on an illegal "factory". But even as the steam roller is about to crush the confiscated watches for the benefit of local press photographers, the counterfeiters will already be setting up shop in a new location and starting production again.

Cutlery, leather, lacquerware

Cutlery made of bronze and porcelain, typical Asian lacquerware, teak and leather goods all make attractive souvenirs.

Ivory

Since the elephant became a protected species under the Washington agreement, genuine ivory is as rare as it is expensive. With the import of ivory being banned by countries which are signatories to the agreement purchases should be confined to the quite authentic-looking imitation ivory craftwork. The same strictures apply to snake and crocodile leather as well as certain other types of animal skin.

TAT recommended shops

Shops recommended by the TAT are under constant scrutiny by the authority. These shops are easily recognised by the TAT logo. If any problems are experienced contact the tourist police or the Tourist Assistance Center (see Emergencies).

Shopping centres

The "General Department Stores", which are to be found in all the larger towns, offer a large range of goods at fixed prices and can be recommended. Addresses can be obtained from hotel receptions.

Duty-free shops

Thai International Airways has a duty-free shop in Bangkok (485 Silom Road, tel. 235 4362).

Dispatch to Europe

Normally for larger purchases, e.g. furniture, the vendor will arrange shipment to Europe and carry out all the necessary customs formalities.

Excess baggage

Most airlines allow only 20kg baggage per passenger free of charge (the exact allowance is printed on the airline ticket). Beyond this limit, applied with varying degrees of strictness, additional weight has to be paid for. This can work out very expensive because as a general rule every kilogram of excess luggage is charged at 1% of the first-class fare for the flight. Providing arrangements are made in good time, however, heavy costs like these can be avoided. All the major airlines flying to Bangkok have air-freight services and will deliver baggage to a passenger's destination at the (considerably lower) standard air-freight rate. To make use of this service contact one of the airlines (see entry) and ask to be put through to their freight office.

Precious stones

See entry

Craftwork

See entry

Markets

See entry

Social Customs

See Thai Society and the Visitor

Souvenirs

See Shopping

Sport

Almost any kind of European-style sport can be enjoyed in Thailand, apart from outdoor winter sports. Some hotels (holiday clubs) employ organisers who advise guests on the choice of sports and introduce them to the rudiments.

Ice-skating

There is even an ice-rink in Bangkok (New Petchaburi Road). Open: Mon.–Fri. noon–10pm, Sat., Sun. and public holidays from 10am.

Golf

In recent years Thailand has become something of a mecca for golfing enthusiasts. There are now golf courses in practically every part of the country, including what is quite possibly the most crazily located course in the world: it is situated between the runways of Bangkok's airport. At the Siam Intercontinental Hotel there is a driving range. TAT offices can provide a free brochure which lists all the golf courses which are open to guest players. If wishing to play at weekends and on public holidays it is best to book in advance. The daily paper "The Nation" gives information about opening times and green fees in the sports section of its weekend edition. Big golf tournaments with international players participating take place regularly in Thailand.

All the important golf courses will have equipment available which a guest player can rent.

Golf courses

The following are a selection of 18–hole courses which have a grading of difficulty of Par 72:

Bangkok

Ekachai Golf & Country Club: (02) 314 6101
Green Valley Country Club: (02) 251 4577–8
Krungthep Kritha Golf Course: (02) 374 0491, 374 6063
Muang-Ake Golf Course: (02) 533 9335–8
Navatanee Golf Course: (02) 374 6127, 374 7077
Rose Garden Golf Course (with hotel): (02) 253 0295–7
Royal Thai Army Golf Course (old course): (02) 521 1184–5
Royal Thai Army Golf Course (new course): (02) 521 1530
State Railway Golf Course: (02) 271 0130
Thai Country Club: (02) 233 7924
UNICO Golf Course: (02) 377 9038, 374 0493

Arrangements to play on any of these courses can be made by contacting: Paradise Golf Plus, 19/354 Juldis Mansion, 19 Soi Juldis, Phetchburi Road; tel. (02) 377 3522

Bang Phra

Bang Phra International Golf Club: (038) 311312, 311149
Panya Resort Country Club: (02) 322370–81

Hua Hin

Royal Hua Hin Golf Course: tel. (032) 511099, 512475

Kanchanaburi

Khao Lam Golf Course: tel. (034) 599077

Sport

Nakhon Ratchasima

Khao Yai Golf Course: tel. in Bangkok (02) 281 3041

Pattaya

Siam Country Club: tel. (038) 428 002 or in Bangkok (02) 215 3334
Sattahip Navy Golf Club: (02) 601185, ext. 2600
Asia Pattaya Golf Course (bookings at hotel reception)

Phuket

Blue Canyon Country Club Phuket: tel. (076) 214748
Phuket Golf & Country Club: tel. (076) 213388
Phuket Golf Course: (076) 213130, 211532

Chiang Mai

Lanna Golf Course: tel. (053) 221911

Marathon run

The "Bangkok Marathon", which takes places every year in December, attracts runners from all over the world. Another marathon run takes place in Phuket. Information can be obtained from the TAT (see Information).

Sports clubs

If the sports facilities in one's hotel are not sufficient, application can be made to the following sports clubs in Bangkok:
International Soccer & Recreation Club, 84 Soi Asoke, Sukhumvit Road; tel. (02) 233 7020 ext. 2287
Student Christian Centre, 328 Phya Thai Road; tel. (02) 281 7222
Thai Red Cross Society, Rajadamri Road; tel. (02) 252 6913.

Diving

The coast and the offshore islands, in particular, are still a paradise for lovers of diving, even if much of the fascinating underwater world has been largely destroyed by the activities of irresponsible divers. The Thai government has passed restrictive laws to protect submarine life and these should be obeyed to the letter. Thus it is strictly forbidden to despoil the coral-reefs around Thailand's shores. Boats are subject to spot checks on returning to land. Officially, harpooning is forbidden, although control of this is almost totally ineffective.

There are many diving schools: before embarking on a course of instruction it is advisable to check that the instructors possess the international training licence. This is particularly important for beginners wanting to gain a diving certificate. Only two organisations offer certificates which can be said to have worldwide currency: the PADI (Professional Association of Diving Instructors) and the NAUI (National Association of Underwater Instructors).

Information about reliable diving schools and bases can be obtained from the following organisations:
Diving Promotion Centre, 219 Mahachai Road, Bangkok 10200; tel. (02) 221 0465
Ocean Rover, 112 Soi Loet Nawa, Krungthep-Kritha Road, Hua Mak, Bangkok 10240; tel. (02) 374 0244
Phuket Marine Biological Centre, Amphoe Muang, Phuket 83000; tel. (076) 391127, 391128
Thailand Sub Aqua Club, 95 Soi Akrapat, Sukhumvit 49, Bangkok 10110

Equipment needed for diving can usually be rented. But be especially careful: diving organisations which are not properly set up will often issue equipment which is not in good working order.

There is excellent diving on the islands off the south-east coast: Koh Larn, Koh Sak and Koh Khrok off Pattaya (diving to a depth of some 20m/66ft); further afield are the islands Koh Klung Badan, Koh Man Wichai and Koh Rin. Round the island of Koh Sikchang off Si Racha diving is possible to 40m/131ft and also diving to wrecks. Diving is also possible near Sattahip on the island Koh Samae San and off Trat near Koh Chang.

In the south the finest areas for diving are around Phuket, on Koh Phi Phi Lay and Koh Phi Phi Don, off Koh Lanta Noi, Koh Yao Yai, Koh Dok Mai (near here is the particularly interesting "Shark Point", an underwater reef, which serves as a sleeping-place for leopard-sharks and stingrays), Koh Miang and several other islands. The marine national park off Koh Similan (80km/50 miles from Phuket) is quite unspoilt, as are the Tarutao Islands (about 160km/100 miles from Phuket).

Tennis

Tennis courts, often with floodlights, are available in many hotels (see Hotels), either free or for a small charge, for the use of guests and usually also for visitors. In the larger resorts such as Pattaya and Phuket there are well-qualified coaches.

Thai boxing

The Thai national sport is Thai boxing and the fights which are transmitted live on television can usually be guaranteed to empty the streets (see Introduction, Traditional Sports). Boxing exhibitions also take place in the tourist resorts, specially designed for visitors to take photographs, although whether it is really the "genuine article" is sometimes debatable.

Water sports

The beach resorts on the coast of the Gulf of Siam offer the most superb conditions for every conceivable type of water-sport. Wind surfing, sailing (also with catamarans), snorkelling, diving, parasailing, motor boats, and of course swimming – and all this all the year round, in water temperatures that people in Europe can only dream of. Equipment for these sports can normally be rented for a fairly modest charge.

It is recommended that care be taken with so-called "water scooters". These powerful vehicles require a certain handling skill. Serious accidents repeatedly occur, usually due to inexpert handling or negligent behaviour. These vehicles are also often in a bad state of repair and the user can find himself held responsible for damage which he has in no way helped to cause. In all cases it is best to follow the instructions of the renter carefully and keep to the permitted areas.

Tailors

Made-to-measure tailoring is a thriving business in Thailand, with immigrant Indian Sikhs holding something of a monopoly. With impeccable skill they will turn out any sort of garment to the customer's measurements. Prices are very reasonable. Bear in mind though that it will take at least three days to make a good suit, for example, and that a minimum of one fitting will be necessary in the process.

Tailor's shops

While good, sometimes even excellent, ladies' and gentlemen's tailors are found in all the hotels (especially the larger ones), the innumerable tailor's shops in the city have just as much to offer. The names of good and reliable tailors are probably best circulated by word of mouth.

Ordering a garment

The quality of the finished article can be judged from the the models in the windows. Anyone daunted by the sheer extent of the choice available can ask to see one of the European fashion magazines which are usually on display.

After making the order and having the measurements taken it is usual to leave a deposit as surety. 20% of the price is sufficient in most cases.

Prices

A gentleman's made-to-measure suit (jacket, waistcoat and trousers) costs between £60 and £100, a pure silk shirt about £10–15. Ladies' clothes cost more but the tailors will go to endless trouble to satisfy individual requirements.

Thai silk

Thailand is justly famous for its excellent silk which is extremely pleasant to wear. It is ideal for men's shirts as well as for ladies' evening wear. Chinese silk is rather more expensive but creases less than the Thai. As well as silk all the good tailors keep an extensive range of other materials suited to European fashion.

Taxis

See Public Transport

Telecommunications

Telephone

In Bangkok in particular telephone lines are overloaded and telephone numbers change quite frequently, sometimes without any prior notice. In the larger towns there are telephone kiosks, although they often have no directory or one that is very old.

International calls

Many large hotels offer a direct dialling service from Thailand to Europe (IDD, International Direct Dialling); otherwise it is necessary to go through the normal international exchange. Telephone calls can be made at all post offices throughout the country. During the day it usually takes about half an hour between booking the call and getting the connection, in the evenings it can be much quicker.

Telephone charges

A three-minute call by satellite to Europe costs about 240 baht. After the first three minutes the operator will ask if one wants to continue the call; the alternative is to state a time limit when booking the call, otherwise the operator can sometimes "forget" about the call.

Local calls from telephone kiosks cost 5 baht, hotels as a rule charge more.

Information

Telephone directories, if they are available at all, tend to be out of date, because the telephone numbers are changed so frequently. The English language directories to be found in hotel rooms and hotel telephone kiosks are the most reliable.

Information in English about inland calls can be obtained by dialling 101, the international service is 100.

Telefax

Telefax machines are fast becoming available in almost every hotel and can generally be used by hotel guests and even visitors. The larger hotels also have a "Business Center" in which business travellers will find all the most up-to-date communication methods.

Thai Society and the Visitor

Despite an ever-increasing exposure to the ways of the West, Thai society still manages to preserve its own distinctive codes of behaviour. If one were to try to describe the Thai national character, then politeness, tolerance and a deep-rooted joy of life would take first place. The Thais also attach much importance to hospitality, a fact greatly in evidence in their dealings with foreigners. That said, visitors also need to observe some basic do's and dont's if they are to avoid giving offence, however unintentionally.

Adults and children alike are naturally curious, and questions about a person's age, partner, children, occupation, etc. are considered a sign of genuine concern and indeed good breeding. A women though may be asked whether she is travelling alone (*kon dee'o*) as a prelude to making advances (or even as a prelude to an attempted handbag snatch). An appropriate response to *kon dee'o* might be *mai chai* (not really), or *bai pop sah-mee* (I am just on the way to meet my husband). Unwanted questions about age can be deflected with *mai bork* (I'm not saying) or *mai sahp* (I don't know), but by far the easiest solution is to say *mai kao jai* (I don't understand). Above all else, however, never stop smiling, and the more negative the answer, the friendlier the smile should be. To show anger, annoyance and irritation by a loud tone of voice is not only impolite but also extraordinarily lacking in respect.

Wai – greeting

To avoid bodily contact, especially between the sexes, the Thai form of greeting, the *wai*, should be used. This involves pressing the palms together in a prayer-like greeting. Bringing the hands up to the level of the forehead (or higher) denotes particularly deep respect, as would be shown to a monk for example. When greeting one's peers or strangers the hands should be level with the chin or nose, and a warm smile is appropriate too. Adults responding to a *wai* from a child ordinarily do so with a *wai* at chest level, though nowadays a nod of the head sometimes takes its place.

Politeness

The Thai notion of politeness is not such as to require a seat on the bus or boat to be given up to the elderly, mothers with babies, or pregnant women, etc. (although seats are sometimes offered to monks and the back seats in buses are usually reserved for them). A European who gets up can expect to be acknowledged with nothing more than a very fleeting, sympathetic smile.

Conversation

Of all Thai habits, however, the one that Westerners tend to find most disconcerting is having their conversation totally ignored – during a meal for instance. Even if all the Thais present speak the relevant foreign language they will only take notice of topics which interest them. It is quite normal to have them interrupt and start up a conversation among themselves in Thai, even when they are in the position of guests.

Invitations

If a Thai married couple are invited out, the wife may well send her apologies, pleading a headache or other engagement. The husband is then likely to arrive accompanied by two or three friends instead.

It is not uncommon for Western visitors to be shown special hospitality in the form of an invitation to visit a Thai home. Thais seldom entertain just a single guest, however, usually inviting several at once to make up as interesting a gathering as possible.

Dress is unlikely to be prescribed (unless for an official occasion). Nevertheless, great care should be taken to arrive suitably attired (never in black because of the association with death). Something more than shorts and a T-shirt is almost certain to be required.

Nine different spirits watch over a Thai house, living both in the garden and in the house itself. There is one in particular, the threshold spirit, which the unwary visitor is liable to offend. If the door has a threshold, be sure to step over it rather than on it. Shoes must also be removed before entering. Small gifts will be expected by the hosts – flowers are normally correct for the lady of the house while children love receiving little toys. Baby clothes should never be taken to expectant mothers – they are thought to bring bad luck.

Endearments

In Thailand a man and a woman should never indulge in any show of affection in the presence of others (not even their own children). Only since the 1973 revolution has it become acceptable for a young couple to hold hands in public. On the other hand it is not at all uncommon to see people of the same sex linking arms or embracing in the street – even uniformed officers.

Taboos

Besides displays of physical contact between the sexes there are deep-rooted taboos connected with the head and the foot. Thais regard the head, the highest part of the body, as sacred, the locus of a person's spiritual being and humanity. No one's head should ever therefore be touched. Even a pat on the head for a child, however well intentioned, will give offence. Passing something over a person's shoulder is equally taboo since their head runs the risk of being touched in the process. Respect for the head also requires that looking down on someone be avoided, especially elders or superiors. This creates difficulties for Europeans who, being for the most part taller than Thais, cannot always help looking down on them. A token gesture, e.g. bending over somewhat, or sitting when the other is standing (though never the reverse), is then appropriate. This taboo is the reason why processions or parades are never watched from upper floor windows or balconies. If the King (above whom no one is permitted to stand) were present for example, taking up such a viewpoint would amount to sacrilege.

Since the feet are the lowest part of the body they are regarded as unworthy, offensive and unclean, the very opposite of the respect afforded to the head. Consequently it is considered rude to point a foot towards another person. The Western habit of crossing legs should therefore be avoided (unless out of sight under the table). Feet being unclean (even when spotless), shoes are deemed even more so, and so are always removed before entering a temple or private home.

Religious taboos

In cosmopolitan Bangkok (as opposed to the provinces) a great deal is capable of being forgiven or at least made light of. This only applies, however, to any infringements of social taboos. Religious taboos in contrast are enshrined in law, and any transgressions are liable to meet with severe punishment in the form of a stiff fine or at worst even imprisonment.

According to article 206 of the penal code it is unlawful to commit, with regard to "any object or place of religious worship of any community, any act by any means whatever in a manner likely to insult the religion concerned".

This means, for example, that Buddhist statues should not be touched or even pointed at with hand or foot (let alone climbed upon). Nor should holiday snaps be posed for in front of statues of Buddha (or in front of pictures of the Royal Family).

These laws apply not only to Buddhism (the religion of the vast majority of Thais) but also to the other faiths represented in the kingdom. Thus to disturb people at their devotions is equally illegal whether in a Buddhist or Hindu temple, a church or a mosque.

There are some basic rules to observe when visiting places of worship or the Grand Palace in Bangkok (see entry):

In general dress neatly. Do not go shirtless or wear shorts, mini-skirts or other unsuitable attire. At Wat Phra Kaeo shoes must be removed before entering the inner bot or temple. Visiting a mosque women should wear a long skirt or slacks, with a long-sleeved blouse buttoned to the neck. Men should wear a hat and women a scarf over their heads. All visitors should remove their shoes before entering. If an act of worship is in progress, leave at once.

Buddhist monks are forbidden to touch or be touched by a woman or to accept anything direct from a woman's hand. If a woman wants to give anything to a monk or novice, she must first pass it to a layman or place it on a piece of cloth (sometimes a handkerchief) which the monk sets down before him.

Royalty

The Thais have a particularly deep devotion to their Royal Family, based on long tradition. Visitors too should accord them the utmost respect, including in conversation. Stand to attention at once when the King's picture is shown in cinemas or whenever the national anthem is played.

Seemingly trivial things can sometimes offend Thai sensibilities in this respect. For example, baht notes, which bear the King's portrait, should never be crumpled up, and certainly not thrown away. Mistreatment of Thai banknotes has led to several unpleasant incidents in recent years involving Western tourists.

Women

See Introduction, Population

Time

Time difference

Bangkok is seven hours ahead of British time (GMT + 7), or six hours ahead when British Summer Time is in force.

Lunar calendar

The lunar calendar was still in use in Thailand until the turn of the century and the dates of traditional and religious festivals continue to be set by it.

For all other purposes the Western calendar is now followed. Monday is also regarded as the first day of the week, appearing as such on bus, train and airline timetables.

The Buddhist year

One important difference all too easy to overlook is in the way the years are reckoned. The year in which Buddha entered Nirvana (543 B.C.) is the Buddhist year 1. So A.D. 1993 corresponds to 2534 on the Buddhist reckoning.

Times of the day

Thais divide the day into four six-hour periods, each marked with a special term. For visitors this can be a rich source of confusion, best avoided by insisting on exact times being given using the twenty-four hour clock.

In Thai *chao* refers to any time between 6 and 11am while *klung wun* is midday. 1pm is *bai mohng* and 2pm *bai sorng*. In the cool of the evening *yen* together with a number gives the hour after 6pm. After 10pm, however, the word *keun* is used, midnight being *klung keun*.

Toilets

The toilet is called *horng nahm* (literally water closet), and in simple hotels and private homes it refers to the bathroom as well. The word for "where", *tee nai*, can probably be avoided by a gesture. If all else fails, saying *soo-um* may well save the day. If the toilets are not clearly marked with a pictogram, ask for *chai* (men) or *ying* (ladies).

Translation and Secretarial Services

The larger hotels in Bangkok offer their guests an interpreting and secretarial service using all available modern methods of communication (indicated under Hotels by the letters BC (business center)). Extra charges will be made for these services.

Apart from the hotels there are numerous firms, particularly in Bangkok, which offer similar services, e.g.:

International Translations (translation agency)
22 Silom Road; tel. (02) 233 7714
Bangkok Business Service (office and courier services)
5/6 Soi Saladaeng, Silom Road; tel. (02) 233 4768
Other addresses can be found in the "Yellow Pages".

Traffic Regulations

See Road Transport

Transport

See Air Transport, Car rental, Ferries, Rail and Bus, Public Transport

Travel Agents

Included in the wide range of services offered by travel agents in all the larger Thai towns are excursions to destinations both close by and further afield, as well as visits to displays of folk music and dancing. Some firms have European proprietors and therefore may have some European personnel. To be sure of dealing with a reputable firm, look for the TAT recommendation (a blue logo on the doors or window).

People on package tours will be able to find out the times when they can speak to their tour operators by asking at the hotel reception. There will usually be staff who can speak English in most travel agencies.

Bangkok
Dialling code: 02

Arlymear Travel, CCT Building, 6th floor, 109 Surawong Road; tel. 236 9317
Arosa Travel Service, Kongboonma Building, 699 Silom Road; tel. 233 4526
Asia Tours Centre, 5th floor, British Airways Building, 113/9 Gaysorn Road; tel. 252 9388
Dee Jai Tours Co. Ltd., 119 Mahesak; tel. 235 9896

Diethelm Travel Co. Ltd., 140/1 Wireless Road (Kian Gwan Building II); tel. 255 9150, 255 9160, 255 9170
Open: Mon.–Fri. 9am–noon, 12.30–5pm, Sat. 8am–noon; emergencies after office hours
Oldest travel agency in Thailand, under Swiss management; extensive range of one-day and longer excursions, including neighbouring countries (Malaysia, Myanmar (Burma), Hong Kong, etc.). Many branches all over the country. Agents for many reputable tour operators.

Exotissimo Travel, 21/17 Sukhumvit Road, Soi 4; tel. 253 5250–1
Sawadee Travel Ltd., 21/6–7 Sukhumvit Road, Soi 23; tel. 258 4366, 258 4334
Songserm Travel Center, 121/7 Soi Chalermia, Phyathai Road; tel. 255 8790–8
World Travel Service (branches throughout the country), 1053 Charoen Krung Road; tel. 233 5900–9

Chiang Mai
Dialling code: 053

Air Booking Center, 255 Thapae Road; tel. 233603
Diamond Travel Service, 29 Ratchamanka Road; tel. 217025
Far East North Tour, 873/8 Phatholyothin Road; tel. 713615

Chiang Rai
Dialling code: 053

Chiangrai Travel & Tour, 869 Permwipak Road; tel. 713314, 713967
Far East North Tours, 873/8 Phaholyothin Road; tel. 713615, 711026

Pattaya
Dialling code: 038

KN Travel, 597/2 South Pattaya Road; tel. 429 134 and 429 143
Exotissimo Travel, Soi Post Office; tel. 422 788, 422 790
Malibu Travel, Soi Post Office; tel. 423 180

Phuket
Dialling code: 076

Songserm Travel Center, 64/2 Rasada Road (in the Rasada Shopping Center); tel. 214272, 214297
Many other travel agencies along Patong Beach.

Surat Thani
Dialling code: 077

Songserm Travel Center, 30/2 M. 3 Bangkung; tel. 285124–6
Samui Tours, 326/12 Talat Mai Road; tel. 282352

Travel documents

Personal papers
Visas

To enter Thailand the visitor must be in possession of a valid passport and an entry permit. For visits of up to 30 days no special visa is required; visas for longer stays need to be applied for from the relevant consulate before departure (see Diplomatic Representation). The passport must be valid for six months beyond the intended departure date.

For stays of longer than 30 days there are 60-day tourist visas and 90-day non-immigrant visas. Visitors who know that they might need to extend their stay in Thailand are advised to obtain the 60-day tourist visa at the outset, as the 15-day visa can only be extended in exceptional circumstances. Even the extension of a 30-day visa costs a disproportionate amount of time and money. For every day that a visitor spends over and above the period of their visa a fee will be exacted on departure.

Visas to visit the neighbouring countries of Myanmar (Burma), Laos and Vietnam can only be obtained in Bangkok and not at the border crossing points (entry to Myanmar is in any case only possible by air). The processing of a visa application can take several days. For Malaysia a visa valid for 90 days is issued at the border crossing or airport. If visitors are leaving Thailand temporarily, for instance on a trip to Hong Kong or Myanmar, with the intention of returning, a special multiple entry visa should be applied for, which allows a maximum of three entries.

The cost of a visa is determined by the number of entries into the country which are planned. At the time of publishing the cost of a transit visa was about £7, a tourist visa £10 and a non-immigrant visa £17 (per entry).

Visa applications

Visa application forms can generally be obtained from travel agencies. Two completed forms are needed together with two photos and the passport. For those travelling on organised tours a confirmation of the booking from the tour company should be enclosed and, when applying by post, a stamped addressed envelope. The visa processing fee must be paid in cash.

Visa extensions

Application for an extension to a visa must be made to the relevant Immigration Department before the period of the initial visa has elapsed. If the stay in Thailand exceeds the period allowed for by the visa by up to six days a charge is payable on departure, at the time of publishing 100 baht per day (not applicable to 15-day short visas).

The main offices of the Immigration Department (open: Mon.–Fri. 8.30am–noon, 1–4.30pm):

Bangkok: Soi Suan Ply, Sathorn Tai Road; tel. (02) 287–3101, 286 4231

Chiang Mai: Sanambin Road (near the airport); tel. (053) 213510

Kanchanaburi: 284/40 Saengchuto Road

Koh Samui: near the post office in Nathon; tel. (077) 421 069

Krabi: Uttarakit Road

Pattaya: Beach Road, Soi 8; tel. (038) 429–409

Phuket: South Phuket Road; tel. (076) 212–108

Surat Thani: Don Nok Road (Surat Thani City Hall); tel. (077) 273 217

Tax Clearance Certificate

Anyone who spends more than 90 days in Thailand in any calendar year is required to present a Tax Clearance Certificate, which absolves the individual from tax liability in Thailand. The certificate is also required from visitors who have a Thai work permit or who have stayed in Thailand for more than 14 days on business. Applications for the certificate need to be made to either the Tax Clearance Sub-Division, Central Operating Division, 1 Chakrapongse Road, Phanakom District, Bangkok, or the Revenue Department, Rajdamnoen Road, Bangkok (tel. 282 9340). Processing applications can take a few days.

Loss of passport

Where a visitor loses a passport and is scheduled to leave Thailand either in the evening or at the weekend the embassies are not in a position to help immediately, as the Immigration Department has to be contacted first in order to arrange replacement entry papers.

Some advice

It is a good idea to travel with some passport-size photos. These often prove useful, for instance when applying for visas to enter neighbouring countries. It is also worth having a photocopy of the important pages of one's passport, e.g. the pages giving personal details and the one with one's entry visa into Thailand. Always keep these photocopies separate from the originals. In the event of the passport being lost, these copies can often make it much easier to obtain replacement documentation while still abroad.

Inoculations

See Health Precautions

Customs regulations: See entry

When to go

High season

The best months for Europeans and others from temperate climes are from November to mid February when temperatures are at their coolest (25–30°C/77–86°F) and the humidity is relatively low (65–70%). This being the peak tourist season, however, prices are at their highest. For Thais on the other hand, the high season – and the only time they go to the beaches – is from March to the end of May when the children are on holiday. From a European point of view Bangkok becomes unbearably hot at this time of year, with up to 95% humidity and temperatures of over 35°C/97°F. Nevertheless, these months are made very interesting by the great number of local festivals.

Out of season

Travelling out of season can be thoroughly recommended. Although flooding has to be contended with in towns and on smaller cross-country roads, the countryside is greener, lusher and more in bloom than at any other time. At this time the north-east, not generally very well blessed in terms of vegetation, although culturally interesting, is a good place to visit. In addition, hotel reservations, which are absolutely necessary in the high season, can usually be dispensed with at this time, good accommodation being easily found at reasonable prices everywhere.

The oppressive humidity is at an end and in central Thailand at least (i.e. in and around Bangkok) it rains only once a day for about 30 to 50 minutes, usually in the late afternoon.

Climate

See Facts and Figures, General

Clothing

See entry

Youth hostels

Besides numerous smaller hotels and hundreds of guest houses, which offer favourably priced accommodation, there are also perfectly adequate youth hostels in the larger towns in Thailand. They are as a rule fairly simple and quite often it is necessary to share a room with one or more fellow-guests. Therefore take great care of personal possessions (thieves are normally other tourists).

It is best to avoid accommodation in seedy or shady areas as these places can often be the meeting-places of drug dealers and are therefore watched by the police and often searched.

Bangkok

YMCA, 27 Sathorn Tai Road (also for families); tel. (02) 286 1936

YWCA, 13 Sathorn Tai Road; tel. (02) 286 1936
Both places offer accommodation which is not exclusively for young people (advance reservation usually necessary).

Bangkok Christian Guest House, 123 Sala Daeng Road, Soi 2; tel. (02) 233 2206

Chiang Mai

YMCA International House, Mengrai-Rasami Road; tel. 221819; 90 r
Youth Hostel, 21/8 Chiang Khlan Road; tel. 236735, 236737; 26 r
Youth Hostel 2, 31 Phra Pok Klao Road Soi 3; tel. 212863 (Reservations in Bangkok: 281 6834); 15 r

Chiang Rai

YMCA International House, 70 Phaholyothin Road; tel. 713785–6, 714336; 50 r

Principal Tourist Sights in Thailand

Index

Imprint

273 illustrations, 16 town plans, 15 general maps, 12 site plans, 6 drawings, 1 large map at end of book

Original German text: Heiner Gstaltmayr, Prof. Dr Wolfgang Hassenpflug, Anita Rolf, Hanna Tichy

Revised and additional text: Heiner Gstaltmayr

Editorial work: Baedeker, Stuttgart (Dr Bernhard Abend)
English language edition: Alec Court

General direction: Dr Peter Baumgarten, Baedeker Stuttgart

Cartography: Harald H. Harms, Erlenbach; Gert Oberländer, München; G. Schiffner/ Christoph Gallus, Hohberg-Niederschopfheim (large map)

Source of Illustrations: J. Beck (12), J. Dittmar (2), K. U. Müller (1), K. Peter (3), Surachit Jamonman (3), TAT (1), Thai Airways International (1); all other photographs by Heiner Gstaltmayr.

English Translation: Wendy Bell, Julie Bullock, David Cocking, Brenda Ferris, Crispin Warren

Revised text: Crispin Warren

2nd English edition 1997

Published in the United States by:
Macmillan Travel
A Simon & Schuster Macmillan Company
1633 Broadway
New York, NY 10019–6785

Macmillan is a registered trademark of Macmillan, Inc.

Distributed in the United Kingdom by the Publishing Division of the Automobile Association, Fanum House, Basingstoke, Hampshire RG21 2EA

A CIP catalogue record of this book is available from the British Library

Licensed user:
Mairs Geographischer Verlag GmbH & Co.,
Ostfildern-Kemnat bei Stuttgart

Printed in Italy by G. Canale & C.S.p.A – Borgaro T.se –Turin

ISBN 0 02 861354 6 USA and Canada
0 7495 1479 5 UK

Notes

Notes

Notes